Educational Media and Technology Yearbook

Michael Orey · V. J. McClendon ·
Robert Maribe Branch
Editors

Educational Media
and Technology Yearbook

Volume 34, 2009

In cooperation with the AECT

 Springer

\# 2694 35948

Editors

Michael Orey
Department of Educational Psychology
   and Instructional Technology
University of Georgia
604 Aderhold Hall
Athens GA 30602
USA
mikeorey@uga.edu

V. J. McClendon
Department of Educational Psychology
   and Instructional Technology
University of Georgia
604 Aderhold Hall
Athens GA 30602
USA
vjmcclen@uga.edu

Robert Maribe Branch
Department of Educational Psychology
   and Instructional Technology
University of Georgia
604 Aderhold Hall
Athens GA 30602
USA
rbranch@uga.edu

ISBN 978-0-387-09674-2   e-ISBN 978-0-387-09675-9
DOI 10.1007/978-0-387-09675-9

Library of Congress Control Number: Applied For

springer.com

Preface

The *Educational Media and Technology Yearbook* has become a standard reference in many libraries and professional collections. Examined in relation to its companion volumes of the past, it provides a valuable historical record of current ideas and developments in the field. Part I, "Trends and Issues," presents an array of chapters that develop some of the current themes listed above, in addition to others. Part II, "Library and Information Science," concentrates upon chapters of special relevance to K-12 education, library science education, school learning resources, and various types of library and media centers—school, public, and academic among others. In Part III, "Leadership Profiles," authors provide biographical sketches of the careers of instructional technology leaders. Part IV, "Organizations and Associations in North America," and Part V, "Graduate Programs in North America," are, respectively, directories of instructional technology-related organizations and institutions of higher learning offering degrees in related fields. Finally, Part VI, the "Mediagraphy," presents an annotated listing of selected current publications related to the field.

For a number of years we have worked together as editors and the sixth with Dr. Michael Orey as the senior editor. Last year as the senior editor, Orey decided to try and come up with a list of the top programs rather than just the list of all the programs. This has proven to be problematic. First of all, bias exists when we are rating a field in which our program is within those to be rated. A second concern is the lack of data available for selecting the top programs which might remove some of this bias. Yet another issue is why a list is needed at all. Finally, an issue we had not foreseen is that there actually several "fields" interested in how technology influences teaching and learning.

Here we attempt to address some of these issues. First, why do this list. In the short period of time we attempted to create such a list, many people have expressed concern. People want to know why their program may have been left out. Our intent was to generate a list of the top programs, without a rank ordered list similar to the method employed by *US News and World Report*. So, why go through this process? There are some good reasons to do this. One is that potential students want to make decisions about which school to attend and a list like this may assist them. Another reason is that often we compete for resources within our colleges and membership among the top programs in the country may provide some leverage. Another reason might be to motivate some departments that are left out to work towards being included in the list. The bottom line is that the last three sections of this book are essentially data and this list provides some analysis for that data.

The inherent weakness in this analysis is its basis in our conversations with others as the sole rubric for judgment. Data has not been analyzed to create this list of top programs. Initially this year we tried to use some measurement for this process. We examined the past two years of issues of the Educational Technology Research and Development (ETRD) journal and counted the number of publications from different Instructional Technology related departments. We counted the institution only once if it had multiple authors from a single institution, but multiple authors from separate institutions, were counted as distinct individuals. This method generated the following list:

5 – Nanyang Technological University in Singapore
4 – University of Georgia
3 – Indiana University, Florida State University, Utah State University
2 – Brigham Young University, University of Miami (Ohio), Virginia Tech, Penn State University

This analysis was sent to some of the people from last year's identified programs of instructional technology. Those universities not in the list immediately began lobbying to be put on the list based on other data such as grant money generated. Others complained that ETRD provides too narrow of a focus and members of organizations such as the International Society for Technology in Education (ISTE), International Conference on the Learning Sciences (ICLS), International Society for Performance Improvement (ISPI), and Association for the Advancement of Computing in Education (AACE) often do not choose to publish in ETRD. Thus we return to the issue of what is the field that concerns itself with technology and how it relates to learning, teaching and education.

The programs participating in ISTE are not the same as the programs participating within our sponsoring organization, AECT. The programs in ICLS are not the same as those participating in ISTE and AECT. Not only do we have various organizations with nuanced differences in focus, but the field itself can be called, "Instructional Technology," "Educational Technology," "Learning Sciences," or "Information Science."

If we are the Learning Sciences, then we are a "… community of researchers and practitioners who use cognitive, socio-cognitive, and socio-cultural approaches to studying learning in real-world situations and designing environments, software, materials, and other innovations that promote deep and lasting learning" (ISLS, 2008). In contrast, AECT says, "Educational technology is the study and ethical practice of facilitating learning and improving performance by creating, using, and managing appropriate technological processes and resources" (Januszewski & Molenda, 2008, p. 1). The former definition points to a more theory driven focus, yet the two definitions seem to have the same focus to us as editors. Library and information science converge with these areas with Information Literacy (IL). The AASL/AECT standards explain that the information literate individual accesses information efficiently and effectively, critically evaluates it, and can use and gather information accurately and creatively and technology is a leading tool in this endeavor today (AASL/AECT, 1998). The bottom line is that there is a great deal of overlap between these allegedly distinct fields. For the sake of convenience, we are going to break the world up into Learning and Information. The former we will label Learning, Design, and Technology (LDT) because this seems to embrace all perspectives. The Information Science field has largely influenced the former School Library Media section, so the other field we will call Information Science. Given this variance in field definitions, and with little comparative data available, we are trying to create a list of the top programs in a field of related studies peopled by organizations such as ISTE, AECT, AACE, ISPI and ISLS for the LDT field. Certainly there are other great programs and we will work towards gathering data for the 2010 edition of EMTY so that will be data driven.

In the meantime, we compiled a list of top LDT programs. You might think of this list as an opinion list and that is okay. We sought and received opinions from about 5 to 10 other faculty members from around the country, but other than the data on publications in ETRD, all of this anecdotal data was opinions. For a while, we had separate categories for those programs that focused most of their efforts at the masters level and those that focused on doctoral education. In the end, we just combined them into a single list. The top 30 LDT programs based on this opinion data *listed alphabetically* are:

Arizona State University
Brigham Young University
Carnegie Mellon University
East Carolina University
Florida State University
George Mason University
Georgia Tech
Indiana University
Miami University of Ohio
MIT Media Lab
Nanyang Technological University
Northern Illinois University
Northwestern University
Penn State University
Purdue University
San Diego State University
Stanford University
Syracuse University
University of California Berkeley
University of California Los Angeles
University of Georgia
University of Memphis
University of Michigan

University of South Alabama
University of Twente
University of Washington
Utah State University
Vanderbilt University
Virginia Tech
Wayne State University

Similarly, we polled just a very few folks working in schools in the area of Information Science. If the LDT list is tentative, this list is even more tentative because fewer people offered opinions. However, we would like to use this list as a starting point for gathering further data next year. We do not want to rank order our list, just have a list of some of the most influential programs. Here is our very tentative list of IS programs that focus on information in the schools *listed alphabetically*:

Drexel University
Florida State University
Rutgers University
San Jose State University
University of British Columbia
University of Georgia
University of Illinois at Urbana-Champaign
University of Maryland
University of North Carolina at Chapel Hill
University of North Texas
University of South Carolina
University of Washington
University of Wisconsin

The audience for the *Yearbook* consists of media and technology professionals in schools, higher education, and business contexts. Topics of interest to professionals practicing in these areas are broad, as the Table of Contents demonstrates. The theme unifying each of the following chapters is the use of technology to enable or enhance education. Forms of technology represented in this volume vary from traditional tools such as the book to the latest advancements in digital technology, while areas of education encompass widely ranging situations involving learning and teaching which are idea technologies.

As in prior volumes, the assumptions underlying the chapters presented here are as follows:

- Technology represents tools that act as extensions of the educator.
- Media serve as delivery systems for educational communications.
- Technology is *not* restricted to machines and hardware, but includes techniques and procedures derived from scientific research about ways to promote change in human performance.

- The fundamental tenet is that educational media and technology should be used to:

1. achieve authentic learning objectives,
2. situate learning tasks,
3. negotiate the complexities of guided learning,
4. facilitate the construction of knowledge,
5. aid in the assessment/documenting of learning,
6. support skill acquisition, and
7. manage diversity.

The Editors of the *Yearbook* invite media and technology professionals to submit manuscripts for consideration for publication. Contact Michael Orey (mikeorey@uga.edu) for submission guidelines.

Athens, USA	Michael Orey
Athens, USA	V. J. McClendon
Athens, USA	Robert Maribe Branch

References

1. ISLS. (2008). *About the International Society of the Learning Sciences.* Accessed July 15, 2008, from http://www.isls.org/about.html
2. Januszewski, A., & Molenda, M. (2008). *Educational technology: A definition with commentary.* New York: Erlbaum.
3. American Association of School Librarians and Association of Educational Communications and Technology. (1998). *Information power.* Chicago: American Library Association.

Contents

Contributors

Doug Achtermann San Benito High School, Hollister, CA, USA
dachterman@sbhsd.k12.ca.us

Xornam S. Apedoe Department of Learning & Instruction, University of San
Francisco, San Francisco, CA, 94117, xapedoe@usfca.edu

Brenda Bannan-Ritland College of Education and Human Development, George
Mason University, Fairfax, VA 22030, USA, bbannan@gmu.edu

Michael Behrmann College of Education and Human Development, George
Mason University, Fairfax, VA 22030, USA, mbehrman@gmu.edu

Joanne P. H. Bentley Department of Instructional Technology, Utah State
University, Logan, UT 84322-2830, USA, Joanne.Bentley@usu.edu

Elizabeth Boling Instructional Systems Technology, Indiana University,
Bloomington, IN 47405-1006, USA, eboling@indiana.edu

Robert Maribe Branch The University of Georgia, Athens, GA 30602-7144,
USA, rbranch@uga.edu

Abbie Brown Library Science and Instructional Technology, East Carolina
University, Joyner Library, Greenville, NC 27858, USA, brownab@ecu.edu

Carol A. Brown , MAEd Instructional Technology, Joyner Library 1102, East
Carolina University, Greenville, NC 27858, USA, BROWNCAR@ecu.edu

Lora Lee Smith Canter East Carolina University, Greenville, NC 27858, USA

Kevin Clark College of Education and Human Development, George Mason
University, Fairfax, VA 22030, USA, kclark6@gmu.edu

Max H. Cropper Department of Instructional Technology, Utah State University,
Logan, UT 84322-2830, USA, maxcropper@comcast.net

Lesley S. J. Farmer California State University, Santa Barbara, Long Beach, CA
90840-2201, USA, lfarmer@csulb.edu

Mary Ann Fitzgerald Ed Psych & Instructional Technology (EPIT), University
of Georgia, Macon, GA 31206, USA, mfitzger@uga.edu

Pamela Fortner The University of Georgia, Athens, GA 30602-7144, USA, phales@uga.edu

Daniel Fuller School of Library and Information Science, San Jose State University, One Washington Square, San Jose, CA 95129-0029, USA, dfuller@slis.sjsu.edu

Chad Galloway The University of Georgia, Athens, GA 30602-7144, USA, cagi@uga.edu

Tim Green California State University, Fullerton, California, USA, tgreen@fullerton.edu

Jackie Hill Lenior County Schools, North Carolina, USA

Douglas R. Holschuh Department of Instructional Technology, College of Education, The University of Georgia, Athens, GA, USA, dholschu@uga.edu

Tara Jeffs East Carolina University, Greenville, NC 27858, USA

Allan C. Jeong Department of Instructional Systems Program, Educational Psychology and Learning Systems, College of Education, Florida State University, Tallahassee, FL 32306, USA, jeong@fsu.edu

Marci Kinas Jerome College of Education and Human Development, George Mason University, Fairfax, VA 22030, mkinas@gmu.edu

Tristan E. Johnson Department of Instructional Systems Program, Educational Psychology and Learning Systems, College of Education, Florida State University, Tallahassee, FL 32306, USA, tjohnson@lsi.fsu.edu

Jami Biles Jones 1108 Joyner Library, East Carolina University, Greenville, NC 27858, USA, jonesj@ecu.edu

Ting-Ling Lai AIMS for 3C Project, National Taiwan Normal University, Science Education Center RM 602, Taipei, 11699 Taiwan, TL.Lai@sec.ntnu.edu.tw; Ting-ling Lai txl166@gmail.com

Susan M. Land Instructional Systems Program, The Pennsylvania State University, University Park, PA 16802-1303, USA, sml11@psu.edu

Xin Mao Department of Instructional Technology, Utah State University, Logan, UT 84322-2830, USA

V. J. McClendon Department of Educational Psychology and Instructional Technology, The University of Georgia, Athens, GA 30602-7144, USA, vjmcclen@uga.edu

Cathy McLeod Libraries, Media, and Television, Seattle Public Schools, Seattle, WA, USA, csmcleod@seattleschools.org

Patricia Miller Programming, Promotion, Education, KNPB Channel 5 Public Broadcasting, Reno, NV 89503, USA, patricimiller2383@sbcglobal.net

Michael Molenda , Instructional Systems Technology, Indiana University, Bloomington, IN 47405-1006, USA, eboling@indiana.edu

Betty J. Morris Jacksonville State University, Jacksonville, AL 36265-1602, USA, bmorris@jsu.edu

Nora Murphy Los Angeles Academy Middle School, Los Angeles, California, USA

Priscilla Norton College of Education and Human Development, George Mason University, Fairfax, VA 22030, USA, pnorton@gmu.edu

Michael Orey The University of Georgia, Athens, GA 30602-7144, USA, mikeorey@uga.edu

Mimi Recker Department of Instructional Technology, Utah State University, Logan, UT 84322-2830, USA, mimi.recker@usu.edu

Frances Reeve Longwood University, Farmville, VA 23909, USA, reevefm@longwood.edu

Thomas C. Reeves Department of Instructional Technology, College of Education, The University of Georgia, Athens, GA, USA, treeves@uga.edu

Shayne Russell Kenneth R. Olson Middle School, Tabernacle, NJ 08088, USA, shayne.russell@gmail.com

Cindy Schmidt Longwood University, Farmville, VA 23909, USA, schmidtcm@longwood.edu

Kerstin Schroder Department of Psychology, Utah State University, Logan, UT 84322-2830, USA, Kerstin.Schroder@usu.edu

Norbert M. Seel Department of Instructional Systems Program, Educational Psychology and Learning Systems, College of Education, Florida State University, Tallahassee, FL 32306, USA, seel@fsu.edu

Valerie J. Shute Department of Instructional Systems Program, Educational Psychology and Learning Systems, College of Education, Florida State University, Tallahassee, FL 32306, USA, vshute@fsu.edu

Joseph B. South Instructional Psychology and Technology, Brigham Young University, Provo, Utah, 84602, USA

J. Michael Spector Department of Instructional Systems Program, Educational Psychology and Learning Systems, College of Education, Florida State University, Tallahassee, FL 32306, USA, mspector@lsi.fsu.edu

Jinn-Wei Tsao The University of Georgia, Athens, GA 30602-7144, USA, miketsao@uga.edu

Shahron Williams van Rooij College of Education and Human Development, George Mason University, Fairfax, VA 22030, USA, swilliae@gmu.edu

Karen S. Voytecki East Carolina University, Greenville, NC 27858, USA

Stephen C. Yanchar Instructional Psychology and Technology, Brigham Young University, Provo, Utah, 84602, USA, stephen_yanchar@byu.edu

Alana M. Zambone Department of Curriculum and Instruction, East Carolina University, Greenville, NC 27858, USA, zambonea@ecu.edu

Part I
Trends and Issues in Learning, Design, and Technology

Introduction

Michael Orey

This is the eighth edition of this book where I have served as the editor of the Trends section. I have used a variety of strategies for organizing this section. Last year, I decided if I could identify the top programs in the field, I could ask each of them to submit a work that might represent the trends in research in the department. Collectively, this would then represent the trends in the field. I began before the 2008 edition with a very short list that I contacted. Most of them then submitted a chapter and also revised my list which I then published in 2008. For this section, I used the expanded list from the 2008 list. Next, year, I will use the now 28 institutions listed in this edition. I was only able to get 6 of those institutions to give me a chapter by the deadline of going to press. Interestingly, the departments at each of these 6 institutions took one of two paths in deciding how to frame trends in the field. One approach was to create a large collaborative document written by all or most of the faculty in the department and they were able to then show a very broad view of the trends in their department. The others followed my recommendation from last year and simply choose one doctoral student dissertation and use it as an example of the work being done within that department. This provides the reader with a much deeper understanding of a single issue, but it also does not complete represent the entire department. I think that this combination of approaches then gives you the reader a broad and sometimes deep view of the field and this is an optimal view for a given year.

In addition to the chapters from the top departments, I also have chosen to continue to include the trends chapter that has been authored by Michael Molenda in the past and is now been taken over by Abbie Brown and Timothy Green. Each year they take a look at the trends in Business and Industry, Higher Education, and K-12 Schools. So this is a different chapter, but it is an important chapter to continue to include in this yearbook to keep track of trends.

Brown and Green begin this section with their chapter, "Issues and Trends in Instructional Technology: Web 2.0, Second Life, and STEM Share the Spotlight." Web 2.0 technologies have dominated the discussion of what is new in Business and

M. Orey (✉)
The University of Georgia, Athens, GA 30602-7144
e-mail: mikeorey@uga.edu

M. Orey et al. (eds.), *Educational Media and Technology Yearbook*,
DOI 10.1007/978-0-387-09675-9_1, © Springer Science+Business Media, LLC 2009

Industry and Higher Education. Some of the technologies have been understood and exploited like YouTube, while others are still be explored to determine how to use the technology like Second Life. In the K-12 arena, while there is some interest in Web 2.0, a refocus on Science, Technology, Engineering and Mathematics (STEM) has dominated the decision making about technology.

The Instructional Systems Technology Faculty's chapter is representative of all of their views. The title of the chapter is, "Research and Theory in Instructional Systems Technology at Indiana University." They characterize their collective work as being focused on "systems thinking" and they use a variety of theoretical frames to explore this primary thread. Those theories include behaviorism, cognitivism, visual perception, social-psychological theories related to learning, instructional organizational behavior and change.

The other collective piece was authored by the faculty at George Mason University. Norton, van Rooij, Jerome, Clark, Behrmann, and Bannan-Ritland describe their program in their chapter, "Linking Theory, and Practice Through Design: An Instructional Technology Program." Whereas the IU program seems to rally around the concept of "systems thinking," the GMU faculty rally around the concept of "design." They have three tracks in their program, one focused on government, military, business and higher education, one focused on technology integration in the schools, and the other track is focused on assistive technologies. All converge on the idea of design for learning, design of software and technology to increase the likelihood that the learner can learn best.

The Florida State University contribution is, "Model-Based Methods for Assessment, Learning, and Instruction: Innovative Educational Technology at Florida State University." Shute, Jeong, Spector, Seel and Johnson describe a large scale collaborative effort to develop a set of tools called Highly Interactive Model-based Assessment Tools and Technologies (HIMATT). These tools assess mental models of learners in various ways. It is a very impressive effort to reveal the deeper conceptual frameworks of learners and promises to be an important contribution to our field.

Brigham Young University has made the list this year and Yanchar and South have contributed a chapter entitled, "Beyond the Theory-Practice Split in Instructional Design: The Current Situation and Future Directions." I have tried to cast our field a bit larger in the Preface of this book. However, the sub-area known as Instructional Technology often points to Instructional Design as its basis. The IU chapter talks about the "systems theory" part of ID and the GMU chapter talks about the centrality of design. The BYU piece looks at the gap between how we teach ID and how people actually use it when they are working in the field. In fact, they suggest a much closer linkage that eliminates the abstractionist approach to academic theory building and suggests an approach that makes theory more concrete based on practical experience.

In the GMU chapter they talked about the program that was designed to help teachers learn more powerful ways to design learning experiences using technology. In the first Utah State University chapter by Mao and Recker, they examine the impact of a professional development workshop that introduced a tool for technology integration. In their chapter, "Effects of a Professional Development on Teacher Integration of Online Resources," Mao and Recker describe a study that made use of Problem-Based Learning within the workshop.

Similarly, the Cropper, Bentley, and Schroder chapter discusses the design of online courses as they relate to Merrrill's theory of instruction. Both of these chapters show a focus on learning and design with technology being a component of the design.

While the USU paper used a mixed methods approach to research, in the Penn State University chapter by Lai and Land entitled, "Supporting Reflection in Online Learning Environments," they use a qualitative research method. Their work shows how important it is to combine scaffolding strategies within a reflection activity to support the kind of deep reflection that can truly impact learning.

In the Apedoe, Holschuh, and Reeves chapter, The Interplay of Teaching Conceptions and a Course Management System Among Award-Winning University Professors, we gain a glimpse of what is happening in higher education and online learning. Interestingly, a massive amount of money have been spent on Course Management Systems (CMSs), but they have not had a huge impact on the teaching approaches of the 5 faculty members examined in this chapter. Not only did the CMS not change their teaching approach, most simply used it as a device for distributing material. Certainly, Apedoe, et al., attempt to examine learning theories in action as the result of the design of a computer tool (CMS) aligns quite well within the LDT framework suggested in this edition of this book.

In the preface, we suggested that there are disparate fields all of whom seem to be interested in learning, teaching and education particularly as it is impacted by technology, both artifact and process technologies. In each of these chapters we see this focus.

Issues and Trends in Instructional Technology: Web 2.0, Second Life, and STEM Share the Spotlight

Abbie Brown and Tim Green

Abstract Comprised of four sections: Overall Developments; Corporate Training and Development; Higher Education; and K-12 Settings, this chapter synthesizes the findings of major annual reports including ASTD's, *State of the Industry Report*; the *EDUCAUSE Core Data Service Fiscal Year 2006 Summary Report; The ECAR study of undergraduate students and information technology;* the fifth annual report on the state of online learning in U.S. higher education; *Education Week's* Technology Counts annual report, and the fifth annual *Speak Up* and *Horizon Report*. The authors describe the state of the economy and its impact on instructional technology and comment on the importance of Web 2.0, Second Life, and Science Technology Engineering and Mathematics (STEM) initiatives.

Keywords Educational technology · Instructional technology · Training · Education · Technology

We continue with the tradition of reporting the issues and trends of instructional technology that have continued or arisen within the past year. This chapter is comprised of four sections: Overall Developments; Corporate Training and Development; Higher Education; and K-12 Settings.

Overall Developments

In the time since the previous review was written (Brown & Green, 2008), the United States economy has weakened considerably. Spurred by the weak housing market due, in part, to subprime mortgages followed by record foreclosures, oil prices reaching over $100 a barrel, and an unstable job market, the economy saw minimal growth (if any growth at all). Overall, for all three sectors—K-12, higher education,

A. Brown (✉)
Library Science and Instructional Technology, East Carolina University, Joyner Library, Greenville, NC 27858
e-mail: brownab@ecu.edu

M. Orey et al. (eds.), *Educational Media and Technology Yearbook*,
DOI 10.1007/978-0-387-09675-9_2, © Springer Science+Business Media, LLC 2009

and corporate—funding for technology expenditures was tight, if not contracted. The financial support of K-12 and higher education suffered due to lower tax revenues generated at the state level. The norm was for schools to work within a budget that had seen overall cuts. While commitment to technology in all sectors remained; new initiatives, were limited. A ray of hope at the end of the review period provides optimism that positive changes are on the horizon.

Web 2.0 Matures

Web-based tools that allow individuals to create and share knowledge, collaborate, and learn together continue to remain popular. Personal broadcasting of personal experiences, information, and events through venues such as You Tube and vlogs has seen an increase in use by students at all levels. The integration of these tools into the classroom by teachers and trainers continues to expand as the tools become more stable and accessible (Horizon Report, 2008; Project Tomorrow, 2008).

Online Learning Continues to Grow

e-Learning and online courses and programs continue to increase in popularity (Allen & Seaman, 2007; Paradise, 2007). Although the increase may not be as extreme as in previous years, it seems that growth in e-Learning and online instruction is maintaining a faster growth rate than traditional, face-to-face instruction. Major consumers of e-Learning and online instruction are members of larger and more dispersed populations of professionals within a single corporate organization (Paradise, 2007) and non-traditional college students (Allen & Seaman, 2007).

Personal Digital Assistants (PDAs) Give Way to Smartphones

On campus, the use of smartphones has increased as the use of PDAs has decreased (Salaway, Borreson, Caruso, & Nelson, 2007). This is probably due to the increased capabilities of smartphones and their abilities to provide much of the same functionality as PDAs along with cellular phone service. Apple's iPhone was named "Invention of the Year" by Time Magazine (Grossman, 2007). AT&T, currently the only service provider for the iPhone gave Apple unprecedented freedom to develop its own specifications for its smartphone, which will undoubtedly have repercussions on the services other cellular phone developers will be able to offer (Grossman).

Second Life Takes a Spotlight

The MUVE (massive multiplayer virtual environment), Second Life received a great deal of attention for its potential as an instructional activity and instructional support system. As of March 2008 there are over 12.8 million Second Life participants worldwide (Linden Labs, 2008), over 1 million of which logged in within the last two months.

Linden Labs, the organization that owns and operates Second Life, has actively solicited the education and training and development community by offering "islands" which can be leased by organizations. These islands provide a level of privacy that allows universities and business organizations opportunities to create and maintain protected environments for their students or employees.

Corporate Training and Development

As had been done in previous issues and trends chapters of the yearbook (Molenda & Bichelmeyer, 2005; Bichelmeyer & Molenda, 2006; Brown & Green, 2008), we continue to track corporate application of instructional technologies primarily by referring to the American Society for Training and Development's (ASTD's), *State of the Industry Report*, (Paradise, 2007). The current ASTD annual report is based on data collected from the Benchmarking Forum (BMF) organizations, ASTD BEST award winners, and responses from users of ASTD's WLP (Workforce Learning and Performance) Scorecard. The report describes the activities of organizations recognized as exemplary in their approach to workplace learning and performance as represented by the BEST award winners; larger, global organizations typically represented by BMF members; and data collected from users of ASTD's WLP Scorecard benchmarking and decision support tool.

Learning Investments

On average, direct expenditure on instruction per employee continues to drop. BMF and BEST organizations' expenditures fell 7.3% (to $1,320) and 5.23% (to $1,531) respectively (Paradise, 2007). The average expenditure as a percentage of payroll remains remarkably stable, having risen a consolidated average of only 0.02% since the previous year (Paradise).

Learning hours used by employees have been stabilizing, with only small gains or declines reported among the various groups from whom data was collected (Paradise, 2007). The costs for both delivery and consumption of learning content is increasing; Paradise attributes this to an increase in the number of full-time employees per organization. This larger number of employees also contributed to an increased reuse ratio (Paradise).

Instructional Content

Profession or industry-specific skills and information was the leading content area in 2006 (Paradise, 2007). Specialized learning is in high demand; this accounted for almost one quarter of the learning hours reported in the BMF sample (Paradise). Processes, procedures, and business practices, followed by managerial and supervisory topics were the next most popular content areas of the consolidated sample (Paradise).

Use of Technology: e-Learning Continues to be Popular and Online Virtual Reality Attracts Interest

e-Learning (instruction delivered via networked computing devices) remains popular and continues its consistent upward trend (Paradise, 2007). Of the learning hours provided in 2006, 30.28% of them were technology-based, and more than 75% of those technology-based hours were delivered online (Paradise). Approximately 80% of online learning in recent years has been self-paced (Paradise).

The online MUVE, (multi-user virtual environment), Second Life has taken the spotlight in the past year, numerous articles devoted to Second Life's potential use for corporate training have appeared in magazines and journals including ASTD's, *Training + Development* (Galagan, 2008; Gronstedt, 2007; Hall & Nguyen, 2007). ASTD currently maintains an "island" within Second Life in order to support its membership and, "...capture the growing audience of learning professionals who are seeking new methods to interact with a larger, more dispersed population" (Harris, 2008, p. 63).

Use of External Services (Outsourcing)

Organizations surveyed by ASTD (Paradise, 2007) reflect a consistent use of external services including content delivery, infrastructure development, translation services and custom content development. Paradise reports, in general, more than one quarter of organizational expenditure for direct learning is allocated to external providers.

Higher Education

We examine universities' information technology use and instructional technology application primarily by referring to the *EDUCAUSE Core Data Service Fiscal Year 2006 Summary Report* (Hawkins & Rudy, 2007). As with the previous year's report, 933 institutions submitted the 2006 survey; the data set was frozen in May of 2007 to prepare the analysis for the summary report released in September of 2007. Undergraduate trends in particular are examined primarily by referring to *The ECAR study of undergraduate students and information technology, 2007*, (Salaway et al., 2007). 27,864 students at 103 two-year and four-year institutions responded to the ECAR survey. Trends in online learning are examined by referring to the fifth annual report on the state of online learning in U.S. higher education, *Online Nation* (Allen &

Seaman), supported by the Alfred P. Sloan Foundation and based on responses from more than 2,500 colleges and universities.

Information Technology Planning on Campus

One of the more significant changes in this year's EDUCAUSE Core Data Service report (or CDS) is the increased diversity of campus constituents who contribute to IT strategies (Hawkins & Rudy, 2007). There was a marked increase in the number of campuses reporting IT strategy input from president's cabinet/councils, system/district offices, student committees, academic/faculty committees, and administrative committees (Hawkins & Rudy). One might speculate this increase is due to the increasing IT sophistication of the campus population in general; as a greater range of individuals become more comfortable with information technologies, they are more likely to request an opportunity to provide input, just as the organization as a whole is more likely to solicit input from an increasingly sophisticated population.

A variety of institutions surveyed cite improved access as their top reason for offering online courses and programs (Allen & Seaman, 2007). While generally not viewed as a way to reduce or contain costs, online course and program offerings do maintain a high appeal for non-traditional students (Allen & Seaman).

Student Computing

Nearly all of the students represented in the ECAR survey (98.4%) own a computer, laptops continue to increase in popularity (Salaway et al., 2007). 65.5% of the students responding to the ECAR survey report ownership of a computer that is less than two years old; 20.4% own a computer four years old or older (Salaway, et al.). Reliance on older computers may cause reliability and performance problems (Salaway, et al.). Furthermore, according to the CDS report, a significant number of students, particularly at public institutions, may not own their own computers and continue to rely on public-access computing stations and campus computer labs.

According to the ECAR survey, undergraduates spend a great deal of time online, and the vast majority of students have access to high-speed connectivity (Salaway et al., 2007). Only 8.4% depend on dial-up access, which marks a decrease since 2005 (Salaway, et al.). Students are using computers to access e-mail, course management systems and library Web sites (Salaway, et al.). 81.6% of those responding to the ECAR survey use social networks (e.g. Facebook) and most do so daily (Salaway et al.).

The use of smartphones has significantly increased, while the use of personal digital assistants (PDAs) has declined, probably as a result of the increased capabilities of the smartphones available (Salaway et al., 2007).

Campus Technology Support

The CDS report indicates that much discussion continues regarding the need for round-the-clock computing support. However, the CDS report reveals only about 7% of institutions with help desks offer 24-hour service. This past year saw minor increases in help desk availability and 24-hour service support in particular (Hawkins & Rudy, 2007).

Over 90% of all institutions responding to the CDS survey report that they currently provide e-mail accounts for students (Hawkins & Rudy, 2007). This is critically important in that it determines whether faculty and administrators can rely on being able to contact all students in a class or on campus via e-mail (Hawkins & Rudy).

Classrooms equipped with computers in general rose about 4% this past year, and Internet connectivity in classrooms has increased as well (Hawkins & Rudy, 2007). Doctoral institutions in particular report a significantly higher percentage of wired classrooms (Hawkins & Rudy). Much of the increase in connectivity at doctoral institutions is related to increased wireless connectivity, and wireless connectivity increased 11% for all schools in the CDS report (Hawkins & Rudy).

Use of Technology for Instruction

Course managements systems (CMS) remain an important and popular aspect of college and university instruction. More than 90% of all campuses reported in the CDS the support and use of one CMS or more, although the use of these systems by faculty is erratic (Hawkins & Rudy, 2007). ECAR respondents generally report favorably on using CMS (Salaway et al., 2007).

Although only 5% of ECAR respondents reported the use of podcasting as part of their course work, students were overwhelmingly positive about podcasts for course support (Salaway et al., 2007).

According to Allen and Seaman (2007), nearly 20% (nearly 3.5 million) of all U.S. higher education students were taking at least one online course in the fall of 2006. This represents a 9.7% increase over the previous years (Allen & Seaman). Two-year associate's institutions indicate the highest growth rates, accounting for over one-half of all online enrollments for the last five years, while baccalaureate institutions maintain the fewest online enrollments and indicate the lowest rates of growth (Allen & Seaman). Non-traditional students in particular seem to find online instruction attractive; a high number of institutions cite growth in professional and continuing education as an objective for offering online courses and programs (Allen & Seaman).

Technology Support for Faculty

Offering faculty training upon request and offering training through scheduled seminars were once again the two most common methods of assisting faculty according to the EDUCAUSE Core Data Service survey (Hawkins & Rudy, 2007). Training upon request was offered by 94% of the campuses surveyed, and training through scheduled seminars was offered by 84% of those campuses (Hawkins & Rudy).

As in previous years, undergraduate students report no particular interest in having faculty incorporate technologies that may be commonplace to young people (e.g. instant messaging) into course work, especially if the perception is that the technology is being used for the sake of using technology instead of appropriately supporting course content (Salaway et al., 2007). It would seem that one approach to technology support for faculty may be to maintain an ongoing discussion on the nature of appropriate use of innovative technologies in the college/university classroom.

Online Virtual Environments: Second Life Becomes a Hot Topic

Although none of the major studies reviewed make mention of online virtual environments specifically, the MUVE (massive multiplayer virtual environment), Second Life, was a hot topic this past year. Academic journals featured a number of articles on the subject of using Second Life for instruction and instructional support in higher education (e.g. American Library Association, 2007; Ananthaswamy, 2007; Bainbridge, 2007; Barack, 2006; Deubel, 2007; Kirriemuir, 2007). Second Life as a method of instruction was featured in a number of articles appearing in the popular press as well (e.g. Bugeja, 2007; Foster, 2007a, 2007b; Lagorio, 2007). The articles focus on a combination of descriptions of specific cases of experiments in teaching using Second Life (e.g. Lagorio, 2007) and of discussing the potential use of online virtual reality for instructional purposes (e.g. Deubel, 2007).

K-12 Education

Although many of the issues regarding instructional technology use in K-12 have persisted from pervious review years (Molenda & Bichelmeyer, 2005; Bichelmeyer & Molenda, 2006; Brown & Green, 2008), one major issue that had wide reaching influence in 2008 took center stage. This issue was the push for improvement in science, technology, engineering, and mathematics (STEM) education. Business leaders and politicians who saw a fragile economy, weak standardized test scores, and a skilled foreign workforce as destabilizing forces to the overall economic health of the U.S. were a driving force behind this push. Congress approved legislation that authorized funding—an estimated $3 billion—for STEM-related federal programs in order to step-up efforts to help students succeed in science, technology, engineering, and mathematics. The states, especially those hit hardest by job losses in manufacturing, viewed this as an opportunity to implement STEM education initiatives in attempt to help strengthen the economy through an educated workforce (Cavanagh, 2008; Technology Counts, 2008).

In 2007, the authors primarily consulted two comprehensive reports—*Education Week's* 9th annual Technology Counts 2006 and *America's Digital Schools 2006: Mobilizing the Curriculum*—in indentifying and helping make sense of data regarding the issues and trends in instructional technology in K-12 education. This year's review again focuses on *Education Week's* Technology Counts annual report in addition to the fifth annual *Speak Up* report and the *Horizon Report*.

The *Education Week's* Technology Counts 2007 issue focuses on a survey of state education representatives conducted by the Editorial Projects in Education Research Center that assesses the status of K-12 educational technology across the nation by tracking state progress in critical areas of technology policy and practice. The three major areas are access to technology, the use of technology, and the ability of teachers to use technology effectively. For the second consecutive year, the report assigned letter grades for all 50 states and the District of Columbia indicating how well each performed in these major areas. As a whole, the nation earned a C+ (the same as in 2007) with West Virginia again leading the nation with the grade of A. Only three states earned a letter grade of A or A– while 13 states earned a grade of B+, B, or B–, 28 earned a C+, C, or C–, and the remaining seven earned D+, D, or D–. The District of Columbia took over the bottom spot from Nevada with a D-grade (*Education Week*, 2008).

The topic headings used to organize this K-12 section mirror those from last year's review (Brown & Green, 2008). They are: funding, student data management using technology, computer-based media, emerging technologies used in K-12, teacher access to and use of technology, teacher training and certification, delivery of online learning, and student access to and use of technology.

Funding

With state tax revenues remaining flat, or in many cases decreasing over the past year throughout much of the U.S., K-12 public education budgets faced cuts across the board. Monies for technology budgets were included in these cuts (Vogel, 2008). The previous issues and trends chapter included information from a report conducted by the Denver-based National Conference of State Legislatures indicating that schools expected to spend nearly 8% more on K-12 education then in the previous year—2006 to 2007—and the spending increase would continue into future years. The expected increases were in addition to the seven percent average states provided K-12 public education during the 2005–2006 budget year (McNeil, 2007). Due to lower state tax revenues, however, these increases were not as predicted.

Despite the lower-than-projected revenues, spending on technology occurred—districts' technology spending averaged $577,100 per district for an estimated total of $4.3 billion in U.S. K-12 education (Dyril, 2008). A majority of district technology monies went toward the usual items of staff, maintenance, and upgrades. For many districts, network hardware upgrades were the biggest IT initiative (Hildebrand, 2007). We predict that spending patterns (both funding levels and items purchased) will remain consistent in the near future until the health of the economy improves considerably.

Using Technology for Student Assessment: Using Data-Management System to Mine Student Data

The use of technology for student assessment remains a dominant trend in K-12 technology use. Accountability, through mandates and initiatives of the No Child Left Behind (NCLB) Act, continues to have states focusing on data-management systems to collect and manage student data systems. Therefore, state monies continue to flow into this area, again making student assessment data plentiful, as in 2007.

Although student assessment data remains plentiful in an electronic format, easy access to the data by teachers to inform their teaching and to improve student learning continues to be an issue. In the 2008 issues and trends chapter, we reported that according to *Technology Counts 2006*, "Only 28 states provide current student state assessment results through a centralized data system that teachers can access. Almost half (24) of the states do not provide systems that allow teachers to track student progress on a year-to-year basis. Only 20 states have systems that allow teachers to compare their school with other similar schools" (Brown & Green, 2008). We have seen some documented improvement in this area—although it is still difficult to determine how individual districts are faring in their efforts to make data more accessible to teachers (Davis, 2008).

The trend we see, therefore, is that data-management systems will begin to focus more on data mining functionalities rather than simply on the collection and storage of student data. Individual teachers need to have the ability to mine student data in order to track student yearly progress. This ability will provide teachers with the opportunity to use testing data to make instructional decisions based on specific student needs in content and skill areas based on state standards. Companies that fail to include usable data-mining functionalities for teacher access and control over student data in their products will see these products fail. Opportunities will continue to exist for companies that can satisfy these needs in a sophisticated manner.

At the federal level, with the increase in funding for STEM education, the call has been made for better tracking and evaluation of STEM education initiatives. According to Cavanagh (2008), in discussing the findings of a report conducted by the American Competiveness Council, wrote that the measures used to evaluate STEM education programs fail to provide specifics on their impact in the classroom. In looking at these programs, federal agencies tend to judge the programs on "inputs" like number of teachers involved or changes in attitude of participants—rather than on measures dealing with whether student learning has improved. A trend we see with federally funded programs is an increase in research on the effectiveness of STEM programs on student learning. This will lead to an increase in the collection, storage, and management of student achievement data. Funding will be available for organizations to be involved in these research activities.

Emerging Digital Tools: The Continued Ubiquity of Networks and Computers along with the Maturation of Web 2.0 Tools

The major trends from this section in last year's chapter have carried over into the current review year: ubiquitous networks and computers—along with the use of collaborative digital tools—have become even more entrenched in the K-12 environment.

Ubiquitous Networks. According to the Consortium for School Networking, the majority of states offer K-12 schools access to a high-capacity network through a partnership with universities. This provides the backbone on which K-12 schools can implement wireless networks (CoSN, 2007). As reported in last year's issues and trends chapter (Brown & Green, 2008), the number of public schools using wireless networks during 2001–2005 increased by 400%. In 2005, 45% of public schools had wireless networks (Borja, 2006). We predict that this percentage has continued to increase with the development of faster and more secure wireless protocols along with the opening up of access to existing networks—such as, cellular networks (Wildstrom, 2008). We also predict that more districts will consider moving toward a single network infrastructure that converges data, voice, video, and wireless traffic as price and stability of these systems improve (eSchool News, 2007).

Ubiquitous Computing. Mobile computing devices continued to remain popular. While current data exists that describes percentages of student ownership of mobile devices, the same type of data is not as available for school ownership. We previously reported (Brown & Green, 2008) that the tablet-PC would be the most likely purchased student appliance by schools (America's Digital Schools, 2006). However, we could not find evidence—empirical or anecdotal—to support this prediction. The most likely purchased student appliance by schools was laptops.

Personal access by students to mobile devices—especially MP3 players, smart phones, and personal digital assistants—exploded since the last review period (Project Tomorrow, 2008). Approximately 60% of all K-12 students have access to MP3 players while close to 47% have cell phone access and 34% have access to laptops. Twenty-two percent of students in grades 3–12 have access to smart phones or personal digital assistants (Project Tomorrow, 2008). The available data strongly suggests that student access to mobile devices will continue to increase. The use of these devices in K-12 schools, however, will rest largely on how teachers and administrators view these devices as tools that can enhance student learning There is no doubt that students have embraced these devices as learning tools.

Web 2.0 Tools. An emerging trend we described in the previous issues and trends chapter (Brown & Green, 2008) was the use of collaborative Web-based digital tools by students primarily to stay connected with friends and peers. Examples of these tools included blogs, IM, social networks, and wikis. While students continue to use these tools for communication purposes, teachers have increased their use these tools for teaching and learning. Sixty-eight percent of teachers surveyed indicated using Web 2.0 tools to help students develop 21st century literacy skills (Project Tomorrow, 2008). We see this trend continue as current Web-based digital tools are enhanced, as additional ones (e.g. data mashups) are developed, and as teachers become more comfortable using these tools.

Teacher Access to and Use of Technology

Data describing teacher access to technology in schools remains inconsistent, if not elusive, from year to year. A significant annual report—*Teachers Talk Tech*—from which extensive teacher use data was pulled from for the previous issues and trends chapter, was not available for the current review period. Therefore, due to the lack of specific data, we infer that the access teachers have to technology in schools mirrors student access levels. According to *Technology Counts 2008*, students per instructional computer averaged 3.8 in the U.S. Utah had the highest ratio at 5.4, while South Dakota came in at the lowest with two students per every instructional computer. Students per high-speed Internet connected computers averaged slightly lower with 3.7 in the entire U.S. Utah again had the highest average at 5.3, while South Dakota had the lowest at 1.9. The percentage of fourth grade students with access to computers was reported at 95%, and the percentage of eighth grade students with access to computers was 83% (Bausell, 2008).

Data regarding teacher use of technology is more readily available. According to the latest *Speak Up* survey, 33% of the teachers surveyed identified themselves as technology experts, with 56% claiming to be average technology users (Project Tomorrow, 2008). When asked, "What do you do regularly with technology?" the teachers indicated that they primarily use technology for e-mail communication. Ninety-three percent reported using e-mail to communicate with colleagues and parents—only 34% reported using e-mail to communicate with students. Using technology to create PowerPoint presentations came in at 59% of the teachers surveyed. Creating or listening to podcasts or videos came in at 35% followed by maintaining a personal Web site at 21%. Teachers (51% surveyed) reported that their number one use of technology to facilitate student learning was to assign homework or practice work (Project Tomorrow, 2008).

With regard to key emerging technologies—such as, educational gaming and mobile devices (specifically, laptops, MP3 players, and smart phones)—teachers were surveyed on their current and potential use of these technologies in the classroom. Fifty percent indicated they would be interested in learning more about integrating gaming technologies into the classroom, and 11% indicated they are currently incorporating some gaming into their instruction. Fifty-two percent stated that mobile devices would most likely increase student engagement in learning. Forty-three percent believed that mobile devices could extend learning beyond the school day, while 42% believed the devices prepare students for the real world. Only 25%, however, see the devices helping students with communication, collaboration, or creativity (Project Tomorrow, 2008).

According to Bausell (2008) citing the EPE Research Center's Annual State Research Policy Report for 2008, 16 states have embedded technology standards into subject area standards. Of these states, fifteen embed them within the four core content areas of English, history, mathematics, and science. States are most likely to integrate technology standards in mathematics and science (Bausell). The overt expectation exists, in several states, for teachers to integrate technology throughout the curriculum to help students meet content standards. We see this trend continuing.

Teacher Professional Development and Teacher Certification Requirements

In the previous review, we were hopeful that with the updated (in June 2007) International Society for Technology in Education technology standards, states would take the opportunity to revaluate their own teacher technology standards and the technology requirements placed on teacher licensure. Our hopes were not realized. The growth has been marginal in the number of states with technology standards for teachers. The current number is 44, up from 40 in 2004—of the 44 states, 35 have state technology standards for administrators (Bausell, 2008).

The numbers are much lower for technology competence and initial technology licensure. Only 19 states require technology course work or the passing of a test (or both) to determine technology competence for initial licensure. The number is actually down two from the last review. We believe it is important to note that nine states require course work or a test for initial licensure for administrators (Bausell, 2008). One trend we predict is the increased integration of technology into content area courses rather than stand-alone courses. This trend should gain momentum the implementation of more STEM education initiatives in teacher education programs.

In last year's chapter, we reported that only nine states required teachers to demonstrate ongoing competence in technology or to complete professional development related to technology before being recertified (*Education Week*, 2006). The number has increased by one. The number of states requiring ongoing technology training or testing for competence for administrators is six, with California only requiring technology-related professional development for principals of low-performing schools (Bausell, 2008).

Overall, according to *Technology Counts 2008*, states averaged a C grade for helping build the capacity of teachers to effectively use and integrate technology in the classroom. This was a slight improvement from last year. Three states (Georgia, Kentucky, and West Virginia) earned A's while five states (Idaho, Montana, Nevada, Oregon, and Utah) and the District of Columbia earned F's. Based on past trends, we predict that the numbers we have reported will again remain relatively consistent.

Delivery of Instruction Online

The number of states with established statewide virtual schools grew from 22 to 25 since the last review (Bausell, 2008). Delivering instruction through online education, therefore, remains a trend. Not surprisingly, student interest and participation in online learning continues to increase. Eight percent of high schools students surveyed by Project Tomorrow through their annual Speak Up project indicated that they had taken an online class. An additional 9% indicated that they had participated in an online component of a traditional face-to-face course. Six percent of students surveyed in grades 9–12 indicated taking an online course for personal reasons outside of school (Project Tomorrow, 2008). This data supports the *America's Digital Schools 2006* report data we included in last year's review indicating that 15.6% of students would take an online course by the year 2011. Student interest in online learning for those with no previous online learning experience is strong. Thirty-three percent of high school students, 24% of middle school students, and 19% of 3–5 grade students surveyed indicated interest in taking an online course (Project Tomorrow, 2008).

With continued student interest and participation in online learning, significant challenges remain for K-12 education to address. One major challenge is teacher training and professional development in using technology in the online teaching and learning environment. The good news regarding this challenge is that teachers have been embracing taking professional development online. Nearly one third of teachers surveyed by the Speak Up survey reported taking online professional development; a 29% increase from 2006 to 2007. Twenty-six percent reported that online professional development was their preferred method for training (Project Tomorrow, 2008). We believe the increasing number of teachers taking online professional development may lead to a higher comfort level and willingness among these teachers to teach online.

Despite the challenges, online education holds a great deal of promise for K-12 education. The potential of online learning remains consistent over the past review. Online learning has the potential of bringing about equity among schools—especially in rural and urban districts—where the online environment provides students with access to resources and courses, such as advanced placement courses, they otherwise would not have access to. Online learning also has the potential for providing a learning environment that may better meet the needs of certain student populations. We continue to see online education being a key trend in K-12 education in the years to come.

Student Access to and Use of Technology

Data on student access to instructional computing has significantly improved since 1999. The ratio of students per instructional computer in the U.S. is on average 3.8 to 1 as compared to 5.7 to 1 in 1999 (Project Tomorrow, 2008). Despite this decrease, state ratios vary considerably with 15 states having ratios above 3.8 to 1. Utah has the highest ratio at 5.4 to 1, while South Dakota has the lowest with two students per every instructional computer. Ninety-five percent of forth grade students have access to instructional computers; the percentage of eighth grade students with access is slightly lower at 83% (Bausell, 2008). When examining the nation as a whole, the U.S. earned a grade of C for student access according to the *Technology Counts 2008* report (Bausell).

Similar to student access to instructional computing, student access to the Internet has drastically improved over the years as well. Virtually all public K-12 schools have access to the Internet. This is up from 35% of public K-12 schools in 1994 (NCES, 2005). Integration of the Internet into the classroom has followed a similar path—in 1994, 3% of classrooms had Internet access, with the percentage increasing to 94% in 2005 (Bausell, 2008). This equates to students per high-speed Internet connected computers in the U.S. averaging 3.7 to 1. In looking at individual state ratios, Utah again had the highest at 5.3 to 1, while South Dakota had the lowest at 1.9 to 1 (Bausell). Relatively significant access differences still exist when comparing urban to nonurban schools. The NCES reported that 88% of inner-city classrooms were equipped with Internet access in contrast to 95–98%of classrooms in nonurban schools (2005). Secondary schools, larger schools, and low minority enrollment schools are slightly more likely to have higher access levels (Bausell, 2008).

As a nation, a trend we see continuing is the steady lowering of the average ratios of students per instructional computer and students per high-speed Internet connected computer. This is a result of a combination of elements—the two most important of these being the continued decrease in computing hardware and software costs and the increased implementation of 1:1 computing initiatives. In last year's issues and trends chapter, we reported that 24% of school districts were in the process of implementing 1:1 computing programs—an increase of 20% since 2004 (*eSchool News*, 2006). Although updated data is not available, examples of new1:1computing programs (some of which included the low cost laptops) that support this increase were introduce this past year in places like Iowa and Birmingham, Alabama (see Associated Press, 2008 and *eSchool News*, 2008).

The data points to students having relatively good access to instructional computing and the Internet in school, and they are making use of these for both schoolwork related and non-schoolwork related activities. According to the latest Speak Up survey (Project Tomorrow, 2008), students in grades 6–12 reported that the top five schoolwork related activities were writing assignments (74%); online research (72%); checking assignments or grades online (58%); creating slideshows, videos, and Web pages for schoolwork (57%); and e-mail or IM with classmates about assignments (44%). The top five non-schoolwork activities were gaming, music downloads, social networking, and communication. Over 64% of students in K-12 reported playing online or electronics-based games regularly. Middle school and high school students reported downloading music as their number one technology related activity. Forty percent of middle school students and 67% of high school students maintain a personal Web site through services such as Facebook, MySpace, or Xanga. The most popular activity on the Web site is communicating with friends. Over fifty percent of high school students reported using email, IM, and text messaging on a regular basis, girls exceeded boys in their use of these tools (an average of 12% higher) (Project Tomorrow, 2008).

In looking at how students view their technology skills, 70% of students in grades 6–12 identified themselves as having "average" tech skills compared to their peers. Twenty-four percent identified themselves as "advanced." Examining the differences between the genders, girls in all grades were more likely to identify themselves as having beginning or average tech skills compared to boys. Girls are also less likely to indicate their skills as advanced (Project Tomorrow, 2008).

Conclusion

Economic uncertainty during the period covered in this review led to decreases in budgets for K-12 and higher education. In corporate America, technology spending was cautious. The actual influence the reductions had in K-12 and higher education remained unclear because the use of technology by students and teachers remained at high levels. This was due, in part, to the increased use of the sophisticated computing tools associated with Web 2.0. Online distance education played an increased role in the delivery of instruction everywhere, and it continues to be an appealing and popular option for learners.

In K-12 education, STEM education programs strongly influenced the use of technology. Revamped technology standards for teachers from the International Society of Technology Educators (ISTE) led states to reconsider the teaching and assessment of technology knowledge and skills for certified teachers. NCLB mandates in K-12 education kept student data-management systems in the forefront of district and school technology initiatives and spending. The promise of these systems to help teachers improve student learning still was not realized.

In higher education, students continue their increased technological sophistication with greater access to hardware including laptops and smartphones, making use of these for social purposes as well as school work. Colleges and universities continue to increase their use of course management systems, but application of these systems by faculty is erratic. Online virtual environments, Second Life in particular, received a great deal of attention this year.

The corporate sector spent less on instructional technology this past year, but employee learning hours are stabilizing. Profession and industry-specific skills and information was the most popular instructional content. e-Learning in the corporate sector continues its upward trend and Second Life was the focus of a great many, high-profile initiatives.

While the economy was not conducive to spending, instructional technologies remained popular in all sectors with Web 2.0, Second Life, and STEM as this year's watchwords.

References

Allen, I. E., & Seaman, J. (2007). *Online nation: Five years of growth in online learning*. The Sloan Consortium.

American Library Association. (2007). ALA/Arts island opens in Second Life. *American Libraries, 38*(4), 12.

Ananthaswamy, A. (2007). A life less ordinary offers far more than just escapism. *New Scientist, 195*(2618), 40.

Bainbridge, W. S. (2007). The scientific research potential of virtual worlds. *Science, 317*(5837), 472–476.

Barack, L. (2006). Virtual stacks go live. *School Library Journal, 52*(12), 26.

Bausell, C. V. (2008). Tracking U.S. trends. *Education Week, 27*(30), 39–42.

Borja, R. R. (2006). Technology upgrades prompt schools to go wireless. *Education Week, 26*(9), 10.

Brown, A., & Green, T. (2008). Issues and trends in instructional technology: making the most of mobility and ubiquity. *Educational multimedia and technology yearbook* (Vol. 33). Westport, CT: Greenwood Publishing Group.

Bugeja, M. J. (2007). Second thoughts about Second Life. *Chronicle of Higher Education, 54*(3), C2–C4.

Cavanagh, S. (2008). States heeding calls to strengthen STEM. *Education Week, 27*(30), 10–16, 22–23.

CoSN. (2007). *Internet2: Inventing the next-generation network*. Retrieved on April 11, 2008 from http://www.cosn.org/resources/compendium/2007Summaries/internet2.pdf

Davis, M. R. (2008, January 23). Finding your way in a data-driven world. *Digital Directions*. Retreived April 9, 2008, from http://www.edweek.org/dd/articles/2008/01/23/3data.h01.html

Deubel, P. (2007). Virtual worlds: A next generation for instruction delivery. *Journal of Instruction Delivery Systems, 21*(2), 6–12.

Dyril, O. E. (2008). *District buying power 2007*. Retrieved on April 11, 2008, from http://www.districtadministration.com/viewarticle.aspx?articleid=1263&p=2#0

Education Week. (2006). *Technology counts 2006, 25*(35).

eSchool News. (2006). 1-to-1 computing on the rise in schools. Retrieved April 11, 2008, from http://www.eschoolnews.com/news/showstory.cfm?ArticleID=6278

eSchool News. (2007). Special report: Converged wireless: New technologies allow convergence of voice, video, and data across wireless networks. Retrieved on April 11, 2008 from http://www.eschoolnews.com/resources/unified-communications/unified-communication-articles/index.cfm?i=46356;_hbguid=f7127943-352d-436f-b0ce-b55a590c9048

eSchool News. (2008). Birmingham schools approve low-cost laptop program. Retrieved April 11, 2008, from http://www.eschoolnews.com/news/top-news/?i=53412

Foster, A. L. (2007a). 'Immersive education' submerges students in online worlds made for learning. *Chronicle of Higher Education, 54*(17), A22.

Foster, A. L. (2007b). Teaching geography in Second Life. *Chronicle of Higher Education, 54*(10), 36.

Galagan, P. (2008). Second that!: Could second life be learning's second chance? *Training and Development 62*(2), 34–37.

Greaves, T. W., & Hayes, J. (2006). *America's digital schools: Mobilizing the curriculum*. Retrieved April 11, 2008, from http://www.ads2006.org/ads2006/index.php

Gronstedt, A. (2007). Second Life produces real training results. *Training and Development, 61*(8), 44–49.

Grossman, L. (2007). Invention of the year: The iPhone. *Time.com*, October 31, 2007. Retrieved March 16, 2008, from http://www.time.com/time/business/article/0,8599,1678581,00.html

Hall, T., & Nguyen, F. (2007). IBM@Play on Second Life. *Training Media Review*, July, 2007.

Harris, P. (2008). See how they learn. *Training and Development, 62*(1), 61–65.

Hawkins, B. L., & Rudy, J. A. (2007). *EDUCAUSE core data service fiscal year 2006 summary report*. Boulder, CO: EDUCAUSE.

Hildebrand, C. (2007). *Technology spending still hot.* Computer Weekly.com Retrieved on April 11, 2008, from http://searchcio.techtarget.com/tip/0,289483,sid182_gci1271922,00.html#;

Horizon Report. (2008). Retrieved on March 12, 2008 from http://www.nmc.org/pdf/2008_Horizon_Report.pdf

Kirriemuir, J. (2007). *A July 2007 "snapshot" of UK higher and further education developments in Second Life.* Eduserv Foundation: http://www.eduserv.org.uk/foundation

Lagorio, C. (2007). Pepperdine in a treehouse. *The New York Times,* January 7, 2007.

Linden Labs. (2008). *Economic statistics.* Retrieved March 16, 2008, from http://secondlife.com/whatis/economy_stats.php

McNeil, M. (2007). As budgets swell, spending choices get new scrutiny. *Education Week 26* (29), 1, 19.

Molenda, M., & Bichelmeyer, B. (2005). Issues and Trends in Instructional Technology: Slow Growth as Economy Recovers. In Orey, M., McClendon, V.J., & Branch, R.M (Eds). *Educational media and technology yearbook 2005:* Volume 30. Englewood, CO: Libraries Unlimited. 3–28.

Molenda, M., & Bichelmeyer, B. (2006). Issues and Trends in Instructional Technology: Gradual Growth Atop Tectonic Shifts. In Orey, M., McClendon, V.J., & Branch, R.M (Eds). *Educational media and technology yearbook 2006:* Volume 31. Englewood, CO: Libraries Unlimited. 3–32.

National Center for Education Statistics (NCES). (2005). *The condition of education 2005.* NCES 2005-094. Washington, DC: U.S. Department of Education.

Paradise, A. (2007). *State of the industry report.* Alexandria, VA: American Society of Training and Development.

Project Tomorrow. (2008). *Speak up 2007 for students, teachers, parents, and school leaders report.* Retrieved April 9, 2008, from http://www.tomorrow.org/

Salaway, G., Borreson Caruso, J., &Nelson M. R. (2007). *The ECAR study of undergraduate students and information technology, 2007.* Boulder, CO: EDUCAUSE.

Technology Counts 2008. (2008). STEM: The push to improve science, technology, engineering, and mathematics. *Education Week, 27*(30).

Vogel, C. (2008). *Budget busters: Trimming district budgets is always challenging.* Retrieved April 11, 2008, from http://www.districtadministration.com/viewarticle.aspx?articleid=1469

Wildstrom, S. (2008, April 7). Breaking wireless wide open. *Business Week,* 112.

Research and Theory in Instructional Systems Technology at Indiana University

Instructional Systems Technology Faculty

Abstract Research and theory-building activities in Instructional Systems Technology at Indiana University revolve around several thematic threads: message design, instructional design/development, technology integration, systemic change in education, and change management and human performance technology. A dozen or more student-faculty research groups are active at any given time on inquiry projects related to these themes. Recent projects, their theoretical bases, and some of their findings are elaborated in this chapter.

Keywords Research · Theory · Faculty · Message design · Systemic change · Instructional design

Overview

Instructional Systems Technology (IST) at Indiana University has long encompassed a large and diverse program, one that often has pushed against the conventional boundaries of the field at the time. However, consistent with its middle name, a "systems" view of the processes of instruction in formal and non-formal settings has for many years dwelt at the heart of the program. This perspective goes back at least to 1969 when the IST label was adopted for what was then a "division" in the School of Education (now a department). The founder of the program, L.C. "Ole" Larson, supported the systems perspective, which had already gained traction at Syracuse University (see Mood, 1964), the University of Southern California (see Silvern, 1963; Heinich, 1965), and Michigan State University (see Barson, 1967). By 1972, the IST curriculum was organized around several emphasis areas: message design, instructional design/development, evaluation and integration, systems design and management, and diffusion/adoption.

Instructional Systems Technology Faculty (✉)
Instructional Systems Technology, Indiana University, Bloomington, IN 47405-1006
e-mail: eboling@indiana.edu

M. Orey et al. (eds.), *Educational Media and Technology Yearbook*,
DOI 10.1007/978-0-387-09675-9_3, © Springer Science+Business Media, LLC 2009

Those themes are echoed in the research-and-theory emphasis areas of IST today: message design, instructional design/development, technology integration, systemic change in education, and change management and human performance technology. The Indiana doctoral program revolves around student participation in research groups working to address these themes. At Indiana, as in many educational technology programs, faculty and students are also often involved in projects to design and develop instructional materials and systems, which are typically evaluated and revised; these might be characterized as "development only" or "primarily development" projects. However, these sorts of activities are not included in this report, focusing instead on research and development work that springs from a theory base and is meant to test and build those theories.

Message Design

Researchers at Indiana University have been in the forefront of inquiry on learning from visuals, exemplified by the early work of Mac Fleming (1967) and Howard Levie (1978). Fleming and Levie also teamed to produce the milestone work on general principles of instructional message design (1978, 1993). The tradition they established is being followed by two current research groups in IST, one working on message design principles for the new digital media, another on instructional illustrations.

Principles of Instructional Message Design for Digital Media

Even as Fleming and Levie were struggling to extract general principles of message design for instructional materials during the decades of the 1960s through the early 1990s (Fleming & Levie, 1978, 1993), media format options were constantly changing and expanding. Message design principles started with the core decisions of how best to present text information and to incorporate images with that text. Soon researchers were adding the complexity of *moving* images with 16 mm films and videos; these media challenged the designer to consider not only the stream of voice narration but to also to couple the moving images i ever changing audio track as well.

Then came hypermedia and the possibility of many unique paths through multimedia information for different learners. The newly popular formats were no longer linear, so the considerations became even more complex. Around this time message design began to fall from Educational Technology curricula, as tools like *Hyper-Card* and *ToolBook* were embraced as the new "best practices" for format and content delivery. In the mid-1990s the hypermedia formats migrated to delivery by the World Wide Web; its exponential growth vastly increased access to these multimedia information delivery formats and led to further rethinking of message design issues (Misanchuk, Schwier, & Boling, 1999).

New media, different paradigms. Today Robert Appelman's message design research group in IST is working to establish principles of message design applicable to the Web 2.0 world—immersive interactive learning environments (IILE) such as games and simulations. The state of the art in these formats surpasses film, video, and hypermedia formats in complexity. In addition, users approach these new media formats with significantly higher level capabilities, not only in interface control, but also in perception and multi-tasking competencies. This places incredible pressure on the message designer to keep up with the levels of sophistication of these new media and their audiences. Nevertheless, even with all these challenges, the goals in message design research are the same as they were when we just had text and pictures to work with. We want to engage the audience with meaningful content, have them be able to perceive the text, images, avatars, music, user interface (UI) elements, and other elements of the "micro-world," such that they would be congruent in dominance with the message we wish to convey. Researchers are finding that most of the principles from the Fleming and Levie era are still applicable to today's IILE, for example:

> 2.3a. Attention is drawn to the parts of a message that stand in contrast to the others. Such contrasts can exist in just about every aspect of the message's content, organization, and modality (Fleming & Levie, 1993, p. 67.)

Contrast is still vitally important to ensure that salient points—whether in auditory, visual, or verbal forms—stand out.

Building a new paradigm. Before one can derive principles of message design in the new media format of an IILE, one must first be able to define what is happening at any point during the users' experience, both cognitively, affectively, and functionally. We must be able to compare one user's experience with another user's along the same criteria (Appelman, 2005; de Vreede, Verbraeck, & van Eijck, 2003; Garris, Ahlers, & Driskell, 2002; Klabbers, 2000; Reigeluth & Schwartz, 1989; Squire & Barab, 2004). To get at these objectives we have created a Virtual Xperience Lab (VX Lab) where we can observe game play, web interactions, and any IILE, be it on a game console or a PC. Through Game Play Analysis methodologies (Appelman, 2007; Zimmermann, Gregory, & Appelman, 2007), we are able to "unpack" the micro interactions and structural changes within the environment on a second-by-second basis. One might think that this level of detail would be over-kill for establishing some broad-based principles for message design, but the pace of interactions and the multiplicity of visual, audio, and functional elements confronting the user are so high, that much would be missed with any other methodology.

Defining the structure of an environment and reporting what happens within it is only a beginning. To design for these new IILEs one must first spend some time learning and playing within them. Thus informed, one can productively begin the instructional design process for an IILE. The path of development (or *pipeline* as it is referred to in the game industry) is an extremely long one, and one that also involves many interdisciplinary collaborators. What we are pursuing is a well defined set of principles to guide teams through the development pipeline for the "serious game." Many see games and other goal-based scenario activities as a viable format for problem-based learning pedagogies within constructivist paradigms (Appelman,

2008; Barab, Thomas, Dodge, Carteaux, & Tuzun, 2005; Hannafin & Hill, 2005; Jonassen, 1999; J. R. Kirkley, S. E. Kirkley, Myers, Lindsay, & Singer, 2003).

Key attributes of IILEs. With previous message design principles, such as Fleming and Levie's, one finds that the principle posits a relationship between a user's (learner's) perception or experience and a particular structural configuration of the mediated environment, e.g. "attention [user perception] ... is drawn to parts of the message [a structural element] ... that contrasts with other elements [the characteristic of the structural element]." The *Experiential Modes Framework* below proposes a typology for message design principles for the new media. It focuses specifically on games and simulations as examples of these new media.

Experiential Modes Framework (EMF)

Player Experience (PX)

1. *Cognition*—encompassing mental activities in both cognitive and affective domains; e.g. the degree of learning as well as the degree of fun, and the "semiotic meaning" of elements.
2. *Metacognition*—encompassing all that the player is aware of: vision, audio, olfactory, kinesthetic, and haptic senses; plus awareness of time, objects, content or information encountered.
3. *Choice*—encompassing the player's perception of degree of control; access to variables and information during game play.
4. *Action*—encompassing the player's perception that they can do things such as: interact with objects, elements within the game, that they have a degree of control; that they have a degree of mobility to move through the virtual environment; that the control interface allows their psychomotor capabilities to effect change.

Game Structure (GS)

1. *Content*—the story, the context, the amount of information available, the degree of concreteness or abstraction of the content, the authenticity, and their variability
2. *Environment*—identifications of the virtual spaces and boundaries, the objects within these spaces and their functionality capabilities, plus any time limits imposed by the game
3. *Formal Characteristics of the Elements*—descriptions of the fidelity, aesthetics, color and audio attributes, and their dominance relative to other elements
4. *Affordances*—encompassing the abilities made available within the game for the player to change, manipulate, and/or to seek alternatives or information

---

Using this framework one might arrive at a message design principle such as: Interaction [PX-Action] with content [GS-Content] that offers the player multiple options [GS-Affordances] will increase player engagement [PX-Cognition]. Such a framework can be used for developing message design principles for web design, distance education, e-learning, games, simulations, and virtually any IILE.

Instructional Illustrations

A fundamental issue for any study of visual media is a basic theory of picture perception. While there is not a consensus among scholars regarding how images are perceived and used, there are a number of schools of thought that provide frameworks for thinking about and studying these issues. Anglin, Towers, and Levie (1996) provide an overview of theories of picture perception as well as a summary of research on learning from visuals. One of the themes that emerges from this research is that while most people in most cultures recognize objects depicted in pictures (Kennedy, 1994; Sless, 1981), they do not necessarily recognize the meaning intended by the creator of the image. Consistent with the theories of Piaget, some scholars have suggested that young children interpret visual information very literally, and that they may not be developmentally ready to understand abstract concepts or representations included in illustrations (Higgins, 1980; Siegel, 1978 as cited by Cooper, 2002). Furthermore, after analysis of numerous studies on children's uses of visual information, Goldsmith (1984) concluded that emphasis on literal interpretation of visual images could interfere with an individual's ability to generalize to a meaning beyond the specific depiction represented in the given illustration, and that the ability to understand complex visuals is a learned capacity.

Interpretation of visual devices. Elizabeth Boling and her Interface Interest and Research Group (IIRG) have pursued a line of inquiry to discover the extent to which various populations interpret the meaning of simple illustrations including graphical devices consistently with the meaning intended by the designer of the illustrations, and to discover something about how individuals make their interpretations. They found that in some cases images with simple graphical devices in them (e.g., arrows, thought balloons) were interpreted differently from the designer's intention by up to 60% of over 600 viewers in groups that included American elementary school students and adult teachers, and college students in the US, Taiwan and Malaysia (Boling, Sheu, Frick, & Eccarius, 2001; Boling, Smith, Frick, & Sheu, 2003; Boling, Eccarius, Smith, & Frick, 2004; Boling, Smith, Frick, & Eccarius, 2007).

Textbook illustrations. Ongoing studies within IIRG include a survey of the page space devoted to images in textbooks from multiple countries and the interpretation of instructional images in learning contexts, including elementary science classrooms and language learning courses for refugees to the U.S. Results to date indicate that page space devoted to images in science textbooks from elementary through high school range from a low of under 10% in some high school texts to a high of almost 40% in several first grade texts, underscoring the importance of understanding how these images are interpreted (Boling, Smith, Eccarius, & Rowe, 2005; Smith, Rowe, & Boling, 2005).

Instructional Design/Development

During the 1960s educationists at a number of different R&D centers were experimenting with ways of applying systems theory to instructional planning. Some of the well-known early efforts included Silvern's courses and monographs (1963) at University of Southern California and Barson's (1967) Instructional Systems Development project at Michigan State University. Meanwhile, Gene Faris and Richard Stowe were working along similar lines at Indiana University's Audio-Visual Center (AVC), leading to their Faris-Stowe instructional development model (Faris, 1968). By the early 1970s the systems approach had been incorporated into the faculty consulting operations at the AVC and into the IST (known at that time as Educational Media) curriculum. In the mid-1980s the AVC research group turned its attention away from instructional development (ID) models and toward an examination of ID as a social process (Schwen, Leitzman, Misanchuk, Foshay, & Heitland, 1984). More recently, IST research groups have continued along the line of critically examining the underlying theories and paradigms of ID.

Instructional Design for the Web 2.0: Participatory Learning

During his graduate studies under Prof. Michael Striebel at University of Wisconsin in the late 1980s, Curt Bonk became interested in the various instructional theories and design approaches that emphasized the social aspects of learning, a concept that did not have an accepted umbrella label at the time. Then Allan Collins produced a technical report with John Seely Brown and Paul Duguid for Bolt, Beranek, and Newman on situated learning and the culture of learning (Brown, Collins, & Duguid, 1988), advocating an apprenticeship approach to learning. A later version published in the *Educational Researcher* (Brown, Collins, & Duguid, 1989) aroused great interest among instructional theorists.

Others such as John Bransford and his colleagues at Vanderbilt University were investigating the use of video as a way to anchor instruction or situate it in a real world context (Cognition and Technology Group at Vanderbilt [CTGV], 1990, 1991). Still, it was the work by Brown et al. on *situated cognition* that provided the theoretical perspective to pull together many seemingly disparate strands of research and thinking related to learning in a social context. Somewhat ironically, exactly two decades after this work on situated learning, Brown published an article which argues for another new perspective for learning, namely, *participatory learning* (Brown & Adler, 2008). In it, he argues that the World Wide Web has created a culture wherein learners can build, tinker with, share, and remix ideas and content.

In effect, the Web has moved from a platform for browsing information content with to an interactive learning environment in which anyone can contribute or participate using tools such as wikis, online shared video, learner generated podcasts and blogs, online photo albums, and virtual worlds such as Second Life.

Curt Bonk and his research groups are pursuing Brown's call for research on the types of participatory learning which the Web 2.0 can now provide. Some of their most recent projects:

Wikibook and Wikibookians. Explores collaboration and community building in Wikibook projects between students at Indiana University and the University of Houston as well as an internationally developed Wikibook; entails surveying and interviewing those who have coordinated, edited, or contributed to Wikibooks (Bonk, Lee, Kim, & Lin, 2008, March).

YouTube and other online videos. Explores online motivational and collaborative factors in watching and generating YouTube videos; also examines participatory forms of learning and pedagogical activities (Bonk, 2008, March).

Blogging in higher education in Korea and China. Explores decentralization, augmented socialization, and the pros and cons of blogging in Asian higher education.

Synchronous and asynchronous online learning. Studies the role of the instructor in synchronous and asynchronous learning environments and the types of online moderation and interaction; aims to develop guidelines for synchronous instruction.

Delphi study of collaborative learning in blended learning. The team is conducting a Delphi study of computer-supported collaborative learning in blended learning with 20–30 experts who contributed to *Handbook of Blended Learning* (Bonk & Graham, 2006).

Massive Multiplayer Online Gaming (MMOG) and role-playing game. Explores the educational and training potential of role-playing games and MMOGs; aims to map out a research agenda related to MMOG for the Department of Defense.

Instructional Design Theories and Effectiveness

In addition to Brown's concept of participatory learning, other recent instructional design theories have stimulated research work in IST. In 2002 M. David Merrill proposed a synthesis of several extant theories of instruction, which he called "first principles of instruction." Merrill (2002) claimed that "there will be a decrement in learning and performance when a given instructional program or practice violates or fails to implement one or more of these first principles" (p. 44). One of Ted Frick's research groups has been working on ways to test the validity of Merrill's claim.

In a MAPSAT pattern analysis the team found that when students in 89 different college courses agreed that First Principles occurred *and* they also agreed that they experienced Academic Learning Time (ALT), they were 9 times more likely to report mastery of course objectives, in contrast to when both were reported to be absent (Frick, Chadha, Watson, Wang, & Green, in press). ALT refers to frequent successful engagement in tasks and activities related to course objectives. ALT is well-documented in the literature as an important variable that predicts student learning achievement.

Chadha, Frick, Watson, Zlatskovksy, and Green (2008) are currently conducting an empirical study of college student ratings of use of First Principles in their classes, their perceived ALT, and their instructors' independent ratings of student mastery of course objectives. Preliminary results indicate that when students agreed that their instructors used First Principles, those students were nearly 3 times as likely to agree that they experienced ALT in the course. Moreover, students who agreed that they experienced ALT were nearly 4 times as likely to be rated as *high masters* of course objectives by their instructors, compared with students who did *not* agree that they experienced ALT. Conversely, students who did *not* agree that they experienced ALT were about 8 times as likely to be rated as *low masters* of course objectives by their instructors, compared with students who did agree that they experienced ALT.

Further studies planned in this research group include a study of teaching and learning quality in Macedonia, and a validation study where classroom observational measures are compared with student teaching and learning quality ratings.

Instructional Theory for Instructional Design/Development

IST researchers have been prominent in building the instructional theories that underlie instructional systems development (ISD). Charles Reigeluth compiled an early synthesis of instructional-design theories (1983), famously known as "the green book." In it, the developers of those theories summarized the current status of each, and Reigeluth added editor's notes to point out commonalities across them. Those same authors each developed a lesson based on their respective theories, each addressing the same objectives to facilitate comparison of the theories (Reigeluth, 1987). About a decade later Reigeluth developed a companion to "the green book" series (Reigeluth, 1999) whose purpose was to summarize a broad range of theories that constitute a "new paradigm" of instruction that is customized to learners' needs and that addresses a much wider range of human learning and development than had traditionally been considered.

Most recently, Reigeluth has been working with a team on another volume in the series, whose purpose is to establish a common knowledge base for instructional-design theory, including a consistent set of terms (Reigeluth & Carr-Chellman, 2009).

Alternative Design Traditions

A team led by Elizabeth Boling and Barbara Bichelmeyer has been studying the ID models used in educational technology in comparison with the "design traditions" that emanate from fields such as engineering, architecture, graphic design, product design, and software design. They have found conceptual overlaps among these varying design traditions, with ID representing a rather narrow and rigid niche by comparison (Bichelmeyer, Boling, & Gibbons, 2006). They are especially concerned with how design is taught in these different traditions, again finding the teaching of ID to be of questionable scope and rigor, in comparison with other fields. Recently members of Boling's research group have been planning and conducting studies on design thinking and design education, including the use of precedent by expert and experienced designers in several disciplines and development of novice instructional designers as design thinkers in basic ISD courses.

Technology Integration

According to a systemic view of education, the design, development, evaluation, and dissemination of new technology does not constitute a complete process. Hardware, software, and new ways of thinking must be accepted, implemented, and maintained in order to truly become part of the solution. In IST, these activities are subsumed under the umbrella of "technology integration," the focus of a research group led by Thomas Brush, Anne Ottenbreit-Leftwich, and Curt Bonk.

Understanding How Teachers Use Technology

Technology integration, "...the incorporation of technology resources and technology-based practices into the daily routines, work, and management of schools" (Technology in Schools Taskforce, 2003, p. 1), is widely recognized as an essential link in the larger process of K-12 education. Whether teachers integrate technology to enhance students' cognitive and affective development or to help students become better prepared for a global society and economy, effective use of technology has become a critical and expected outcome for students in our schools. Kleiman (2004) proposes that the appropriate uses of technology in K-12 education can "...expand opportunities for students, broaden the information they have available, better connect them with real-world issues and activities, provide them with opportunities for creativity, extend how they communicate and collaborate, and in general, better prepare them for the lives they will lead in the technology-rich 21st century" (p. 248).

The National Educational Technology Plan (U. S. Department of Education, 2004) further supports this notion, detailing the need for students and teachers to become technology savvy in an attempt to maintain an internationally competitive society. Research has indicated that although schools are currently equipped with adequate technological resources, teachers are still not utilizing those resources in their classrooms in a way commensurate with the need (U.S. Department of Education, 2003). The National Educational Technology Plan suggests that "The problem is not necessarily lack of funds, but lack of adequate training and lack of understanding of how computers can be used to enrich the learning experience" (U.S. DOE, 2004, p. 22).

Preparing Future Teachers to Integrate Technology

Concerns about shortcomings in the meaningful integration of technologies within K-12 schools have led stakeholders at the higher education and governmental levels to place greater emphasis on technology skills for in-service and pre-service teachers. For example, the U.S. Department of Education's "Preparing Tomorrow's Teachers to Use Technology" (PT3) program provided grants to teacher education programs to incorporate best practices for preparing teachers to use technology in their classrooms. From its genesis in 1999 until 2003, the PT3 program dedicated over $750 million to projects focusing on new methods for preparing future teachers to effectively integrate technology into their teaching (Pellegrino, Goldman, Bertenthal, & Lawless, 2007).

Although education and government leaders have promoted the need for better preparation of teachers to integrate technology, and extensive funds have been expended to support these efforts, there is little research examining the actual methods used across teacher education institutions to prepare future teachers to use technology, the impact these methods are having on teaching practices in K-12 settings, and the empirical basis for implementing these methods (Hew & Brush, 2007; Pellegrino et al., 2007; Lawless & Pellegrino, 2007). Recently, researchers have called for renewed efforts in exploring both what knowledge should be taught in pre-service teacher education programs with regard to technology, and how to best prepare teachers to effectively use that knowledge to support student learning. To this point, research that has examined these issues has tended to rely heavily on self-reported survey data and tended to examine how technology was incorporated into teacher education programs at only a superficial "course" level. Finally, there are few detailed cross-institutional studies available that can provide more generalizable implications regarding how to best prepare prospective teachers to effectively use technology.

The technology integration research group focuses on addressing the knowledge gap regarding how teacher education programs prepare teachers to integrate technology into their teaching. They examine experiences related to technology integration included in pre-service teacher education programs and the impact these experiences have on teaching practices in K-12 classrooms. They are currently partnering with the Granato Group in Washington DC on a major research project funded by the U.S. Department of Education's Office of Educational Technology. The first phase is an overall assessment of the extent to which technologies are being used in American schools. A later phase involves a national study of how teacher preparation programs instruct future teachers on how to best integrate technology for enhanced student learning.

Systemic Change in Education

Advocates of a systems perspective contend that incremental improvements in education systems, such as just adding new media to old classroom structures, seldom lead to dramatically better results. They contend that formal education could be far more efficient, effective, and satisfying if it were designed and managed as a total system, with its interdependent parts aligned according to the goals of the system and educational needs of its communities (See von Bertalanffy, 1968; Banathy, 1968).

Systemic Transformation of Public Education

One of the IST research groups is focused on systemic transformation of public education, in the sense of a fundamental paradigm change. The current paradigm of education was developed for the educational needs and conditions of the Industrial Age and is inadequate for the very different educational needs and conditions of the Information Age. Using systems theory as a guide, Charles Reigeluth and his team have documented that the predominant form of work has changed from manual labor to knowledge work, requiring that many more students be educated to much higher levels and that they be prepared to be lifelong learners, problem solvers, critical thinkers, and team players.

The team also uses systems theory to identify some of the major differences in features for an Information-Age paradigm of education compared to the Industrial-Age paradigm: customization rather than standardization, initiative rather than compliance, diversity rather than uniformity, collaborative relationships rather than adversarial, attainment-based progress rather than time-based, criterion-based assessment rather than norm-based, and a learning-focused system rather than sorting-focused system (Reigeluth, 1992).

However, paradigm change is far more difficult and time-consuming than piecemeal reform, requiring understanding of the systemic change process itself. Thus, the team has been working to advance both descriptive theory (complex causal dynamics) and design theory (means to accomplish desired ends) to help school districts engage in successful paradigm change. Theory building began in the early 1990s (Reigeluth, 1993, 1995), leading to a set of guiding principles: the Guidance System for Transforming Education (GSTE) (Jenlink, Reigeluth, Carr, & Nelson, 1998).

After working with several schools in Indiana, the researchers realized that the school district must be the unit of change, not the individual school, due to strong systemic interrelationships between schools and their district. Thus, in 2001 they began facilitating a district-wide systemic transformation effort in an Indianapolis-area school district, both using and conducting research on the GSTE. Between 2003 and 2006 the group integrated some of the work of Prof. Francis Duffy of Gallaudet University in the GSTE, and in 2006 the group began collaborating with

Duffy to merge their theories into the School System Transformation (SST) Protocol (Duffy & Reigeluth, 2008).

In their work with the school district, the Systemic Change research team has completed seven research studies to improve the SST Protocol (for example, Joseph, 2006; Joseph & Reigeluth, 2005; Lee & Reigeluth, 2007; Pascoe, 2008; Richter & Reigeluth, 2006; Watson & Reigeluth, in press), and has produced an additional 16 conceptual publications about various aspects of this theory (for example, Joseph & Reigeluth, in press; Reigeluth, 2008; Reigeluth, Carr-Chellman, Beabout, & Watson, 2007; Reigeluth & Stinson, 2007a, 2007b, 2007c, 2007d; S. L. Watson, W. R. Watson, & Reigeluth, 2008), with more in progress.

This research group is currently working on a rapid prototyping process to be incorporated into the SST Protocol. The group is dedicated to advancing knowledge about this and other approaches for making the systemic transformation process quicker, easier, and less painful for all people involved.

Simulating Education Systems

Another research group is using systems theory as a foundation for developing computer simulations to teach systems thinking. Axiomatic Theories of Intentional Systems (ATIS), developed by Thompson (2005a, 2005b), has been important for both designing simulations of education systems and for measuring systemic change (MAPSAT, described below). A research group led by Ted Frick has designed and tested a prototype board game called Simulation Game on Technology Integration in Education (*SimTIE*). Under development is a simulation called *SimEd Math: Modeling Differentiated Instruction in Mathematics. SimEd Math* and *SimTIE* give preservice teachers the opportunity to select learning activities in a simulated classroom and to experience the consequences of those decisions. Preservice teachers learn to think systemically in order to be successful in the simulations. They must also understand instructional theory to select student learning activities that are most likely to succeed with students in their simulated classroom, based on those students' profiles. To ultimately succeed in the simulation, teachers are challenged to utilize available resources to best individualize instruction that maximizes student learning of mathematics.

Research Methodologies for Systems Issues

The systems perspective demands a different set of inquiry tools than traditional educational research. MAPSAT (Map & Analyze Patterns & Structures Across Time) is a new set of relation mapping and analysis methods. MAPSAT contains two methodologies: Analysis of Patterns in Time (APT) and Analysis of Patterns in Configuration (APC). APT detects *temporal* relations that linear statistical models cannot, nor can Bayesian networks. APC measures *structural* properties that are determined from axiomatic theory, unlike social network analysis (SNA). APC can measure hypergraphs of multiple affect-relation sets, setting it apart from other forms of network analysis. Both APT and APC have mathematical foundations in graph theory.

Traditional quantitative research methods that are based on algebraic linear models typically yield separate measures of variables, and then researchers statistically analyze relations among measures. That is, they *relate measures*. Alternatively, they could *measure relations* directly. This is not a play on words, but a significant conceptual shift in thinking about research problems and how we collect and analyze data. Frick (1990) invented a procedure called Analysis of Patterns in Time (APT) in order to map temporal relations. Phenomena are observed and coded with categories in classifications. The resulting temporal maps are then queried for temporal sequences of events. The queries are specifications of temporal relations, and the results of such queries then indicate the relative frequency and duration of such observed phenomena. In a study of academic learning time of elementary school children, Frick (1990) found that if interactive instruction was occurring, the likelihood of student engagement was very high (*APTprob* = 0.97). However, when non-interactive instruction was occurring, then students were engaged much less (*APTprob* = 0.57). Regression analysis of the same data was only able to predict 32% of the variance in student engagement.

Thompson's (2008) ATIS Graph Theory provides us a way to measure 17 structural properties of systems, including: compactness, centrality, complexity, flexibility, interdependence, strongness, vulnerability and wholeness. This approach is called Analysis of Patterns in Configurations (APC). A recent study of a Montessori classroom indicated that some structural properties were markedly different in two different types of learning settings: head problems and morning work period. In the latter, for example, there was much more interdependence with respect to affect-relation sets for choice of learning activities and guidance of learning (Koh & Frick, 2007).

Change Management and Human Performance Technology (HPT)

Change Management

In the 1970s vision of IST the "systems design and management" curriculum area embodied the notion that human performance depends very much on arrangements made at the level of the whole organization. New instructional products, new training interventions, and new motivational campaigns would be effective only insofar as they were aligned with and supported by the organization's overall policies and practices. These insights continue to be part of IST's core curriculum, under the heading of "change management."

Theories supporting change management. In addition to systems theory, theories from psychology have contributed to the change management perspective. Festinger's theory of cognitive dissonance (1957) analyzes the distressing mental state that arises when people find that their beliefs are inconsistent with their actions and the deep-seated need to reduce cognitive dissonance by changing either their actions or their beliefs. In organizations, people need to understand how their actions affect the organization and to believe that it is worthwhile for them to participate in change efforts.

The most wide reaching theoretical contribution comes from the work of B. F. Skinner (1969) and a generation of adherents of reinforcement theory who successfully extended his theories into social psychology and economics. Organizational development is based on the principle that reporting structures, operational processes, and measurement procedures—setting targets, measuring performance, and granting financial and non-financial rewards—must be consistent with the behavior that people are asked to carry out. When an organization's goals for new behavior are reinforced, members are more likely to adopt it consistently.

The sort of behavioral change that is of greatest direct interest to educational technologists is that of accepting and using technological innovations. The psychological processes of how people come to accept or reject new ideas have been explored over four decades by Everett Rogers (1962, 1995, 2003). Rogers considers the main elements in the diffusion of new ideas to be: "(1) an innovation, (2) which is communicated through certain channels, (3) over time, (4) among the members of a social system" (1995, p. 35). He pioneered in analyzing case study data to discern a pattern in the individual's innovation-decision process, finding that an individual passes through the stages of knowledge, persuasion, decision, implementation, and confirmation (1995, p. 36). He also found that individuals played different roles vis-à-vis the spread of innovations—formal leaders, opinion leaders, gatekeepers, and so on. This understanding can enlighten change management work by arranging activities that assist people in moving from earlier to later stages of acceptance, and targeting different people to play different roles in the unfolding drama.

Rogers' theories of diffusion of innovations provided a major theoretical foundation for the "diffusion and adoption" curriculum emphasis area begun at Indiana in 1969. Rogers' and others' theories of change management have continued to inspire R&D activity in IST.

IST research and development in change management. To study the application of Rogers' theory, Ted Frick led a group of students to develop an interactive Web version the *Diffusion Simulation Game (DSG)*, based on the original board version created by Michael Molenda and Patricia Young in the 1970s. In this simulation game users practice applying the strategies derived from diffusion theory, allowing researchers to analyze the efficacy of different strategies. Approximately 3,000 students at Indiana University have played the *DSG* since it went online in 2002. Due to popular demand, a limited version of the *DSG* was made available to the general public in late 2006. Since then, the *DSG* has been played over 4,000 times worldwide at www.indiana.edu/~istdemo. The number of requests for licenses for the full version of the *DSG* has been increasing for use in business and education settings.

Human Performance Technology

A label that overlaps considerably with "change management" but has its own history and theory base is "human performance technology" (HPT). This construct evolved in the mid-1970s out of the work of instructional developers in corporate training, initially guided primarily by B. F. Skinner's (1969) theories of learning. Joe Harless (1973) found that even after well designed and executed training programs trainees sometimes stopped using the knowledge, skills, or attitudes they supposedly had mastered. In response, he developed a hypothesis that performance was affected by several factors other than learned skills, especially by being given appropriate incentives and tools. Underlying this insight is Kurt Lewin's "field theory" (1951), which proposes that human behavior is a function of both a person's activity and the environment in which the activity takes place. In one of the seminal works of HPT, Tom Gilbert (1978) adds "management" to Lewin's formula, suggesting that the focus should be on the "worth" of activities people perform in organizations.

Thus the concept of HPT is broader than educational technology; it includes educational interventions and also all other sorts of performance improvement interventions, such as incentive programs and provision of better tools. In that sense, it falls outside the conventional boundaries of the department. However, HPT is treated as a *related* concept, one that is highly interconnected with instructional technology when it comes to application in the workplace. Therefore it occupies a substantial place in the curriculum and research agenda of IST.

A research group that includes Barbara Bichelmeyer and James Pershing, recently joined by professors Ray Haynes and Yonjoo Cho, has been involved in a range of R&D activities related to change management and HPT. All, through consulting relationships or other work experiences, have investigated problems of workplace performance in Fortune 500 companies and similar organizations. Bichelmeyer, for example, recently evaluated HPT activities at the Centers for Disease Control and Prevention, after carrying out similar evaluations at Procter & Gamble, Sprint, and the U.S. Coast Guard, among other client organizations. She and fellow research team members recently completed a four-year evaluation study for Cisco Systems (Dennis et al., 2007).

Further, Bichelmeyer and Horvitz (2006) have proposed a conceptual framework, building on the insights of Lewin and Harless, that allows both practitioners and researchers to develop theory-based approaches by using logic models for the design, implementation and evaluation of human performance technology interventions.

Haynes has analyzed business process reengineering within Fortune 500 corporations nationally. He recently applied change management principles and collaboratively developed a competency model to guide the selection, assessment, development, and performance of K-12 principals in the state of Kentucky. Additionally, he recently developed a methodology for evaluating organizational mentoring and succession management programs using the Strategic Collaboration Model (Haynes & Ghosh, 2008).

Meanwhile, Yonjoo Cho previously analyzed, developed, and evaluated numerous performance interventions while serving as senior researcher in the Division of Human Resource Development (HRD) for Korea Telecom (Cho, Park, & Wager, 1999). She is currently engaged in a research project focused on a comparative study of HRD practices in the IT industry in South Korea and India (Cho & McLean, 2008).

Pershing collaborated over a ten-year period with training and HRD managers at the LG Group of Korea to develop and test a model to guide performance improvement interventions, including the design of instruction—the Strategic Impact Model (Molenda & Pershing, 2004). This model-building continued, culminating in another model, the Pershing Performance Improvement Process (Pershing, 2006, p. 15).

Pershing's research team is currently conducting survey research among HPT experts on the status of and future trends in HPT as part of a larger national project to develop an exemplary curriculum and research agenda for HPT (Pershing, Lee, & Cheng, 2008a, and in press). In two related projects, (1) they surveyed HPT professionals to validate the performance standards established for Certified Performance Technologist (Hale & Pershing, 2008), and (2) they are replicating an earlier study of professional practices and compensation among members of a leading HPT association (Pershing, Cheng, & Foong, 2006, August).

Conclusion

Individually and in teams, faculty and students in IST at Indiana University have been engaged in a wide range of research and development projects stimulated by an array of theoretical and conceptual frameworks. "Systems thinking" provides a conceptual framework for the whole enterprise, but under that umbrella specific programs of research are guided by a number of different theories. Prominent among them are: behaviorist and cognitivist theories of learning and instruction, Gestalt and symbol-systems theories of visual perception, general-systems theory, diffusion of innovations theory, and social-psychological theories of organizational behavior. These theories have generated an abundance of questions, the pursuit of which has led to numerous advances in theory and practice. Through activities such as these, IST intends to maintain its traditional leadership position in building the theoretical structures and the knowledge base in educational technology.

References

Anglin, G. K., Towers, R. L., & Levie, W. H. (1996). Visual message design and learning: The role of static and dynamic illustrations. In D. H. Jonassen (Ed.), *Handbook of research for educational communications and technology* (pp. 755–794). New York: Macmillan Library Reference USA.

Appelman, R. (2005). Designing experiential modes: A key focus for immersive learning environments. *TechTrends, 49*(3), 64–74.

Appelman, R. L. (2007, September). *Experiential modes of game play.* Paper presented at the Digital Games Research Association (DiGRA), Tokyo, Japan.

Appelman, R. L. (2008, February). *The challenges of interdisciplinary pedagogy.* Paper presented at the Game Developers Conference, San Francisco, CA.

Banathy, B. (1968). *Instructional systems.* Palo Alto, CA: Fearon.

Barab, S., Thomas, M., Dodge, T., Carteaux, R., & Tuzun, H. (2005). Making learning fun: Quest Atlantis, a game without guns. *Educational Technology Research & Development 53*(1), 86–107.

Barson, J. (1967). *Instructional systems development, a demonstration and evaluation project.* U.S. Office of Education, Title II-B project OE 3-16-025. E. Lansing, MI: Michigan State University.

Bichelmeyer, B., Boling, E., & Gibbons, A. S. (2006). Instructional design and technology models: Their impact on research and teaching in instructional design and technology. In M. Orey, V. J. McClendon, & R. M. Branch (Eds.), *Educational media and technology yearbook* 2006 (Vol. 31). Westport, CT: Libraries Unlimited.

Bichelmeyer, B., & Horvitz, B. (2006). Comprehensive performance evaluation: Using logic models to develop a theory-based approach for evaluation of human performance technology interventions. In J. A. Pershing (Ed.), *Handbook of human performance technology* (3rd ed., pp. 1165–1189). San Francisco, CA: Pfeiffer.

Boling, E., Eccarius, M., Smith, K., & Frick, T. (2004). Instructional illustrations: Intended meanings and learner interpretations. *Journal of Visual Literacy, 24*(2), 185–204.

Boling, E., Sheu, F.-R., Frick, T., & Eccarius, M. (2001). *Perceived meanings relative to intended meanings of common graphical elements in instructional illustrations: U.S. and Taiwanese college students compared.* Paper presented at the 2nd Annual IST Conference at Indiana University, Bloomington, IN, March 22, 2001.

Boling, E., Smith, K., Eccarius, M., & Rowe, D. (2005, October). *Illustrations in textbooks and the classroom: Textbook content and teacher's perspectives.* Paper presented at annual convention of Association for Educational Communications and Technology, Orlando, FL.

Boling, E., Smith, K., Frick, T. & Eccarius, M. (2007). *Graphical devices in instructional illustrations: Designers' intentions and viewers' interpretations.* Paper presented at the annual meeting of the American Educational Research Association, Chicago, IL.

Boling, E., Smith, K., Frick, T., & Sheu, F. (2003). *Visual representations to support learning: Effectiveness of graphical elements used to extend the meaning of instructional illustrations.* Paper presented at Association for Educational Communications and Technology (AECT) annual convention, Anaheim, CA.

Bonk, C. J. (2008, March). *YouTube anchors and enders: The use of shared online video content as a macrocontext for learning.* Paper presented at the American Educational Research Association (AERA) 2008 Annual Meeting, New York, NY.

Bonk, C. J., & Graham, C. R. (Eds.). (2006). *Handbook of blended learning: Global perspectives, local designs.* San Francisco, CA: Pfeiffer Publishing.

Bonk, C. J., Lee, M., Kim, N., & Lin, G. (2008, March). *The tensions of transformation in cross-institutional wikibook projects: Looking back twenty years to today.* Paper presented at the American Educational Research Association annual convention, New York, NY.

Brown, J. S., & Adler, R. P. (2008, January/February). Minds on fire: Open education, the long tail, and learning 2.0. *EDUCAUSE Review, 43*(1), 16–32. Retrieved February 23, 2008, from connect.educause.edu/Library/EDUCAUSE+Review/MindsonFireOpenEducation/45823

Brown, J. S., Collins, A., & Duguid, P. (1988). *Cognitive apprenticeship, situated cognition, and social interaction* (Technical Report No. 6886). Bolt, Beranek, and Newman, Inc.

Brown, J. S., Collins, A., & Duguid, P. (1989). Situated cognition and the culture of learning. *Educational Researcher, 18*(1), 32–41.

Chadha, R., Frick, T., Watson, C., Zlatskovksy, E., & Green, P. (2008). *Improving course evaluation to improve instruction.* Presentation at the 8th Annual IST Conference, Bloomington, IN, February 29, 2008.

Cho, Y., & McLean, G. (2008, February). *A comparative study of IT firms' HR practices in South Korea and India*. Paper presented at Academy of Human Resource Development (AHRD) International Research Conference, Panama City, Florida.

Cho, Y., Park, H. Y., & Wager, S. (1999, May). Training in a changing Korea. *Training & Development, 53*, 98–99.

Cognition and Technology Group at Vanderbilt. (1990). Anchored instruction and its relationship to situated cognition. *Educational Researcher, 19*(6), 2–10.

Cognition and Technology Group at Vanderbilt. (1991). Technology and the design of generative learning environments. *Educational Technology, 31*(5), 34–40.

Cooper, L. Z. (2002). Consideration in cross-cultural use of visual information with children for whom English is a second language. *Journal of Visual Literacy, 22*(2), 129–142.

de Vreede, G.-J., Verbraeck, A., & van Eijck, D. T. T. (2003). Integrating the conceptualization and simulation of business processes: A modeling method and arena template. *SIMULATION, 79*(1), 43–55.

Dennis, A., Duffy, T., Bichelmeyer, B., Cakir, H., Oncu, S., Paul, K., & Bunnage, J. C. (2007). *Success of the CCNA program: Six-month follow-up* (White Paper WP 07-01). Bloomington, IN: Kelley Executive Partners, Indiana University.

Duffy, F. M., & Reigeluth, C. M. (2008). The school system transformation (SST) protocol. *Educational Technology, 48*(4), 41–49.

Faris, G. (1968, November). Would you believe. . .an instructional developer? *Audiovisual Instruction, 13*(9), 971–973.

Festinger, L. (1957). *A theory of cognitive dissonance*. Stanford, CA: Stanford University Press.

Fleming, M. (1967) Classification and analysis of instructional illustrations. *AV Communication Review, 15*(3), 246–248.

Fleming, M., & Levie, W. H. (1978). *Instructional message design: Principles from the behavioral sciences*. Englewood Cliffs, NJ: Educational Technology Publications.

Fleming, M., & Levie, W. H. (1993). *Instructional message design: Principles from the behavioral sciences* (2nd ed.). Englewood Cliffs, NJ: Educational Technology Publications.

Frick, T. (1990). Analysis of patterns in time (APT): A method of recording and quantifying temporal relations in education. *American Educational Research Journal, 27*(1), 180–204.

Frick, T., Chadha, R., Watson, C., Wang, Y., Green, P. (in press). College student perceptions of teaching and learning quality. *Educational Technology Research and Development*.

Garris, R., Ahlers, R., & Driskell, J. E. (2002). Games, motivation, and learning: A research and practice model. *Simulation & Gaming, 33*(4), 441–467(427).

Gilbert, T. F. (1978). *Human competence: Engineering worthy performance*. New York: McGraw-Hill.

Goldsmith, E. (1984). *Research into illustration: An approach and a review*. New York: Cambridge University Press.

Hale, J., & Pershing, J. A. (2008). *Certified Performance Technologist (CPT): Setting the standard*. Paper presented at annual conference of International Society for Performance Improvement, New York, NY.

Hannafin, M. J., & Hill, J. R. (2005). Epistemology and the design of learning environments. In R. Reiser & J. Dempsey (Eds.), *Trends and Issues in Instructional Technology*. Upper Saddle River, NJ: Prentice Hall.

Harless, J. (1973). An analysis of front-end analysis. *Improving Human Performance, 2*, 229–244.

Haynes, R. K., & Ghosh, R. (2008). Mentoring and succession management: An evaluative approach to the strategic collaboration model. *Review of Business, 28*(2), 3–12.

Heinich, R. (1965). *The systems engineering of education II: Application of systems thinking to instruction*. Los Angeles: School of Education, University of Southern California.

Hew, K., & Brush, T. (2007). Integrating technology into K-12 teaching and learning: Current knowledge gaps and recommendations for future research. *Educational Technology Research and Development, 55*(3), 223–252.

Jenlink, P. M., Reigeluth, C. M., Carr, A. A., & Nelson, L. M. (1998). Guidelines for facilitating systemic change in school districts. *Systems Research and Behavioral Science, 15*(3), 217–233.

Jonassen, D. (1999). Designing constructivist learning environments. In C. M. Reigeluth (Ed.), *Instructional-design theories and models* (Vol. II). Hillsdale, NJ: L. Erlbaum.

Joseph, R. (2006). The excluded stakeholder: In search of student voice in the systemic change process. *Educational Technology, 46*(2), 34–38.

Joseph, R., & Reigeluth, C. M. (2005). Formative research on an early stage of the systemic change process in a small urban school system. *British Journal of Educational Technology, 36*(6), 937–956.

Joseph, R., & Reigeluth, C. M. (in press). The systemic change process: A conceptual framework. *Journal of Educational Change.*

Kennedy, J. M. (1994). Picture perception. In T. Sebeok & J. Umiker-Sebeok (Eds.), *Advances in visual semiotics: The semiotic web* (pp. 185–215). Berlin and New York: Mouton de Gruyter.

Klabbers, J. H. G. (2000). Learning as acquisition and learning as interaction. *Simulation & Gaming, 31*(3), 380–406(327).

Kleiman, G. M. (2004). Myths and realities about technology in K-12 schools: Five years later. *Contemporary Issues in Technology and Teacher Education, 4*, 248–253.

Kirkley, J. R., Kirkley, S. E., Myers, T. E., Lindsay, N., & Singer, M. J. (2003). *Problem-based embedded training: An instructional methodology for embedded training using mixed and virtual reality technologies.* Paper presented at the Interservice/Industry Training, Simulation, and Education Conference (I/ITSEC) 2003, Orlando, FL.

Koh, J., & Frick, T. (2007). Measuring system structural properties of autonomy-support in a Montessori classroom. *Proceedings of the Association for Educational Communication and Technology,* Anaheim, CA. Available online at: www.indiana.edu/~tedfrick/montessori_AECT2007_proceedings_koh_frick.pdf

Lawless, K. A., & Pellegrino, J. W. (2007). Professional development in integrating technology into teaching and learning: Knowns, unknowns, and ways to pursue better questions and answers. *Review of Educational Research, 77*(4), 575–614.

Lee, S. K., & Reigeluth, C. M. (2007). Community involvement in Decatur's Journey toward Excellence. In F. M. Duffy & P. Chance (Eds.), *Strategic communication during whole system change: Advice and guidance for school district leaders and PR specialists.* Lanham, MD: Rowman & Littlefield Education.

Levie, W. H. (1978). A prospectus for instructional research on visual literacy. *Educational Communication and Technology Journal, 26*, 25–36.

Lewin, K. (1951). *Field theory in social science: Selected theoretical papers.* D. Cartwright (Ed.). New York: Harper & Row.

Merrill, M. D. (2002). First principles of instruction. *Educational Technology Research & Development, 50*(3), 43–59.

Misanchuk, E. R., Schwier, R. A., & Boling, E. (1999). *Visual design for instructional multimedia.* Paper presented at ED-MEDIA World Conference on Educational Multimedia, Hypermedia and Telecommunications, Seattle, Washington.

Molenda, M., & Pershing, J.A. (2004, March, April). The strategic impact model: An integrative approach to performance improvement and instructional systems design. *TechTrends, 48*(2), 26–32.

Mood, A. (1964, April). *Some problems inherent in the development of a systems approach to instruction.* Paper presented at Conference on New Dimensions for Research in Educational Media Implied by the Systems Approach to Education, Syracuse University, Syracuse, NY.

Pascoe, S. M. (2008). *Factors influencing attendance for a leadership team in a school district.* Unpublished doctoral dissertation, Indiana University, Bloomington.

Pellegrino, J., Goldman, S., Bertenthal, M., & Lawless, K. (2007). Teacher education and technology: Initial results from the "what works and why" project. *Yearbook of the National Society for the Study of Education, 106*(2), 52–86.

Pershing, J. A. (2006). Human performance technology fundamentals. In J. A. Pershing (Ed.), *Handbook of human performance technology* (3rd ed., pp. 5–34). San Francisco: Pfeiffer.

Pershing, J. A., Cheng, J., & Foong, K. P. (2006, August). International society for performance improvement professional practices survey: A report. *Performance Improvement, 45*(7), 39–49.

Pershing, J. A., Lee, J.-E., & Cheng, J. L. (2008a). Current status, future trends, and issues in Human Performance Technology, Part 1: Influential domains, current status, and recognition of HPT. *Performance Improvement, 47*(1), 9–17.

Pershing, J. A., Lee, J.-E., & Cheng, J. L. (2008b). Current status, future trends, and issues in Human Performance Technology, Part 2: Models, influential disciplines, and research and development. *Performance Improvement 47*(2), 7–15.

Reigeluth, C. M. (1983). *Instructional-design theories and models: An overview of their current status.* Hillsdale, NJ: Lawrence Erlbaum Associates.

Reigeluth, C. M. (Ed.). (1987). *Instructional theories in action: Lessons illustrating selected theories and models.* Hillsdale, NJ: L. Erlbaum Associates.

Reigeluth, C. M. (1992). The imperative for systemic change. *Educational Technology, 32*(11), 9–13.

Reigeluth, C. M. (1993). Principles of educational systems design. *International Journal of Educational Research, 19*(2), 117–131.

Reigeluth, C. M. (1995). A conversation on guidelines for the process of facilitating systemic change in education. *Systems Practice,* 8(3), 315–328.

Reigeluth, C. M. (Ed.). (1999). *Instructional-design theories and models: A new paradigm of instructional theory* (Vol. II). Mahwah, NJ: Lawrence Erlbaum Associates.

Reigeluth, C. M. (2008). Chaos theory and the sciences of complexity: Foundations for transforming education. In B. Despres (Ed.), *Systems thinkers in action: A field guide for effective change leadership in education.* New York: Rowman & Littlefield.

Reigeluth, C. M., & Carr-Chellman, A. A. (Eds.). (2009). *Instructional-design theories and models: Building a common knowledge base.* New York: Routledge.

Reigeluth, C. M., Carr-Chellman, A. A., Beabout, B., & Watson, W. R. (2007). Creating shared visions of the future for K-12 education: A systemic transformation process for a learner-centered paradigm. *The Journal of Educational Alternatives, 2*(3), 34–66.

Reigeluth, C. M., & Schwartz, E. (1989). An instructional theory for the design of computer-based simulations. *Journal of Computer-Based Instruction, 16*(1), 1–10.

Reigeluth, C. M., & Stinson, D. (2007a). The Decatur story: Reinvention of a school corporation – Collaboration: Developing partners in education. *The Indiana School Boards Association Journal, 53*(3), 13–15.

Reigeluth, C. M., & Stinson, D. (2007b). The Decatur story: Reinvention of a school corporation – Culture and climate: The personality of school governance. *The Indiana School Boards Association Journal, 53*(4), 11–13.

Reigeluth, C. M., & Stinson, D. (2007c). The Decatur story: Reinvention of a school corporation – Leadership and empowerment in Decatur's school transformation. *The Indiana School Boards Association Journal, 53*(2), 13–15.

Reigeluth, C. M., & Stinson, D. (2007d). Mission and values for Decatur's school transformation. *The Indiana School Boards Association Journal, 53*(1), 17–19.

Richter, K. B., & Reigeluth, C. M. (2006). A systemic change experience in Decatur Township. *TechTrends, 50*(2), 35–36.

Rogers, E. M. (1962). *Diffusion of innovations.* New York: The Free Press of Glencoe.

Rogers, E. M. (1995). *Diffusion of innovations* (4th ed.). New York: The Free Press.

Rogers, E. M. (2003). *Diffusion of innovations* (5th ed.). New York: The Free Press.

Schwen, T. S., Leitzman, D. F., Misanchuk, E. R., Foshay, W. R., & Heitland, K. M. (1984). Instructional development: The social implications of technical interventions. In R. K. Bass & C. R. Dills (Eds.), *Instructional development: State of the art, II* (pp. 40–50). Dubuque: IA: Kendall/Hunt.

Silvern, L. C. (1963). *Systems engineering in the educational environment.* Hawthorne, CA: Northrop Norair Division of the Northrop Corp.

Skinner, B. F. (1969). *Contingencies of reinforcement: A theoretical analysis.* New York: Appleton-Century-Crofts.

Sless, D. (1981). *Learning and visual communication.* New York: Halstead Press.

Smith, K., Rowe, D., & Boling, E. (2005, October). *Images and instruction: How do learners interpret what they see?* Paper presented at annual conference of International Visual Literacy Association, Orlando, FL.

Squire, K., & Barab, S. (2004). Replaying history: Engaging urban underserved students in learning world history through computer simulation games, *Proceedings of the 6th International Conference on Learning Sciences* (pp. 505–512). June 22–26, 2004, Santa Monica, CA.

Technology in Schools Task Force. (2003). *Suggestions, tools, and guidelines for assessing technology in elementary and secondary education.* Retrieved February 20, 2008, from the National Center for Education Statistics Web site: nces.ed.gov/pubs2003/tech_schools/chapter7.asp

Thompson, K. R. (2005a). "General system" defined for A-GSBT. *Scientific Inquiry Journal, 7*(1), 1–12. Retrieved July 4, 2007, from www.iigss.net/Scientific-Inquiry/THOMPSON-1.pdf

Thompson, K. R. (2005b). Axiomatic theories of intentional systems: Methodology of theory construction. *Scientific Inquiry Journal, 7*(1), 13–24. Retrieved July 4, 2007, from www.iigss.net/Scientific-Inquiry/THOMPSON-2.pdf

Thompson, K. R. (2008). *ATIS graph theory.* Columbus, OH: System-Predictive Technologies. Retrieved April 15, 2007, from www.indiana.edu/~aptfrick/reports/11ATISgraphtheory.pdf

U.S. Department of Education. (2003). *Federal funding for educational technology and how it is used in the classroom: A summary of findings from the Integrated Studies of Educational Technology.* Office of the Under Secretary, Policy and Program Studies Service: Washington, D.C. Retrieved April 30, 2006, from www.ed.gov/about/offices/list/os/technology/evaluation.html

U. S. Department of Education. (2004). *Toward a new golden age in American education: How the internet, the law and today's students are revolutionizing expectations.* Office of Educational Technology: Washington, DC.

von Bertalanffy, L. (1968). *General system theory: Foundation, development, applications.* New York: George Braziller.

Watson, S. L., & Reigeluth, C. M. (in press). Community members' participation in a school district wide systemic transformation effort 'Journey Toward Excellence'. *Journal of Organisational Transformation and Social Change.*

Watson, S. L., Watson, W. R., & Reigeluth, C. M. (2008). Systems design for change in education and training. In J. M. Spector, M. D. Merrill, J. J. G. van Merrienboer, & M. P. Driscoll (Eds.), *Handbook of research on educational communications and technology* (3rd ed.). New York: Routledge.

Zimmermann, K., Gregory, M., & Appelman, R. (2007). *Game play analysis: Bounty Hunter. VX Lab: Game play analysis research, 9.* Bloomington, IN: Indiana University, Instructional Systems Technology department. Retrieved April 14, 2008, from www.indiana.edu/~games/GPA_reports.html

Linking Theory and Practice Through Design: An Instructional Technology Program

Priscilla Norton, Shahron Williams van Rooij, Marci Kinas Jerome, Kevin Clark, Michael Behrmann, and Brenda Bannan-Ritland

Abstract   In the College of Education and Human Development at George Mason University, we have created three independent strands or tracks—each with its own mission, its own target population, and its own connections and collaborations with external organizations and institutions. Track 1 is the Instructional Design and Development (IDD) track, serving those with educational interests primarily in government, military, business, and higher education. Track 2 is the Integrating Technology in Schools (ITS) tract, serving public and private school teachers and school divisions. Track 3 is the Assistive Technology (AT) track, serving those with disabilities in public schools and local, state, and federal agencies. Even though these tracks appear to be three unique programs, we have found a unifying center in the field of design. This paper explores the concept of design as it can be applied to understanding the teaching/learning enterprise regardless of context, goal, and audience. It then discusses how this concept informs curriculum and processes in each track.

Keywords Instructional technology · Graduate education · Design · e-Learning · Technology integration · Assistive technology

Introduction

Programs in instructional technology are interesting outliers in academia. First, they are relatively new. They are not part of the centuries old academic tradition of philosophy, literature, or mathematics but rather newer 20th and 21st century programs. Second, informed by a myriad of academic disciplines, instructional technology programs frequently struggle with identity issues as these they are often confused with information technology and the like. Articulating its identity as a distinct discipline,

P. Norton (✉)

College of Education and Human Development, George Mason University, Fairfax, VA 22030

e-mail: pnorton@gmu.edu

M. Orey et al. (eds.), *Educational Media and Technology Yearbook,*
DOI 10.1007/978-0-387-09675-9_4, © Springer Science+Business Media, LLC 2009

given that it is grounded in systems theory, communication theory, educational theory and practice as well as current technology, it is challenging for instructional technology to "find its place" in academe. Third, who is instructional technology's target audience? Candidates include such organizations as government, military, business, higher education, K-12 public schools, and social services agencies. The problems and responsibilities faced by educators who serve learners within each of these environments may be more different than they are alike. Fourth, when an instructional technology program is part of a school or college of education, it remains unclear with whom the program should be most closely aligned - adult education, elementary and secondary education, educational foundations, or educational leadership—to name a few. Finding its "place" in academia remains a challenge for many instructional/educational technology programs.

In the College of Education and Human Development at George Mason University, we have been part of and influenced by all of these debates. Early on, we answered the challenge by creating three independent strands or tracks—each with its own mission, its own target population, and its own connections and collaborations with external organizations and institutions. Track 1 became the Instructional Design and Development (IDD) track, serving those with educational interests primarily in government, military, business, and higher education. Track 2 became the Integrating Technology in Schools (ITS) tract, serving public and private school teachers and school divisions with an eye to the K-12 learner. Track 3 became the Assistive Technology (AT) track, serving those who work on behalf of individuals with disabilities in public schools and local, state, and federal agencies. For most of our history, we coexisted as related yet parallel and distinct domains, uncomfortably accepting the absence of a unifying core.

What might unify an academic program in instructional technology? One way to define an academic program is to view it as a confederation of faculty, courses, requirements, and students. In this case, unity derives from routines and policies. Another is to understand instructional technology as an attempt to bring insights to a central question: how can technology be used to solve educational problems? Perhaps a center might be found in a focus on a particular application—e-learning or hypermedia, for instance. The unifying focus then becomes mastery and study of educational artifacts in general or in particular. Alternately, a conceptual center might be discovered in a particular model (e.g., ADDIE) or a particular philosophical perspective (e.g., constructivism). Each of these perspectives offers possibilities and focus to a disparate program, yet each limits the others in unacceptable ways.

Design as a Unifying Concept

Anything that is not naturally occurring is in some way designed. If the principles that guided the design are robust, flexible, grounded in theory and practice, articulated, and reusable, the design has applicability and usability and presents a positive solution to a problem. The union of a design process and design principles can support a course of study, research, and learning. Not all educational problems may be solved with the same design process since there is a relationship between process and product with each informing the other. Similarly, design principles are not universal as each educational problem has its own unique audience, goal, and context. Yet each educational solution ought to be the result of a thoughtful design process and set of principles that inform that process. The field of design—its decision-making processes, its varied principles, and its study—can frame the teaching/learning enterprise regardless of context, goal, and audience.

Design has been defined as the generation of an idea and the process of giving "form, structure and function to that idea" (Nelson & Stolterman, 2003, p. 1). The process of design includes locating relevant information, structuring a problem, inducing creative insight, proposing a solution, and evaluating that solution (Lawson, 2004). Using the primary lens of the design process rather than theoretical perspective provides insight into how decisions are made and factors that may impact the complex, ill-structured, and human act of design.

Those involved in the act of design including professionals in architecture, engineering, computer, product design, learning sciences design, instructional design disciplines, among others seem to agree that design is a complex, yet practical journey. Design is often referred to as selection of tradeoffs in decision-making, where the constraints are continually changing and need to be considered and reconsidered in relation to the overall problem and proposed solution (Preece, Rogers, & Sharp, 2002). In studies of architects' work, design is described as an act that closely integrates analysis or understanding of the applied problem with synthesis or generation of a solution (Lawson, 2004). Architects engaged in design continually generate new goals and redefine constraints throughout the process. These descriptions illustrate the challenges and complexity as well as the integration of pragmatic, dynamic, and generative processes of design.

As a program, we have found that the demands inherent in the act of design exceed those described by a traditional focus on systematic design procedures and push us toward other perspectives on this complex process. For instance, Doblin (1987) characterized the design process as consisting of a current, beginning state, followed by a design process which contains analysis, genesis, and synthesis activities and finally culminates in a different state. These states dynamically change and evolve as decisions are made and design paths are selected and may require different forms of decision-making and evaluation at different points in the process. These states can be described as different "problem states" that engender interpretive, evaluative, or analytical processes and then prompt corresponding "design moves."

The act of design can also be viewed as a balance between the tensions of the theoretical and the practical. Nelson and Stolterman (2003) discuss this tension in distinguishing between reactive and proactive stances in design by "'finding meaning' in things that happen and 'making meaning' by causing things to happen" (p. 49). Designers are tasked with the dual challenge of attempting to make meaning through deliberately causing things to happen through the act of design and development while also trying to find meaning in analyzing the consequences of that action to generate knowledge about teaching and learning.

As we have come to understand the complexities of learning, we have come to understand that our students will not be challenged by "tame" problems—those problems with a clear mission, one best solution, and easy and accurate determination of when the problem is solved. Instead, today's educational dilemmas and the nature of learning in classrooms and other complex situations resonate more with the need to solve "wicked" problems—those problems that can be characterized as cyclical, complicated, contentious, and—at times, even destructive (Rittel & Webber, 1973). Helping educators in each of our tracks bring knowledge of the design process and design principles to bear on the solution to these "wicked" problems unifies our program.

Thus, regardless of track, students learn to consider the characteristics of their learners, the demands of their contexts, the complexities of learning goals and outcomes, and the ways in which learning resources and tools can be leveraged—all in the service of designing solutions to today's educational problems. They learn to attend to design as a process informed by principles. They learn not "what" to do but "how" to do it. They learn to study teaching and learning designs not only to judge their outcomes but to derive principles that inform their practice and illuminate and/or contribute to theory.

Design Embedded in Three Domains of Inquiry

Track 1: Instructional Design and Development (IDD)

The IDD track of the instructional technology program provides the knowledge and skills to craft effective solutions to instructional and performance challenges including the design and development of technology-based solution systems and learning environments using the latest educational technologies and design processes. Graduates of this track are prepared to assume instructional design responsibilities in public, private, government, and educational contexts. Program options include a part-time Master's degree program, a full-time Master's degree program (Immersion), a doctoral emphasis, and an e-learning certificate.

Immersion Program. Track 1 IDD implements and teaches design through a theoretical framework based on action learning and project-based instructional design experiences (Bannan-Ritland, 2001). This approach to design is implemented through courses and is best exemplified by our full-time, one-year intensive Master's program called Immersion. The nature of the Immersion program requires a new and distinct model of teaching involving the investigation and exploration of content, theory, and process related to the project at hand. Teaching in this "just-in-time" fashion can involve various methods of instruction including lecture, discussion, collaborative group activities, and guest experts as well as student-initiated presentations and contributions. This instructional approach is supported by an electronic infrastructure that provides Web-based resources often created by students as well as instructors in order to complement and reinforce teaching or project management activities.

The Immersion program modifies the traditional instructional design process of analysis, design, development, implementation, and evaluation to reflect an applied, theory-to-practice approach. The Immersion program incorporates, constructs, and processes from instructional design, usage-centered design, usability, and performance-centered design as well as other fields. The program experience includes the following stages: performance analysis; usage-centered design that includes the development of role models, use cases, and interface content models; wire frame modeling; and prototyping. If we characterize the Immersion method in terms of the traditional instructional design model, the analysis is accomplished in the performance analysis stage, design is accomplished in the usage-centered design stage, development is accomplished in the creation of the wire frame model and the prototype, and the evaluation process is similar to traditional instructional design models.

The Immersion program is designed to allow students the opportunity to participate in an authentic, project-based guided instructional design experience. Given that knowledge and application are different levels of learning, the program allows students to assimilate, utilize, and practice their instructional design knowledge in an applied context. Additionally, in this type of experience, other required skills become apparent such as a team-based orientation, clear communication, and negotiation skills. The Immersion program allows students to practice and explore necessary skills of practitioners as well as integrate and internalize instructional design processes.

At the center of our approach is the concept of usage-centered design. Usage-centered design is founded on a set of basic guidelines to assist designers in making reasonable decisions and developing usable systems (Constantine & Lockwood, 1999). Usage-centered design includes the development of role models, task models, and content models in a streamlined but systematic approach that closely aligns to the genuine needs of users. Role models focus on the relationship between the user and the system. Task models are representations of the tasks that users will need to accomplish. Content models focus on the tools and materials supplied by the user interface.

Usage-centered design uses abstract models to solve concrete problems by allowing the designer to focus their attention on the larger picture rather than on the details. According to Muller et al. (1995), abstract user interface models facilitate bifocal modeling, which helps designers move between a panoramic overview and close-in, detailed views of designs. Case models are an essential part of usage-centered design that help the designer solve problems in a technology-free, idealized, abstract manner. By using this approach, designers can construct models that are free of limitations or restrictive assumptions. This results in design models that are more flexible, robust, and accommodating to changing technologies. Additionally, the use of case models enables the design of better user interfaces by identifying and representing the essential aspects of the user's requirements and their relationship to the system. In usage-centered design, the user interface is constructed by examining how all of the interface components integrate into a complete system that is understandable to the user.

e-Learning Certificate. The e-learning certificate program is designed to prepare e-learning practitioners to apply the appropriate technologies to solve instructional problems in educational, corporate, government agency, or community settings. Program participants include (a) trainers and consultants, (b) instructional and Web designers, (c) faculty and faculty support staff interested in e-learning, and (d) e-learning program developers and related support staff. To be successful with these audiences, an e-learning program must marry instructional design with the appropriate use of technologies, so that e-learning professionals can create a positive learning experience in their chosen career environments. The strength of our e-learning certificate program lies in its solid foundation in research-based research-validated instructional design principles that generate e-learning by design.

With the evolution of the knowledge-based economy and increasing globalization comes the need to acquire new knowledge and skills in an efficient and timely manner. e-Learning—instruction delivered via electronic means that are dependent on computer networks operating through a variety of channels and technologies (Wentling et al., 2000; Moore, 2003; Zhang, Zhao, Zhou, & Nunamaker, 2004)—provides opportunities for the personalized, flexible learning essential to a well-educated, well-trained workforce. The core of e-learning is learning, irrespective of the specific technologies, and requires a solid grounding in design. Learning results from applying sound instructional strategies and designing with the right instructional methods regardless of how the lesson will be delivered (Clark & Mayer, 2003; Song, Singleton, Hill, & Koh, 2004). In building on processes that are research-based and validated in a body of literature, our e-learning certificate program models a framework that is credible to researchers, educators, and policy-makers (McCombs & Vakili, 2005).

Essential to a well-designed e-learning program is the ability to offer a variety of opportunities for learners to obtain a design team experience similar to what they will encounter in the world of work. That experience includes not only the acquisition of a strong knowledge base but also the application of diverse social, communication, and cooperation skills that today's employers expect (McLoughlin & Luca, 2002). The ability to work in teams and to communicate effectively in visual, written, and oral form is deemed an essential competency by the International Board of Standards for Training, Performance, and Instruction (IBSTPI, 2000). This is particularly important when design team members are dispersed across multiple locations and are meeting—whether regularly or occasionally—in a virtual environment.

Our e-learning graduate certificate program models the virtual team experience by including virtual team projects as one of its instructional methods. Project-based learning with virtual teams not only assists with knowledge generation and application but also helps learners acquire the special skills, including an understanding of human dynamics across functional and cultural boundaries, necessary to lead and work in virtual teams in many organizations (Duarte & Tennant Snyder, 2001).

Track 2: Integrating Technology in Schools (ITS)

The ITS track provides the knowledge and skills needed to effectively integrate technology with the teaching/learning process. The focus of this program is on the K-12 learning environment. The ITS track prepares teachers to assume leadership roles in implementing, supervising, managing, and integrating technology resources in schools. Graduates of this track frequently become the local expert and change agent for technology in schools. Track 2 includes a course of study structured by the cohort process. Groups of twenty-four students are selected each year and study together for five consecutive semesters. Track 2 also offers a doctoral emphasis, a 15-hour online certificate focusing on specific tools and their integration with K-12 learning, a 15-hour online certificate focusing on teaching virtual high school students, and a Master's cohort that prepares students to design and teach in virtual high school environments. Similar design processes and guiding design principles are taught throughout all the options.

There is some controversy and a great deal of discussion these days about the role of the K-12 classroom teacher. Some refer to a teacher as a "sage on the stage." Others would describe the role of a teacher as a "director." More recently, alternative descriptors of the K-12 educator's role have emerged. A teacher is a facilitator; a teacher is a coach; a teacher is a cognitive mentor. These descriptors reflect the notion that students, not the teacher, are the locus of the learning act. This suggests that as learners what students need is a "guide on the side"—a provocateur and support system.

There is, however, a much more fundamental but less discussed role: The teacher as designer. The teacher as designer recognizes the centrality of planning, structuring, provisioning, and orchestrating learning. While the role of designer may be the least observed or recognized teacher role, the intellectual analysis of content filtered through an understanding of learning and learners and the subsequent construction of learning opportunities for students underpins all robust and worthwhile K-12 learning opportunities.

While it is possible for teachers to rely on the learning designs of others—the textbook publisher, the instructional materials provider, or the lesson plan idea book, only teachers know their particular community of learners, the unique personalities of their learners, and the context and requirements of their context. Only the classroom teacher understands the conditions of their classroom, the prior experiences and content-related comprehension of both teacher and students, the group dynamics of a particular group of learners, and the resources available for teaching and learning.

Thus, teachers are and ought to be designers. And they must come to understand that they are designers and learn theories and principles that guide their ability to create designs that promote opportunities to learn. Their ability to design focuses on the ways in which they learn to craft answers to six guiding questions: (a) What foundations of learning do today's students most need to learn? (b) What activities should designers choose to ensure that students become actively engaged in learning through construction? (c) What contents, ideas, and/or concepts afford a context for student learning? (d) What tools might a designer choose to best support and enhance student learning? (e) What systems of assessment might a designer construct to appropriately assess student learning? (f) How might learning environments be constructed to complement the overall learning design?

With these questions as guides, an educator can begin the dynamic process of designing opportunities for students to learn. The Track 2 program focuses on the mastery of several design processes and related design principles as well as the conditions under which each is likely to be appropriate. Unlike some instructional design settings, the work of a K-12 educator must keep an eye not only on learners but on the learning that came before and the learning that is to come after. Today's teachers are charged with designing opportunities to learn a broad and long history of cultural understanding, a specific and targeted set of skills, and generalizable habits of mind. Local and state mandates highlight specific content objectives such as understanding the Civil War or reading text with a certain level of comprehension while broader social institutions demand life-long learning habits and intellectual competencies that transfer among contents (i.e., Partnership for 21st Century Skills, 2008). Design for the K-12 teacher is simultaneously specific to a grade level and generalizable to future work and local, national, and global citizenship.

In the domain of global goals for K-12 learners, Track 2 teachers learn to design opportunities for K-12 learners that promote problem-solving, information using, community participation, knowledge, and literacy as they meet content standards established by local, state, and professional organizations. They learn to create designs for learning that promote the language of thinking, thinking dispositions, mental management, higher order knowledge, transfer of knowledge, and a strategic spirit (Tishman, Perkins, & Jay, 1994). Students learn the difference between information getting and having and information using. They learn to include searching, sorting, creating, and communicating in their designs (Norton & Sprague, 2001). Teachers learn to design opportunities for learning that teach learners about being part of a community through cooperation, collaboration, democratic principles, and virtual learning (Norton & Wiburg, 2003). Teachers learn to create opportunities for learning that focus on the structures and processes inherent in disciplinary knowledge (Bruner, 1960). Teachers learn that literacy is "the power to encode and decode meaning through any of the forms that humans use to represent what they have come to know" (Eisner, 1994, p. xii) and to include multiple symbolic forms within their designs for learning.

In the domain of affordances and uses of a range of technologies, Track 2 teachers study a broad range of technology tools not so much for how they work but for what they bring to the teaching/learning process and how they structure information and thinking. For instance, they study principles of layout and design—contrast, repetition, alignment, and proximity (Williams, 2008)—in order to teach their students to use and create desktop publishing documents and web pages. Teachers learn to choose and assign graphic representations based on their purpose—decorate, represent, organize, explain, or transform (Levin, 1989)—in order to design learning opportunities that capitalize on graphics programs, web graphics, and print graphics. Teachers learn to guide the construction of meaning in a range of environments by structuring learning designs and student activities using DEAPR—design, encode, assemble, publish, and revise (Norton & Wiburg, 2003)—in order to design lessons that allow their students to structure knowledge and communicate meaning with word processors, hypermedia programs, podcasts, or videos.

Teachers learn ACTS (Norton & Sprague, 2001) and FACTS (Norton & Wiburg, 2003) as design processes for creating lessons and units respectively. Much of what teachers are asked to teach has little relevance to their students, and often, neither teachers nor students are clear on why they are charged with teaching or learning specific content or skills. Teachers must learn to design in ways that bring relevance to learning. Track 2 teachers learn to design learning opportunities for their students that anchor instruction in authentic problems—that situate learning in the context of its use (Brown, Collins, & Duguid, 1989). They learn to link authentic problems with clear outcomes and to embed in their learning designs lessons that empower young learners to become designers themselves. Track 2 teachers learn to design opportunities for student learning that weave together intellectual competence, authentic, background building, constructing and sharing activities, and content mastery as they select and provide the best tools for learning.

Track 3: Assistive Technology (AT)

The AT track provides a tiered approach for individuals interested in the area of applying assistive technology to help individuals with various disabilities and across all ages with ways to adapt or accommodate to the functional limitations that the disability imposes upon them. The program offers an undergraduate minor, a graduate certificate, a Master's degree, and a doctorate.

The certificate and minor programs are designed to provide practical training to apply AT solutions at school, work, home, or community settings. Enrollees in the programs include (a) general and special educators, (b) related service personnel, (c) instructional and web designers, (d) rehabilitation counselors, (e) adult service providers, and (f) family and care givers who work with various individuals with disabilities.

The focus of the Master's degree program is on developing specialists in AT with knowledge and skills in assessment, collaboration, and training as well as the fundamentals of assistive technology devices and services provided in the certificate. Graduates of this track are prepared to incorporate technology in schools and various workplace environments as educators, related service providers, AT consultants, hardware/software and web designers, and school-based technology coordinators. Students at the doctoral level focus on research, policy, and leadership in AT in higher education, public agency, and school administrative positions.

The program philosophy reflects the goals of three major pieces of federal legislation. The Technology Related Assistance Act of 1988 (now the Assistive Technology Act of 1998 and 2004) provided definitions of assistive technology devices (improve, maintain, or increase functional skills) and services (assessment, acquisition, maintenance, funding, etc.) that have been incorporated into the Americans with Disabilities Act of 1990 (ADA) as well as the Individuals with Disabilities in Education Act (IDEA) of 1990 (now the Individuals with Disabilities in Education Improvement Act of 2004). As a result of these laws, individuals with disabilities are guaranteed either a free appropriate public education in the least restrictive environment or, as adults, a "reasonable accommodation" for their disability. Under IDEA, services—including assistive technology—are mandatory for individuals who have disabilities that have an adverse effect on their education. Under the ADA, adults have the right not to be discriminated against but are only "eligible for services" and must be their own advocates and ask for support services.

The AT track at George Mason University embodies several overarching principles/philosophies: (a) social justice and inclusion, based in civil rights, and (b) universal design and universal design for learning to enhance accessibility. Fundamental to the program is the belief that all individuals have the capability to learn and use technology to increase, maintain, or improve their functional skills and empower their lives. We also believe that they have the rights to use assistive technologies to access their living, learning, working, and recreational activities and that those environments should be constructed using the principles of universal design or universal design for learning.

Universal design (UD) was initially used in architecture to reference accessible building design that could benefit all individuals such as automatic door openers and curb cuts. Universal design is the "design of products and environments to be usable by all people, to the greatest extent possible, without the need for adaptation or specialized design" (The Center for Universal Design, 1997, p. 1).

Universal design for learning (UDL) expands the concept of universal design in architecture to the field of education. UDL stresses the development of general education curricula that are conceived, designed, developed and validated to achieve results for the widest spectrum of students, including those with disabilities, without the need for subsequent adaptation or specialized design (Hitchcock & Stahl, 2003).

The AT program addresses these underlying principles throughout the curriculum; however, there is varying emphasis on different elements within specific courses. The minor and certificate courses are designed to ensure that the program provides breadth of knowledge of characteristics and needs of persons with disabilities from birth to death, matching those needs to available technology. Initially, we focus on teaching our students to understand the needs of individuals with disabilities through specific applications of AT. However, we also begin to provide a broad understanding across disabilities of commonalities and differences in functional and learning needs with the intent of finding the "universal" solutions to meeting as many of the common needs of individuals with varied disabilities in single products (often Web based), thus minimizing the need to provide highly customized assistive technology devices and services to individuals.

The principles of UD and UDL are specifically taught in different classes, most directly in EDSE 610: Designing Adaptive Environments. This capstone course provides an overview of environmental adaptations for people with disabilities to increase their access to community, workplace, and school activities. The course also covers legal issues within the ADA for adapting environments and addresses programmatic and physical access issues. The culminating project for the class is to research, develop, and present an adaptation plan for an environment of a real client. At the Master's level, Web accessibility (which utilizes a systematic application of principles of UDL) is another major emphasis area. In that course, students experience the issues related to addressing federal 508 compliance standards, experiencing disabilities through simulation and developing web sites that are accessible to individuals with varying disabilities.

Our Master's and doctoral students are constantly challenged with the principles of access through UD and UDL as well as AT and the need to constantly evaluate and adapt. Following principles of UD and UDL, the products, environments, and curricula they develop or use should allow for the broadest use up front, thus minimizing the need for specialized adaptation whether technological or not. However, we can never fully remove that barrier as individuals will always have specific needs (Hitchcock & Stahl, 2003). We must keep in mind that those individuals have the right to have us strive to provide the necessary accommodations to enable them to be the most productive members of our society that they can be. With that, we have strived to develop a comprehensive program that educates practitioners, users, specialists, and leaders whose goal is to provide AT services to individuals with various disabilities across the spectrum of ages and environments, helping them to increase, maintain or improve their functional skills.

Conclusion

Our instructional technology programs are graduate programs and, thus, our students are generally practicing professionals in military, government, higher education, or business contexts, in public and private K-12 schools, or with social service agencies. They are familiar with how their organizations operate, with the general routines and practices associated with their context, and with professional expectations. What unites them and brings them to our instructional technology programs is the drive to use technology to solve educational problems. By linking theory and practice with design, our goal is to ensure that our graduates are able to connect rigorous design processes and principles with carefully and wisely chosen technologies. Armed with this know how, they are prepared to serve as educational problem-solvers and decision-makers in their respective professions.

References

Americans with Disabilities Act of 1990, 42 U.S.C. § 12101 *et seq*. Retrieved May 10, 2008, from http://uscode.house.gov/download/pls/42C126.txt

Assistive Technology Act of 2004, 29 U.S.C. §3001 *et seq*. Retrieved May 10, 2008, from http://frwebgate.access.gpo.gov/cgibin/getdoc.cgi?dbname=108_cong_public_laws&docid=f:publ364.108

Bannan-Ritland, B. (2001). Teaching instructional design: An action learning approach. *Performance and Improvement Quarterly, 14*(2), 37–52.

Brown, J. S., Collins, A., & Duguid, P. (1989). Situated cognition and the culture of learning. *Educational Researcher, 18*, 32–41.

Bruner, J. (1960). *The process of education.* Cambridge, MA: Harvard University Press.

The Center for Universal Design. (1997). *The principles of universal design, version 2.0.* Raleigh, NC: North Carolina State University.

Clark, R., & Mayer, R. (2003). *E-learning and the science of instruction: Proven guidelines for consumers and designers of multimedia learning.* San Francisco: Pfeiffer.

Constantine, L., & Lockwood, L. (1999). *Software use: A practical guide to the models and methods of usage-centered design.* New York: ACM Press.

Doblin, J. (1987). A short, grandiose theory of design. *STA Design Journal, Analysis and Intuition,* 6–16. Chicago: Society of Typographic Arts.

Duarte, D., & Tennant Snyder, N. (2001). *Mastering virtual teams* (2nd ed.). San Francisco: Jossey-Bass.

Eisner, E. W. (1994). *Cognition and curriculum re-considered.* New York: Teachers College Press.

Hitchcock, C., & Stahl, S. (2003). Assistive technology, universal design, universal design for learning: Improved opportunities. *Journal of Special Education Technology, 18*(4), 45–52.

Individuals with Disabilities Education Improvement Act of 2004, 20 U.S.C. §1400 *et seq.* Retrieved May 10, 2008, from http://frwebgate.access.gpo.gov/cgi-bin/getdoc.cgi?dbname=108_cong_public_laws&docid=f:publ446.108

International Board of Standards for Training, Performance and Instruction (IBSTPI). (2000). *Instructional design competencies.* Retrieved January 5, 2007, from http://www.ibstpi.org/competencies.htm

Lawson, B. (2004). *What designers know.* Burlington, MA: Architectural Press.

Levin, J. R. (1989). A transfer-appropriate-processing perspective of pictures in prose. In H. Mandl & J. R. Levin (Eds)., *Knowledge acquisition from text and pictures* (pp. 83–100). Amsterdam: Elsevier.

McCombs, B., & Vakili, D. (2005). A learner-centered framework for e-learning. *Teachers College Record, 107*(8), 1582–1600.

McLoughlin, C., & Luca, J. (2002). A learner-centered approach to developing team skills through web-based learning and assessment. *British Journal of Educational Technology, 33*(5), 571–582.

Moore, M. G. (2003). This book in brief: Overview. In M. Moore & W. Anderson (Eds.), *Handbook of distance education* (pp. xiii–xxii). Mahwah, NJ: Lawrence Erlbaum Associates, Inc.

Muller, M., Tudor, L. G., Wildman, D. M., White, E. A., Root, R. W., Dayton, T., et al. (1995). Bifocal tools for scenarios and representations in participatory activities with users. In J. M. Carroll (Ed.), *Scenario-based design.* New York: Wiley.

Nelson, H. G., & Stolterman, E. (2003). *The design way: Intentional change in an unpredictable world, foundations and fundamentals of design competence.* Englewood Cliffs, NJ: Educational Technology Publications.

Norton, P., & Sprague, D. (2001). *Technology for teaching.* Needham, MA: Allyn & Bacon.

Norton, P., & Wiburg, K. (2003). *Teaching with technology* (2nd ed.). Belmont, CA: Wadsworth Publishing.

Partnership for 21st Century Skills. (2008). *Framework for 21st century learning.* Retrieved May 11, 2008, from http://www.21stcenturyskills.org/documents/frameworkflyer_072307.pdf

Preece, J., Rogers, Y., & Sharp, H. (2002). *Interaction design.* New York: Wiley.

Rittel, H. W. J., & Webber, M. M. (1973). Dilemmas in a general theory of planning. *Policy Sciences, 4*, 155–169.

Song, L., Singleton, E., Hill, J., & Koh, M. (2004). Online learning: Student perceptions of meaningful and challenging characteristics. *The Internet and Higher Education, 7*(1), 59–70.

Tishman, S., Perkins, D., & Jay, E. (1994). *The thinking classroom: Learning and teaching in a culture of thinking.* New York: Allyn & Bacon.

Wentling, T. L., Waight, C., Gallaher, J., La Fleur, J., Wang, C., & Kanfer, A. (2000). *e-learning: A review of the literature*. Research report of the Knowledge and Learning Systems Group, National Center for Supercomputing Applications. Retrieved April 7, 2008, from http://learning.ncsa.uiuc.edu/Publications.html.

Williams, R. (2008). *The non-designers design book* (3rd ed.). Berkeley, CA: Peachpit Press.

Zhang, D., Zhao, J., Zhou, L., & Nunamaker, J. (2004). Can e-learning replace classroom learning? *Communications of the ACM, 47*(5), 75–79.

Model-Based Methods for Assessment, Learning, and Instruction: Innovative Educational Technology at Florida State University

Valerie J. Shute, Allan C. Jeong, J. Michael Spector, Norbert M. Seel, and Tristan E. Johnson

Abstract   In this chapter, we describe our research and development efforts relating to eliciting, representing, and analyzing how individuals and small groups conceptualize complex problems. The methods described herein have all been developed and are in various states of being validated. In addition, the methods we describe have been automated and most have been integrated in an online model-based set of tools called HIMATT (Highly Interactive Model-based Assessment Tools and Technologies; available for research purposes at http://himatt.ezw.uni-freiburg.de/cgi-bin/hrun/himatt.pl and soon to be available on a server at Florida State University). HIMATT continues to expand in terms of the tools and technologies included. Our methods and tools represent an approach to learning and instruction that is now embedded in many of the graduate courses at Florida State University and also at the University of Freiburg. We call our approach model-based because it integrates representations of mental models and internal cognitive processes with tools that are used to (a) assess progress of learning, and (b) provide the basis for informative and reflective feedback during instruction.

Keywords   Belief networks · Causal diagrams · Cognitive modeling · Concept mapping · Mental models · Model-based assessment · Technology-based assessment

Introduction

> Knowledge is no longer an immobile solid; it has been liquefied. It is actively moving in all the currents of society itself (Dewey, 1915, p. 25).

This quote by John Dewey nearly 100 years ago is particularly relevant now. That is, in our increasingly technological society, understanding the ebb and flow of

V.J. Shute (✉)
Instructional Systems Program, Educational Psychology and Learning Systems Department, College of Education, Florida State University, Tallahassee, FL 32306, USA
e-mail: vshute@fsu.edu

M. Orey et al. (eds.), *Educational Media and Technology Yearbook*,
DOI 10.1007/978-0-387-09675-9_5, © Springer Science+Business Media, LLC 2009

mental models, and figuring out how to help people develop and hone good mental models—alone and in collaboration with others—are important goals with potentially large educational and economic benefits (e.g., Seel, 1999a; Shute & Zapata-Rivera, 2008; Spector, Dennen, & Koszalka, 2006).

Mental models have been researched extensively over the past several decades, and have been implicated in many phenomena that are fundamental parts of human cognition, such as the ability to reason—inductively and deductively—about complex physical and social systems, to generate predictions about the world, and to form causal explanations for what happens around us (e.g., Gentner & Stevens, 1983). As part of the Instructional Systems program at FSU, we have been building on the theoretical and empirical foundations of mental model research. Currently, we're using a model-based approach to design and develop innovative educational technologies to (a) represent mental models (i.e., externalized constructions of internalized structures), (b) analyze their changes over time, and (c) create instructional interventions to support learning. We have also been developing tools to aggregate mental model representations, compare those representations, and identify the reasons for change. We call our approach model-based because it integrates representations of mental models and internal cognitive processes with tools that are used to assess progress of learning, and provide the basis for informative and reflective feedback during instruction.

This chapter focuses on the role of internal representations (i.e., mental models) in interpreting experience and making sense of things. While internal representations are not available for direct and immediate observation, we accept the general notion that the quality of internal representations is closely associated with the quality of learning. So, to help instructional designers and educational technologists improve support for learning, we have devised a theoretical foundation and a collection of tools to facilitate assessment and to provide personalized, reflective, and meaningful feedback to learners, particularly in relation to complex and challenging problem-solving domains.

We first review the foundations of our model-based approach to assessment, learning, and instruction. Then we discuss a variety of tools and technologies that we have been developing and validating in a number of different problem-solving domains. We expect these tools and technologies to evolve and perhaps be replaced with other tools and technologies. We also expect that the underlying foundations will evolve as scientists learn more about specific human learning mechanisms. However, in the near-term we believe that a model-based approach to learning and instruction supported by the kinds of tools described here are important for progress in educational technology research.

Foundations of Our Model-Based Approach

Our model-based research and development rests on two foundations: (1) mental models research and systems thinking (*internal* constructs and processes), and (2) concept maps and belief networks (*external* representations and entities). We aim to assess the quality of the former via aspects of the latter.

Internal Constructs: Mental Models and Systems Thinking

As philosophers have long argued, we create internal representations of things that we experience. The most direct statement of this capability can be found in Wittgenstein's Tractatus Logico-Philosophicus: *"We make to ourselves pictures of facts"* (Wittgenstein, 1922; for an online version, see http://www.kfs.org/~jonathan/witt/tlph.html). Psychologists have expanded and elaborated this notion of internal representations in the last several decades to include the key constructs of mental models and schema. Because these internal constructions are vital to how people come to make sense of and learn about the world, we place particular emphasis on such internal representations as the basis for developing proper support for learning.

What is the nature of these internal constructs? We each hold many different beliefs about the world based on our unique experiences, and we can conceive of these beliefs as structures or networks of concepts (nodes) and their relationships (links). Some beliefs may be more accurate than others, depending on the existence and quality of the underlying evidence. Some beliefs may be more or less firmly held, depending on the strength of the links. As educators, we would like to be able to make valid inferences about what a person knows and believes. Beliefs are not fixed and unchanging. [1] Instead, belief structures or mental models: (a) are incomplete and constantly evolving; (b) may contain errors, misconceptions, and contradictions; (c) may provide simplified explanations of complex phenomena; and (d) often contain implicit measures of uncertainty about their validity that allow them to used even if incorrect (e.g., Ifenthaler & Seel, 2005; Seel, 2003). So knowledge and beliefs can change, but seldom randomly—there are typically triggering events that provide the impetus for change. We will explore this in more detail later when we describe our tools that model evolving belief networks, and attempt to identify the basis for change.

Mental models also play a key role in qualitative reasoning. For example, Greeno (1989) argued that model-based reasoning in specific situations (e.g., physics, economics, and so on) occurs when an individual interacts with the objects involved in a situation in order to manipulate them mentally so that the cognitive operations simulate (in the sense of thought experiments) specific transformations of these objects which may occur in real-life situations. In line with symbolic models of cognition, it is widely recognized that the construction of mental models necessarily presupposes the use and manipulation of signs (used as index, icon, or symbol) to the extent that mental models are used to organize the symbols of experience and thinking to achieve a systematic representation of this thinking as a means of understanding and explanation (Seel & Winn, 1997; Seel, 1999a). Accordingly, in cognitive and educational psychology, mental models are considered *qualitative mental representations which are developed by individuals (or groups) on the basis of their available world knowledge (or beliefs) aiming at solving problems or acquiring competence in a specific domain.*

---

[1] To illustrate, your belief that *Pluto is a planet* likely changed in 2006 when the International Astronomical Union decided to re-classify Pluto as a "dwarf planet."

In short, mental models are cognitive artifacts; that is to say they are inventions of the mind that represent, organize, and restructure a person's knowledge and beliefs in such a way that even complex phenomena of the (observable or imagined) world become plausible. For our purposes, complex phenomena include social, technological, and natural systems, whereby a system is understood as a designed entity (designed by humans or by nature) that maintains its existence and functions as a whole through the dynamic interaction of its parts. A system's interdependent parts form a unified whole, driven by a purpose; and the various parts generally attempt to maintain stability or equilibrium through feedback (examples of such systems include human respiration, energy consumption in a hybrid vehicle, and the caucus system to determine U.S. presidential nominations). The ability to understand and reason about such complex systems is often called *systems thinking* and has been identified as an essential skill for the 21st century (Federation of Scientists, 2006). The International Board of Standards for Training, Performance and Instruction also regards systems thinking as a fundamental skill (see http://www.ibstpi.org).

External Entities: Concept Maps, Causal Models, and Belief Networks

As we mentioned earlier, our high-level goal is to infer the quality of presumed internal constructs and processes (mental models and systems thinking) via valid techniques that seek to externalize internal, invisible structures. This task is made simpler because humans have developed an amazing ability to talk about (or otherwise represent) their private, internal representations (thoughts, feelings, beliefs). Discourse is a vital component of most learning experiences, and Wittgenstein (1953) recognized the criticality of discourse in his later work, referring to this ability as engaging in what he termed *language games*. A language game is specific to a group of people who share a common purpose or enterprise. A language game is context specific as well as specific to a community of speakers. Key aspects of a language game include a common vocabulary, a set of accepted conventions and rules, and sets of expected statements and responses. This notion is relevant to our focus on assessing learning in complex domains. That is, what people say and how they relate various aspects of a problem situation are indicative of their understanding. Examining these external representations, then, provides evidence of the nature and quality of the internal representations that are the basis for action. These external representations come in (and can be shaped into) various forms including concept maps, causal models, and belief networks.

A *concept map* is a diagram showing the relationships among concepts. Concepts are connected with labeled arrows, often in a hierarchical structure. The relationship between concepts is specified via linking phrases, such as, "results in," "is required by," or "is part of." Concept mapping is the term used for visualizing the relationships among different concepts. Concept maps are frequently used to examine and assess learners' understanding of complex domains and their progress towards increased understanding (e.g., Spector & Koszalka, 2004). However, many of the current studies on concept maps focus on well-defined problems (Freeman & Urbaczewski, 2001; Ruiz-Primo & Shavelson, 1996) and are restricted to a closed format where concepts are provided by the evaluator (Zele, 2004). This closed format, while making it easy to score, provides little insight into the actual process of learning, or more specifically, the cognitive processes underlying the changes learners make to their concept maps. To examine the underlying processes of concept mapping, researchers can provide learners with the opportunity to create and annotate nodes and links in their concept maps (Alpert, 2003), yielding richer and more accurate maps (Spector et al., 2006). These annotated maps enable researchers to access, study, and determine some of the cognitive processes that underlie, trigger, and explain changes (both good and bad) in learners' mental models.

A *causal model* is like a concept map, only instead of allowing any type of link between nodes or concepts, it uses cause and effect logic to describe the behavior of a system. In traditional causal modeling, a network of variables is developed and the causal relationships between variables are explicitly delineated. It is a model in which the variables of interest (the dependent variable or variables) are related to various explanatory variables (or causal variables) based on a specified theory.

A *belief network* is a probabilistic graphical model that represents a set of variables and their probabilistic independencies. This goes beyond causal models (e.g., "*A causes B*") in that belief networks allow for the specification of degree or level of relationships (e.g., "*If A occurs, that will strongly influence B*"). Belief networks are in line with our goal of wanting to represent individuals' understanding of complex phenomena (e.g., systems thinking), and encompass a wide range of different but related techniques which deal with reasoning under uncertainty. Both quantitative (mainly using Bayesian probabilistic methods) and qualitative techniques can be used to interpret belief networks. Our approach involves representing a learner's (or group of learners') current set of beliefs about a topic by overlaying Bayesian networks (Pearl, 1988) on top of students' causal maps. Again, this allows us to model and to question the degree to which relationships among concepts/nodes hold as well as the *strength* of the relationships. In addition, prior probabilities can be used to represent preconceived beliefs. A probabilistic network provides us with a richer set of modeling tools that we can use to represent the degree to which people ascribe to a particular belief structure (for more, see Shute & Zapata-Rivera, 2008).

Figure 1 illustrates a simplified example of the progression from concepts, to causal maps, to belief nets when Bayesian networks are overlaid to specify structure, node size, and links (i.e., type, directionality, and strength of association). Furthermore, evidence can be attached to each node-relationship which either supports or counters a given claim.

The *size* of the node in the belief network indicates a given node's marginal probability (e.g., p(node 1 = True) = 0.55—a medium node with a slightly better-than-average probability of being true). *Links* illustrate the perceived relationships among the nodes in terms of *type, direction,* and *strength. Type* refers to the probabilistic or deterministic representation—defining the nature of the relationship (in this case, causes). The *strength* of the relationship is shown by the thickness of the

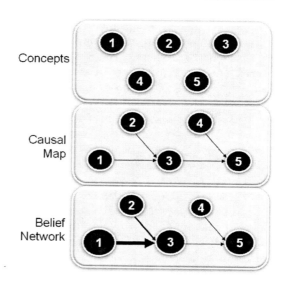

Fig. 1 Progression from concepts to causal map to belief network (from Shute & Zapata-Rivera, 2008)

link, and the *direction* indicates that the relationship has an origin and a destination. The belief structure in Fig. 1 models the beliefs of a person (or group of people) that, for example: (a) nodes 1 and 2 exist, (b) the current probability of node 1 is greater than node 2, and (c) there is a positive and strong relationship between nodes 1 and node 3 (represented by a thick line).

When comparing two belief nets (e.g., the same student at different points in time; a student with an expert), they may contain the same concepts, but the size of the respective nodes, the directionality of relations, and/or the strength of the links may be very different. Because we have chosen to use Bayesian networks to

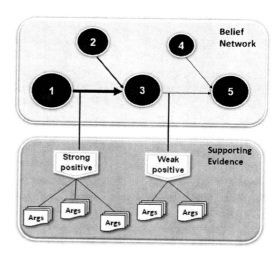

Fig. 2 Supporting evidence underlying an example belief network

represent belief structures, this enables us to examine not only (a) the structure of the map, but also (b) the content (nodes and links), as well as (c) the underlying evidence that exists per structure (and per node). That is, as part of creating a current belief structure, the student arranges concepts and establishes links, and he or she includes specific evidence (sources) per claim (i.e., arguments and relevant documentation in support of, or in opposition to a given claim). Figure 2 shows a generic belief network with its supporting evidence attached.

Tools and Technologies

The complexity and quantity of data that can be produced in relation to concept maps, causal models, and belief networks has motivated our design and development of new software tools and methods. These tools are designed to produce numerical indices (e.g., structural similarity between a pair of maps) as well as visual representations (often automatically generated) that can simultaneously reveal: (a) global patterns emerging in the maps and the cognitive processes, events, and/or conditions that trigger changes in the maps; (b) the extent to which the changing patterns are progressing toward a target model; and (c) detailed and precise information on what and where changes are occurring within the maps.

To date, we have developed six tools and technologies, detailed in this section, for purposes of assessing mental models and using that information as the basis to improve learning. The names of the six tools are: DAT, jMap, DEEP, ACSMM, SMD, and MITOCAR. The last four have been integrated in a Web-based assessment tool kit called HIMATT (Highly Interactive Model-based Assessment Tools and Technologies), while DAT and jMap are in the process of being integrated. These tools are currently available at http://himatt.ezw.uni-freiburg.de/cgi-bin/hrun/himatt.pl) and soon will be available on a server at Florida State University. The six tools are summarized below.

DAT (Discussion Analysis Tool)

As described earlier, belief networks represent and analyze links and nodes in causal maps. Similarly, sequential analysis (Bakeman & Gottman, 1997) has been used to model and analyze *sequential links* between behavioral events to determine how likely one given event is followed by another given event. Jeong (2004, 2005) developed DAT to compute the transitional probabilities between dialog moves observed in online debates. For example, DAT produces a transitional probability matrix to report the percentage of replies to stated arguments (ARG) that are challenges (BUT) vs. explanations (EXPL) vs. supporting evidence (EVID); and the percentage of replies to challenges that are counter-challenges vs. explanations vs. supporting evidence (see Fig. 3).

The matrix shown in Fig. 3 represents actual data from an online debate. The circled number indicates that 48% of all replies to opposing arguments (−ARG) were

	+ARG	+BUT	+EXPL	+EVID	-ARG	-BUT	-EXPL	-EVID	Replies	No Replies	Givens	Reply Rate	% replies	% givens
+ARG	.02	.03	.25	.17	.00	.49	.00	.04	213	21	127	.83	.25	.10
+BUT	.00	.10	.05	.10	.00	.66	.06	.03	135	162	289	.44	.16	.23
+EXPL	.00	.02	.08	.15	.00	.67	.06	.02	52	64	112	.43	.06	.09
+EVID	.00	.00	.10	.13	.00	.71	.00	.06	31	50	84	.40	.04	.07
-ARG	.00	(.48)	.03	.02	.00	.02	.26	.19	174	21	124	.83	.20	.10
-BUT	.00	.61	.11	.02	.00	.08	.08	.09	157	185	328	.44	.18	.26
-EXPL	.00	.56	.13	.00	.00	.04	.17	.10	52	56	102	.45	.06	.08
-EVID	.00	.62	.05	.03	.00	.00	.15	.15	39	49	81	.40	.05	.06

Fig. 3 Transitional probability matrix produced by DAT

challenges (+BUT), for this group of students. DAT also produces a corresponding z-score matrix to identify and automatically highlight transitional probabilities that are significantly higher/lower than expected probabilities to determine which behavioral sequences can be considered a "pattern" in a group's behaviors.

To visually and more efficiently convey the complex data revealed in the transitional probability matrix, DAT converts the observed probabilities into transitional state diagrams (see Fig. 4). Potential differences in behavior patterns between experimental groups—such as groups with students that are high vs. low in intellectual openness (Jeong, 2007)—can be easily seen by juxtaposing state diagrams and observing the differences in the thickness of the links between events (signifying the strength of the transitional probabilities between given events).

Once specific patterns and differences are identified between particular events, DAT automates the process of tabulating raw scores that reveal, for example, how

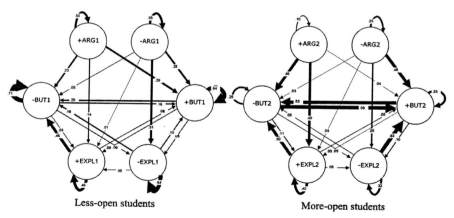

Less-open students   More-open students

Fig. 4 Transitional state diagrams of response patterns produced by less- vs. more-intellectually open students

many challenges are elicited by *each* argument, or how many explanations are elicited by *each* challenge. These raw scores can then be used to test for differences in the mean number of challenges elicited per argument and the mean number of explanations elicited per challenge between two or more experimental groups using two-way analysis of variance.

jMap

Another tool we have recently developed is an Excel-based software application called *jMap* (Jeong, 2008; Shute, Jeong, & Zapata-Rivera, 2008), designed to accomplish four specific goals: (1) elicit, record, and automatically code mental models; (2) visually and quantitatively assess changes in mental models over time; (3) determine the degree to which the changes converge towards an expert's or the aggregated group model; and (4) measure how specific social and/or cognitive events and processes (e.g., degree to which evidence is presented, degree to which the merits of presented evidence is thoroughly cross-examined) trigger changes in mental models.

Using jMap, students (and experts, as warranted) individually create their causal maps using Excel's *autoshape* tools. Causal link strength is designated by varying the densities of the links. The strength of evidentiary support for a link (not shown in Fig. 5) is designated by dashed lines where longer dashes convey stronger evidence. jMap automatically codes each map into a transitional frequency matrix by inserting two values into each matrix cell—*causal strength* of the links between nodes

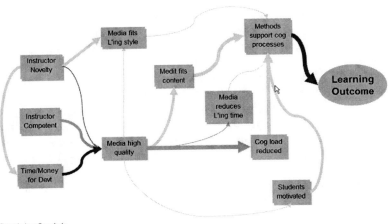

Fig. 5 Student's causal map superimposed over an expert's map

Fig. 6 Transitional state
diagrams revealing how
absence vs. presence of
evidentiary support affects
how causal link strengths
change over time

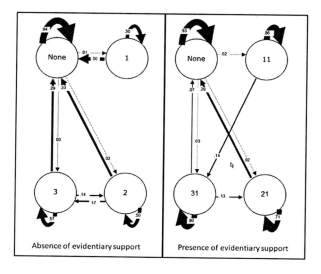

Absence of evidentiary support   Presence of evidentiary support

(1 = weak, 2 = moderate, 3 = strong) and *strength of evidentiary support* underlying the links (0 = none, 1 = weak, 2 = moderate, 3 = strong). Figure 5 shows a student's map overlaid on an expert's map.

Once maps are tabulated, *jMap reproduces and presents each student's map using a standardized map template* (e.g., based on an expert's map). Using this approach, the maps of two or more learners and/or experts can be superimposed over one another. Visual comparisons can be performed between: (a) student A's map produced at time 1 vs. time 2; (b) student A's map vs. an expert's map; and (c) a group map (produced by aggregating all maps across all students) vs. an expert's map. Users (e.g., teachers, researchers, students, etc.) can rapidly toggle between maps produced over different times to animate and visually assess how maps change over time and the extent to which the changes are converging toward an expert or collective group map. Additional jMap tools enable users to compile raw scores to: (a) compare quantitative measures (e.g., test the rate of change in the number of matching links); and (b) sequentially analyze and identify patterns in the way causal link strengths change over time using both jMap and DAT software combined. Figure 6 shows state diagrams for two groups of students—those who did not include evidentiary support in their causal maps (left) and those who did (right). The presence of evidence appears to stabilize students' causal maps.

ACSMM

Our next tool is called Analysis Constructed Shared Mental Model (ACSMM). This methodology was developed primarily as a way to assess *team processes* and predict team performance by determining the degree of overlap or "sharedness" of mental models among team members (O'Connor & Johnson, 2004; Johnson & O'Connor, 2008). The ACSMM methodology is based on the understanding that: (1) teams with similar ways of thinking are likely to work more effectively together than teams with different ways of thinking (Cannon-Bowers & Salas, 1998; Guzzo & Salas, 1995; Hackman, 1990), and (2) the degree to which a team shares similar conceptualizations is seen as a key indicator of overall team performance (Salas & Cannon-Bowers, 2000). That is, as teammates interact with one another, they begin to share knowledge. This knowledge sharing enables them to create cues in a similar manner thus helping them to make compatible decisions and to take proper actions (Klimoski & Mohammed, 1994; Mathieu, Heffner, Goodwin, Salas, & Cannon-Bowers, 2000). Shared knowledge can help team members understand what is occurring with regard to the task at hand, develop accurate expectations about future member actions and task states, and communicate meanings efficiently.

A common method for assessing team knowledge has been via concept maps (e.g., Herl et al., 1999; Ifenthaler, 2006; O'Connor & Johnson, 2004; O'Neil, Wang, Chung, & Herl, 2000). Through concept mapping, similarity of mental models can be measured in terms of the proportion of nodes and links shared between one concept map and another (Rowe & Cooke, 1995). Utilizing qualitative techniques with an aggregate method of creating an analysis constructed shared mental model (ACSMM), we can capture a more descriptive understanding than by using only quantitative techniques. Specifically, ACSMM can retain not only the logical structure, but also a general semantic meaning of the shared mental models.

How does it work? ACSMM involves a methodology where individually-constructed mental models (ICMMs) are elicited, and then a technique is used such that the sharedness is determined not by the individuals who provided their mental models, but by an analyst or analytical procedure. That is, ACSMM provides a set of heuristics to code the individual maps and then transform the ICMMs into a team map (i.e., the ACSMM) without losing the original perspective of the individual (see Fig. 7).

The methodology includes several phases: elicitation design and preparation, elicitation of individual team member mental models, coding of individual data, analysis of data to determine what is shared among team members, and construction

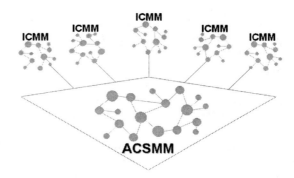

Fig. 7 Relationship between ICMMs (Individual Constructed Mental Model) and ACSMM (Analysis Constructed Shared Mental Model)

of the team conceptual representation (i.e., the team map). One of the key features of ACSMM is that this method accounts for map relatedness at the concept, link, and cluster levels. Because individual maps are so unique, the coding strives to reduce the spatial, structural, and logical information thereby permitting comparisons among maps. The coding process involves documenting the *explicit* information on the maps as well as making assessments regarding *implicit* information, which allows for explication of implicit relationships by considering the spatial, structural, and logical information in the map. The process of coding each ICMM is much like the process of interpretation. That is, each map is analyzed and then the researcher codes her interpretation in a spreadsheet (or other appropriate tool). At least one of two congruency guidelines must be satisfied before coding implicit clusters or links: (1) logical and spatial congruency, or (2) logical and structural congruency.

This technique was initially carried out by hand, but there are parts of the methodology that are automated and can be carried out in HIMATT. ACSMM is designed to quickly and easily capture mental models and that is the extent at intervening in the teams' activities. An alternative approach (not addressed by the ACSMM methodology) involves the team members themselves co-constructing a team mental model.

DEEP

The Dynamic Evaluation of Enhanced Problem-solving (DEEP) (Spector & Koszalka, 2004) methodology is based on the notion that learning in a complex domain implies becoming more like an expert (Ericsson & Smith, 1991) and more skilled in higher-order causal reasoning and problem solving (Grotzer & Perkins, 2000). A fundamental assumption is that it is possible to predict performance and assess progress of learning by examining a person's conceptualization of the problem space that person associates with a representative problem. Representations can then be compared with other representations using the analytic methods of MITO-CAR (Model Inspection Trace of Concepts and Relations Methodology) and SMD (Surface, Matching and Deep Structure Methodology), described later in this section. Moreover, these representations can be created by small groups, as well as individuals, and then analyzed using the ACSMM (Analysis Constructed Shared Mental Model) methodology or jMAP procedure, discussed earlier.

In DEEP, learners are presented with a short problem scenario and then asked to identify the most relevant factors influencing the problem situation. Next, learners are asked to describe each factor and indicate how it is related to other factors, again describing the nature of each identified relationship. These representations amount to annotated causal maps used in system dynamics to elicit expert models of complex, dynamic systems (i.e., intended to reflect systems thinking); although DEEP also allows for non-causal links (e.g., correlations, steps in a procedure, examples, and formulas). A sample DEEP representation is shown in Fig. 8 .

Two reflection questions are asked to complete the problem conceptualization: (1) What else would you need to know in order to actually resolve this problem situation? and, (2) What assumptions have you made in responding to this problem

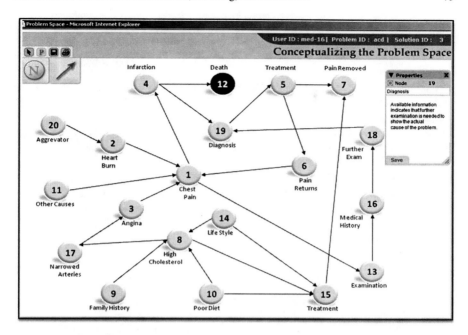

Fig. 8 A sample DEEP problem representation

situation? One strength of this methodology is that it is relatively simple to use and understand, minimizing the influence of the elicitation method on the representation.

The annotated causal representations in DEEP can be compared with prior representations and with those of experts, using some of the other tools described in this section (e.g., ACSMM, jMap, SMD, etc.). Three general levels of analysis can be applied to these representations: surface, structural, and semantic. A unique aspect of the DEEP methodology is that it is intended for complex problems involving causal relationships that are interrelated and that may change over time. Moreover, a variety of graphical representations (e.g., semantic networks, flowcharts, causal diagrams, etc.) can be accommodated in this methodology. The graphical representations are converted into standard networks for analysis (e.g., causal maps or belief networks). The reason for using causal representations as the basis for analysis is that such representations reflect internal relationships among factors and components (i.e., problem dynamics), and causal representations can be derived from many other graphical representations when the appropriate documentation is provided (e.g., the descriptions of individual factors).

SMD

The SMD (Surface, Matching, and Deep Structure) methodology (Ifenthaler, 2006, 2007) takes graphical representations in the form of causal diagrams (e.g., DEEP, jMap) or association networks (e.g., MITOCAR) as inputs and provides *similarity metrics* for purposes of analysis of mental model development and progress of learning. The similarity metrics are derived from graph theory, and allow for comparisons among surface, matching, and deep structures.

Surface structure analysis is based on the sum of all propositions (node-link-node) in a particular representation. *Matching* structure is based on an analysis of the shortest path between the most distant nodes of the representation (Harary, 1974; Ifenthaler, Masduki, & Seel, 2008). *Deep* structure is based on an analysis of the semantic similarity of propositions (Tversky, 1977) between a domain-specific expert representation and a particular representation. The automated, on-the-fly analysis of SMD enables instructors to give learners immediate feedback during the learning process or while solving complex problems. The same metrics also provide researchers with powerful tools to analyze causal representations and association networks created using DEEP and MITOCAR, described next.

MITOCAR

The Model Inspection Trace of Concepts and Relations (MITOCAR) methodology (Pirnay-Dummer, 2006, 2007) is the final tool in our current HIMATT collection. And like the others, it is based on mental model theory (Seel, 1991). One of the unique features of MITOCAR is its ability to dig deeper into the semantics of various representations. Towards that end, MITOCAR operates in two phases—an assessment phase and an inferential phase.

During the assessment phase of MITOCAR, students usually respond in two rounds. In the first round they only provide a number of natural language phrases (usually sentences, and the program currently accepts English and German language as input) about a specific subject matter or problem area. The program's parser then extracts the most frequent concepts from the text corpus and creates an internal network of pairs of concepts from which a proximity vector is constructed. These data allow one to derive graphical models from text and compare them in several ways (Fruchterman & Reingold, 1991; Ganser & North, 1999; Maedche, Pekar, & Staab, 2002).

Like SMD, MITOCAR provides a variety of analysis measures based on graph theory and Tversky-Similarity (Tversky, 1977). For example, concept matching (surface level) compares the use of terms between different models, and structural matching introduces an algorithm that compares concepts maps in relation to (a) structure only (e.g., providing a testing ground for hypotheses about the structure of expertise), and (b) several density measures (Pirnay-Dummer, 2006).

In the second round of assessment, the students are asked to rate how close the concepts, output by MITOCAR, are to their current conceptualization (i.e., confidence in the validity of the MITOCAR assessment). The participants also cluster their concepts from a random list into a list of groups—a method that is sometimes used in knowledge tracking (Janetzko, 1996). Finally, they are asked to rate the plausibility of their fellow group members' source phrases.

Table 1 Summary of six model-based assessment tools to support learning

Method	Data collection	Analysis	Data conversion	Comparison(s)
DAT	Annotated natural language from discussion or debate	Quantitative analysis—analysis is calculated using tools	Structural decomposition of event sequences and mean response scores (e.g., mean number of times X elicits Y)	Produces diagrams for visual comparison; produces raw scores for performing statistical comparisons
jMAP	Concept maps, causal maps, or belief networks	Quantitative analysis—analysis is calculated using tools	Structural decomposition into link strengths between causal factors and evidentiary strength	Superimposes maps of individual ($n=1$) and group of learners ($n = 2+$) over a specified target map
ACSMM	Concept map	Qualitative with descriptive statistics. Analysis is done mostly by hand.	Structural decomposition into 3 categories (manual), structural re-composition into 1 representation (team map)	Unlimited comparisons, showing details relative to concepts.
DEEP	Annotated causal maps	Quantitative/qualitative—analysis is done mostly by hand	Structure decomposition into 3 categories (automatic)	Unlimited comparisons, showing details relative to concepts
SMD	Concept map or natural language	Quantitative—analysis is calculated using tools.	Structural decomposition into 3 categories (manual and semi-automatic)	Unlimited comparisons.
MITOCAR	Natural language	Quantitative—analysis included multiple calculations using tools	Structural composition into 1 category (automatic)	Paired comparisons for semantic and structural model distance measures

While the semantic comparison of MITOCAR uses traditional measures of similarity (Tversky, 1977), the technology of structural comparison is unique to MITO-CAR and can compare models from different subject domains (Pirnay-Dummer, 2006). The outputs of MITOCAR are graphical representations created from individual and group statements about a problem domain or situation. MITOCAR provides similarity measures, or a researcher can import MITOCAR outputs (graphs) into SMD for analysis.

Table 1 summarizes each of the six tools described in this chapter in relation to its (a) data collection requirements, (b) primary form of analysis, (c) data conversion procedure, and (d) permissible comparisons.

Conclusions

At any given time, students hold various beliefs about concepts, procedures, and other phenomena, which are all unobservable. Educators need valid, reliable, and efficient ways to externalize students' internal beliefs in order to accurately assess understanding and provide timely and meaningful assistance. Our chapter has presented a set of tools and technologies we are developing to support this assessment of individual and group mental models in different instructional contexts (e.g., problem-centered modules, discussion forums, informal settings).

In general, our tools aim to produce external representations (i.e., concept maps, causal models, and belief networks) that provide insight into internal constructs and processes (e.g., mental models and systems thinking). These external representations can provide useful information on how well students are conceptualizing some content area; and then teachers or automated instructional systems can adjust instructional supports appropriately. In addition to helping instructors and researchers, our tools can also help students to adjust their learning strategies and enhance their metacognitive skills if they are permitted to view, compare, and otherwise interact with their maps. Open or visible student models, as they're called, have been used to support knowledge awareness, student reflection, group formation, student modeling accuracy, and student learning (Bull & Pain, 1995; Kay, 1998, Hartley & Mitrovic, 2002; Zapata-Rivera & Greer, 2004). Finally, the tools can provide instructional designers with valuable information on which to base specific modifications to the structure and sequence of various learning activities.

As society becomes more complex, and new educational tools and technologies are being developed to keep pace with these changes, there is a growing need for assessment tools that can capture and measure mental models. Research in this area, however, must be based on sound theoretical foundations, and employ validated, scalable, and easy-to-use assessment tools. Moreover, these tools need to allow for measurement of change—one of the central problems of mental model research (Seel, 1999b). Towards that end, we have been designing and developing tools to allow for an assortment of comparisons between maps/models, of individuals and groups, and at various points in time—to show not only where students began, but also their learning trajectories, similar to the benefits of motion pictures over still photographs.

References

Alpert, S. R. (2003). Abstraction in concept map and coupled outline knowledge representation. *Journal of Interactive Learning Research, 14*(1), 31–49.

Bakeman, R., & Gottman, J. (1997). *Observing interaction: An introduction to sequential analysis.* Cambridge: University Press.

Bull, S., & Pain, H. (1995). Did I say what I think I said, and do you agree with me?: Inspecting and questioning the student model. *Proceedings of the Artificial Intelligence in Education (AACE),* Charlottesville, VA, pp. 501–508.

Cannon-Bowers, J. A., & Salas, E. (Eds.). (1998). *Making decisions under stress: Implications for individual and team training.* Washington, DC: American Psychological Association.

Dewey, J. (1915). *The school and society.*(2nd ed.). Chicago: University of Chicago Press.

Ericsson, K. A., & Smith, J. (Eds.). (1991). *Toward a general theory of expertise: Prospects and limits.* New York: Cambridge University Press.

Freeman, L. A., & Urbaczewski, A. (2001). Using concept to assess students' understanding of IS. *Journal of Information Systems Education, 12,* 3–8.

Fruchterman, T. M. J., & Reingold, E. M. (1991). Graph drawing by force-directed placement. *Software – Practice and Experience, 21*(11), 1129–1164.

Ganser, E. R., & North, S. C. (1999). An open graph visualization system and its applications to software engineering. *Software – Practice and Experience, 00*(S1), 1–5.

Gentner, D., & Stevens, A. (1983). *Mental Models.* Hillsdale, NJ: Erlbaum.

Greeno, J. G. (1989). A perspective on thinking. *American Psychologist, 44*(2), 134–141.

Grotzer. T. A., & Perkins, D. N. (2000). *A taxonomy of causal models: The conceptual leaps between models and students' reflections on them.* Paper presented at the National Association of Research in Science Teaching (NARST), New Orleans, LA, 28 April–1 May 2000.

Guzzo, R. A., & Salas, E. (1995). *Team effectiveness and decision-making in organizations.* San Francisco, CA: Jossey-Bass, Inc.

Hackman, R. A. (1990). *Groups that work (and those that don't): Creating conditions for effective team work.* San Francisco, CA: Jossey-Bass.

Harary, F. (1974). *Graphentheorie.* München: Oldenbourg.

Hartley, D., & Mitrovic, A. (2002). Supporting learning by opening the student model. *Proceedings of ITS 2002,* pp. 453–462.

Herl, H. E., O'Neil, H. F., Jr., Chung, G. L. W. K., Bianchi, C., Wang, S., Mayer, R., et al. (1999). *Final report for validation of problem solving measures* (CSE Technical Report 501). Los Angeles: CRESST.

Ifenthaler, D. (2006). *Diagnosis of the learning-dependent progression of mental models. Development of the SMD-Technology as a methodology for assessing individual models on relational, structural and semantic levels.* Freiburg: Universitäts-Dissertation.

Ifenthaler, D. (2007). *Relational, structural, and semantic analysis of graphical representations and concept maps.* Paper presented at the Annual Convention of the AECT, Anaheim, CA.

Ifenthaler, D., Masduki, I., & Seel, N. M. (2008). *Tracking the development of cognitive structures over time.* Paper presented at the AREA 2008, New York.

Ifenthaler, D., & Seel, N. M. (2005). The measurement of change. Learning-dependent progression of mental models. *Technology, Instruction, Cognition and Learning, 2*(4), 317–336.

Janetzko, D. (1996). *Knowledge tracking. A method to analyze cognitive structures.* Freiburg: IIG-Berichte 2.

Jeong, A. (2005). A guide to analyzing message-response sequences and group interaction patterns in computer-mediated communication. *Distance Education, 26*(3), 367–383.

Jeong, A. (2007). The effects of intellectual openness and gender on critical thinking processes in computer-supported collaborative argumentation. *Journal of Distance Education, 22*(1), 1–18.

Jeong, A. (2008). *jMap.* Retrieved May 5, 2008, from http://garnet.fsu.edu/~ajeong

Jeong, J. C. (2004). *Discussion Analysis Tool (DAT).* Retrieved March 4, 2008, from http://garnet.fsu.edu/~ajeong/DAT

Johnson, T. J., & O'Connor, D. L. (2008). Measuring team shared understanding using the analysis-constructed shared mental model methodology, *Performance Improvement Quarterly, 21,* 113–134.

Kay, J. (1998). *A scrutable user modelling shell for user-adapted interaction.* Ph.D. Thesis, Basser Department of Computer Science, University of Sydney, Sydney, Australia.

Klimoski, R., & Mohammed, S. (1994). Team mental model – Construct or metaphor. *Journal of Management, 20*(2), 403–437.

Maedche, A., Pekar, V., & Staab, S. (2002). Ontology learning part one – On discovering taxonomic relations from the web. *Proceedings of the Web Intelligence Conference,* pp. 301–322, Springer.

Mathieu, J. E., Heffner, T. S., Goodwin, G. F., Salas, E., & Cannon-Bowers, J. A. (2000). The influence of shared mental models on team process and performance. *Journal of Applied Psychology, 85*(2), 273–283.

O'Connor, D. L., & Johnson, T. E. (2004). *Measuring team cognition: Concept mapping elicitation as a means of constructing team shared mental models in an applied setting.* First International Conference on Concept Mapping, September 14–17, 2004, Pamplona, Spain.

O'Neil, H. F., Wang, S., Chung, G., & Herl, H. E. (2000). Assessment of teamwork skills using computer-based teamwork simulations. In H. F. O'Neil & D. H. Andrews (Eds.), *Aircrew training and assessment* (pp. 244–276). Mahwah, New Jersey: Lawrence Erlbaum.

Pearl, J. (1988). *Probabilistic Reasoning in Intelligent Systems: Networks of Plausible Inference.* San Mateo, CA: Morgan Kaufman Publishers.

Pirnay-Dummer, P. (2006). *Expertise und Modellbildung: MITOCAR.* Freiburg: Universitäts-Dissertation.

Pirnay-Dummer, P. (2007). *Model inspection trace of concepts and relations. A heuristic approach to language-oriented model assessment.* Paper presented at the AERA 2007, Division C, TICL SIG, April 2007, Chicago.

Rowe, A. L., & Cooke, N. J. (1995). Measuring mental models: Choosing the right tools for the job. *Human Resource Development Quarterly, 6*(3), 243–255.

Ruiz-Primo, M. A., & Shavelson, R. J. (1996). Problems and issues in the use of concept maps in science assessment. *Journal of Research in Science Teaching, 33,* 569–600.

Salas, E., & Cannon-Bowers, J. A. (2000). The anatomy of team training. In S. Tobias & J. D. Fletcher (Eds.), *Training & retraining: A handbook for business, industry, government, and the military* (pp. 312–335). New York: Macmillan Reference.

Seel, N. M. (1991). Weltwissen und mentale Modelle *[World knowledge and mental models].* Göttingen, Germany: Hogref.

Seel, N. M. (1999a). Semiotics and structural learning theory. *Journal of Structural Learning and Intelligent Systems, 14*(1), 11–28.

Seel, N. M. (1999b). Educational diagnosis of mental models. Assessment problems and technology-based solutions. *Journal of Structural Learning and Intelligent Systems, 14*(2), 153–185.

Seel, N. M. (2003). Model-centered learning and instruction. *Technology, Instruction, Cognition and Learning, 1*(1), 59–85.

Seel, N. M., & Winn, W. D. (1997). Research on media and learning: Distributed cognition and semiotics. In R. D. Tennyson, F. Schott, S. Dijkstra, & N. M. Seel (Eds.), *Instructional design international perspectives: Vol. 1. Theories and models of instructional design* (pp. 293–326). Hillsdale, NJ: Lawrence Erlbaum Associates, Publishers.

Shute, V. J., Jeong, A., & Zapata-Rivera, D. (2008). *Assessing mental models and discourse patterns with evidence-based flexible belief networks.* Paper presented at the American Educational

Research Association conference for the Technology, Instructional, Cognition and Learning (TICL) Symposia, New York, NY.

Shute, V. J., & Zapata-Rivera, D. (2008). Using an evidence-based approach to assess mental models. In D. Ifenthaler, P. Pirnay-Dummer, & J. M. Spector (Eds.), *Understanding models for learning and instruction: Essays in honor of Norbert M. Seel*. New York: Springer.

Spector, J. M., Dennen, V. P., & Koszalka, T. (2006). Causal maps, mental models and assessing acquisition of expertise. *Technology, Instruction, Cognition and Learning, 3*, 167–183.

Spector, J. M., & Koszalka, T. A. (2004). *The DEEP methodology for assessing learning in complex domains (Final report the National Science Foundation Evaluative Research and Evaluation Capacity Building)*. Syracuse, NY: Syracuse University.

Tversky, A. (1977). Features of similarity. *Psychological Review, 84*(4), 327–352.

Wittgenstein, L. (1922). *Tractatus logico-philosophicus* (C. K. Ogden, Trans.). London: Routledge and Kegan Paul.

Wittgenstein, L. (1953). *Philosophical investigations* (G. E. M. Anscombe, Trans.). London: Blackwell.

Zapata-Rivera, D., & Greer, J. E. (2004). Interacting with inspectable Bayesian models. *International Journal of Artificial Intelligence in Education, 14*, 127–163.

Zele, E. C. (2004). Improving the usefulness of concept maps as a research tool for science education. *International Journal of Science Education, 26*(9), 1043–1064.

Beyond the Theory-Practice Split in Instructional Design: The Current Situation and Future Directions

Stephen C. Yanchar and Joseph B. South

Abstract   The authors provide an overview of the theory-practice split in instructional design by reviewing the nature and limits of six prominent attempts to connect these disparate aspects of the field. The authors then suggest an alternative viewpoint in which theory and practice are not fundamentally distinct, but rather two ways of interpreting experience, taking account of phenomena, and guiding action. While theory is primarily based on abstractions (e.g., explanatory constructs, variables, models), practice is primarily based on the concrete meanings of everyday life (e.g., implicit assumptions and values, tacit knowledge, and inarticulate "theories"). A re-conceptualized view of theory can help obviate the theory-practice split by emphasizing concrete meanings and avoiding abstractions that are difficult to apply. In conclusion, the authors offer several implications for theory and inquiry in the field.

Keywords   Theory-practice split · Practice theory · Abstract meanings · Concrete meanings · Facilitative theory

Formal theories of learning and instructional design have grown in abundance over the last several decades (see, for example, Driscoll, 2000; Jonassen & Land, 2000; Reigeluth, 1983, 1999). While this proliferation of theory has yielded a variety of interesting perspectives on the processes of learning and instruction, it is worthwhile to query into the extent to which these theories have proven beneficial to practicing designers. General discontent regarding theory across many fields suggests that the potential of theoretical understanding to facilitate practice often goes unrealized (e.g., Fealy, 1997; Fishman, 1999; Polkinghorne, 2004; Raines, 2004; Rowe, 2004; Schön, 1987). Some have suggested that the disjunction between theory and practice does not merely constitute a failure on the part of practitioners to make adequate use of theories, but points to a failure on the part of theories (and accompanying research) to inform everyday application (e.g., Fishman, 1999; Polkinghorne,

S.C. Yanchar (✉)
Instructional Psychology and Technology, Brigham Young University, Provo, Utah, 84602
e-mail: stephen_yanchar@byu.edu

M. Orey et al. (eds.), *Educational Media and Technology Yearbook*,
DOI 10.1007/978-0-387-09675-9_6, © Springer Science+Business Media, LLC 2009

2004). If theories of learning and instructional design within the field cannot withstand scrutiny of this sort, then scholars who produce them must either rise to the challenge of developing more useful conceptual resources or face the reality that their theoretical work is, and will continue to be, largely irrelevant to practicing designers. With these concerns in mind, we state our main questions in frank terms: (a) To what extent has the theory-practice split rendered scholarly work irrelevant to the applied world of instructional design, human performance improvement, training, and so on? (b) What efforts have scholars in the field made to overcome the theory-practice split? (c) What remains to be done?

In framing these questions, we are aware that debate regarding the theory-practice split has a long history in education (e.g., Bruner, 1966; Dewey, 1900, 1929; Mayer, 2003; Randi & Corno, 1997) and in the subdiscipline of instructional design and technology (e.g., Dick, 1997; Reigeluth, 1983, 1999; Seels, 1997a; Snelbecker, 1974). Indeed, one of our purposes in this chapter is to briefly review such prior discussion concerning the theory-practice split, including the major concerns regarding theory's contribution to practice in the design of instruction (or lack thereof) as well as proposals and progress made by scholars to address those concerns. We will also suggest, however, that the gap between theory and practice has yet to be satisfactorily resolved and that an alternative way of thinking about this long-standing problem, and about theory per se, can offer additional resources in the attempt to generate useable theoretical understanding. As we explicate this alternative perspective, we will suggest several of its implications for future theorizing and inquiry in the field.

Brief Overview of the Theory-Practice Split

In academic and scholarly work, theory matters. Major contributions to disciplinary knowledge typically come in the form of theories and models, and prominent figures in scholarly fields are typically those who make lasting theoretical contributions. This can be seen, for example, in education and psychology where leading scholars are known primarily for the introduction of influential ideas (e.g., Dewey, Thorndike, Skinner, Piaget, Vygotsky, Bruner, Bandura, and so on). The reason for this emphasis on theory is not difficult to identify—theory functions as the main vehicle for scholarly communication, understanding, and, ultimately, progress (for more on the nature and kinds of theories in the field, see Seels, 1997b). More specifically, theory is viewed as the principal means by which broad perspectives on phenomena can be taken (Dick, 1997), the source of guidelines for decision making and problem solving (Dick, 1997; Driscoll, 2000; Reigeluth, 1999; Winn, 1997), and the basis for the generation of taxonomies (Seels, 1997b), new ideas and understandings (Wilson, 1997), research hypotheses (Seels, 1997b), frameworks for interpreting data, links between disparate variables or phenomena, and scientific description and explanation (Wilson, 1997). Theories are, in this sense, the driving force and unifying element behind systematic views of the world; they are, through their continual development, revision or refinement, and sometimes replacement, what allows a scholarly field to advance knowledge.

However, theoretical progress in science, scholarship, and academics does not necessarily translate into helpful applications and more effective practices. Early in his work, Dewey (1900) discussed the lack of theory-based and scientifically-informed pedagogy. He identified assumptions that tended to limit the effectiveness of teachers and suggested that scientific findings and theory of the time could help ameliorate this situation. Interestingly, Dewey (1929) also contended that everyday practice is what provides science its basic questions and subject matter in the first place, even if it is not always recognized for doing so, and that viewing science as the main driver of practice was simplistic and unhelpful. Decades later, Bruner (1966) contended that theories of instruction were needed because basic theories of learning and development could not adequately relate to or inform actual teaching practices. As he stated, "A theory of instruction, in short, is concerned with how what one wishes to teach can best be learned, with improving rather than describing learning" (p. 40). And from the literature of instructional technology, Snelbecker (1974) argued that, "...neither educators nor psychologists have yet found widely accepted procedures for using psychological theories to plan and to improve educational practice" (p. 4). These observations are consistent with the contemporary view that theory is not typically or substantively used by a majority of practitioners (e.g., Christensen & Osguthorpe, 2004; Reigeluth, 1997; Rowland, 1992; Wilson, 1997).

It is important to note that the disjunction between theory and practice involves both major types of theorizing in the field—*descriptive* and *prescriptive* (Reigeluth, 1983, 1999; see also Bruner, 1966). The former of these are constructed for the purpose of describing, or in some inquiry-based way, mapping, the dynamics of a phenomenon or process (such as animal learning) as it occurs naturally in the environment; there is no attempt here to describe or map how an intervention into that process would alter its normal functioning or dynamics. Such theory is well-known to resist easy translation into practical applications (e.g., Bruner, 1966; Dewey, 1900; Perez & Emery, 1995; Reigeluth, 1997, 1999; Sandoval, 2004; Snelbecker, 1974). Oddly enough, the second kind of theory—which is specifically constructed to facilitate interventions into natural processes (e.g., instructional design theories such as Elaboration Theory) and take on a much more practical or "prescriptive" role—is subject to similar difficulties regarding application. Indeed, scholars in the field have increasingly noted that prescriptive theories are inadequate to meet the demands of instructional design practice and that more practitioner-oriented resources are needed (Christensen & Osguthorpe, 2004; Perez & Emery, 1995; Rowland, 1992; Schwier, Campbell, & Kenny, 2004; Tessmer & Wedman, 1990; Wedman & Tessmer, 1993; Winer & Vazquez-Abad, 1995). Perhaps Wilson captured the sentiment best when he concluded: "It's no wonder ID theories aren't more used, because they tend to be static and abstract, not fitting the situations very well" (personal communication, November 2, 2006).

A similar conclusion has been reached by many regarding instructional design process models, namely, that they tend to be disconnected from the ways that designers actually perform their craft and offer limited help in practical situations (Christensen & Osguthorpe, 2004; Kenny, Zhang, Schwier, & Campbell, 2005; Kirschner, Carr, van Merrienboer, & Sloep, 2002; Zemke, 1985). Christensen and Osguthorpe (2004), in summarizing a review of the literature by Kirschner et al. (2002), concluded that "...practitioners selectively complete traditional instructional design tasks according to the needs and circumstances of the context in which they work, frequently deviating from traditional ISD process models and practices" (p. 46). These findings are consistent with Zemke's (1985) survey of the readers of *Training* magazine, which suggested that designers typically complete only 50% of 14 common elements of a systems approach to ID and that only 11% of respondents surveyed complete eight key steps all of the time (that would, according to the authors, make their approach "textbook"). As one set of commentators argued, "...the primary model of instructional design in the field of IDT does not guarantee quality, is not efficient, is out of date, and doesn't reflect the real work of instructional design" (Bichelmeyer, Boling, & Gibbons, 2006, p. 36).

Under these circumstances, there is little reason to expect that practitioners would pursue theoretical understanding and attempt to make significant use of it in their work. And given constraints under which designers typically operate (deadlines, budgets, stakeholder needs, etc.), there would seem to be little motivation for them to study theories that require considerable time and energy to translate into principles that may be only marginally helpful or occasionally applicable. To the extent that this problem cannot be resolved—that is, to the extent that scholarly work in the applied field of instructional design cannot produce theoretical knowledge that meets the demands of practice—it is difficult to see how practitioners could consider theory as anything but largely superfluous. From a scholarly standpoint, on the other hand, default disregard for theoretical resources that may actually be helpful in guiding decision making and problem solving, particularly in complex design situations, could only be viewed as immature and imprudent (Winn, 1997). Ultimately, the oft-stated notion that there is nothing so practical as a good theory may be true and scholars have simply not yet found the most fruitful means of connecting theory with practice.

Current Positions on Overcoming the Theory-Practice Split

A variety of responses to the theory-practice split have been offered in the literature, suggesting that many scholars are far from unconcerned about the tenuous relationship between their work and the demands of practice. Six that are most visible in this disciplinary discussion are: (a) renewed emphasis on scientific-technical theorizing; (b) the development of "linking" theories; (c) theoretical eclecticism; (d) development of theories-in-context through design-oriented research strategies; (e) development of practice-based knowledge by describing what designers actually do; and (f) more practical instructional design training. We will describe these responses and briefly outline the contributions and limitations of each.

Renewed emphasis on scientific-technical theorizing. One response to the theory-practice split, rooted in the "received view" of science (Polkinghorne, 1983, p. 59), calls for the use of "interventions based firmly on sound scientific theory, principles, and measurement" (Clark & Estes, 1998, p. 8)—what might be termed scientific-technical theorizing (see also Schön, 1987). This scientific-technical view, emphasizing theory developed through traditional experimental, quasi-experimental, and correlational research, continues to be advocated and used by many within the broad field of education (e.g., Mayer, 2000; Slavin, 2002), and in the subfield of instructional design and technology (Clark & Estes, 1998; Dick, 1997; Merrill, Drake, Lacy, Pratt, & the ID$_2$ Research Group, 1996). Moreover, current trends in educational discourse and funding perpetuate this view of method and science, seen perhaps most notably in the emphasis on randomized drug trial-style research design to experimentally determine "what works" in educational practice (e.g., Slavin, 2002). In one way or another, advocates of this position (e.g., Clark & Estes, 1998; Dick, 1997; Merrill et al., 1996) state that genuine advances in instructional design and technology will occur through the rigorous scientific testing of theories and design principles, and in order to be part of the solution, practitioners should also take part in this scientific-technical project (e.g., carefully use these substantiated theories and principles).

Efforts on the part of these scholars to produce rigorous knowledge and substantiated theories is surely laudable; and however the field proceeds, it will need to make research a central part of its work. However, the plausibility of this particular strategy, at least as the primary response to the theory-practice split, seems severely challenged by the long history of estrangement between scientific-technical progress, on the one hand, and applied needs and know-how on the other. As a growing number of commentators have argued, such research has not fulfilled the promise of generating highly useful findings and theories that can significantly improve learning and instruction in practical situations (e.g., Bensimon, Polkinghorne, Bauman, & Vallejo, 2004; Mishler, 1979, Olson, 2004; Schön, 1987). As these authors have argued, this approach to research typically begins with researchers formulating questions that follow from a research literature that is detached from the concerns and dynamics of actual practice. Further, the research process often results in abstract models and statistical patterns—typically justified by p-values, measures of effect size, and other numeric indices—that offer little insight to the practicing designer, project manager, technologist, or teacher. The search for received-view knowledge, including complex models of, or conclusions about, theoretically interesting "variables" ultimately provides a body of literature that might best be described as academic (Bensimon et al., 2004; Danziger, 1990; Mishler, 1978).

Given the abstract-objectivist knowledge often generated by researchers, it is understandable that practitioners do not rely on academic venues of dissemination such as research conferences and scholarly publications. There is a sort of disengagement between the creators of abstract, often mathematized knowledge and practitioners that will not be overcome by the generation of still more abstract knowledge following from the empirical literature (Bensimon et al., 2004). In order for findings to be helpful they must be perceived as current, beneficial, feasible, and in a form conducive to application (Richey, 1998). Ultimately, research and theory produced under the received view—through its emphasis on highly technical and abstract solutions—results in a retrenchment of the theory-practice split it sought to overcome.

The development of "linking" theories. A second response to the theory-practice split involves the development of models, theories, or other conceptualizations that are essentially translations of basic theories of learning (or elements of those basic theories) into applicable design and instruction principles, what one theorist termed "linking" theories (Tennyson, 2002, p. 52). As Tennyson (2002) suggested, such a linking theory might distill practical principles from cognitive, behavioral, and constuctivist perspectives and then suggest how each principle might be applicable when pursuing certain learning objectives. Another way to "link" theory and practice involves designed environments that instantiate basic theories, what another author termed "embodied conjectures" (Sandoval, 2004, p. 215). The call to link theory and practice in this way can be traced at least to the work of Dewey (1900), as Reigeluth (1997) pointed out. As a proponent of both rigorous science and humane social practice, Dewy suggested that an interplay must be achieved between the results of science and scholarly theory, on the one hand, and the pedagogical activities that emerge in the midst of everyday schooling experiences on the other. He contended that actual practice has much to learn from the abstract theory and laboratory-based findings of scientific psychology, but that this is unlikely to occur without some sort of "linking science" (1900, p. 6) that can actuate the potentially fruitful relation between theorist-inquirers and practitioners, and do so in a way that does not turn teachers into mechanical implementers of scientific and theoretical principles (for a review of research on teacher implementation of curricula, instructional packages, and principles, see Randi & Corno, 1997).

While contemporary attempts to link theory and practice in this way are hardly monolithic—for example, some boil down to the development of instructional design theories (Tennyson, 2002) while others come in the form of design elements that are instantiations of basic theory (Sandoval, 2004)—they are all constructed to deal in some productive way with the abstractness and inapplicability of basic theories through the creation of still more theories and models. Surely theorizing at this intermediate level can provide tangible benefits; however, as we described above, theories and models of instructional design themselves often entail a degree of generality and abstractness that renders them difficult to apply in specific design situations. Instantiations of basic theory within designed environments (i.e., embodied conjectures) are obviously more concrete and offer considerable potential in making theory useable, but little guidance is given to practitioners regarding how to actually derive an instantiation from a theory when not working directly with the theorist-researchers themselves. Interestingly, in such cases, the nature of scholarly theorizing per se is not examined or called into question. It is assumed that such a theory will be, by its very nature, abstract and detached from actual contexts of practice, and that steps—often laborious and difficult ones—must be taken to draw from it any particular relevance.

Theoretical eclecticism. A third response to the theory-practice split involves using elements of various learning and instructional design theories strategically in order to optimize instructional effectiveness (e.g., Christensen & Osguthorpe, 2004; Reigeluth, 1997; Visscher-Voerman & Gustafson, 2004; Wilson, 1999). Given that theories are often too abstract and inflexible to be used as originally disseminated in the scholarly literature, practitioners can select from them whatever is helpful for their purposes and not feel obliged to employ a theory whole cloth or be constrained by rigid adherence to a particular theoretical viewpoint, model, or paradigm. Some have argued that broad knowledge of theory is needed so that the theoretical principles, from any given theory, can be applied to solve instructional problems as needed (Christensen & Osguthorpe, 2004; Wilson, 1999). One set of researchers further suggested that not having this berth of knowledge, and not having the capability to use theories in this way, may amount to a form of designer incompetence (Visscher-Voerman & Gustafson, 2004).

Theoretical eclecticism is persuasive in its conviction that theories are essentially tools to be used in whatever ways seem appropriate, rather than as rigid conceptual structures that map reality or mandates on how design must proceed. As Christensen and Osguthorpe (2004) suggested, this eclectic approach may very well describe the leanings of most practicing instructional designers; if they use theory at all, they use it eclectically and in conjunction with other practical resources (expert advice, templates, past work, etc.). The reason for this approach seems fairly obvious—when elements of theories may offer some value, yet theories as wholes seem too abstract and impractical to apply, picking and choosing whatever might help is the obvious alternative; it leaves practitioners free of theoretical bias or rigidity as they approach their work (at least on the face of it) and affords them the flexibility needed to solve complex instructional problems.

Critical examinations of theoretical eclecticism, however, have suggested that the surface appeal of this position tends to obscure deeper problems. For one, the apparent unrestrictiveness of eclecticism is belied by a general set of underlying assumptions that will, like any underlying assumptions, bias the practitioner toward or away from certain views and practices. Some of these assumptions include the following: that no single theory is adequate by itself, that elements of theories are in some way self-contained and able to be extracted from the larger theory without implication, that eclectic combinations will meld together into harmonious and effective instructional strategies, and that eclecticism is the main (or only) alternative to theoretical rigidity. Any of these beliefs may or may not be true, and in a given situation, any one may lead practitioners toward inferior instructional design. For instance, the combination of two instructional techniques from contradictory theories could lead to the dilution of the efficacy of both, if neither one were given the emphasis and structure needed for it to create its intended effect. In general, eclecticism commits practitioners to a particular (theoretical) view regarding the role of theory and practice within instructional design processes—a view that should be treated like any other view—cautiously, reflectively, and with an awareness of its limitations.

Moreover, it might be asked how eclectically-oriented designers would actually make design decisions in a given situation; that is, what considerations would lead eclectic designers to a particular configuration of features, activities, and experiences in the design of a course or learning environment? Obviously, there are situational constraints (which we have already noted, for example, time, budget, and managerial mandates) that will shape the design process to some degree. But beyond these basic constraints there seem to be two general possibilities: one involves randomness, caprice, or brute trial and error; the other involves a conceptual background—that is, implicit assumptions, values, and biases about learning and instruction—that influences how designers will interpret instructional problems and frame potential solutions (Osguthorpe & Osguthorpe, 2007). While the former of these two possibilities is not likely to be recommended by most experienced designers and scholars of the field, the latter is not free of complications. Indeed, as critics of eclecticism have argued, an overtly eclectic stance taken by practitioners tends to obscure the implicit background that will guide decisions and thus precludes the possibility that this background will be acknowledged and critically examined (e.g., Slife, 1987; Yanchar & Williams, 2006). Even criteria for success or "what works" in a given situation will refer back to some prior conception of what counts as a good outcome, and diverse theoretical positions on learning and instruction tend to come with diverse views regarding the ideal outcomes of learning (Yanchar & Williams, 2006).

From this perspective, theoretical eclecticism—which calls for no critical check on these background assumptions and implicit theoretical leanings—could hardly count as best professional practice (for more on this type of critical thinking, see Osguthorpe & Osguthorpe, 2007; Slife & Williams, 1995). Indeed, once a background of theoretical assumptions is acknowledged, the practitioner's stance no longer functions as eclectic, but rather as a type of personal theory that possesses at least some degree of coherence. The best of these personal understandings, it has been argued, will be explicated (to the extent possible), critically evaluated, and flexibly adapted and revised over time (Osguthorpe & Osguthorpe, 2007; Slife & Williams, 1995).

Development of theories-in-context through design-oriented research strategies. A fourth response to the theory-practice split involves the development of research strategies that facilitate the construction and refinement of theory in real-world contexts. Most prominent among these strategies are formative research (Reigeluth & Frick, 1999), design-based research (Barab 2006; Brown, 1992; Kelly, 2003), and design and development research (Richey & Klein, 2007). Common among all these approaches is the selection of a particular theory or set of theories to investigate in practice, a research team that includes practitioners (usually instructional designers or teachers or both) as well as researchers, a practical setting, and an iterative cycle of analysis, design, implementation, and revision with implications for both theory and practice. Despite these similarities, Richey and Klein (2007) point out that each approach tends to have a different focus.

Formative research is defined by Reigeluth and Frick (1999) as "a kind of developmental research or action research that is intended to improve design theory for designing instructional practices or processes" (p. 633). The most common type is the "designed case" in which the "theory is intentionally instantiated (usually by the researcher)" (p. 637) and the "design instance is based as exclusively as possible on the guidelines from [the] theory [being studied]" (p. 636). Because formative research is focused on improving a theory by researching its instantiation, the improvement of the design theory for practical purposes is the major focus.

The second design-oriented research strategy—design-based research—is defined by Wang and Hannafin (2005) as "a systematic but flexible methodology aimed to improve educational practices through iterative analysis, design, development, and implementation, based on collaboration among researchers and practitioners in real-world settings, and leading to contextually-sensitive design principles and theories" (pp. 6–7). Its goal, according to Barab (2006), is to advance "theory-in-context" (p. 156). He elaborates:

> The phrase 'theory-in-context' communicates the conviction that the theory is always situated in terms of local particulars. Drawing on Gibson's (1986) ecological psychology terminology, the phrase includes both a relatively invariant aspect, the theory, and a variant aspect, the context. Accounts of DBR [design-based research] should describe both the theory and the particulars in a way that allows others to understand how to recontextualize the theory-in-context with respect to their local particulars. (p. 156)

Design-based research, then, focuses on the improvement of learning programs in applied settings, and their underlying theories, by providing contextual accounts of the application and refinement of both over time. Its theoretical focus can extend to instructional-design theory and learning theory, depending on the approach of the researcher. Typically, the researcher and the practitioner identify a learning situation or curriculum in need of improvement and collaborate to determine which theory or set of theories might offer the most benefit. A theoretically-aligned approach is then implemented and both the theory and its instantiation may be adjusted through multiple iterations until a satisfactory outcome is achieved (Barab, 2006; Brown, 1992; Kelly, 2003).

The third design-oriented research strategy—design and development research—is defined by Richey and Klein (2007) as "the systematic study of design, development and evaluation processes with the aim of establishing an empirical basis for the creation of instructional and non-instructional products and tools and new or enhanced models that govern their development" (p. xv). It is divided into Type 1 and Type 2 research (Richey, Klein, & Nelson, 2004). Type 1 research, also called "Product and Tool Research," focuses on "the study of specific product or tool design, development, or use projects leading primarily to context-specific conclusions" (Richey & Klein, p. 159). Type 2 research, also called "Model Research," focuses on "the study of the development, validation, and use of design and development models, leading primarily to generalized conclusions" (p. 158). These forms of research, then, focus either on product and tool improvement or on model improvement, but not on both at the same time. In each case, a single product or tool or a single model is selected for study and improvement through iterative implementation.

While the focus across these three approaches may vary, the role of researchers and practitioners in each is similar: a researcher initiates the study of a particular theory or model (or set of theories or models) and collaborates with practitioners to achieve the goals of improved learning, improved theories or models, and so forth. This kind of research has provided insight into the challenges and issues faced when theory is applied in a practical setting, and represents a significant step forward in resolving the theory-practice split. However, such an approach does not illuminate how theories are understood and implemented by instructional designers in everyday work settings. All three research strategies require collaboration with practitioners who either agree to implement the theory (or set of theories) or who negotiate with researchers the theoretical approaches to be investigated. In this way, the researcher's agenda significantly impacts the theoretical thrust of the implementation. With this research strategy it is difficult, if not impossible, to understand how a practitioner might select and implement theories without researcher involvement. Indeed, the vast majority of design situations entail teams of practitioners working independently of scholarly input. It is for this reason that inquiry into how well practitioners ordinarily avail themselves of theory is valuable. An important way to study and improve theory, then, is not only to use researcher-practitioner teams, but also to study how designers use, struggle with, or don't use theories in realistic situations and allow those results to help inform theory development. This would seem to be what Reigeluth and Frick (1999) had in mind when they described the "naturalistic formative research study" (p. 645). However, this particular research strategy, and examples of it in use, are seldom discussed in the literature.

Development of practice-based knowledge by describing what designers actually do. A fifth response to the theory-practice split, involving the construction of bodies of formalized design knowledge based on descriptions of practitioners' ways of knowing and doing, have been advocated by numerous authors in the literature (e.g., Kenny et al., 2005; Perez & Emery, 1995; Pieters & Bergman, 1995; Wedman & Tessmer, 1993). The principal assumption behind this strategy is that considerable practical wisdom, tacit knowledge, and expert skill are located in everyday design contexts which, once explicated, can be used to inform practice more effectively than traditional theories and research findings. As Schwier et al. (2004, p. 69) asserted:

> ...much of the extensive work describing theoretical models of instructional design (ID) has not been drawn from the practice of the instructional designer and, consequently, instructional design theory is not grounded in practice. It is important to draw on the professional experience of instructional designers, their personal understanding of and values related to learning with technology, and the relation of these to their practice.

Interestingly, none of the authors who advocate the formalization of designer knowledge have discussed the possibility that new, more practical theories could emerge from empirical-descriptive work of this sort. It is also interesting that few of these authors suggested that novel insights and forms of design practice should be continually pursued from outside the field. In this sense, this reply to the theory-practice split is based on a type of conservativeness regarding best practices, where the "ought" of optimal design work is strongly guided by the "is" of what designers already do. However, this sort of conservativeness regarding what is formalized and disseminated as best practice, based on observations of extant practice, may well limit the possibilities that the field envisions for itself. It seems that attempts to "naturalize" the models and practices of the field by recording what typically goes on would be most informative when balanced against attempts to pursue the open exploration of ideas and practices outside of the field. Moreover, none of this empirical-descriptive work could be done in an atheoretical, impartial fashion—merely describing the "facts" about "what works"—as is almost universally agreed upon in the history and philosophy of science literature (Curd & Cover, 1998). Thus, empirical work of this sort would need to be conducted in conjunction with an explicit (and continually examined) conceptual framework to guide judgments of "what works," "best practice," "expert knowledge," and so on (for more on this argument, see Yanchar & Williams, 2006).

More practical instructional design training. A sixth response to the theory-practice split involves designer training that would combine intensive real-world experiences with theoretical understanding (e.g., Bannan-Ritland, 2001; Christensen & Osguthorpe, 2004; Perez & Emery, 1995; Quinn, 1994; Visscher-Voerman, Kuiper, & Verhagen, 2007). Such training would not only help students of the field learn to apply theories, but also afford them an opportunity to accrue "strategic knowledge" about how to solve instructional problems in practical settings (e.g., Perez & Emery, 1995, p. 94). Quinn (1994) described a graduate program in instructional design and technology based on these ideas and reported favorable student outcomes. In describing the program's purpose and structure, he stated:

> It was intended that such an integration of education and practice occur through providing students with experience in the world of practice under the close guidance of an expert (a faculty member). Working in teams, students were required to design, produce, implement, and evaluate instruction for a client under the supervision of the instructor. In addition, students were encouraged to reflect on how their practice relates to the technical knowledge which forms the basis of the discipline of instructional design, the limitations of such knowledge, and if and how such knowledge needs to be transformed in the transition from education to practice. (p. 72)

Designer training that offers these immersive experiences, and that reduces some of the abstractness involved in teaching and learning about theory, would provide a valuable step beyond the theory-practice split. Through this educational process, students could gain a mature sense of what theories mean and how (and when) to use various aspects of them in conjunction with the development of other relevant skills.

Programs such as this would be predicated on the notion that it is worthwhile to translate abstract theoretical knowledge into practical applications and that this process would become at least somewhat transparent to students as they study and work. However, given that many theories are not readily applicable to particular situations, and that motivation to use theory may not always be high, student learning could be seriously curtailed and the distance between theory and practice would not be reduced. In such a case, which is likely to be common, the role and importance of theory in facilitating practice would need to be explicated as students are mentored—is theory a scientific-technical resource expected to produce good outcomes when followed carefully (e.g., Clark & Estes, 1998), a heuristic for solving design problems (Perez & Emery, 1995), a general source of ideas (Wilson, 1997), all of these, some of these, something else? Answers to these general questions, whatever they may entail, would presuppose something about the theory-practice split and how it should be overcome, which is the basic problem that such programs were, at least in part, intended to solve in the first place. In this sense, a graduate program (or individual faculty members) cannot avoid the deleterious influence of the theory-practice split in their program without a conceptual solution to guide their efforts (either implicit or explicit). But such conceptual solutions are precisely what has been at stake in disciplinary discussions of theory and practice to this point. The responses we described above could help inform graduate training that overcomes the theory-practice gap, but which ones and why? Moreover, it is not yet clear that these responses have offered all that is needed in this regard.

Implications and Future Directions

Based on our review and analysis, it seems clear that the theory-practice gap in instructional design and technology will not go away easily and that responses to it—while helpful in moving the field toward a more workable theory-practice relationship—are limited in their ability to foment the changes envisioned by many. Given the pervasiveness of this historical problem, it may be more plausible to seek continual movement toward an improved theory-practice relationship, making advances where possible, than to expect the not-so-distant realization of some ideal solution. In this sense, the responses we have already reviewed provide potentially useful ideas for making incremental progress toward tighter theory-practice connections. However, it also seems clear that these responses offered in the literature, to this point, have not exhausted the ways that theory and practice might be reconciled and do not give reason to assume that the theory-practice gap will soon be closed.

In the remainder of this chapter, we will describe an alternative perspective that may offer additional assistance in grappling with the theory-practice split. While we do not expect that this alternative will offer a quick and easy solution to theory-practice problems at all levels, it provides some potentially fruitful ways of thinking about theory per se, the relation between theory and practice in applied settings, and accompanying research practices. As we contended above, alternative viewpoints not only offer new insights and potentially useful strategies for connecting theory with practice, but also provide a useful point of comparison and contrast for the assessment of all perspectives involved.

The alternative we have in mind is consistent with the practice turn in philosophy and social theory—a movement usually associated with philosophical hermeneutics (Gadamer, 1975; Heidegger, 1962; Taylor, 1985; Wittgenstein, 1958) and practice theory (e.g., Schatzki, Knorr Cetina, & von Savigny, 2000). While no monolithic "practices" approach has issued from the work of these theorists, their related arguments have been influential on work in social sciences such as psychology (Polkinghorne, 2004; Richardson, Fowers, & Guignon, 1999; Slife, 2004; Westerman, 2006), sociology (Bourdieu, 1977; Giddens, 1976), and anthropology (Geertz, 1973; Lave, 1988). While the perspective we offer is based on this admittedly variegated body of work, it is not meant to be a strict dissemination of any particular thinker's rendition; rather it is our interpretation extrapolated from the arguments of these scholars, and brought together, we hope, into a coherent picture. Because this (or any) form of practice theory is complex and multifaceted, we can briefly describe only a few basic contentions that are particularly relevant to the theory-practice split in instructional design and technology.

Practices. From a practice theory perspective, human action is inevitably enmeshed in *practices*, or more specifically, practical involvement in historical forms of life that give rise to the meanings of everyday existence. These meanings are said to be "concrete" (Westerman, 2006, p. 198), in that they are part and parcel of the rich and familiar activities of life in its "everydayness" (Heidegger, 1962, p. 383)—working, solving problems, interacting with people, and the day to day affairs of life. Concrete meanings are instantiated in the language, categories, views, and values by which people interpret experience and engage in activities. Such meanings stand in opposition to abstract meanings associated with endeavors like mathematics (meanings as expressed in axioms, complex formulas, functions, etc.) and positivist-oriented social science (meanings as expressed in constructs, forces, averages, latent variables, etc.).

Although abstract meanings of one sort or another are inevitable (e.g., language itself entails a sort of abstraction; see Slife & Williams, 1995) and are useful in certain ways, they become problematic when they are taken to be more fundamental than the concrete meanings by which people live and are assumed to offer a privileged access to the nature of human existence (for more on abstractionism in social science, see Slife, 2004; Westerman, 2006). Indeed, from a practice theory perspective, there is no "deeper" reality (behavioral laws, constructs, natural forces) that is more fundamental than the concrete meanings of everydayness, so theoretical constructs—as abstract theoretical explanations (e.g., retrieval failure as an explanation of forgetting)—could be viewed as metaphors at best, but perhaps dangerous ones because they often become reified and taken to be the basic reality that stands "behind" and governs the world of experience (Slife & Williams, 1995; Westerman, 2006). From a practice theory perspective, then, humans are not natural objects or conglomerations of variables to be explained through rigorous research and theorizing, but contextually embedded agents operating against a backdrop of shared meaning and historical practices. To understand human action, from this perspective, is to understand it as a meaningful, purposive, and ongoing part of larger social practices, not as an instantiation of abstract processes and forces. As Westerman (2006, p. 197) argued in this regard, "practical activity is bedrock."

Practice as theoretical. From a practice theory perspective, people are involved in their work assumptively and tacitly (Heidegger, 1962; Polanyi, 1967; Taylor,

1985; Westerman, 2006). That is, much of what they do, and the concrete meanings by which they live their lives, are based on inarticulate but vitally important background understandings. From this standpoint, it might be said that these background understandings provide the basic conditions for all knowing, interpretation, and action (Gadamer, 1975). For example, implicit assumptions and beliefs about human development, social norms, relationships, conduct, moral action, the purpose of life, and related concerns are likely to play into child rearing, and might coalesce into a "personal theory" of this activity, even if such assumptions have never been explicitly acknowledged and examined by a parent. That is, for one to engage in certain parenting practices, she or he will have assumed something particular about the activity in question (e.g., corporal punishment is permissible and the only way to teach a child a certain lesson)—even if that conduct has long since reverted to habit.

This is the case for professional practice just as it is for human practices more generally. For example, tacit understandings surely play a part in the practice of instructional design, where much will be assumed about learners and instruction—both in terms of relatively obvious issues (e.g., learner background, interests, abilities, etc.) and more basic ones (e.g., how humans learn in general, whether or not minds construct knowledge, how much control people have over their learning, etc.). Again, such tacit understandings provide the basic conditions for action and knowing; they are what enable practitioners to interpret a given situation and make reasonable efforts to produce instruction. Such tacit understandings function as theories of a sort—albeit informal and largely inarticulate ones—in that they are views of the topic in question that enable work to get done. These informal and largely inarticulate theories are concrete meanings derived from, and developed within, everyday contexts of life, often expressed in the form of practical wisdom, expert knowledge, and advice. As informal and inarticulate theoretical frameworks for making sense of experience, these concrete meanings become the basis for craftsman-like practice. Indeed, the notion that designers are craftspersons (e.g., Osguthorpe & Osguthorpe, 2007; Rowland, 1993) presupposes the concrete meanings and inarticulate theories central to this view of practice.

Theory as practice. This understanding of practice as theoretical suggests that a fundamental theory-practice schism does not exist; rather, one appears only when abstractions are emphasized in ways that formalize tacit understanding and basic insights into abstract theories that are not intimately connected with, or perhaps even relevant to, the concrete meanings of lived experience and practical involvement. Like the tacit understandings of everyday activity, such formalized theories offer ways of interpreting experience and engaging in activities through the language, concepts, categories, perspectives, and possibilities they afford. But formalized theories and their abstract meanings tend to be general, rigid, remote from actual practice, not applicable to particulars, and impractical. That is, the abstract meanings of formalized theory—which are undoubtedly rooted in practical concerns at some level—only faintly reconnect with the concrete meanings of practice and, as a result, are not readily applicable in real contexts.

If the view of practitioner as craftsperson has merit, then formal theory might offer insights and suggestions that facilitate the work of practitioners; but it wouldn't be put forth as offering fundamental explanations or descriptions of phenomena, and it wouldn't be presented as well-ordered procedures for designing instruction. Indeed, some have suggested that prescriptive theory was never intended to provide firm procedures and that whatever help it might offer (for example, as an "idealized guide") could be disregarded in favor of "intuitive shortcuts" and "improvisation" as deemed appropriate in context (especially by expert designers; Molenda, Pershing, & Reigeluth, 1996, p. 268). If this is so, then scholarly theorizing better suited to the facilitation of flexible, innovative, and reflective design practice would seem to be a reasonable goal—that is, *facilitative*, rather than descriptive or prescriptive, theory.

Such theories would be rooted partly in understandings of practical involvement with theory and design (through inquiry on practices which we describe below) and partly in scholars' evolving conceptions of the world of practice. Moreover, such theories would attempt to convey concrete meanings rather than abstract ones, or more specifically, offer a means of understanding situations and phenomena in ways that do not, in a sense, reduce the world of practical involvement to abstractions (processes, explanatory constructs, fundamental causes, etc.) that make little connection with everyday design work. Such theories would attempt to facilitate practice (not direct it in a strong sense) by providing "raw material" that would orient practitioners to relevant but unacknowledged aspects of their own experience for critical examination and refinement, and help practitioners develop their personal theories and understandings in ways that improve their craft. For example, coming into contact with a theory that focused concretely on human experiences of freedom, choice, and responsibility (e.g., Westcott, 1988) might alert designers to questionable biases or beliefs they have previously made in the design process and suggest alternative forms of practice that better reflect their modified understanding. In this sense, theory would be, as much as anything else, a tool for self-development and an important factor in the evolution of one's professional identity over time. While theories of this sort could come in many forms, work in narrative theory (e.g., Clandinin, 2007; Polkinghorne, 1988) and on participatory models (Westerman & Steen, 2007) offer potentially useful resources for the construction and articulation of facilitative theories.

Research on practices and concrete meanings. What kind of research could deal in concrete meanings and support the development of non-abstractionist theorizing? It is likely that design-oriented research would be helpful, provided that studies of this sort were conducted in order to generate understandings for practitioners and theorists interested in concrete meanings. As we stated above, however, inquiry that explores practitioners' ordinary ways of knowing and doing (through tacit understanding, personal theories, etc.) would also be helpful in the formation of deeper understandings of practice and theories more capable of facilitating it. Indeed, as we stated above, it is important to understand the concrete meanings involved in ordinary design situations—that is, design without scholarly direction or collaboration—since most design work does not involve close practitioner interaction with scholars. Such inquiry, which would emphasize practical involvement with theory in real design contexts, would be similar in some ways to research that pursues practice-based knowledge (by describing what designers actually do); but what we recommend would have researchers focus on everyday theory use per se (a relatively uncommon research focus in this literature) and involves detailed exploration of this activity through case studies, ethnographic methods, and other forms of interpretive inquiry. Increasingly effective research strategies that emphasize concrete meanings and practical involvement could be used to understand designers' general ways of thinking about and using theory.

Perhaps more importantly, however, would be intensive studies of designers' practical involvement with a particular theory—for example, studying how insights drawn from cognitive apprenticeship were involved in a designer's evolving view of her work, or how she applied this approach to solve certain instructional problems. More generally, research of this sort would be primarily concerned with how a theory was and was not used, the insights it offered, its limitations and weaknesses, how it helped designers broaden their perspective or refine their skills, and so on. Such inquiry would help provide the kind of data—indeed, the concrete meanings—required to understand the theoretical nature of practice and the practical nature of theory; and understandings of this sort may go a long way in rendering the traditional theory-practice distinction obsolete.

Conclusion

We have suggested that theory and practice are not fundamentally different, but actually both ways of interpreting experience and guiding engagement in activities. Theory becomes disconnected from practice when it takes an abstractionist form and loses much of its relevance to the concrete meanings of everyday life. The main purpose of non-abstractionist theory, then, would be to thematize and clarify concrete meanings in ways that do not lose their connection with practical activities; such theory could facilitate design work by offering insights and guidance that may facilitate specific design tasks as well as the continual development of practitioners' views of their work and their professional identity. While the notion of non-abstractionist, facilitative theory that deals in concrete meanings needs to be better developed, and examples of it need to be offered in the context of instructional design, it raises a possibility not widely discussed in the literature—that the very idea and nature of theorizing might be part of the historical theory-practice problem, and that an alternative view of theory per se could be part of the solution.

References

Bannan-Ritland, B. (2001). Teaching instructional design: An action learning approach. *Performance Improvement Quarterly, 14*(2), 37–52.
Barab, S. (2006). Design-based research: A methodological toolkit for the learning scientist. In R. K. Sawyer (Ed.), *The Cambridge handbook of the learning sciences* (pp. 153–169). New York: Cambridge University Press.

Bensimon, E. M., Polkinghorne, D. E., Bauman, G. L., & Vallejo, E. (2004). Doing research that makes a difference. *The Journal of Higher Education, 75*, 104–126.

Bichelmeyer, B., Boling, E., & Gibbons, A. S. (2006). Instructional design and technology models: Their impact on research and teaching in instructional design and technology. In M. Orey, V. J. McClendon, & R. M. Branch (Eds.), *Educational media and technology yearbook* (Vol. 31, pp. 33–73). Littleton, CO: Libraries Unlimited, Inc.

Bourdieu, P. (1977). *Outline of a theory of practice*. New York: Cambridge University Press.

Brown, A. L. (1992). Design experiments: Theoretical and methodological challenges in creating complex interventions in classroom settings. *Journal of the Learning Sciences, 2*(2), 141–178.

Bruner, J. S. (1966). *Toward a theory of instruction*. Cambridge, MA: Harvard University Press.

Christensen, T. K., & Osguthorpe, R. T. (2004). How do instructional design practitioners make instructional-strategy decisions? *Performance Improvement Quarterly, 17*(3), 45–65.

Clandinin, J. (Ed.). (2007). *Handbook of narrative inquiry: Mapping a methodology*. Thousand Oaks, CA: Sage Publications.

Clark, R. E., & Estes, F. (1998). Technology or craft? What are we doing? *Educational Technology, 38*(5), 5–11.

Curd, M., & Cover, J. A. (1998). *Philosophy of science: The central issues*. New York: W. W. Norton & Company.

Danziger, K. (1990). *Constructing the subject: Historical origins of psychological research*. New York: Cambridge University Press.

Dewey, J. (1900). Psychology and social practice. *The Psychological Review, 7*, 105–124.

Dewey, J. (1929). *The sources of a science of education*. New York: H. Liveright.

Dick, W. (1997). Better instructional design theory: Process improvement or reengineering? *Educational Technology, 37*(5), 47–50.

Driscoll, M. P. (2000). *Psychology of learning for instruction* (2nd ed.). Boston: Allyn and Bacon.

Fealy, G. M. (1997). The theory-practice relationship in nursing: An exploration in contemporary discourse. *Journal of Advanced Nursing, 25*, 1061–1069.

Fishman, D. B. (1999). *The case for pragmatic psychology*. New York: NYU Press.

Gadamer, H. G. (1975). *Truth and method* (2nd ed.). New York: Continuum.

Geertz, C. (1973). *The interpretation of cultures*. New York: Basic Books.

Gibson, J. J. (1986). *The ecological approach to visual perception*. Hillsdale, NJ: Lawrence Erlbaum.

Giddens, A. (1976). *New rules of sociological method*. New York: Basic Books.

Heidegger, M. (1962). *Being and time*. New York: Harper and Row.

Jonassen, D. H., & Land, S. M. (Eds.). (2000). *Theoretical foundations of learning environments* (pp. 57–88). Mahwah, NJ: Lawrence Erlbaum Associates, Publishers.

Kelly, A. E. (Ed.). (2003). Theme issue: The role of design in educational research. *Educational Researcher, 32*(1).

Kenny, R. F., Zhang, Z., Schwier, R. A., & Campbell, K. (2005). A review of what instructional designers do: Questions answered and questions not asked. *Canadian Journal of Learning and Technology, 31*(1), 9–26.

Kirschner, P., Carr, C., van Merrienboer, J., & Sloep, P. (2002). How expert designers design. *Performance Improvement Quarterly, 15*, 86–104.

Lave, J. (1988). *Cognition in practice: Mind, mathematics, and culture in everyday life*. New York: Cambridge University press.

Mayer, R. E. (2000). What is the place of science in educational research? *Educational Researcher, 29*(6), 38–39.

Mayer, R. E. (2003). Theories of learning and their application to technology. In H. F. O'Neil, Jr. & R. S. Perez (Eds.), *Technology applications in education: A learning view* (pp. 127–157). Mahwah, NJ: Lawrence Erlbaum Associates.

Merrill, D. M., Drake, L., Lacy, M. J., Pratt, J., & the ID_2 Research Group. (1996). Reclaiming instructional design. *Educational Technology, 36*(5), 5–7.

Mishler, E. G. (1978). Meaning in context: Is there any other kind? *Harvard Educational Review*, *49*, 1–19.

Molenda, M., Pershing, J. A., & Reigeluth, C. R. (1996). Designing instructional systems. In R. Craig (Ed.), *The ASTD training and development handbook* (4th ed.). New York: McGraw-Hill.

Olson, D. R. (2004). The triumph of hope over experience in the search for "what works": A response to Slavin. *Educational Researcher, 33*(1), 24–26.

Osguthorpe, R. T., & Osguthorpe, R. D. (2007). Instructional design as living practice: Toward a conscience of craft. *Educational Technology, 47*(4), 13–23.

Perez, R. S., & Emery, C. D. (1995). Designer thinking: How novices and experts think about instructional design. *Performance Improvement Quarterly, 8*(3), 80–94.

Pieters, J. M., & Bergman, R. (1995). The empirical basis of designing instruction. *Performance Improvement Quarterly, 8*(3), 118.

Polanyi, M. (1967). *The tacit dimension*. London: Routledge & Kegan Paul.

Polkinghorne, D. E. (1983). *Methodology for the human sciences: Systems of inquiry*. Albany: State University of New York Press.

Polkinghorne, D. E. (1988). *Narrative knowing and the human sciences*. Albany: State University of New York Press.

Polkinghorne, D. E. (2004). *Practice and the human sciences: The case for a judgment-based practice of care*. Albany: State University of New York Press.

Quinn, J. (1994). Connecting education and practice in an instructional design graduate program. *Educational Technology Research and Development, 42*(3), 71–82.

Raines, J. C. (2004). Evidence-based practice in school social work: A process in perspective. *Children & Schools, 26*(2), 71–85.

Randi, J., & Corno, L. (1997). Teachers and innovators. In B. J. Biddle, T. L. Good, & I. F. Goodson (Eds.), *International handbook of teachers and teaching* (Vol. 3, pp. 1163–1221). Dordrecht, Netherlands: Kluwer Academic Publishers.

Reigeluth, C. M. (Ed.). (1983). *Instructional-design theories and models: An overview of their current status*. Hillsdale, NY: Lawrence Erlbaum Associates.

Reigeluth, C. M. (1997). Instructional theory, practitioner needs, and new directions: Some reflections. *Educational Technology, 37*(1), 42–47.

Reigeluth, C. M. (Ed.). (1999). *Instructional-design theories and models: A new paradigm of instructional theory* (Vol. 2). Mahwah, NJ: Lawrence Erlbaum Associates.

Reigeluth, C. M., & Frick, T. W. (1999). Formative research: A methodology for creating and improving design theories. In C. M. Reigeluth (Ed.), *Instructional-design theories and models: A new paradigm of instructional theory* (Vol. 2, pp. 633–651). Hillsdale, NJ: Lawrence Erlbaum Associates.

Richardson, F. C., Fowers, B. J., & Guignon, C. B. (1999). *Re-envisioning psychology: Moral dimensions of theory and practice*. San Francisco: Jossey-Bass.

Richey, R. (1998). The pursuit of useable knowledge in instructional technology. *Educational Technology Research and Development, 46*(4), 7–22.

Richey, R. C., & Klein, J. D. (2007). *Design and development research: Methods, strategies, and issues*. Mahwah: Lawrence Erlbaum.

Richey, R.C., Klein, J. D., & Nelson, W. (2004). Developmental research: Studies of instructional design and development. In D. Jonassen (Ed.), *Handbook of research for educational communications and technology* (2nd ed., pp. 1099–1130). Bloomington, IN: Association for Educational Communications and Technology.

Rowe, D. (2004). Contemporary media education: Ideas for overcoming the perils of popularity and the theory-practice split. *Journal of Media Practice, 5*, 43–58.

Rowland, G. (1992). What do designers actually do? An initial investigation of expert practice. *Performance Improvement Quarterly, 5*(2), 65–86.

Rowland, G. (1993). Designing and instructional design. *Educational Technology Research and Development, 41*(1), 79–91.

Sandoval, W. A. (2004). Developing learning theory by refining conjectures embodied in educational designs. *Educational Psychologist, 39*, 213–223.

Schatzki, T. R., Knorr Cetina, K., & von Savigny, E. (Eds.). (2000). *The practice turn in contemporary theory*. Florence, KY: Routledge.

Schön, D. A. (1987). *Educating the reflective practitioner: Toward a new design for teaching and learning in the professions*. San Francisco: Jossey-Bass.

Schwier, R. A., Campbell, K., & Kenny, R. (2004). Instructional designers' observations about identity, communities of practice, and change agency. *Australasian Journal of Educational Technology, 20*(1), 69–100.

Seels, B. (Ed.). (1997a). Special issue: Examining the role of theory development in the field of educational technology. *Educational Technology, 37*(1).

Seels, B. (1997b). Taxonomic issues and the development of theory in instructional technology. *Educational Technology, 37*(1), 12–21.

Slavin, R. E. (2002). Evidence-based education policies: Transforming educational practice and research. *Educational Researcher, 31*(7), 15–21.

Slife, B. D. (1987). The perils of eclecticism as a therapeutic orientation. *Theoretical and Philosophical Psychology, 7*, 94–103.

Slife, B. D. (2004). Taking practice seriously: Toward a relational ontology. *Journal of Theoretical and Philosophical Psychology, 24*, 157–178.

Slife, B. D., & Williams, R. N. (1995). *What's behind the research? Discovering hidden assumptions in the behavioral sciences*. Thousand Oaks, CA: Sage Publications.

Snelbecker, G. E. (1974). *Learning theory, instructional theory, and psychoeducational design*. New York: McGraw-Hill.

Taylor, C. (1985). *Philosophy and the human sciences: Philosophical papers* (Vol. 2). New York: Cambridge University Press.

Tennyson, R. D. (2002). Linking learning theories to instructional design. *Educational Technology, 42*(3), 51–55.

Tessmer, M., & Wedman, J. F. (1990). A layers-of-necessity instructional development model. *Educational Technology Research and Development, 38*(2), 77–86.

Visscher-Voerman, I., & Gustafson, K. L. (2004). Paradigms in the theory and practice of education and training design. *Educational Technology Research and Development, 52*(2), 69–91.

Visscher-Voerman, I., Kuiper, W., & Verhagen, P. (2007). Educating educational designers: The University of Twente case. In M. Simonson (Ed.), *Proceedings of the association for educational communication and technology* (Vol. 2, pp. 332–343). Anaheim, CA: AECT.

Wang, F., & Hannafin, M. J. (2005). Design-based research and technology-enhanced learning environments. *Educational Technology Research and Development, 53*(4), 5–23.

Wedman, J., & Tessmer, M. (1993). Instructional designers' decisions and priorities: A survey of design practice. *Performance Improvement Quarterly, 6*(2), 43–57.

Westcott, M. (1988). *The psychology of human freedom: A human science perspective and critique*. New York: Springer-Verlag.

Westerman, M. A. (2006). Quantitative research as an interpretive enterprise: The mostly unacknowledged role of interpretation in research efforts and suggestions for explicitly interpretive quantitative investigations. *New Ideas in Psychology, 24*, 189–211.

Westerman, M. A., & Steen, E. M. (2007). Going beyond the internal-external dichotomy in clinical psychology: The theory of interpersonal defense as an example of a participatory model. *Theory & Psychology, 17*, 323–351.

Wilson, B. G. (1997). Thoughts on theory in educational technology. *Educational Technology, 37*(1), 22–27.

Wilson, B. G. (1999). *The dangers of theory-based design*. Retrieved April 14, 2008, from http://it.coe.uga.edu/itforum/paper31/paper31.html

Winer, L., & Vazquez-Abad, J. (1995). The present and future of ID practice. *Performance Improvement Quarterly, 8*(3), 55–67.

Winn, W. (1997). Advantages of a theory-building curriculum in instructional technology. *Educational Technology, 38*(1), 34–41.

Wittgenstein, L. (1958). *Philosophical investigations* (3rd ed., G. E. M. Anscomb, Trans.). New York: MacMillan.

Yanchar, S. C., & Williams, D. D. (2006). Reconsidering the compatibility thesis and eclecticism: Five proposed guidelines for method use. *Educational Researcher, 35* (9), 3–12.

Zemke, R. (1985, October). The system's approach: A nice theory but.... *Training, 22*, 103–108.

Effects of a Professional Development on Teacher Integration of Online Resources

Xin Mao and Mimi Recker

Abstract   The purpose of this study was to investigate the impact of a professional development (PD) workshop on teachers' knowledge and use as related to the integration of online resources. In addition, this study attempted to examine whether teachers' aptitude was a moderating factor in the impact of the PD workshop. Moreover, it explored how teachers used online resources in their practice and how teachers' aptitude might affect their behavior. Based on problem-based learning, the PD workshop was designed to teach in-service teachers the use of a software tool, the Instructional Architect, and the integration of online resources into instructional activities intended for student use. This mixed-method study employed both quantitative and qualitative methods. A quantitative phase of research, a nonequivalent control group pretest-posttest design, as well as a qualitative phase of research, was employed. A repeated measures MANCOVA indicated that the PD workshop had a significant impact on improving teachers' knowledge and use. On the other hand, aptitude was not a moderating factor in the impact of the workshop. In addition, the qualitative phase suggested that while different aptitude teachers behaved similarly regarding how they used online resources, low aptitude teachers appeared to have the most positive attitudes toward the workshop.

Keywords   Teacher professional development · Technology integration · Online learning resources · Mixed-method study

Introduction

Professional development of teachers is now recognized as a vital component of policies to enhance the quality of teaching and learning in schools (Ingvarson, Meiers, & Beavis, 2005). With the increasing use of technology in classrooms,

M. Recker (✉)
Department of Instructional Technology, Utah State University, Logan, UT 84322-2830
e-mail: mimi.recker@usu.edu

M. Orey et al. (eds.), *Educational Media and Technology Yearbook*,
DOI 10.1007/978-0-387-09675-9_7, © Springer Science+Business Media, LLC 2009

there is a need for effective professional development that improves teachers' technology integration knowledge and use that ultimately increases student learning outcomes (Lawless & Pellegrino, 2005; Russell, Bebell, O'Dwyer, & O'Connor, 2003). Several studies have suggested that problem-based learning (PBL), an instructional method in which learners learn through engaging authentic and challenging problems in cooperation with their group members (Barrows, 1996), might be an effective approach to train teachers, providing evidence that PBL has the potential to improve teachers' knowledge and use (Albion, 2003; Albion & Gibson, 2000; Butler & Wiebe, 2003; Levin, Hibbard, & Rock, 2002; Ochoa, Kelly, Stuart, & Rogers-Adkinson, 2004). However, a review of the literature found that those studies in the domain of teacher education mostly only used qualitative method. The only quantitative study (Gülseçen & Kubat, 2006) found by the review in this domain did not suggest that PBL-based PD was better than lecture-based PD, although there are quantitative studies showing favorable outcomes for PBL with adult learners in other domains (Doucet, Purdy, Kaufman, & Langille, 1998). Meanwhile, as documented by the research, teachers' aptitude may have a moderating role in the impact of PBL-based PD on teachers' knowledge and use (Hmelo-Silver, 2004). Additional research is needed to employ methods beyond the qualitative method and consider teachers' aptitude as an influencing factor.

On the other hand, recently researchers have stated that the widespread availability of online learning resources on the World Wide Web, as one kind of educational technology, hold great potential for transforming education (Lawless & Pellegrino, 2005; Recker, Dorward, Dawson, Mao, et al., 2005). "Through interacting with Web content, students can now engage in highly personalized learning experiences, instead of relying on the one-size-fits-all textbook" (Recker, Dorward, Dawson, Mao, 2005, p. 197). In recognition of this, many digital libraries have been developed to provide teachers with catalogued collections of high quality online resources (Recker et al., 2007). The NSF-funded National Science Digital Library (NSDL.org), as a prominent example, is intended to increase the use of online learning resources and ultimately improve teaching and learning, specifically in science, technology, engineering, and math (STEM) disciplines (Recker et al., 2007). However, few studies have investigated how teachers' knowledge and use are changed as a result of their interactions with these online resources, and how teachers adapt, design, and reuse the resources in their classrooms (Recker, Dorward, Dawson, Mao, et al., 2005; Recker et al., 2007).

This chapter presents a mixed-method study, employing both quantitative and qualitative methods, which investigated teachers' changes in knowledge and use after they participated in a PBL-based professional development workshop that taught them integration of online resources. We looked for evidence of whether teachers had increased in their knowledge and use of online resources, how they designed and implemented instructional activities around online resources, and whether and how their aptitude influenced the impact of the PD workshop on their knowledge and use. This study was part of the Utah State University's Digital Libraries go to Schools ((DLConnect.usu.edu) project (Recker et al., 2007)

Teacher Technology: The Instructional Architect

Teachers participating in this study learned to use the Instructional Architect (IA.usu.edu) as part of the professional development activities. The IA is a simple end-user authoring service, which allows teachers to use, find, and share online resources from the National Science Digital Library and the Web, and create engaging and interactive instructional activities or IA projects around the online resources (Recker, Dorward, Dawson, Halioris, et al., 2005). Figure 1 shows an example of an IA project created by teachers using the IA tool. The foreground of the figure shows one of the teacher's selected online resources. The background shows the output of using IA: a web page containing the content created by the teacher, consisting of activities and annotations for online resources (referred to by links).

Teachers can use the IA in several ways. In the "My Resources" area of the IA, teachers can directly search for and save STEM resources from the NSDL Data Repository (NDR). Teachers can also select any Web resource including interactive and Web 2.0 content (such as RSS feeds and podcasts), and add it to their list of saved resources. In the "My Projects" area, teachers can design web pages in which they select a look and feel for their project, input selected online resources and provide accompanying text. Finally, teachers can "Publish" their projects for only their students, or the wider web world.

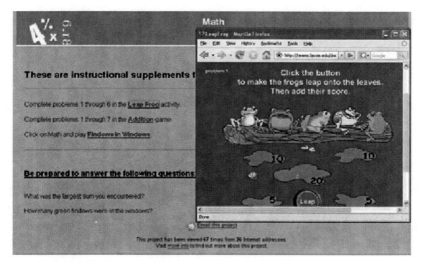

Fig. 1 Demonstration of an IA project and within online resources The author's name of the project has been removed to protect his/her privacy.

Theoretical Framework

In this section, firstly we introduce the framework for this study. Then we describe the professional development model used in this study. Furthermore, we introduce the design continuum we adopted to analyze how teachers designed instructional activities using online resources.

Because mixed methods research can incorporate the strengths of both quantitative and qualitative methodologies (Johnson & Onwuegbuzie, 2005), this study employed them both. Figure 2 shows the framework for this study. As seen in Fig. 2, the PBL-based PD workshop was used as the intervention. The construct "knowledge" was quantitatively measured in terms of the participants' understanding of the concepts about online resources and use of the IA. The construct "use" was both quantitatively and qualitatively measured. First, it was quantitatively measured in terms of the participants' self-reported use of online resources. Then, it was qualitatively examined in terms of how the participants designed and implemented their IA projects. The participants' aptitude as related to their knowledge, comfort, and experience with technologies was assumed to be a moderating factor in the impact of workshop participation on their knowledge and use of online resources.

PBL-Based Professional Development

The main focus of the PBL-based PD workshop was to teach the teachers to design and implement classroom instructional activities (or IA projects) through using the Instructional Architect. By blending technological skills with classroom practice, the PBL-based workshop not only prepared the teachers to master the basic technology skills such as searching for online resources, and creating an IA project, but was also intended to promote the teachers' pedagogy as related to strategies for the integration of online resources in their classrooms.

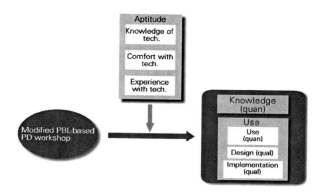

Fig. 2 Framework for the study

By following Barrows' PBL framework (Barrows, 1996), the workshop provided the teachers with problems that were authentic and situated in their practices, opportunities to direct their learning, and collaborative opportunities to discuss and share their experiences and practices. Meanwhile, several modifications were implemented, also called modified PBL strategies, primarily following Jonassen's (2000) problem solving framework and van Merriënboer et al.'s 4C/ID model (van Merriënboer, Clark, & de Croock, 2002).

First, Barrows' framework of PBL suggested presenting a problem at the beginning. Instead, this workshop presented the introduction of the IA and the basic steps involved in creating an IA project first. Second, Barrows advocated for a very specific and purposeful selection and sequencing of problems to promote learning. This workshop provided various small problems that ranged from more structured and simple (e.g., creating a simple IA project) to more ill-structured and complex (e.g., designing an advanced IA project). And the teachers selected the problems on their own. Third, as stated in Barrows' framework of PBL, learners should work cooperatively in groups to seek solutions to real world problems. However, the group processes in this workshop were not as involved as in a standard PBL implementation. During this workshop, the teachers were involved in a variety of group processes such as reflection on problem solutions to interact with peers, but there was no meaningful interaction in terms of working collaboratively to find out problem solutions. Fourth, Barrows' framework of PBL provided learners with minimal guidance. This workshop provided scaffolding (e.g., checklist, just-in-time help) to support the teachers' learning. As the problems became more complex, as teachers presumably gained more skill, the scaffolding decreased. Fifth, different from Barrows' framework of PBL, this workshop provided the teachers with opportunities to reflect on their practice. The final reflective phase (e.g., revising previous IA project based on the feedback from group members) asked them to summarize what has been learned and to integrate it with their prior knowledge.

Design Continuum

Brown and Edelson's perspective (2003), teaching as design, was used to explore how the participants designed their IA projects by incorporating online resources. Brown and Edelson (2003)'s perspective of "teaching as design" suggested that teachers designed instruction by using the curriculum resources as resources. They defined teachers' use of curriculum resources on a continuum, ranging from offloading to adaptation to improvisation. In offloading, the curriculum resources are adopted essentially unchanged. While in improvisation, the teacher flexibly borrows and customizes pieces. The adaptation category represents the mid point of the continuum. Online resources, representing one kind of curriculum resources, could support and constrain the instructional activities designed by teachers. By adapting Brown and Edelson (2003)'s framework to the context of online resource usage, this study defined the design continuum as Table 1 shows.

Table 1 Descriptions and examples of the design continuum

	Description
Offloading	There was little added teacher-created content beyond the links of resources. Use tends toward simple links to resources with added navigational information.
Adaptation	A midpoint, with some of the elements listed below.
Improvisation	The objectives of the instructional activity are clear;
	The project has a clear structure as an instructional activity, as comprised of objectives, the links of resources, teacher-added instructional content, and assessment;
	The instructions on how to use the resources are clear.

Purpose of the Study

The purpose of this study was to investigate the impact of a PBL-based professional development workshop on teachers' knowledge and use. Specifically, this study addressed the following three research questions.

1. Was there an impact of the modified PBL-based PD workshop on improving teachers' knowledge and use with regard to their integration of online resources?
2. Was teachers' aptitude a moderating factor in the impact of the modified PBL-based PD workshop on their knowledge and use?
3. How did teachers use online resources in their practice as a result of participating in the workshop? How did teachers' aptitude moderate the impact of the workshop on their behavior?

This study is significant in that it contributed to research on the impact of PBL-based PD workshops. First of all, it used a design of mixing quantitative and qualitative methods and approaches, as well as different data collection approaches. Moreover, it directly linked the goal of the modified PBL-based PD workshop to teachers' learning outcomes. With regard to the existing studies, while the objectives of the professional development programs were helping teachers improve their knowledge and use, the studies usually did not examine teachers' learning outcomes (Fishman, Marx, Best, & Tal, 2003). In addition, this study added to the knowledge base by considering teachers' aptitude when investigating the effects of the modified PBL-based professional development.

Methods

Design

This study adopted a mixed-method and mixed-model design (Johnson & Onwuegbuzie, 2005), employing a quantitative phase of research and a qualitative phase of research, as well as mixing quantitative and qualitative approaches within each phase. According to the five major purposes of conducting mixed method research proposed (Greene, Caracelli, & Graham, 1989), the purpose of such a design was primarily expansion. That is, it sought to expand the breadth and range of research by using different methods for different inquiry components.

A quantitative phase of research was used to address the first two research questions and a qualitative phase of research was used to address the third research question. The quantitative phase of research, a nonequivalent control group pretest-posttest design, consisted of a treatment group ($N = 48$) and a control group ($N = 41$). The participants enrolled in two online courses formed the treatment group. They were trained using the modified PBL-based professional development workshop. The control group was comprised of participants enrolled in one other online course. The control group only took the four-part pre-survey and two-part post-survey, without receiving any training using the modified PBL-based PD workshop. The independent variable was the group assignment. The dependent variables were the participants' knowledge and skills. And the participants' self-reported aptitude was used as a covariate.

With regard to the qualitative phase of research, we performed an in-depth analysis on the treatment group participants' use of online resources. Specifically, the content and use of participants' IA projects, reflection papers, and discussion posts, were analyzed. A case study was further conducted by purposively selecting seven participants for an in-depth analysis of their implementation. Moreover, the qualitative phase of research was used to explore how different aptitude participants behaved differently.

Participants

The participants in the quantitative phase of study were those who enrolled in three online courses at a state university during the fall semester of 2006. They mostly consisted of in-service elementary, secondary, high, and post-secondary school teachers. One of the 48 treatment group participants did not complete the workshop. Of the remained 47 treatment group participants, 38 (79%) participants finished both the pre-survey and the post-survey. Of the 41 control group participants, 15 (37%) participants finished both surveys. Because some participants did not have opportunities to use online resources in classrooms and some participants' responses to the pre-survey and the post-survey did not meet the timeline requirement, we further limited these participants by examining their responses to the demographic survey (i.e. as one part of the pre-survey). 22 treatment group participants and 13 control group participants remained for the quantitative phase of research. Table 2 displays the participant demographics.

Treatment

The treatment was the PBL-based PD workshop offered to the treatment group participants, inservice K-12, post-secondary, and seminary teachers. The instructional

Table 2 Demographic characteristics of the participants

Characteristics	Treatment group ($N = 22$)	Control group ($N = 13$)
Teaching Years		
5 or less	12 (54.55%)	6 (46.15%)
6–10	5 (22.73%)	4 (30.77%)
11–15	4 (18.18%)	3 (23.08%)
16 or more	1 (4.54%)	0
Occupations		
K-12 classroom teachers	12 (54.55%)	11 (84.62%)
K-12 librarians/media specialists	8 (36.36%)	0
College instructors	2 (9.09%)	2 (15.38%)
Grade Levels		
Elementary	7 (31.82%)	1 (7.70%)
Secondary	13 (59.09%)	10 (76.92%)
College	2 (9.09%)	2 (15.38%)

condition was conducted in a WebCT, a learning management system. The treatment materials consisted of primarily three sections, the syllabus, the content module, and the discussion board, all of which were conducted as a WebCT course. The syllabus provided the participants with an introduction to the workshop and its expectations. The content module was the primary section of the workshop curriculum. It included the following sections: introduction to the IA and how to browse IA projects, create an IA account, basic steps to create an IA project, connect to core curriculum, online resources, design IA projects, implement IA projects, comment on others' IA projects, modify IA projects, and conclusion. The discussion board allowed the participant to share, discuss information and experiences with his/her group members, while he/she worked individually on the workshop problems and activities.

Each participant was asked to create at least one IA project for implementation in a classroom setting. Moreover, the participant needed to modify the implemented project or create a new project during the workshop. Then the participant was required to post the URL of the projects he/she created or modified/re-created to the discussion board. In addition, each participant was asked to submit a reflection paper to the discussion board upon the completion of the workshop. In the reflection paper, the participants primarily provided an image of how they implemented their IA projects in an instructional situation, along with some design issues.

Instrument

There were four instruments used in the study (see Table 3). In the following discussion of the instruments, we describe the design parameters for each, as well as efforts to establish validity and reliability.

Table 3 Instruments

Name	Construct	Time period	No. of items	Type	Reliability coefficients
Demographic survey	Demographic info	Pre-survey	8	Short answer	/
Aptitude survey	Prior aptitude	Pre-survey	16	Likert scale	Cronbach's alpha $= 0.899$
Knowledge test	Knowledge	Pre-survey and post-survey	5 (pre) 5 (post)	Combination of multiple choice and open-ended response	Pearson's $r = 0.978$ (pre) & 0.966 (post)
Use survey	Use	Pre-survey and post-survey	4	Combination of Likert scale and open-ended response	Cronbach's alpha $= 0.703$

Demographic survey. This instrument, as part of the four-part pre-survey, was designed to understand the treatment and control group participants' demographic characteristics. This included: (a) years of teaching experience, (b) grade level taught, and (c) position at schools.

Aptitude survey. This instrument, as part of the four-part pre-survey, was designed to measure the entering aptitude of the treatment and control group participants as related to self reports of their (a) knowledge of computers and the Internet, (b) comfort with computers and the Internet, and (c) experience with computers and the Internet in their professional life. In terms of the first subset and the second subset, the five responses that the teachers could choose from ranged from $0 =$ very low to $4 =$ very high. Four responses ranged from $0 =$ very low to $3 =$ very high for the third subset. The highest possible mean score was 3.69 (59/16) and the lowest possible mean score was 0.

This instrument was adapted from the surveys developed by Becker and Anderson (1998) and Russell and his research group (Russell, Bebell, & O'Dwyer, 2003). In an effort to test the reliability of this instrument, we conducted a test of internal consistency using a Cronbach Alpha test. It reported that the reliability of this instrument was high with 0.899 as the reliability coefficient.

Knowledge test. We developed this instrument to test the knowledge of the treatment and control group participants. Specifically, this test measured their understanding of the concept of online resources, searching techniques, criteria for determining high-quality online resources, and the Instructional Architect. The participants responded by selecting from a multiple choice list or by typing in a short answer. The posttest for this section was basically the same as the pretest of this section. The only difference between them was that one item was replaced in the posttest to see whether the teachers had acquired knowledge regarding online resources and the IA after the treatment. The strongest total score was both 8 points for the pretest and the posttest.

This instrument was developed by the IA team. It was reviewed by a panel of 6 professionals, which included those who are professionals in the online workshop content and those who are professionals in educational assessment. Upon review by the panel, slight changes were made for greater clarity. With regard to the reliability of this instrument, two raters scored half of the tests and had negotiations on the scoring key to determine the interrater reliability of this knowledge test. In calculating the interrater reliability, the ultimate reliability coefficient was 0.978 and 0.966 for the pretest and the posttest, respectively.

Use survey. The use survey was intended to measure the participants' use of online resources and online lessons before and after the treatment. This instrument was a combination of Likert scale and open-ended questions that collected self-reported data from both the treatment group and the control group. The post-survey for this section was identical to the pre-survey of this section. The two Likert scale items had anchors from $0 =$ very low to $4 =$ very high. The two open-ended questions asked the participant to self report how often he/she presented online resources to his/her students in the last two weeks and how often he/she let the students use online resources in the last two weeks. Because there was a need to examine the participants' responses for the four items on the same scale, we scaled the participants' responses for these two items to 0–4 Likert scale, that is, $0 =$ none, $1 = 1$–5, $2 = 6$–10, $3 = 11$–15 and $4 =$ more than 15. The highest possible mean score was 4 and the lowest possible mean score was 0.

This instrument was adapted from the survey developed by the IA team. Therefore, the construct validity of this instrument was anchored in literature. In an effort to test the reliability of this instrument, we conducted a test of internal consistency using a Cronbach alpha test on the pre-survey and the post-survey, respectively. The reliability coefficient was 0.703 by using the reliability for the pre-survey. This suggested that the reliability of this instrument was good as there were only four items.

In addition to the data collection described on the preceding pages, we employed an analysis of IA projects to understand how the participants designed IA projects using online resources across time. We also analyzed the participants' reflection papers and discussion posts to explore how they implemented their IA project(s) in a classroom setting.

Data Analysis

Quantitative Phase of Study

In an effort to address the first two research questions, a repeated measures multivariate analysis of covariance (MANCOVA) testing two-way interaction and a repeated measures MANCOVA testing three-way interaction were conducted using SPSS. The between-groups variable was the intervention (i.e., represented as group). The covariate was the aptitude (i.e., represented as aptitude). The within-groups variable was time, time1 and time 2 (i.e., represented as time). The two dependent variables were the total scores on the knowledge test (i.e., knowledge) and the average scores on the use survey (i.e., use).

Qualitative Phase of Study

The data analysis for the qualitative phase of research was comprised of an analysis of IA projects and a case study analysis of several participants. In terms of the former, the purpose was to explore how the participants incorporated online resources into IA projects as designers. With regard to the latter, we were interested in understanding how the participants implemented their projects in classrooms. Moreover, how the participants' aptitude related to their design and implementation of IA projects was explored. The data analysis involved processes such as organizing the data, coding the data, converting the data, generating patterns, offering interpretations, and writing the report. Mixed approaches were employed, for example, the qualitative data (i.e., via coding) were converted to numerical codes that could be represented quantitatively.

Results and Findings

Repeated Measures MANCOVA

A repeated measures MANCOVA was conducted to answer the first two research questions: (a) was there a significant interaction effect between time and group? and (b) was there a significant interaction effect between time, group, and aptitude?

First, in order to address the first research question described above, a repeated measures MANCOVA was performed testing the interaction between group and time with aptitude as a covariate. The results suggested that there was a significant interaction between time and group on knowledge and use as a whole ($F = 5.18$, $p < 0.05$, $ES = 0.25$; see Table 4). This indicated that changes with regard to knowledge and use across time were significantly different for the teachers in the two groups.

Moreover, the univariate effects of the interaction between time and group on both knowledge ($F = 4.99$, $p < 0.05$, $ES = 0.135$) and use ($F = 7.035$, $p < 0.05$, $ES = 0.18$) were significant (see Table 4). In terms of the effect on the teachers' knowledge, both the treatment and control group teachers increased their knowledge while the treatment group scores (from 3.32 to 5.14) increased more than those of the control group (from 2.46 to 3; see Table 5). With regard to the effect on their use, as both groups had a similar entering average score, 1.51 and 1.52, respectively, mean scores for the treatment group increased to 1.80 after the intervention, while the control group decreased to 1.36 over time (see Table 5). Specifically, the treatment group increased 20% (from 1.5 to 1.8) regarding their use of online resources.

On the other hand, in an effort to address the second research question, a repeated measures MANCOVA was performed testing the three-way interaction between time, group, and aptitude. The results indicated that

Table 4 Univariate and multivariate interaction and main effects for a repeated measures MANCOVA testing two-way interaction

Effects	Univariate				Multivariate		
	Dept. var.	F	P	ES	F	P	ES
Time × Group	Knowledge	4.99	0.033*	0.135	5.18	0.011*	0.25
	Use	7.035	0.012*	0.18			
Time	Knowledge	4.178	0.049*	0.115	2.893	0.07	0.157
	Use	2.522	0.122	0.073			
Group	Knowledge	23.436	0**	0.423	15.364	0**	0.498
	Use	3.319	0.078	0.094			

* $p < 0.05$
** $p < 0.01$

Table 5 Group means (SD) at pre-survey and post-survey for variables (N = 22 in treatment group, N = 13 in control group)

Variable	Data collection point	
	Pre-survey	Post-survey
Aptitude survey		
Treatment group	2.37 (0.62)	–
Control group	2.46 (0.57)	–
Knowledge test		
Treatment group	3.32 (1.04)	5.14 (1.46)
Control group	2.46 (1.05)	3 (0.91)
Use survey		
Treatment group	1.51 (0.66)	1.80 (0.53)
Control group	1.52 (0.75)	1.36 (0.62)

both the multivariate ($F = .760$, $p > 0.05$, $ES = 0.05$) and univariate effects (knowledge: $F = 0.630$, $p > 0.05$, $ES = 0.04$; use: $F = 1.177$, $p > 0.05$, $ES = 0.07$) of interaction between time, group, and aptitude were not significant (see Table 6). In addition, as seen from Table 6, there was not a significant time-by-group interaction any more, because the inclusion of the three-way interaction weakened this effect and there was not enough test power (sample size) to retain the significance.

In summary, the modified PBL-based PD workshop had a significant impact on improving the teachers' knowledge and use. However, the teachers' aptitude did not significantly moderate the impact of the workshop on their knowledge and use.

Findings of the Analysis of IA Projects

The emphasis in the analysis of IA projects was on investigating the ways the participants designed with online resources. It also examined whether there were changes between the projects created at time1 and those created or modified at time 2. It

Table 6 Univariate and multivariate interaction and main effects for a repeated measures MAN-COVA testing three-way interaction

Effects	Dept. var.	Univariate			Multivariate		
		F	P	ES	F	P	ES
Time × Group x Aptitude	Knowledge	0.630	0.539	0.039	0.760	0.556	0.05
	Use	1.177	0.322	0.071			
Time × Group	Knowledge	0.003	0.955	0	0.002	0.998	0
	Use	0.001	0.980	0			
Time	Knowledge	4.203	0.049*	0.119	3.044	0.063	0.169
	Use	2.819	0.103	0.083			
Group	Knowledge	0.975	0.331	0.031	1.006	0.378	0.063
	Use	0.682	0.415	0.022			

$^*p< 0.05$

should be noted that the time 2 version of the projects was identified by examining the last version of the projects re-created or modified during the workshop. Finally, the relationship between the participants' aptitude and their behavior was explored.

Analysis of aptitude level. We classified each treatment group participant into high, medium, or low aptitude level to understand how the participants with different aptitude levels performed differently with regard to the design and implementation of IA projects. The 25th percentile (2.0625) and the 75th percentile (2.89) were used as the thresholds for the high and low aptitude level, respectively. Therefore, the mean aptitude that was 2.0625 or lower was defined as the low aptitude level; the mean aptitude that was 2.89 or higher than defined as the high aptitude level; the medium aptitude level referred to the mean aptitude that was between 2.0625 and 2.89. In summary, six participants had high aptitude levels, 13 participants had medium aptitude levels, and seven participants had low aptitude levels.

Analysis of IA projects. By examining the projects the participants submitted, it turned out that 10 (38%) participants revised their previous projects, eight (31%) participants created new projects, three (12%) participants both revised and re-created projects, and five (19%) participants neither revised nor re-created their projects. Therefore, 13 (10+3) projects between time1 and time 2 showed differences in terms of revision and 11 (8+3) projects were re-created. We separately analyzed 13 revised projects and each of the 11 re-created projects at both their time1 and time 2 versions. Moreover, the five projects without revision or re-creation were analyzed for their time1 version. Specifically, these projects were coded into one category of the design continuum (offload, adaptation, or improvisation, see Table 1). The aptitude level of the author (participant) corresponding to each project was also coded into one category of the aptitude continuum (low, medium, or high).

In order to test the reliability of coding the data, two coders used the design continuum to code the time1 version and time 2 version of each of 13 randomly selected projects that experienced revision or re-creation. Although there were discrepancies in the beginning regarding the ways in which the two coders coded the projects, they were resolved after a discussion and a 100% inter-rater reliability was achieved. Finally, we applied the final coding scheme on the remaining projects.

The two coders clarified during the coding procedure that: (1) in terms of the improvisation category, the assessment was accepted when it was evident that students using the IA projects were asked to submit some work to the participant (i.e. the project author), such as reflection papers, answer sheets, and so forth; (2) in terms of the improvisation category, it was required that there were instructions on use of resources. This focused on whether it was clear regarding how to use those online resources. Therefore, although in some project links to resources were listed, the project was classified as improvisation since the purpose was to ask students to discover information from those resources and the project author had made it clear how to use them; (3) in terms of the offloading category, links to resources were provided primarily for student view. The project contained few instructional elements.

Table 7 shows the number and percent of projects falling into each category of both the design and aptitude continuums. As Table 7 shows, while most participants appeared to master the incorporation of online resources into IA projects, there were little changes between time1 and time 2 with regard to the design continuum. When connecting the participants' aptitude to their projects on the design continuum, there were interesting findings. All of the low aptitude participants made changes to their projects. The high and medium aptitude participants tended to revise projects while the low aptitude participants tended to re-create projects. This suggests that low aptitude participants were more willing to invest time and effort in the workshop than medium and high participants.

Table 7 Number (%) of projects in design and the aptitude continuums for time1 and time 2

No. of projects		Time1					Time 2			
5 projects		L	M	H[1]	Total	–				
	O	0	0	0	0	–				
	A	0	1(20)	1(20)	2(40)	–				
	I[2]	0	2(40)	1(20)	3(60)	–				
		0	3(60)	2(40)		–				
13 revision Projects		L	M	H	Total		L	M	H	Total
	O	0	2(15)	0	2(15)	O	0	2(15)	0	2(15)
	A	2(15)	1(8)	1(8)	4(31)	A	2(15)	1(8)	1(8)	4(31)
	I	1(8)	4(31)	2(15)	7(54)	I	1(8)	4(31)	2(15)	7(54)
		3(23)	7(54)	3(23)			3(23)	7(54)	3(23)	
11 re-creation projects		L	M	H	Total		L	M	H	Total
	O	0	0	0	0	O	1(9)	1(9)	0	2(18)
	A	4(36)	1(9)	1(9)	6(54)	A	3(27)	1(9)	0	4(36)
	I	3(28)	2(18)	0	5(46)	I	3(28)	1(9)	1(9)	5(46)
		7(64)	3(27)	1(9)			7(64)	3(27)	1(9)	

[1]L, M, and H represent low, medium, and high aptitude level, respectively.
[2]O represents offloading, A represents adaptation, and I represents Improvisation.

It is important to note that the analysis of IA projects as discussed above was primarily aimed at describing how the participants incorporated online resources into their projects across time, rather than assessing the quality of those changes. Therefore, the design continuum was not a quality continuum, and, as such, improvisation doesn't necessarily imply a higher quality project than adaptation and offloading.

Findings from the Case Study

We also conducted a case study on several purposively selected participants to provide an image about the context surrounding the IA project(s) each of them implemented, and how the participants implemented the project(s) in their classrooms, as well as the relationship between their aptitude and implementation. In this analysis, we selected seven participants based on a stratified purposeful sampling procedure (Gall, Borg, & Gall, 1996), using the participants' aptitude as the stratification variable. As described previously, we first conducted an analysis of aptitude level. Then we randomly selected 25% participants (cases) from each aptitude level. Information was collected from the document analysis of reflection papers describing a variety of issues related to the selected participants' application. In addition, the analysis of the selected participants' IA projects and discussion threads were corroborated with the analysis gathered from their reflection papers. There were two major themes emerged from the analysis.

Facilitating and improving student learning. As the participants stated in their reflection papers, the IA projects or instructional activities implemented by them seemed to facilitate and improve student learning. First, they reported that the students enjoyed using online resources to tackle real-world tasks. One participant reported that "some of the students liked doing the project and were diligent about looking at the websites and completing the assignment." Another participant commented that "the students were engaged in the websites and the information within those websites" (quotes from the reflection paper), and they all completed the task easily. A survey conducted by a participant indicated that her students generally had positive attitudes toward the IA project or instructional activity. Moreover, the students had a gain of knowledge or skills throughout the instructional activities. Another participant reported that overall her students improved their skills, which she attributed the gain to the project she implemented. These indicated that the participants' implementation were relatively successful.

Holding different attitudes with different aptitude levels. Perhaps the most intriguing issues to emerge from this case study analysis of selected participants were those associated with the themes which focus on the relationship between the participants' aptitude and their attitudes. The low aptitude participants appeared to be the most active participants in the workshop module, and the participants who expressed the most interest in the Instructional Architect. One low aptitude participant thought the workshop was very helpful. Two low aptitude participants commented that the IA bypassed time-consuming and unproductive processes, most notably searching for resources. And they both had fun doing these projects. The high aptitude participants, by contrast, appeared to be the most inactive participants in the workshop. Some of them were not satisfied with IA functionality, as they expected more features to be able to design their projects. The medium-aptitude participants, neither held attitudes as positively as the low-aptitude participants toward the IA nor appeared to be uninterested in the IA as the high aptitude participants. The findings indicated that different aptitude participants exhibited different attitudes towards the workshop. However, there was little evidence to suggest that which level of aptitude participants might benefit more than other aptitude participants from the workshop with regard to their knowledge and use.

Conclusions and Discussion

Because the mixed-method and mixed-model design was an expansion design, the first two research questions and the third research question investigated different inquiry components. The data collected during the course of the inquiry point to four conclusions. The first two conclusions shed light on the research questions 1 through 2 which seek to understand whether there was an impact of the workshop on improving teachers' knowledge and use, and whether teachers' aptitude was a moderating factor. In seeking to answer these two questions, a quantitative phase of research was conducted and the analyses yielded the following conclusions.

First, as indicated by a repeated measures MANCOVA testing the interaction between time and group, the modified PBL-based PD workshop had a significant impact on improving teachers' knowledge and use. This is consistent with what the research suggested. It has been documented that PBL might be an effective instructional approach (Dochy, Segers, Van den Bossche, & Gijbels, 2003; Gijbels, Dochy, Van den Bossche, Segers, 2005). One quantitative study showed significantly favorable outcomes for a PBL group in the domain of adult education (Doucet, Purdy, Kaufman, & Langille, 1998).

Second, a repeated measures MANCOVA testing the three-way interaction between time, group, and aptitude did not show that teachers' aptitude significantly influenced the impact of the workshop on their knowledge and use. While some research suggested that learners' aptitude might influence their performance in a PBL learning environment (Mergendoller, Bellisimo, & Maxwell, 2000; Mergendoller, Maxwell, & Bellisimo, 2006), the small sample size especially for the control group ($N = 13$) could account for this result.

The final two conclusions addressed the research question 3. In seeking to answer this question, a qualitative phase of research was conducted and the analyses yielded the following conclusions.

Third, the analysis of IA projects revealed that many teachers incorporated online resources into their IA projects by adding necessary instructional content instead of only listing online resources.

Fourth, while different aptitude teachers behaved similarly with regard to the way they designed and implemented IA projects by incorporating online resources, low aptitude teachers appeared to have more positive attitudes toward the modified problem-based learning environment than high aptitude teachers.

In summary, the findings from the qualitative phase of research were in line with the results of the quantitative phase of research. The analysis of the IA projects suggested that all the teachers appeared to master the skills of incorporating online resources into IA projects, although there were little changes between the projects designed across time. The case study revealed that most of the teachers agreed that the students learned what they needed to learn, indicating that the teachers' design and implementation were relatively successful. Therefore, the qualitative phase of study also indicated that the workshop had a positive impact on teachers' knowledge and use. Despite this, more evidence is needed to indicate that those positive behaviors resulted from the workshop. Firstly, there was a lack of a comparison of the behaviors between the treatment group and the control group. Secondly, there was a lack of sustained investigations regarding how those teachers used online resources in practice. As Lawless and Pellegrino (2005) suggested, sustained or follow-up studies on teachers' behaviors in practice are important to reveal the impact of a workshop model.

With regard to the role of teachers' aptitude in the impact of the workshop, the qualitative phase of research echoed the quantitative phase of research, showing that different aptitude teachers behaved in similar ways regarding the way they incorporated online resources into IA projects and how they implementation IA projects in classrooms. We did find that high aptitude teachers did not create any offloading projects. However, this only suggested that high aptitude teachers were different from low and medium aptitude teachers at the entering level, since the analyses did not reveal any changes to the projects designed across time between different aptitude teachers. Interestingly, there was an emergent finding from the qualitative phase of research, suggesting that low aptitude teachers seemed to have the most positive attitudes toward the workshop and the IA. Previous research suggested that learners with high aptitude may be more willing to accept ill-structured treatments (e.g., low external control, implicit sequences and components) such as PBL than low aptitude learners (Kirschner, Sweller, & Clark, 2006; Snow & Swanson, 1992). One response to the contradictory finding is that the PBL-based PD workshop in this study was a modified PBL-based workshop, and not a true ill-structured treatment. Another implementation is that there needs to be further evidence as few empirical studies have investigated this issue.

Acknowledgments   This material is based upon work supported by the National Science Foundation under Grants No. 0333818 & 0434892, and Utah State University. Any opinions, findings, and conclusions or recommendations expressed in this material are those of the authors and do not necessarily reflect the views of the National Science Foundation. We thank the teachers who participated in our studies. Moreover, we would like to express our thanks to Dr. Andrew Walker, Dr. Jim Dorward, Dr. Kerstin Schroder, and Dr. Yanghee Kim, for their thoughtful comments and questions during this study. We also acknowledge the Instructional Architect team members, Deonne Dawson, Bart Palmer, Sam Halioris, Jaeyang Park, Ye liu, Brooke Robertshaw, and Heather Leary, who shared their thoughts and practice with us.

References

Albion, P. R. (2003). Pbl + imm = pbl2: Problem based learning and interactive multimedia development. *Journal of Technology and Teacher Education, 11*(2), 243–257.

Albion, P. R., & Gibson, I. W. (2000). Problem-based learning as a multimedia design framework in teacher education. *Journal of Technology and Teacher Education, 8*(4), 315–326.

Barrows, H. S. (1996). Problem-based learning in medicine and beyond: A brief overview. In L. Wilkerson & W. Gijselaers (Eds.), *Bringing problem-based learning to higher education: Theory and practice* (pp. 3–12). San Francisco: Jossey-Bass.

Becker, H. J., & Anderson, R. E. (1998). *Teacher's survey: Combined versions 1–4*. Irvine: Center for Research on Information, University of California, Irvine.

Brown, M., & Edelson, D. (2003). *Teaching as design: Can we better understand the ways in which teachers use materials so we can better design materials to support their change in practice? (design brief)*. Evanston, IL: Center for Learning Technologies in Urban Schools.

Butler, S. M., & Wiebe, E. N. (2003). Designing a technology-based science lesson: Student teachers grapple with an authentic problem of practice. *Journal of Technology and Teacher Education, 11*(4), 463–481.

Dochy, F., Segers, M., Van den Bossche, P., & Gijbels, D. (2003). Effects of problem-based learning: A meta-analysis. *Learning and Instruction, 13*(5), 533–568.

Doucet, M. D., Purdy, R. A., Kaufman, D. M., & Langille, D. B. (1998). Comparison of problem-based learning and lecture format in continuing medical education on headache diagnosis and management. *Medical Education, 32*, 590–596.

Fishman, B. J., Marx, R. W., Best, S., & Tal, R. T. (2003). Linking teacher and student learning to improve professional development in systemic reform. *Teaching and Teacher Education, 19*(6), 643–658.

Gall, M. D., Borg, W. R., & Gall, J. P. (1996). *Educational research: An introduction* (6th ed.). White Plains, NY: Longman.

Gijbels, D., Dochy, F., Van den Bossche, P., & Segers, M. (2005). Effects of problem-based learning: A meta-analysis from the angle of assessment. *Review of Educational Research, 75*(1), 27–61.

Greene, J. C., Caracelli, V. J., & Graham, W. F. (1989). Toward a conceptual framework for mixed-method evaluation designs. *Educational Evaluation and Policy Analysis, 11*, 255–274.

Gülseçen, S., & Kubat, A. (2006). Teaching ict to teacher candidates using pbl: A qualitative and quantitative evaluation. *Educational Technology & Society, 9*(2), 96–106.

Hmelo-Silver, C. E. (2004). Problem-based learning: What and how do students learn? *Educational Psychology Review, 16*(3), 235–266.

Ingvarson, L., Meiers, M., & Beavis, A. (2005). Factors affecting the impact of professional development programs on teachers' knowledge, practice, student outcomes and efficacy. *Education Policy Analysis Archives, 13*(10), 1–26.

Johnson, R., & Onwuegbuzie, A. (2005). Mixed methods research: A research paradigm whose time has come. *Educational Researcher, 33*(7), 14–26.

Jonassen, D. (2000). *Toward a Design Theory of Problem Solving*. Educational Technology Research and Development *48*, 63–85.

Kirschner, P. A., Sweller, J., & Clark, R. E. (2006). Why minimal guidance during instruction does not work: An analysis of the failure of constructivist, discovery, problem-based, experiential, and inquiry-based teaching. *Educational Psychologist, 41*(2), 75–86.

Lawless, K., & Pellegrino, J. (2005). *A prospectus for design of evaluation studies of the usdoe eett program: Professional development of teachers in the integration of technology into teaching and learning*. Unpublished manuscript, Chicago, IL.

Levin, B., Hibbard, K., & Rock, T. (2002). Using problem-based learning as a tool for learning to teach students with special needs. *Teacher Education and Special Education, 25*(3), 278–290.

Mergendoller, J. R., Bellisimo, Y., & Maxwell, N. L. (2000). Comparing problem-based learning and traditional instruction in high school economics. *Journal of Educational Research, 93*(6), 374–382.

Mergendoller, J. R., Maxwell, N. L., & Bellisimo, Y. (2006). The effectiveness of problem-based instruction: A comparative study of instructional methods and student characteristics. *The Interdisciplinary Journal of Problem-Based Learning, 1*(2), 49–69.

Ochoa, T. A., Kelly, M. L., Stuart, S., & Rogers-Adkinson, D. (2004). The impact of pbl technology on the preparation of teachers of English language learners. *Journal of Special Education Technology, 19*(3), 35–45.

Recker, M., Dorward, J., Dawson, D., Halioris, S., Liu, Y., Mao, X., et al. (2005). *You can lead a horse to water: Teacher development and use of digital library resources.* Paper presented at The Joint Conference on Digital Libraries, New York.

Recker, M., Dorward, J., Dawson, D., Mao, X., Liu, Y., Palmer, B., et al. (2005). Teaching, designing, and sharing: A context for learning objects. *Interdisciplinary Journal of Knowledge and Learning Objects, 1,* 197–216.

Recker, M., Giersch, S., Walker, A., Halioris, S., Mao, X., & Palmer, B. (2007). *A study of how online learning resource are used.* Paper presented at the Joint Conference on Digital Libraries, New York.

Russell, M., Bebell, D., & O'Dwyer, L. (2003). *Use, support, and effect of instructional technology study: An overview of the useit study and the participating districts.* Boston: Technology and Assessment Study Collaborative.

Russell, M., Bebell, D., O'Dwyer, L., & O'Connor, K. (2003). Examining teacher technology use: Implications for preservice and inservice teacher preparation. *Journal of Teacher Education, 54*(4), 297–310.

Snow, R. E., & Swanson, J. (1992). Instructional psychology: Aptitude, adaptation, and assessment. *Annual Review Psychology, 43,* 583–626.

van Merriënboer, J. J.G., Clark, R. E., & de Croock, M. B. M. (2002). Blueprints for complex learning: The 4C/ID-model. *Educational Technology Research and Development, 50*(2), 39–64.

How Well Do High-Quality Online Courses Employ Merrill's First Principles of Instruction?

Max H. Cropper, Joanne P.H. Bentley, and Kerstin Schroder

Abstract   The purpose of this study was to evaluate the reliability and validity of Merrill's five star system using award-winning online courses. We compared Merrill's rubric with other recognized rubrics to explore the convergence of course awards with high scores on the Merrill's system, and convergence of scores on the Merrill system with relevant scores on the other evaluation tools. This was an exploratory study which attempted to see how high-quality courses employ Merrill's first principles of instruction. From our results we believe that Merrill's first principles should be included in the myriad of criteria for determining online course quality. Award-winning courses tend to use Merrill's first principles, and it seems likely that there is still significant room for improvement of even award-winning courses.

Keywords   Course quality · Evaluation · First principles of instruction

Introduction

Merrill's *first principles of instruction* (Merrill, 2002a) were distilled through a life-time synthesis of theories, models, and methods in the search for universal instructional principles. As a design heuristic, it was intended to identify universal principles of instruction that are common to the various instructional design theories. The instructional principles he identified apply to all teaching and learning, no matter what learning theory or educational philosophy is employed.

According to Merrill, his first principles of instruction involve a four-phase cycle of instruction "consisting of activation, demonstration, application, and integration (see Fig. 1). Effective instruction involves all four of these activities repeatedly as required for different problems or whole tasks. Perhaps as important as the 4-phase cycle of instruction is the notion that effective instruction is problem-centered." This

M.H. Cropper (✉)
Department of Instructional Technology, Utah State University, Logan, UT 84322-2830
e-mail: maxcropper@comcast.net

M. Orey et al. (eds.), *Educational Media and Technology Yearbook*,
DOI 10.1007/978-0-387-09675-9_8, © Springer Science+Business Media, LLC 2009

Fig. 1 Phases of Effective
Instruction. (Merrill, 2002a)

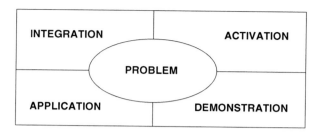

type of instruction contains individual instructional components (information, parts, concepts (kinds), procedures (how-to), and principles (what-happens). These components "are most effectively taught in the context of a progression of a real-world problem where the student is shown the problem, then taught the components, and then shown how the components are used to solve the problem or do the whole task" (Merrill, 2002a, 2002c).

The purpose of this study was to evaluate the reliability and validity of Merrill's five star system. We decided to evaluate award-winning online courses with Merrill's rubric and some other recognized rubrics, to determine (a) interrater reliability of Merrill's five star system and comparison of the reliability of other evaluation instruments; (b) convergence of teaching awards with high scores on the Merrill's system to establish criterion validity, and (c) comparison of scores based on Merrill's five star system with relevant scores on other evaluation tools. This was an exploratory study which went through two distinct iterative phases in its attempt to see how well high-quality courses employ Merrill's first principles of instruction.

Course Selection

We selected seven high-quality online courses to evaluate for instructional quality. We chose to use online courses because of their stability in capturing instructional methods for evaluation purposes. These courses covered a range of diverse topics and represent a variety of types of learning content (i.e., facts, concepts, procedures, principles, systems) as well as a variety of types of cognitive processes (i.e. understanding, remembering, creating/designing, low and high-level problem solving, and evaluating). By evaluating a variety of topics and types of learning involved in the courses, we hoped to be able to determine if Merrill's first principles are intuitively applicable to all types of learning outcomes.

We decided to use award-winning courses as part of our evaluation, presuming that the courses would be of better-than-average quality. We hypothesized that award-winning courses should score high on instructional principles if these are indeed relevant for high-quality education and if the assessment instruments are valid. Low scores of award-winning courses would indicate that (a) either the principles are less relevant than presumed, (b) the assessment instruments are not reliable or valid (though the principles might be), or (c) even award-winning courses have not achieved an instructional quality that measures up to the generally recommended principles of high-quality instruction.

In order to locate award-winning online courses, we searched for recognized award-granting organizations and the winners of their awards. We were already aware of three well-known awards. These awards were (1) the WebCT Exemplary Course Project, (2) the ISPI Outstanding Product or Intervention, and (3) the Brandon Hall Excellence in Learning. We also did a Google search using "Online Course Award" and found some other prominent awards. These included United States Distance Learning Association (USDLA) Awards Presented for Excellence in Distance Learning, University Continuing Education Association (UCEA) Best in its Class Award, Instructional Technology Council (ITC) Outstanding Online Courses Award, and Canadian Society for Training and Development (CSTD) External E-Learning Program Award. We also found some additional award granting institutions, but either their selection process was not rigorous enough, or the courses winning awards did not meet our criteria. We selected approximately 20 courses as candidates for potential review. For the most part, we selected courses from recent award winners. We eliminated some courses from consideration because we were unable to get contact information for the courses developers. Other courses were eliminated because they were no longer available online.

We received permission to use approximately ten of the courses that we identified as suitable for the study. We decided not to use two college courses and one commercial course because of lack of access to critical portions of the course. That left us with seven courses for our evaluation. Our final selection of courses included three college and four commercial courses. In addition we were able to use a NETg Excel Scenario-Based course, which was developed based upon Merrill's first principles, as a baseline course.

Rubric Selection

Merrill's 5 Star Instructional Design Rating (Merrill, 2001) served as our baseline evaluation rubric. We then looked for other reputable rubrics with similar levels of detail that focus on instructional methods. We were aware of online course evaluation rubrics which had been developed by WebCT (WebCT, 2005), Brigham Young University (BYU) (Petersen, 2005), Michigan Virtual University (MVU) (Michigan Virtual University, 2002) and American Society for Training and Development (ASTD) (Sanders, 2003). Incidentally, Merrill assisted with the early development stages of the ASTD e-Learning Courseware Certification Standards prior to formalizing his own evaluation criteria. We knew Hirumi was an expert on online course standards, so we contacted him, and were referred to the Texas IQ online course standards which he helped develop (Region 4 Education Service Center, 2005). We also did a Google search on online course standards and rubrics and found the Checklist for Online Interactive Learning (COIL) (D. W. Sunal, C. S. Sunal, Odell, & Sundberg, 2003) and the Southern Regional Education Board's (SREB) Criteria for Evaluating Online Courses (Southern Regional Education Board, 2005). When we checked with representatives of Brandon Hall about evaluating courses that had won their award, they subsequently offered us the use of their rubric for our study. We also used a motivational rubric developed by Patricia Brouwer of Twente University for her master's thesis.

We selected rubrics which focused primarily on instructional strategies and methods. Another selection criteria for the study was that the rubric existed in, or could easily be converted to, a checklist style format, making it easy for a course evaluator to use. We added a five point likert scale to all of the rubrics so variation in quality could be more easily compared and exposed. We also created a description for each rating value (from 1–5) for each question in order that multiple raters could more easily understand the meaning of each rating value. We used Merrill's 5 Star Instructional Design Rating as a Baseline Rubric. For rubrics developed primarily to evaluate online school courses, we used the Texas IQ rating form, The WebCT Exemplary Course Project 2005 Nomination Instructions and Form, and the Southern Regional Education Board's Criteria for Evaluating Online Courses (SREB). For rubrics developed primarily to evaluate online commercial courses, we used The ASTD Institute E-Learning Courseware Certification (ECC) Standards and the Brandon Hall Excellence in Learning award rating form.

Because we were mostly focusing on instructional strategies in the study, we wanted to use rubrics which concentrated primarily on instructional strategies. Under the instructional strategy umbrella, we included instructional methods, media use, interactivity, communication, and collaboration, etc. In other words, we included factors that were implemented by the instructor or instruction that could directly influence the effectiveness of the learning experience. We excluded administrative factors as relating primarily to increased satisfaction but not significantly to increased learning. In some cases, when rubrics focused on both instructional strategy and administrative factors, we used only the portions of rubrics which focused on instructional strategies. The common thread used in rubric choice was the focus on instructional strategies for achieving high quality online instruction.

A comparison of the rubrics used reveals that the various rubrics provide emphasis on different areas depending on how and why they were developed. For example, Merrill's 5 Star rubric provides emphasis on its problem-centered focus, on the various aspects of activation, on the specific strategies for demonstration and on application for various kinds of content (information-about, parts-of, kinds-of, how-to, what-happens), and upon real-life integration (see Table 1). The other rubrics emphasize objectives, course requirements, appropriate use of media, content, practice consistent with objectives, practice followed by corrective feedback, collaboration, and effective use of online technology. Please note that in Table 1 each "1" indicates that a question for the given criterion was included on the rubric. Multiple 1's indicate that multiple questions on that criterion were included on that rubric.

It is interesting to observe that most of the award rubrics do not emphasize problem-centeredness, activation, specific strategies for demonstration or application of various types of content, or for integration by the learner of what has been

Table 1 Comparison of the various online course evaluation rubrics. Italics indicate subcategories.

Merrill (2002a) 1st Principles	5 Star rating	WebCT	Texas IQ	SREB	Brandon Hall	ASTD	Other guidelines
Problem Centered	1						
Learners are shown the task, rather than just given objectives	1	111	1	1	1	111111	
Learners are engaged at problem or task level	1		1		1		
Learners solve progression of problems	1						
Activation	1						
Learners recall previous knowledge, experience	1					1	
Help learner see relevance and have confidence in their ability to gain knowledge and skill	1						
Use a procedure to select the right content for each learner	1		111		11	111	
Learners given new experience for knowledge foundation	1						
Learners recall structure for organizing knowledge	1	1	1		11	1	Engagement techniques
			1				Support to prepare for entry level
			11				Test for entry-level skills
		1	111111111	1			Syllabus/Course Requirements
Demonstration							
Demonstrate (show examples of) what is to be learned	1	11		1	1	1	
Demonstration consistent with learning goal	1	1	11		1	1	

Table 1 (continued)

Merrill (2002a) 1st Principles	5 Star rating	WebCT	Texas IQ	SREB	Brandon Hall	ASTD	Other guidelines
Examples and non-examples for kinds–of (Concepts)	1						
Demonstrations for how-to (procedures)	1						
Visualizations for what-happens (processes)	1						
Appropriate learner guidance	1						
· Learners directed to relevant information	1						
· Multiple representations used and compared	1						
Learners assisted to relate the new information to the structure that was recalled or provided	1						
Relevant media used	1	1111 / 1	11111111 / 111	1 1 1	‖‖‖‖‖‖‖‖‖	1 / 1111	Adequate content and resources to meet learning goals and objectives
Application	**1**						
Practice is consistent with objectives	1				1111	111	
Information -about practice requires learners to recall or recognize information.	1	11	11				
Parts-of practice requires the learners to locate, name, and/or describe each part.		1					
Kinds-of practice requires learners to identify new examples of each kind.	1	1					
How-to practice requires learner to do the procedure.	1	1					
What-happens practice requires learner to predict a consequence of a process given cognition, or to find faulted conditions given an unexpected consequence.	1	11	1				

Table 1 (continued)

Merrill (2002a) 1st Principles	5 Star rating	WebCT	Texas IQ	SREB	Brandon Hall	ASTD	Other guidelines
Practice followed by corrective feedback and an indication of progress, not just right-wrong feedback.	1	1	111111	11111	1	1111	
Diminishing coaching	1					1	
Varied problems	1	1	1	1			The content and requirements are as demanding as a face-to-face course.
		1					Assignments and projects that require students to make appropriate and effective use of external resources
		1		1		1	Clearly communicated assignments
		1					Explicitly communicated expectations, including deliverables
Integration							
Public demonstration of knowledge	1						
Reflection, discussion, defending knowledge	1	1					
Creation, invention, exploration of ways to apply knowledge	1						

Table 1 (continued)

Merrill (2002a) 1st Principles	5 Star rating	WebCT	Texas IQ	SREB	Brandon Hall	ASTD	Other guidelines
Implementation							
The instruction facilitates navigation	1	1	11		111		Effective use of online technology
The degree of learner-control is appropriate for the learning goals and the learners	1		1		11		Provision is made for students with special needs
Collaboration is used effectively	1	111111	111111	1111			Is the interactivity creative—Are expert design practices used?
Instruction is personalized	1	1111	1111111111				The course provider's credentials are available for review.
				1	1		Has the course been developed by a qualified team consisting of content experts and instructional designers?

Each "1" indicates that a question for the given criterion was included on the rubric. Multiple 1s indicate that multiple questions on that criterion were included on the rubric.

learned. However, they do include other criteria generally recognized for general online course quality such as clear objectives and appropriate use of media.

Phase I: Analysis of Courses Using Multiple Instruments

In the initial phases of the online course quality study, two graduate evaluators trained each other on the use of the rubrics in iterative cycles of clarification under the direction of two faculty. As part of the training they both evaluated the *Research for the Classroom Teacher* course using all seven rating forms. They reconciled their ratings, and Kappa interrater reliability for their reconciled ratings of this course, across the seven forms, was calculated at 0.64. They then rated the rest of the courses using all of the instruments. No reconciliation was completed on the other course ratings.

The raters had some problems with interrater reliability. The kappa interrater reliability was adequate for the Texas IQ (0.4638), WebCT (0.4887), SREB (0.4254), and Motivation (0.4190) rubrics, but not for the Merrill 5 Star (0.2464), ASTD (0.1836) or Brandon Hall (0.2567) rubrics. For the courses, the interrater reliability was adequate for Research for the Classroom Teacher (0.6427), SAT, Landscape Design (0.4009), and Cashier Training (0.5092) courses, but not for the Psychology of Communication (0.3564), Digital Craft (0.3594), Evaluating Training Programs (0.2853), or Excel Scenario-Based (0.1294) courses. The scores above 0.4 indicate adequate levels of interrater reliability.

The lack of interrater reliability may have been partially a result of ambiguous items on the rubrics or lack of follow-up training/reconciliation after the first course. Also, one rater was not an instructional design expert, and spoke English as a second language. This may have caused some problems with precision on the ratings. In addition, they rated the Excel course online in their country of origin. The course included multiple resources in unique formats which possibly lead to some additional confusion as to how different portions of the materials applied to rubric questions. It was uncertain whether the rater was able to access all course materials, which could have affected the ratings.

Any conclusions from an ANOVA with such low interrater reliability are preliminary at best, but served as encouragement to continue to the next phase of this study. An ANOVA of courses and instruments shows significant difference between courses ($f = 6.065$, sig. $= 0.000$) and instruments ($F = 10.443$, sig. $= 0.000$). Bonferroni post hoc tests showed that Merrill's 5 Star rating does not score courses significantly differently than the other rubrics. The Brandon Hall rubric gave the highest average rating (3.994) and the motivation rubric gave the lowest average rating (3.372).

We believe that the rubrics that give courses significantly lower scores do so because they have stricter criteria. Graphs visually depict the difference in ratings between rubric scoring of all the courses and between course ratings (see Fig. 2).

In Fig. 2, the graph on the right shows visually how the courses compare in quality. Post hoc tests comparing course quality show that the Landscape Design

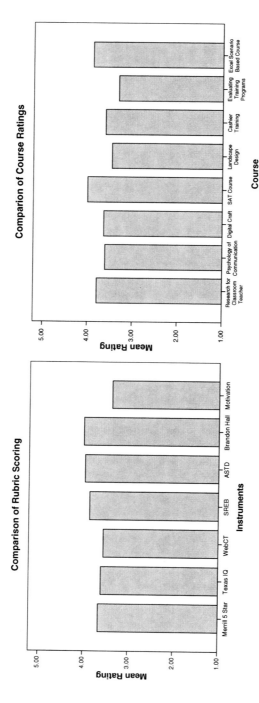

Fig. 2 The first graph shows the relative scoring of all seven rubrics. Merrill's 5-star rating is listed first, the three school instruments are listed next, then the two commercial instruments are listed, and finally the motivation instrument. Merrill's rubric doesn't score the courses significantly differently than the other rubrics. However, the commercial rubrics do score courses higher than the Texas IQ and WebCT rubrics, and the motivation rubric scores courses significantly lower than the commercial and SREB rubrics. The second graph compares the various courses that were included in the study. Notice that all of the courses score fairly high, with only the landscape design and evaluating training program courses scoring significantly lower than the baseline Excel Scenario Based (NETg) course

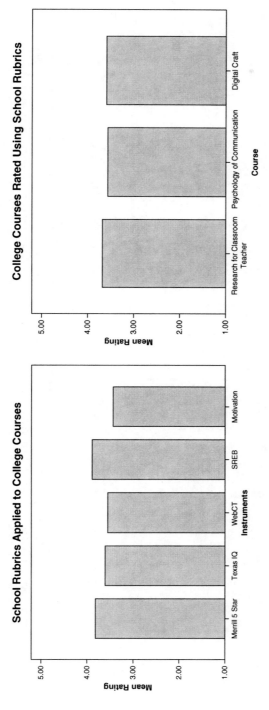

Fig. 3 The first graph demonstrates that the ratings of the school rubrics, including the 5 Star and motivation rubrics, are not significantly different. The second graph shows that ratings of the college courses using the school rubrics are almost identical

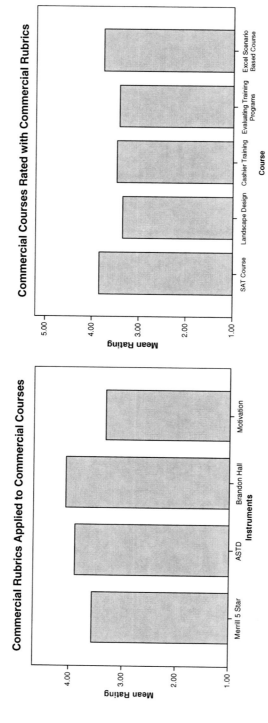

Fig. 4 The first graph shows the commercial rubric ratings for commercial courses. The Brandon Hall rubric scored the commercial courses significantly higher than the 5 Star rubric and the motivation rubric. Perhaps this occurred because the Brandon Hall rubric focuses on media, appearance, and interactive design more than instructional design. The second graph demonstrates a significant difference between the ratings for the SAT course and the Landscape Design course. However, there is no significant difference in ratings between the baseline Excel course and the other courses

and Evaluating Training Programs courses are the only ones that score significantly lower than the baseline NETg Excel course (which was designed using 5 star principles). Research for the Classroom Teacher, Psychology of Communication, Digital Craft, the SAT course, and Cashier Training were not significantly different from the Excel course in their scoring, meaning they were all of similar high quality.

Up to this point, we have been grouping school and commercial rubrics together and school and commercial courses together. Because school rubrics are intended to evaluate school courses and commercial rubrics for commercial courses, the mixing of the rubrics and courses may have confounded the data analysis. Therefore we decided to look at school courses as rated by school rubrics and commercial courses as rated by commercial rubrics. We also included Merrill's rubric and the motivation rubric for school and commercial courses. There is no significant difference between the school rubrics (including the Merrill and motivational rubric). A graph of the comparison between school rubrics visually demonstrates the similarity between school ratings (see Fig. 3). The second graph shows how the college courses were rated by the school instruments (see Fig. 3). The rating appears to be almost identical for the three courses. A Bonferroni post hoc test confirms that there is no significant difference.

When we analyzed the commercial courses as rated by the commercial course rubrics we discovered that the Brandon Hall rubric scored the courses significantly higher than Merrill's 5 Star rubric (mean difference $= 0.4988$, se;0.132, sig. $= 0.01$) and higher than the motivation rubric (mean difference $= 0.7429$, se $= 0.11377$, sig. $= 0.00$). The first graph in Fig. 4 visually depicts this difference.

However, when the commercial courses are rated by the commercial rubrics, including the 5 Star and motivation rubric, there is no significant difference between the baseline Excel course and the other courses (see the second graph in Fig. 4). By analyzing the school courses and rubrics and the commercial courses and rubrics separately, most of the significant differences between courses and rubrics have been eliminated. This is appropriate because an award-winning school course should score high on school course ratings and award-winning commercial courses should score high on commercial course ratings.

The tentative conclusions from this phase of the study are that award-winning online college and commercial courses rate fairly high on the respective rubrics and that they do tend to follow Merrill's First Principles of Instruction. The conclusions are tentative for this exploratory study because we are keeping in mind the inconsistent interrater reliability for a low number of courses and evaluators with a low amount of variation in course quality.

Phase II: Analysis of Courses Using Merrill's 5 Star Rubric

From Phase I we established the need to re-evaluate the reliability of the Merrill instrument with more experienced raters. We determined from the first phase of the study that both the school and commercial rubrics tend to rate courses approximately the same as Merrill's rubric. Therefore, we had reason to believe there was at least a tentative relationship between Merrill's rubric and the two types of rubrics. Phase II was an attempt to go more in-depth by estimating the reliability for each of Merrill's principles separately. Moving forward, we chose to focus on ratings using Merrill's rubric and felt we didn't need to include the other rubrics for a closer examination of Merrill's 5 star system. We did this because the overall study focus is on the 5-star instructional design rating and Merrill's first principles of instruction.

We added three expert evaluators, each with 10 or more years of experience as instructional designers. After being trained on Merrill's 5-Star Rating/First Principles of Instruction, the new evaluators evaluated sample modules from six of the courses from the initial phase of the study (we eliminated the Psychology of Communication and Landscaping courses from the study because they were no longer available for review). In the data analysis we included the ratings of the three new evaluators, plus the original ratings from Phase I.

Interrater Reliability

To calculate interrater reliability, we use intraclass correlation. Intraclass correlation is a scale reliability measure that is often used for interrater reliability between multiple raters and is like a measure of internal consistency. When we calculated intraclass correlation reliability over courses, for each principle separately, we found that there is high interrater reliability among raters (0.620–0.766) for all of the principles except the problem-centered principle, which had a Cronbach alpha of 0.123 (see Table 2). The interrater reliability may be low for the problem-centered principle because the definition of "real-world problems," may be confusing to raters.

Raters must decide to what degree significant contrived problems, which will be solved within the online class environment, can be classified as real-world problems. Perhaps some raters are too strict, and others are too lenient with their definition of real-world problems.

When we calculated intraclass correlation reliability over principles for each course separately, we found that there is high interrater reliability (0.568–0.847) for the raters across all of the courses except the SAT course, which had a rating

Table 2 Reliability over courses, for each principle separately. The problem-centered principle has low interrater reliability, while the other principles have high interrater reliability

Reliability statistics		
Principle	Intraclass correlation	N of raters
problem centered	0.123	5
activation	0.690	5
demonstration	0.600	5
application	0.766	5
integration	0.620	5

Table 3 Reliability over principles, for each course separately. All of the courses have relatively high interrater reliability except the SAT course

Reliability statistics		
Course	Intraclass correlation	N of raters
research for the classroom teacher	0.617	5
digital craft	0.568	5
SAT-course	0.453	5
cashier training	0.847	5
evaluating training programs	0.668	5
NETg excel scenario based exercise course	0.700	5

of 0.453 (see Table 3). The raters may have had a problem rating the problem-centeredness of the SAT course because although as a college entrance test course it provides questions that are problems, it is debatable whether there is a progression of problems, and whether the contrived problems on the test could qualify as real-world problems.

Results

With significantly improved interrater reliability from Phase I, we more confidently used ANOVAs to determine how the courses compared, how the raters compared, and how the use of Merrill's five principles compared. An ANOVA of principles, courses and principles∗courses shows that there is a significant difference between ratings of principles ($f = 12.835$, sig. $= 0.000$), between course ratings ($f = 7.664$, sig. $= 0.000$), and within the interaction of principles and courses ($f = 2.718$, sig. $= 0.000$).

A Bonferroni Post Hoc Comparison of Courses showed that there is a significant difference between the baseline NETg Excel course, the Digital Craft course (mean difference $= 0.63$, sig. 0.002) and Evaluating Training Programs course ratings (mean difference $= 0.84$, sig. 0.000). There is no significant difference between the NETg Excel course and the Research for the Classroom teacher, SAT, and Cashier Training courses. The first graph in Fig. 5 visually depicts these differences.

The Comparison of Use of Merrill's First Principles graph (see Fig. 6) shows that the problem-centered principle is used significantly more in the courses than all of the other principles. In addition, integration is used significantly less than demonstration or application.

Three of five of the award-winning courses rate high on the use of Merrill's First Principles. The Research for the Classroom Teacher Course, the SAT course, and the Cashier Training course do not rate significantly lower than the NETg Excel course. The Digital Craft Course and the Evaluating Training Programs Course do rate significantly lower.

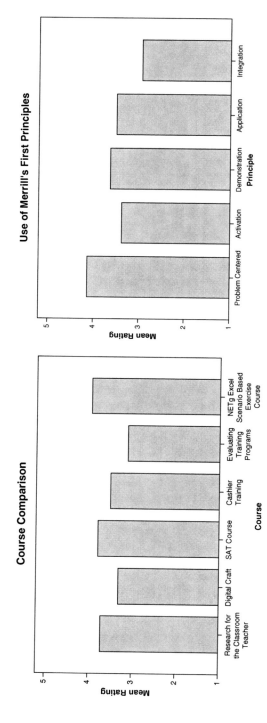

Fig. 5 The course comparison graph (*left*) visually shows that the Digital Craft course and the Evaluating Training programs course are the only ones that are rated significantly lower than the NETG Excel baseline course. The Comparison of Use of Merrill's First Principles graph (*right*) shows that the problem-centered principle is used significantly more than the other principles

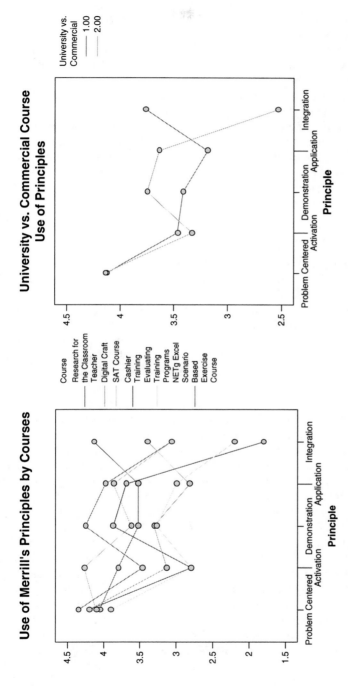

Fig. 6 The plot on the *left* shows that all of the courses are problem-centered. They implement demonstration effectively, but with some variation. They implement application a little less, and with some varying degrees, from high implementation to very low implementation. The graph on the *right*, University vs. Commercial Course Use of Principles, shows that university and commercial courses have high and similar levels of problem-centeredness, and lower and similar levels of activation. The commercial courses have higher levels of demonstration and application than the college courses. However, the commercial courses have dramatically lower levels of integration. This last difference can be explained by the fact that commercial courses are self-contained, have no interaction with the instructor, and the course contains no way of requiring students to integrate what they learn on the job or in the real world

A plot of individual principles used in each of the courses (see Fig. 6) reveals that there is a wide variation in the use of activation, application, and especially integration. However, most of the variation in integration can be explained by the fact that college courses can require students to apply their learning outside the classroom. Self-contained commercial courses do not have that capability (See Fig. 6, University vs. Commercial Course Use of Principles).

We can see by our analysis of the use of Merrill's first principles, that most courses are problem-centered; there is a variety of levels of activation, some variety of demonstration, some variety of application, and a wide variety of integration. The big difference in the use of integration can be explained by the fact that college courses can require integration, while commercial courses are often self-contained and don't have any way of requiring learners to implement their learning in real-life situations.

Conclusions

From phase I of the study we learn that some differences in instruments and courses are eliminated when college courses are aligned with school rubrics, and commercial courses with commercial rubrics. There were no significant differences between the school rubrics and the Merrill and motivation rubrics. However, there were some differences between the commercial rubrics and the commercial courses. We were able to tentatively conclude that award-winning courses do tend to use Merrill's first principles, but not to the extent we expected. We can only make tentative conclusions because of the low interrater reliability on some of the instruments and on some of the courses.

From phase II of the study we learn that award-winning courses tend to intuitively use Merrill's first principles, but with a pronounced variation in degree of application. This is not wholly unexpected as Merrill's principles are a composite of good instructional design principles. All courses rated high on the problem-centered principle, but had variation in ratings on the other principles. College courses scored high on integration, presumably because they can require students to integrate learning in real-life situations. Commercial courses scored lower on integration, presumably because they are more self-contained, and cannot require learners to integrate learning into the real world.

Also from phase II we learn that raters achieved high interrater reliability for all of the principles except the problem-centered principle. The interrater reliability may be unexpectedly low for the problem-centered principle because the definition of "real-world problems" may be confusing to raters. The characteristics of a real world problem need to be more clearly defined. Raters achieved high interrater reliability (0.568–0.847) across all of the courses except the SAT course. The raters had difficulties rating the problem-centeredness of the SAT course because although it uses questions that are problems, it is debatable whether there is a progression of increasing complexity within the problems, and whether the contrived problems on the test could be described as "real-world."

From this study we learn that accounting for individual differences in conceptual understanding between raters is very challenging for emerging areas of understanding. It appears that even award-winning courses can rate relatively low on Merrill's 5 star system when it comes to real-world tasks. Instructional support for integration of new knowledge is difficult to judge because many courses struggle with how to require integration of knowledge in the limited classroom setting. There is no doubt that we need a more concise, operationalized definition of the terms "problem-based" or "task-centered" before experts can agree on how well a course meets that 5 star requirement and before further validity tests can be performed. The reliability of the instrument has to be addressed before we can fully test the validity.

Merrill's instrument definitely has some problems, however, for now the face validity of Merrill's 5 star system still stands. From these results it does seem likely that there is still significant room for improvement of even award-winning courses. From the results to date we believe that Merrill's first principles should be included in the myriad of criteria for determining online course quality. Award-winning courses tend to use Merrill's first principles and we tentatively conclude that the use of Merrill's first principles is linked in some fashion to high-quality instruction. Once the problem with definitions has been addressed, then additional studies need to be done which correlate the use of Merrill's first principles with courses of a wide range of quality.

Appendix: Description of Rating Forms Used in this Study

1. **Merrill's 5 Star Instructional Design** Rating
2. The **Texas IQ rating form**. The Investigating Quality of Internet Course (IQ) Project was initiated under the direction of the Texas Education Agency (TEA) during the fall of 2001. The purpose of the project was to develop a tool that could be used to improve the quality of Internet-based course for Texas students.
3. The WebCT Exemplary Course Project 2005 Nomination Instructions and form. The **WebCT Exemplary Course Rubric** can be used by course authors to evaluate their course in preparation for submission for the award.
4. The Southwest Regional Education Board's Criteria for Evaluating Online Courses. The Southwest Regional Education Board's Criteria for Evaluating Online Courses is based on the SREB Essential Principles of Quality and is designed to assist states in determining the quality and effectiveness of Web-based courses.
5. The **ASTD Institute E-Learning Courseware Certification (ECC) Standards**. The ASTD Certification Standards Committee, composed of e-learning experts, academicians, instructional systems design practitioners, and other learning leaders in the industry, created The ASTD Institute E-Learning Courseware Certification (ECC) Standards. The standards are supported by examples, clarifications, definitions, scoring criteria, and other supporting information (ASTD, 2005)

6. **Brandon Hall Excellence in Learning award rating form**. The Brandon Hall Excellence in Learning Awards is entering its 13th year of recognizing the best in online learning from around the world.
7. **Motivational rubric**, which was developed by Patricia Brouwer of Twente University for her master's thesis in online motivational strategies.

References

ASTD. (2005). *The ASTD institute e-learning courseware certification (ECC) standards.* Retrieved 3/15/2005, 2005, from http://workflow.ecc-

Merrill, M. D. (2001, April 27, 2001). *5 Star Instructional Design Rating*, from http://cito.byuh.edu/merrill/text/papers.htm

Merrill, M. D. (2002a). First principles of instruction. *ETR&D, 50*(3), 43–59.

Merrill, M. D. (2002c). A pebble-in-the-pond model for instructional design. *Performance Improvement, 41*(7), 39–44.

Michigan Virtual University. (2002). *Standards for quality online courses.* Retrieved 3/14, 2005, from http://standards.mivu.org/index.tml

Petersen, M. (2005). Quality review criteria rubric. In J. Bentley (Ed.). Provo: BYU Independent Study.

Region 4 Education Service Center. (2005), *Quality of Service Guidelines for Online Courses Evaluation Matrix.* Retrieved 4-12-2005, 2005, from http://www.iqstandards.info

Sanders, E. (2003). *E-Learning courseware certification standards (1.5). Alexandria, Virginia: ASTD Certification Institute.*

Southwest Regional Education Board. (2005). *Criteria for evaluating online courses.* Retrieved 3/14, 2005, from http://www.sret.sreb.org/criteria/online.asp

Sunal, D. W., Sunal, C. S., Odell, M. R., & Sundberg, C. A. (2003). Research supported best practices for developing online learning. *The Journal for Interactive Online Learning* (2.1).

WebCT. (2005). *WebCT Customer Success Exemplary Course Project Nomination/Ruberic Form.* Retrieved 4-7-2005, 2005, from http://www.webct.com/exemplary

Supporting Reflection in Online Learning Environments

Ting-ling Lai and Susan M. Land

Abstract   Reflection is essential to deep learning and problem solving. From a socio-cultural perspective, reflection is developed through social interaction and semiotic mediation (Vygotsky, 1978; Wells, 1999). To reflect, students need to be given opportunities to review their own and others' mental processes and to use techniques such as writing or verbal reports to organize and revise thoughts (Cobb, Boufi, McClain, & Whitenack, 1997). This paper reviews strategies for supporting reflection in online environments, primarily focusing on journaling / blogging and small group asynchronous discussion. We discuss how these strategies support reflection, and survey studies that investigate the effectives of the two strategies. We also provide suggestions for guidance and evaluation of reflection with online learning environments.

Keywords   Reflection · Online journaling · Online discussion · Large-size classes

Introduction

Recent research has investigated how reflection supports learning in a variety of contexts. A number of instructional techniques can support reflection, such as weekly reports (e.g., May & Etkina, 2002; Palmer, 2004), concept maps, question prompts (e.g., Lin & Lehman, 1999), teacher-led classroom discussions (e.g., Cobb et al., 1997), or computer-supported collaborative learning environments (see for example, Hmelo, Guzdial, & Turns, 1998; Loh et al., 1997; Scardamalia, Bereiter, McLean, Swallow, & Woodruff, 1989; Schwartz, Brophy, Lin, & Bransford, 1999). Lin, Hmelo, Kinzer, and Secules (1999) summarized several uses of technology to support reflection, including process displays, process prompts, process models, and reflective social discourse.

T.-l. Lai (✉)
National Taiwan Normal University, Science Education Center RM 602, Taipei, 11699 Taiwan
e-mail: TL.Lai@sec.ntnu.edu.tw

M. Orey et al. (eds.), *Educational Media and Technology Yearbook*,
DOI 10.1007/978-0-387-09675-9_9, © Springer Science+Business Media, LLC 2009

Dewey (1938) claimed that "We do not learn from all experiences; we only learn from the experiences on which we reflect." (p. 78). Recent efforts to support student reflection have used technology to help learners reflect upon and organize ideas and make thinking more explicit and "visible" (Davis & Linn, 2000). One area of research involves helping learners *individually* to process and reflect upon their own and others' learning experiences more productively. Another area of research emphasizes the social nature of reflection, and the use of dialog and social interaction with others as a means for articulating and reflecting on multiple perspectives. Consequently, this chapter reviews research related to two primary means of supporting reflection: learning journals and collaborative peer discussion. This chapter will review the theoretical background of reflection strategies, followed by assessment, guidance, and implications for design.

Journal Writing as a Reflective Activity

Writing is a well-known instructional strategy that supports learning and thinking. From a socio-cultural perspective, writing is a psychological tool rather than an activity in its own right (Wells, 1999). By engaging in writing, students are required to employ deep cognitive processing, for example, systematically organize concepts, discover, review, and retain ideas (Emig, 1977; Fulwiler, 1987; Langer & Applebee, 1987). Teachers use writing to serve three main purposes: (1) to draw on relevant knowledge and experience in preparation for new activities; (2) to consolidate and review new information and experiences; and (3) to reformulate and extend knowledge (Langer & Applebee). According to Vygotsky, the process of writing requires writers to develop a more conscious and intentional status to transfer inner speech into written text. The writing process promotes deliberation and systematic thinking; it is also a process of problem solving (Scardamalia et al., 1989). A number of writing activities, such as note taking, summarizing, answering, and essay questions, have been shown to support learning (Keys, 1999; King, 1994). Qualitative studies have indicated that expressive writing, especially journal writing, plays a key role in developing personal understandings of science material (Powell & Lopez, 1989; Roth & Rosaen, 1991).

Traditionally, journals are used in literature and language arts classes to help writers experiment with language and document their progress (Fulwiler, 1987). Recently, journal writing has become an effective writing exercise that is used in connecting thoughts, feelings, experiences and actions for self-development, professional education, and literacy. Learning journals can be described as a "written document that students create as they respond to various concepts, events, or interactions over a period of time for the purpose of gaining insights into self-awareness and learning." (Thorpe, 2004, p. 328). The distinguishing features of learning journals are that students are able to (1) express their observations, opinions and experiences informally in a loose structure and in first-person voice; (2) keep entries over a period of time; (3) summarize and evaluate their learning process and product; and/or (4) elaborate concepts they learned from class (Lai & Land, 2007).

How Journal Writing Supports Reflection

Journal writing can support learning and reflection in both cognitive and metacognitive domains. When students are composing entries, they recapture what they have learned in class. Frequent review and connection between new information and prior knowledge promotes integration and organization of knowledge (Weinstein & Mayer, 1986). Studies have found that use of written journals leads to better learning outcomes. For instance, Jurdak and Zein (1998) report that middle school students who spent 7–10 minutes at the end of each math class summarizing the course content and listing difficulties performed better on conceptual understanding, procedural knowledge, and mathematical communication than students who took drill and practice at the end of each math class. Meel (1999) found that college students in a calculus class who emailed their weekly journal to the instructor had higher averages on the unit test, proficiency exam, and final. May and Etkina's (2002) similarly found that students with high conceptual gains had better reflection than students with lower conceptual gains.

Self-verbalization can promote self-regulated learning (Harris, 1990). Similarly, reflective journal writing is associated with improving capacities of metacognitive awareness. Studies have shown that journal writing can support metacognitive awareness. McCrindle and Christensen (1995) investigated college students' metacognitive level between journal writing and a scientific report group. Freshmen in a biology class recorded their reflections on the course content and the process of that content each week. Mostly, students reflected on what they learned in the lab session, strategies they used, and evaluations or recommendations for their future use. The results indicated that journal writers used more advanced strategies for learning and had greater metacognitive awareness about their task. Also, students in the journal group were more likely to use elaboration strategies, while students in the scientific report group were more likely to use rehearsal strategies. The journal writers performed better than the science-report group on the class examination and had more developed knowledge structures. As for their conceptual learning, students in the journal group had more complex and abstract understandings than the science report group.

The process of reviewing and revising journal entries also helps students to reflect. In Palmer's (2004) study, engineering students kept weekly online reflection journals for an engineering management course. Students in the study reported that journal writing was most useful for continuous revision of course material, and in comparing their understanding of the course material with that of other students.

Students reflect not only on personal experiences, but also from observation of peers' performance or correct models (Moreno & Mayer, 2005). Students benefit from opportunities to reassess the efficacy of strategies and procedures used in problem solving (Mezirow, 1990). College students in May and Etkina's study (2002) reported that reading peers' journals helped them to understand concepts. Similar results were also found in teacher training research (e.g., Hammersley-Fletcher & Orsmond, 2005).

Teachers usually assign journals for a variety of practical reasons, such as to (1) help students find personal connections to the material they are studying in class and text books, (2) provide a place for students to think about, learn, and understand course matter, (3) collect observations, responses, and data, and (4) allow students to practice their writing before handing it in to be graded (Fulwiler, 1987, p. 6). Journals have been used in several ways, such as to summarize what students have learned from lectures, readings, or course assignments (e.g., Ballantyne & Packer, 1995), to list difficulties in learning tasks (e.g., Jurdak & Zein, 1998), to apply course concepts to life experiences (e.g., Connor-Greene, 2000), or to evaluate a course.

Journal Writing in Online Learning Environments

With Web 2.0 technology, students can now easily write journal entries via electronic mail, blogging sites, or discussion forums (e.g., Andrusyszyn & Davie, 1997; Meel, 1999; Nückles, Schwonke, Berthold, & Renkl, 2004). Students can submit their weekly journal entries to instructors, or post their reflections online to share with peers. One example of a Web-based journal is a Weblog (blog). A blog is a personal publishing system that contains many short posts organized in reverse chronological order. Posts may include text, images, audio, video clips and any other digital formats that can be served on the Internet. Students can work individually or collaboratively to write their own personal reflection, document their learning process and problems, filter information found on the Internet, or comments on the news (Blood, 2002; Buggetun & Wasson, 2006). Compared to traditional journals, blogs enable more features for reflection. For example, blog writers can label each post and *categorize* it according to their own knowledge structure. This category function serves as a metacognitive tool which allows writers to review and re-organize their own knowledge structure.

Blogs extend individual, private, one-way written discourse to a collaborative, interactive, multimedia presentation. Blogs are not only used for reflection, but are also used for personal portfolio development, knowledge management, and community building (Oravec, 2003; Wang, Fix, & Bock, 2005; William & Jacobs, 2004). Blog writers can decide the interactive level by allowing readers to leave comments in each post, to use *RSS* to subscribe to blogs, or to cite the content. Bloggers can directly or indirectly intend to invite the community for conversation (Wrede, 2003, cited in Buggetun & Wasson, 2006). On the other hand, readers can use aggregators to collect these blog posts, so that they can organize new information according to their needs.

Like paper-based journals, blogs have also been used in educational settings. Students are encouraged to use blogs to document the design process (MacColl, Morrison, Muhlberger, Simpson, & Viller, 2005); to review and discuss teaching practices (Tan, 2006), or to use as a preparation for further peer discussion (Wang et al., 2005). Ferdig and Trammell (2004) compared blogs with other asynchronous discussion forums, such as newsgroups and bulletin boards, and proposed that blogs may be more successful in promoting conversational interactivity and active learning. Blogs may foster critical and analytical writing, as they prompt students to contemplate their own opinions and how their views might be interpreted by others (Williams & Jacobs, 2004).

Guidance to Support Reflective Journaling

A number of instructional strategies that provide guidance for reflective journaling have been proposed. Most include a summary of weekly course content to link theory and practice with observations of real world cases, elaborated from the learner's own opinions and report of learning progress. Studies indicated that students need to be provided with explicit instruction in order to compose reflective journal entries (Thorpe, 2000). Models are also suggested for students to look at specific examples of journal entries.

Moon (1999b) suggests to structure journal entries to include the following characteristics: (1) a description of observations or issues; (2) new information or revision of a former theory; (3) personal reflection—relating experiences, reinterpreting from different points of view, including different contextual factors, or linking theory to practice; and (4) action plans that resolve problems that conflict with existing knowledge. These processes go on to add either more reflection, reach a resolution, or return to the description of an event due to reviewing a new purpose against the original.

As for the format, journals can be students' individual journals that are submitted during or after classes; a dialogue journal, which is a two-way communication with instructors (e.g., Hanrahan, 1999), or a group journal, in which a group of students completes a project (e.g., Abrams, 2001).

Another factor affecting reflective journal writing includes the quantity and quality of teachers' and peers' feedback (Paterson, 1995). Studies have shown that journal writers benefit from both instructors' and peers' feedback. Instructors who provide regular feedback to prompt and reinforce analytic responses may likely maintain a high level of cognitive engagement throughout the course (Ballantyne & Packer, 1995). The feedback can model thinking processes, offer ways of organizing or expanding upon ideas, direct students to a relevant direction, and ease students' learning anxiety (Meel, 1999). Discussing entries in small groups would also contribute to shaping students' responses from different perspectives (Ballantyne & Packer, 1995).

Collaborative Peer Discussions to Support Reflection

In the past few decades, peer discussion has been employed in various learning contexts. The learning mechanisms involved in the group context are generally framed by two perspectives (Webb & Palincsar, 1996)—social interaction and cognitive conflict. Social interaction is an internalization of social processes to fit the individual's cognitive systems. Social interactions allow the learner to activate underdeveloped cognitive functions that enable him/her to perform on a higher cognitive level (Salomon, Globerson, & Guterman, 1989). Vygotsky emphasized that learning does not merely occur when the individual participates in social interaction; rather, the individual's intrapsychological plane also affects the internalized process of social interaction (Wertsch, 1991).

Based on Piaget's (2001) concept of "disequilibrium," cognitive conflict is another mechanism in the group process. Cognitive conflict arises when the learner perceives a contradiction between his/her formed experiences and present understanding. This conflict leads learners to question their beliefs and try to find new meaning. Cognitive conflict is essential to the development of knowledge. Sometimes this perspective also involves social-cognitive conflict, which results from the learner's social exchanges (Webb & Palincsar, 1996). Chan (2001) compared grade 9 and grade 12 students working with peers and individually on different levels of conceptual conflict problems. The study found that peer discussion was more beneficial for older students and students in most conceptual conflict groupings.

According to Piaget, cognitive conflicts are more likely to arise when learners work with peers than when they work with adults or advanced learners, because learners do not cooperate equally with advanced learners and do not exercise mutual control over the interaction. Studies found that peer discussion is more generative and exploratory than teacher-guided discussion (Hogan, Natstasi, & Pressley, 2000) and is more likely to use active reasoning than discussion with adults (De Lisi & Golbeck, 1999).

Peer Discussion to Support Knowledge Construction and Reflection

In a group learning context, learners talk to each other to present their ideas and perspectives. They may ask questions, provide information, and suggest plans of action. Peer discussion requires learners to (1) articulate thoughts; (2) recognize the differences among peers' perspectives, values, and general understandings; (3) negotiate meanings; and (4) refine the perspective to agreed-upon meanings and understandings. Scholars assert that even without any responses from peers, students can "think aloud," which helps the students to clarify their own ideas, elaborate them, evaluate existing knowledge for accuracy and gaps, integrate and reorganize knowledge, or in some other manner reconceptualize the material (Brown & Campione, 1986).

When learners make their thinking explicit, they may discover that their own perspectives, facts, assumptions, values, and general understandings of the material differ to a greater or lesser extent from those of their peers. To reconcile the discrepancies, the group members may negotiate understanding and meaning with each other. The negotiations occur when learners explain concepts to each other, defend their own views, ask thought-provoking questions, hypothesize, speculate about alternative interpretations, evaluate suggestions for feasibility, revise plans, and in general arrive at agreed-upon meaning and plans. These processes of meaning negotiation with others are continually reorganizing and restructuring learners' own knowledge and thinking processes. Working alone would not typically result in the same extent of cognitive development.

Webb (1989) reported that students who gave detailed elaborate explanations achieved more in peer discussion groups. King (1989) also found that students who have more verbal interaction are more likely to succeed in problem solving. Further, students who asked more task-related questions of each other reached higher levels of strategy elaboration than did unsuccessful pairs.

Asynchronous Online Discussion to Support Reflection

Online discussion is a way for learners using networked computers to exchange messages as they discuss a topic of mutual interest (Gunawardena, Lowe, & Anderson, 1997). Asynchronous online discussion supports reflection in several ways. For example, learners are able to compose their responses over elapsed time. Thus, students have more time to think and organize their thoughts (Harasim, 1993). Further, network technology enables learners' reasoning and thinking to be made visible by displaying, tracing, and recording students' arguments, including how thoughts change through the help of others (Hmelo et al., 1998; Lin et al., 1999; Scardamalia et al., 1989). Many computer-supported collaborative learning environments embed peer discussion as one important component to support students' reflection. These learning environments foster a community environment that supports students in communicating with each other, sharing notes, and commenting and building on each other's arguments. Another advantage of network technology is that it supports learners from different cultures to communicate and share different perspectives (Lin et al., 1999).

Similar to face-to-face discussion, students in asynchronous online discussion are able to make their ideas explicit and compare their ideas to those of peers (Pena-Shaff, Martin, & Gay, 2001). Previous studies have found that discussants in computer-mediated learning environments tended to spend more time monitoring and reflecting on ideas than in face-to-face interactions alone (Cohen & Scardamalia, 1998; Dillon, 1994) and generated more task-related ideas and perspectives than in face-to-face conditions (Jonassen & Kwon, 2001). Hawkes (2001) compared in-service teachers' reflection levels on a problem-based learning curriculum with face-to-face and asynchronous discussion. He found that teachers in an asynchronous discussion group were more reflective by reviewing the purposes of the task and products of discussion, while teachers in the face-to-face discussion group were task-focused.

In Cohen and Scardamalia's (1998) study, there were similar amounts of self-monitoring in both face-to-face and computer-supported collaborative learning conditions, and little coordinating of others in either condition. There was a higher portion of metaprocess (i.e., monitoring one's own ideas, monitoring ideas of others, and coordinating the ideas of all participants to create a more integrated framework for their work) in the face-to-face condition. Students were more likely to monitor others' ideas and experiments when using the computer-supported collaborative condition, while in face-to-face conditions, students were more likely to monitor their own ideas and past work.

Format of Discussion

Research findings related to online discussion have revealed a number of principles for fostering effective discussion and reflection. Examples include selecting discussion topics that relate to learners' experiences (Hsi & Hoadley, 1997), asking higher-order questions (Hara, Bonk, & Angeli, 2000), designing discussions around an anchor, such as a case or a question (Hmelo et al., 1998), and providing explicit scaffolding to encourage collaboration and reflection (Land & Dornisch, 2001).

Studies suggest that explicitness of task instruction is more important than task format (Lamy & Hassan, 2003). Gilbert and Dabbagh (2005) found that evaluation rubrics, such as the requirement of even distribution of postings and increased grade weights, have a positive impact on online discourse. That is, students who received evaluation rubrics had more peer interaction posts and made more inferences. However, if the discussion protocols mandated reading citations or limiting the length of posts, students' posts dropped and showed a lower level of cognitive processing.

Drawbacks of Online Discussion to Foster Reflection

Although online discussion holds promise to foster high-order thinking, some drawbacks have been reported. For example, Kanuka and Anderson (1998) indicated that unstructured asynchronous forums can provide metacognitive reflection and exposure to multiple perspectives, but they may not promote the application of new knowledge. In other words, students can monitor, plan, and judge different perspectives, but cannot always formulate or revise their own perspectives. Murphy (2004) examined an online asynchronous discussion via a six-level framework—social presence, articulating individual perspectives, accommodating or reflecting on the perspectives of others, co-constructing shared perspectives and meanings, building shared goals and purposes, and producing shared artifacts. She found that participants engaged primarily in processes related to social presence and articulating individual perspectives. Also, there was little evidence of accommodating or referring to the perspectives of others, which is consistent with other studies (e.g., Henri, 1992) showing that many participants in online discussions are engaged in monologues rather than in a genuine interaction.

Also, discussion can be limited in depth and breadth, and individual understanding can be unrelated to the group's understanding or to some opinion leaders in the group (Bianchini, 1995). Chen and Hung (2002) purported that online discussion forums lack the facility to support personalized knowledge representation. It is not easy to develop ownership of most discussion issues. One may mistakenly assume that all students who contributed to the collection have learned from it.

Assessing Level of Reflection During Journal Writing and Online Discussion

One of the main issues with using journal writing and online discussion as a significant classroom practice is related to how to effectively assess students' reflection. This section describes various approaches to assess and evaluate depth of reflection.

Self-Report Survey

One method to assess general reflection is a self-report survey. Kember et al. (2000) developed a 5-point Likert survey based on Mezirow's (1990) critical reflection model that includes the following categories: *habitual action, understanding, reflection, and critical reflection*. Questions from *reflection* categories included: "I often reflect on my actions to see whether I could have improved on what I did," and "I often re-appraise my experience so I can learn from it and improve for my next performance." Critical reflection questions focus more on whether the learner changes original concepts. *Critical reflection* questions included: "The course has challenged some of my firmly held ideas," "As a result of this course I have changed my normal way of doing things," and "During this course I discovered faults in what I had previously believed to be right." This type of instrument is designed to assess gains in perceived reflection during the scope of a course. Typically, students take the questionnaire at the beginning of the course and then again at the end of the course to assess the extent to which students perceive that their reflection has increased.

Content Analysis of Written Discourse

Assessing level of reflection during online discussion can be complex. Many researchers use content analyses of discussion posts to analyze level of reflection. Coding schemes for content analysis differ according to the purposes and content of the discussion. For example, Henri (1992) proposed five key dimensions—participation rate, interaction type, social cues, cognitive skills and metacognitive skills and knowledge. Gunawardena, Lowe, and Anderson (1997) developed a five-stage coding scheme to examine the knowledge construction process—sharing/comparing of information; discovery and exploration of dissonance or inconsistency among ideas, concepts, or statements; negotiation of meaning; testing and modification of proposed synthesis; and agreement statements.

Sparkes-Langer, Simmons, Pasch, Colton, and Starko (1990) reported seven levels of reflection that distinguish types of language and thinking: (1) no descriptive language; (2) simple, layperson description; (3) events labeled with appropriate terms; (4) explanation with tradition or personal preference given as the rationale; (5) explanation with principle/theory given as the rationale; (6) explanation with principle/theory and consideration of context factor; and (7) explanation with consideration of ethical, moral, and political issues. Although the coding scheme mirrors Gagne's (1968) hierarchy of thinking, it is aligned primarily to the linguistic structure of discourse than to a model of reflective thinking.

Hatton and Smith (1995) developed a series of rubrics to assess reflective writing for teacher training, including *no reflection, descriptive reflection, dialogic reflection,* and *critical reflection. No reflection* is a level in which students simply describe the action without relating it to their explanation, meaning, or judgment. *Descriptive reflection* focuses on one's own perspective. *Dialogic reflection* not only includes multiple perspectives, but also analyzes and integrates factors and perspectives. In this level, students may recognize inconsistencies and provide deliberate rationales and critique. *Critical reflection* includes multiple perspectives, influenced by multiple historical and socio-political contexts. Based on Hatton and Smith's (1995) and others' coding schemes, Maclellan (2004) added three categories to comprise three elements of the reflective process—the conceptualization, the implication, and the veracity of the issue; and four hierarchical levels of reflection: technical, descriptive, dialogical, and critical. The two coding schemes have been used to analyze written discourse in professional training.

Conclusion

This chapter reviewed current research related to two primary strategies for fostering student reflection: written journals and collaborative peer discussion. Research shows that, regardless of the specific strategies used, reflection needs guidance. Without guidance, reflection can be unfocused and superficial. By supporting students to reflect and build upon each other's work and to engage the collaborative knowledge building process, increased reflection is more likely to be realized. More research is needed, however, in advancing our understanding of what strategies best support reflection and how to measure reflection in contexts that are scalable to most practices of online education—particularly those that support large class sizes.

References

Abrams, Z. I. (2001). Computer-mediated communication and group journals: Expanding the repertoire of participant roles. *System, 29,* 489–503.

Andrusyszyn, M., & Davie, L. (1997). Facilitating reflection through interactive journal writing in an online graduate course: A qualitative study. *Journal of Distance Education, 12,* 103–126.

Ballantyne, R., & Packer, J. (1995). The role of student journals in facilitating reflection at the doctoral level. *Studies in Continuing Education, 17*(1–2), 29–45.

Bianchini, J. A. (1995). *Groupwork in middle school science: A case study of scientific knowledge and social process construction.* Paper presented at the annual meeting of the American Educational Research Association, San Francisco.

Blood, R. (2002). *The weblog handbook: Practical advice on creating and maintaining your blog.* Cambridge, MA: Perseus.

Brown, A. L., & Campione, J. C. (1986). Psychological theory and the study of learning disabilities. American Psychologist, *14,*1059–1068.

Buggetun, B., & Wasson, W. (2006). Self-regulated learning and open writing. *European Journal of Education, 41*(3–4), 453–472.

Chan, C. K. K. (2001). Peer collaboration and discourse patterns in learning from incompatible information. *Instructional Science, 29,* 443–479.

Chen, D. T., & Hung, D. (2002). Personalized knowledge representations: The missing half of online discussions. *British Journal of Educational Technology, 33*(3), 279–290.

Cobb, P., Boufi, A., McClain, K., & Whitenack, J. (1997). Reflective discourse and collective reflection. *Journal for Research in Mathematics Education, 28*(3), 258–277.

Cohen, A., & Scardamalia, M. (1998). Discourse about ideas: Monitoring and regulation in face-to-face and computer-mediated environments. *Interactive Learning Environments, 6*(1–2), 93–113.

Connor-Greene, P. A. (2000). Making connections: Evaluating the effectiveness of journal writing in enhancing student learning. *Teaching of Psychology, 27*(1), 44–46.

De Lisi, R., & Golbeck, S. (1999). The implications of Piagetian theory for peer learning. In A. O'Donnell & A. King (Eds.), *Cognitive perspectives on peer learning.* Mahwah, NJ: Lawrence Erlbaum Associates.

Davis, E. A., & Linn, M. (2000). Scaffolding students' knowledge integration: Prompts for reflection in KIE. *International Journal of Science Education, 22* (8), 819–837.

Dewey, J. (1938). *Experience and education.* New York: Collier, Kappa Delta Pi Series.

Dillon, J. T. (1994). *Using discussion in classrooms.* Buckingham: Open University Press.

Emig, J. (1977). Writing is a mode of learning. *College Composition and Communication, 28,* 122–128.

Ferdig, R. E., & Trammell, K. D. (2004). Content delivery in the "Blogosphere." *T.H.E. Journal, 31*(7), 12–20.

Fulwiler, T. (1987). *The journal book.* Portsmouth, NH: Boynton/Cook.

Gagne, R. M. (1968). Learning hierarchies. *Educational Psychologist, 6,* 1–9.

Gilbert, P. K., & Dabbagh, N. (2005). How to structure online discussions for meaningful discourse: A case study. *British Journal of Educational Technology, 36*(1), 5–18.

Gunawardena, C. N., Lowe, C. A., & Anderson, T. (1997). Analysis of a global online debate and the development of an interaction analysis model for examining social construction of knowledge in computer conferencing. *Journal of Educational Computing Research, 17*(4), 397–431.

Hammersley-Fletcher, L., & Orsmond, P. (2005). Reflecting on reflective practice within peer observation? *Studies in Higher Education, 30*(2), 213–224.

Hanrahan, M. (1999). Rethinking science literacy: Enhancing communication and participating in school science through affirmational dialogue journal writing. *Journal of Research in Science Teaching, 36*(6), 699–717.

Hara, N., Bonk, C. J., & Angeli, C. (2000). Content analyses of on-line discussion in an applied educational psychology course. *Instructional Science, 28*(2), 115–152.

Harasim, L. (1993). Collaborating in Cyberspace: Using computer conferences as a group learning environment. *Interactive Learning Environments, 3*(2), 119–130.

Harris, K. (1990). Developing self-regulated learners: The role of private speech and self-instructions. *Educational Psychologist, 25*, 35–50.

Hatton, N., & Smith, D. (1995). Reflection in teacher education: Towards definition and implementation. *Teaching and Teacher Education, 11*(1), 33–49.

Hawkes, M. (2001). Variables of interest in exploring the reflective outcomes of network-based communication. *Journal of Research on Computing in Education, 33*(3), 299–315.

Henri, F. (1992). The process of distance learning and teleconferencing assisted by computer: An analytic essay. *Canadian Journal of Educational Communication, 21*(1), 3–18.

Hmelo, C. E., Guzdial, M., & Turns, J. (1998). Computer-support for collaborative learning: Learning to support student engagement. *Journal of Interactive Learning Research, 9*(2), 107–129.

Hogan, K., Natstasi, B. K., & Pressley, M. (2000). Discourse patterns and collaborative scientific reasoning in peer and teacher-guided discussions. *Cognition and Instruction, 17*(4), 379–432.

Hsi, S., & Hoadley, C. M. (1997). Productive discussion in science: Gender equity through electronic discourse. *Journal of Science Education and Technology, 6*(1), 23–36.

Jonassen, D., & Kwon, H. I. (2001). Communication patterns in computer-mediated vs. face-to-face group problem solving. *Educational Technology Research and Development, 49*(10), 35–52.

Jurdak, M., & Zein, R. A. (1998). The effect of journal writing on achievement in and attitudes toward mathematics. *School Science and Mathematics, 98*(8), 412–419.

Kanuka, H., & Anderson, T. (1998). On-line social interchange, discord and knowledge construction. *Journal of Distance Education, 13*(1), 57–74.

Kember, D., Leung, D. Y. P., Jones, A., Loke, A. Y., Mckay, J., & Sinclair, K. (2000). Development of a questionnaire to measure the level for reflective thinking. *Assessment and Evaluation in HigherEducation, 25*(4), 381–395.

Keys, C. W. (1999). Language as an indicator of meaning generation: An analysis of middle school students' written discourse about scientific investigations. *Journal of Research in Science Teaching, 36*(9), 1044–1061.

King, A. (1989). Verbal interaction and problem-solving within computer-assisted cooperative learning groups. *Journal of Educational Computing Research, 5*(1), 15.

King, A. (1994). Guiding knowledge construction in the classroom: Effects of teaching children how to question and how to explain. *American Educational Research Journal, 31*(2), 358–368.

Lai, T-L., & Land, S.M. (2007, April). The Effects of Using Peer Discussion, Learning Journal and Question Prompts to Support Reflection in a Distance Learning Environment. *Paper presented at the annual conference of the American Educational Research Association*, Chicago, IL.

Lamy, M. N., & Hassan, X. (2003). What influences reflective interaction in distance peer learning? Evidence from four long-term online learners of French. *Open Learning, 18*(1), 39–59.

Land, S. M., & Dornisch, M. M. (2001). A case study of student use of asynchronous bulletin board systems (BBS) to support reflection and evaluation. *Journal of Educational Technology Systems, 30*(4), 365–377.

Langer, J. A., & Applebee, A. N. (1987). *How writing shapes thinking: A study of teaching and learning* (NCTE Research Report No. 22). Urbana, IL: National Council of Teachers of English.

Lin, X., Hmelo, C., Kinzer, C. K., & Secules, T. J. (1999). Designing technology to support reflection. *Educational Technology Research and Development, 47*(3), 43–62.

Lin, X., & Lehman, J. D. (1999). Supporting learning of variable control in a computer-based biology environment: Effects of prompting college students to reflect on their own thinking. *Journal of Research in Science Teaching, 36*(7), 837–858.

Loh, B., Radinsky, J., Reiser, B. J., Gomez, L. M., Edelson, D. C., & Russell, E. (1997). The progress portfolio: Promoting reflective inquiry in complex investigation environments. In R. Hall, N. Miyake, & N. Enyedy (Eds.), *Proceedings of computer supported collaborative learning '97* (pp. 169–178). Toronto, Ontario, Canada.

MacColl, I., Morrison, A., Muhlberger, R., Simpson, M., & Viller, S. (2005). *Reflections on reflection: Blogging in undergraduate design studios.* Blogtalk Downunder Conference, 2005

Maclellan, E. (2004). How reflective is academic essay? *Studies in Higher Education, 29*(1), 75–89.

May, D. B., & Etkina, E. (2002). College physics students' epistemological self-reflection and its relationship to conceptual learning. *American Journal of Physics, 70*(12), 1249–1258.

McCrindle, A., & Christensen, C. (1995). The impact of learning journals on metacognitive process and learning performance. *Learning and Instruction, 5*(3), 167–185.

Meel, D. E. (1999). Email dialogue journals in a college calculus classroom: A look at the implementation and benefits. *Journal of Computers in Mathematics and Science Teaching, 18*(4), 387–413.

Mezirow, J. (1990). Fostering critical reflection in adulthood: A guide to transformative and emancipatory learning. San Francisco: Jossey-Bass Publishers.

Moon, J. A. (1999b). Learning journals: A handbook for academics, students and professional development. London: Kogan Page.

Moreno, R., & Mayer, R. E. (2005). Role of guidance, reflection, and interactivity in an agent-based multimedia game. *Journal of Educational Psychology, 97*(1), 117–128.

Murphy, E. (2004). Recognizing and promoting collaboration in an online asynchronous discussion. *British Journal of Educational Technology, 35*(4), 421–431.

Nückles, M., Schwonke, R., Berthold, K., & Renkl, A. (2004). The use of public learning diaries in blended learning. Journal of Educational Media, 29, 49–66.

Oravec, J. A. (2003). Blending by blogging: Weblogs in blended learning initiatives. *Journal of Educational Media, 28*(2/3), 225–233.

Palmer, S. (2004). Evaluation of an online reflective journal in engineering education. *Computer Applications in Engineering Education, 12,* 209–214.

Paterson, B. L. (1995). Developing and maintaining reflection in clinical journals. *Nurse Education Today, 15*(3), 211–220.

Pena-Shaff, J., Martin, W., & Gay, G. (2001). An epistemological framework for analyzing student interactions in computer-mediated communication environments. *Journal of Interactive Learning Research, 12*(1), 41–68.

Piaget, J. (2001). *Studies in reflecting abstraction.* Hove, UK: Psychology Press.

Powell, A. B., & Lopez, J. (1989). Writing as a vehicle to learning mathematics: A case study. In P. Connally & T. Vilardi (Eds.), *Writing to learn mathematics and science* (pp. 157–177). New York: Teachers College Press.

Roth, K. J., & Rosaen, C. L. (1991). *Writing activities in conceptual change science learning community: Two perspectives.* Paper presented at the annual meeting of the National Association for Research in Science Teaching, Lake Geneva, WI.

Salomon, G., Globerson, T., & Guterman, E. (1989). The computer as a zone of proximal development: Internalizing reading-related metacognition from a reading partner. *Journal of Educational Psychology, 81*(4), 620–627.

Scardamalia, M., Bereiter, C., McLean, R. S., Swallow, J., & Woodruff, E. (1989). Computer-supported intentional learning environments. *Journal of Educational Computing Research, 5*(1), 51–68.

Schwartz, D. L., Brophy, S., Lin, X., & Bransford, J. D. (1999). Software for managing complex learning: Examples from an educational psychology course. *Educational Technology Research and Development, 47*(2), 39–59.

Sparkes-Langer, G., Simmons, J., Pasch, M., Colton, A., & Starko, A. (1990). Reflective pedagogical thinking: How can we promote and measure it? *Journal of Teacher Education, 41,* 23–32.

Tan, A. (2006). *Does scaffolded blogging promote preservice teacher reflection? Examining the relationships between learning tool and scaffolding in a blended learning environment.* Unpublished Dissertation, Indiana University.

Thorpe, K. (2004). Reflective learning journals: From concept to practice. *Reflective Practice, 5*(3), 327–343.

Thorpe, M. (2000). Reflective learning and distance learning—made to mix by design and by assessment. *Information Services & Use, 20*(2–3), 145–158.

Vygotsky, L. S. (1978). *Mind in society: The development of higher psychological processes* (M. Cole, V. Jogh-Steiner, S. Scribner, & E. Souberma, Eds. & Trans.). Cambridge, MA: Harvard University.

Wang, M., Fix, R., & Bock, L. (2005). The use of blogs in teaching, knowledge management, and performance improvement. In Richards, G. (Ed.), *Proceedings of world conference on e-learning in corporate, government, healthcare, and higher education 2005* (pp. 3192–3199). Chesapeake, VA: AACE.

Webb, N. M. (1989). Peer interaction and learning in small groups. *International Journal of Educational Research, 13*, 21–39.

Webb, N. M., & Palincsar, A. S. (1996). Group process in the classroom. In D. C. Berliner & R. C. Calfee (Eds.), *Handbook of educational psychology* (pp. 841–873). New York: Simon & Schuster Macmillan.

Weinstein, C. E., & Mayer, R. E. (1986). The teaching of learning strategies. In M. Wittrock (Ed.), *Handbook of research on teaching* (3rd ed., pp. 315–332). New York: Macmillan.

Wells, C. G. (1999). *Dialogic inquiry: Towards a sociocultural practice and theory of education.* Cambridge, UK; New York: Cambridge University Press.

Wertsch, J. V. (1991). *Voices of the mind.* Cambridge, MA: Harvard University Press.

Williams, J. B., & Jacobs, J. (2004). Exploring the use of blogs as learning spaces in the higher education sector. *Australasian Journal of Educational Technology, 20*(2), 232–247.

Wrede, O. (2003). *Weblog and discourse: Weblogs as a transformational technology for higher education and academic research.* Blogtalk Conference paper, Vienna, May 23–24, 2003. http://weblogs.design.fh-aachen.de/owrede/publikationen/weblogs_and_discourse

The Interplay of Teaching Conceptions and a Course Management System Among Award-Winning University Professors

Xornam S. Apedoe, Douglas R. Holschuh, and Thomas C. Reeves

Abstract   As the use of course management systems (CMSs) becomes nearly ubiquitous in higher education, it is imperative that we consider their impact and influence on instructional methods and the learning environments. Moves to incorporate more student-centered models of teaching and learning, and integrating technology such as CMSs, are unlikely to be successful without understanding the relationship between the teaching conceptions of faculty and their adaptations of the technological tools available to them. The purpose of this study was to examine (a) how CMSs influence teaching methods, and (b) how faculty members' conceptions about teaching and learning are supported by the functions available in CMSs. Results indicate that use of a CMS had very little influence on faculty members' teaching practices or conceptions of teaching. Additionally, faculty reported using CMSs primarily for information dissemination, regardless of their conceptions of teaching. The results of this study have implications for administrators and faculty in higher education, as well as designers of CMSs.

Keywords   Course management systems · Learning management systems · Teaching methods · Higher education

The Internet has been a part of university life for far longer than it has been in use in the general population. Indeed, its first real population of users came primarily from the ranks of university professors and researchers (Hafner & Lyon, 1996). Early adopters of the Internet in teaching higher education courses primarily utilized e-mail, internet relay chat (IRC), and Usenet newsgroups. However, it wasn't until the creation of the World Wide Web and the mass propagation of Web browsers and Internet access that the capacity to use Internet technologies for teaching was opened up to the larger population of faculty who were not among the pioneers. But the mass adoption of the World Wide Web wasn't enough by itself to push the

X.S. Apedoe (✉)
Department of Learning & Instruction, University of San Francisco, San Francisco, CA, 94117
email: xapedoe@usfca.edu

M. Orey et al. (eds.), *Educational Media and Technology Yearbook*,
DOI 10.1007/978-0-387-09675-9_10, © Springer Science+Business Media, LLC 2009

use of Internet technologies in higher education to a critical mass. There needed to be an easy and efficient way for instructors to put their courses online, and this became the catalyst for the development of numerous course management systems (CMSs) such as WebCT, Blackboard, and Desire2Learn. The large-scale adoption of commercial CMSs by universities and colleges across North America suggests that this push has been well received by higher education decision-makers and that the movement to put courses online or to augment courses with online components is proceeding apace (Pittinsky, 2003).

In a different vein, there has been a movement, albeit slowly, away from traditional lecture-heavy methods of instruction where information transmission and student memorization are considered the keys to academic success. Over the past two decades, constructivist and student-centered notions of teaching and learning have worked their way into the college curriculum, and although they have been rarely adopted in full, concessions towards them, such as having small group study sessions and more discussion opportunities, are increasingly common, even in lecture courses with scores or even hundreds of students (Bransford, Brown, & Cocking, 2000).

These two developments create a complex picture wherein faculty are trying to incorporate constructivist learning principles while at the same time moving much or all of their courses to an online environment. Faculty members' ability to succeed at these two goals is dependent both on the capacity of the technology to foster a constructivist learning experience as well as on the instructor's conceptions of knowledge (Howard, McGee, Schwartz, & Purcell, 2000) and teaching (Laurillard, 2002).

Literature Review

Course management systems (CMSs) have been promoted as an easy way for faculty to integrate Web technology into their traditional classroom instruction, or even to transition completely into online teaching (Maeroff, 2003; Mann, 2000). CMSs are software packages that reside on an Internet server and provide various functions such as storing course-related information online (Oliver, 2001). Popular systems include Blackboard (www.blackboard.com), Desire2Learn (www.desire2learn.com) and WebCT (www.webct.com). These systems are designed specifically for faculty who lack experience with Web development or file management on Internet servers. These systems typically provide templates for developing Web pages and tools for faculty to upload course material for access by students using a Web browser. Current versions have been criticized as providing faculty with tools to develop and deliver content, for example, online readings (Oliver, 2001) using a traditional instructivist (teacher-centered) perspective (Herrington & Standen, 2000) rather than enabling interaction. However, CMSs typically include discussion boards, chat rooms, and sometimes electronic workgroup areas, which can be used to promote constructivist (learner-centered) learning goals (Perkins, 1991).

Online learning, which may make content delivery *per se* more efficient and less expensive, is not necessarily pedagogically advanced (Reeves, 2003), and it certainly does not equate with constructivist learning (Weigel, 2002). As Cuban (2001) noted, the majority of university faculty fail to use the technology available to them, and the few who do adopt technology use it primarily to maintain existing classroom practices.

Oliver (2001) categorizes three common uses of the Web for online teaching: (a) quick dissemination, (b) Web-enabled supplements, and (c) Web-engaged activity. Quick dissemination is characterized by its focus on delivering information to anyone at anytime. It typically involves the use of text documents or slide presentations placed on the Web for students to access. This use of the Web in teaching is to provide students who may miss a class (or lose the information) with important course resources such as lecture notes, assignment sheets, course syllabus, and so on. Providing Web-enabled supplements is another strategy employed for online teaching. Here the focus is on providing students with access to resources they would otherwise not have the opportunity to view or study. Finally, creating Web-engaged activities to promote students' higher order thinking is another teaching strategy that is utilized. Studies by Britto (2002) and Dehoney and Reeves (1999) found that information (quick) dissemination uses of course Web pages were far more common than supplements or interactive activities.

The different uses of the Web in online teaching can be related to instructors' conceptions about teaching and learning. The term "conception," which is often used interchangeably with the term "beliefs," can be defined as the

> ... specific meanings attached to phenomena which then mediate our response to situations involving those phenomena. We form conceptions of virtually every aspect of our perceived world, and in so doing, use those abstract representations to delimit something from, and relate it to, other aspects of our world. In effect, we view the world through the lenses of our conceptions, interpreting and acting in accordance with our understanding of the world. (Pratt, 1992, p. 204)

With respect to teaching, conceptions of teaching may be envisioned as being the lens through which the process of teaching and learning is viewed and shaped. Research (e.g., Kember, 1997; Kember & Kwan, 2002) suggests that there is an important relationship between teaching conceptions and approaches to teaching. Kember (1997) has stated that "At the level of the individual teacher, the methods of teaching adopted, the learning tasks set, the assessment demands made and the workload specified are strongly influenced by the orientation to teaching" (p. 270).

Conceptions of teaching. In Kember's (1997) review of the literature, he concludes that university lecturers' conceptions of teaching fall into one of two orientations: teacher-centered or student-centered. A teacher-centered orientation has a focus on communication of defined bodies of content or knowledge, whereas a student-centered orientation focuses on student learning and taking a developmental approach to students' conceptions of knowledge. Each orientation can be further characterized by conceptions of teaching. The conceptions are as follows:

1. Imparting Information: This is the most teacher-centered conception, and has a focus on delivering information to students. In this conception, teaching is viewed merely as the presenting of information, and the focus is on the lecturer.

2. Transmitting Structured Knowledge: As with the imparting information conception, the emphasis is on delivering information to the students but in a structured way so that students have a better chance of receiving the knowledge. Much more emphasis is placed on how the information is presented, and teaching may be viewed as a stage performance.
3. Student-Teacher Interaction: This is a transitional conception that recognizes the importance of student-teacher interactions. There is less emphasis on the lecturer's knowledge base, and more emphasis on students' understanding. Often, there is a "tension between not taking everything at face value and telling them the (right) outcome" (Kember, 1997, p. 267).
4. Facilitating Understanding/Learning Facilitation: This conception falls under the student-centered orientation. The role of the teacher is to help the student reach specific learning goals. The desired outcome of the teaching process under this conception is student understanding, which is demonstrated by applying knowledge, not regurgitating it.
5. Conceptual Change/Intellectual Development: This conception is the most student-centered. It may have two facets, changing student conceptions and holistic developmental processing resulting in interpersonal relationships between teachers and students.

More recent research (Kember & Kwan, 2002; Samuelowicz & Bain, 2001) has challenged Kember's (1997) identification of the "student-teacher interaction" conception, yet the validity of the other conceptions proposed by Kember remains intact. Although there is a relationship between conceptions of teaching and observable teaching approaches, Kember (1997) notes that the relationship is not always automatic. Rather it is believed that the selection of a teaching approach can be described as having a preferred or relational nature (Kember & Kwan, 2002). That is, instructors are likely to have a predominately preferred teaching approach, but will adopt an alternative approach if the teaching environment demands it. For example, an instructor that has a primarily student-centered teaching orientation may occasionally still engage in teaching practices that may appear inconsistent with this orientation, such as lecturing. However, this does not imply that the instructor's beliefs have changed, rather, it suggests that the use of a more teacher-centered practice, in this case lecture, is used as one element of an overall teaching approach to facilitate learning. In any case, it appears that the preferred approach to teaching is likely determined to a large extent by the faculty member's conceptions of teaching (Kember & Kwan, 2002). Kember (1997) states that:

> A lecturer who holds an information transmission conception is likely to rely almost exclusively upon a unidirectional lecture approach. Even classes designated as tutorials are likely to end up largely as monologues. It is hard to see anyone holding such beliefs engaging in more interactive teaching methods such as dialogue or role play. (p. 270)

Teaching Conceptions and CMSs. There are two issues that arise regarding the use of CMSs in relation to conceptions of teaching and learning. First, uses of Web technologies are promoted by researchers, developers, and commercial interests for their capabilities to provide more interaction and enhance student engagement (Oliver, 2001; Pittinsky, 2003). Higher education instructors are encouraged to develop online course components, with CMSs being the preferred method for doing so. Yet, in the promotion of using these Web technologies (CMSs in particular), little consideration is given to faculty members' conceptions of teaching and learning. Unless a faculty member holds a conception of teaching compatible with student-centered learning (i.e., facilitating deep understanding or conceptual change/intellectual development), then CMSs are unlikely to be used in a manner that promotes such learning.

The second issue that arises pertaining to use of CMSs and faculty's conceptions of teaching relates to the tools available in CMSs. Despite the popularity of CMSs, a major concern of some critics and researchers is that they most strongly promote one purpose of online teaching: information dissemination (Britto, 2002; Oliver, 2001). Because of the strong relationship between teaching conceptions and teaching approaches, faculty who hold teaching conceptions other than information dissemination may not perceive CMSs as obviously helpful in their attempts to facilitate student learning. Although there is evidence that CMSs can offer powerful interactive tools for instructors who wish to use them to support constructivist learning environments centered around authentic tasks (Herrington, Oliver, & Reeves, 2003), CMSs may promote traditional teaching methods simply because many of their basic functions are described in commonplace instructional terms such as presentations, readings, quizzes, and grades.

Present Study

The purpose of this study was to understand faculty members' experiences teaching with course management software. We examined (a) how course management systems influence teaching methods, and (b) how faculty members' beliefs about teaching and learning are supported by the functions available in the course management system that they use. The specific research questions of interest were:

1. What are faculty members' conceptions of teaching?
2. How are faculty members' conceptions of teaching and/or practices influenced by the integration of course management systems into their teaching practice?
3. How are faculty members' conceptions of teaching supported by the tools available in course management systems?

Method

Context and Participants

This study was conducted at a large research university in the southeastern USA from spring 2003 to spring 2004. The university has been using WebCT since 1997, and was at one time the largest single adopter of WebCT. It still ranks as one of the largest users of WebCT, and the CMS is used in virtually every academic department on campus. Even so, WebCT use at the university is still pedagogically immature.

Participant Descriptions. Research participants were senior and junior faculty members from various departments, who have been (a) formally recognized for their excellent teaching, and (b) have been users of WebCT. A total of five senior and junior faculty members participated in this study. A brief description of each participant follows.

- Dr. Andrews has been a professor in the business side of a science related field for 17 years. At the time of the interview, he was an associate professor and the undergraduate coordinator for his department. Dr. Andrews has taught the courses he discussed in his interview throughout his time at the university, and has been nominated for and received numerous teaching awards. Dr. Andrews is a long time user of the Web, and has been putting his course syllabus and notes online since 1997. Dr. Andrews reports that he came to use WebCT primarily because he believes that students have come to expect it. As the undergraduate coordinator for his department he encourages his colleagues to use WebCT in their courses.
- Dr. Barnes is an assistant professor in the business college at the university. He has been teaching at the university for 4 years, and has already received one award for his teaching. Dr. Barnes attributes his use of WebCT to the need to find a way to provide students with notes and information that they demanded he provide them ahead of class time.
- Dr. Halloway is a member of a professional school at this southeastern institution. He has worked in the professional school for 13 years, and has been recognized for his teaching excellence. Dr. Halloway claims, "there's a big gulf here in terms of generations between me and the people who are using computers," and identifies himself as a novice user of technology for instructional purposes. Dr. Halloway chose to begin using WebCT primarily because it was the platform of choice at the university, and it was one way to offer the course that he was teaching, which was primarily online.
- Dr. McBurton received his Ph.D. in 1980, in a science related field. He has taught at the university for 19 years. He is a full professor, and has received numerous teaching awards. Dr. McBurton reports using technologies such as overhead projectors, 8 mm movies, and digital movies in his classroom teaching. He is a new user of both WebCT and PowerPoint for instruction. Dr. McBurton reports that he came to use WebCT as a result of administrative pressure to reduce his photocopying costs.
- Dr. Samuels is an assistant professor in a professional school at the university and has already been recognized for her teaching excellence. Dr. Samuels states that although she was familiar with WebCT, her inspiration to really begin using WebCT in her own teaching was from observing a colleagues extensive use of the system for teaching.

Data Collection and Analysis

The primary method of data collection was semi-structured interviews. All recent recipients of teaching awards were contacted through email and asked to participate in an interview study examining teaching and the use of WebCT. Faculty members who volunteered to participate were then contacted again through email and a face-to-face interview was scheduled. Interviews were audio-taped and lasted approximately 45 minutes. All interviews were transcribed by the researchers.

Interview transcripts were analyzed on multiple passes by the researchers (Miles & Huberman, 1994). In one pass, researchers coded the interviews against the *a priori* codes taken from Kember (1997). In a second pass, researchers coded against the research questions. In a third pass, researchers coded against the interview questions. The three coding passes allowed the researchers to conduct detailed, cross-coded searches for themes and categories.

Results and Discussion

What Are Faculty Members' Conceptions of Teaching?

Participants' statements were categorized using Kember's (1997) conceptions of teaching. As these were all award-winning teachers, we must admit that we expected all of them to fall toward the student-centered end of Kember's scale. This did not turn out to be the case for every participant, and perhaps it is our own subjectivities as members of a discipline (instructional technology as sub-discipline of the larger education field) that has become so heavily student-centered and constructivist over the last decade that gave us this false preconception. As we ventured out into the larger university community, we discovered that even award-winning faculty members held different views on teaching from our own.

Dr. Andrews' teaching conceptions. Based on his statements, it appears that Dr. Andrews' conception of teaching can be best characterized as being that of Transmitting Structured Knowledge. It appeared that his concern was focused on presenting students with information, and that his focus was not on engaging students in the learning process using techniques such as discussion.

In describing his teaching Dr. Andrews, often spoke of presenting knowledge:

> I kind of see myself as presenting new ideas and new materials and new kinds of tools to use and so I like to have the students first of all be presented with the material but then also to use the material in some context.

Dr. Andrews also spoke of giving his students detailed notes so that they would be able to follow along with what he was trying to convey:

> They come to class with this set of notes and I go over it, and then they ask questions if there are any problems, but a lot of times they just sit there like a bump on a log, not many of them write.

Dr. Barnes' teaching conceptions. Facilitating Understanding/Learning Facilitation best captures the sentiments expressed by Dr. Barnes in his interview. Dr. Barnes spoke primarily about getting his students to first learn the content matter, and then understand, with a heavy emphasis on being able to apply their knowledge. All of these goals are characteristic of the facilitating understanding conception of teaching. Dr. Barnes described his objectives for his course:

> I want them to understand that, to be critical thinkers of information and also be able to actually start to develop skill in using ways to influence other people.

His focus on understanding and applying concepts is evidenced in these statements:

> Really it's a lot of questioning trying to get them to understand when something might apply, or when it may not apply. . .That's the in-class way that I try to meet those objectives. They know its not just memorizing, they are going to need to be able to recognize it in a situation, and they are going to need to be able to apply it in a situation. . .So you not only need to know it, I tell them, but you have to start to develop the skills of diagnostics to be able to tell when a certain principle or a certain practice needs to be applied.
> I really want to push it past memorization. I want to try to get it so that they are actually practicing something. Because I think learning happens through practice.

Dr. Halloway's conceptions. Dr. Halloway was a bit of an anomaly for our study because the course that he described throughout his interview was a graduate level course that was conducted primarily online, whereas the other interviewees all described undergraduate courses that regularly met face-to-face. It may be safe to assume that the goals and methods used in teaching a graduate level course are typically quite different from the goals and methods used to teach an undergraduate course. With that being said, Dr. Halloway, primarily spoke of his teaching using phrases that could be categorized as Facilitating Understanding/Learning Facilitation. Dr. Halloway spoke of the goals for his course as being:

> I'm trying to get them to understand the relationship between general education and the philosophy and purposes of the technical school and clearly the community college that they were evolving to. . .

Dr. Halloway also spoke of his philosophy of teaching as trying to encourage curiosity among his students, and providing opportunities for them to develop skills to use in other contexts:

> I think besides just transmitting knowledge which includes in my mind a point of view. . .the transfer of knowledge or experience from somebody who has done some of it to somebody who is just starting to do it and then to incite some curiosity and some interest in the subject even if they're not interested in the subject so that they at least have working knowledge of what its all about and the ability to recognize when in fact that material applies to the situation whether its intended to or not so that they carry away some knowledge, skills, and tools that will intellectually or professionally help them.

Dr. McBurton's teaching conceptions. Dr. McBurton appears to hold the Conceptual Change/Intellectual Development conception of teaching, in which his focus is on helping students' intellectual development and conceptual development. He spoke frequently of trying to encourage his students to think, and providing them with tools to learn how to do so. In describing his course and his teaching methods Dr. McBurton used phrases such as: "prompt thinking; a lot of focus on learning and thinking." In describing the objectives of his course, Dr. McBurton stated:

So I want the students to know what is known, to be able to look at the cartoons in the textbook, but I also want them to know where the information came from, because if we don't know where something came from how can we question, how can we think?

Dr. McBurton also stated:

So if we can't start teaching them to how to think and appreciate what their knowledge is, what they actually know, then I think we're not doing our jobs for the students.
My teaching philosophy is to challenge the students to learn and grow. Severely challenge them and then empower them with tools and self-confidence so that they can meet the challenge and then go forth with newly found abilities and knowledge and self-confidence.

Dr. Samuels' conceptions. From Dr. Samuels' interview, she can best be described as primarily holding a Conceptual Change/Intellectual Development of teaching. Because Dr. Samuels is in a professional studies field, we believe that the nature of the material that she teaches may contribute to the way she speaks about teaching. Dr. Samuels described the objectives of her course:

The objectives are to learn the fundamentals, fundamentals of practice... They've already had, in the communication class, we introduce interviewing, ... and so they are to take what they know about that and then take what they, they're also getting human behavior and so they are to begin to integrate all of those things with what they're learning about issues and problems and people and begin to be able to do assessments and begin to be able to make case plans, umm, begin to struggle with what's an ethical dilemma...For example, one of the things that our students really struggle with are gay issues, gay and lesbian issues, how do you put what may be your religious beliefs aside and deal with a person as opposed to an act, for example.

Dr. Samuels' conception of teaching as being primarily to influence conceptual change and/or intellectual development in her students is evidenced in statements such as:

I think teaching is a mutual journey between the teacher and the student. I think that the teachers can learn as much from the student as the students can ever learn from the teacher. Um, I think that if you go in as a teacher and you don't respect what the student brings then you've lost what you're there to do before you've even started. Umm, I like to think of it, I have knowledge and expertise to offer but I need to present it in a way that challenges you to think about it. I need to be open to and respectful of different opinions... But in general to me it's a glorious journey, for both of us. And I tell my students that if they'll let themselves there will never be a client that they won't learn something from. And I think that there is never a class that we don't learn something about ourselves from. We just have to be open enough to listen to that. And students will, students aren't reticent to tell you, if you'll listen.

How Are Faculty Members' Conceptions of Teaching and/or Practices Influenced by the Integration of Course Management Systems into Their Teaching Practice?

From faculty members' stated uses of WebCT, it does not appear that their conceptions of teaching, or teaching practices, have been greatly influenced by integrating WebCT into their courses. Both Dr. Andrews and Dr. McBurton provided notes to their students prior to the introduction of WebCT into their teaching. The introduction of WebCT into their instruction merely offered another method of providing information to their students.

Dr. Andrews.

I always had a Web site. . .I have had the notes on the Web probably since '97 maybe or '98, I mean whenever the Web really got going there. So I've always had the Web site with the notes.
The WebCT has not changed the way I teach. . .in fact I still have a separate, I have two Web sites, one is our departmental Web site with everything the same as WebCT. The only difference is WebCT they can look at their grades.

Dr. McBurton.

And I always wanted the students to have a very good chance to learn and an equal chance to learn so I always came to class with a large printed handout for every student. . .with 6 or 8 pages and mention things that were in the book and some figures.
[In response to: "it sounds like not a lot has changed?"]
No, I think the biggest positive change for the learning is that the students can study the lecture before class. . ..

Dr. Samuels, made use of the discussion feature in WebCT for her class. For Dr. Samuels, the use of the WebCT discussions was viewed as "icing on the cake," to her regular class instruction, and a way to extend the learning experience of her students. However, the .integration of WebCT did not change her conceptions of teaching, or her teaching practices in any significant way.

Because, see, we were in class 4 days a week and so, and this [WebCT discussions] was used to just, almost like icing on the cake, and to think about what we've done during this week. . .
. . . I think one of the biggest positives for me is that it does require everybody to think, and speak, ummm, because try as I might, there are always one or two students who I can't get to talk otherwise. And I think it's good for the students because I believe that it allows them to speak in a way that they probably wouldn't otherwise. . .

Dr. Halloway remained skeptical about the appropriateness of Web-based learning technologies even after using WebCT in his instruction. He acknowledged that the use of WebCT has its advantages, but was still a strong advocate of face-to-face instruction.

I have a much more positive attitude about it now than I did the first time. I'm too old of a dog to learn this kind of a trick. I guess I would have to say I'm an advocate of it now in the right circumstances, it clearly gives us an opportunity we didn't have before. And I think there are a lot of opportunities for it to really enhance the face to face that I've probably been reluctant ever to say can be completely replaced, I think it does give it a chance to enhance that. Now I'm not skilled enough really to be able to pull it off, I know how I would like to do it but I'm not in a position to do it myself and without a lot of help.

... why we could have done this interview, on using something, some facility like WebCT, basically the same concept, but it's not the same, and that's the way, I guess that's the way I feel about the teaching. . .

Although for Dr. Barnes a change in teaching conceptions did not result as a consequence of using WebCT, it appears that a change in teaching conceptions directly led him to seek out the use of WebCT.

My first semester I learned through the retribution of MBA students that I was to provide them with something. That to simply talk and to take notes like when I was a student wasn't what students were used to. The expectation was that you would provide them with some sort of notes outline or whatever else. And so that's when I first came up with, you know using PowerPoint more and having some outline of that PowerPoint that I would provide to them. And I can't even remember at this point if maybe in that first semester I simply made, I probably did, simply made copies of those PowerPoint slides and would pass them out before I would cover a chapter. And then umm, I came to find out about WebCT and basically was able to load if you will those PowerPoint slides onto WebCT. That was really the primary reason I wanted to use it, so that then students could access those before hand and um be prepared for class that way.

How Are Faculty Members' Conceptions of Teaching Supported by the Tools Available in Online Course Management Systems?

To answer this question, statements regarding how the faculty used WebCT were examined in light of each faculty members' conceptions of teaching. Dr. Andrews, Dr. McBurton, and Dr. Barnes all reported using WebCT primarily for information dissemination purposes.

Dr. Andrews.

I use WebCT the same way as I do in the other class, mainly for information posting. I put all my notes up there, my assignments I put up there.

...When you get 150 students handing out a lot of paper is a lot of paper and again, they can always go in here and if they lose something and print it out. . .

Dr. McBurton.

And so this semester for the first time I'm using WebCT. And what is happening is that all of these notes that I used to give out in class are being posted on WebCT.

Dr. Barnes.

A lot of what I use WebCT for is to get things out to the students so I don't have to make copies of them. And so previous to that, I just didn't provide them with stuff. . .

For Dr. Andrews, whose conception of teaching falls within the Transmitting Structured Knowledge category, the tools available in WebCT clearly supported his conception of teaching and learning. He made full use of the tools available to distribute information to his students in an efficient and timely manner. However, it would have been expected that Drs. McBurton, and Barnes would be using more student-centered tools in WebCT, such as the discussion tools, since their conceptions of teaching were characterized as Facilitating Understanding/ Learning Facilitation. While both Dr. Halloway and Dr. Samuels, who also share student-centered orientations to teaching, made use of the discussion tools available in WebCT, both Dr. McBurton and Dr. Barnes primarily relied on the use of the information dissemination tools. There are a number of possible explanations for this, one being that both Dr. McBurton and Dr. Barnes expressed that they had limited knowledge of the other available features in WebCT, and thus could not make use of them. A second possible explanation is that Drs. McBurton and Barnes chose to use the technology (WebCT) as just one of numerous teaching methods that they used in helping to facilitate their students' understanding, and thus employed more student-centered teaching approaches that did not involve the use of WebCT. Interestingly, regardless if it appeared that the tools available in the CMS did, or did not, support faculty members' conceptions of teaching, all faculty members reported feeling satisfied with their use of WebCT.

Implications of the Study

The results of our study suggest that faculty members from diverse disciplines who have won teaching awards embrace the ideas and principles of constructivism, as four out of five participants' teaching conceptions were much more student-centered rather than teacher-centered. Despite this tendency toward learner-centered teaching, participants in this study chose to primarily use a CMS for information dissemination purposes, which is considered a very teacher-centered practice. Our results provide support to Oliver's (2001) claim that CMSs may promote the pedagogy of information dissemination as well as Britto's (2002) finding that faculty perceived the benefits of teaching a course using WebCT as pertaining primarily to the convenience and efficiency of course administration and management. Our findings also lend support to the notion that an instructor's learner-centered conceptions of knowledge and teaching may not be sufficient to allow them to perceive the affordances of a CMS for supporting student learning with technology. Technological tools such as CMSs may need to be redesigned to more clearly communicate their capabilities for supporting constructivist pedagogical dimensions (Herrington et al., 2003).

These findings have implications for both administrators and faculty in higher education, as well as future designers of CMSs. Administrators who encourage the wholesale adoption of CMSs should be aware of the strong influence of faculty's teaching conceptions in the design and creation of learning environments and the relatively weak influence of CMSs. If the administration's motive for encouraging the use of CMSs is to stimulate the creation of constructivist learning environments, both the characteristics of the technological tools and the teaching conceptions of the faculty should be taken into consideration. Likewise, for designers of future CMSs, serious consideration should be given to the types of tools, and their ease of use, that are included in CMSs to ensure that an instructivist pedagogy such as information dissemination is not inadvertently promoted. A positive development is that open source CMSs such as Moodle (www.moodle.org) are explicitly designed to support social constructivist pedagogy (Dougiamas & Taylor, 2003).

Conclusion

As the use of CMSs becomes nearly ubiquitous in higher education environments, it is imperative that we consider their impact and influence on instructional methods and the learning environment. Moves to modify existing teaching practices in higher education by incorporating current educational learning theories such as constructivism and situated cognition, and integrating technology, such as CMSs and wireless computing, are worthy goals. However, these initiatives are unlikely to be successful without understanding the influence and relationship between the teaching conceptions of faculty and their adaptations of the technological tools available to them. This relationship remains ambiguous although the results of this study suggest that assumptions that learner-centered instructors will automatically adopt CMSs to promote constructivist learning online are unwarranted.

References

Blackboard, Inc. (2003). *Blackboard* [On-line]. Available: http://www.blackboard.com/

Bransford, J. D., Brown, A. L., & Cocking, R. R. (2000). *How people learn: Brain, mind, experience, and school.* Washington, DC: National Academy Press.

Britto, M. (2002). *An exploratory study of the development of a survey instrument to measure the pedagogical dimensions of web-based instruction.* Unpublished doctoral dissertation, The University of Georgia.

Cuban, L. (2001). *Oversold and underused: Computers in the classroom.* Cambridge, MA: Harvard University Press.

Dehoney, J., & Reeves, T. C. (1999). Instructional and social dimensions of class web pages. *Journal of Computing in Higher Education, 10*(2), 19–41.

Dougiamas, M., & Taylor, P. C. (2003). Moodle: Using learning communities to create an open source course management system. *Proceedings of the EDMEDIA 2003 Conference,* Honolulu, Hawaii. Norfolk, VA: Association for the Advancement of Computing in Education.

Hafner, K., & Lyon, M. (1996). *Where wizards stay up late: The origins of the internet.* New York: Simon & Schuster.

Herrington, J., Oliver, R., & Reeves, T. C. (2003). Patterns of engagement in authentic online learning environments. *Australian Journal of Educational Technology, 19*(1), 59–71.

Herrington, J., & Standen, P. (2000). Moving from an instructivist to a constructivist multimedia learning environment. *Journal of Educational Multimedia and Hypermedia, 9*(3), 195–205.

Howard, B. C., McGee, S., Schwartz, N., & Purcell, S. (2000). The experience of constructivism: Transforming teacher epistemology. *Journal of Research on Computing in Education, 32,* 455–465.

Kember, D. (1997). A reconceptualization of the research into university academics' conceptions of teaching. *Learning and Instruction, 7*(3), 255–275.

Kember, D., & Kwan, K.-P. (2002). Lecturer's approaches to teaching and their relationship to conceptions of good teaching. In N. Hativa & P. Goodyear (Eds.), *Teacher thinking, beliefs and knowledge in higher education.* New York: Kluwer Academic.

Laurillard, D. (2002). *Rethinking university teaching: A conversational framework for the effective use of learning technologies* (2nd ed.). London: Routledge/Falmer.

Maeroff, G. I. (2003). *A classroom of one: How online learning is changing our schools and colleges.* New York: Palgrave/Macmillan.

Mann, B. L. (Ed.). (2000). *Perspectives in web course management.* Toronto: Canadian Scholar's Press.

Miles, M. B., & Huberman, A. M. (1994). *Qualitative data analysis: An expanded sourcebook* (2nd ed.). Thousand Oaks, CA: Sage.

Oliver, K. (2001). Recommendations for student tools in online course management systems. *Journal of Computing in Higher Education, 13*(1), 47–70.

Perkins, D. (1991). Technology meets constructivism: Do they make a marriage? *Educational Technology, 31*(5), 18–23.

Pittinsky, M. S. (Ed.). (2003). *The wired tower: Perspectives on the impact of the internet on higher education.* Upper Saddle River, NJ: Prentice Hall.

Pratt, D. D. (1992). Conceptions of teaching. *Adult Education Quarterly, 42*(4), 203–220.

Reeves, T. C. (2003). Storm clouds on the digital education horizon. *Journal of Computing in Higher Education, 15*(1), 3–26.

Samuelowicz, K., & Bain, J. D. (2001). Revisiting academics' beliefs about teaching and learning. *Higher Education, 41*, 299–325.

WebCT. (2003). *WebCT* [On-line]. Available: http://www.webct.com/

Weigel, V. B. (2002). *Deep learning for a digital age: Technology's untapped potential to enrich higher education.* San Francisco: Jossey-Bass.

Part II
Trends and Issues in Library and Information Science

Introduction

V. J. McClendon

A brave new connected world is upon us, made possible by the ever-evolving Internet, using Web 2.0 social and communication technologies. The problem is the world is changing and the Internet is molding the context for that change, by ignoring these changes, some educators feel out of touch or outdated. Many educators wonder what the relevance of such technologies is to education. Business embraces new Web 2.0 technologies because these new communication avenues address ease of information access which is relevant to many fields—business, education, and social networks. For education increasing the quality of service delivery now keys on the smart use of Web 2.0 applets. The chapters included in this year's Library and Information Science section address many trends, technologies, and implementation ideas for K-12, academic, public, and special libraries, as well as information science and instructional technology education programs. These chapters provide a sense of the world we live and work in, and give ideas on how we, as educators, may respond to our constantly evolving, technology-enhanced world.

Events unfold at Internet speeds these days, with reactions and ramifications sprinting around the world in record time. As of December 2007, there were 1.3 billion documented users of the Internet (Miniwatts Marketing Group, 2008). Friedman (2006) proclaims that the Internet and its Web capabilities are systemically flattening our entire world, speeding the exchange of international goods and services. According to Friedman, more than ever before, "the spread of the Internet and the coming to life of the Web" (p. 91) connects a record number of people and businesses. Communication changes rise to importance because customers, namely students, parents and faculty, ubiquitously use the Internet and demand timely delivery of goods and services—including education and information access. We, as educators, miss opportunities to more effectively communicate and update our students/customers if we cannot use the tools they use.

Dawkins (1989) coined the phrase "meme" to describe this cultural transformation, defined as a "self-propagating unit of cultural evolution" (Wiktionary.com). In

V.J. McClendon (✉)
Department of Educational Psychology and Instructional Technology, University of Georgia, Athens, GA 30602-7144, USA
e-mail: vjmcclen@uga.edu

M. Orey et al. (eds.), *Educational Media and Technology Yearbook*,
DOI 10.1007/978-0-387-09675-9_11, © Springer Science+Business Media, LLC 2009

transition between members of a culture changes the "meme" or item or behavior becomes transformed itself. This year many notable events transform our physical and cultural world. These include the flood in Iowa and the heartland, record fires in California, continued U.S. war with Iraq, spiraling fuel prices, galloping inflation, weakening global economies, the end of the (second) Bush era and minority candidates for U.S. President—all of these documented and discussed avidly in the new "meme" of the Web 2.0 world. New virtual worlds are available online daily. Facebook and other programs allow users to create their own cities. Google's new Lively allows users to create rooms where they can chat with friends and these integrate into other online systems like Facebook. Such Internet interface interoperability is called a "mashup" or a web application "combining data from more than one source into a single integrated tool" (Wikipedia, 2008). Unique pieces, called widgets, provide the blocks which build user designed pages such as iGoogle, myYahoo, and more. What are the origins of the Web 2.0 concept and where is it taking us in the future of education, teaching and learning, and information literacy? What do these tools offer information and education delivery?

As a term, Web 2.0, coined by O'Reilly, was a way of defining the shift from static web pages built and controlled by an administrator, toward increased user-controlled content, and greater user interaction online. O'Reilly (2005) explains the meme of Web-user driven content as radical extension between trusting users to create their own myYahoo type information to extending broading trust to inherent in Wikipedia and related wiki technologies democratically built by and for the general population. This awareness of content helps users, web developers, and educators by promoting the use of "tag clouds" (Sinclair, 2008, p. 15) a visual use of what librarians long ago termed indexing or search terms. Imagine yesterday's indexing as today's cool tag cloud![1,2] Imagine students, faculty, staff, and parents being interested in making content more searchable. As software and widgets allow a reduced learning curve toward embracing new technologies, more educators are trying environments often viewed as entertainment.

For example, some instructors are beginning to explore multi-user, virtual environments (MUVE). Educational conferences increasingly house demonstrations and discussions on MUVE-based teaching. Museums, libraries, galleries and cultural sites are finding new interest in MUVE environments such as *Second Life* (e.g., Urban, 2007). Educators explore the possibilities of increased learning through inquiry by teaching via such graphically stimulating virtual locations (e.g., Ketelhut, Clarke, Dede, Nelson, & Bowman, 2008). In other applications, business and education groups use social presence marketing[3] as a way to invest in existing customers and those customers at convenient points of need. For example, OCLC launched a Facebook page[4] providing discussion of its services and boasts

---

[1] Sinclair (2008) provides a greater understanding of social networks and tagging for improved searching in "The folkonomy tag cloud: When is it useful?".

[2] For a cool use of a tag cloud check out NASA at http://www.nasa.gov/.

[3] http://freetraffictip.com/traffic-thursdays-what-is-social-presence-marketing.php

[4] http://www.facebook.com/pages/OCLC/20530435726?ref=s

632 "fans". Adding a link onto a Facebook page to OCLC's page will generate content automatically fed each time the user logs in. Similarly many libraries provide instant messaging chat services or provide chat widgets to plug into students' "mycollege" webpages. These tools provide news feeds to personal webpage interface and stand ready to answer user questions on demand. The chapters which follow embrace a number of these ideas as well as addressing a wide variety of other educational issues such as challenges of meeting at-risk students needs, learning disabilities, meeting the special needs of girls through e-gaming, administrative support and academic recognition for library professionals, as well as the use of library generated data to prove the strength and contribution of the media center towards meeting curriculum-wide goals. Importantly, many authors broach the difficult topic of education and library professional reticence in accepting Web 2.0 tool and concepts as a legitimate part of the our changing world. Each chapter provides useful insight into ways to manage our changing technology-infused world better.

In the first chapter, Dr. Mary Ann Fitzgerald wades into the fray regarding Wikipedia and its value for education and learning. At a recent conference, Dr. Fitzgerald found herself seated among a sea of disapproving library professionals when a speaker used Wikipedia for a working definition. She notes Badke (2008) states, "If you want to get five opinions from four information professionals, just mention Wikipedia." Fitzgerald examines the value in Wikipedia with its democratic method of building content and weighs its limitations and strengths. Lastly Fitzgerald urges educators to consider the successes of such wiki-based web sites as opportunities to increase critical thinking skills among students to evaluate as they should regardless of the content medium. Questioning and critical thinking lay at the heart of life-long learning, which information professionals seek to encourage in all our customers.

The second chapter, *High-tech tools for the Library Media Center* by Dr. Dan Fuller, Doug Achtermann, and Cathy McLeod, attempts a deeper understanding of the shift between early web pages—or Web 1.0—and the significant shift which created the current Web 2.0 technologies. The authors go further to compare library tools in a similar shift, explaining Library 2.0 tools and practical uses to extend the reach of libraries beyond their physical walls into the virtual lives of digital natives.

The third chapter comes from Shayne Russell, a practicing media specialist with years of experience and a wide variety of interests. Russell challenges librarians everywhere to consider the development of Web 2.0 skills necessary for both schools and students. The author provides reasons and applications for school libraries to consider the potential for pushing services and access forward with these new technologies as ways to better prepare students for the connectedness demanded by businesses of today and beyond.

Brown and Hill explain the various technologies available through Web 2.0, including blogs, wikis, podcasts, social bookmarking, and multi-user virtual worlds such as Second Life. The authors explain the transition from using Internet information to controlling and developing information as self-publishers of Web content. Further, Brown and Hill surveyed over 130 K-12 library media websites to provide readers with a summary of the current uses of Web 2.0 tools among schools. In addition, the authors push one step further linking potential Web 2.0 applications in meeting American Association of School Librarians' (ASSL) learning standards.

Chapter five, *The Turnaround School Library Program,* was written by the dynamic writing and research team of Jones and Zambone from East Carolina University. In *The Turnaround School Library Program,* the authors provide a framework for creating a nurturing program within the media center to help at-risk students increase academic performance. Jones and Zambone first explain at-risk factors for students nearing failure. Later, the authors discuss the strong correlation between increased student academic success and supportive efforts housed in the school library media center. Lastly, they provide strategies for creating and continuing a "turnaround" program in any school to offer lasting assistance for at-risk populations.

Dr. Lesley Farmer provides a valuable contribution yet again this year. Each year, Dr. Farmer offers her latest work via the Educational Media and Technology Yearbook. As an award winning author and educator, we avidly look forward to her latest research results. In chapter six, Farmer works with Murphy, a practicing teacher librarian (TL), to explore the concerns of gender equity in school libraries by extending e-gaming as a viable interest point for young teens. Despite historically being a male dominated "sport," Farmer and Murphy suggest that TLs may provide a welcoming and stimulating environment in the media center, encouraging girls and boys with e-gaming strategies to reinforce interests and as an entrée into the learning center. This supportive environment can help girls find a legitimate stronghold toward critical thinking and career-oriented technologies through the collaborative help of TLs and teachers.

Supporting special needs students marks a common function in media centers today among their broader support of programs across the curriculum. Zambone, Canter, Voytecki, Jeffs, and Jones explain the confusion that often exists with administration and teachers about the purpose of the media center and its programming. Yet, clearly research and test scores show strong support for media centers creates a powerful formula for school success. Extending this discussion, Zambone et al. propose library media specialists may convert research and local data collection methods to advocate for even greater administrative support for library goals and programming.

A problem in today's schools is "the 65% solution." According to the American Library Association (2008), this solution is a funding mandate tying 65% of state educational funds toward classroom functions. At first this legislation sounds appropriate for today's schools, fighting to meet "Adequate Yearly Progress" results. Yet, the media center functions as a classroom as well, but many suffer from funding cuts resulting from this legislative "solution." Chapter eight, by Drs. Schmidt and Reeve, supports the previous chapter that a disconnect exists between perceptions of the media center and its professionals and the actual impact well-funded programs actually have on schools and test results. To help fight for adequate support and funding, the authors argue library professionals must prove their impact and worth to turn the problem around. Schmidt and Reeve offer suggestions on collecting data and formulating persuasive arguments in support of the school library media center as a valid classroom used by the whole curriculum.

In the last chapter, Dr. Morris' research finds that principal support is critical for creating exemplary school library media programs. Discussing the results of a pilot study, the author explains the crucial role of librarian and teacher collaboration in creating a synergy for learning in Georgia's schools. Morris' research works toward the development of an understanding of the necessary elements for creating and supporting exemplary library programming in Georgia schools. This research supports earlier works such as the Lance state studies (2002), but goes further to begin a survey of practitioners in developing an understanding of what exemplary library programming means for Georgia schools and the key role that principals play in fostering an atmosphere of collaborative teaching excellence.

Taken individually each chapter offers practices useful for any library or media center regardless of service populations. Read as a body, these chapters capture the breadth of activity going on in libraries and library education today. Libraries are active centers, not only for student learning but for extending technology and professional development and collaboration in colleges, schools, and communities across the United States. Library professionals must act as a vanguard in embracing change to reach students and promote life-long learning across the curriculum and via the library physical space and virtual environments as well.

References

American Library Association. (2008). *What is the 65% Solution?* Retrieved May 25, 2008, from http://www.ala.org/ala/issues/65rule.cfm

Badke, W. (2008). What to do with Wikipedia [Electronic version]. *Online, 32*(2). Retrieved April 1, 2008, from http://www.infotoday.com/online/mar08/Badke.shtml

Dawkins, R. (1989). Memes: The new replicators. *The selfish gene* (2nd ed.). Oxford: Oxford University Press.

Friedman, T. L. (2006). *The world is flat: A brief history of the twenty-first century* (2nd ed.). New York: Farrar, Straus and Giroux.

Ketelhut, D. J., Clarke, J., Dede, C., Nelson, B., & Bowman, C. (2008). *Inquiry teaching for depth and coverage via multi-user virtual environments.* Retrieved April 19, 2008, from http://muve.gse.harvard.edu/rivercityproject/documents/muvenarst2005paperfinal2.pdf

Lance, K. (2002, February). Impact of *school library media* programs on academic achievement. *Teacher Librarian, 29*(3), 29.

Miniwatts Marketing Group. (2008). *Internet world stats: Usage and population statistics.* Retrieved March 14, 2008, from http://www.internetworldstats.com/stats.htm

O'Reilly, T. (2005). *What is web 2.0: Design patterns and business models for the next generation of software.* Retrieved March 18, 2008, from http://www.oreillynet.com/pub/a/oreilly/tim/news/2005/09/30/what-is-web-20.html

Sinclair, J. (2008). The folkonomy tag cloud: When is it useful? *Journal of Information Science, 34*(1), 15–29.

Urban, R. (2007, August/September). Second Life, serious leisure, and LIS. *Bulletin of the American Society for Information Science & Technology, 33*(6), 38–40.

Wikipedia. (2008). Retrieved April 29, 2008, from http://en.wikipedia.org/wiki/Main_Page

Wikipedia: Adventures in the New Info-Paradigm

Mary Ann Fitzgerald

Abstract   School library media specialists, along with other librarians, are often reluctant for students to use Wikipedia in their school work. This chapter argues against this perspective, citing the values of the free online encyclopedia, and suggesting strategies for exploiting its weaknesses to help students develop critical thinking skills.

Keywords   Wikipedia · Web 2.0 · Higher order thinking skills

> *If you want to get five opinions from four information professionals, just mention Wikipedia. (Badke, 2008)*

Seated in a darkened convention hall, we enthusiastically listened to an inspiring speaker. Offhandedly, he mentioned looking up something in Wikipedia, in relation to a story he was telling. Suddenly, the auditorium roiled with sounds of disapproval—polite but distinct "tssks" and mutters of complaint. I hardly believed my ears. This meeting was a national convention of school media specialists—surely the most progressive in the profession, considering the expense and effort required to attend the conference. How could they scorn this powerful new tool, containing more information than any encyclopedia ever before? Many audience members were likely as taken aback as I, but the muttering seemed widespread. Likewise, around the world, many librarians and academics debate the pros and cons of new collaborative reference tools, and opinions seem fervent on both sides (e.g., the JESSE listserv archives, winter of 2008). Certainly, worthy arguments grace both sides of this debate.

Although surprised at the audience's vehement reaction, I also understand their frustration. School librarians provide marvelous databases for learners, loaded with numerous scholarly articles and authoritative citations. They are dedicated to help any patron—student or adult—negotiate the mysteries of Boolean and keyword searching in online public access catalogs. They prepare comprehensive annotated

M.A. Fitzgerald (✉)
Ed Psych & Instructional Technology (EPIT), University of Georgia, Macon, GA 31206
e-mail: mfitzger@uga.edu

M. Orey et al. (eds.), *Educational Media and Technology Yearbook*,
DOI 10.1007/978-0-387-09675-9_12, © Springer Science+Business Media, LLC 2009

bibliographies on any topic that a teacher could possibly wish, and configure library computer web pages to provide easy access to state-funded virtual libraries and other carefully selected resources (Mardis & Perrault, 2008). And yet, students regularly circumvent all of these efforts with admirable dexterity to access the mighty Google first, followed by Wikipedia second. Students do this, even in schools where such access is forbidden and computers locked against illicit use. School librarians justifiably worry about the credibility and efficiency of these tools, especially when more trustworthy resources are available.

The reluctance of librarians (public, academic, and school) to endorse resources such as Wikipedia is understandable. After all, anyone can write or edit a Wikipedia article. Most libraries provide authoritative alternatives, such as the venerable and valuable *Encyclopedia Britannica* or the beloved *World Book*. Why, still, do students insist on using the less trustworthy Wikipedia?

Wikipedia is possibly the most prominent representative of a host of new tools designed for what Jenkins calls "participatory culture" (2006, p. 60). While some feel threatened by this paradigm shift in online activity, others are inspired (Hargadon, 2008). My point of view in this chapter is that we must overcome the outrage expressed in that auditorium while at the same empathizing with its causes. We must join the scholarly community and examine the usefulness of new tools from an academic point of view, as others are beginning to do (e.g., Lih, 2004; Rosenzweig, 2006). In this chapter I will present several arguments in favor of new tools, while simultaneously pointing out several weaknesses and dangers to users. In the end, I strongly believe that Wikipedia can help students become wiser users of all resources, online and off. I will conclude with ideas about how to apply such tools constructively with learning objectives in mind.

Strengths of Wikipedia

Wikipedia regularly, if not almost always, inhabits the top ten list of websites visited worldwide (Cohen, 2008). The definitive reasons for user behavior may be hard to establish, but there are at least four powerful reasons to use Wikipedia instead of traditionally vetted resources: ease of use, accessibility, volume, and the power of collaborative wisdom. While there are certainly other reasons, I will focus on these four in this section.

Ease of Use

Wikipedia is a model of easy usability, at least at first glance. Most users lose patience with Boolean operators and protracting searching when a question needs an answer. Some call this tendency laziness. On the other hand, there is much to be said for efficiency. Many of us enjoy the one-box simplified searching exemplified by Google, and Wikipedia works as easily as Google in terms of searching.

Novice users need neither workshops nor manuals to perform a successful first search of Wikipedia. Unfortunately, many of the powerful, professionally-crafted subscription databases cannot be so easily used on the first attempt. While their interfaces have vastly improved, the common result "no records found" still indicates to the layman that these databases are difficult to use. Strongly-motivated users will persevere, but ease of use will often cause the default choice to be Google and Wikipedia over scholarly databases.

Accessibility

In this area, Wikipedia provides an even greater advantage over traditional encyclopedias. With the important exception of filtered terminals (a topic that deserves its own discussion), Wikipedia is available wherever an online Internet terminal is available, and increasingly on mobile devices via cellular networks as well. Print encyclopedias are too heavy to carry anywhere, except for one limited volume at a time. Online traditional encyclopedias have greatly improved in terms of providing off-campus accessibility through password protocols, but many still require subscriptions or institutional purchase. These charges add up rapidly. Under-funded libraries must make difficult choices regarding which resources, if any, can be offered. Cost-related problems inevitably lead to decreased access to expensive tools in some learning environments.

Those of us in Academia with powerful and comprehensive access to commercial scholarly databases and other university-purchased resources often underestimate the value of no-cost resources. Many states provide databases and high-quality encyclopedias for K-12 users through their virtual libraries, but this level of access pales in comparison to higher education. Some believe that free resources will eventually edge out the subscription-based ones due to new economic models. Anderson (2008) provides intriguing glimpses of how these new models may work. Wikipedia is leading the way in this regard. For many users, the free encyclopedia may be the only viable encyclopedia.

Volume

Wikipedia clearly wins any contest with other encyclopedias when articles, words, languages, or topics are counted. No other encyclopedia comes close to matching the number of articles in Wikipedia. Whatever qualms may exist about article quality, any evaluator must consider that many Wikipedia articles have no parallels in other encyclopedias. For example, the baseball player Victor Starffin has an interesting article in Wikipedia but not in *Encyclopedia Britannica*. Admittedly, Mr. Starffin was probably not important enough to merit a *Britannica* entry. However, in Wikipedia space is no issue and devoted baseball fans may find him interesting.

Along with volume comes currency. Current events are often quickly accompanied by corresponding articles in Wikipedia that keep pace with the news. The evolution of these "breaking" Wikipedia articles is easily watched through the revision histories of each article. For example, the Reverend Jeremiah Wright figured prominently in news coverage of the 2008 Presidential election. A search of *Encyclopedia Britannica Online*, Academic version (http://search.eb.com/) provided no relevant hits. The same search, entered directly through the Google box as "jeremiah wright" led directly to an article of that name in Wikipedia.[1] No traditional encyclopedia approaches this level of currency, a problem known as the "knowledge gap" in journalism (Lih, 2004, p. 5).

The Power of Collaboration

As Fallis (2007) suggests, much depends upon a user's epistemology. He discusses the argument (along with its counterargument) that consensus has epistemological validity. Often called the "wisdom of crowds" principle (Surowiecki, 2004), this difference exemplifies a revolution in the infosphere. In theory, the attention of many minds can create an information product superior to that created by one and edited by another. The structures that long gave encyclopedias their credibility—expertise and editing—give way to collaborative construction in the Web 2.0 world. In other words, the majority rules. Most of the time, or so the theory proposes, the group will produce the best answer—democracy, after all, is founded on this principle. Further, at least one author disputes that Wikipedia is authored by a crowd, citing evidence that much of the work is done by "bots," bits of software which automatically detect patterns of destructive behavior and quickly revert those changes (Wilson, 2008). Still, little doubt exists that the intellectual content of Wikipedia results from the collective work of a large number of humans. As Jenkins writes in his blog, "...there's no question that there is more knowledge in the combined readership of this article than I have at the time I am writing it" (Jenkins, 2007b).

What are the Problems?

Wikipedia presents information challenges along with its great power. Some of these problems are thoroughly described in the scholarly literature across several disciplines. In this section, I briefly recount several of the most significant: inaccuracy, unbalanced coverage, and inappropriate use.

In a world where any literate, computer-savvy person may contribute to Wikipedia, the potential for inaccuracy is significant. Denning, Horning, and Parnas, Weinstein (2005) argue that traditional encyclopedia gatekeeping mechanisms are useful and necessary, and that Wikipedia "cannot attain the status of a true

---

[1] http://en.wikipedia.org/wiki/Jeremiah_Wright

encyclopedia without more formal content-inclusion and expert review procedures" (p. 152). Inaccuracies may take the form of misinformation (mistakes due to a large number of reasons, including insufficient expertise) or disinformation (lies or deliberate information vandalism). Certainly, evidence for both exists (e.g., Seigenthaler, 2005). Along with downright mistakes come a range of other problems like bias (despite the Wikipedia requirement for neutral point of view), over- or under-specificity, and the unfortunately common poor writing, grammar, and spelling.

A good example of Wikipedia inaccuracy problems is the Middlebury College (Vermont) case. The history department at that institution made a policy that students could not "cite Wikipedia as a source in exams and papers" (Cohen, 2007; Middlebury, 2007). This policy was established after a consistent inaccuracy among student exams was traced to a Wikipedia entry. Although a similar incident could have resulted from use of a low-credibility website, the comprehensiveness of Wikipedia may lead to an assumption of trustworthiness among students (Cohen, 2007). It is important to note that Middlebury did not ban the *use* of Wikipedia (Middlebury, 2007), which would have arguably been a violation of students' intellectual freedom.

Giles (2005) compared the credibility to Wikipedia to that of *Britannica*. This found Wikipedia to be less accurate, but to a modest degree. Further, even the scholarly peer-reviewed journal press has often experienced problems with falsified research and other inaccuracies (e.g., Guterman, 2008). As a dynamic entity, however, Wikipedia will likely always present a significant possibility of inaccuracy.

Another problem is unbalanced coverage of topics despite relative importance. Because creators compose entries about topics of personal interest, entries are numerous in some arcane areas while not thoroughly representative in other important areas. Topics of great popular interest, but arguably little importance, may be covered in great detail. An example of this phenomenon cited by Cohen (2008) is the topic "John Locke." John Locke, the 17th-century philosopher whose ideas influenced the founding of the US, has an article of 4,694 words at the time of this writing. John Locke, a fictional character in the popular television show *Lost*, has an article of 5,150 words. From a cultural point of view, this emphasis on the popular is interesting. From an information quality perspective, however, the emphasis seems skewed and likely to give a false impression of lasting importance. It disturbs many people that a biography of a prominent historical figure receives less attention than a fictional character of a television show when the two are compared side by side. In theory, this imbalance between the two articles will work itself out over time. For today's user, however, the problem is of some significance.

Other problems about Wikipedia could certainly be explored. For example, users may be consciously or unconsciously subject to the idea that some benign, wise authority edits Wikipedia and evaluates its information accordingly. Perhaps this assumption will fade over time as the population educated to believe in gatekeeping authority ages. However, it is commonplace for news media and other trusted information sources to cite Wikipedia, although we could certainly debate the trustworthiness of standard media sources as well. It is not common for such fleeting references to caution listeners to "consider the source."

For this discussion, the final problem regarding Wikipedia is a traditional academic one. Encyclopedias are designed to be general sources of information with a wide scope and shallow coverage, useful for overviews and descriptions. The entries are themselves syntheses of various sources of information, never meant to stand as original sources on their own. Wikipedia certainly follows this pattern, and its size and accessibility makes it even more tempting to abuse than its traditional counterparts. Students and scholars should never rely on any encyclopedia as a scholarly source for research.

Educational Use of the Forbidden

Despite the significant problems listed above, I believe Wikipedia plays a valuable role in the educational enterprise. There are at least three reasons in favor of its educational use: its inherent motivational power, its usefulness, and its ability to stimulate thinking.

Motivation

Preservice teachers are taught to seek out the things that students are naturally interested in, and to integrate these inherently motivational elements into curriculum as much as possible. It makes little sense to invent motivational strategies or set up elaborate coercion schemes to reward learning behavior when students already have natural curiosities and attractions to elements of popular culture. Although some student interests are not suitable for educational use, many technology-rich ones are. At the end of the first decade of the 21st century, social networking technology is wildly popular among teens and young adults. This trend is exemplified by a Pew study indicating that "93% of teens use the Internet" and "64% of online teens ages 12–17" have created online content (Lenhart, Madden, Macgill, & Smith, 2007, p. i). Jenkins (2007a) explored reasons for this pervasive participation in his blog, listing "relatively low barriers to . . . expression and civic engagement" along with support and mentorship, and invitation into communities where "members feel that their contributions matter." It is highly likely that rapidly evolving technology, widely labeled "Web 2.0" will increasingly make entry barriers lower, accompanied by strong social incentives. In short, this trend has staying power. Instead of fighting it, educators must harness this power.

Wikipedia, on the leading edge of Web 2.0 from its earliest emergence, has progressed from trendy to ubiquitous. For the foreseeable future, we must exploit its popularity along with that of other collaborative resources. Otherwise, our digital-native students will see us as increasingly irrelevant to their world.

Utility

In addition to its ease of use, Wikipedia is truly useful. Anyone with a readily available Internet connection knows that many questions of everyday life can be beneficially researched using Wikipedia, at least as a starting point. Wikipedia's currency and accessibility make it an essential ready reference tool. On balance, this usefulness far outweighs its inaccuracies and irrelevancies. Given the cautions above and implementation strategies listed below, I believe that educators must abandon their dismay over its problems and accept this basic fact.

Higher-Order Thinking Required

Many educators believe that public education has been crippled by the testing focus of the No Child Left Behind (NCLB) legislative philosophy (e.g., Valenza, 2008). One of its most damaging legacies has been unintended production of graduates who may be effective multiple-choice test-takers but crippled in their higher-order thinking skills. Most of all, I encourage the use of Wikipedia because it has the potential to encourage thinking, especially critical thinking.

Thompson (2003) poses the question of whether college students are "lazy" or information-illiterate in their observed failure to evaluate web information competently. Flanagin and Metzger (2000) discuss the significant levels of motivation required to evaluate online information. It is tempting to conclude that people *are* lazy in their information seeking and prescribe that they simply work harder in evaluating information and other propositions. I believe that this point of view is simplistic, and instead that people are inundated with an indigestible amount of information daily. Further, critical thinking takes a great deal of both energy and skill. Therefore, I believe that a more measured approach is warranted—people should consider how important a search is and how much depends upon the accuracy of the resulting information. According to the risk of inaccurate information, information seekers should spend a proportionate amount of energy executing strategies to evaluate the relevant information. I believe that *all* information forms require evaluation when the questions are truly important (e.g., Flanagin & Metzger, 2000).

Wikipedia, along with most social tools, provides another important opportunity for higher-order thinking: creating original content. "The school expects every student to master the same content, while Wikipedia allows students to think about their own particular skills, knowledge, and experience" (Jenkins, 2007b). Certainly, young people may write Wikipedia articles themselves, and many are doing so. This is another inherently motivating aspect of 2.0 vehicles. Some 2.0 authors (young or not) may fail to take their creative responsibilities seriously, intentionally or unintentionally adding to online misinformation. However, when students become authors with the ability to publish instantaneously, they assume the responsibilities of authority: checking the facts, synthesizing a point of view, and presenting reasonable arguments. As Jenkins asserts: "Participating in the Wikipedia community helps young people to think about their own roles as researchers and writers in new ways" (2007b). Educators should help young authors understand the implications of irresponsible publication.

In summary, I agree with Parry (2008):

> And this is why digital literacy is so crucial for educational institutions: we do a fundamental disservice to our students if we continue to propagate old methods of knowledge creation and archivization without also teaching them how these structures are changing, and, more importantly, how they will relate to knowledge creation and dissemination in a fundamentally different way. (p. X) You have ended with a long quote – should you add at least one sentence to unpack and make your own?

Using Wikipedia Constructively

Many times Wikipedia provides quick, concise answers to precise, closed-ended questions. When the questions are important, users must adopt the practice of verifying answers from more than one source, and applying several evaluative strategies to judge the quality of the information found. When the question is less important, we must ask: "What if this is not the truth?" It may not matter much, but the user must be the one to make this judgment.

There are many excellent website evaluation checklists available online. While helpful, few users will realistically consult them consistently at the point of need. In short, these two strategies may help users deal with most information situations:

1. Assume that all information, regardless of source, is flawed to some degree.
2. When the situation is important, take the time to verify crucial aspects of the information.

Bloggers such as Hargadon, Valenza, and Harris (each active in 2008) frequently emphasize that a paradigm shift is taking place in the infosphere and that information professionals, including school library media specialists, must capitalize on the associated changes. We need waste no more time arguing about if and whether, but move on to how. This list of implementation strategies may help encourage the use of online tools for educational enhancement:

- Integrate the use of new media, including Wikipedia, into all appropriate educational goals. The very higher-order thinking skills that are underserved within the NCLB paradigm lend themselves to expression through creative uses of new, motivational media such as Wikipedia.
- Likewise, promote the new tools as intrinsic motivators, helping to solve one of the most intractable problems we have in education—apathy.
- Use Wikipedia as a way to explore bias. Assign students topics to examine for compliance with the rule of neutral point of view (Jenkins, 2007b), and to write articles that apply it. Understanding point of view is one building block of good critical thinking. Extend the discussion of bias to the traditional media. Build

the ability to respect multiple perspectives by requiring students to debate arguments from the opposite of their own point of view. This ability to empathize with another perspective is critical to our multicultural and globally "flat" future (Friedman, 2007).

- Fight the filters. Protest the wholesale blocking of useful online tools, while working within established rules and policies. Use diplomacy and reasonable arguments to help decision-makers understand the shortsightedness and futility of tightly locked terminals.
- Beyond elementary grades, students should not cite encyclopedias. Use Wikipedia alongside traditional encyclopedias to explain and explore their usefulness as general, introductory sources for most topics.
- Recruit students to use Wikipedia along with a range or authoritative resources in checking the accuracy of textbook information, and vice versa. When Wikipedia is incorrect, encourage them to contribute corrections. When the textbook is incorrect, encourage students to contact the publishers.
- Train students to study the revision history of Wikipedia articles to discover how online vandalism occurs and is corrected, along with the evolution (or devolution) of article quality.
- Although it seems precocious for young students to write Wikipedia articles, local history is one area currently under-represented. Organize student projects to develop encyclopedia articles about local topics such as:

  - Infamous local crimes of long ago
  - War-time home front events from any war
  - Biographies of local prominent people
  - Place (buildings and sites) histories in relation to broad historical events
  - Significant artists and artistic and cultural events
  - Local biology, habitats, plants, and animals
  - Local customs and cultural characteristics

These ideas offer a small sampling of the many ways to incorporate the power of Wikipedia into an educational mission. In this age of technology, we have inherited and invented wondrous tools and resources. It is up to educators to harness these tools for the benefit of students of all ages.

References

Anderson, C. (2008, February 25). Free! Why $0.00 is the future of business [Electronic version]. *Wired, 16*(3). Retrieved May 27, 2008, from http://www.wired.com/techbiz/it/magazine/16-03/ff_free

Badke, W. (2008). What to do with Wikipedia [Electronic version]. *Online, 32*(2). Retrieved April 1, 2008, from http://www.infotoday.com/online/mar08/Badke.shtml

Cohen, N. (2007, February 21). A history department bans citing Wikipedia as a research source [Electronic version]. *New York Times*. Retrieved May 29, 2008, from http://www.nytimes.com/2007/02/21/education/21wikipedia.html

Cohen, N. (2008, March 16). Start writing the eulogies for print encyclopedias [Electronic version]. *New York Times.* Retrieved March 18, 2008, from http://www.nytimes.com/2008/03/16/weekinreview/16ncohen.html?pagewanted=1&ei=5070&en=85f96efb61addf41&ex=1206504000&emc=eta1

Denning, P., Horning, J., Parnas, D., & Weinstein, L. (2005). Wikipedia risks. *Communications of the ACM, 48*(12), 152.

Fallis, D. (2007, October 31). *The epistemology of Wikipedia* [podcast]. Retrieved February 21, 2008, from http://milton.sbs.arizona.edu/%7Esirls/20071031fallis.html and http://milton.sbs.arizona.edu/%7Esirls/20071031fallis.pdf

Flanagin, A. J., & Metzger, M. J. (2000). Perceptions of internet information credibility. *Journalism & Mass Communication Quarterly, 77*(3), 515–540.

Friedman, T. L. (2007). *The world is flat: A brief history of the twenty-first century.* New York: Farrar, Straus & Giroux.

Giles, J. (2005). Internet encyclopedias go head to head. *Nature, 438*(7070), 900–901.

Guterman, L. (2008, February 22). *Indian chemist is found to have plagiarized and falsified articles. Chronicle of Higher Education News Blog.*Retrieved March 18, 2008, from http://chronicle.com/news/article/4019/indian-chemist-is-found-to-have-plagiarized-and-falsified-articles

Hargadon, S. (2008, March 4). Web 2.0 is the future of education [blog entry]. Retrieved March 24, 2008, from http://www.stevehargadon.com/2008/03/web-20-is-future-of-education.html

Harris, C. (2008). *Digital Reshift* [blog hosted by *School Library Journal*]. Retrieved May 30, 2008, from http://www.schoollibraryjournal.com/blog/840000284.html

Jenkins, H. (2006). *Fans, bloggers, and gamers: Exploring participatory culture.* New York: New York University Press.

Jenkins, H. (2007a, June 26). What Wikipedia can teach us about new media literacies (part one). *Confessions of an Aca-Fan: The official Weblog of Henry Jenkins.* Retrieved April 7, 2008, from http://henryjenins.org/2007/06/what_wikipedia_can_teach_us_ab.html

Jenkins, H. (2007b, June 27). What Wikipedia can teach us about new media literacies (part two). *Confessions of an Aca-Fan: The official Weblog of Henry Jenkins.* Retrieved April 7, 2008, from http://henryjenkins.org/2007/06/what_wikipedia_can_teach_us_ab_1.html

Archives of JESSE@Listserv.utk.edu. (2008). Retrieved June 1, 2008, from http://listserv.utk.edu/archives/jesse.html

Lenhart, A., Madden, M., Macgill, A. R., & Smith, A. (2007). *Teens and social media.* Pew Internet & American Life Project. Retrieved May 30, 2008, from http://www.pewinternet.org/pdfs/PIP_Teens_Social_Media_Final.pdf

Lih, A. (2004). *Wikipedia as participatory journalism: Reliable sources? Metrics for evaluating collaborative media as a news resource.* Paper presented at the 5th International Symposium on Online Journalism, University of Texas, Austin, April.

Mardis, M., & Perrault, A. M. (2008). A whole new library: Six "senses" you can use to make sense of new standards and guidelines. *Teacher Librarian, 35*(4), 34–38.

Middlebury College. (2007, March 23). *Wikipedia in academia: History department decision still fueling debate.* Retrieved May 29, 2008, from http://www.middlebury.edu/about/newsevents/archive/2007/newsevents_633084484309809133.htm

Parry, D. (2008, February 11). Wikipedia and the new curriculum: Digital literacy is knowing how we store what we know. *Science Progress, 3.* Retrieved February 19, 2008, from http://www.scienceprogress.org/2008/02/wikipedia-and-the-new-curriculum/

Rosenzweig, R. (2006). Can history be open source? Wikipedia and the future of the past. *The Journal of American History, 93*(1). Retrieved March 12, 2008, from http://www.historycooperative.org.proxy-remote.galib.uga.edu:2048/journals/jah/93.1/rosenzweig. html

Seigenthaler, J. (2005, November 30). A false Wikipedia "biography." *USA Today.*

Surowiecki, J. (2004). *The wisdom of crowds: Why the many are smarter than the few and how collective wisdom shapes business, economies, societies, and nations.* New York: Doubleday.

Thompson, C. (2003). Illiterate or lazy: How college students use the web for research. *Libraries and the Academy, 3*(2), 259–268.

Valenza, J. (2008, February 6). Saving Tinkerbell! On the importance of clapping. *Neverendsearch* blog, *School Library Journal*. Retrieved February 12, 2008, from http://www.schoollibraryjournal.com/blog/1340000334/post/390021439.html?nid=3714

Wilson, C. (2008, February 22). The wisdom of the chaperones: Digg, Wikipedia, and the myth of Web 2.0 democracy [Electronic version]. *Slate*. Retrieved March 18, 2008, from http://www.slate.com/id/2184487/pagenum/all/#page_start

High-Tech Tools for the Library Media Center: The Future from a Low-tech Point of View

Daniel Fuller, Doug Achtermann, and Cathy McLeod

Abstract Change and technology seem to be synonymous with the library media center. The Web 2.0 tools such as blogs, wikis, RSS, podcasts, and social tagging change the dynamic from a passive collection of resources to an interactive relationship with learners. The authors propose a trajectory to describe the relationship of libraries to the interactive tools from the pre-Internet to the post Internet future. Library 2.0 tools are defined and discussed with suggestions for practical use. The concept of digital natives is examined in the context of support for student learning and the implications for user interactions with traditional content to create new information and knowledge. To assist educators to embrace and understand the tools, a del.icio.us link to all tools and examples is provided.

Keywords Web 2.0 · Blogs · Wikis · RSS · Podcasts · Social tagging · Library 2.0

Science fiction authors have affection for the Rip Van Winkle metaphor where the unsuspecting character from the past awakens befuddled by the changes of the day. In the twenty-first century, library media specialists (LMS) may feel the same way. Almost overnight students are using strange names for new tools and describing them as both nouns and verbs—like Google, Googled, and Googling. The sense of confusion created the same sensation: the world changed and many of us have to catch up. Students are using their thumbs to send messages on cell phones and prefer only information found online.

Educators, and especially the library media specialists, may feel as if we have awakened in a new world where our skills are marginalized and may be seen as irrelevant. While school libraries traditionally focused on information and student learning, the tools have changed again. Today interactive learning tools claim the stage in the form of blogs, wikis, podcasts, and social tagging. Tomorrow, these tools will be replaced by even greater possibilities—and so change goes. Our task is to understand how these new technologies leverage the media center toward increased

D. Fuller (✉)
School of Library and Information Science, San Jose State University, San Jose, CA 95129-0029, USA
e-mail: dfuller@slis.sjsu.edu

M. Orey et al. (eds.), *Educational Media and Technology Yearbook*,
DOI 10.1007/978-0-387-09675-9_13, © Springer Science+Business Media, LLC 2009

student achievement. With a willingness to change and explore new emerging tools, the LMS will successfully contribute to student learning outcomes as the future awakens.

The Pace of Technological Change

Embracing technology is the hallmark of the LMC. As a result of a series of technology applications, by the turn of the 21st century 95% of all school libraries utilized a computer card catalog (Fuller, 2006). At the same time, innovative technology has been a critical part of the lives of students outside the classroom. Unfortunately, classroom teachers, though sophisticated users of technology in their personal lives, tend not to use the same level of technology in the classroom learning environments (Levin & Arafeh, 2002). According to Levin and Arafeh, the failure to match the pace of technological change for integration into educational practice produces a mismatch with the perception in the eyes of some educators of how students use the Internet and the actual findings of student use.

The world is more connected today than ever before. The technology connections are matched by social connections unimagined even a decade ago. The phenomenon identified as Web 2.0 is a convergence of the Internet world with a variety of new tools promoting interactivity and communication. Nova Spivack described a trajectory of the growth of technological and social connections in a seemingly endless upward direction (Spivack & RadarNetworks, 2007).

Spivack used the term "semantics of information connections" to describe the technological innovations and "semantics of social connections" to identify the interactivity and communication tools (Spivack & RadarNetworks, 2007, ¶ 1). The result is a prediction of a future technology platformdevelopment with intervals called Web 3.0, Web 4.0, and so on. Spivak describes these intervals as time periods. Using the jargon of education and library media centers, the same concept is easily translated into LMC and educational technology. In Fig. 1, the x-axis represents the changing learning environment over time and the y-axis represents the tools students are using. As time passed, learners' increased familiarity with digital information technologies moved the LMC from the basic stand alone computer to LMC 1.0 in the mid-1990s and now LMC 2.0.

The LMC is poised on the edge of LMC 3.0. The interactive tools and technologies of LMC 2.0 point towards greater personalization in digital spaces. Increasingly, the creation of digital products by learners fuels more change, requiring more collaboration and interaction in ever more virtual spaces. To better understand why the future appears to be an LMC 3.0, consider how learners, educators, and the LMC evolved into its present state. Perhaps no other technology played a greater role in Web 2.0 world than email. Email allowed for individuals to communicate and share across space and time. Next were personal Web pages. The Web page development allowed a one-way communication from the creator to the reader. Today, the online journal named weblog (blog) allows Interactive dialog between author and reader.

Learning
Environments

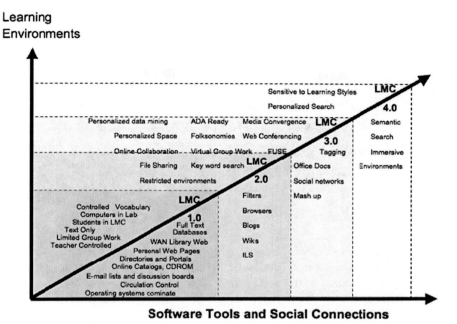

Software Tools and Social Connections

Fig. 1 Trajectory from LMC 1.0 to the future

The ability to store files on a remote server where others access them allows file sharing. Files, including Photos, videos, and music, stored remotely are available to others simply for sharing. The convergence is closely related to social communication and collaboration goals. The convergence is not about the products and tools used.

In the terms of the LMC, a passive repository with limited communication between the LMC to the learner is disappearing. The essential educational link between learners and the resources of the LMC is interactive. Because of increased connectivity, learners have greater options for access to digital information resources. Figure 2 demonstrates the contrast between how learners use libraries and LMC organization using technology is greater than it has ever been in the past.

The contrasts between LMC 1.0 and LMC 2.0 begin with access to materials. In LMC 1.0, the needs of learners adjusted to the physical collection. The collection changed slowly attempting to adapt to the needs of the curriculum and the needs of learners in a time of constant change. In response, learners found a dynamic, digital world in the Internet and adopted it. LMC 2.0 recognizes the needs the learners as they have defined them. The access has to be without the constraints of a physical collection and the learner determines the time it is accessed. LMC 2.0 collection is robust and dynamic resources including print and electronic materials.

Technology allowsthe learner, rather than the expert, to select from a wide variety of print and electronic resources. The experts who created LMC 1.0 must teach the

LMC 1.0	LMC 2.0
Collection centered	Learner centered
Technology enabled	Technology driven
One way communication	Interactive
Pre-defined search methodologies	Constructivist searching
Qualified selection of resources	Learner selected resources
Access limited to physical space	LMC without walls
Time defined by LMC	Time defined by user

Fig. 2 Comparing LMC 1. 0 to LMC 2.0

learner to critically analyze and select resources. The learner has created a learning environment and the expert has to take a constructivist approach to be successful. As the expert ventures into the learner's world, he or she has to be ready to teach the learner to identify and select resources based on factors of creditability and validity rather than what is easy or the learner likes. It is based on mutual trust and is an almost constant dialogue to select from an almost unlimited amount of data.

How does the expert engage and interact with the learner? The process begins by embracing the tools the learner prefers in Web 2.0 and actively uses them within LMC 2.0. The answer involves getting on the trajectory of the tools and demonstrating the relevance of the LMC to the learner. The resulting constructivist collaboration between the expert and the learner addresses the needs of both in an interesting and complicated world.

The Myth of Digital Natives

If the LMS may be Rip Van Winkle, a digital immigrant, then the learners the serve are the digital natives. The digital native appears to be part of a generation born with an innate understanding of all things digital and particularly adept at manipulating small electronic devices. The difference is quite simply practice (Williams, 2006). The new generation took the time to learn something new. What can the LMS do? The answer is practice, plain and simple. The digital immigrant need not wait until the new version is released. Classes can help, but practice refines the learning.

The tech savvy say Web 2.0 is nothing new. The technologies that allowed Web 1.0 to happen such as web browsers, HTML, and high-speed connectivity merged with digital audio and video creating new tools. At the same time, interfaces became simpler, requiring lower and lower thresholds of experience to use them. The tools of Web 2.0 are more about imagination than technical revolution. Bandwidth and infrastructure, the boring topics of technology geeks and politicians, are as responsible for Web 2.0 as the imbedding of microchips in the brains of learners.

LMC 2.0 emerged from the same convergence of technologies. Again the newness is the old technologies interacting with each other to create new possibilities. Over a decade ago, the plethora of CD-ROM databases and other research products caused the world of information professionals to whine for a common user interface. The dominance of the Internet and high-speed bandwidth converged to allow meta-search to happen. The learners prefer it, desiring to find all of their information resources in one place displayed in a simple and attractive manner.

The LMS needs to become more interested in the Web 2.0 tools and interested in what the learners are using them to do. To understand the tools the digital immigrants need to try them out and to use them. Practice is the quickest and most instructive way to gain competence and failing is learning.

Embracing Web 2.0 Tools and Catching up to LMC 2.0

So how does the LMS make sense of all of the tools? The first step is exploration. The volume of information is huge and the LMS is not required to learn everything? Learning today is not bounded by age. The LMS teaches life-long learning and must model life-long learning.

The answer to how to catch up has five characteristics: Look, Play, Think, Practice and Do, and Revise. Before you make any decision about the utility of the Web 2.0 tools, you must see them. Next, begin with play, because with play comes experimentation, a willingness to fail, and a sense of fun without much risk attached. This attitude will help you discover aspects of new technologies you might not uncover if you pose as a serious A+ student all the time. Try things and give yourself permission to fail. After play, give yourself time to think about the experience. Use your personal lens and the view of an outsider. When you find something then take it to the practice and do stage. After you have created a product—revise and refine. Share if you like, because sharing is the whole point of Web 2.0.

The trick is to set a deadline. Promise the faculty you will give them a workshop on a topic such as blogging. Once you accept the commitment, reframe failure to trial and error learning. Most blogs are not widely read nor are the intended to be. If you create a blog for family and friends, you are doing what most bloggers do. Another approach is to follow a blog or a blog topic in which you have a personal interest. One reason young learners appear successful is they manipulate the various technologies as a group. Everyone else is there and they want to be there too. Social networking appears vain to some adults, but young learners see it as a communication device, a living rolodex of friends and acquaintances available from any networked computer.

Find a friend and agree to do it together. The key is to find something to share. Embracing the Web 2.0 tools requires sharing and using the interactivity of the tools. The opportunity is available through professional communities. The California School Library Association (CSLA) provided a good example in an online tutorial developed in the spring of 2007. *School Library Learning 2.0* (http://schoollibrarylearning2.blogspot.com/) is a free online tutorial for the Web 2.0 tools. The CSLA 2.0 Learning Team, a virtual group with sixty collaborators, modified Helen Blowers' Learning 2.0 course under a Creative Commons license (Blowers, 2006). Over 275 people registered for the course resulting in a second version entitled *Classroom Learning 2.0* designed for the classroom teacher.

The first step is to just try. No one approach works for everyone, but trial and error with the mantra "practice, dude" is the road to success. Change is constant and unending. Web 2.0 and the resulting technology tools are simply evidence of this fact of life. When change happens, embrace it and deal with it.

Merging the Old with the New

Another way to look at the Web 2.0 applications is to consider them as evolutions of familiar paper 20th century tools. Figure 3 provides a list of common tools, the Web 2.0 equivalent, and applications for their use. As an example, journaling is almost as old as writing itself. Blogging is new. It is a journal but it is also a journal to be shared with others on a large scale. Further, a blog is interactive and the reader has the ability to respond to the thinking of the author and contribute their own content. Blogs are used as newsletters, information sources before, during and after conferences, and as reflective instruments for book clubs. The *School Library Learning 2.0* initiatives uses a blog to provide instructions and feedback.

In a school setting, blogs are a constructivist tool for learning. They are searchable. Student work remains relevant and is archived for the future. A blog creates

20th Century	21st Century	Application
Journaling	Blogging	Journals, Newsletters, Readers advisor
Vertical File	Wiki	Content management, course work, Projects
Photograph Album	Photobucket, Flickr	Community, Store digital images, Sharing
Bulletin Boards	MySpace, Facebook	Interactive bulletin boards, communication
Phone calls	IM, Texting	Communication, Messages, Reference Q&A
Videotape	YouTube, TeacherTube	PR, Tutorials, Community, Sharing
Course Reserves	Blackboard, Moodle	Course Management system, Sharing
Collage	Mashup	Communication of new knowledge
Tape Recording	Podcast	PR, tutorials, community, sharing

Fig. 3 Genealogy of Web 2.0 tools

a connection to the larger community of learners and support the different learning styles while teaching a wide variety of literacies.

Another Web 2.0 tool is the wiki. A wiki is a website where anyone can edit anything at anytime they want. Wikipedia is the most famous example of the application of a wiki, demonstrating the relevant features of the wiki technology. The learner has the ability to hyperlink plus add, delete, and edit content on the page. The technology tracks every change made the page and has a place to discuss what is happening on the page.

The wiki is an excellent tool to organize content from a variety of resources and work with a group of learners. In the world of the LMC, the wiki can be used for something as simple as a common sign up sheet or it can be used to organize complex projects such as a curriculum review.

Photobucket and Flickr allow the user to store and share photos and other images with others. Rather than send a dozen photos to a dozen people, a link to the photo site is sent instead. It is a photo album that everyone can view. Mashups are collages of the digital world. Instead in paste and paper, learners use multiple digital sources to create new images.

The goal for the LMS is to be the interface between the world libraries have always occupied and the rip, mix and burn world of today and tomorrow. The tools libraries used to organize the first information revolution are useful, but those rules are incomplete for the second information revolution. Putting Web 2.0 technologies into context is a challenge without first trying the tools. Take time to plan a project engaging students, faculty and staff. Experiment with different tools and test their ability to meet your goals. Provide shared owner ship and collaboration. Collect data to validate the effect of the tools on student outcomes.

The Trajectory to LMC 3.0

Finding the future is the focus of LMC 2.0. Not just the future users of the LMC, but also the future technologies. The tools provide services bind the learners to the LMC. Figure 4 provides a list of potential services in future versions of LMC 3.0.

Future learners demand personalization of services. The track record of the target group of learners demonstrates this need for personalization. LMC 3.0 must reconcile the long-standing philosophical practice of shielding the system from knowledge of specific learners with the demand of the new learner for tools to personalize learner resources and search for information in a way they can call their own. The popularity of social networking tools and the use of collaboration as a preferred learning style is not a strange occurrence but a logical progression of the tools in the inherently social nature of the new learner.

The new learner demands to be connected to the world at any and all times. The existence of the network is assumed—not an option to the new learner to be purchased. Without communication via the network, the tools become meaningless. The network allows the most important aspect of communication they seek, instant

Integrated Library System 3.0	Addressing multiple forms of literacy Addressing multiple learning modalities Personalization Use defined by the learner
Interactive Learning Tools of LMC 3.0	Data mining Personalized abstracts and indexing User defined smarter searching Folksonomies
Wireless Access Devices	Three digit cell phone access Voice activated search File sharing downloads Persistent network access
Learner/LMS Interactivity	Constructivist Learning Creating new knowledge Communication

Fig. 4 Learning and LMC 3.0

communication. An example would be a three digit number automatically connecting them to the LMC or any other library via the learners cell phone, say 027. The learner uses their personalized saved searches to view the newest music in the CD collection and determine if the video they reserved is in stock. Of course, schools and libraries would have to recognize the potential of a networked device for learning rather than the current bans on cellular devices.

In the midst of all of the tools is a rich source of media content larger than any available to learners in any previous time in history. A body of research assembled over the last half of the 20th century tells us the learner needs a variety of modalities to communicate and understand information. The learner knows this intuitively. They understand the need to use the modalities to reach the emotional levels where their personal learning exists.

The new learner is motivated by personalization, socialization, media content, and network. The four characteristics lead them to their goal to communicate in many forms and format whenever and wherever they wish. The services are indispensable to the new learners. It refutes a fundamental and basic half-truth of libraries and learning—there is a library and then everything else. Everywhere is a library to the new learner and learning is constantly occurring outside of the school day. The new learner shifts time and shapes LMC 3.0.

Conclusion

Why use Web 2.0 tools? The first reason is to provide deeper learning opportunities for your students. Students need their classrooms to challenge and engage them. They need learning environments on how to work with others, and to create new knowledge through this collaboration. Web 2.0 tools provide this necessary environment.

Web 2.0 tools stimulate student and staff creativity. The knowledge products they create allow them to share the ownership and enjoy collaborative learning. In the experience, they make the global connections between many different ideas and a wide variety of communications methods. The learning environment using Web 2.0 tools allows the student and staff to produce knowledge products easily. The tools remove the obstacles to collaborative learning. The communication makes the collaboration transparent to students and staff. The environment for learning is the focus and not reasons why it cannot be done. To view an example of the phenomena at this web site is available online: http://del.icio.us/hightechlowtech. This site holds a wide variety of applications of Web 2.0 tools and articles related to the topic. This del.icio.us site grew from the collaborative efforts among the authors and dozens of LMS attending a session at the AASL biennial conference in Reno, Nevada in 2007. The site began as the hand out materials for the 2007 presentation and has grown as participants in the session have added additional resources.

In the end, educators and the LMS want to make a difference in the lives of students. Schools with a myopic focus on testing need alternative learning environments. Learning environments need to focus on social interaction in creating new knowledge. The future is in working together with teachers and students to create new knowledge together.

References

Blowers, H. (2006). *Learning 2.0.* Retrieved March 28, 2008, from http://plcmcl2-about. blogspot.com/

Eden, B. (2007, November/December). Library 2.0. *Library Technology Reports, 43*(6), 41–46.

Fuller, D. (2006). School Library Journal & San Jose State University 2006 automation survey. *School Library Journal, 52*(10), 48–52.

Levin, D., & Arafeh, S. (2002). *The digital disconnect, the widening gap between internet savvy students and their schools.* Pew Internet and American Life Project, Washington, DC.

Spivack, N., & RadarNetworks. (2007, February 9). *How the WebOS evolves?* Msg #1 Message posted to http://novaspivack.typepad.com/nova_spivacks_weblog/2007/02/steps_towards_a.html

Williams, J. F. (2006, November). *Making sense of the future.* Paper presented at the School Library Journal Leadership Summit, Chicago, IL.

Taking Care of Business: Authentic Use of Web 2.0 in Schools

Shayne Russell

Abstract   A new generation of web-based tools, referred to as Web 2.0, allows users to organize information, to create and edit content, and to collaborate with others. The skills developed and practiced through the use of these tools are the same skills valued by 21st century employers. Web 2.0 tools offer schools the potential to engage students in assignments demonstrating authentic uses of technology. While students have embraced these tools in their personal lives, school districts remain hesitant to adopt Web 2.0 applications due to safety concerns. This chapter explores potential and actual uses of Web 2.0 in schools, the changes occurring in the business world as a result of these new technologies, and the implications for today's students and educational systems.

Keywords   Educational technology · Web 2.0 · Information literacy · Educational change · Online social networks

Many educators remember the early days of Internet access in schools. The 1990s saw many districts involved in major projects to connect schools to the Internet, and educational literature was rife with predictions of how the Internet would revolutionize education. The educational community viewed the introduction of Internet access as a positive development, with the major concern being one of equity. The term "digital divide" described an inequity in access to technology based on economic factors, geography and race (Gunkel, 2003, p. 501). Concern that students in wealthier school districts may realize advantages and benefits from new technology not available to students in less affluent areas remains a concern today.

Following the initial growth in Internet connectivity and use, the nature of the Web itself changed, evolving from a static environment to one characterized by interactivity. The new Web environment, referred to as Web 2.0, offers tools that enable Web users to create and publish new content, to gain an authentic audience

S. Russell (✉)
Kenneth R. Olson Middle School, Tabernacle, NJ 08088, USA
e-mail: shayne.russell@gmail.com

for that content, and to collaborate with others in online social networks. These powerful new tools are changing the way that young people interact with information and with the Internet, reshaping how companies conduct business on a global scale, and redefining the skills necessary to succeed in the 21st century workplace. How schools respond to the promise and pitfalls of Web 2.0 environments will determine how well students can compete in a new, collaborative economy.

Students and Technology: In and Out of School

Today's students have embraced Web 2.0 and the opportunities it affords to connect with other Internet users. School districts, due largely to safety concerns, have given Web 2.0 a less enthusiastic reception. The result is a disconnect between the way students use technology at school and outside of school. Dubbed "digital natives" (Prensky, 2001, p. 1), today's students live in a world defined by connectivity through the use of a wide range of digital and electronic devices. Contrast this technologically rich existence with the school environment, where cell phones must be turned off and the web-based tools young people rely on outside of school are off-limits. "In most schools, blogs are banned, wikis are scorned and social networks are taboo" (Richardson, 2007, p. 23). Prensky (2008) uses the phrase "powering down" to describe the student's response to the school environment (p. 42). In 2007, Wesch and his Kansas State University Cultural Anthropology class created a YouTube video capturing the contrast between these two worlds and the boredom inspired by traditional schooling. In the video, students sitting in a large lecture hall display signs such as "I will read 8 books this year, 2300 Web pages and 1281 Face-Book profiles" that reflect the influence of the Internet and other technologies in their lives. The students' messages illustrate their use of and learning from digital technologies in ways yet to be recognized by the public education system.

Students have probably always experienced some degree of boredom during the school day, and the disparity between the educational environment and real life is nothing new. In 1907, Dewey observed a similar situation:

> From the standpoint of the child, the great waste in the school comes from his inability to utilize the experiences he gets outside the school in any complete and free way within the school itself; while, on the other hand, he is unable to apply in daily life what he is learning at school. That is the isolation of the school – its isolation from life. When the child gets into the schoolroom he has to put out of his mind a large part of the ideas, interests, and activities that predominate in his home and neighborhood. So the school, being unable to utilize this everyday experience, sets painfully to work, on another tack and by a variety of means, to arouse in the child an interest in school studies. (pp. 89–90)

The 21st century version of this problem may have more serious repercussions for students than the educational "isolation from life" of Dewey's era. The skills students could be learning and practicing in school through the use of Web 2.0 tools are skills increasingly valued by 21st century employers.

Web 2.0 in the Workplace

Business leaders report that knowledge of core content is still necessary, but no longer sufficient for success in a competitive world. "Even if all students mastered core academic subjects, they still would be woefully under-prepared to succeed in postsecondary institutions and workplaces, which increasingly value people who can use their knowledge to communicate, collaborate, analyze, create, innovate and solve problems" (International Society for Technology in Education, State Educational Technology Directors Association, & Partnership for 21st Century Skills, 2007). These are the same skills that businesses demand for Web 2.0 applications for online presence and marketing.

Businesses employ Web 2.0 technologies for internal problem solving, to recruit employees, and to connect with customers. Wikis provide scalable project management, industry news tracking, meeting agenda management, corporate policies posting, and research storage and sharing (King, 2007). Many organizations, including the CIA, use Facebook, a popular social networking site, to post job openings (Roberts, 2008). A poll conducted by Forrester Research indicates that most American companies are considering Web 2.0 technology investments, with 54% using or interested in blogs, 63% in podcasts, 64% in wikis, and 68% in Rich Site Summary, or RSS (Womack, 2007). Web 2.0 technologies improve communication and boost efficiency, earning a positive appraisal by business leaders.

According to Tapscott, author of *Wikinomics* (2006), collaboration models will dominate the 21st century marketplace. The ability to adapt to mass collaboration within a global economy may mean the difference between success and failure for businesses. Business leaders also recognize that the 80 million children of baby boomers now entering the workforce expect collaboration tools in the workplace. In fact, the availability of Web 2.0 and similar collaborative tools to the digital natives in their places of work may well become a recruitment and retention issue for businesses. Industry information leaders recognize that companies lacking the technology demanded by new workers stand to lose those employees to companies who can provide these tools (Havenstein, 2007). Such collaborative tool skill represents a marketable asset for job seekers now and in the future.

Web 2.0 Use in Education

The business world has always adapted to change more rapidly than the education world. The education system moves forward through the efforts of early adopters who recognize both the promise and importance of incorporating new technologies. Often these educators learn about new tools by applying them first in useful ways to their own personal or professional lives. This chapter explores four popular Web 2.0 resources and current and potential application in schools: photosharing, social bookmarks, blogging, and wikis. Authentic application of these tools in the school environment commands attention in light of the value placed by the business sector on these tools and the skills associated with their use. Early adopters in the education world view Web 2.0 as a powerful force both for restoring relevance to education, and for preparing students to compete in a global economy that is based increasingly on communication and information skills.

Photosharing

The sharing of personal photographs provided one of the earliest and most basic uses of the internet. Yahoo's Flickr™, launched in February 2004, represents one of the first Web 2.0 tools. Google introduced Picasa™ later in the same year and a variety of other photosharing services have followed. Photosharing represents an ideal entry point to Web 2.0 for educators and students. This chapter uses Flickr™ to illustrate how teachers and students may use these services.

With a free Flickr™ account, a teacher can upload 100 megabytes of photos to the Web per month. Account features allow teachers to assign titles and captions and to organize groups of photos into sets for sharing. By designating photos as public or private, teachers can control viewers, restricting access to enrolled students or other legitimate groups.

Teachers can use a Flickr™ set to establish a Web presence for a school library or classroom. No Web-editing software or HTML knowledge is needed to create an attractive connection with parents and community members. Photo sets offer an ideal venue to share views of the facility, special events, or student projects.

An option to view a photo set as a slideshow makes Flickr™ useful as a presentation tool. Students may present information using their own photographs to illustrate their points. This type of presentation could be a refreshing alternative to text-heavy PowerPoint slides. However, it is also possible to upload PowerPoint slides to Flickr™. Students or teachers can annotate their slides and share their presentations online. For educators, this feature offers a method to share the content of conference or professional development presentations, while allowing students to share school projects with distant family members.

Notes can be added to Flickr™ photographs. Using the cursor, a student drags a rectangular outline around an item in the photograph. With a mouse-over, a text box containing additional information provided by the student pops up. The content of a note may be quite lengthy, including embedded hyperlinks and more, thus enabling students to organize and present information in a non-linear fashion.

As a member of the Web 2.0 family of tools, Flickr™ includes features to foster community building. Perhaps the most powerful community building technique shared by Web 2.0 applications is *tagging*. Tagging is the practice of assigning descriptive labels to online content. The labels are natural language terms chosen by Web users, creating what has been dubbed a *folksonomy*—or user-generated taxonomy (Wikipedia, 2008).

Tagging is an important concept because these keywords are what make Web content searchable. The idea of tagging becomes more accessible to students when they assign keywords to describe their own photographs. Flickr™ becomes a building block for an important understanding that can later be applied to other Web 2.0 tools.

Since tagging makes the entire Flickr™ community searchable, Flickr™ is a valuable resource for pictures for school projects and assignments. Both in terms of quality and appropriateness of content, Flickr™ can be preferable to a Google image search. Flickr™ employs content filters and users assign safety levels to all pictures that are uploaded. Photographs are designated as safe, moderate, or restricted. The default search level for Flickr™ is SafeSearch, which will retrieve only safe content. Many of the images posted to Flickr™ come from professionals or represent near-professional quality—superior to most of the results of a Google image search.

Flickr™ users also assign copyright licenses to their photos, choosing from six levels of Creative Commons licensing, all of which are explained on the site. Copyright permissions are easy to determine for any photo, creating an opportunity to educate students about intellectual property rights. It is easy to identify the owner of a photograph, and Flickr™ members are able to contact each other through a feature called FlickrMail™ without an individual's email address being displayed. Thus, requesting permission to use a photograph is a simple matter, and students should be encouraged to make it a habit to do so.

Social Bookmarks

Once students have grasped the concept of tagging through Flickr™, they're ready to graduate to another Web 2.0 tool. Social bookmarking services answer several of the problems inherent in browser bookmarks. Browser bookmarks reside on the computer used to bookmark the site, while social bookmarks are web-based. As long as an Internet connection exists, the sites bookmarked are as well. Students access sites found at school from their home computers, and vice versa, through their social bookmark service. The social bookmark arena is a crowded one, with del.icio.us (http://del.icio.us), StumbleUpon (http://www.stumbleupon.com), Digg (http://digg.com/), Furl (http://www.furl.net/), and Simpy (http://www.simpy.com/) among the current favorites. Del.icio.us is the best known and most heavily subscribed of the social bookmark services, and as a result is focused upon in this chapter.

The concept of shared online bookmarks dates back to 1996, but in 2004 del.icio.us introduced tagging and "social" bookmarks (Wikipedia, 2008). Tagging adds an additional layer of organization to saved bookmarks. Instead of creating lengthy lists of saved sites, from which it is often difficult to retrieve resources, tags allow searching by keyword. For instance, I would not be likely to remember the title or URL of a saved site about campsites on the Green River. But I could think of the tags I most likely assigned to it: camping, canoeing, Green River, Utah, river trips, and summer vacation. Searching any of these tags within my own del.icio.us account leads me to the site desired.

In the school library, del.icio.us offers an alternative to creating Web pages that guide students to online resources. With no HTML knowledge, Web-editing software, or server space, a librarian can generate a list of appropriate sources with tags that represent the assigned topics. The addition of annotations transforms the list into an online pathfinder.

Sharing the account's password with the students allows them to tag and add their own finds to the class collection. Each student helps to build a shared resource from which the entire class can benefit. There is no longer any need to hoard information. By using their first names as one of the tags they assign, students are able to view a list of all the resources they have selected for their project. This list may include resources found by others, to which they have attached their own names as an additional tag.

As in Flickr™, del.icio.us users can designate their bookmarks as public or private. Del.icio.us displays the number of users who have saved each site, making it possible to identify popular resources. Communities of people with like interests can be built and educators can browse the public bookmarks of others to discover new resources. One del.icio.us user may even subscribe to the tags of another user with similar interests and continue to reap the benefits of that person's finds. This is a phenomenon common to many Web 2.0 tools, and is referred to as tapping into the wisdom of the crowd.

Del.icio.us bookmarks can also be shared between colleagues and friends. A teacher can share a site with a colleague by tagging it with *for: username*. The site will then appear on the "links for you" page in the colleague's del.icio.us account. This feature aids in organization and lessens the likelihood that a useful link becomes lost amid an overcrowded email box.

Within any profession, individuals with innovative ideas rise to the forefront. In the library world, these same people are frequently the early adopters of technology. These leaders may share their latest del.icio.us bookmarks by posting a linkroll on personal blogs or websites. Others in the profession view or subscribe to these public bookmarks or add these innovators to their personal network. In this way, del.icio.us helps leaders to build influence, contact, and inform others in the profession regarding current issues.

Blogs

The movers and shakers in the education and library world are often bloggers as well. Writing a blog is a useful professional development experience requiring wide reading, information processing, and current practice implementation. The best professional blogs offer reflective and critical thinking, providing insight into the current issues. Professional blog content then may be used in practice and in the classroom as content.

The use of blogs with students has been controversial. However, young people embrace this Web 2.0 tool in their own personal lives. Only 7% of adult Internet users create their own blogs, compared to 19% of Internet users between the ages of 12 and 17—a group comprised of approximately 4 million people (Lenhart & Madden, 2005). Also, young people are more likely to read blogs than adults: 38% as compared to 27%. Schools ignoring or avoiding such new technology rather than teaching its ethical use lose the opportunity to provide students with a current and authentic communication skill.

In recognition of the value of blogging in education, a number of services designed specifically for use with students continue emerging. These sites include Class Blogmeister (http://classblogmeister.com), Gaggle.net (http://gaggle.net), and ePals SchoolBlog (http://schoolblog.epals.com). All of these sites offer safety features that address some common concerns of school administrators. What if a student posts something inappropriate? A setting can be activated to require teacher approval of all posts. Filters can also be applied to block offensive text. Teachers can moderate comments, or disable comments completely if the prospect of allowing community members to respond to student work is perceived as a safety threat. As a more extreme measure, a teacher can password protect the pages which display student work, or password protect the entire blog so that only password-holders may view the protected content. Unfortunately this option deprives the students of an audience for their work, which is one of the features that make Web 2.0 tools attractive to both students and educators.

Examples of the successful use of blogs in schools demonstrate their value as a tool for fostering communication. A well-known application of educational blogging is the exchange between Will Richardson's high school literature class (Hunterdon Central Regional High School, 2002) and author Sue Monk Kid. For students reading her book *The Secret Life of Bees*, the author agreed to answer questions online. Although the dialogue could have been conducted via email, the use of a public blog enabled students and fans throughout the world to benefit from the larger, expanded conversation.

A blog can be used as an online newsletter to inform parents of school, class, or library events. Some school leaders have chosen to use a blog as the platform for the school's website because blogs can be updated so easily. A frequently cited example is the website of Mabry Middle School (2007) in Marietta, Georgia. Under the leadership of then-principal, Dr. Tim Tyson, the school's website was overhauled and rebuilt largely as a collection of blogs, with each staff member also authoring a personal blog. The site remains archived at http://mabryonline.org/.

Originating as online journals, blogs continue to be useful for student reflection. An example from my school involved a seventh grade social studies project. Students researched Revolutionary War artifacts as a part of the curriculum. Their blog entries informed their teacher of ongoing progress. In addition to the facts posted, students were required to respond to prompts each week detailing the research process and reflecting on its development.

Week 3

I have finished my hockey season so now I have every day open. I plan to research at least 3 times a week. Using delicious really helps me and I found out that I have been helping some others that have the same artifact as me. Some keywords that I have been using was [*sic*] Gadsden, Continential [*sic*] Army flag, and Hopkins to find out more about my artifact. No bumps in my research yet. All smooth. (Nick, 2007a)

Using Class Blogmeister, the teacher responded to each student's posts with comments only visible to that student. The resulting interaction provided a more complete picture of each student's progress than ascertainable during a 40-minute class period. Each student received equal time, in contrast to class time potentially monopolized by needier or more assertive students. Despite the challenging research, students responded positively to the project.

Week 5

I only have one more thing to tell you about the artifact. That's how it impacted the colonists. The colonists were moe [*sic*] confident and stood up for themselves. Each flag was inspiring to them and made them feel great about themselves. This project is awesome! (Nick, 2007b)

The blog format supported open communication between classmates and between each student and the teacher. The resulting interaction and connectivity kept students engaged throughout the project.

Wikis

In 2004, *Webster's Dictionary* named *blog* the word of the year. By December of that year, *Forbes.com* posted an article stating, "Blogs are so last year. The next big thing, according to Web junkies, is the 'wiki'" (Rand, 2004). Most students and educators are familiar with wikis due to the popularity of *Wikipedia*, an online encyclopedia to which anyone can contribute or edit content.

Through the use of a wiki, many people can share in the creation of content by contributing new information and editing existing information. The ability to make changes represents a major departure from blogs in the management of information. While readers may comment on the content of a blog, they cannot change it. Wiki users also engage in teamwork and negotiation. These elements make wikis suitable for different types of educational uses than blogs.

In the Revolutionary War social studies project discussed above under *Blogs*, students researching the same artifact used a wiki to collaborate. For the final product, students combined their work, producing one article per artifact, describing how each reflected the time period and influenced the outcome of the war. Each seventh grade student contributed. Using a wiki, students shared their information in one place, discussed items for inclusion and established order, and drafted the article. Students used the wiki to work on the project asynchronously, from home or during school, effectively eliminating the need for face-to-face meetings and the associated scheduling and transportation difficulties. Because wikis log and identify individual author contributions and edits, the teacher assesses individual participation within the group, solving another common accountability problem.

This example demonstrates a type of project suited uniquely for wikis, but this tool may be employed for similar purposes discussed for other Web 2.0

tools as well. For instance, an educator may create a class or library Web page using a wiki. One example is the *Welcome to Room 15 Wiki!* (http://mrlindsay. pbwiki.com/). This wiki provides documents, videos, graphics and audio files uploaded online. Similarly, student work showcases are demonstrated by the Village Elementary School wiki (http://villagewiki.pbwiki.com/Digital+Stories). In addition, the Plymouth Regional High School Library wiki (http://prhslibrary.pbwiki.com/) illustrates how a wiki creates and maintains resource lists and pathfinders, rather than using del.icio.us for this purpose.

Other services of education use may be found in wiki forms online. Examples of such education-friendly wikis include Wikispaces (http://www.wikispaces.com/), PBwiki (http://pbwiki.com/), Wetpaint (http://www.wetpaint.com/), and EditMe (http://www.editme.com). These and other wiki services offer the same advantages as other types of Web 2.0 tools—free or low-cost accounts for educators, security features, and sites free from advertisements. Like other Web 2.0 tools, wikis are easily created, requiring no HTML knowledge, Web-editing software, or space on a school district server.

Conclusion

Authentic, educationally sound uses of Web 2.0 tools with teacher supervision should mitigate some of the safety concerns voiced by administrators regarding the Web. While the dangers of online predators, cyberbullying, and threats to networks and equipment remain real, the risks may be alleviated by employing good judgement in the Web 2.0 environment. Students are adept at learning collaborative tool use, but need guidance to discern safe practices and issues of ethical use. As in other curriculum areas, teachers must provide students with the information necessary to choose wisely, and a safe, supervised environment for practice. With prudent safety measures in place, the integration of Web 2.0 tools into the curriculum provides powerful implications for education beyond the classroom walls and timeframe.

For the first time in history, educators work to prepare students for a future we cannot clearly describe. The jobs students will hold in ten years may not even exist today, but we can anticipate that those jobs will be information driven in a digital world (e.g., Warlick, 2004). The education system must take its cues from the corporate world in moving toward an environment of mass communication and collaboration. The collaborative tools used in business are the same tools currently used by students daily. The missing link is the integration of these same applications within the school environment. Just over 100 years ago, Dewey (1907) recognized a disconnect between a child's learning in school and his experiences outside of school. Teaching students to be responsible and ethical Web 2.0 contributors provides an important step towards finally bridging that gap between the school and the authentic world beyond while preparing them for the challenging future ahead.

References

100,000 Wikis in the Classroom. (2008). *Wikispaces*. Retrieved April 29, 2008, from http://www.wikispaces.com/site/for/teachers100K

Del.icio.us. (2008). Retrieved April 28, 2008, from http://del.icio.us/

Dewey, J. (1907). Waste in education in *The school and society* (pp. 89–90). Chicago: University of Chicago Press.

EditMe. (2008). Retrieved April 29, 2008, from http://www.editme.com

Flickr. (2008). Retrieved April 28, 2008, from http://flickr.com/

Folksonomy. (2008, April 23). *Wikipedia, the free encyclopedia*. Retrieved April 13, 2008, from http://en.wikipedia.org/w/index.php?title=Folksonomy&oldid=207704897

Gunkel, D. G. (2003, December 1). Second thoughts: Towards a critique of the digital divide. *New Media and Society*, *5*(4), 499–522. Retrieved May 21, 2008, from Sage Journals Online database.

Havenstein, H. (2007, December 17). IT faces stiff challenge from emerging workforce. *ComputerWorld*, *41*(51), 16–17.

Hunterdon Central Regional High School. (2002, November 25). *The secret life of bees*. Retrieved April 20, 2008, from http://weblogs.hcrhs.k12.nj.us/bees/

International Society for Technology in Education, State Educational Technology Directors Association, & Partnership for 21st Century Skills. (2007). *Maximizing the impact: The pivotal role of technology in a 21st century education system*. Retrieved April 28, 2008, from http://www.picnet.net/basecamp/partnershipfor21stcenturyskills/supportretainer/SIP tech paper.pdf

King, R. (2007, March 12). No rest for the wiki. *Business Week Online*. Retrieved May 10, 2008, from EBSCO Business Source database.

Lenhart, A., & Madden, M. (2005, November 2). *Teen content creators and consumers*. Retrieved April 17, 2008, from the Pew Internet and American Life Project website at http://www.pewinternet.org/pdfs/PIP-Teens_Content_Creation.pdf

Mabry Middle School. (2007). *MabryOnline.org*. Retrieved April 20, 2008, from http://mabryonline.org

Nick, F. (2007a, March 13). *Week 3*. Weblog entry posted to http://classblogmeister.com/blog.php?blogger_id=74240&l=1209070771

Nick, F. (2007b, March 13). *Week 5*. Weblog entry posted to http://classblogmeister.com/blog.php?blogger_id=74240&l=1209070771

PBwiki. (2008). Retrieved April 29, 2008, from http://pbwiki.com/

Prensky, M. (2001, October). Digital natives, digital immigrants. *On the Horizon*, *9*(5), 1–6.

Prensky, M. (2008, March). Turning on the lights. *Educational Leadership*, *65*(6), 40–45.

Rand, M. (2004, December 13). Extreme blogging. *Forbes.com*. Retrieved April 21, 2008, from http://www.forbes.com/best/2004/1213/bow001.html

Richardson, W. (2007, Fall/Autumn). Locked in an irrelevant system? Network building and the new literacy. *Education Canada*, *47*(4), 23–25. Retrieved May 10, 2008, from WilsonWeb OmniFile Full Text Mega database.

Roberts, B. (2008, March). Social networking at the office. *HR Magazine*, *53*(3), 81–83.

Social Bookmarking. (2008, May 30). *Wikipedia, the free encyclopedia*. Retrieved June 3, 2008, from http://en.wikipedia.org/wiki/Social_bookmarking

Tapscott, D., & Williams, A. D. (2006). *Wikinomics: How mass collaboration changes everything*. New York: Portfolio.

Warlick, D. F. (2004). *Redefining literacy for the 21st century*. Worthington, OH: Linworth.

Wesch, M., & The Students of Introduction to Cultural Anthropology, Class of Spring, 2007. (2007, October 12). *A vision of students today* [Video file]. Video posted to http://www.youtube.com/watch?v=dGCJ46vyR9o

Wetpaint. (2008). Retrieved April 29, 2008, from http://www.wetpaint.com/

Womack, B. (2007, August 21). Firms using wikis, RSS as enterprise 2.0 grows. *Investor's Business Daily.* Retrieved May 10, 2008, from http://www-03.ibm.com/industries/financialservices/doc/content/news/magazine/3197768103.html

Connecting Media Specialists, Students, and Standards Through Web 2.0

Carol A. Brown and Jackie Hill

Abstract Web 2.0 is more than an Internet buzzword. This new platform provides transition from static informational pages to dynamic portals for connecting and sharing of information. School library media specialists can use the read/write tools to ensure students are prepared to work in digital environments that are already commonplace. Blogs, wikis, podcasts, social bookmarking sites, and virtual worlds make it possible for readers to also become authors and publishers. Following a review of over 130 school websites, the authors describe common uses by media specialists and make recommendations in how Web 2.0 can be used to support the Library and Learning Standards published by the American Association of School Librarians.

Keywords Web 2.0 · School library · Digital environments · Blogs · Wikis · Podcasts · Social bookmarking · Virtual worlds · Learning standards

The 21st Century Library Learning Standards (American Association for School Librarians [AASL], 2008) describe many competencies that require communicating and connecting with others. Although these skills are not new, we have learned that online mediums for communication are very new. The new century introduced a new rage of social networking through the Web 2.0. By using this new platform, students and teachers can co-author a book review on their favorite writer, or contribute an encyclopedia article through wikis. Instead of writing to our congressmen, we send personalized pleas for governmental change through YouTube© videos. No longer do we sign one another's class yearbook; rather, young people connect by logging to one another's blogs, viewing podcasts, or listening to podcasts automatically downloaded by RSS feeds. Instead of trading favorite movie or sports magazines, students share and talk about favorite websites through social bookmarking.

C.A. Brown (✉)
East Carolina University, Greenville, NC 27858
e-mail: BROWNCAR@ecu.edu

And, we easily share our favorite snapshots through websites for multimedia photo albums. These activities present potential for new approaches in teaching information and reading literacy in K12 schools. Mastering this new Web 2.0 medium allows teachers to collaborate with students as readers now may become authors and publishers. These interactive experiences using Web 2.0 could be included in the design of instructional activities for meeting national standards in information literacy. The new information literacy standards robustly extend and promote uses of information for problem solving, reflection, and shared learning experiences. This chapter provides recommendations in how school library media specialists and teachers may use the interactive read/write Web, known as Web 2.0, in meeting new information literacy standards. These recommendations are based on an analysis of school library websites, a review of the literature with current reports on what is working in school libraries and the frequency of use by school librarians. It begins a review of the literature with definitions of commonly used tools available through Web 2.0.

Schools across the United States clearly evidence the new age of learning with digital information. Most schools maintain, at the very least, a simple webpage hosted by a service or on a school server. Many schools provide sophisticated websites that provide open portals to every resource within the campus. Web portals allow open doors to the schools, the teachers and administrators, and the culture of the community. Synchronous communication tools such as instant messaging or chat provide an immediate response from a topical expert or fellow researcher (Lawson, 2005). Because of the interactive nature of Web 2.0, students may contribute to the content of the web, thus enhancing literacy skills for both reading and writing.

Growing at a rapid pace, blogging represents a popular new trend among Internet users. In a report from the American Life Project, 80,000 blogs are created each day, equaling a new blog per second (Pew, 2007). People have a lot to say, thus take advantage of the read-write Web to communicate their knowledge, opinions, and personal aspirations. A "blog" is a frequently updated Web page that includes stream-of-consciousness entries by a single writer or group of writers. The term blog comes from weblog or, a log of journalistic writings by the originator/author of the blogsite. Weblogs have been called "digital paper" (Oatman, 2005, p. 37), or referred to as online journals and venues for reflective writing (Ray & Hocutt, 2006). Blog entries or posts are usually marked with the time and listed in reverse-chronological order. Blogs include links to news sites, other blogs, email, online advertisements, video and audio files, or other online content. Links are often embedded in the text of entries or appear in the sidebars (Martindale & Wiley, 2004). Blogs may also include an autobiography of the writer, archived posts, a search mechanism, comments, and a blogroll listing the author's favorite Web sites. The blogger controls subject, style, and length of blog posts (Nelson, 2006). Blogs represent tools for professional networking within a true learning community in which the participants can share ideas and experiences. Contexts established in a blog represent distinctive qualities of a community. Like-minded individuals easily connect with persons of similar ideas and concerns. According to blog expert Will

Richardson (2007), 21st century lifestyles place great value on being clickable as well as approachable.

In his blog, Richardson says: ". . .the fact that I am 'clickable' or find-able to this extent gives me tremendous opportunities to connect to other people, many of whom may have much to teach me" (2007, para. 2). Whether electronically or otherwise, students like being connected and Web 2.0 tools make these connections possible.

The wiki Web page, similar to blogs, provides a method for students to continually update, revise, and create original documents in a shared learning environment (McPherson, Wang, Hsu, & Tsuei, 2007). Similar to blogs, wiki spaces on library pages provide an opportunity for book reviews and requests for students to respond with comments on their current reading, however, blogs differ from wikis due to the original author's ownership of the blog site. Bloggers make decisions about contents for the site, whereas wiki spaces are openly collaborative with proactive contribution from others. Classes for language arts and literature can post group projects to the wikis and use the interactive functions for writing and revision, making this a useful tool for collaborative learning in middle and secondary school environments (New Media Consortium, 2008).

Ease of use for photoblogs and electronic scrapbooks make it possible for students and teachers to become Web publishers (Lamb, 2005). Professional looking websites can be designed without use of programming code and complex protocol for transferring files. Webhosting services such as eScrapbooking, Flickr, Photostream, and VoiceTread display still images, slideshows and streaming video on the school webpage (Hauser, 2007; New Media Consortium, 2008).

Although social networking tools like Flickr should be distinguished from blog sites, many of the electronic scrapbooking sites provide a quick and easy widget for adding the slide presentation to the library's blog (Kroski, 2008). A widget is an interactive device usually displayed on a blog screen or from the popular website YouTube©.

Educators frequently share what they consider their best and most useful information sources. Social bookmarking connects students and teachers with educational resources through sites like del.icio.us, Furl, or Diigo. Social bookmarks make possible a worldwide bookshelf of information for student assignments (Hargadon, 2007). Members of social bookmarking sites have convenient access to recommended resources that can be categorized according to personal needs and preferences. The functionality for both gathering and sharing information is characteristic of social bookmarking and supports information literacy skills for 21st century learners. Highly valued in the new century workplace are skills for generating new ideas within a collaborative environment (U.S. Department of Labor, 1991; Weis, 2004). Tools for social bookmarking may be useful for developing these special skills.

Podcasts, in the form of audio or video, provide access to multimodal communication for learners in many different settings. Research in the design of multimedia has long supported use of multimodality in instruction (Yerrick, 2006). Since the early days of dual coding theory (Paivio, 1986) instructional developers have enhanced educational resources by placing supporting images adjacent to textual messages. For example, visualization of scientific phenomena has been used to teach processes not easily understood through verbal explanation (Velazquez-Marcano, V. M. Williamson, Ashkenazi, Tasker, & K. C. Williamson, 2004).

Video often communicates a more powerful message that inspires, affirms, enhances, and persuades, when compared to the same information in textual format alone. The audio/video podcasts add warmth to the educational web missing up until now. The sound of the human voice comes into the classroom with a personal presence that causes the learner to respond in new and different ways (Mayer, 2003). Podcasting tools, along with blogging tools, contribute to the ease of uploading video and audio files. The popularity of YouTube© Website is an example of the rapid growth in the recreational use of podcasting further supporting the idea that learners respond favorably to messages that are both viewed and/or heard.

The Global Kids Project (MacArthur Foundation, 2007) reported uses of digital media and the Internet by young people ages 14–19. Two hundred youth participated in online discussion threads to describe their current use and understanding of what digital media means to them personally. According to the American Life Project,[1] a growing number of teens use multi-channel forms of communication (Pew, 2007). In this report, 59% of teens surveyed participate in some form of online content creation. Content creation includes all the tools for social media—blogging, wikis, video-sharing, and electronic scrapbooking tools. Based on results of this, and similar research, it could be concluded that students, aged 14–19 in the U.S., commonly use some type of interactive technology throughout their day. The report also suggests there may be a need for increased use of interactive tools in K12 classrooms. Others in the literature report serious concerns in school environments becoming irrelevant to students' way of life (Spires, Lee, Turner, & Johnson, 2008).

Results of focus groups and student surveys report growing discontent with differences between in-school and out-of-school technologies. Use of cell phones, iPods, and fast speed internet has generated a society with 24/7-connected lifestyles. Children growing up in the information age consider themselves digital natives with multitasking activity a normal process throughout the day (Prensky, 2007). Special interest groups such as the Partnership for 21st Century Skills urge educators to adopt teaching methods that include strategic use of digital information that is representative of new century workplaces (Partnership for 21st Century Skills, 2007). Systemic changes are needed to ensure students are prepared to be ready for a world that is global in perspective, collaborative in relationships, and fluent with use of digital information sources. Whether for good or ill, these changes may be an indication that more dynamic methods for learning and literacy should be investigated for the 21st century.

With the increasing need for Web 2.0, precautionary use of such tools remains a concern. According to Johnson (2008), online chat rooms pose the greatest threat for online sexual solicitation. The most recent studies report a greater threat from teens who engage in bullying and other inappropriate dialog through the Internet. A growing problem with young people uploading images and video often places them

---

[1] Pew Internet & American Life Project is the source of the data for teens' social use of technology. The Project bears no responsibility for the interpretations presented or conclusions reached based on analysis of the data.

in negative situations. These online photos and video can be viewed forever, even by future employers or college admissions officers. Johnson says, "To put it simply, the danger to kids in Web 2.0 comes not from what they may find online, but from what they may put online for others to find" (p. 50).

Thus, it seems very important that educators, in particular the school librarian, should clearly and consistently include standard 3.1.6 "use information and technology ethically and responsibly" in the writing of the school mission statement and curriculum (Owens, 2004). A review of the literature devoted to teaching methods and tools for 21st century classrooms consistently promotes the safe and appropriate use of digital resources. Ideally, knowledgeable teachers and specialists guiding students to use information appropriately and successfully also guard these access points in and beyond the doors of the school. Just as students must learn defensive driving skills for the road, so must they become skilled in the use of digital information that will become part of their future workplace.

Despite these changes evident in the culture of our youth and their methods for communication, a random review of school library websites in North Carolina revealed very few school websites displaying the read/write activities commonly found on Web 2.0. An expanded review of schools and libraries in other states also resulted in a limited number of Web 2.0 tools being implemented. Many school systems filter most, or block all, of the more dynamic tools such as blogs and wikis. This seems to add concerns reported by instructional and information specialists that methods for teaching and learning in our K12 schools grows more and more irrelevant. Students are living in the 21st century yet learning in 20th century environments. We began this investigation to identify ways school media specialists use Web 2.0 and discover how these resources might be used to support standards for teaching new information literacy skills so that all students are future-ready for the new century.

Methodology

As a professor of instructional technology and a high school media specialist, we created this study based on a shared interest in emerging technologies for K12 schools. We also needed to determine how these are being implemented in school libraries for meeting the new standards for the 21st century learner (American Association for School Librarians, 2008). Three methods in data collection allowed the identification of Web 2.0 use by school library media specialists in K12 schools. First, review of school websites listed with the state departments of education; second, review of school websites returned from search engines using keywords related to blogs, podcasting, and other terms associated with Web 2.0; and third, purposeful selection of schools linked to educational blogs and wikis.

The investigation began with a review of school websites accessed through the North Carolina Department of Public Instruction. Our original investigation, how North Carolina school library media coordinators used Web 2.0 tools to meet state K12 Information Literacy Skills (North Carolina Department of Public Instruction, 2008), revealed very limited use in North Carolina. We expanded the search to include a review of schools across the United States. The National Center for

Education Statistics (NCES) and the link to State Education Agencies (nces.ed.gov/) provided access to school libraries. Both qualitative and quantitative methods were used to analyze the content of school library websites. Following the recommendation of Silverman (2005), categories were established to identify frequency of use for specific tools defined as Web 2.0 and interactive.

Qualitative analyses included evaluative investigation of methodologies used by school library media specialists and pedagogical use of the interactive tools. During the qualitative evaluation, we asked the following questions.

1. Are tools being used for interactive learning?
2. What evidence suggests consistent contribution by students?
3. Does use of the tools align with new information literacy standards?

Analyses for school websites began with a random sample from each state accessed through the state agencies listed in the NCES website. Because the investigation intended to identify possible instances and use in schools, the selection method included schools located through online searches using keywords blog, podcast, wiki, virtual and school library. Using a purposive sampling method (Patton, 1990), we reviewed 174 Web pages, in fifty five schools from the following states Alabama, Arizona, California, Georgia, Hawaii, Illinois, Kentucky Maine, Massachusetts, Michigan, Minnesota, New Hampshire, New Jersey, New York, North Carolina, Ohio, Oregon, Pennsylvania, South Carolina Tennessee, Texas and Washington. Web pages were accessed through use of search engines or through review of indexes to social networking websites. Analyses included innovative school libraries in Canada, Hong Kong, New Zealand, and Manila. We included these in the analyses because of innovative ideas that support learning in K12 libraries and classrooms.

Excel spreadsheets were used to record use of blogs, wikis, podcasts, streaming video, audio only, portfolios, bookmarking, and scrapbooking. Each instance of a tool on a school website was entered for each category. Tallies were calculated and recorded. We individually entered personal observations regarding use of the tools.

By comparing our two perspectives, college professor and library media specialist, a reasonable level of inter-rater reliability was possible. In most instances, evaluation of the schools was consistent between the researcher (professor) and the practitioner (school media specialist). Comments were then summarized and used to identify common themes and uses for all tools identified in the school websites.

Results and Discussion

Web 2.0 categories defined for this study include forums for reading and writing, tools for multimedia development, online services for shared resources, virtual worlds, and opportunities for reflective writing.

The chart in Table 1 presents several popular tools typically associated with Web 2.0 and correlated with AASL standards for the school library programs. The

Table 1 Commonly used Web 2.0 resources that align with the 21st Century Library and Learning Standards for school libraries (AASL, 2008)

Web 2.0 Genre	Example of tool	Standard	Standard
Reading/writing	Blogger.com wikispaces.com	2.1.5 Collaborate with others to interchange ideas, develop new understandings, make decisions, and solve problems.	3.1.2 Participate and collaborate as members of a social network of learners.
Design/development multimedia	eScrapbook.com Flickr.com	4.1.8 Use creative and artistic formats to express personal learning.	4.3.1 Participate in the social exchange of ideas, both electronically and in person.
Shared Resources	Google bookmarks (Google.com/bookmarks/) LibrayThing.com De li cious Social Bookmarking (del.icio.us/)	4.1.6 Organize personal knowledge in a way that can be called upon easily.	4.1.7 Use social networks and information tools to gather and share information.
Virtual Worlds	Whyville (www.whyville.net/smmk/nice) Teen Second Life (teen.secondlife.com/)	1.2.3 Demonstrate creativity by using multiple resources and formats.	3.3.5 Contribute to the exchange of ideas within and beyond the learning community.
Reflective Writing	Task Stream [ePortfolios] (www.taskstream.com/pub/) wikis and blogs	3.4.1 Assess the processes by which learning was achieved in order to revise strategies and learn more effectively in the future.	4.4.5 Develop personal criteria for gauging how effectively own ideas are expressed.

organizational framework, as defined in this table, could be a useful taxonomy for the selection of appropriate resources when designing instruction. Based on the literature describing trends for Web 2.0 tools, we generated these categories as representative of what many schools are using with library websites. Most often, they represent a method for communicating with students and the community.

A checklist that included each of the tools was used during analysis of the 174 school library Web sites. Blogs, wikis, social bookmarking, and multimedia podcasting emerged as the most commonly used tools available on Web 2.0.

As can be seen in Fig. 1, blogs and podcasts appeared most often, with some instances of bookmarking, scrapbooking, wikis, and streaming video resources. Of the entire number websites ($N=174$) reviewed for this study, 63 provided instances of a blog displayed in a prominent place on the school website. Common uses included booktalks and book reviews with uploaded images from book jackets and links to authors' websites. Interactive discussions invited students to post comments about what they were currently reading. In addition to posts by students, comments by publishers, authors, and other experts in the publishing profession provide 21st century innovations for these digitally formatted book reports. With Web 2.0 the personal viewpoints and life experiences of authors are much more accessible for readers. The elaborate design for many of the blogs included content related pathfinders compiled by the library media specialist. Some included resources carefully planned and displayed in complex taxonomies. A number of the blogs displayed personable images of the students, teachers, and school projects.

Many schools replaced authoring software or complex html coding with use of tools provided by blog sites. Librarians used their blog pages to create well designed library homepages. Use of these tools seems to provide advantages related

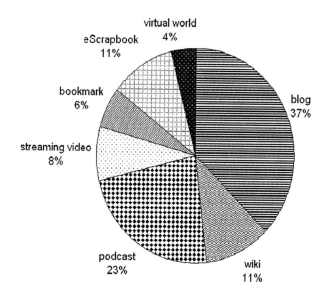

Fig. 1 Use of Web 2.0 tools sample of K12 schools ($N = 174$)

to time and efficiency in the development of webpages because collaborative building removes some authorship burden. Thus, such tool-use provides teachers and librarians more time to plan activities for research and information literacy instruction.

Blogs and Information Literacy Standards

Blogs devoted to book talks by the librarian, and book reviews by students, provide an open forum for the educational community to communicate their opinion on popular fiction and interpretation of the classics. These interactive environments could heighten the quality of the traditional book report. Potential for timely and thoughtful feedback from peers is one advantage for the blogger/student book reviewer.

Throughout many of the blog posts, students' comments voiced a personalized connection with characters in book reports. The opportunity for complex thinking that evaluates the writing of others could be another important advantage in use of Web 2.0. During our qualitative evaluations, it was noted that blogs with active ongoing dialog, containing substantive comments, followed a particular pattern in their design. First, blogs written to

> **Standard 3.1.2 Participate and collaborate as members of a social and intellectual network of learners.**

include open-ended questions posted by the author/publisher of the blog seemed to illicit more reflective comments from students. By modeling the reflective writing process, students observe the teacher or librarian under the guidance of cognitive apprenticeships (Brown, 2000, 2006). According to Brown, *cognitive apprenticeship* is a step-by step- approach in thinking and problem-solving. Thinking processes required for writing, for example, might be an analysis of fictional events or characters. With repeated writing samples, students seemed to follow the model of their librarian or teacher for their own writings. Secondly, for motivation and aesthetic appeal, blogs that included images from book jackets commonly appeared in the sample of schools. Often the book authors themselves provided a short greeting and personal photo.

Many of the blogs provided a template with a structured format for book reviews and reports. Many of those using the template approach resulted in well written reviews that included articulate discussions on plot, characters, and setting. The use of online templates could be of special advantage to schools with middle and primary age students. Last, blogs in which the teacher or librarian modeled enthusiasm for the topic with detailed comments in their reviews most often resulted in student postings with some merit. Dull and boring blogs are no different than dull and boring textbooks, magazine, or webpages. To maintain interest, students should be guided to write for clarity, creativity, and literary appeal.

In the late 20th century, students created posters, presented oral book reports, or created electronic slides. Consequently, presentations designed for one-way communication result in limited opportunity for students to respond with feedback. The use of blogs transforms the traditional book report into a collaborative interactive experience with teachers and students. With the traditional book report, students communicate what has been read. Book reviews published to a blog promote constructed learning based on the student's experience with a book. Traditional book reports tell; blogger's reviews are experiential.

Many of the blogs included topics associated with community events, making it possible for students to connect reading with personal life-issues. For example, books on obesity, blended families, and death of a friend linked to local happenings such as death of a classmate, growing concerns for poor nutrition, and conflicts at home.

According to the Pew Institute (2005), a majority of 12–18 year olds use multichannel forms of communication. Students in middle and high school call each other on the phone, send text messages, post comments to blogs, upload their pictures to photoblogs, and exchange email. When properly monitored, school library blogs provide a safe forum for interactive discussions related to national and state events, and community issues (Johnson, 2008). A key advantage is in using a form of communication widely used by many students and similar to informal environments outside of school. In one library media center for middle school students, blog topics devoted to becoming a "good web citizen" provided opportunity for students to express viewpoints on social and ethical issues referenced in national standards.

> Standard 4.3.1 Participate in the social exchange of ideas, both electronically and in person.
>
> Standard 4.3.4. Practice safe and ethical behaviors in personal electronic communication and interaction

In Fig. 2, a student describes appropriate and responsible behavior on the Internet when posting to the school blog. At this particular school, the library media specialist modeled the thinking processes for describing the characteristics of a good web citizen, "what does one look like and what does a good citizen not look like?" Students responded with informed and articulate comments demonstrating unusually mature perspectives for this particular student population. Interactive blogs could

🖂CSS Library said...
To be a good digital citizen is to not cyber-bully, not to plagiarize, and don't use silly excuses to get out of trouble like, "Everyone does it," or "It wasn't me it was my online character". But the big message in this thing is, we all know better so just take a few seconds to think before you click!
SMM
11:19 AM

Fig. 2 Blog post describing characteristics for "a good digital citizen"

be an excellent tool for teaching legal and social issues related to Internet and the importance of safety in electronic communication.

Podcasting and National Standards

Through this investigation we discovered many innovative uses for podcasting in school libraries. Content management systems make it easy for students to express ideas using multimedia presentations published to the Web. For example, students using VoiceThread.com may upload a personal image and record voice comments to clarify, elaborate, or critique their message. This facilitates the sharing of ideas with the viewer's option for responding, not within a text blog, but by inserting a personal audio clip. A draw tool allows the person sending the comment the capability for drawing marks on a still image from the video clip.

Standard 3.2.1 Demonstrate leadership and confidence by presenting ideas to others in both formal and informal situations.
Standard 3.3.4 Create products that apply to authentic, real-world context.

In Fig. 3 a screen shot from VoiceThread.com displays an example of Video Doodling, a unique tool used by many of the school websites. Sons of a Dr. Skip Via, at University of Alaska Fairbanks, describe excavation sites for native caribous.

Fig. 3 Example of video doodling published to Video.com

A response to their photo and message comes from another student who inserts a voice message and line drawings to clarify the question.

Yerrick (2006) describes several strategies for use of podcasting in teaching science. Many of these could be used in other curriculum areas originating from the library media center. Experts in science, social studies, or civics can be used to bring timely information directly to teachers and students.

In Fig. 4 is an example of a science podcast linked to one of the libraries reviewed for this study. Through the use of RSS feeds, science related audio podcasts can periodically be sent directly to the subscriber's iTunes© reader. In this example, an RSS feed is available for "Why? The Science Show for Kids", created by Dr. Dave Brodbeck (2008).

Through the use of an iTunes© aggregator, the subscriber receives "web feeds" directly to the student's computer without the need for browsing the author's website. Brodbeck serves as an online science expert by answering students' science-related questions. Students can hear their own, and questions from others, by listening to the podcast.

In other curriculum areas podcasts sent via RSS feeds might include authors' book reviews, syndicated news, and personal biographies for well know scientists, authors, political candidates, and other public figures. Many of the library websites included podcasts with student book reviews. The majority of the podcasts were audio only, however a large number included video presentations with covers of the book jacket displayed in a streaming video file. In addition to book reviews, students authored original books and published these as podcasts. The ease of content management systems for uploading images, video, and audio make publication of multimedia very accessible for K12 students.

Fig. 4 Example of resource provided by RSS feeds

Photoblogs, eScapbooking, and Slide Presentation

Many of the websites used the scrapbook as a tool for introducing their teacher or technology/media specialist while others used the scrapbook to give a face to special community projects. Because of the special appeal to students, scrapbooking can be used to elevate classroom PowerPoint® projects to online presentations automatically published to the Web (escrapbooking.com, 2008). Students upload personal documents as well as download primary sources from distant sites.

> Standard 1.1.7 Make sense of information gathered from diverse sources by identifying misconceptions, main and supporting ideas, conflicting information, and point of view or bias.

Other examples from this study include students' use of collected images of phenomena in nature from Cornell University webcam (2008) and presentations exploring diverse perspectives through investigation of digital primary source documents (Library of Congress, 2008). The emergence of web based, desktop browsing functions simplifies search and access tasks allowing students to focus more on content and conclusions and less on technical glitches. Concerns with debugging software and breakdowns with the school's local network can be serious distracters to the learning environment (Mandefrot, 2001). Multimedia presentation resources like *Flickr* and *VoiceThread* illustrate easy to use content management tools that automatically publish to an approved community of learners. The ability to post comments to another student's multiple-content slides, regardless of location, provides a far-reaching environment for cooperative learning.

Any use of blogs, wikis, or podcasts should include careful instruction in copyright laws and regulations. An information media consultant for Oakland Schools in Waterford, Michigan, Hauser (2007) recommends including Creative Commons' Podcasting Legal Guide (2008) or Electronic Frontier Foundation's Legal Guide for Bloggers (2008) when instructing students in use of read/write tools. These resources support authentic

> Standard 1.3.1 Respect copyright/intellectual property rights of creators and producers.
> Standard 1.2.3 Demonstrate creativity by using multiple resources and formats.
> Standard 2.1.6 use the writing process, media and visual literacy, and technology skills to crate products that express new understandings.
> Standard 3.1.2 Participate and collaborate as members of a social and intellectual network of learners.
> Standard 3.1.6 Use information and technology ethically and responsibly.

methods for teaching responsible use of intellectual property.

These resources could be used by the library media specialist in teaching lessons on copyright regulations or possible integration strategy, for teachers in staff professional development workshops.

Bookmarking

Social bookmarking sites provide a specialized Web 2.0 service for archiving, categorizing, and evaluating websites submitted by members of the community. Use of these services could address at least two of the 21st Century Standards for Learners. Shared bookmarks extend the boundaries of the local school media center and classroom book collection to schools, teachers, and librarians anywhere in the world. Think of a typical school library collection, usually numbering around 10,000–15,000 titles. Members of a particular social bookmarking community may share reviews for millions of books and access to hundreds of thousands of online reading materials. Functions within social bookmarking websites make it possible to share comments about resources, ideas and best practices.

> Standard 1.1.5 Evaluate information found in selected sources on the basis of accuracy, validity, appropriateness for needs, importance, and social and cultural context.
> Standard 4.4.6 Evaluate own ability to select resources that are engaging and appropriate for personal interests and needs.

The most commonly identified sites—*Del.icio.us, Yahoo Bookmarks, Google Bookmarks* and *Diigo* promoted learning communities with common interests through shared reading, comments, and the option for posting evaluation and recommended uses for websites. Social bookmarking communities lend themselves to skills for evaluating and sharing of information beyond the student's local learning community (standard 3.3.5). Based on the theories of Vygotsky (1978), learning is enhanced when supported by social interaction, with guidance from a mentor, and mediated by appropriate resources. Social bookmarking could be one of the more powerful tools on Web 2.0 making it possible to engage in social learning experiences supported by a limitless variety of resources.

LibraryThing.com website provides a tool for entering book and media titles, tags, and personal comments about the school library's collection. These may be stored and retrieved from the LibraryThing server. LibraryThing will match the titles entered with information on Amazon.com and Library of Congress for the librarian's personal catalog, which then becomes linked

> Standard 1.1.8 Demonstrate mastery of technology tools for accessing information and pursuing inquiry.
> Standard 1.2.2 Demonstrate confidence and self-direction by making independent choices in the selection of resources and information.

to the school's library blog. The widget with LibraryThing displays booklists, annotations, and personal comments by the librarian. This provides students with a selection of highly recommended books, reviews, and other information. Library-Thing.com provides a social online catalog personalized to meet the needs of a particular community or school. Del.icio.us or LibraryThing, as tools for socially constructed learning, could be used to help students become more self-directed users of information, capable of making independent choices in the selection and evaluation of reading and information sources

Virtual Worlds

Results of this investigation show only four percent of schools currently use virtual reality. However, many public libraries use virtual worlds with interactive capabilities for learning communities and social networking (Tenopir, 2007). The world of avatars and virtual villages can be

Standard 1.1.9 Collaborate with others to broaden and deepen understanding.

connected to the therapeutic value of fiction to help readers relate to traumatic events in the imaginary life of a book character (Regan & Page, 2008). Much of the research in early childhood development discusses free play and the imaginary worlds of children (Singer & Singer, 2006). Healthy play, especially when guided by an adult, can be strongly associated with positive social development in later years. Troubled teens and children may find solace in the make-believe virtual worlds now available on the web. The most well known, Teen Second Life (TSL) provides a safe environment where young people can act out wholesome fantasy, connect with their peer group, and indulge in creative digital design. Participants in virtual worlds like TSL create icons of their self-image called avatars. Through the use of interactive tools students engage in a fanciful creation of personal hair style, clothing, body shape, skin color and other identifying characteristics.

According to Czarnecki and Gullett (2007), virtual travel through Teen Second Life is entirely safe with strictly enforced community standards – no vulgar language, sexual content, or negative bullying practices. TSL includes the virtual Camp Global Kids encouraging young people to become active thinkers and participants in public policy and international affairs (MacArthur Foundation, 2007). One such fund-raising project uses TSL linden dollars to fight the effects of teenage sex trafficking, a common social problem in many economically depressed areas of the world (Finnegan, 2008). This same group participated in the focus groups used by the MacArthur Foundation to gather information on use of Web 2.0 by urban teens. The report suggests that many Internet-using students learn within immersive experiences not possible through the one dimensional experiences of reading or listening to audio reports.

Virtual worlds can provide experiential simulations for schools and libraries. The virtual *Land of Lincoln* (SecondLifeInsider, 2008) is designed to teach about life in 19th-century America. Features include the Lincoln White House, his Springfield home, and even a Memorial Cemetery with gravestones telling stories about the deceased.

Standard 4.3.4 Practice safe and ethical behaviors in personal electronic communication and interaction.
Standard 4.4.6 Evaluate own ability to select resources that are engaging and appropriate for personal interests and needs.

In another example, the University of Chicago (2008) library provides a virtual world to explore ancient Mesopotamia. Students may travel to other parts of the world for archeological digs, collect artifacts, and keep records of the quest.

The development and source of *Mesopotamia—DigIntoHistory* was presented at a virtual conference in the Second Life conference center, with an avatar speaker presenting *DigIntoHistory!* The creators designed this virtual world in order to promote an attitude for persistent search techniques for young researchers who may be searching for artifacts and primary sources documents related to ancient history concepts. Characteristic of most games and simulations, persistence is required to solve the mystery and win the game. Virtual worlds designed specifically for K12 users and audiences may provide excellent simulations that engage students in learning experiences not possible in the real-world. Even young children can experience interaction within virtual worlds. A preteen friendly world, Whyville.com provides a place for children and younger teens to visit, interact, and explore a variety of topics and curriculum areas. Similar to Teen Second Life, the user enters Whyville, creates a personalized avatar and then participates in hot air balloons rides, the local civic life, runs for office in the Whyville Senate or becomes a journalist for the Whyville Times. Money presents no problem because salaries or clams can be earned by participating in educational activities. Students are motivated to participate in discussions using fanciful characters that are self-designed. Opportunity to connect with others in a safe virtual environment clearly fits with AASL standard 4.3.4 Practice of safe and ethical behavior in electronic communication and interaction. Whyville.com is highly rated virtual world that is both safe and interactive (Weir, 2004).

Conclusions

Web 2.0 tools may be used for ensuring students meet standards for 21st century learning by providing a diversity of ideas, outreach to world community, opportunity for constructing knowledge and sharing resources never before possible with

Web 1.0. In addition to opportunity for reflective reading, speed in access and currency of content provide strong justification in use of new Web 2.0 tools. Along with advantages to quick access, is the important responsibility for identifying bias and editorial abuse that is becoming rampant in the news media (Sullivan, 2005). Based on a review of websites and uses of the Web 2.0 platform, we recommend that students be carefully mentored and guided in use of these new tools. For many decades, educators taught young people to use proper term paper citations, punctuation and grammar. We, as teachers, taught students to write with clarity, accuracy, and good form. Use of the new tools requires that we also teach appropriate selection and evaluation of digital information, strategies for building online collaboration, and open minds for making the best use of resources from across the globe. Based on the concerns of parents and educators about dangers lurking in the digital shadows, we must also teach proper precautions in use of these resources. Just as when taking a group of children on any field trip, we also need to prepare students to balance their selection and use of reading and writing venues. Guiding students in the selection and use of digital resources that result in reflective thinking processes that transfer to future lives beyond the classroom is foundational to new century standards. Our charge, and responsibility as educators, is to ensure proper balance, discretion, and assessment of 21st century learners' literacy skills and achievement.

Howard Gardner (2008), noted author in the study of multiple intelligences, warns the loss of 20th century literacy in the new digital age:

> Many of us enjoyed long summer days or solitary train rides when we first discovered an author who spoke directly to us. Nowadays, as clinical psychologist Sherry Turkle has pointed out, young people seem to have a compulsion to stay in touch with one another all the time; periods of lonely silence or privacy seem toxic. If this lust for 24/7 online networking continues, one of the dividends of book reading may fade away. The wealth of different illiteracies and the ease of moving among them—on an iPhone for example—may undermine the once-hallowed status of books. (p. B01)

There is a responsibility for ensuring that students use blogs, podcasting, and virtual worlds to share their own discoveries from solitary times of reading and reflection. Discussing literary work allows depth of thought and feeds the soul within Web 2.0. Critical reflection involves giving reasons for posting a comment and this requires complexity of thought. This type of social learning (e.g., Bandura, 1977) is more likely to occur when students learn in a comfortable setting. Students need a safe environment enabling self-revelation within that space. Interaction within virtual worlds and journalistic blogging may provide ideal environments for the kind of metacognitive processes that help students make the connection between theory and practical experience.

In the final analysis it is concluded that the interactive tools available on the new Web can be powerful for teaching and learning. It may also be concluded that, as with the first written words on the walls of a cave, the printing press, or email— these tools require careful planning and guidance. Without this, we risk damage to the children and youth whom we have committed to teach and nurture for the 21st century.

References

American Association for School Librarians (AASL). (2008). *Standards for the 21st century learner.* Retrieved April 5, 2008, from http://www.ala.org/ala/aasl/aaslproftools/learningstandards/standards.cfm

Bandura, A. (1977). *Social learning theory.* Englewood Cliffs, NJ: Prentice-Hall.

Brodbeck, D. (2008) *Why? The science show for kids podcasts.* Retrieved April 5, 2008, from, http://feeds.feedburner.com/whyscience

Brown, J. S. (2000). Growing up digital. *Change, 32*(2), 10–21.

Brown, J. S. (2006). New learning environments for the 21st century: Exploring the edge. *Change, 38*(5), 18–25.

Cornell University. (2008). *Watch birds.* Retrieved April 5, 2008, from http://watch.birds. cornell.edu/nestcams/home/index

Creative Commons' Podcasting Legal Guide. (2008). Retrieved April 5, 2008, from http://wiki.creativecommons.org/Main‑Page

Czarnecki, K., & Gullet, M. (2007). Meet the new you. *School Library Journal, 53*(1), 36–39.

Electronic Frontier Foundation's Legal Guide for Bloggers. (2008). Retrieved April 5, 2008, from http://w2.eff.org/bloggers/lg/

eScrapbooking.com. (2008). *eScrapbooking.* Retrieved April 5, 2008, from http://www.escrapbooking.com/overview.html

Finnegan, W. (2008). The countertraffickers. *New Yorker, 64*(12), 44–59, 16p, 1c.

Gardner, H. (2008, February 17). The end of literacy? Don't stop reading. *The Washington Post,* P. B01.

Hargadon, S. (2007). Cool tools: Best of social bookmarking. *School Library Journal, 53*(12), 20.

Hauser, J. (2007). Media Specialists can learn Web 2.0 tools to make schools more cool. *Computers in Libraries, 27*(2), 6–7, 47–49.

Johnson, D. (2008). Staying safe on the Read-Write Web. *Library Media Connection, 26*(6), 48–52.

Kroski, E. (2008). Widgets to the rescue. *School Library Journal, 54*(2), 41–43.

Lamb, A. (May, 2005). Escrapbooking and SLM centers. *Educapes.com.* Retrieved April 5, 2008, from http://eduscapes.com/librarians/escrapbooking.htm

Lawson, R. (2005). Real-time solutions for online learning: Using synchronous communication tools for right-now learning, *Campus Technology.* Retrieved June 4, 2008, from http://www.campustechnology.com/article.aspx?aid=40259

Library of Congress. (2008). *American memory project.* Retrieved April 5, 2008, from http://lcweb2.loc.gov/learn/

MacArthur Foundation. 2007. *Digital media and learning.* White paper funded by MacArthur Foundation and the Pew Institute. Retrieved April 5, 2008, from http://digitallearning. macfound.org/default.html

Mandefrot, K. (2001). An embarrassment of technology: Why is learning still difficult? *Journal of Research on Computing in Education, 33*(5), 1–34.

Martindale, T., & Wiley, D. (2004). Using weblogs in scholarship and teaching. *TechTrends, 49*(2), 55–61.

Mayer, R. E. (2003). The promise of multimedia learning: Using the same instructional design methods across different media. *Learning and Instruction, 13*, 125–139.

McPherson, S., Wang, S.-K., Hsu, H.-Y., & Tsuei, M. (2007). New literacies instruction in teacher education. *TechTrends, 51*(5), 24–31.

Nelson, M. (2006). The blog phenomenon and the book publishing industry. *Publishing Research Quarterly, 22*(2), 3–26.

New Media Consortium, & Educause. (2008). *The Horizon report.* Retrieved May 24, 2008, from http://horizonproject2008.wikispaces.com/

North Carolina Department of Public Instruction. (2008). *Information literacy skills curriculum.* Retrieved April 5, 2008, from http://www.ncpublicschools.org/curriculum/information/

Oatman, E. (2005). Blogomania. *School Library Journal, 51*(8), 36–39.

Owens, B. B. (2004). *Student performance studying ethics in the context of Internet use*. Paper presented at NECC, 2004. Retrieved June 9, 2008, from http://www.iste.org/Content/ Navigation-Menu/Research/NECC_Research_Paper_Archives/NECC_2004/Owens-Boucher-NECC04.pdf

Paivio, A. (1986). *Mental representations: A dual coding approach*. New York: Oxford University Press.

Partnership for 21st Century Skills. (2007). P21Skills white paper. *Building 21st century skills*. Retrieved June 11, 2008, from http://www.21stcenturyskills.org/route21/images/ stories/epapers/skills_foundations_final.pdf

Patton, M. Q. (1990). *Qualitative evaluation and research methods* (2nd ed.). Newbury Park, CA: Sage Publications.

Pew Internet & American Life Project. (2005). *Family friends and community*. Retrieved April 5, 2008, from http://www.pewinternet.org/ppf/r/166/report_display.asp

Pew Internet & American Life Project. (2007). *Teens and social media*. White paper presented for the PewInternet.org. Available 1615 L ST., NW – SUITE 700 WASHINGTON, D.C. 20036. Retrieved April 5, 2008, from http://www.pewinternet.org

Prensky, M. (2007). Listen to the natives. *Educational Leadership, 63*(4), 8–13.

Ray, B. B., & Hocutt, M. M. (2006). Reflection and the Middle School Blogger: Do blogs support reflective practices? *Meridian: A Middle School Computer Technologies Journal, 9*(1). Retrieved April 5, 2008, from http://www.ncsu.edu/meridian/win2006/MS_blogs/index.htm

Regan, K., & Page, P. (2008). Character building: Using literature to connect with youth. *Reclaiming Children & Youth, 16*(4), 37–43.

Richardson, W. (2007). *On being clickable*. Retrieved June 4, 2008, from http://weblogged.com/2007/on-being-clickable/

SecondLifeInsider. (2008). *Land of lincoln*. Retrieved May 23, 2008, from http://www.secondlifeinsider.com/2007/10/24/land-of-lincoln-to-come-to-sl/

Silverman, D. (2005). *Doing qualitative research: A practical handbook* (2nd ed.). London: Sage.

Singer, J. L., & Singer, D. G. (2006). Preschoolers' imaginative play as precursor of narrative consciousness. *Imagination, Cognition & Personality, 25*(2), 97–117.

Spires, H. A., Lee, J. K., Turner, K. A., & Johnson, J. (2008). Having our say: Middle grade student perspectives on school, technologies, and academic engagement. *Journal of Research on Technology in Education, 40*(4), 497–515. Retrieved June 11, 2008, from Research Library Core database. (Document ID: 1490343921).

Sullivan, M. (2005). Media bias is real finds UCLA political scientist. *UCLA Newsroom*. Retrieved June 10, 2008, from http://newsroom.ucla.edu/portal/ucla/Media-Bias-Is-Real-Finds-UCLA-6664.aspx?RelNum=6664

Tenopir, C. (2007). Living the virtual library life. *Library Journal, 132*(16), 24.

U.S. Department of Labor. (1991). *What work requires of schools: A SCANS report for America 2000*. SCANS Report by the U.S. Department of Labor.

University of Chicago. (2008). *DigintoHistory*. Retrieved May 18, 2008, from http://mesopotamia.lib.uchicago.edu/interactives/DigIntoHistory.html

Velazquez-Marcano, A., Williamson, V. M., Ashkenazi, G., Tasker, R., & Williamson, K. C. (2004). The use of video demonstrations and particulate animation in general chemistry. *Journal of Science Education and Technology, 13*(3), 315–323.

Vygotsky, L. S. (1978). *Mind in society*. Cambridge, MA: Harvard University Press.

Weir, L. (2004). Get a life: Students collaborate in simulated roles. *Edutopia*, Retrieved May 18, 2008, from http://www.edutopia.org/forward/5258

Weis, J. P. (2004). Contemporary literacy skills: Global initiatives converge. *Knowledge Quest, 32*(4), 12–15.

Yerrick, R. (2006). Globalizing education one podcast at a time. *T.H.E. Journal*. Retrieved April 5, 2008, from http://www.thejournal.com/the/newsletters/smartclassroom/archives/

The Turnaround School Library Program

Jami Biles Jones and Alana M. Zambone

Abstract   For many students, particularly for those who are at-risk for school failure, an emphasis on instructional strategies without including the resiliency-building factors will not increase academic achievement. Students thrive academically when instructional practices are effective and the environment in which they learn is nurturing and supporting. The "turnaround" school library integrates effective instruction into a supportive, nurturing environment. This chapter provides a framework for creating a "turnaround" school library program to increase the academic success of students who are at-risk for failure. Through nurturing, mentoring and development of individual strengths, the "turnaround" school library program and the media specialist can provide powerful supports for students at-risk for school failure. The chapter begins with a discussion of the factors that predict who is at risk for school failure. The research findings which validate a positive correlation between school library programs and student achievement are summarized, as is the research on resiliency. Principles and practices of a school library program that turns students who are a failing into successes are provided Evidence-based principles and strategies for increasing students' resiliency and competence are described. Media specialists are provided with the principles and a set of strategies for creating a "turnaround" school library program.

Keywords   At-risk · Resiliency · Holistic school library programs

There are numerous indicators that America's schools are failing to meet the needs of all students, despite ongoing reform efforts. An average of 1.2 million students drop out every year and many of those dropouts remain inadequately prepared for college (Strong American Schools [SAS], 2008). Forty percent of high school seniors lack the seventh and eighth grade math skills required to learn a trade and reading scores declined by six points between 1990 and 2005 (National Center for Education Statistics, 2007; SAS, 2008). Yet, research illustrates the potential power

J.B. Jones (✉)
1108 Joyner Library, East Carolina University, Greenville, NC 27858
e-mail: jonesj@ecu.edu

M. Orey et al. (eds.), *Educational Media and Technology Yearbook*,
DOI 10.1007/978-0-387-09675-9_16, © Springer Science+Business Media, LLC 2009

of the school library program to "turn around" students treading a path toward academic failure and dropping out of school.

This chapter provides an overview of students at-risk for failure and summarizes the research on the power of school library programs to help students succeed. The chapter also presents the research on increasing the resiliency of students who are at-risk and implications for media specialists. The authors share effective practices and principles for increasing academic performance and strengthening students, and provide suggestions on building a "turnaround" school library program. In addition, the chapter outlines strategies to help media specialists plan for and create a holistic school library program, concluding with a discussion of the seven principles of a "turnaround" school library program.

Students At-Risk for School Failure

School reformers seeking to understand at-risk students often employ an "ecological systems" perspective, and take into account environments and circumstances of both students and schools separately and in relation to each other (e.g., Jones & Zambone, 2008; Smink & Schargel, 2004; Williams, 2003). School personnel adopting an eco-logical systems perspective recognize that neither students nor schools develop in isolation or function in a vacuum. When identifying at-risk students, school prac-tices require examination as well as students' individual characteristics (Orfield, Losen, Wald, & Swanson, 2006).

The families of students most "at-risk" for school failure comprise the lowest socioeconomic strata in the U.S. These families have "low socioeconomic status" (SES), meaning "limited income and educational levels," (Almeida, Cassius, & Steinbert, 2006, p. 2). Additional risk factors include racial or ethnic minority status, most notably African-Americans and Latinos; immigrant status, particularly those with limited English proficiency; and parents or students with disabilities (Almeida et al., 2006; SAS, 2008). Children and families experiencing trauma are also at-risk for school failure (Duplechain, Reigner, & Packard, 2008; Perry, 1999).

"The key indicator for dropping out" of school is low socioeconomic status (SES) (Almeida et al., 2006, p. iii). Four factors determine SES: family income, parental education level, parental occupation, and social status in the community. Contacts within the community, group associations, and the community's perception of the family determine social status. Families with low SES lack the financial, social, and educational support that higher SES families enjoy. Low SES families may have inadequate or limited access to community resources that promote and support chil-dren's development and school readiness. Poverty is a distinguishing characteristic of low SES. Latino, African American and Native American families experience poverty at twice the rate of Caucasian and Asian families (Capps et al., 2007).

Members of racial or ethnic minority groups, particularly those who are Latino or African-American often enter school facing conditions that put them at-risk for failure. Latinos and African-Americans are less likely than Asian and Caucasian children to attend preschool and more likely to be: (a) categorized as low SES;

(b) retained in one or more grades; (c) enrolled in courses that do not prepare them for college; (d) misidentified as disabled and placed into special education; and (e) drop-out of school (Capps et al., 2007; Orfield et al., 2006, Kozol, 2005).

Over the past 20 years, immigration contributed to the dramatic increase in student diversity (Taylor & Whittaker, 2003). If current trends continue, immigrants and persons of color will comprise 40% of the population by the year 2050. Effective school reform recognizes that changes in community demographics necessitate a change in the policies and practices for including families in the school community (Zambone, Howard, & Elliott, 2002, p. 12). Twenty-five percent of students identified as low SES are children of immigrants (Pong, 2003). When compared to their Caucasian peers, immigrants remain poorer, achieve less formal education, master only limited English proficiency, and access fewer resources such as health care and jobs (Pong, 2003).

In 2007, the graduation rate for students receiving special education services reached 52%, notably lower than that of any other population (US Department of Education). Numerous factors influence this rate, including low expectations resulting in limited opportunities to learn and the stigma associate with special education services (Orfield et al., 2006). Many students receiving special education services exhibit high skill sets but learn in different ways or require accommodation and support to demonstrate their knowledge and abilities. When expectations are low and adequate accommodations are not provided, many of these students miss the opportunity to learn and succeed.

An estimated five million students experienced trauma such as violence, disaster, abuse or severe illness (Perry, 2006). According to Perry, nearly forty percent of this group will develop a long-term neuropsychological disorder potentially impairing their academic, social, and emotional functions. In some cases, school personnel may know that the child is traumatized, in others they may not. Many students exhibiting other risk factors, such as low SES and immigrant status, also experience trauma. Traumatized students often suffer stress, depression, or family complications which challenge their achievement in school.

All at-risk students require particular attention and support to build resiliency and increase the likelihood of success in school. As reviewed in the next section, research indicates that the media specialist and the school library program offer important factors in student academic success. For the at-risk student, the school library program, building on this history, holds a greater likelihood of turning around the at-risk student's school experience than perhaps any other program.

The School Library Program's Impact on Academic Achievement

Sixty years of research validates the claim that school library programs lead to increased student achievement (Lonsdale, 2003). "Library media predictors almost always outperformed other school characteristics, such as teacher-pupil ratio and per pupil expenditures" in improving student achievement, once SES was accounted for (Lance, Welborn, & Hamilton-Pennell, 1993, p. 34). The number of media specialists and the size of the collection significantly influence the power of the school library program to improve student achievement (Lance & Loertscher, 2005; Todd & Kuhlthau, 2005; Lance et al., 1993). Additional characteristics of school library programs and the roles of media specialists that positively influence student achievement comprise the following list:

- Ongoing collaboration and planning in the areas of instructional delivery, information literacy
- Collections designed to support the curriculum
- Integration of state-of-the-art technology into teaching processes
- Cooperation between the media specialist and other types of librarians, especially public librarians
- Staffing of the school library by a professional media specialist and assisted by support personnel
- Collaborative efforts between the media specialist and teachers
- Information technology that extends the reach of the school library program into classroom and labs
- Allocation of a well-organized budget (Lance, Robins, & Hamilton-Pennell, 2005).

Student feedback and performance further substantiates the school library program's potential to increase students' success in school, particularly for those considered at-risk. For example, while female students rate the helpfulness of school library programs for their academic success somewhat higher than male students, both groups indicate that accessing technology for learning is the most important function of the school library (Todd & Kuhlthau, 2005). A skilled media specialist at the helm proves to impact student success even more than the collection and technology supplied by the school library program.

Media specialists realize their potential to significantly impact students' academic success when they assume an instructional role within the school (Lance & Loertscher, 2005; Todd & Kuhlthau, 2005; Lonsdale, 2003; Lance et al., 1993, p. 30). Findings which indicate the school library program is a primary factor in reading improvement, particularly for African-American students further support the education function of the media specialist (Todd & Kuhlthau, 2005). Specifically, media specialists who ensure that the school library program positively influences student achievement, such as reading improvement, also shape the school library collection, partner with classroom teachers, and provide guidance and direction to teachers and students. Figure 1 summarizes these findings by organizing the role of the media specialist in student achievement into three broad principles: leadership, collaboration, and technology. Representative activities and characteristics that positively influence academic achievement are identified for each principle.

Effective media specialists function as leaders and strive to form partnerships with others. These media specialists find that "leadership translates to higher

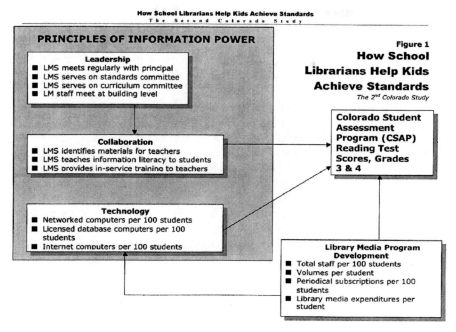

Fig. 1 How school librarians help kids achieve standards: the second Colorado study
Source: Lance, Rodney, and Hamilton-Pennell (2000). Reprinted with permission.

collaboration with teacher(s) in creating quality learning experiences that, in turn, have a direct impact on academic achievement (Lance & Loertscher, 2005, p. 48). Leaders meet regularly with administrators; serve on standards committees and curriculum committees; attend school staff meetings; and hold regular library staff meetings in the event that the staff is larger than one person. Proactive collaborators plan instruction with teachers; teach information literacy; and push digital information beyond the media center (Lance & Loertscher, 2005). Collaboration also encompasses information literacy instruction and motivational reading-based activities for students, as well as in-service training for teachers. A proactive media specialist is imperative for a successful school library (Todd & Kuhlthau, 2005). Through leadership and collaboration, the proactive media specialist implements evidence-based practices to improve students' academic achievement. These practices, discussed more fully below, positively affect all students' achievement, particularly those students who are at-risk for failure.

Effective Practices to Improve Academic Achievement

Employing effective teaching strategies creates the best route to improving academic achievement. "If we follow the guidance offered from 35 years of research, we can enter an era of unprecedented effectiveness for the public practice of education—one in which the vast majority of schools can be highly effective in promoting student learning" (Marzano, 2003a, p. 1). Marzano synthesizes the research on effective strategies into three categories: school-level factors; teacher-level factors; and student-level factors (2003b).

School-level factors furthering academic achievement involve: a guaranteed and viable curriculum; challenging goals and effective feedback; parent and community involvement; a safe and orderly environment; and collegiality and professionalism. Teacher-level factors increasing academic achievement encompass: application of evidence-based instructional strategies; effective classroom management; and relevant classroom and curriculum design. Student-level factors encompass: a supportive home environment; learned intelligence; and sufficient background knowledge and experience. Leadership and collaboration enables the medial specialist to realize school level and teacher level factors, and activate student level factors through the school library program.

The student-level factors require the media specialist to provide students who are at-risk for school failure with ever-increasing knowledge and skills; in other words, by building students' vocabulary and expanding their background knowledge. Such students' poor literacy skills often affect their learning and performance across the curriculum. Literate students possess the language to understand ideas, concepts, and experiences and communicate those to others. Conversely, many at-risk students come to school without the background knowledge to support vocabulary development. Even the most carefully chosen collection inadequately affects this situation without a proactive media specialist to build background knowledge and champion student success through instruction and mentoring.

Identified as the most significant protective factor in resiliency research, mentoring increases reading performance (Werner & Smith, 2001). Mentoring occurs when a caring adult forges a one-to-one relationship with a student needing support. Mentoring effectively broadens students' background knowledge by exposing them to new ideas and concepts. Effective mentoring occurs in the nexus between the relationship and the opportunities provided to the student. Through a caring relationship with the student, the media specialist identifies opportunities for beneficial new experiences and connects students with people who help them articulate and realize goals.

Although travel and field trips throughout the community, such as to museums and art galleries, offer another effective approach to increase background knowledge, these may be expensive and present coordination difficulties. As an alternative, media specialists can build students' background knowledge by using technology and resources for virtual field trips and experiences.

Concurrent vocabulary instruction and repeated practice further improve reading scores and increase a student's connectedness to school. Vocabulary development offers another approach for increasing background knowledge. The linguist, Chomsky (1965), argued compellingly that language and thought are linked. Building vocabulary strengthens thinking and anchors concepts and ideas. Media specialists assist students to acquire the words and phrases necessary to understand curricular content. Students learn vocabulary best when exposed multiple times to new words in the context of the experience or concept represented by the word. The power of repeated practice using new vocabulary is enhanced when students have the opportunity to express their understanding of new words by conjuring up mental images and representing the word in pictures or symbols as well as in writing.

Effective media specialists also understand the culture and values of the student's family and community. Culturally relevant curriculum and instruction engages and motivates students and activates their background knowledge and experiences in the learning process (Thompson, 2004). Boykin (2002) developed a model for cultural relevance to improve the academic achievement of African-American students which benefits all students, regardless of their race, ethnicity, or class. Boykin's model contains eight components:

- High standards for all students
- Multiple assessments to determine students' strengths and success
- Approaches that build on students' assets
- A developmentally appropriate education
- An active, constructivist approach to learning
- A thematic and interdisciplinary curriculum
- Preparation for the demands of the 21st century
- A caring school community focused on students' academic and personal well-being. (p. 87)

By applying these principles, media specialists boost the competence of students who might otherwise disengage from learning because of pessimism about their likelihood of success. In this way, media specialists realize the support of the school library program for at-risk students. Students' strengthen their resiliency, which in turn furthers their academic achievement. The next section suggests effective practices that both improve academic achievement and amplify student resiliency.

Effective Practices to Strengthen At-Risk Students

Between one-half and two-thirds of children who are poor, abused or otherwise at-risk, overcome these hardships to become productive adults with meaningful lives and relationships (Edwards, 2000, p. 15). Developing resiliency effectively overcomes hardships. Benard (1993) defines resiliency as the ability to "bounce back successfully despite exposure to severe risks" (p. 44). Researchers concur that resilient children have both internal and external assets that protect them from the long-term deleterious consequences of adversity (Werner & Smith, 2001, 1992). In fact, most individuals develop protective factors, enabling them to resolve crises and recover from trauma—and become wiser and more compassionate in the process of doing so (Henderson, 2007). Three clusters of protective factors represent critical markers for an individual's resiliency (Werner & Smith, 2001, 1992):

- Cluster 1: Average or above average cognitive skills and a pleasing and sociable disposition that causes others to respond favorably to the youth.
- Cluster 2: Affectionate ties with adults who help the youth develop trust, autonomy, and initiative. Many resilient children cite a supportive and encouraging teacher as a major influence for their success in adulthood.
- Cluster 3: Access to and reliance on supportive organizations such as churches, youth groups, and schools.

Increasing student's cognitive skills through effective academic instruction and their social skills by creating authentic and meaningful opportunities for interaction lessens the impact of risky situations. When adults cloak students in a supportive environment and mentor them, students can recover from at-risk conditions and acquire trust, autonomy and initiative.

Furthermore, research indicates that resilient youth develop good reading and reasoning skills in elementary school, regard education positively, set realistic vocational plans in high school, and engage in a hobby or interest which their peers respect (Werner & Smith, 2001; Sameroff, 1998). "Nowhere were the differences between the resilient individuals and their peers with problems in adolescence more apparent than in the goals they had set for themselves for their adult lives" (Werner & Smith 2001, p. 68).

Resilient youth believe in their capacity to shape their own life through the actions they take. They also believe that difficulties are surmountable. Furthermore, the research demonstrates that close bond with at least one emotionally supportive adult nurtures and sustains students' belief in their abilities (Werner & Smith, 2001; Sameroff, 1998). Oftentimes, this mentor was a "teacher who had become a role model, friend, or confidant" (p. 57). Because resilient youth participate in more extracurricular activities than their troubled peers, they experience opportunities to develop competence and forge positive relationships with adults. The nature of the school library program enables media specialists to incorporate many of the protective factors that the research identifies. "The Resiliency Wheel" (Henderson, 2007, p. 10), Figure 2, provides a graphical representation of the elements that ideally surround each person, family and organization to create an environment that reduces risk and increases resiliency for students. Protective factors added to the environment increase resiliency. Likewise, the impact of risk factors are lessened. A "turnaround" school library program incorporates each of the six factors in the wheel. The highlighted dimension, caring and support, is achieved both by implementing the other components and by including mentorship within the school library program.

Adding protective factors to the environment represents the first strategy for building resiliency and minimizing risk. Caring and supportive relationships, high expectations, and opportunities for meaningful participation help strengthen at-risk youth. Caring and supportive relationships are the most important of these protective factors. "Providing oneself and others with unconditional positive regard, love, and encouragement is the most powerful external resiliency-builder" (Henderson, 2007, p. 10).

Fig. 2 The Resiliency Wheel
Source: Nan Henderson and
Resiliency in Action at
<www.resiliency.com>.
Reprinted with permission.

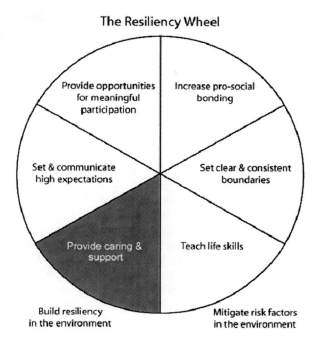

The Resiliency Wheel

Provide opportunities for meaningful participation

Increase pro-social bonding

Set & communicate high expectations

Set clear & consistent boundaries

Provide caring & support

Teach life skills

Build resiliency in the environment

Mitigate risk factors in the environment

Source: Nan Henderson, www.resiliency.com

Increasing pro-social bonding, setting clear and consistent boundaries, and teaching life skills encompass the second strategy to lessen risk factors in the environment. Hosting activities which facilitate collaboration among students and encourage friendships increases pro-social bonding. An example is "The Lunch Bunch." [1] This award-winning program was created by Martin, a media specialist in Florida, when she noticed that the same students sat alone in the school library during lunch day after day. Martin discovered that most were new to the school and had not yet made friends. To help their transition, Martin permitted these students to bring their lunch to the library and eat together in an out-of-the-way spot. She purchased games for them to play, and assigned them minor chores around the library. In her application for the Amanda Award, Martin described how students flourished as they developed friendships within the group and connected to the school through the library. If media specialists recognize the importance of helping youth develop social skills, make friends, and establish connections, they will replicate Martin's program or develop a similar one.

---

[1] Martin was awarded the Florida Association for Media in Education's (FAME) first annual Amanda Award in 2002 in recognition of her efforts to strengthen youth by developing programs to promote resiliency.

Media specialists strengthen students by applying the resiliency-building approaches identified in "The Resiliency Wheel" and establishing caring and nurturing programs such as Martin's. Although no hard and fast rules or formulas exist for resiliency-building school library programs, an open and caring attitude towards students inaugurates each.

The Turnaround School Library

Students thrive academically when provided effective instructional practices in nurturing and supportive environments. The turnaround school library offers both effective instruction and nurturance focused on the affective needs of students. Many students at-risk for failure face multiple challenges such as poverty, discrimination, deprivation, or inconsistent parenting—each of which can stand in the way of learning. Overcoming challenges will not occur solely by improving instructional strategies. Any effective effort to address academic failure boosts feelings of well-being and connectedness to others. Figure 3, The Library Ladder of Resiliency, visually represents a model that addresses both the affective and academic needs of the student who is at-risk for school failure. The Library Ladder of Resiliency strengthens students by helping them move "up the ladder" from making connections to developing hobbies and interests. Each rung of the ladder corresponds to a protective factor found in the most resilient youth (Werner & Smith, 2001, 1992; Sameroff, 1998).

When media specialists create a holistic school library program to increase students' competence and resiliency, in essence "turn their lives around." The "turnaround" or holistic school library attends to students' affective as well as academic needs. The media specialist appreciates the interrelatedness of an individual's emotional and academic well-being and therefore strives to both improve academic achievement and strengthen the resiliency of students facing the challenges discussed in this chapter.

Fig. 3 Library Ladder of Resiliency
Source: Jami Biles Jones.
Reprinted with permission
from the author.

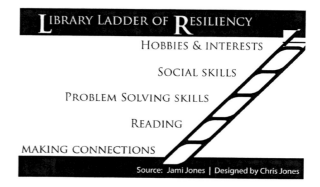

LIBRARY LADDER OF RESILIENCY

HOBBIES & INTERESTS

SOCIAL SKILLS

PROBLEM SOLVING SKILLS

READING

MAKING CONNECTIONS

Source: Jami Jones | Designed by Chris Jones

Holistic is a term most often used in the health realm to describe care that recognizes the interrelatedness of the physical, mental, and spiritual aspects of the individual. When the notion of resiliency is integral to a holistic school library program, the media specialist enhances human achievement through nurturing, mentoring, and developing individual strengths. For many students, particularly those considered at-risk, the resiliency-building factors cited in Fig. 2 are critical for academic success. Effective instructional strategies alone are not adequate.

The holistic school library embraces the ecological systems perspective, by recognizing that a student's development and learning is a function of all of the environments in which the student participates, rather than assuming that failure rests entirely with the student or family (Wilson, 1998). Media specialists who adopt this perspective recognize the outside forces, such as funding and school climate, which influence how they are able to operate the school library and respond to students' needs; and seek to identify those forces in the school that contribute to the student's success or failure.

Longitudinal research indicates that students' resiliency increases when they establish just one strong and supportive relationship with an adult and find one place where they feel welcome and competent (Sameroff, 1998; Werner & Smith, 1992). Turnaround school libraries create an environment and culture that provides all students in the school "somewhere to walk and someone to walk with" (Jones, 2007, p. 495).

Creating a Turnaround School Library Program

Media specialists who adopt an ecological systems perspective create environments for students that are supportive and nurturing. By recognizing the outside forces that influence their programs, they identify others with whom to collaborate in order to gain the expertise and resources required for a "turnaround school library." These partnerships exponentially increase the creativity and intelligence of the media specialist's efforts to build students' resiliency.

When creating a vision of the school library as a place that increases students' resiliency, media specialists begin by reflecting, with their team, on their dreams and their role in the school library. The characteristics of resiliency discussed in this chapter and the protective factors identified in the Resiliency Wheel (Fig. 2) suggest a framework for media specialists' vision of the "turnaround" school library. The mission statement evolves when media specialists articulate how the school library program will implement each of the six dimensions of the Resiliency Wheel.

The next step is to compare the vision of the "turnaround school library program" with its reality. Media specialists can use program evaluation approaches to determine the difference between their vision and the program's reality. The plan to build on the program's successes to close that gap evolves from the evaluation results. Program evaluation is a tool that, like assessment of students, guides the future of the school library. The media specialist will therefore want to continue the evaluation process to guide their journey and ensure that they are achieving their goals. Below is a framework for program evaluation:

- With others, identify questions to be addressed in the evaluation process. Questions can be determined through consideration of the components of the Resiliency Wheel (Fig. 2)
- Prioritize the questions that are most important for answering the primary question of whether the school library program builds resiliency and mitigates risk factors for students
- Define and clarify questions so that they can be answered with evaluation data such as the amount of time students who are successful are spending in the school library and what they are doing while there
- Choose measurement tools and strategies to answer the questions. Noonan & Henderson note that "most variables … in program evaluation fall into one of the following categories: attitudes, knowledge, skills, behavior, or environmental factors. This data can be collected by self-reports, interviews, surveys, and records in archival sources, observations and/or current records" (p. 54)
- Design the evaluation, describing how data will be collected to answer each question
- Implement the evaluation plan after trying out the measurements to make sure they will provide the necessary data to determine any needed changes in order to realize the vision and achieve the mission
- Organize and analyze the data, making adjustments in measurements or addressing new questions
- Share the results with the team and other key individuals such as administrators in order to guide the systems change plan and generate the support necessary to implement it
- Start all over again with new questions to evaluate whether the plan is working (Noonan & Henderson, 2007, pp. 51–56).

Sharing the vision and results of the initial evaluation with colleagues creates the collective expertise to build student's resiliency because the media specialist and colleagues pool their knowledge and experience and learn new things together. This team will identify the "tipping point" for realizing their vision—the first small change that will bring about great change … "much like a small tug boat can turn a large ship once it finds the point along the hull to begin pushing" (Jones & Zambone, 2008, p. 90). Together, the media specialist and team generate an effective plan that includes ways to overcome barriers and constraints and the steps to take to create the "turnaround school library program."

Principles of a "Turnaround" School Library Program

While each media specialist creates a vision that reflects the unique "ecology" of the schools in which they operate and the students whom they serve, seven principles should be evident in every "turnaround" school library plan:

- Identify at risk students early. Media specialists want to know who the struggling students are. Talk to teachers, review student data, and identify students reading below grade level. Target these students and learn their interests.
- Closely examine new and existing school library policies and procedures to determine how current policies and procedures impact the most at-risk populations. Do these policies and procedures keep students from using the school library or do they reflect an understanding of the generation that they serve, rather than the generation that created the program? Policies and procedures should be created in partnership with the community, families and students served by the school library. In this way, the program will respond to students' interests and needs, creating a place that is safe and welcoming. Policies and procedures that recognize challenges students encounter (e.g. losing control over their books because they are moving between parents' separate homes) will respond with a safe place in which to resolve these conflicts.
- Build strong community partnerships with public libraries, bookstores, museums and other organizations that help students broaden their experience and develop vocabulary. At the same time personalize the school library for students by making relationships a priority. For example, the school library program can help students develop hobbies and interests through partnerships with hobbyists.
- Create structured opportunities for students to interact, collaborate, and assist others and reduce social isolation. Use books to develop empathy. Initiate projects and other opportunities to increase students desire to give back to the community.
- Manage both small and large student transitions. Use routines and rituals to establish a transition process between the school library and the classroom or other school environments. When students move to a new school, connect them with the media specialist there. Invite the middle school or high school media specialist to meet with students to understand their interest. Take students to visit college libraries and other resources.
- Create options and implement creative interventions. Draw on the expertise in the school and community, such as special educators and other specialists, parents, and community experts to support positive behavior and encourage students to succeed. Partner with coaches and others to motivate students. Provide a variety of media and print materials on topics and activities of interest to students and encourage students to exchange the knowledge they gain from exploring these, without being penalized because of language limitations or other constraints.
- Build parent/family relationships and communicate with parents in ways and at times that are accessible to them. Have a reception during open house or host a "library night." Provide students with incentives to bring a family member to see the school library. For example, one inner-city school media specialist received a donation from a local store to hold an ice cream 'social' for all of the students and their families who came into the media center at least once during a month. Proactively reach out to parents, e.g. form a parent/family advisory board.

In essence, the seven principles repeat the research findings and strategies shared throughout the chapter. Knowing students, evaluating the current program, collaborating with others, and reaching out to the community are all part of making the school library program responsive to students' affective as well as academic needs. By following the seven principles identified above, media specialists construct a school library that supports students holistically. Proactive media specialists assess the academic deficiencies of students and to mentor and nurture the whole child, thereby addressing students' affective and academic needs.

While this chapter opened with a bleak picture of the growing number of students at-risk for failure, it also offers a message of hope. The school library program can be a powerful force for all students, particularly those at-risk. Media specialists touch every student in a school through a "turnaround" school library program. Every adult in the school is a potential partner in this effort. A survey of eighteen to twenty-four year olds conducted by Jones asked students to reflect on their school library experiences. The response given most often indicated that these adults associated the school library with assignments they disliked and skills, such as research, about which they felt inept. Many cited negative experiences with school library programs and media specialists because of policies and procedures perceived as controlling and punitive, while others claimed little interest in the materials and resources offered through their school library programs. Students perceived the media center as unwelcoming and of little benefit.

Media specialists, however, occupy a unique position from which they teach research skills, provide resources, and create a haven of learning and success for students. Media specialists can collaborate with teachers, share their expertise to supplement curriculum and instruction, and develop assignments that are doable and interesting for students. When media specialists respect and respond to the interests and characteristics of the students in the school and provide opportunities and support, they changes the way current and future students will remember their school library program and perceive themselves. Most importantly, these medial specialists will build the resiliency and increase the success of all students, particularly those who are at-risk for school failure and therefore most likely to drop out.

References

Almeida, C., Cassius, J., & Steinbert, A. (2006). *Making good on a promise: What policy makers can do to support the educational persistence of dropouts*. Boston, MA: Jobs for the Future – JFF.

Benard, B. (1993). Fostering resiliency in kids. *Educational Leadership, 51*(3), 44–48.

Boykin, A. W. (2002). Talent development, cultural deep structure, and school reform: Implications for African immersion initiatives. In S. J. Denbo & L. M. Beaulieu (Eds.), *Improving schools for African American students: A reader for educational leaders* (pp. 81–94). Springfield, IL: Charles C. Thomas.

Capps, R., Fix, M., Murray, J., Ost, J., Passel, J., & Herwantoro, S. (2007). *The new demography of America's schools: Immigration and the No Child Left Behind Act*. Washington, DC: The Urban Institute.

Chomsky, N. (1965). *Aspects of the theory of syntax*. Cambridge, MA: MIT Press.

Duplechain, R., Reigner, R., & Packard, A. (2008). Striking differences: The impact of moderate and high trauma on reading achievement. *Reading Psychology*, *29*(2), 129–136.

Edwards, C. H. (2000). Moral classrooms communities for student resiliency. *Education Digest*, *37*(2), 441–478.

Henderson, N. (2007). *Resiliency in action: Practical ideas for overcoming risks and building strengths in youth, families, & communities.* Ojai, CA: Resiliency in Action.

Jones, J. L. (2007). Somewhere to walk and someone to walk with. *Voice of Youth Advocates*, *29*(2), 495–498.

Jones, J., & Zambone, A. (2008). *The power of the media specialist to improve academic achievement and strengthen at-risk students.* Columbus, OH: Linworth Books.

Kozol, J. (2005). *The shame of the nation: The restoration of apartheid schooling in America.* New York, NY: Crown publishers.

Lance, K. C., & Loertscher, D. (2005). *Powering achievement: School library media programs make a difference: The evidence* (3rd ed.). Salt Lake City, UT: Hi Willow Research & Publishing.

Lance, K. C., Rodney, M. J., & Hamilton-Pennell, C. (2000). *How school librarians help kids achieve standards: The second Colorado study.* San Jose, CA: Hi Willow Research and Publishing.

Lance, K. C., Welborn, L., & Hamilton-Pennell, C. (1993). The impact of school library media centers on academic achievement. Castle Rock, UT: Hi Willow Research & Publishing.

Lonsdale, M. (2003, February 20). *Impact of school libraries on student achievement: A review of the research* (Australian Council for Educational Research). Retrieved February 15, 2008, from http://www.asla.org.au/research/index.htm

Marzano, R. J. (2003a). Direct vocabulary instruction: An idea whose time has come. In B. Williams (Ed.), *Closing the achievement gap* (pp. 48–66). Alexandria, VA: Association for Supervision and Curriculum Development.

Marzano, R. J. (2003b). *What works in schools: Translating research into action.* Alexandria, VA: Association for Supervision and Curriculum Development.

National Center for Education Statistics. (2007). *Mapping 2005 State Proficiency Standards onto the NAEP Scales.* Washington, DC: U.S. Government Printing Office.

Noonan, C., & Henderson, N. (2007). An introduction to program evaluation: A step-by-step guide to getting started. In N. Henderson (Ed.), *Resiliency in action: Practical ideas for overcoming risks and building strengths in youth, families, and communities* (pp. 51–56). Ojai, CA: Resiliency in Action.

Orfield, G., Losen, D., Wald, J., & Swanson, C. (2006). *Losing our future: How minority youth are being left behind by the graduate rate crisis.* Washington, DC: The Urban Institute.

Perry, B. (1999). *Stress, trauma, and post-traumatic stress disorders in children: An introduction.* Retrieved April 1, 2006, from http://www.childtrauma.org

Pong, S. (2003). *Immigrant children's school performance.* Front Royal, VA: Population Research Institute. Retrieved May 23, 2008, from http://www.pop.psu.edu/general/pubs/working_papers/psu-pri/wp0307.pdf

Sameroff, A. (1998). Environmental risk factors in infancy. *Pediatrics*, *102*(5), 1287–1292.

Smink, J., & Schargel, F. (Eds.). (2004). *Helping students graduate: A strategic approach to dropout prevention.* Larchmont, NY: Eye on Education.

Strong American Schools. (2008). *A stagnant nation: Why American students are still at risk.* Washington, DC: Author.

Taylor, L., & Whittaker, C. (2003). *Bridging multiple worlds: Case studies of diverse educational communities.* Boston, MA: Allyn & Bacon.

Thompson, G. L. (2004). *Through ebony eyes: What teachers need to know but are afraid to ask about African American students.* San Francisco, CA: Jossey-Bass.

Todd, R., & Kuhlthau, C. (2005). Student learning through Ohio school libraries, Part 1: How effective school libraries help students. *School Libraries Worldwide*, *11*(1), 63–88.

U.S. Department of Education. (2007). *27th annual report to Congress on the implementation of the Individuals with Disabilities Education Act, 2005*. Washington, DC: Government Printing Office.

Werner, E. E., & Smith, R. (1992). *Overcoming the odds: High risk children from birth to adulthood*. Ithica, NY: Cornell University Press.

Werner, E. E., & Smith, R. (2001). *Journeys from childhood to midlife: Risk, resilience, and recovery*. Ithaca, NY: Cornell University Press.

Williams, B. (Ed.). (2003). *Closing the achievement gap: A vision for changing beliefs and practices* (3rd ed.). Alexandria, VA: Association for Supervision and Curriculum Development.

Wilson, W.J. (1998). The role of the environment in the black-white test score gap. In C. Jencks & M. Phillips (Eds.), The black-white test score gap (pp. 501–510). Washington, D.C.: Brookings Institution Press.

Zambone, A., Howard, C., & Elliott, K. (2002). *The ABLE guidebook: Achieving better learning through equity*. Newton, MA: Education Development Center.

Girls and Egaming Engagement: Optimizing Gender Equity in School Libraries

Lesley Farmer and Nora Murphy

Abstract   Egaming reveals gender-linked issues that need to be addressed explicitly in order to ensure gender equity when incorporating egames and egaming elements into school library programs. Egaming traditionally connoted male dominance. Teacher librarians (TL) should consider factors in egaming that repel and attract females in order to can set up conditions for learning that can address the needs and interests of both sexes. TLs can help girls counter those societal messages by substituting positive attitudes and practices by offering fun, low-stress egaming environments, providing girl-friendly, egaming resources that resonate with girls, encouraging girl-oriented egaming, facilitating girl egaming creation, and incorporating egaming principles into instruction. Egaming addresses student awareness of and affinity for information literacy skills related to collaboration, pursuit of personal interests, evaluation of information, and information sharing. TLs may help girls experience egaming comfortably and develop an interest in other technologies.

Keywords   Egaming (gaming) · Gender studies · Teacher librarians · Instruction · Collection development · Information literacy

Teacher librarians (TL) are hotly discussing egaming. Should TLs incorporate egaming into school library resources and services? Where does egaming fit into information literacy? Where K-12 settings previously banned all games on the Internet and eschewed collecting game guidebooks, teacher librarians (TL) now often reconsider their policies, holding gaming tournaments, and locating core gaming collection lists to help guide collection development for viable titles and even equipment purchases. However, not every school library currently joins this shift, but the library world certainly serves as a curriculum focal point engaged in current conversations regarding gaming. Within the last two decades, these same school libraries addressed concerns over of cardboard games. For this reason, in this chapter the

L. Farmer (✉)
California State University, Santa Barbara, Long Beach, CA 90840-2201
e-mail: lfarmer@csulb.edu

M. Orey et al. (eds.), *Educational Media and Technology Yearbook*,
DOI 10.1007/978-0-387-09675-9_17, © Springer Science+Business Media, LLC 2009

term "egaming" differentiates these electronic game forms from more traditional print counterparts.

Increasingly, TLs pro-actively reach out to their audiences, meeting youth in its own territory. For example, when graphic novels attained higher status relative to less valued comic books, librarians started paying more attention to this new genre. While egames technically predated Web 2.0, the convergence of Internet interactivity and increasingly popular MMORPGs (Massively Multiplayer Online Role Playing Game) led to their consideration by many TLs. Rather than fight the technological flood, TLs grapple with ways to embrace the phenomenon and legitimately link these to the curriculum and learning. A certain "cool" factor played a part in this endeavor illustrating a link between school libraries and recreational options as well as meeting academic demands. Some TLs "translate" egaming skills into information literacy skills helping students to bridge life at school and life at home.

Why do school librarians want to incorporate egaming into school libraries? Most commonly, this addition is used to attract more boys. Particularly since boys tend to read less—and less well than girls (Smith & Wilhelm, 2002), TLs try to encourage non-traditional reading matter, such as gaming books. Thus boys become engaged, and begin practicing and developing an enjoyment of reading. Additionally, TLs hope that boys will choose positive participatory leisure habits, including carefully selected egames such as Dance Dance Revolution™ and City of Heroes™. Even though more females than males now play role playing games (RPG), egaming currently remains largely a male bastion—a fact not lost on females (Neilsen, 2007).

Although different library activities appeal to different population segments, be it calligraphy, video-editing or literature circles, TLs should consider factors in egaming potentially repelling and attracting girls. By addressing girls' needs, TLs may foster environments that optimize learning, equally addressing the differing needs and interests of both sexes.

Current Egaming Practice

At this point, egames have substantially penetrated U. S. households. In terms of console games (i.e., games played on dedicated equipment, such as Playstation, Xbox, Nintendo), 71% of households with boys or girls owned video consoles, and 80% of households with teenagers owned consoles (Neilsen, 2007). A 2007 Pew Internet study indicated that 93% of teens go online, and 60% of teens own two or more technological gadgets; teens prefer desktop computers the most, and choose cell phones second-most.

As early as 2001, the National Institute of Media and Family found that most children either played egames or knew others who did. By 2003, two-thirds of college students reported playing egames occasionally or regularly (Jones, 2003). A 2005 Kaiser Foundation study showed that 63% of boys and 40% of girls engaged with video games each day; youth between the ages of 8 and 14 played the most. Minors constitute almost one-third of the most frequent console gamers and one-quarter of the most computer gamers (Entertainment Software Association, 2008). Boys tend to play more video games for longer periods of time, while girls prefer shorter computer or handheld games (e.g., Simpson, 2005; Amory, Naicker, Vincent, & Adams, 1999). Indeed, of the total number of hours played counted only 6% of 2–11 year-old girls and 4% of teenage girls accounted for the total video game audience, as opposed to 21% of 2–11 year-old boys and 20% of teenage boys (Neilsen, 2007).

Gendered Egaming Practices

Girls enter adolescence at the same time engagement in egaming drops. Teens start to explore their sexual identity, and egaming connotes masculinity, despite some continued female gamers. The culture of technology remains male-dominated and mechanical (Graner Ray, 2004), so girls try to distance themselves from that stereotype, particularly since peer perception is so important to them. Another reason that girls play egames less is because they choose to spend their time in other ways, such as reading. In addition, they tend to have more household responsibilities than boys (Fromme, 2003).

Males and females also tend to master egames differently. Boys are more likely to ask peers for help and consult cheat sheets and guides. Girls tend to work out problems independently or to ask a male for help. Rather than consult a manual, girls will reset the level or start the game over (Hayes, 2007). Cooper and Weaver (2003) also noted that in coed settings, boys outperformed girls in playing egames, but when physically separated, girls performed equally well or better than boys, particularly if the game offered personalized textual feedback (boys, on the other hand, prefer icon-based help). Indeed, Hargittai and Shafer (2006) found that females' online skills equaled males, but that the former under-estimated their expertise. Part of the issue is based on attrition theory (e.g., Cooper & Weaver, 2003). When girls experience success with computers, they tend to attribute that success to the machine. When they are not successful, girls tend to blame themselves. In contrast, boys tend to praise their own prowess when technologically successful, and often blame the computer when unsuccessful (Cooper & Weaver, 2003). In terms of the physical experience, boys enjoy mastering complex hand-eye coordination itself, while girls prefer to focus on concrete goals. If the navigation protocols are difficult to figure out or distract from achieving the goal, girls often walk away from the egame (Cooper & Weaver, 2003).

Non-users tend to express gendered behaviors and attitudes about egames most strongly. Non-gamer girls will assert that egames are a waste of time. When they first see an egame, girls may confuse the look of the game (the quality of its graphics, for instance) and its playability. Because girls tend to take risks less than boys, females are more likely to give up on a complicated game than their male counterparts. Furthermore, boys are more likely to value game play socially than girls (Carr, 2005). On the other hand, when girls find satisfaction accomplishing a gaming goal, they will continue to game, just as boys persist (Forssell, 2008). Furthermore, as gamers become more experienced, gendered differences tend to fade. Particularly for RPGs, both sexes enjoy the sense of community and socialization, they like to experiment with various identities, they like to compete against themselves or to meet a goal, and they like to explore virtual environments (Taylor, 2003). On a negative note, if girls have negative first experiences, they are less likely to become successful long-term gamers.

Choice of Egames

Amory et al. (1999) discovered that students found adventure and strategy games highly appealing, rating sound, graphics, and storyline as highly important. DeKanter (2005) found that strategy games rated as the most popular PC games. In Rosen and Weil's (2001) study of southern California youths aged 10–25, solitaire and other card games dominated computer games, and Super Mario™ ranked as the favorite video game. Nevertheless, sex-linked preferences emerged. Boys' favorite egame was Grand Theft Auto, and they frequently chose titles targeted for older gamers. Boys preferred action and fighting games (33%), sport games (21%) and platform games (17%), while girls preferred logic and puzzle games (20%) (Fromme, 2003). This difference in selections illustrates boys' risk-taking behaviors.

Indeed, girls shy away from many types of egames. Most egame motifs tend to be competitive, and many are combative, both of which stress girls. Boys, on the other hand, find such games stress relievers. Nor do girls like intense problem-solving or high-stakes risks; they prefer to explore open-ended settings (Hayes, 2005; Schott & Horrell, 2000). On the other hand, girls enjoy games with nuanced characters, strong story lines, good graphical features, high collaborative interactivity, and engaging contexts. Girls self-report that ideal games offer user-friendly interfaces, are challenging yet fun, encourage goals quickly accomplished using logic, foster relationships, and mesh concrete characters and locales (Kafai, 1996). Fortunately, both sexes enjoy role-playing games (RPGs). This genre actively engages students, it provides both textual and visual cues, it often requires collaboration in order to accomplish a task, it often demands clear communication, it can facilitates problem-solving skills, it provides immediate feedback, and it fosters attention to detail (Gros, 2003).

In general, females feel uncomfortable about the appearance of egame characters or avatars. Designers on the whole have not paid enough attention to this detail and its connotations. In a study of preteen boys, Harrison and Bond (2007) found that Caucasian boys were motivated by gaming magazines to aspire to the muscular images of egame characters. Also notable, preteen boys preferred gaming magazines over all other magazine genres, and favored magazines over books and newspapers. Fewer female characters are featured, even in RPGs, and the default figures represent stereotypical images that probably attract males more than females; furthermore, fewer variations among female images exist than for male images (Taylor,

2003). Lara Croft represented one of the first strong female gaming characters, and she has highly sexualized features. Particularly when preteen girls play these RPGs, they may feel uncomfortable about their avatar options, and may even think that they will need to grow up having that busty figure to be considered feminine. Women gamers tend to "bracket" their characters, distancing themselves from online visual identities, but younger girl players are still trying to determine their *real* identity, so may succumb to the coded societal messages (Agosto, 2004; Graner Ray, 2004; Taylor, 2003). For that reason, girls tend to favor animal characters (Schott & Horrell, 2000). Although a social network rather than an RPG or egame *per se*, GaiaOnline (http://www.gaiaonline.com/) provides a happy alternative; incorporating anime and other graphic elements. This site's introduction invites girls to "make a little clone of your real-life self, or create a crazy style you could never pull off in the real world. Go ahead, express yourself" (GaiaOnline, avatars ¶ 1).

Because of the nature of most egames, and girls' less frequent gaming behavior, girls are likely to be disadvantaged if egames are summarily introduced into school library settings (Agosto, 2004; Hargittai & Shafer, 2006). Furthermore, according to the 2006 of the American Association of University Women, if girls do not use computers by sixth grade, they are likely never to pursue science or technology. Therefore, TLs need to pay attention to individual students' experiences and interests if they are to insure that egaming is to benefit the school community.

Benefits of Egaming

Certainly, egames attract and engage youth, sometimes even to the detriment of academics. On the other hand, egames reflect 21st century literacy skills: information literacy, multimedia manipulation, creative problem solving, collaboration, and effective communication (Armstrong & Warlick, 2004). In terms of academic success, egames can introduce students to technology through motivating activities. Indeed, computer gaming significantly predicts college success (Wilson, 2002). Increased practice with video games improved girls' spatial skills, and collaborative work in computer grams improved girls' mathematics problem-solving (Agosto, 2004). Social gaming leads to positive identity assets: self-esteem, self-employment, personal sense of purpose, and personal positive future orientation (Helmrich & Neiburger, 2007).

In sum, games, particularly PRGs, offer a rich learning environment in which to explore and achieve specific goals (Myers, 2008). The characteristics of gaming informing instruction include the following list:

- use of fixed, equitable rules
- clear roles and expectations
- internally-consistent environment where everything is possible
- clear goals within a rich context that gives goals personal meaning and relevance
- opportunities to explore identities

- cognitive and affective engagement
- (usually) multiple ways to achieve them through constructivist strategies
- specific, timely feedback
- sense of control and personal investment
- situated learning
- sense of reward for effort, including trial and error
- structured interaction between players, and between players and the game
- blend of cooperation and competition. (e.g., DeKanter, 2005; Deubel, 2006; Gee, 2007; Simpson, 2005; Squire, 2006; Lee & Young, 2008)

All of these elements can resonate with girls. Indeed, gender-sensitive implementation predicts egaming's successful implementation.

Games in School and Public Libraries

School library mission statements most often include support of the school and district's curriculum initiatives, promotion of a love of reading and learning, providing access to quality resources, and developing efficient and effective users of information. In some cases, school libraries diverge slightly from these goals, like Weymouth High School in Massachusetts, which strives to be the "intellectual center of the school", linking the school to "an ever wider circle of...knowledge and information" (Weymouth High School, 2008). The Sherwood School District in Missouri hopes to "help students with recreational needs" as well as "develop positive attitudes toward library" and "promote a lifelong use of libraries" (Sherwood High School, 2008). These variances from the most common mission of school libraries align with many public libraries, which more commonly strive to serve the personal and recreational needs of patrons, "improve quality of life of patrons" (MHLS, 2005), to be "tuned in to the people" served (Seattle Public Library, 2008), and "empower" patrons (Los Angeles Public Library, 2008).

In direct opposition to this recreational interest, classroom, school site, or school district policies restrict most forms of video and computer games. In an attempt to isolate skills needed to raise test scores, teachers give students few opportunities to develop personal interests, create authentic products, or find alternative ways to express their ideas in an academic setting. Now that games are making legitimate inroads into educational settings, more school library program need to reflect the ways in which exemplary school programs are using students' recreational interests to develop skills that will transfer to academic achievement, engage them in the school community, and encourage them to pursue information for personal gain and enrichment.

In a survey of 78 school libraries, Nicholson found that while 51% allowed web-based games on library computers, and 37% allowed locally-installed games to be played, 33% allowed no games at all in the school library (Nicholson, 2007). The school libraries participating in Nicholson's study had a wide variety of goals for their gaming programs, including: attracting new patrons, serving existing patrons, creating a school community hub, recognizing the cultural significance of games, allowing users to hone skills, raising funds, addressing new literacies, and keeping patrons occupied (Nicholson, 2007). Nevertheless, school library media centers might not serve the recreational and personal interests of its patrons to the fullest extent possible (Nicholson, 2007).

Levine's 2006 case study of a Downers Grove High School gaming event, which included board games as well as video games, showed that, for students who do not value the traditional services of the school library, gaming events provided a way for them to reconsider the library as a place offering programs sensitive to their personal worlds. In many cases, library patrons attending a gaming event returned to the library later for other non-gaming services (Nicholson, 2007). Neiburger and Gullett (2007) pointed out that library gaming events offer players more positive benefits than those experienced at home. This conducive environment made a social event out of video game consumption, and offered community engagement as an alternative to solitary absorption/isolation.

Potentially, the role of the school library can include "creating an environment that makes visitors feel welcome—and keeps them coming back" and "creating a library that serves as an alternate space—a third place—that's different than students' homes and classrooms" (Kenney, 2008, p. 11). Nevertheless, girls' participation in these gaming resources and services garners little attention. However, school libraries may potentially provide safe environments to experience egaming, particularly since a majority of TLs are female.

Library as Portal

School libraries can act as a portal to gaming affinity spaces, providing dedicated time for gamers to congregate around egames, to provide gaming magazines and strategy guides, to publicize gaming events and resources, and to provide online access to gaming resources. Eminent video game scholar James Gee (2007) suggests that a portal can serve as an access point to a gaming affinity space. To that end, he makes the following recommendations regarding library portals:

- adding console-specific 'official' gaming magazines to the periodical collection.
- adding gaming strategy guides to the general collection.
- adding student-created content, such as game reviews, to the school website.
- adding game-related displays that include game art, game-related fiction, and information about careers in gaming.

Developing the library collection to include the recommended gaming resources offers another point of access for students to gain entry to the library's wider services. Girls can participate in this part of the library portal by contributing game reviews and displays.

Choosing Games

Nicholson (2007) notes that librarians may need guidance (and perhaps the guidance of patrons) to select games that will lead to a successful program, and to make sure that no students are left out, games in other formats may need to be included at gaming events (board, trivia, card, and physical games). The Douglass Project at Rutgers (Agosto, 2008) developed the following list of criteria for evaluating websites that affirm girls' ways of knowing:

- *confidence*: encourage and support girls' abilities
- *collaboration*: facilitate working together
- *personal identification*: relate to personal life
- *contextuality*: present information in narrative or story form
- *flexibility/motility*: offer several navigational paths
- *social connectivity*: facilitate interpersonal connections
- *inclusion*: portray diverse populations
- *multimedia presence*: meld high-quality graphic, motion and audio elements. (p. 1)

Using the Douglass Project evaluation guidelines provides a rubric for examining egaming for girls as well as these ideas easily transfer.

Halverson (2005) distinguished between exogenous games, which uses technology to organize information, and endogenous games, which drives the content via the technological environment. The latter typology facilitates greater exploration. Halverson also identified four learning environments for egames: learner-centered to help users to apply knowledge, assessment-centered, knowledge-centered to help users learn, and community-centered to build social skills. These categories help guide TLs as they choose egames; exogenous games tend to facilitate instruction. Librarians should focus on endogenous games, aligning them with desired educational goals.

Many studies conducted using games address historical content, such as Civilization, Revolution, and Age of Mythology. These games proved intellectually engaging, highly challenging, and complex learning activities (e.g., DeKanter, 2005; Gee, 2007; Squire & Jenkins, 2003), perhaps making them best suited to the high school and university settings in which researchers conducted the studied. Two recent educational multi-user virtual learning environments, River City Project (http://muve.gse.jarvard.edu/riversityproject/) and Dimension M (http://tabuladigita.com), offer ways for students to investigate authentic problems and learn academic concepts constructively. Many egames fuse educational and recreational components (Nicholson, 2007), and it is important to note that in order to be engaging to students, games should be both fun and interactive (Amory et al., 1999). Girls need egaming protocols that are easy and intuitive so they can focus on the content rather than on navigating through virtual space (Cooper & Weaver, 2003).

TLs might also consider acquiring game-creation application software. Student creation of egames ramps up their skill sets, draws upon their knowledge of egaming protocols and allowing critical thinking and transference of existing knowledge to new applications. Particularly since girls tend to like to work collaboratively on a concrete project, egame construction can be a productive and fulfilling activity. Regarding egame development, Myers (2008) detailed teen engagement and success in public library settings experienced using Scratch and Game Maker programming tools.

Social Aspects of Gaming in Libraries

Developing an egaming program to establish new or promote existing communities among students may allow the school library to attract new patrons, enhance services provided to existing patrons, and act as a model for the school community as it molds and changes with new technologies and ways of learning. Student gamers already belong to an affinity space, defined by Gee (2007) as a space where people interact because of a common endeavor. Student gamers interact while playing egames; by reading gaming magazines, blogs, or websites; by discussing games; by drawing gaming characters on their notebooks; and by making references to games in classroom discussions. While egames provide a common framework for discussion, each player experiences something different (Squire & Jenkins, 2003). In addition, gaming opens communication between teachers and students (Amory et al., 1999; Simpson, 2005). When students are allowed access to egame-related services in the library, they are entering a portal to their egaming affinity space where they can interact, socialize, learn, and contribute to a larger information-based community (Gee, 2007).

Because girls value the social aspect of gaming *per se*, school libraries can optimize those elements in several ways:

- providing enough space at each computer station to allow two people to sit together
- allowing students to play games that build on social interaction, such as RPGs
- offering a online venue to play RPGs so that gamers of different ages and sexes can interact safety and anonymously
- providing a venue for reviewing egames and sharing egaming experiences.

Playing egames at school can also improve student-teacher relationships. Egames allow teachers and students to get to know each other better, and offer teachers new ways to relate to students, reminding that teachers have a kid inside them.

Egames and Instruction

Instruction can intersect with egaming in a couple of ways: (1) linking personal egaming interest and skill to academics; (2) incorporating egames in learning activities; and (3) using egaming elements into instruction.

Changing current practices to accommodate gaming students requires that educators find out how students spend their time outside of school hours and how they self-identify their literacies (Alvermann et al., 2007). For example, students may seek information and problem-solve within the community but may be bored at school, seeing no relevance in what or how they are being asked to learn (Alvermann et al., 2007; Simpson, 2005). By "translating" egaming behaviors such as asking expert advice or persevering until success is achieved, into academic competences, educators are acknowledging and leveraging students' personal expertise as it applies to their formal learning environments. As noted before, girls who communicate effectively in RPGs can use that skill in collaborative schoolwork, for instance.

Schools may tap into students' true abilities better by providing more access to their recreational affinity spaces. For example, for after-school hours, school libraries may consider providing access to online games. This approach appeals to those teachers potentially uncomfortable with egaming during school time. Such a stratey lessens the academic pressure some girls may feel when "forced" to deal with technology protocols that distract from the content learning. Especially for girls with less access to technology at home, providing time and equipment to enjoy egames recreationally increases comfortable with these technologies, and may bolster their social value. Moreover, all youth need to balance academic and recreational activities (Alvermann et al., 2007), so making egames part of a mandatory assignment during class time potentially ruins them for some students (Squire & Steinkuehler, 2005). Moreover, social transgression explains to a large part of the enjoyment of games, and transgressive behavior is usually unaccepted in school settings. Even manufacturers of gaming consoles stay away from games that sound too educational (DeKanter, 2005; Prensky, 2006), which may suggest that libraries should do the same when first initiating egaming services. School libraries can optimize effective service by providing a portal to existing gaming affinity spaces. Even so, offering games, especially purely recreational games, in the school library program raises technological issues; most school computers are not configured for multimedia egaming (i.e., advanced video cards, high resolution large screens, and high-volume RAM).

Egaming, specifically game simulations, incorporates gaming design into the knowledge building process rather than simply providing a way to organize information (Halverson, 2005). This kind of structural interactivity may intimidate teachers, who must overcome a "certain fear factor" in order to embrace video games in the classroom (DeKanter, 2005). Squire (2006) showed that many students find games more difficult than school; contemporary pedagogical practice creates "learned helplessness" by providing students with short, solvable problems with all information laid out. Game-based learning, on the other hand, begins with failure; students must build skills and knowledge over time by accessing new information, evaluating circumstances, and through practice (Gee, 2007; Squire, 2006).

Educators would do well to try a few egames in order to understand some of the underlying principles of egaming techniques, which largely echo Vygotsky's activity theory. Accordingly, in his book on gaming and learning, Shaffer (2006) asserted that instruction can incorporate these principles, even without using egames themselves, by:

- providing student choice (which topic to study)
- offering opportunities for low-pressure situations
- emphasizing the importance of memorizing and mastering basics of a concept before applying the knowledge
- encouraging collaborative work
- providing extra help for struggling students
- providing extension activities for students who excel
- evaluating effort rather than product
- using alternative and authentic assessments—designing demo games, tests based on mastery levels (not everyone takes the same tests).

Fortunately, these principles resonate for girls, regardless of their attitudes about egaming. Thus, both girls and boys excel when these instructional practices are used.

Information Literacy and Gaming

Seeing the library as an access point to a gaming affinity space provides an opportunity to engage students in the practice of information literacy skills, specifically. Paralel to information literacy, games establish an information goal, require the user to locate resources, evaluate them, and move towards the goal by using found information (Simpson, 2005). Egames may be considered a new medium for communication, as television and film once were; games differ, though, in that they depend upon the concept of agency (Becker, 2007). Students involved in gaming must actively participate in decoding and manipulate language as they play the game Prospero's Island (Squire & Jenkins, 2003). In the same study, Squire and Jenkins also looked at student reactions to highly involved games such as Civilization, noting that games do not replace traditional games, but that students are motivated to keep playing in order to succeed; the games acted as a gateway to the search for further knowledge on a particular subject.

Games require the use of information tools, collaboration, and trial and error (Simpson, 2005; Squire & Jenkins, 2003; Gee, 2007) as well as promoting constructivist learning environments (DeKanter, 2005). Games provide contexts for peer-to-peer teaching and emergence of learning communities (Squire & Jenkins, 2003); students consult peers and guides (print and non-print) to help them be successful in their gaming efforts. Nicholson (2007) noted that games promote critical thinking skills, logic, and planning: all components of information literacy, if not traditional content-area curriculum. Students involved in gaming may access hints, tips, codes on the Internet, post reviews or experiences, or create game-related drawings (Prensky, 2006), all of which require a variety of information literacy skills. Acting at a higher level of information literacy, Gee points out that players start overtly to realize that their choices in their gaming reflect their behaviors in real life, and they begin reflecting on and questioning those real life choices (Gee, 2007).

Information literacy is in many ways aligned with gaming literacy, and the library program can offer instruction and guidance, both formally and informally, for students already involved with these literacies. To embed information literacy into gaming activities in an informal manner, the library program should provide students regular opportunities to collaborate in order to produce shared information about games, such as Frequently Asked Questions, game reviews, and game guides published on the library website. This could be done in the form of contests with game-related prizes for the best-quality product.

Several aspects of egaming potentially resonate for girls relative to information literacy. In their discussion of gaming and information competency, the Association of College and Research Libraries (2007) asserted that librarians need to make sure that egames include the following attributes to help girls gain information literacy skills:

- just-in-time verbal or textual feedback when the gamer wants it
- affirmation of effort as it leads to performance and competence
- incorporation of the affective domain, particularly as it relates to personal priorities
- consideration of systems and relationships as they impact information analysis and use
- emphasis on distributed knowledge and cross-functional information-seeking teams
- acknowledgement and leveraging of multiple perspectives
- empathy of complex information systems.

Observing these concepts will improve the player/learner in entering the increasing complex digital world of information literacy today.

To formally address information literacy skills and gaming, the library program could offer a short course on gaming, which could include the girl-friendly following information literacy aspects:

- collaborative writing about gaming
- interviews given to student and staff gamers
- creation of game-related art or game design ideas
- research and compilation of gaming tips and tricks for shared use.

By offering a formal training opportunity, TLs demonstrate the importance of technology, and provide a school-endorsed way to scaffold technology learning.

Conclusion

Egaming speaks volumes about youth. Egaming also reveals some gender-linked issues that need to be addressed explicitly in order to insure gender equity when incorporating egames and egaming elements into school library programs.

Egaming also continues to reflect male dominance. This stereotype is outdated as witnessed by the number of females engaged in RPG games in particular, but also realizing that females now constitute the majority of Internet users (Macgill, 2007). TLs can help girls counter those societal messages by substituting positive attitudes and practices. TLs can encourage girls to take intellectual risks and boost their self-efficacy by offering fun, low-stress egaming environments. Specifically, TLs can provide egaming resources that resonate with girls, encourage technology use among girls, offer girls-only egaming opportunities, invite girls to talk and write about gaming, and facilitate girl egaming creation.

Egaming reveals student needs in a school setting, and girls can benefit significantly in this discussion. Youth emphasis on choice, authentic activities, mastery, and differentiation indicate a clear need to look closely at the way instruction is currently delivered and student progress is evaluated. Egaming also addresses student awareness of and affinity for information literacy skills related to collaboration, pursuit of personal interests, evaluation of information, and information sharing. Existing egaming practices provides the library program a point of entry to engage students in leveraging their personal skills for academic success. Girl gamers can profit from this strategy because TL affirmation can validate their behaviors, which are usually not socially acceptable among their peers. Furthermore, girls not experienced at egaming may feel more comfortable exploring this technology, and develop an interest in other technologies as a result of this exposure. In any case, egaming principles hold promise for *all* students.

References

Agosto, D. (2004). Girls and gaming: A summary of the research with implications for practice. *Teacher Librarian, 31*(3), 8–14.

Agosto, D. (2008). Evaluating materials. *Girls Tech.* Retrieved June 7, 2008, from http://girlstech.douglass.rutgers.edu/gt1b.html

Alvermann, D., Hagood, M., Heron-Hruby, A., Hughes, P., Williams, K., & Yoon, J. (2007). Telling themselves who they are: what one out-of-school time study revealed about underachieving readers. *Reading Psychology, 28*, 31–50.

American Association of School Librarians and Association of Educational Communications and Technology. (1998). *Information power.* Chicago: American Library Association.

Amory, A., Naicker, K., Vincent, J., & Adams, C. (1999). The use of computer games as an educational tool: identification of appropriate game types and game elements. *British Journal of Educational Technology, 30*, 311–321.

Armstrong, S., & Warlick, D. (2004). The new literacy. *TechLearning, 25*(2), 24–31.

Association of College and Research Libraries. (2008, September). Gaming, information literacy, and the college student. *C&RL News,* Vol. 69, No. 9.

Becker, K. (2007). Digital game-based learning once removed: Teaching teachers. *British Journal of Educational Technology, 38*, 479–488.

Carr, D. (2005). Context, gaming pleasures, and gendererd preferences. *Simulation & Gaming, 36*(4), 464–482.

Cooper, J., & Weaver, K. (2003). *Gender and computers: Understanding the digital divide.* Nawah, NJ: Erlbaum.

DeKanter, N. (2005). Gaming redefines interactivity for learning. *TechTrends, 49*(3), 26–31.

Deubel, P. (2006, January). Game on. *T.H.E. Journal, 33*(6), 30–41.

Entertainment Software Association. (2008). *Game player data.* Retrieved June 7, 2008, from http://www.theesa.com/facts/gameplayer.asp

Forssell, K. (2008). Girls, games, and getting interested in technology. In K. McFerrin, et al. (Eds.), *Proceedings of society for information technology and teacher education international conference 2008* (pp. 991–996). Chesapeake, VA: American Association of Computer Education.

Fromme, J. (2003). Computer games as a part of children's culture. *Game Studies, 3*(1). Retrieved June 7, 2008, from http://www.gamestudies.org/0301/fromme/

Gee, J. (2007). *What video games have to teacher us about learning and literacy* (2nd ed.). Palgrave, England: Macmillan.

Graner Ray, S. (2004). *Gender inclusive game design: Expanding the market.* Hingham, England: Charles River Media.

Gros, B. (2003, July). The impact of digital games in education. *First Monday.* Retrieved June 7, 2008, from http://www.firstmonday.dk/issues/issue8_7/xyzgros/

Halverson, R. (2005). What can K-12 school leaders learn from video games and gaming? *Innovate, 1*(6). Retrieved June 7, 2008, from http://www.innovateonline.info

Hargittai, E., & Shafer, S. (2006). Differences in actual and perceived online skills: The role of gender. *Social Science Quarterly, 87*(2), 432–448.

Harrison, K., & Bond, B. (2007). Gaming magazines and the drive for muscularity in preadolescent boys: A longitudinal examination. *Body Image, 4*(3), 269–277.

Hayes, E. (2005). Women, video gaming, & learning: Beyond stereotypes. *TechTrends, 49* (5), 23–28.

Hayes, E. (2007). Women, video gaming & learning: Beyond stereotypes. *TechTrends, 49*(5), 23–28.

Helmrich, E., & Neiburger, E. (2007). Video games as a service: Three years later. *VOYA, 30*(2) 113–115.

Jones, S. (2003). *Let the games begin: Gaming technology and entertainment among college students.* Washington, DC: Pew Internet & American Life Project.

Kafai, Y. (1996). Video game design by girls and boys: Variability and consistency of gender differences. In J. Cassell & H. Henkins (Eds.), *For Barbie to Mortal Kombat: Gender and computer games* (pp. 90–114). Cambridge, MA: MIT Press.

Kaiser Family Foundation. (2005). *Generation M: Media in the lives of eight to eighteen year olds.* Menlo Park, CA: Kaiser Family Foundation.

Kenney, B. (2008, January). The power of place. *School Library Journal, 54*(1), 11.

Lee, J., & Young, C. (2008). Middle level educators and online social gaming. In K. McFerrin, et al. (Eds.), *Proceedings of society for information technology and teacher education international conference 2008* (pp. 1726–1732). Chesapeake, VA: American Association of Computer Education.

Levine, J. (2006). Gaming and libraries. *Library Technology Reports, 42*(5), 5–30.

Los Angeles Academy Middle School. (2006). *Accountability Report Card (SARC) for school year 2005–2006.* Retrieved June 7, 2008, from http://search.lausd.k12.ca.us/cgibin/

Los Angeles Public Library. (2008). *Mission statement.* Retrieved June 7, 2008, from http://www.lapl.org/about/mission.html

Macgill, A. (2007). *Parent and teen internet use.* Washington, DC: Pew Internet & American Life Project.

Myers, B. (2008). Minds at play: Teens gain 21st-century literacy skills designing their own computer games. *American Libraries, 39*(5), 54–57.

National Institute on Media and the Family. (2001). *11th annual mediawise video game report card.* Retrieved June 7, 2008, from http://mediafamily.org/research/report_vgrc_2006.shtml

Neiburger, E. (2007). *Gamers...in the library?!* Chicago: American Library Association.

Neiburger, E., & Gullett, M. (2007, Winter). Out of the basement: The social side of gaming. *Young Adult Library Services, 5*(2), 34–38.

Neilsen Company. (2007). *The state of the console.* Chicago: Neilsen.

Nicholson, S. (2007). *The role of gaming in libraries: Taking the pulse*. Retrieved June 7, 2008, from http://boardgameswithscott.com/pulse2007.pdf

Prensky, M. (2006). *Don't bother me mom – I'm learning!* St. Paul, MN: Paragon House.

Rosen, L., & Weil, M. (2001). *Are computer, video and arcade games affecting children's behavior? An empirical study.* Retrieved June 7, 2008, from the Technostress Web site: http://www.technostress.com/ADHDVideoGames3.htm

Schott, G., & Horrell, K. (2000). Girl games and their relationship with the gaming culture. *Convergence, 6*(4), 36–53.

Seattle Public Library. (2008). *About the library: Mission statement.* Retrieved June 7, 2008, from http://www.spl.org/default.asp?pageID=about_mission

Shaffer, D. (2006). *How computer games help children learn.* New York: Palgrave Macmillan.

Sherwood Cass R-VIII School District. (2008). *Library media center mission statement.* Retrieved June 7, 2008, from http://sherwood.k12.mo.us/high%20school/libraryweb/mission_statement.htm

Smith, M., & Wilhelm, J. (2002). *Reading don't fix no Chevys: Literacy in the lives of young men.* Portsmouth, NH: Heinemann.

Squire, K. (2006). From content to context: Videogames as designed experience. *Educational Researcher, 35*(8), 19–29.

Squire, K., & Jenkins, H. (2003). Harnessing the power of games in education. *Insight, 3*, 5–33.

Squire, K., & Steinkuehler, C. (2005, April). Meet the gamers. *Library Journal, 130*(7), 38–41.

Simpson, E. (2005). Evolution in the classroom: What teachers need to know about the video game generation. *TechTrends, 49*(5), 17–22.

Taylor, T. (2003, May). Multiple pleasures: Women and online gaming. *Convergence, 9*, 21–46.

Weymouth High School. (2008). *Library/media center.* Retrieved June 7, 2008, from http://www.weymouth.ma.us/schools/commercial/library.asp?id=305

Wilson, B. (2002). A study of actors promoting success in computer science including gender differences. *Computer Science Education, 12*, 141–164.

The School Library Benefits Everyone: Technology, Approaches, and Resources for Serving Students with Special Needs

Alana M. Zambone, Lora Lee Smith Canter, Karen S. Voytecki, Tara Jeffs, and Jami Biles Jones

Abstract   Teachers serving students with disabilities often rely on the school library because of the diversity of resources, its positive association for many students, and the perception that it facilitates individualized attention. Media specialists and educators report that teachers typically send students with disabilities to the school library during "class-time" to complete individual or small group projects; reduce classroom disruptions; provide an opportunity to focus or "calm down;" provide access to alternative curriculum and instruction; and as a reward for positive behavior. The power of the school library program and the media specialist to improve student achievement is well documented. While this research does not specifically address students with special needs, it is highly likely that they can experience the same positive impact as their non-disabled peers if the school library has adaptive technology and the media specialist provides instructional accommodations to meet their needs. This chapter presents the impact of different disabling conditions on students' learning and functioning, and discusses evidenced-based solutions for meeting the needs of exceptional students. The chapter summarizes the current literature on assistive technology for the school library program and describes informative resources, essential technologies, and implementation strategies. The chapter concludes with resources and approaches for collaborating with special educators and other specialists on behalf of students with special needs.

Keywords   Assistive technology, special education, disability, exceptionality, adaptations, impairments, challenges, accommodations, modifications, media center, school library

All students, including those with disabilities, receive essential services from the school library. Media specialists, like all school personnel, must fulfill the legal mandates of the Individuals with Disabilities Education Improvement Act (IDEA) (2004) and No Child Left Behind (NCLB) (2001) to serve students with special

A.M. Zambone (✉)
Department of Curriculum and Instruction, East Carolina University, Greenville, NC 27858
e-mail: zambonea@ecu.edu

M. Orey et al. (eds.), *Educational Media and Technology Yearbook*,
DOI 10.1007/978-0-387-09675-9_18, © Springer Science+Business Media, LLC 2009

needs. Teachers of students with disabilities perceive the school library as a supportive environment for their students. These teachers rely on the school library for its diversity of resources and its positive association for many students. In surveys and interviews conducted by the authors, both media specialists and educators report that teachers often send students with disabilities to the school library during "class-time" to complete individual or small group projects; reduce classroom disruptions; provide an opportunity to focus or "calm down"; provide access to alternative curriculum and instruction; and reward for positive behavior.

The power of the school library program to improve the achievement of typical students is well documented (Lance & Loertscher, 2005; Lonsdale, 2003; Lance, 2002). Students who do not have disabilities report that the school library program helps them to learn and complete school projects; and that it positively impacts their level of engagement and academic success in classroom activities (Todd & Kuhlthau, 2005). While this research does not specifically address students with special needs, it is highly likely that students with disabilities experience the same positive impact. When the school library is equipped with assistive technology, students with disabilities experience increased success (Downing, 2006). This chapter provides an overview of the effects of different disabling conditions on students' learning and functioning; and discusses the ways that assistive technology in the school library enhances their achievement. The chapter concludes with considerations for integrating assistive technology into the school library center and supporting school personnel in this effort.

Impact of Disabilities on Learning and Functioning

Students with disabilities often become motivated, learn, and experience success in the school library (Jones & Zambone, 2008). The school library media center allows students with disabilities to disassociate from the failure or frustration of the classroom. It provides access to a variety of materials that complement their learning strengths; presents opportunities to work independently or in smaller groups; and empowers choices, such as working at an area other than a typical classroom desk and/or making selections from varied resources. These elements all contribute to the students' positive response toward the school library and the media specialist (Smith, 2006; Wesson & Kief, 1995). Accomplishments in the school library encourage students with disabilities to work and succeed across the curriculum in a variety of settings.

When media specialists become familiar with the characteristics of different disabling conditions they have a framework for understanding individual students' special needs and can explore ways to facilitating learning and functioning. Media specialists must keep in mind that students and youth with disabilities are people first. It is easy to lose sight of the person when learning about their disabling conditions and the ways these conditions can impact development and learning. Additionally, how a student's disability affects his development, learning and functioning varies, depending on the student's individual characteristics and experiences.

While IDEA specifies criteria for determining that a student requires special education services, some students may be wrongly determined to have a disability, others with disabilities remain unidentified, and still others' disabilities are misidentified. In addition, a great deal of variability within and across disability categories remains. Consequently, students with disabilities form an exceedingly heterogeneous group. Some prominent learning characteristics, however, cross disability categories. These characteristics typically manifest in similar academic, social, and behavioral challenges in school, regardless of the student's disability label.

Students in public schools are considered eligible for special education services if they exhibit the criteria specified for one or more of the thirteen disability categories recognized in IDEA. IDEA typically organizes the thirteen categories of disabilities listed in the law into two groups: high incident and low incident disabilities. High incident disabilities appear most often in the general population. These include:

- Learning Disabilities
- Mild or moderate Mental Retardation, currently referred to as Intellectual Disability
- Emotional Impairments
- Speech or Language Impairments

Low incidence disabilities occur at a lower rate in the general population and include:

- Hearing Impairments
- Visual Impairments
- Deaf-Blindness
- Severe or profound Intellectual Disability
- Multiple Impairments
- Orthopedic and Neurological Impairments
- Traumatic Brain Injury
- Autism
- Chronic Illness or Other Health Impairments

Regardless of the specific disability label, in order to qualify for services under IDEA, the disability must impede students' achievement in school to the extent that they require accommodations, support, and/or specialized instruction.

When working with students with disabilities, professionals do not need to become familiar with all the characteristics of each category of exceptionality, because children with different disability labels share similar traits. Professionals working with them should be familiar with the learning characteristics evident in the more global domains of cognitive function; academic performance; social/emotional function; behavioral skills; physical and neurological function; and speech/language/communication skills. Also, it is important to note that individuals may concurrently have more than one type of specific disability. For instance, a student with a learning disability may also have an emotional disorder. Figure 1

Functions	Impairments or Challenges	Disability Categories Manifesting these Challenges
Cognitive	Cognitive deficits or differences such as sequencing, abstract understanding, and/or generalizing what is learned to new tasks or environments	Learning Disabilities Mental Retardation Traumatic Brain Injury More severe forms of Autism Spectrum Disorders
	Metacognitive deficits (e.g. thinking strategies, such as planning)	Learning Disabilities Emotional Disorders Traumatic Brain Injury Autism Spectrum Disorders
	Short or long-term memory deficits	Learning Disabilities Intellectual Disabilities Traumatic Brain Injury
	Attention deficits and/or hyperactivity	Attention Deficit Disorder Learning Disabilities Emotional Disorders
	Perceptual deficits (e.g. visual or tactual/kinesthetic perceptions, visual motor integration, visual or auditory memory)	Learning Disabilities Neurological Impairments Intellectual Disabilities Autism Spectrum Disorders
Academic Performance	Decoding or comprehending print	Learning Disabilities Intellectual Disabilities Hearing Impairments
	Phonological awareness for decoding and spelling	Learning Disabilities Speech/Language Disorders Hearing Impairments
	Deficits in the visual/motor aspects of handwriting	Learning Disabilities Neurological Impairments
	Deficits in the content or structure of written expression	Learning Disabilities Neurological Impairments Speech or Language Impairments
	Math computation	Learning Disabilities
	Gaps in knowledge and skills in various academic areas	Other Health Impairments Visual Impairments Neurological Impairments
Social/Emotional	Poor social skills	Learning Disabilities Intellectual Disabilities Emotional Disorders Autism Spectrum Disorders
	Low self-esteem	All disability areas
	Limited self-regulation	Learning Disabilities

Fig. 1 Overview of learning challenges

		Intellectual Disabilities Traumatic Brain Injury Emotional Disorders Autism Spectrum Disorders
	Low motivation	All disability areas
	Incapacitating mood states (e.g. anxiety)	Emotional Disorders Traumatic Brain Injury
Behavioral	Adaptive behavior deficits (social interaction, self-care, social coping, application of motor and other skills)	All disability areas
	Disruptive behavior in response to frustration and other emotions	Behavioral/Emotional Disorders Communication Disorders Learning Disabilities Intellectual Disabilities
	Withdrawal	Emotional Disabilities
Physical & Neurological	Missing or limited use of extremities	Neurological Impairments (e.g. Cerebral Palsy) Physical Impairments
	Difficulty controlling motor movements or balance and position of the body or extremities	Neurological Impairments Sensory Impairments Physical Impairments
	Strength and stamina	Health Impairments Sensory Impairments Neurological Impairments Physical Impairments
Speech/Language/ Communication	Difficulty speaking clearly or rhythmically (e.g. stuttering)	Speech Impairment
	Difficulty processing and/or responding to spoken or print language	Learning Disability Autism Spectrum Disorders Neurological Impairments
	Difficulty using language (e.g. using names and labels)	Learning Disability Language Impairment
	Difficulty using one or more symbolic forms of language (e.g. written, spoken)	Learning Disability Language Impairment Intellectual Disabilities
	Difficulty reading social cues and using language socially	Autism Spectrum Disorders Learning Disabilities Emotional Disabilities Neurological Impairments

Fig. 1 (continued)

overviews impairments or challenges and the disability labels typically associated with them (Mercer & Mercer, 2005).

Problems in each of the aforementioned domains reciprocally influence each other, putting the child at risk for stunted personal and interpersonal development as well as poor scholastic success. For example, students with learning disabilities often exhibit higher rates of challenging behaviors than their peers in the general population (Mercer & Mercer, 2005; Bender & Wall, 1994). Efforts to hide an academic weakness, avoid failure on an academic task, or underdeveloped social or communication skills typically lead to the problem behaviors these students exhibit. Students with reading disabilities frequently struggle in math and science classes because of their limitations in using print to learn in these subjects. Technology makes it possible to meet the needs of students with learning challenges, such as those described in Figure 1, because it can support instructional practices (Egbert, 2008).

The Role of Assistive Technology and Strategies for Students with Disabilities

Teaching and learning for students with disabilities can be broadly organized into three major aspects: (1) motivation and engagement; (2) content instruction; and (3) learning strategy and skill acquisition (Mercer & Mercer, 2005). Whether they are receiving instruction in basic functional or academic skills, motivation and engagement in learning pose a significant challenge for students with special needs and their teachers. While many typical students lack motivation as well, students with disabilities grapple with connections between different content and skills, and seldom see the curriculum's relevance. Frequently, these students find their impairments interfere with their ability to engage in instructional activities, which further undermines their motivation. Since many students with a disability enjoy assistive technology, they actively engage in the learning process and perceive instruction as relevant through its use. Furthermore, technology gives students the opportunity to master content in a way that meets their needs and to practice skills until they experience success. Because assistive technology compensates for their limitations and capitalizes on their strengths, the struggle to engage in learning is reduced while success is increased (Poel, 2007).

Students with disabilities must acquire learning strategies in order to acquire content knowledge. Assistive technology creates a "floor of opportunity" for these students to achieve because it facilitates application of learning strategies to master content (Parette & Peterson-Karlan, 2007). Not only does assistive technology increase students' motivation, it also provides the tools they need to acquire and use learning strategies in order to master content (e.g., assistive technology can be used as a tool that allows students with disabilities to access the Internet).

Integrating assistive technology into the school library program and into the media specialist's teaching practice facilitates differentiation of instruction for diverse learners, increases the student's independence, and promotes positive interdependence with peers in the teaching and learning process (Hopkins, 2006; Wojahn, 2006). Incorporating assistive technology into instruction makes it possible to extend and increase academic and social expectations of students with disabilities. Assistive technology extends, supplements, and individualizes special education instructional strategies and approaches for students with disabilities (Starkman, 2007).

Most special education practices are not really "specialized." Rather, special education elaborates teaching those practices that are proven effective for all students and individualizes the practice according to each student's strengths and needs. Direct instruction is one technique that exemplifies an effective and researched teaching practice for students with disabilities, largely because it integrates learning strategies and content instruction (Dean & Kuhn, 2007; Flores & Ganz, 2007). The National Institute for Direct Instruction describes DI as a model for teaching that "emphasizes well-developed and carefully planned lessons designed around small learning increments and clearly defined and prescribed teaching tasks. It is based on the theory that clear instruction eliminating misinterpretations can greatly improve and accelerate learning." DI is characterized by systematically structured and prescriptive curriculum design; explicit and progressive instruction; and routine and predictable presentation. The key elements of DI include a clearly articulated curriculum and a form of instruction referred to as "faultless communication" where instructional conversation is pattern-based and oft times scripted (Bartholomew, 2007). DI provides a framework for establishing a learning community in any setting. DI approach relies on explicit definitions of concepts presented to students in the form of precise examples referred to as propositions (or rule relationships). DI demonstrates the logical interconnection and empirical tests of propositions or rule relationships. Table 1 identifies seven steps to incorporate assistive technology into DI learning activities. By following these steps, professionals effectively present and promote content acquisition, application, and generalization for students with disabilities.

Incorporating some of the principles underlying DI into other instructional approaches such as discovery learning, problem-based learning, and authentic learning increases students' with disabilities likelihood of success. For example, students with disabilities attain new knowledge and skills, regardless of the instructional approach used, when teachers correct the students' errors immediately, structure students' responses and interaction with peers, and prompt them when the students struggle to grasp large or abstract concepts (Engelmann, 2007).

In addition to instructional approaches such as DI, various learning strategies improve students' performance and achievement (Berthold, Nuckles, & Renkl,

Table 1 Seven steps of direct instruction

1 *Analyze the objective(s) into knowledge components.*
2 *Teach the identified knowledge components **before** you work on a new objective that **requires*** (because it *consists* of) these knowledge components.
3 *Review and assess comprehension* of the knowledge components (prerequisites) ***before*** initial instruction on the new objectives.
4 *Use model-lead-test to teach the new knowledge unit/objective.*
5 *Provide a range of examples and nonexamples* that sample the *range of application. Juxtapose some of these* examples and nonexamples to reveal sameness and difference.
6 *Present a formal acquisition test*—using exactly the same examples and non-examples utilized in #5.
7 *Immediately correct (and note) every error.*

2007). Understanding the various learning strategies in the field of special education helps media specialists and other professionals select appropriate technology to help students' acquire and apply the most effective strategies. Examples of learning strategies include using graphic organizers to organize information and using mnemonic devises to retain and recall information (Fontana, Scruggs, & Mastropieri, 2007). When students with disabilities master learning strategies their interaction with students who are not disabled improves. Other evidence-based approaches to help students develop and apply learning strategies as they master content include (Berthold et al., 2007; Fontana et al., 2007):

- segmenting material to avoided information overload
- providing immediate positive feedback and reinforcement
- modeling metacognitive processes through think-alouds
- helping students develop advanced organizers to increase predictability
- providing directions verbally and in writing
- having students paraphrase discussion points or answers to questions
- incorporating multi-sensory approaches to address a variety of learning modalities
- using questioning techniques to access prior knowledge

Assistive technology enhances instructional techniques such as DI and encourages students to apply learning strategies (Puckett, 2006). For example, guided web-quests (e.g. book-marking key sites ahead of time and providing step-by-step guides for the quest); brainstorming and mapping software such as *Inspiration* and *Kidspiration* software[1] for creating graphic organizers or developing outlines; and/or the use of word processing and note-taking tools such as the *Neo-AlphaSmart*[2], *Braille Lite Millenium*[3], or *BrailleNote*[4] serve to support content learning because they help students with disabilities use learning strategies. Furthermore, assistive technology insures that learning opportunities are accessible to students who may have difficulty with traditional academic tasks because of conditions such as learning disabilities or physical or sensory impairments (Jeffs, Behrmann, & Bannan-Ritland, 2006).

Successfully researching and learning new information poses a particular challenge for students with disabilities. The following guidelines for integrating assistive technology with effective instructional design address this challenge (Egbert, 2008, p. 50):

---

[1]For sources and an overview of *Inspiration* and *Kidspiration* software: http://www.Inspiration.com

[2]For sources and information on the *Neo-AlphaSmart*: http://www.alphasmart.com/index.html

[3]For sources and information on the *Braille Lite Millenium*: https://sales.freedomscientific.com/

[4]For sources and information on the *BrailleNote*: http://www.humanware.com

- Incorporate just-in-time learning: plan supplementary lessons, such as a lesson on how to find the main idea, by preparing mini-lessons and bookmarking websites that provide needed information or skill instruction.
- Use different technologies to differentiate instruction so that students who need more visual than language based information, or an opportunity to interact with learning tactually or kinesthetically, can do so.
- Teach in a culturally responsive manner by connecting with parents to understand student's home cultures and supports; and sending technology home to share with families.
- Adapt materials and establish a data base that teachers can access to identify materials and technology for use in presenting content in ways that are accessible and understandable for students with varying ability levels.
- Balance content and tools by choosing the simplest technological solutions then adding features and extensions to challenge students with diverse capabilities.

Assistive technology also facilitates creativity while reinforcing learning strategies. Learners brainstorm, plan, and organize ideas in visually meaningful ways through tools such as *Inspiration* software[1] and *Spark Space* idea mapping software[5]. These programs easily convert text to outline form with a click of the mouse. With resources such as these, students see their ideas and make meaningful additions and changes. Likewise, object generator software[6] helps students develop ideas in a topic area and guides questions and interaction with the information in unique ways. Students organize and express their knowledge and ideas in various formats that match their learning styles, preferences, and interests with story starters and publishing software, such as *Storybook Weaver*[7], *Imagination Express*[8], and *Clicker*[9].

As a powerful tool for teaching and learning, assistive technology increases media specialists' success with students who have disabilities (Hopkins, 2006). The following section outlines principles and practices for selecting assistive technology for school library programs and suggests tools, hardware, and software that may prove particularly useful to media specialists.

Assistive Technology in School Library Programs

IDEA defines assistive technology as "...any items, piece of equipment or product system, whether acquired commercially off the shelf, modified, or customized

---

[5]For sources and information on *Spark Space* idea mapping software: http://www.enablemart.com/Catalog/Visual-Learning

[6]A fairly comprehensive list of generators can be found at http://generatorblog.blogspot.com, although not all may be appropriate for the school library or classroom.

[7]For information and sources for *Storybook Weaver* software: learningcompany.com

[8]For information and sources for *Imagination Express* software http://www.synapseadaptive.com/edmark/edmark_software_products.htm

[9]For information and sources for *Clicker* software: http://www.cricksoft.com/

that is used to increase, maintain or improve functional capabilities of students with disabilities" (300.5). Devices and software can support many of the challenges that students with disabilities experience, including: communication; accessing information through their senses; committing information to memory; and completing academic tasks such as math problems, reading and writing. IDEA requires that the students with disabilities have access to any assistive technology devices and services they may need (Alper & Raharinirina, 2006).

Media specialists should determine who will use the assistive technology and how they will be use it prior to selecting devices and software. Teachers and related service specialists, such as occupational therapists, typically analyze the individual student's assistive technology needs. Many school districts also employ an assistive technology specialist who participates in this process. The media specialist should request these assessment results and work with the team to select assistive technology for the school library. The media specialist can choose from a wide range of assistive technology resources. The following list provides examples of assistive technology devices and software, and their relationship to the disabilities that students using the school library may have (Egbert, 2008; Neal & Elbert, 2006).

Cognitive/ Perceptual Disabilities

More and more technology is being stored on convenient flash drives. The programs operate from these drives and never alter the computer systems in which the drives are being used. Students simply check out the flash drives for in library use. These flash drives could include programs such as:

- Concept/mind mapping software (i.e. *Inspiration* or *Spark Space*)
- Text readers (i.e. *Text Help Read & Write* or *Kurzweil 3000*)
- Voice recognition software
- Word prediction programs
- Universally designed software (i.e. *eReader* or *Thinking Reader*)
- Ebooks (i.e. *DAISY* or *Dolphin EaseReader*)
- Reading and math pens (i.e. *Reading II*)

Mobility Impairments

A designated computer station could include:

- Assorted keyguards
- Assorted activation switches
- Alternative keyboards (i.e. *Intellikeys)*
- Touch screen
- Head mouse
- Voice recognition software

Hearing Impairments

Assistive technologies could include:

- Personal amplification devices (i.e. *PocketTalker Pro)*
- Teletypewriters (TTY) and Telecommunication Devices for the Deaf (TDD)
- Real-time video captioning systems
- Signing avatars

Visual Impairments

Assistive technologies could include:

- Closed Circuit Television systems (CCTVs)
- Video magnifiers
- Screen magnification software (i.e. *ZoomText*)
- Braille translation software (i.e. *Duxbury*)
- Braille embossers
- Screen reader software (i.e. *JAWS*)

Varying Impairments

- Adjustable Work Stations
- Listening Stations
- Interactive White Boards (i.e. *SMART Board or Promethean Board*)

Once the assistive technology has been selected and made available, media specialists can afford opportunities for the users to explore and interact with the various components and software. Both the media specialist and the students who will use the assistive technology should receive training in its use.

Managing Assistive Technology

There are three actions media specialists can take to efficiently manage assistive technology in the school library program. First, categorize assistive technology equipment and software needs either as a "necessity" or as an "extra." Necessities are basic equipment and software that are required to complete productive tasks by the majority of school users, including but not limited to students with disabilities. Extras are equipment and software used with basic equipment to increase ease of use and productivity, particularly for a student with a disability.

Second, develop and maintain an equipment inventory of the "necessity" and "extra" items of available assistive technology. Such a listing facilitates sharing technology resources with teachers, families, and students particularly when linked to a system for tracking the location and use of equipment and software. Connecting the equipment inventory list and the tracking system identifies patterns of use and the need to update or replace items. The inventory also informs program evaluation, funding applications, and decisions on future assistive technology acquisitions.

The third consideration for managing assistive technology in school library programs is placing the equipment in accessible areas that encourage both its use and the users' interaction with others. Assistive technology can promote the success of a student with disabilities if its location meets the learner's mobility and modality needs.

The Media Specialist's Role in Special Education and Supportive Collaborative Partnerships

Media specialists are not solely responsible for the success of students with disabilities or the assistive technology requirements discussed within this chapter. As leaders, media specialists know that "collaboration with teachers in creating quality learning experiences . . . have a direct impact on academic achievement" (Lance & Loertscher 2005, p. 48). Collaboration ensures that media specialists contribute their unique knowledge and skills to students' special education teams and know each student's requirements for success. Furthermore, the team helps media specialists gain access to any supports they may need to become proficient with adaptive technology and its use for students with disabilities. This section elaborates on the role of collaboration in creating a technology-rich school library program to respond to the needs of students with disabilities.

The mandate that general education personnel participate in determining whether a student is eligible for special education services and the nature of those services is a major change in the 2004 reauthorization of IDEA. A "pre-referral process" is required prior to evaluating students to determine if they have a disability. The goal of the pre-referral process is to resolve the behavioral or learning challenges a student may experience by making changes in the classroom environment and instruction. This process rules out other possible reasons a student may have difficulties besides the presence of a disability and helps identify strategies that may be helpful for the student, even if it is determined that the student is disabled. Media specialists may consult on a pre-referral team that is supporting the general education teacher, provide some of the services to increase the student's success, and offer input into the assessment process based on their knowledge of the student and how he or she functions in the classroom and school library. Media specialists assume an important role on the pre-referral team because of their knowledge of resources and technology, and because the school library is often a place where students who are not successful in the classroom feel welcome and can find materials that are meaningful and useful to them (Jones & Zambone, 2008).

If, despite providing extra help and changing the way we educate and support the student, the student continues to struggle, the team determines whether he has a disability that requires services and develops the Individualized Education Plan (IEP). The IEP, a legal document describing the services, accommodations, and supports the student with disabilities will receive, is generated by a team which includes the family. The media specialist should participate on the IEP team because the supports, adaptations, and modifications mandated in a student's IEP must be available in the school library as well as in the classroom.

While the media specialist provides expertise to greatly enhance the effectiveness of school personnel during pre-referral and development of the IEP, these partners and resources also help integrate assistive technology into the school library program. Figure 2 provides an overview of potential collaborators and the types of expertise they can contribute to the media specialist and the school library program.

Collaborative Partners	Contributions
Special Educators	Student characteristics, strengths & needs Effective learning strategies and approaches Software that supports and reinforces students' learning and performance Curriculum and instruction design and delivery
Occupational Therapists	Sensory regulation and integration strategies Functional arrangements of technology aids (e.g. optimal placement of computer keyboard for a student with cerebral palsy) Recommendations for assistive technology that increases students' functionality Strategies for supporting students' engagement in learning and use of assistive technology
Physical Therapists	Positioning and handling of students Placement, seating and other aspects of incorporating assistive technology into the school library
Assistive Technology Specialists	Sources of hardware and software Set-up and maintenance of hardware and software Assessment of student's technology needs Recommendations of hardware and software Training for the media specialist and student in use of equipment and software Sources for funding and support
School Administrator	Funding and support Alignment of the IEP with the school library program to ensure special education provides needed hardware and software
Students with and without disabilities & their Families	Students strengths, needs, interests and preferences Input and support for use and management of assistive technology

Fig. 2 Collaborative partners and their contributions

Collaboration allows media specialists to make informed choices regarding assistive technology and its application to their school library programs. The Assistive Technology Act of 1988 established grant programs to increase the availability of assistive technology for students with disabilities. The amount of information on funding sources, regulations and assistive technology itself is "almost overwhelming" (Balas, 1999, p. 40). Collaboration enables the media specialist and other school members to develop "collective expertise" about resources and effective approaches for students with disabilities in the school library program. Appendix presents sources of information on assistive technology and accessibility for school library programs.

Conclusion

The school library and media specialists are in a unique position to make assistive technology available for students and teachers because it is the focal point of many schools (Neal & Ehlbert, 2006). While it is impossible to list every potentially useful resource, media specialists need to be "both current and forward-looking when it comes to selecting and using equipment, procedures, and devices that will make the educational experience for students with disabilities more efficient and rewarding" (p. 119). Forward-looking media specialists request the professional development and collaboration they need to embrace this mission. More than being able to enter a facility or room, accessibility means students with disabilities fully participate in ways that are meaningful them (Cox & Lynch, 2006). As masters of information technology and as teachers, media specialists are in an optimal position to determine the ways in which students learn best and the tools that will help them do so (Zabala, 2005). Research indicates that the school library increases students' success in school. When the school library program includes assistive technology for students with disabilities, they too will achieve success in school.

Appendix: Resources for Assistive Technology Application in the School Library

For information about effective practices in implementing the assistive technology mandate of IDEA, visit www.wati.org

For information and Assistive Technology (Most of the material on this page has gathered from the Oregon Assistive Technology Project). http://www.otap-oregon.org/OtapAssistiveTech.htm

ABLEDATA: http://www.abledata.com

AccessIT: National Center on Accessible Information Technology in Education http://www.washington.edu/accessit/index/php

American Library Association. (2004a). The future is here – The choice is yours. *Library Technology Reports, 40*(3), 78–80.

American Library Association. (2004b). Information access for people with disabilities. *Library Technology Reports, 40*(3), 10–31.

CAST: Center for Applied Special Technology http://www.cast.org/

*Closing the Gap: Assistive Technology Resources for Children and Adults with
Special Needs* http://www.closingthegap.com/

Education World's *Teaching Special Kids: Online Resources for Teachers*
http://www.education-world.com/a_curr/curr139.shtml

International Center for Disability Resources on the Internet http://www.icdri.
org/

ISTE's Educator Resources—Grant Sources http://www.iste.org

Jossey-Bass: Technology Funding for Schools http://www.josseybass.com/
WileyCDA/WileyTitle/productCd-0787950408.html

Merlot's articles, videos, and tools on accessibility http://www.merlot.org

National Center to Improve Practice in Special Education through Technology,
Media, and Materials—Videos and resources http://www2.edc.org/NCIP/

NASA's Learning Technologies Project http://learn.arc.nasa.gov/grants/index.
html

10 Technology Funding Sources in NCLB: May 2003: *THE Journal* http://
thejournal.com/articles/16369

UCP: Assistive Technology Funding Search Tips http://www.ucp.org/ucp_
channeldoc.cfm/1/14/86/86-86/2938

Grants/Funding Sources http://www.technologygrantnews.com/grant-funding-
sitemap.html

Electronic School: Searching for Technology Funding http://www.electronic-
school.com/199901/0199f1.html

Funding Your Technology Dreams http://www.cpsb.org/Scripts/abshire/grants.asp

Office of Educational Technology (OET) http://www.ed.gov/about/offices/
list/os/technology/index.html

Grants.gov http://www.grants.gov/aboutgrants/awards.jsp

References

Alper, S., & Raharinirina, S. (2006). Assistive technology for individuals with disabilities: A
review and synthesis of the literature. *Journal of Special Education Technology, 21*(2), 47–64.

Balas, J. (1999). Online resources for adaptive information technologies. *Computers in Libraries,
19*(6), 34–35.

Bartholomew, B. (2007). Why we can't always get what we want. *Phi Delta Kappan, 88*(8),
593–598.

Bender, W.N., & Wall, M.E. (1994). Social-emotional development of students with learning disabilities. *Learning Disability Quarterly, 17,* 323–341.

Berthold, K., Nuckles, M., & Renkl, A. (2007). Do learning protocols support learning strategies
and outcomes? The role of cognitive and metacognitive prompts. *Learning and Instruction,
17*(5), 564–577.

Cox, J., & Lynch, D. (2006). Library media centers: Accessibility issues in rural Missouri. *Intervention in School and Clinic, 42*(2), 101–106.

Dean, D., & Kuhn, D. (2007). Direct instruction vs. discovery: The long view. *Science Education*, *91*(3), 384–397.

Downing, J. (2006). Media centers and special education. Introduction to the special issue. *Intervention in School and Clinic*, *42*(2), 67–77.

Egbert, J. (2008). *Supporting learners with technology: Essentials of classroom practice*. Columbus, OH: Pearson/Merrill/Prentice Hall.

Engelmann, S. (2007). Student-program alignment and teaching to mastery. *Journal of Direct Instruction*, *7*(1), 45–66.

Flores, M., & Ganz, J. (2007). Effectiveness of direct instruction for teaching statement inference, use of facts, and analogies to students with developmental disabilities and reading delays. *Focus on Autism and Other Developmental Disabilities*, *22*(4), 244–251.

Fontana, J., Scruggs, T., & Mastropieri, M. (2007). Mnemonic strategy instruction in inclusive secondary social studies classes. *Remedial and Special Education*, *28*(6), 345–355.

Hopkins, J. (2006). Assistive technology: 10 things to know. *Library Media Connection*, *25*(1), 12–14.

Jeffs, T., Behrmann, M., & Bannan-Ritland, B. (2006). Assistive technology and literacy learning: Reflections of parents and children. *Journal of Special Education Technology*, *21*(1), 37–44.

Jones, J., & Zambone, A. (2008). *The power of the media specialist to improve academic achievement and strengthen at-risk students*. Columbus, OH: Linworth Books.

Lance, K. (2002). Impact of school library media programs on academic achievement. *Teacher Librarian*, *29*(3), 29–34.

Lance, K., & Loertscher, D. (2005). *Powering achievement: School library media programs make a difference: The evidence* (3rd ed.). Salt Lake City, UT: Hi Willow Research & Publishing.

Lonsdale, M. (2003). *Impact of school libraries on student achievement: A review of the research*. Australian Council for Educational Research. Retrieved 20, Mar 2008, from www.asla.org.au/research/index.htm

Mercer, C., & Mercer, A. (2005). *Teaching students with learning problems* (7th ed.). Columbus, OH: Pearson/Merrill/Prentice-Hall.

Neal, J., & Elbert, D. (2006). 20 ways to add technology for students with disabilities to the library or media center. *Intervention in School and Clinic*, *42*(2), 118–123.

Parette, H., & Peterson-Karlan, G. (2007). Facilitating student achievement with assistive technology. *Education and Training in Developmental Disabilities*, *42*(4), 387–397.

Poel, E. (2007). Enhancing what students can do. *Educational Leadership*, *64*(5), 64–66.

Puckett, K. (2006). An assistive technology toolkit: Type II applications for students with mild disabilities. *Computers in the Schools*, *22*(3–4), 107–117.

Smith, E. (2006). *Student learning through Wisconsin school library media centers: Case study report*. Madison, WI: Wisconsin Department of Public Instruction.

Starkman, N. (2007). Assistive technology: Making the impossible possible. *T.H.E. Journal*, *34*(1), 27–32.

Todd, R., & Kuhlthau, C. (2005). Student learning through Ohio school libraries, Part 1: How effective school libraries help students, *School Libraries Worldwide*, *11*(1), 63–88.

Wesson, C., & Kief, M. (1995). *Serving special needs students in the school library media center*. Westport, CT: Greenwood Press.

Wojahn, R. (2006). Everyone's invited: Ways to make your library more welcoming to children with special needs. *School Library Journal*, *52*(2), 46.

Zabala, J. (2005). Ready, SETT, go! Getting started with SETT framework. Closing the gap. *Computer Technology in Special Education and Rehabilitation*, *23*(6), 1.

Prove It! Using Data to Advocate for School Library Media Programs

Cindy Schmidt and Frances Reeve

Abstract   Research studies reveal that many administrators, classroom teachers, students, and parents have misconceptions about the role of library media specialists (LMSs) and how they impact student learning. Conversely, there is a growing body of evidence that demonstrates a strong correlation between quality school library media programs staffed by qualified LMSs and higher student achievement on standardized tests. Therefore, it is apparent that a disconnect exists between the perceived and real impact of school library media programs. In order to address this disconnect, LMSs can use data to advocate for their programs and for their profession. By combining results of published research studies in conjunction with data collected about their own programs, LMSs can prove the impact of their programs on student achievement and garner respect and support from their service populations.

Keywords   School library media specialists · School library media programs · Advocacy · Public relations · Marketing · Student achievement · Evidence-based practice · Data-driven decision-making

Library media specialists (LMSs) are often frustrated by a lack of support and understanding of their role in and contributions to the educational process. Research reveals administrators, teachers, parents, and students often regard the LMS negatively or as serving in an auxiliary capacity. These perceptions conflict with a growing body of research demonstrating the positive impact of a qualified, successful LMS on student achievement.

In a data-driven educational climate, data may bridge this gap between user misconceptions and the research base documenting the strong impact of LMSs on student achievement. LMSs need to be aware of the research documenting their impact. In addition, LMSs critically need to know what and how to collect data about their

C. Schmidt (✉)
Longwood University, Farmville, VA 23909
e-mail: schmidtcm@longwood.edu

M. Orey et al. (eds.), *Educational Media and Technology Yearbook*,
DOI 10.1007/978-0-387-09675-9_19, © Springer Science+Business Media, LLC 2009

program and how to disseminate that data to various library media center audiences. By combining published research findings with local data, LMSs can strongly advocate their vital role in the educational process.

Perceptions vs. Reality

Research reveals that many administrators, classroom teachers, students and parents hold misconceptions about the role of LMSs and how LMSs impact student learning. In fact, a 2002 survey found that the number one challenge facing LMSs continues to be gaining respect among administrators (Ishizuka, Minkel, & St. Lifer, 2002). In addition, principals believe that material selection constitutes the most important task of LMSs (Olson, 1996). Conversely, LMSs consider information literacy instruction to be their main function (Kolencik, 2001). Furthermore, only 47% of the principals believe a direct link exists between effective libraries and increased student achievement, while only 41% understood that libraries have a positive effect on students' standardized test scores (Lau, 2002).

Groups other than principals hold skewed perceptions of LMSs. *A Report of the Findings from Six Focus Groups with K-12 Parents, Teachers, and Principals, as Well as Middle and High School Students* (American Association of School Librarians, 2003) revealed that the "perceived value of the school library and librarians is lower for middle and high school students than for elementary students—particularly among parents and students" (p. 3). Furthermore, "many, especially parents and students, do not see librarians as educated professionals who play an active role in the academic community" (p. 4). Especially disconcerting is the view reported by high school students who "tend to associate the library with mostly negative thoughts: a nagging/yelling librarian, absolute silence required, an irritating need to show their ID in order to use the school library, and restricted Internet access and checkout limits" (p. 7). The study also found the following:

> Parents . . . do not seem to have a clear picture of how their children interact with the librarian, what their children are doing in the library, nor how often they are going. . . . [They] tend to rely on their own image of school libraries and librarians from their youth. When asked what they see as the value of school librarians for their children today, several immediately respond, "Nothing!" These parents see their children utilizing resources outside the school library more frequently and efficiently. (p. 13)

This study demonstrates the importance of establishing an inviting atmosphere to meet the needs of the students. Proactively educating parents and students regarding the available services, resources, and expertise ensures that they understand the value of the library in the overall educational experience.

One reason these misconceptions exist is, "Librarians have done everything so right that they have made themselves invisible" (Wallace & Van Fleet, 1994, p. 6). The primary goal of the LMS is to teach students how to locate, access, evaluate, analyze, and synthesize information. Rather than simply providing students with information, the LMS strives to help students acquire skills to become independent users of information. If the LMS is successful with this endeavor, it may result in the impression that she is not critical in that growth. Even when students become successful, independent users of information, the school still needs a qualified LMS to build a strong collection that supports the curriculum and encourages students to explore personal interests. Collection development is just one of the many vital but unseen tasks that the LMS does to build a successful and strong school library media program. In order to be recognized for the contributions made to student learning, the LMS needs to find ways to become more visible and to document her impact on student achievement.

Administrators often overlook the importance of qualified LMSs due to their lack of training on the instructional and collaborative roles of LMSs. In addition, many administrators have preconceived notions due to their own experiences as students, classroom teachers, or administrators. Negative, non-instructional, or non-collaborative experiences likely result in decreased respect, appreciation, and support of LMSs (Church, 2007, p. 104).

Yet, despite these misconceptions regarding the roles and contributions of LMSs, a growing body of evidence demonstrates a strong correlation between quality school library media programs and higher student achievement on standardized tests. Twenty-one U.S. and Canadian studies document a correlation between student reading achievement and qualified LMSs who establish strong, successful programs supporting and enhancing the curriculum (*School Libraries Work!*, 2008; Small, Snyder, & Parker, 2008). Additional research shows similar correlations between successful LMSs and science achievement (Mardis, 2007). Furthermore, a U. S. National Center for Education Statistics (NCES) longitudinal study demonstrates students with low to middle standardized test scores utilized fewer library resources for assignments, projects, and research papers than did students with high scores (Scott, 2004). This finding further validates the notion that increased use of school library media resources contributes to greater student academic achievement.

Despite such validation, a disparity still exists between the actual impact of LMSs and the perception held by administrators, parents, and students regarding the value of LMSs. Many may wonder if the various studies made any impact at all. Kaplan (2006) notes the studies documenting the impact of school libraries on student achievement affect individual schools but such results did not proliferate. We content that LMSs must advocate for their programs and for their profession. Using findings of published research studies in conjunction with local data demonstrates the impact of LMSs on student achievement, garnering respect and support. Todd (2003) explains, "Principals, teachers, and parents want to hear of local successes; they want to know how their students—not other schools—are benefiting. Local outcomes matter" (¶ 5). Therefore, if LMSs want to transform perceptions and gain support, they need to collect local data and compare it with published research findings proving their impact on student learning.

Unearthing the Evidence

Collecting data remains a critical component in proving local impact on student learning. Depending on the purpose or issue addressed, use various methods for collecting data. These include conducting surveys, focus groups, and interviews; tracking collaboration and instruction; collecting usage statistics; and utilizing collection mapping and analysis.

Surveys, Focus Groups, and Interviews

Conduct surveys, interviews, and/or focus groups to garner patron feedback. Surveys can assess the perceptions that patrons have about the library media center and the contributions they feel it makes to student achievement while also providing information on the needs, interests, or use of the library media center. Conduct surveys in print or online formats for either a limited time period or as an ongoing data collection tool. The design of the surveys should reflect the attention and abilities of the intended audience. Even kindergartners can complete surveys by coloring a smiley face, a neutral face, or a sad face when the classroom teacher or LMS reads statements regarding the library media center. In addition to considering the audience, word questions carefully to ensure collection of useful information. Include at least one open-ended question such as "Please explain and give examples of how the library media center has been useful to you this year." This type of question should generate helpful quotes that can be used for documenting and reporting the impact of the LMS. The surveys can be given to the entire library media center population or target groups such as teachers, students in a particular grade level, or some other group that has common interests or needs. Targeting surveys to particular patron groups helps the LMS identify and meet diverse patron needs. This can also be accomplished by using focus groups.

A focus group is a sampling of individuals that represent a certain user population, such as parents, teachers, students, or a cross-section of all patrons. The groups can be further subdivided by other characteristics such as grade level, gender, ethnicity, socio-economic status, special needs students, ESL/LEP students, subject area teachers, or any other group whose members share similar characteristics and/or needs. Focus groups usually meet face-to-face with a facilitator. These meetings can generate dialog and provide useful feedback. There is the potential risk that members of the group will hesitate to voice their opinions or will be easily swayed by opinions presented by others. This is especially true when dealing with students. It may be helpful to either interview members individually and/or to have someone other than the LMS serve as facilitator.

A combination of methods is often the best way to ensure that conclusions will represent the general consensus of the target population group. For instance, conduct a survey and follow up with a focus group or individual interviews to clarify findings from the survey. In addition to gauging patron perceptions, these techniques can also assess patron needs or identify strengths and weaknesses in the collection, program, or services. While gathering data on patron perceptions and needs is vital, the LMS should also document the ways she currently impacts student learning. Tracking collaboration and instruction is one way to accomplish this.

Tracking Collaboration and Instruction

When determining the impact on student learning, library media center services, instruction, and activities must directly connect to learning objectives. These can be curriculum-driven learning objectives, information literacy skill objectives, or a combination. The LMS must document library media center instruction and track lesson objectives supporting or enhancing the curriculum using various methods. Record objectives from the lesson plan book and/or track instruction by teacher, subject area, and grade level through Microsoft Excel™ or Access™. *IMPACT!*™, an Excel-based program, allows the LMS to easily track collaboration. All of these programs generate supporting charts and graphs.

Time & Task Tracker™, another Excel-based program, allows the LMS to track the amount of time spent on various tasks. The program categorizes each task into one of the four roles of the LMS (teacher, instructional partner, information specialist, or program administrator) as outlined in *Information Power* (AASL & Association for Educational Communications and Technology, 1998). *Time & Task Tracker*™ subdivides these four broader categories into specific daily tasks, including collaborative planning and teaching, and then generates graphics to illustrate the various roles the LMS assumes daily. Since it is impractical to collect this type of data every day, record the data periodically during the year for seven to ten days to provide a fairly accurate reflection of time spent on various tasks. These or other programs provide an excellent way to document and generate data to demonstrate how the LMS supports or enhances the curriculum to impact student achievement. In addition to tracking collaboration and instruction, usage statistics can also help demonstrate the impact of the LMS on student learning.

Usage Statistics

Usage statistics include traffic counts, circulation records, subscription database use, and equipment and facility use. Traffic counts, physical or virtual, may be conducted in a variety of ways. Simply recording tick marks on a sheet or calendar divided by class periods tracks visits by individuals to the library media center. A sign in/out sheet of time and purpose provides more information than the tick mark method. If teachers appear reluctant to sign in, explain this record keeping helps to improve staffing and services in the library media center. Physical traffic counts may be conducted randomly or periodically throughout the year, generating snapshots of typical library usage.

Counters on each library Web page provide virtual traffic counts. Tracking the number of visitors per page assists in determining usefulness and utility. Many of these pages contain pathfinders that support particular class projects or curricular units. Documenting the number of patron visits to these pages during the specific time students study those topics prove how library resources support students in their academic endeavors.

Circulation statistics provide another snapshot of usage. Automated library systems track circulation by patron types (faculty or student) or by grade levels to provide such statistics. These systems tabulate the average number of items per patron type circulating monthly and yearly. Scanning resources used in-house into the circulation system generates more accurate statistics of collection use, especially for reference resources often heavily used but rarely circulated. Statistics from specific areas of the collection also provide useful data. These statistics help determine circulation for resources on a particular topic during the time students study it. For instance, the number of resources related to Native Americans circulated during a sixth-grade assignment provides circulation statistics for associated Dewey number areas.

In addition to statistics for circulation of print resources, vendor reports for electronic subscription resources track the use of the databases by library patrons. Determine if usage increases during the periods students are working on specific projects and/or following instruction on the use of the databases.

Tracking the use of various pieces of equipment and use of the facility itself can prove the value of the resources and the facility. After providing in-service workshops on specific types of equipment, determine whether or not circulation of the equipment increased as a result of the training. Increased use of equipment can prove that the LMS impacts student learning by facilitating the use of technology in the school.

By tracking various types of usage data, prove that the collection, resources, programs, services, and facility are necessary and vital in supporting and enhancing student achievement. In addition to seeking patron feedback, tracking data on collaboration and instruction, and compiling usage statistics, evaluating the collection can prove how well it supports the curriculum and instruction.

Collection Mapping and Analysis

Use collection mapping to determine which library resources align with specific learning objectives of the school. This data can prove the support already in place or demonstrate the need for additional funding. Consult professional resources for collection mapping examples and guidance (Loertscher, Woolls, & Felker, 1999; Loertscher, 1996; Lowe, 2001).

While collection mapping examines the support for specific curriculum objectives, collection analysis examines the general condition of the collection to reveal strengths and weaknesses, identify the average age of the collection, and compare the collection to benchmark standards. Many vendors offer free collection analysis to their customers, enabling the LMS to compare results from more than one source. Both collection mapping and analysis document the status of the collection and prove that the LMS is building a relevant, current collection to meet curricular needs.

Deciphering and Disseminating the Data

Collecting local data, combining it with published research, and disseminating it to the community create an informed service population. A survey designed to measure the impact of advocating for the school library media program found that respondents reported a positive effect on their relationships with their principals and teachers (Lance & Callison, 2005). Eighty-one percent of respondents reported sharing the research with their principals. Many others disseminated the information to their superintendents, other administrators, technology staff, and/or parents while 66% shared it with teachers. As a result of sharing this information, the survey revealed that almost half reported "their students now have access to more electronic information (48%) and larger collections (45%)" (Lance & Callison, 2005, ¶ 22). "Two out of five respondents reported that classes and other groups now visit their school libraries more frequently (40%) and on more flexible schedules (39%)," and "more than a third of respondents (37%) report increased library visits by individuals" (Lance & Callison, 2005, ¶ 22).

After collecting data on various aspects of the program, create charts and reports to indicate the number of collaborative lessons, document how well the collection supports the curriculum, and/or demonstrate the need for additional funding. Incorporate usage statistics in combination with actual collaboration and instructional lessons to illustrate that the library media center impacts many on an individual basis. Most importantly, use the statistics and comments from the surveys, focus groups, and interviews to further reinforce the impact that the library media center has on the students' success as reported by teachers and students.

Once the data has been collected and deciphered, the LMS can disseminate it to appropriate audiences: classroom teachers, building-level administrators, district administration, local policy makers, and parents. Spread the message in a variety of ways. Present at faculty, PTO, school board, and board of supervisors meetings. Provide information for local newspapers and school newsletters. Create infomercials on the local cable channel, library newsletters, program brochures, and Web site announcements. Host special events for the community. Provide free workshops and training for classroom teachers, administrators, and parents.

It is important for the LMS to share the information collected beyond the local level. She can contact state and national policy makers; present at regional, state, and national conferences attended by classroom teachers, reading specialists, and principals; and publish articles in professional publications directed toward teachers and administrators.

The LMS who seeks and achieves National Board Certification adds further validity to her instructional role and contributions to student learning. Not only does achieving National Board Certification help teachers, parents, and administrators view the LMS as a qualified teacher, it also helps the LMS think reflectively and articulate how all activities in the school library media center impact student learning.

When disseminating the information, consider the intended audience. For instance, consider the leadership style of the principal as well as her knowledge and perception of the school library media center and her overall vision for the school. Johnson notes, "People don't buy a quarter-inch drill bit because they want a quarter-inch drill bit. They buy a quarter-inch drill bit because they want to create a quarter-inch hole" (Hartzell, 2002, p. 31). Likewise, principals want good school libraries and increased student achievement. Busy classroom teachers often focus on student performance via standardized tests. The LMS provides information to teachers by focusing on helping students perform better on these high-stakes tests. By demonstrating past successes with other teachers, use data to demonstrate how collaboration saves instructional time and shares the instructional responsibility. In addition, this paired instruction incorporates information literacy skills and curriculum standards maximizing student achievement.

Conclusions

Collecting data about one's program and citing the findings of research studies on the impact of the LMS on student learning and sound reasonable, but does this process really work? Examples from practicing LMS reports[1] demonstrate that collecting data and linking it to student learning does make a difference. For instance, when LMS Gordon's school district in Nevada received a bond to update the schools, the computer specialist informed her that he planned to use most of the money for two new computer labs but that he would "give" her $3,000. Before the committee met to decide on the disbursement of the funds, Lee pulled together data for her library media center. Lee said,

> I had been at the school about ten years and had end-of-year reports and stats for all ten years. I could show the collection age of the 500s and 600s was 1973 (the year the school was built), and it was now 1995 ... I charted the stats, made handouts showing budget allocations, age and percentage of the collection, dropping circulation in those areas, etc.

Lee reported that, when she concluded her report on how she needed the bond money to improve the science section of the collection to better support the curriculum and positively contribute to student achievement, there was a "stunned silence" followed by the committee's decision to award $20,000 of the bond money to Lee's library media center to update the science collection!

---

[1] Library Media Specialists were interviewed via email. Reported results originate from personal correspondences received February 28, 2008.

Davis, a high school library media specialist in Virginia, collects data on her program to demonstrate the impact on student learning by combining circulation statistics with library media center traffic. She collects traffic data via a clip-board sign-in sheet to track student visits that are in addition to the classes scheduled for library instruction or research. She reports that she has been able to successfully use the data with her principal to reinforce how much she and her staff support student learning. As an added bonus, because he knows how busy the library media center is as a result of this data, Betsy reports that "he doesn't ever ask us to cover classes or to do duties that many of our colleagues are asked to do."

Cavender at the American School of Doha in Doha, Qatar, used data to illustrate how vital her library media center is on student learning to gain more staffing. After collecting information on traffic counts, purpose for visits, scheduled classes, and circulations, Cavender stated, "All information is kept in tables and graphs and included in both monthly and annual reports. All of this is a lot of work, but with it I was able to prove . . . [that] our monthly circulations were equal to the annual circulation in the middle/high school library." Cavender exclaimed, "Having the numbers to prove we needed more help was invaluable!" As a result of these figures, staffing increased from one LMS and one assistant to two LMSs and three and one-half assistants.

Shaw, a district administrator in charge of school libraries in Anchorage, Alaska, successfully used data on collection age to demonstrate the need for increased funding. Shaw reported, "The final result was a community-approved bond for $3 million to refurbish the school library collections!" These funds made it possible to improve the collections to better accommodate student needs and support the curriculum.

These examples verify that using data makes a significant difference when proving the LMS's impact on student learning. Administrators, parents, and policy makers respond to facts and figures. Data can prove the importance, quality, and quantity of contributions to student learning and illustrate the need for increased funding for collection and staffing. While collecting data certainly takes time, such investment justifies requests and documents the LMS as a vital team-player in educating the nation's 21st-century learners.

References

American Association of School Librarians. (2003). *A report of the findings from six focus groups with K-12 parents, teachers, and principals, as well as middle and high school students*. Washington, DC: KRC Research.

American Association of School Librarians & Association for Educational Communications and Technology. (1998). *Information power: Building partnerships for learning*. Chicago: ALA.

Church, A. P. (2007). *Elementary school principals' perceptions of the instructional role of the school library media specialist*. Unpublished doctoral dissertation, Virginia Commonwealth University, Richmond.

Hartzell, G. (2002). The hole truth: Librarians need to emphasize what they have to offer. *School Library Journal, 48*(7), 31.

Ishizuka, K., Minkel, W., & St. Lifer, E. (2002). Biggest challenges for 2002. *School Library Journal, 48*(1), 50–53.

Kaplan, A. G. (2006). Benign neglect: Principals' knowledge of and attitudes towards school library media specialists (Doctoral dissertation, University of Delaware, 1990). *Dissertations Abstracts International, 67,* 1998.

Kolencik, P. L. (2001). Principals and teacher-librarians: building collaborative partnerships in the learning community (Doctoral dissertation, University of Pittsburg, 2001). *Dissertations Abstracts International, 62,* 1784.

Lance, K. C., & Callison, D. (2005). Enough already?: Blazing new trails for school library research: An interview with Keith Curry Lance, Director, Library Research Service, Colorado State Library & University of Denver. *SLMR, 8.*

Lau, D. (2002). What does your boss think about you? SLJ's survey reveals principals' lack of knowledge about the role of school librarians. *School Library Journal, 48*(9), 52–55.

Loertscher, D. (1996). *Collection mapping in the LMC: Building access in a world of technology.* Salt Lake City, UT: Hi Willow Research and Publishing.

Loertscher, D., Woolls, B., & Felker, J. (1999). *Building a school library collection plan: A beginning handbook with internet assist.* Salt Lake City, UT: Hi Willow Research and Publishing.

Lowe, K. (2001). *Resource alignment: Providing curriculum support in the school library media center.* Millers Creek, NC: Beacon Education Consulting Services.

Mardis, M. (2007). School libraries and science achievement: A view from Michigan's middle schools. *SLMR, 10.*

Olson, R. (1996). Principals give short shrift to librarians' curricular role. *School Library Journal, 42*(1), 12–13.

School libraries work! (3rd ed.). (2008). New York: Scholastic. Retrieved April 30, 2008, from http://www2.scholastic.com/content/collateral_resources/pdf/s/slw3_2008.pdf

Scott, L. (2004). *School library media centers: Selected results from the education longitudinal study of 2002.* National Center for Educational Statistics. Retrieved April 30, 2008, from http://nces.ed.gov/pubsearch/pubsinfo.asp?pubid=2005302

Small, R. V., Snyder, J., & Parker, K. (2008). *New York State's school libraries and library media specialists: An impact study, preliminary report.* New York: Syracuse University. Retrieved April 30, 2008, from http://www.nyla.org/content/user_19/Preliminary_Report_Small.pdf

Todd, R. J. (2003). School libraries & evidence: Seize the day, begin the future. *Library Media Connection, 22*(1), 12–18.

Wallace, D. P., & Van Fleet, C. (1994). The invisible librarian. *RQ, 34,* 6–9.

Recommended Resources

Baule, S. M. (2004). Politips for school librarians: Or, working with your administrators. *Knowledge Quest, 33*(1), 24–25.

Borsche, J. (2005). Marketing the school library. *PNLA Quarterly, 69*(3), 6, 26–28.

Bradburn, F. B. (1999). *Output measures for school library media programs.* New York: Neal-Schuman.

Burkman, A. (2004). A practical approach to marketing the school library. *Library Media Connection, 23*(3), 42–43.

Cassidy, A. (2002). No invisible librarians allowed: Visiting your library as a patron. *PNLA Quarterly, 66,* 5–6.

Church, A. P. (2002). Leverage your library program: What an administrator needs to know. *Library Media Connection, 22*(6), 32–33.

Church, A. P. (2003). *Leverage your library program to help raise test scores: A guide for library media specialists, principals, teachers, and parents.* Worthington, Ohio: Linworth.

Dempsey, K. (2002). Visibility: Decloaking "the invisible librarian". *Searcher, 10,* 77–81.

Everhart, N. (1998). *Evaluating the school library media center: Analysis techniques and research practices.* Westport, CT: Libraries Unlimited.

Fisher, J. D., & Hill, A. (2002). *Tooting your own horn: Web-based public relations for the 21st century librarian.* Worthington, OH: Linworth.

Fisher, P. H., & Pride, M. M. (2006). *Blueprint for your library marketing plan: A guide to help you survive and thrive.* Chicago: ALA.

Gallagher-Hayashi, D. (2001). Engaging your principal in your school library program. *Teacher Librarian, 28*(5), 13–17.

Hart, K. (1999). *Putting marketing ideas into action.* London: Library Association Publishing.

Hartzell, G. (1997). The invisible school librarian: Why other educators are blind to your value. *School Library Journal, 43*(11), 24–29.

Hartzell, G. (2002). Principals of success: Getting the boss's attention is crucial to your effectiveness. *School Library Journal, 48*(4), 41.

Hartzell, G. (2003). *Building influence for the school librarian: Tenets, targets & tactics* (2nd ed.). Worthington, OH: Linworth.

Hartzell, G. (2003). The power of audience: Effective communication with your principal. *Library Media Connection, 22*(2), 20–22.

Hartzell, G. (2003). Why should principals support school libraries? *Teacher Librarian, 31,* 21–23.

Howard, J. K., & Eckhardt, S. A. (2005). *Action research: A guide for library media specialists.* Worthington, OH: Linworth.

Jones, P., & Muller, K. (Eds.). (1991). *Great library promotion ideas VI: JCD library public relations award winners and notables 1990.* Chicago: ALA.

Junion-Metz, G., & Metz, D. L. (2002). *Instant web forms and surveys for children's/YA services and school libraries.* New York: Neal-Schuman.

Langhorne, M. J. (2005). Evidence-based practice: Show me the evidence! Using data in support of library media programs. *Knowledge Quest, 33*(5), 35–37.

McGhee, M. W., & Jansen, B. A. (2005). *The principal's guide to a powerful library media program.* Worthington, OH: Linworth.

Nebraska Educational Media Association. (2000). *Guide for developing and evaluating school library media programs* (6th ed.). Englewood, CO: Libraries Unlimited.

Oberg, D. (2006). Developing the respect and support of school administrators. *Teacher Librarian, 33*(3), 13–18.

Pitcher, S. M., & Mackey, B. (2004). *Collaborating for real literacy: Librarian, teacher, and principal.* Worthington, OH: Linworth.

Reed, D. (2005). Marian the Librarian meets NCLB. *Library Media Connection, 23*(7), 56–58.

Schrock, K. (2003). The ABC's of marketing. *School Library Journal, 49*(11), 36–37.

Weeks, A. C. (2001). Stop the whining. *School Library Journal, 47*(9), 56–57.

Weingand, D. (1997). *Customer service excellence: A concise guide for librarians.* Chicago: ALA.

Wilson, P., & MacNeil, A. J. (1988). In the dark: What's keeping principals from understanding libraries? *School Library Journal, 44*(9), 114–116.

Wilson, P. P., & Lynders, J. A. (2001). *Leadership for today's school library: A handbook for the library media specialist and the school principal.* Westport, CT: Greenwood Press.

Helpful Links

How to Write a Good Survey http://www.accesscable.net/~infopoll/tips.htm

School Library Impact Studies (Library Research Service – Keith Curry Lance) http://www.lrs.org/impact.php

The School Library Media Specialist (Gary Hartzell) http://eduscapes.com/sms/overview/hartzell.html

Selling Yourself and Your Services: Marketing the School Library. www.library.uq.edu.au/schools/slaq_marketing_2004.pdf

Survey & Questionnaire Design http://www.statpac.com/surveys/

The Survey System http://www.surveysystem.com/sdesign.htm

What is a Survey? http://www.whatisasurvey.info/

Your School library Media Program and No Child Left Behind (American Association of School Librarians) http://www.ala.org/ala/aasl/aaslpubsandjournals/aaslbooksandprod/aaslbooksproducts.cfm#nclb

Principal Support of Media Specialist and Teacher Collaboration: A Research Study

Betty J. Morris

Abstract   This descriptive research study examined principal support of collaboration in Georgia schools designated as having exemplary library media programs from the perspective of media specialists, classroom teachers and principals. A pilot study generated a survey instrument to be used for the exemplary school media program study. The literature on collaboration is well covered; however, literature about the principal's influence on collaboration is becoming an issue of concern. The purpose of this study established principal support of collaboration between media specialists and classroom teachers in Georgia schools with exemplary library media programs. Twelve schools, designated as meeting this criteria, received questionnaires mailed to media specialists, classroom teachers and principals. The hypothesis of the study explored schools with exemplary media programs and principals who support collaboration between media specialists and classroom teachers. The findings for the study supported the hypothesis. Based on the conclusions of the study, principals need to identify improvements to be made in their support of collaboration.

Keywords   School Library Media · Teacher Collaboration · Library Support · Academic Achievement · School Principal Leadership

Introduction and Literature Review

Effective school principals, unique as instructional leaders in their schools, guide teachers in better developing their teaching roles. Because principals identify themselves as teachers, they are knowledgeable about what teachers do and how to support them; however, the same is not true when they need to support the media specialist as a collaborator with classroom teachers in instruction. The role of the media specialist in the instructional process is, unfortunately, not thoroughly understood by most school principals because they lack similar background. Hartzell

B.J. Morris (✉)
Jacksonville State University, Jacksonville, Alabama 36265-1602
e-mail: bmorris@jsu.edu

M. Orey et al. (eds.), *Educational Media and Technology Yearbook*,
DOI 10.1007/978-0-387-09675-9_20, © Springer Science+Business Media, LLC 2009

(2002) lists reasons for the importance of principal support in school library media programs stating: "Principals should support school libraries because it is in both their students' and their own best interest to do so. Quality library media programs can enhance student achievement, and informed, committed librarians can help principals enhance their own administrative practice" (p. 1). Principals benefit when they support school media centers, as well as media specialists and classroom teachers, because they are perceived as effective administrators who involve all faculty in instruction and because student achievement is improved.

The principal is responsible for encouraging and facilitating collaboration among classroom teachers and media specialists. Collaboration is enabled when the principal places emphasis on the school culture that fosters a harmonious working environment. The principal fosters this environment most by supporting resource based learning and learner engagement with instructional tools such as the Internet, current information, and Web 2.0 collaborative tools, such as wikis, blogs, and other technological innovations.

According to Hartzell (2002), school library media specialists may have a "discernibly positive impact on student achievement" as supported by fifty years of supporting research (p. 1). Yet principals continue to ignore this evidence. Wilson and Blake (1993) contend this failure to recognize school library media specialist's potential because such data is not covered in administrator journals. There is evidence in the literature that collaboration has not been defined properly so that everyone who practices it will be striving to do the same kind of collaboration. Normally, it is defined in three stages.

Stages/Levels of Collaboration

Hughes-Hassell and Wheelock (2001) define collaboration in three stages: cooperation where the media specialist serves as the provider of resources for the teacher and not co-teaching with the classroom teacher; coordination where the media specialist is the provider of resources for the teacher with some minimal teaching; and finally collaboration brings together the media specialist and classroom teacher planning instruction, developing instructional materials, evaluating students' work and teaching the lessons. The subject of this research is the last stage of collaboration described above.

Two earlier books set the stage for the initial development of collaboration between school library media specialists and classroom teachers. Turner (1988) wrote *Helping Teachers Teach*, the first instructional design book written specifically for school library media specialists to collaborate with classroom teachers. Three levels of collaboration noted in this book include: passive participation level, the reaction level and the action/education level. The name of the levels changed in later editions of the book to initial, moderate and in-depth. Loertscher (1988) showed eight levels of the teacher taxonomy. At the higher levels, that taxonomy portrays the teacher and media specialist as partners in the instructional process.

Information Power: Partnerships for Learning (AASL & AECT, 1998), the national school library guidelines, supports the concept of the media specialist working as a partner with other educators. At least two principles in the guidelines reinforce the idea that media specialists need support of the principal in collaborative planning with teachers. For example, Principle 3: Learning and Teaching notes, "The library media specialist models and promotes collaborative planning and curriculum development" (p. 4). Principle 4: Program Administration: explains, "An effective library media program requires ongoing administrative support" (p. 100). The new AASL Standards for 21st Century Learners (2007) continue to support collaboration as a practice for media specialists, concluding: "School librarians collaborate with others to provide instruction, learning strategies, and practice in using the essential learning skills needed in the 21st century" (p. 3). Since *Information Power* (1988), the standards continue to provide support for collaboration between media specialists and classroom teachers. A major concern in the literature is the principal's support of collaboration and its effect on the process.

Leadership of the Principal

When the principal works to facilitate school library media specialists and classroom teacher collaboration, student achievement improves according to research (Lance, Rodney, & Hamilton-Pennell, 2000; Lance, Rodney, & Hamilton-Pennell, 2005; Baughman, 2000; Baumbach, 2003). Thus, it is crucial that principals support such collaborative instruction. Communication and a harmonious working environment, where there is a feeling of trust and mutual respect (Brown, 2004; Buzzeo, 2002), encourage collaboration. For that reason, principals need to communicate that collaboration is expected through both written and spoken words as well as by their deeds (Hay & Henri, 1995; Haycock, 1999; Oberg, 1997; Pounder, 1998; Tallman & van Deusen, 1994a, 1994b). Futhermore, principals should clearly communicate methods for measuring teacher/media specialist collaboration. For example, media specialists may document teacher planning meetings or showcase student work. Principals may ask teachers for documentation of collaboration projects partnered with the media specialist in their annual evaluations. According to Bishop and Larimer (1999), administrative support is essential because the likelihood of collaboration being practiced is greater when principals ask classroom teachers how they are using the expertise of the media specialist in their teaching. Morris (2004) suggests that the principal may offer substitutes for teachers to collaboratively plan with the media specialist. This action clearly shows principal support of the practice.

Principal support of collaboration is evidenced by verbal rewards that promote instructional activity. The principal seals this message by physically attending collaborative events. A culture of collaboration is encouraged by open communication among all faculty members. Repeating this message in written communications provides an added impetus for teachers and media specialists to continue their work together. As far back as 1944, Liderman recognized principal support as a vital educational component, a truism which remains valid today.

Research on Collaboration and Its Effect on Student Achievement

According to Champlain and Loertscher (2003), "good things happen" when collaboration includes two or more teachers working together and when all educators can offer their professional expertise (p. 67). In this case, students have the support of two or more teachers instead of one and double or triple the expert content knowledge. Research has supported that collaboration increases student achievement.

According to Lance (2001), there have been approximately 75 studies on the impact of school library media programs on academic achievement over the past twenty-five years. Research done in 15 states indicates that student achievement scores can be increased when certain components are in place, one of which is collaboration between library media specialist and classroom teachers (Lance et al., 2005; Lance, Rodney, & Hamilton-Pennell, 2002; Lance, 2001; Lance et al., 2000). According to Champlain, Loertscher, and Eib (2004) in schools where student achievement is improved, the media specialist serves as an information coach and a learning consultant collaborating with teachers to build information and technology-rich environments. In these schools, the principal "plays a significant role in financial support and leadership" (p. 55). It is this kind of support and leadership that is examined in this research study of exemplary library media programs.

Background and Purpose

The purpose of the research study determined principal support of collaborative efforts between school library media specialist and classroom teachers in Georgia schools with exemplary school library media programs. The hypothesis of the study suggested that schools with exemplary school library media programs would exhibit strong collaboration of school library media specialists and classroom teachers because principals in those schools would be supportive of collaborative efforts. This assumption, based on a statement by Haycock (1982), stated that "exemplary school resource centers are characterized by strong administrative support" (p. 39). The researchers expected that exemplary school library media programs would exhibit strong collaboration between school library media specialists and classroom teachers because principals in those schools would be supportive of collaboration. These exemplary school library programs would provide a backdrop setting where principal support for collaboration could be examined in depth.

Exemplary Media Programs in Georgia

Schools with exemplary library media programs in Georgia, chosen by the State Department of Education, possess a level of quality and quantity of service beyond that of other schools. Entry-level media specialists in Georgia are required to hold a master's degree in library media. Their role as a media specialist requires them to collaborate with teachers in:

- designing instruction
- providing flexible scheduling so that collaboration can take place
- promoting reading
- integrating technology into the curriculum
- providing a comprehensive collection of library resources in a variety of learning styles
- administering the school library media program
- teaching information literacy for lifelong learning.

A school may nominate itself or be nominated by another school as one worthy of being designated as an exemplary school library media program. A school committee evaluates the school's library media program using a rubric on a Likert scale of basic, proficient, and exemplary programs using 18 target indicators. To meet such criteria, a school must demonstrate that it meets the proficiency level of all the target indicators and at least 14 of the indicators showing evidence of meeting the exemplary level indicators. An exemplary program meets the following target indicators as described below:

1. Fosters critical thinking skills and independent inquiry;
2. Promotes instructional collaboration between classroom teachers and media specialists;
3. Uses a variety of teaching styles to meet diverse learning needs of students;
4. Establishes a critical element in the school's reading program;
5. Designs activities in collaboration that leads to student achievement;
6. Uses a variety of collaboratively designed tools for assessing student achievement;
7. Employs a full-time media specialist and a full-time paraprofessional available throughout the school day;
8. Maintains flexible scheduling to allow collaboration between media specialist and teachers;
9. Exceeds minimum square footage requirements to accommodate large and small groups and individuals working simultaneously;
10. Meets Georgia electronic distribution system requirements;
11. Provides access to databases, Internet, and other library media resources on a LAN throughout the school;
12. Utilizes OPAC resources in MARC format available on LAN throughout school;
13. Provides instruction in using Galileo (virtual library) in an organized manner;
14. Maintains communications among media specialists in the school district;
15. Takes a leadership role (principal) in encouraging teachers to integrate library media resource into the curriculum and fostering a climate of collaboration;

16. Establishes a library media committee effective in the development of library media policy, for example, budget, technology plans, acquisition of resources and reconsideration of materials;
17. Sets clear and comprehensive policies that are reviewed annually by a media advisory committee;
18. Serves as a partner (media specialist) in planning the budget with administrators;
19. Enhances media specialist's professional skills by attending conferences and planning staff development workshops[1] (Georgia Department of Education, 2008).

Schools meeting these criteria exhibit quality library media program standards that exceed those met in the average school in Georgia.

Methodology

Information Power (AASL & AECT, 1998) provided a foundation for the pilot study determining 10 main category questions and subheadings to be used in the questionnaire. Three schools participated in the pilot study (one elementary, one middle and one high school) to determine the appropriateness of the survey questions at each level. The validity of the questionnaire, established by media specialists in the pilot study, offered feedback for wording and category changes. The reliability of the questionnaire, tested using a Cronbach's alpha, resulted in 0.978. Cronbach's alpha measures the reliability consistency of a survey instrument. With the 10 questions and subheadings determined, 207 questionnaires were mailed to 12 Georgia schools with exemplary school media programs as awarded by the Georgia State Department of Education. Three different participants in the study (principals, media specialists and 15 teachers in each identified school) received questionnaires gathering quantitative data for the study. The following chart illustrates the number of surveys mailed and returned as well as the number of respondents in each category (Table 1):

Table 1 Demographics of surveys numbers sent to Georgia Exemplary Media Schools

Recipents	Surveys sent	Surveys returned
Media Specialist	15	12 (80%)
Principal	12	12 (100%)
Teacher	180	78 (44%)

---

[1] The rubric is available at: http://www.glc.k12.ga.us/passwd/trc/ttools/attach/mediaspec/exemplary/Rubric07.pdf.
Nominations may be made online. The Georgia State Department of Education selects six outstanding media programs annually, two each at the elementary, middle, and high school level (Georgia Department of Education, 2008).

The return rate for surveys mailed showed media specialists (80%), principals (100%), but lower for teachers (44%).

Findings

The survey contained ten main questions to determine how supportive the three respondents perceived principal support of collaboration between school library media specialists and classroom teachers. Within each of the ten questions, subcategories existed. All three respondents, basically asked the same questions, identified different perceptions of the respondents. Questions for the study are identified below and problem areas precede the significant findings reported in the tables between the three different respondents: principals, media specialists and teachers. A Kruskal-Wallis ANOVA, used comparing multiple independent variables, measured ordinal data, such as the Likert scale used in the study. In the cases of no significant difference, all three respondents perceived the principal to be supportive of collaboration between media specialists and classroom teachers.

Question One dealt with how supportive the principal is in these several areas:

a. Supporting collaboration between the media specialist and the classroom teacher;
b. Recommending collaboration in faculty meetings;
c. Attending grade/subject level meetings;
d. Expecting school library media specialists to attend grade level/subject level meetings;
e. Evaluating teachers on collaborative activities with media specialists;
f. Supporting flexible scheduling in school library media center;
g. Asking teachers and media specialists to collaborate or work together on projects.

Table 2 Finding of significance with principal support with question 1f

Question	Position	N	Mean Rank	Chi-Square	Df	Sig.
1f. Supporting flexible scheduling in school library media center				7.84	2	0.020
	Media Specialist	12	66.50			
	Principal	10	55.7			
	Teacher	77	46.69			

Media specialists and principals perceived the principal as supporting flexible scheduling to a greater extent than did the teachers. All other categories were perceived to be supported by the three respondents.

Question 2 series demonstrated no disagreement on any of the questions about "How supportive is the principal of teachers and media specialists in the following activities":

a. Planning content lessons together;
b. Teaching content lessons together;
c. Teaching information literacy skills (research) together;
d. Evaluating lessons taught together.

Because the three respondents identified the principal as supportive of the four categories above, it shows agreement of the activities they perceive as collaborative between the media specialist and classroom teachers.

Question 3 series also found no disagreement on any of the questions about "What level of support does the principal show the school library media center by:"

a. Attending program events;
b. Reading to students during story time;
c. Being present in the school library media center for events;
d. Offering substitutes so classroom teachers and media specialists can plan collaboratively;
e. Evaluating school library media specialist and teacher collaboration as part of annual review.

The principal was perceived by all three respondents as supportive in the five categories noted.

Question 4 series found a significant difference between the media specialist and the principal when compared to the teacher on questions about how much support does the principal show the school library media specialist by: sub questions 4a, 4e, and 4f (see Table 3) were found to be statistically different.

a. Appointing to leadership positions in the school;
b. Becoming actively involved in the media advisory committee;
c. Planning together how the whole school might collaborate;
d. Promoting the information literacy (research) curriculum of the school library media specialist;
e. Giving the school library media specialist leadership responsibilities that promote visibility within the school and so forth;
f. Communicating to teachers the school library media center's contribution to student learning.

The principal was perceived by all three respondents to be supportive in the three sub-questions 4b, 4c, and 4d.

Table 3 Responses to "How much support does the principal show the school library media specialist by"

Question	Position	N	Mean rank	Chi-square	Df	Sig.
4a. Appointing to leadership positions in the school				12.379	2	0.002
	Media Specialist	12	68.0			
	Principal	10	63.2			
	Teacher	77	45.5			
4f. Giving the school library media specialist leadership responsibilities that promote visibility within the school and so forth.				8.98	2	0.011
	Media Specialist	12	68.5			
	Principal	10	59.00			
	Teacher	79	47.3			
4g. Communicating to teachers the school library media center's contribution to student learning				10.2	2	0.006
	Media Specialist	12	70.63			
	Principal	10	60.55			
	Teacher	79	46.81			

In all three categories in the above table, the media specialist and the principal when compared to teachers perceived the principal as more supportive than did the teachers.

Question 5 series demonstrated no disagreement on any of the questions about how well does the media specialist do the following:

a. Show an interest in teachers and their curriculum;
b. Actively invite classroom teachers to collaborate on curriculum projects;
c. Show enjoyment in working with classroom teachers.

The media specialist was perceived by all three respondents to be supportive in the three categories above.

Question 6 only showed two sub-questions to be of significant difference. In both questions the difference was between the media specialist and the teachers (see Table 4). The major question was "How well do collegial partnerships between school library media specialist and classroom teachers":

a. Show a positive influence on the instructional program of the school;
b. Connect content standards (QCC) and information literacy standards (ALA) in planning lessons;
c. Show a variety of resources used in teaching, including media in many formats;
d. Promote sharing of teaching duties;
e. Promote the philosophy that the school library media specialist is central to the learning process;
f. Promote school library media specialists as proactive leaders in instruction.

Table 4 How well do collegial partnerships between school library media specialist and classroom teachers

Question	Position	N	Mean rank	Chi-square	Df	Sig.
6e. Promote the philosophy that the school library media specialist is central to the learning process				6.14	2	0.046
	Media Specialist	12	63.63			
	Principal	10	58.55			
	Teacher	77	46.77			
6f. Promote school library media specialists as proactive leaders in instruction				6.54	2	0.038
	Media Specialist	12	64.46			
	Principal	10	57.80			
	Teacher	77	46.73			

The collegiality of classroom teachers and media specialists were perceived by all three respondents to be supportive in the four sub-questions 6a, 6b, 6c and 6d above.

In the two categories in the above table, the media specialists perceived that more collegiality was supported by principals than did teachers.

Question 7 series demonstrated no disagreement on any of the questions about How well does the school library media specialist display the following characteristics that are needed for collaboration with teachers to take place:

a. Takes initiative for initial contact for collaboration;
b. Shows confidence in abilities to work with classroom teachers;
c. Possesses excellent communication skills;
d. Encourages classroom teachers to collaborate on planning lessons.

All respondents perceived that the media specialist displayed the above four characteristics when collaborating with teachers.

Question 8 "How well does the principal make collaboration attractive to classroom media specialists and classroom teachers by:" (Had one sub question where both media specialist and principal answered significantly different than did the responding teachers (see Table 5)).

a. Helping both teachers and classroom teachers to develop similar instructional goals;
b. Providing meeting structure where classroom teachers and school library media specialist can share ideas for student learning;
c. Creating an environment of trust and mutual respect between school library media specialists and classroom teachers;
d. Encouraging collaborative curriculum planning between school library media specialists and classroom teachers;
e. Encouraging school library media specialists to be proactive leaders in the school.

Table 5 Principal support making collaboration attractive to classroom media specialists and teachers by

Question	Position	N	Mean rank	Chi-square	Df	Sig.
8e. Encouraging school library				7.341	2	0.025
media specialists to be	Media					
proactive leaders in the	Specialist	12	65.88			
school	Principal	10	61.85			
	Teacher	78	46.68			

All respondents perceived the principal to be supportive of the four sub questions 8a, 8b, 8c, 8d.

Both the media specialist and the principal perceived the principal as being more encouraging than did teachers in sub-question 8e.

Question 9 How well does the principal promote any or all of the environmental factors that affect collaboration: found significant differences between how media specialist and principals were perceived when compared to teachers on three sub questions (see Table 6).

a. Scheduling common planning times of school library media specialists and classroom teachers;
b. Supporting collaborative meetings for planning between classroom teachers and school library media specialists;
c. Supporting impromptu discussions about lessons between the school library media specialist and classroom teachers;
d. Defining roles within the collaborative group;

Table 6 Principal promotion of any or all of environmental factors affecting collaboration?

Question	Position	N	Mean rank	Chi-square	Df	Sig.
9b. Supporting collaborative				10.80	2	0.005
meetings for planning	Media					
between classroom teachers	Specialist	12	65.54			
and school library media	Principal	10	69.0			
specialists.	Teacher	77	45.11			
9c. Supporting impromptu				11.37	2	0.003
discussions about lessons	Media					
between the school library	Specialist	12	70.67			
media specialist and	Principal	10	62.85			
classroom teachers	Teacher	77	45.11			
9e. Supporting a flexible	Media	12	69.25 46.40	7.716	2	0.021
schedule for the media center	Specialist	10	46.79			
so collaboration can take	Principal	76				
place.	Teacher					

Table 7 Promoting the school library media specialist as a proactive team leader

Question	Position	N	Mean rank	Chi-square	Df	Sig.
10a. Promoting the school library media specialist as a proactive team leader				11.14	2	0.004
	Media Specialist	12	67.00			
	Principal	10	62.65			
	Teacher	77	45.71			

e. Supporting a flexible schedule for the media center so collaboration can take place;

f. Providing full-time clerical assistance so the school library media specialist has the opportunity to collaborate with classroom teachers.

All three respondents perceived that the principal provided support in environmental factors that affect collaboration in sub-questions 9a, 9d and 9 f.

In all three categories in Table 6, when compared to teachers, the media specialist and the principal perceived the principal as more supportive than did the teachers in supporting environmental factors that affect collaboration.

Question 10 How well does the principal support the following social factors that affect collaboration? Had one subset of questions between how media specialist and principals and teachers responded to the sub question (see Table 7).

a. Promoting the school library media specialist as a proactive team leader;

b. Sharing vision of learning with collaborative team;

c. Promoting open communication between classroom teachers and school library media specialists;

d. Cultivating trust and mutual respect between school library media specialists and classroom teachers.

All three respondents perceived the principal as supporting social factors that affect collaboration in sub-questions 10b, 10c, and 10d.

Both the principal and the media specialist perceived the principal as promoting the media specialist as a proactive team leader than did the teacher.

Conclusions

The findings of the study reveal the following conclusions: (a) Principals in schools with exemplary library media programs show support for collaboration between media specialists and classroom teachers. (b)Exemplary library media programs may be exemplary because of strong collaboration support of the principal. (c) The principal support offered has an effect on collaboration. (d) Principals perceive themselves positively as supportive; however, (e) media specialists and principals perceive more positive aspects of collaboration than teachers. (f) Although teachers and media specialists perceive the principal as supportive of collaboration; it is the media specialist who gives the principal a higher rating. (g) Principals need to make improvements in how they communicate and support collaboration with classroom teachers. Each conclusion is presented below with the connections to the literature.

Principals in schools with exemplary library media programs show support for collaboration between media specialists and classroom teachers. There may be a connection between collaboration in these schools and their being chosen as having exemplary library media programs. This finding supports the hypothesis of the study. Obviously, principals in these schools became knowledgeable about media centers' contribution to student achievement and fostering of exemplary programs. According to Kachel (2006), this knowledge is not common because most school administrators know very little about school media centers and their relationship to student achievement or how to cultivate an outstanding library media program. Few stakeholders fully understand nor acknowledge the role of the library media center's role in student achievement (Todd, 2008). However, in these exemplary schools, principals are knowledgeable.

Exemplary library media programs may be exemplary because of strong collaboration support of the principal. There are many factors that define "exemplary" but strong evidence exists illustrating collaboration support may be a benchmark in selection of the schools designated as exemplary.

Principal support affects collaboration in schools. According to Hartzell (2002), it is in their own best interest as the instructional leader of the school to support collaboration because it can enhance student achievement. Hay and Henri (1995) suggest that the principal is responsible for ensuring that all teachers in the school are actively and effectively involved in the instructional program. According to Dorrell (1995), the principal must understand the role of the media specialist in the instructional process in collaboration with teachers and offer support to assist in student learning.

Media specialists and principals perceive more positive aspects of collaboration than teachers. The library media specialist is in a better position to determine principal support than teachers because they have a wide-angle view as the initiator of collaboration, whereas, teachers are more passive in seeking to collaborate. The principal and media specialist are more aware of the principal's involvement in flexible scheduling and monetary support because they are factors that are directly related to the library media center.

Principals in schools with exemplary library media programs perceive themselves positively as supporting collaboration between school library media specialists and classroom teachers. It is the leadership of the principal that determines the level of collaboration possible and that develops a school environment conducive to supporting effective teaching and learning. Within this school environment, student library use and classroom teacher/library media specialist collaboration are both valued and promoted (Campbell & Cordiero, 1996; Wilson & Lyders, 2001). Also critical to this school environment is a flexible schedule controlled by the principal

allowing for collaboration (McGregor, 2002; van Deusen & Tallman, 1994). Therefore, the principal influences the learning environment and enhances instructional
partnerships between classroom teachers and media specialists.

*Teachers and media specialists perceive the principal as supportive of collabo-
ration; however, it is the media specialist who gives the principal a higher rating.*
Media specialists are more aware of principal support of collaboration because it is
reflected in how the media center functions, the services it provides, and its staffing
that allows collaboration to occur. Classroom teachers may be unaware of collaborative efforts of the principal in certain instances; however, the media specialist may
be fully aware which would account for the media specialists giving the principal
higher ratings than classroom teachers.

*Principals need to make improvements in how they communicate and support
collaboration with classroom teachers.* Because teachers did not perceive the principal as supportive of collaboration as much as media specialists, an exerted effort
needs to be made to show evidence of principal support for teachers as they agree
to collaborate. The principal must provide activities that cultivate trust and mutual
respect between media specialists and teachers by making it clear that much can
be gained through increased student achievement when they collaborate. Principals
need to clearly define the roles of the teachers and the roles of the media specialists
when collaboration takes place so they know what to expect and how they need to
proceed when collaborating with each other. The principal can show great support of
collaboration by physically attending grade/subject level meetings when classroom
teachers and media specialists are planning collaboratively.

Findings for this research study support ideas from the literature. This study did
not look at student achievement as it relates to collaboration such as those studies
done by Lance and others. (Baughman, 2000; Baumbach, 2003; Lance et al., 2000;
Lance, 2001; Lance et al., 2002, 2005). This study looked at exemplary library
media programs and perceptions of media specialists, principals, and teachers of
principal support of collaboration. All of these studies are related because collaboration affects student achievement and principal's support affects collaboration.
This study confirms the idea that communication, mutual trust and respect are factors (Brown, 2004; Buzzeo, 2002) that the principal controls in the school environment when collaboration is practiced. The hypothesis of the study that principals in
schools with exemplary library media programs support collaboration proved to be
valid in this study.

Further Research

This research study needs to be extended in three ways. This study needs to be
replicated in schools where national board certified media specialists are employed
to determine principal support of collaboration compared to the current study. As a
replication study, it will ask the same questions of principals, media specialists and
teachers as the current study. A general sample of schools employing certified media

specialists should be compared with studies of exemplary library media programs such as this one, asking the same questions. Further, a qualitative study could provide insight on specific methods employed for collaboration in exemplary schools and its effect on student achievement. This type of study would enhance a more in-depth coverage of what types of support are most effective for generating greater collaboration at the school level.

References

American Association of School Librarians. (2007). *Standards for the 21st-century learner.* Retrieved June 9, 2008, from http://www.ala.org/aasl/standards

American Association of School Librarians and Association of Educational Communication and Technology. (1988). *Information power: Guidelines of the school library media program.* Chicago: American Library Association.

American Association of School Librarians and Association of Educational Communication and Technology. (1998). *Information power: Partnerships for learning.* Chicago: American Library Association.

Baughman, J. C. (2000). *School libraries and MCAS scores.* Retrieved June 9, 2008, from http://web.simmons.edu/~baughman/mcas-school-libraries/Baughman%20Paper.pdf

Baumbach, D. (2003). *Making the grade: The status of school library media centers in the sunshine state and how they contribute to student achievement.* Retrieved June 9, 2008, from http://132.170.176.110/makingthegrade/summary.pdf

Bishop, K., & Larimer, N. (1999, October). Literacy through collaboration. *Teacher Librarian, 27*(1), 15–20.

Brown, C. (2004, October). America's most wanted: Teachers who collaborate. *Teacher Librarian, 32*(1), 6 & 13. Retrieved June 9, 2008, from http://www.teacherlibrarian.com/tlmag/v_32/v_32_1_brown.html

Buzzeo, T. (2002, September). Disciples of collaboration. *School Library Journal, 48*(9), 34.

Campbell, B. S., & Cordiero, P. A. (1996). *High school principal roles and implementation themes for mainstreaming information literacy instruction* (ERIC Document Reproduction Service No. ED399667). Paper presented at the annual meeting of the American Education Research Association, New York City.

Champlain, C., & Loertscher, D. (2003, March). Reinvent your school's library and watch student achievement increase. *Principal leadership.* Retrieved on June 9, 2008, from http://www.indianalearns.org/downloads/principalleadership.pdf

Champlain, C., Loertscher, D. V., & Eib, B. J. (2004, April). Creating a digital-age school library. *Principal leadership.* Retrieved on June 9, 2008, from http://www.indianalearns.org/downloads/digitalagelibrary.pdf

Dorrell, L. D. (1995). What are principals' perceptions of the school library media specialist? *NASSP bulletin.* Retrieved on June 9, 2008, from http://bul.sagepub.com/cgi/content/abstract/79/573/72

Georgia Department of Education. (2008). *Georgia's exemplary library media center program.* Retrieved on June 9, 2008, from http://www.glc.k12.ga.us/pandp/media/exemplary.htm

Hartzell, G. (2002, November). Why should principals support school libraries? *ERIC digest.* Retrieved on June 9, 2008, from http://www.ericdigests.org/2003-3/libraries.htm

Hay, L., & Henri, J. (1995). *Leadership for collaboration: Making vision work.* Paper presented at 61st IFLA General Conference, August 20–25, 1995. Retrieved on June 9, 2008, from http://www.ifla.org/IV/ifla61/61-hayl.htm

Haycock, K. (1982). Getting to first base: Developing support from school principals. *School Libraries in Canada, 1*(3), 17–18.

Haycock, K. (1999). Fostering collaboration, leadership, and information literacy: Common behaviors of uncommon principals and faculties. *NAASP bulletin, 83*(605), 8287. (ERIC Document Reproduction Service No. EJ585580).

Hughes-Hassell, S., & Wheelock, A. (2001). *The information-powered school.* Chicago: American Association of School Librarians.

Kachel, D. E. (2006, November). Educating your principal. *School Library Media Activities Monthly, 23*(3), 48–50.

Lance, K. C. (2001). Proof of the power: Quality library media programs affect student achievement. *Multimedia schools.* Retrieved on June 9, 2008, from http://www.infotoday.com/mmschools/sep01/lance.htm

Lance, K. C., Rodney, M. J., & Hamilton-Pennell, C. (2000). *How school libraries help kids achieve standards.* Denver, CO: Denver Library Research Service. Retrieved on June 9, 2008, from http://www.lrs.org/impact.php

Lance, K. C., Rodney, M. J., & Hamilton-Pennell, C. (2002). *Making the connection: Quality school library media programs impact student achievement in Iowa.* Bettendorf, Iowa: Mississippi Bend Area Education Agency. Retrieved on June 9, 2008, from, http://www.iowaaeaonline.org/about/Make%20The%20Connection1.pdf

Lance, K. C., Rodney, M. J., & Hamilton-Pennell, C. (2005). *Powerful libraries make powerful learners: The Illinois study.* Retrieved on June 9, 2008, from http://www.alliancelibrarysystem.com/illinoisstudy/TheStudy.pdf

Liderman, W. B. (1944). What should a librarian expect of the school principal? *The School Review,* 611–617.

Loertscher, D. V. (1988). *Taxonomies of the school library media program.* Englewood, CO: Libraries Unlimited.

McGregor, J. (2002). Flexible scheduling: How does a principal facilitate implementation? *School Libraries Worldwide, 8*(1), 71–84.

Morris, B. J. (2004). *Administering the school library media center* (4th ed.). Westport, CT: Libraries Unlimited.

Oberg, D. (1997). The principal's role in empowering collaboration between teacher-librarians and teachers: Research findings. *Scan, 16*(3), 6–8.

Pounder, D. G. (Ed.). (1998). *Restructuring schools for collaboration: Promises and pitfalls.* Albany, NY: SUNY Press.

Tallman, J., & van Deusen, J. (1994a). Collaborative unit planning-schedule, time and participants. *School Library Media Quarterly, 23*(1), 33–37. (ERIC Document Reproduction Service No. EJ493343).

Tallman, J., & van Deusen, J. (1994b). External conditions as they relate to curriculum consultation and information literacy skills instruction by school library media specialists. *School Library Media Quarterly, 23*(1), 27–31. (ERIC Document Reproduction Service No. EJ493342).

Todd, R. (2008, April). The evidence-based manifesto. *School Library Journal, 54*(4), 39–43.

Turner, P. (1988). *Helping teachers teach.* Englewood, CO: Libraries Unlimited.

van Deusen, J., & Tallman, J. (1994). The impact of scheduling on curriculum consultation and information skills instruction. *School Library Media Quarterly, 23*(1), 17–25. (ERIC Document Reproduction Service No. EJ493341).

Wilson, P. J., & Blake, M. (1993). The missing piece: A school library media center component in principal-preparation programs. *Record in Educational Leadership, 12*(2), 65–68.

Wilson, P. P., & Lyders, J. A. (2001). *Leadership for today's school library: A handbook for the library media specialist and the school principal.* Westport, CT: Greenwood Press.

Part III
Leadership Profiles

Introduction

Robert Maribe Branch

The purpose of this section is to profile individuals who have made significant contributions to the field of educational media and communication technology. Leaders profiled in the *Educational Media and Technology Yearbook* have typically held prominent offices, composed seminal works and made significant contributions that have influenced the contemporary vision of the field. The people profiled in this section have often been directly responsible for mentoring individuals, who have themselves, become recognized for their contributions in one way or another.

There are special reasons to feature people of national and international renown. This volume of the *Educational Media and Technology Yearbook* profiles an individual who continues to uphold the tradition of leadership in educational media and communication technology. The leader profiled this year is:

Addie Kinsinger

The following people [alphabetically listed] were profiled in earlier volumes of the *Educational Media and Technology Yearbook*:

John C. Belland	Kent Gustafson
Robert K. Branson	John Hedberg
James W. Brown	Robert Heinich
Bob Casey	Stanley A. Huffman
Betty Collis	Harry Alleyn Johnson
Robert E. De Kieffer	Roger Kaufman
Robert M. Diamond	Jean E. Lowrie
Walter Dick	Wesley Joseph McJulien
Frank Dwyer	M. David Merrill
Donald P. Ely	Michael Molenda
James D. Finn	David Michael Moore
Robert Mills Gagné	Robert M. Morgan
Castelle (Cass) G. Gentry	Robert Morris
Thomas F. Gilbert	James Okey

R.M. Branch (✉)
The University of Georgia, Athens, GA 30602-7144
e-mail: rbranch@uga.edu

M. Orey et al., *Educational Media and Technology Yearbook*,
DOI 10.1007/978-0-387-09675-9_21, © Springer Science+Business Media, LLC 2009

Ronald Oliver   Howard Sullivan
Tjeerd Plomp   William Travers
Rita C. Richey   Constance Dorothea Weinman
Paul Saettler   Paul Welliver
Wilbur Schramm   Paul Robert Wendt
Charles Francis Schuller   David R. Krathwohl
Don Carl Smellie

There is no formal survey or popularity contest to determine the persons for whom the profiles are written. People profiled in this section are usually emeritus faculty who may or may not be active in the field. You are welcome to nominate individuals to be featured in this section. Your nomination of someone to be profiled in this section must also be accompanied by the name of the person who agrees to compose the leadership profile. Please direct comments, questions and suggestions about the selection process to the Senior Editor.

Addie Kinsinger: Leader Among Leaders

Patricia Miller

Any conversation with Addie Kinsinger about her profession as an educator begins with her passion for the importance of leadership development. While her career path has taken her in several directions over the years, the focus of her professional mission has remained intact: the value of the human element in teaching and learning. Whether the setting was a classroom, a library/media center, or a television station, Addie inspired students and colleagues to explore, take risks, and grow.

P. Miller (✉)
KNPB Public Television, Reno, Nevada
e-mail: patricimiller2383@sbcglobal.net

M. Orey et al. (eds.), *Educational Media and Technology Yearbook*,
DOI 10.1007/978-0-387-09675-9_22, © Springer Science+Business Media, LLC 2009

Thus, her contribution to the field of education has been manifested through the thousands of lives she has touched and the contributions of the educational technology professionals who have benefitted from her mentoring have served to strengthen and expand the field worldwide. Addie's career path has taken her in three distinct directions, from classroom teacher to library/media specialist to instructional television professional.

Addie's roots as a leader go back to her years as a classroom teacher. Soon after her graduation from Hiram College, Addie began teaching mathematics in public middle schools in the Midwest and upstate New York. During these early years as an educator, Addie spent several years in Holland, as a teacher and librarian at the International School in The Hague. Upon returning to Michigan, Addie was encouraged by her mentor, Dr. Elwood "Woody" Miller, to establish a media center in the Okemo School District, home to many faculty at Michigan State University. Soon Addie's media center became a model for instructional leadership, both for students and for other teachers. Graduate faculty at Michigan State University and University of Michigan used Addie's media center, equipped with computers and other technologies, as a laboratory. And Addie earned her Master's Degree in Library Science from Western Michigan University. While she was never to return to public school teaching, Addie frequently cited the leadership skills she learned as a classroom teacher.

During her Michigan years as Library/Media Specialist, Addie thrived within the changing field of educational technology. In the role of instructional leader, Addie discovered opportunities to shape the changing education environment, finding herself advising school administrators and school board members to a new vision of education that encouraged learners to explore and grow using new technology resources to access a world of resources through the media center. At the same time, Addie began to reach out to other library/media specialists through what was one of two strong professional membership organizations in Michigan. Addie was able to work with other professionals to influence a merger of these two professional organizations of librarians and media specialists. MAME, the Michigan Association of Media Educators, joined together to form what is today one of the strongest professional organizations for school library/media specialists in the country.

The next logical step for Addie's development as a leader in the field was membership in AECT, the Association for Educational Communications and Technology. Once again encouraged by her mentors, Addie soon found herself in a variety of leadership positions in AECT, from planning chair for the AECT annual international convention to chairing the AECT Government Relations committee. In 1992 Addie was elected President of AECT, a three-year responsibility for presenting the annual international convention, managing the programmatic and fiscal responsibilities of the volunteer Board of Directors, and providing leadership development. During Addie's presidency, AECT was faced with difficult decisions requiring intense work in planning strategically. A plan, "Vision 2000," developed during Addie's presidency resulted several years later in moving the organization headquarters from Washington, D.C. to Bloomington, Indiana, and redesigned AECT staffing operations and fiscal management systems.

Over these years, Addie did not abandon her roots as a librarian, maintaining active roles in ALA and AASL as well as in AECT. In the early 1980s Addie was presented with an opportunity to lead, this time to influence direction-setting through a national project. As a result of her leadership in professional organizations, Addie was nominated to serve on the writing team for "Information Power," a new set of guidelines for libraries and media centers as instructional resources. Addie's participation on this writing team drew upon her expertise, not only as a library/media specialist, but also as an educator in general. Her knowledge and understanding of the power of books and media resources in an age that was clearly moving from a focus on industrial development to a culture hugely reliant on access to information provided an invaluable perspective to the team of writers. Since publication of "Information Power" in 1987, Addie has been recognized by AECT and by her peers for her vision and her service to the field.

After a full career as a library/media specialist in Michigan, Addie and her family moved to Arizona in the early 1980s. What might have been retirement for another person was not anything of the sort for Addie Kinsinger. Addie had become involved as an educator in the work of her local public television station in Michigan, so when she moved to Scottsdale, Arizona, she contacted Arizona State University licensee KAET—TV to find out what opportunities might be available to use her skills. Thus began Addie's third career as instructional television specialist. KAET's management team had been exploring development of a statewide instructional television organization as a support service of the resources available to educators through public television. Soon Addie was on the team that conducted a feasibility study and developed a pilot project toward that end. The result was the establishment of ASSET, Arizona School Services through Educational Technology. During her years with ASSET, Addie's leadership took her throughout the state of Arizona, training teachers to use instructional technology as part of their classroom curriculum. ASSET grew from a pilot project in 1984 to a service that today remains the primary source of instructional technology resources for Arizona K—12 teachers and students.

After a second retirement, this time from ASSET, Addie's leadership with AECT continued, this time as a member of the Board of Trustees for the ECT Foundation, the non-profit philanthropic arm of AECT. As a dedicated member of AECT, Addie led the way to establish a "Human Capital Campaign," designed to increase AECT membership The campaign encourages AECT members to fund dues for first-time AECT members, thus introducing emerging leaders in the field of educational technology to the AECT professional community. Soon thereafter, as ECT Foundation President, Addie championed establishment of a capital campaign to build the ECT endowment corpus. True to Addie's commitment to leadership development, these funds support scholarships for emerging leaders to participate in AECT activities and awards to honor achievement among AECT members.

Addie's vision continues to inspire leadership among her peers. She has served on task forces to conduct needs assessment and draft language for the AECT Strategic Plan and presented sessions at numerous conferences over the years. She is recognized among public television education leaders for her work both at station and at regional levels. She is frequently consulted by the professional community she has served so well. Indeed, she has lived the vision she described in the 1998 issue of *Media Spectrum*: "...creative people are attracted to opportunities that provide them with new experiences, presumably in the hope that these new experiences lead to a further burst of new imaginative and creative efforts." People follow Addie's leadership quite naturally—the sign of a true "Leader Among Leaders."

Part IV
Organizations and Associations
in North America

Introduction

Michael Orey

Introduction

Part V includes annotated entries for associations and organizations, most of which are headquartered in North America, whose interests are in some manner significant to the fields of instructional, educational, or learning technology or media. For the most part, these organizations consist of professionals in the field or agencies which offer services to the educational media community. In an effort to only list active organizations, I deleted all organizations who had not updated their information since 2006. Any readers are encouraged to contact the editors with names of unlisted media-related organizations for investigation and possible inclusion in the 2010 edition.

Information for this section was obtained through e-mail directing each organization to an individual web form through which the updated information could be submitted electronically into a database created by Michael Orey. Although the section editors made every effort to contact and follow up with organization representatives, responding to the annual request for an update was the responsibility of the organization representatives. The editing team would like to thank those respondents who helped assure the currency and accuracy of this section by responding to the request for an update. Figures quoted as dues refer to annual amounts unless stated otherwise. Where dues, membership, and meeting information are not applicable such information is omitted.

M. Orey (✉)
The University of Georgia, Athens, GA 30602-7144
e-mail: mikeorey@uga.edu

M. Orey et al. (eds.), *Educational Media and Technology Yearbook,*
DOI 10.1007/978-0-387-09675-9_23, © Springer Science+Business Media, LLC 2009

United States and Canada

Alphabetical listing of 87 organizations related to the general field of Instructional Technology.

Name of Organization or Association – Adaptech Research Network

Acronym – n/a

Address – Dawson College, 3040 Sherbrooke St. West

City – Montreal

State – QC

Zip Code – H3Z 1A4

Country – Canada

Phone Number – 514-931-8731 #1546

Fax Number – 514-931-3567 Attn: Catherine Fichten

Email Contact – catherine.fichten@mcgill.ca

URL – http://www.adaptech.org

Leaders – Catherine Fichten, Ph.D., Co-director; Jennison V. Asuncion, M.A., Co-Director; Maria Barile, M.S.W., co-director.

Description – Based at Dawson College (Montreal), we are a Canada-wide, grant-funded team, conducting bilingual empirical research into the use of computer, learning, and adaptive technologies by postsecondary students with disabilities. One of our primary interests lies in issues around ensuring that newly emerging instructional technologies are accessible to learners with disabilities.

Membership – Our research team is composed of academics, practitioners, students, consumers and others interested in the issues of access to technology by students with disabilities in higher education.

Dues – n/a

M. Orey et al. (eds.), *Educational Media and Technology Yearbook*, 319
DOI 10.1007/978-0-387-09675-9_24, © Springer Science+Business Media, LLC 2009

Meetings – n/a

Publications – Fossey, M. E., Asuncion, J. V., Fichten, C. S., Robillard, C., Barile, M., Amsel, R., et al. (2005). Development and validation of the Accessibility of Campus Computing for Students with Disabilities Scale (ACCSDS). *Journal of Postsecondary Education and Disability, 18*(1), 23–33. Jorgensen, S., Fichten, C. S., Havel, A., Lamb, D., James, C., & Barile, M. (2005). Academic performance of college students with and without disabilities: An archival study. *Canadian Journal of Counselling, 39*(2), 101–117. Fichten, C. S., Asuncion, J. V., Barile, M., Fossey, M. E., Robillard, C., Judd, D., et al. (2004). Access to information and instructional technologies in higher education I: Disability service providers' perspective. *Journal of Postsecondary Education and Disability, 17*(2), 114–133.

Name of Organization or Association – Agency for Instructional Technology

Acronym – AIT

Address – Box A

City – Bloomington

State – IN

Zip Code – 47402-0120

Country – US

Phone Number – (812)339-2203

Fax Number – (812)333-4218

Email Contact – info@ait.net

URL – http://www.ait.net

Leaders – Charles E. Wilson, Executive Director

Description – The Agency for Instructional Technology has been a leader in educational technology since 1962. A nonprofit organization, AIT is one of the largest providers of instructional TV programs in North America. AIT is also a leading developer of other educational media, including online instruction, CDs, videodiscs, and instructional software. AIT learning resources are used on six continents and reach nearly 34 million students in North America each year. AIT products have received many national and international honors, including an Emmy and Peabody award. Since 1970, AIT has developed 39 major curriculum packages through the consortium process it pioneered. American state and Canadian provincial agencies have cooperatively funded and widely used these learning resources. Funding for other product development comes from state, provincial, and local departments of education; federal and private institutions; corporations and private sponsors; and AITs own resources.

Membership – None.

Dues – None.

Meetings – No regular public meetings.

Publications – None.

Name of Organization or Association – American Association of Community Colleges

Acronym – AACC

Address – One Dupont Circle, NW, Suite 410

City – Washington

State – DC

Zip Code – 20036-1176

Country – US

Phone Number – (202)728-0200

Fax Number – (202)833-9390

Email Contact – nkent@aacc.nche.edu

URL – http://www.aacc.nche.edu

Leaders – George R. Boggs, President and CEO

Description – AACC is a national organization representing the nations more than 1,195 community, junior, and technical colleges. Headquartered in Washington, DC, AACC serves as a national voice for the colleges and provides key services in the areas of advocacy, research, information, and leadership development. The nations community colleges serve more than 11 million students annually, almost half (46%) of all U.S. undergraduates.

Membership – 1,195 institutions, 31 corporations, 15 international associates, 79 educational associates, 4 foundations.

Dues – vary by category

Meetings – Annual Convention, April of each year; 2009: April 4–7 Phoenix, AZ

Publications – Community College Journal (bi-mo.); Community College Times (bi-weekly newspaper); Community College Press (books, research and program briefs, and monographs).

Name of Organization or Association – American Association of School Librarians

Acronym – AASL

Address – 50 East Huron Street

City – Chicago

State – IL

Zip Code – 60611-2795

Country – US

Phone Number – (312)280-4382 or (800) 545-2433, ext. 4382

Fax Number – (312)280-5276

Email Contact – aasl@ala.org

URL – http://www.ala.org/aasl

Leaders – Julie A. Walker, Executive Director

Description – A division of the American Library Association, the mission of the American Association of School Librarians is to advocate excellence, facilitate change, and develop leaders in the school library media field.

Membership – 9,500

Dues – Personal membership in ALA (beginning FY 2009, 1st yr., $65; 2nd yr., $98; 3rd and subsequent yrs., $130) plus $50 for personal membership in AASL. Student, retired, organizational, and corporate memberships are available.

Meetings – National conference every two years; next national conference to be held in 2009.

Publications – School Library Media Research (electronic research journal at http://www.ala.org/aasl/SLMR) Knowledge Quest (print journal and online companion at http://www.ala.org/aasl/kqweb) AASL Hotlinks (e-mail newsletter) Non-serial publications (http://www.ala.org/ala/aasl/aaslpubsandjournals/aaslpublications.cfm).

Name of Organization or Association – American Educational Research Association

Acronym – AERA

Address – 1430 K Street, NW, Suite 1200

City – Washington

State – DC

Zip Code – 20005

Country – US

Phone Number – (202)238-3200

Fax Number – (202)238-3250

Email Contact – outreach@aera.net

URL – http://www.aera.net

Leaders – Lorraine M. McDonnell, President of the Council, 2008–2009

Description – The American Educational Research Association (AERA) is the national interdisciplinary research association for approximately 25,000 scholars who undertake research in education. Founded in 1916, AERA aims to advance knowledge about education, to encourage scholarly inquiry related to education, and to promote the use of research to improve education and serve the public good. AERA members include educators and administrators; directors of research, testing, or evaluation in federal, state, and local agencies; counselors; evaluators; graduate students; and behavioral scientists. The broad range of disciplines represented includes education, psychology, statistics, sociology, history, economics, philosophy, anthropology, and political science. AERA has more than 160 Special Interest Groups, including Advanced Technologies for Learning, NAEP Studies, Classroom Assessment, and Fiscal Issues, Policy, and Education Finance.

Membership – 25,000 Regular Members: Eligibility requires satisfactory evidence of active interest in educational research as well as professional training to at least the masters degree level or equivalent. Graduate Student Members: Any graduate student may be granted graduate student member status with the endorsement of a voting member who is a faculty members at the students university. Graduate Students who are employed full-time are not eligible. Graduate Student membership is limited to 5 years.

Dues – vary by category, ranging from $35 for graduate students to $120 for voting members, for one year. See AERA website for complete details: www.aera.net

Meetings – 2009 Annual Meeting, April 13–17, San Diego, California.

Publications – Educational Researcher; American Educational Research Journal; Journal of Educational and Behavioral Statistics; Educational Evaluation and Policy Analysis; Review of Research in Education; Review of Educational Research. Books: Handbook of Research on Teaching, 2001 (revised, 4th edition). Ethical Standards of AERA, Cases and Commentary, 2002 Black Education: A Transformative Research and Action Agenda for the New Century, 2005 Studying Teacher Education: The Report of the AERA Panel on Research and Teacher Education, 2006 Standards for Educational and Psychological Testing (revised and expanded, 1999). Co-published by AERA, American Psychological Association, and the National Council on Measurement in Education.

Name of Organization or Association – American Foundation for the Blind

Acronym – AFB

Address – 11 Penn Plaza, Suite 300

City – New York

State – NY

Zip Code – 10001

Country – US

Phone Number – (212)502-7600, (800)AFB-LINE (232-5463)

Fax Number – (212)502-7777

Email Contact – afbinfo@afb.net

URL – http://www.afb.org

Leaders – Carl R. Augusto, Pres.; Kelly Parisi, Vice Pres. of Communications

Description – The American Foundation for the Blind (AFB) is a national non-profit that expands possibilities for people with vision loss. AFB's priorities include broadening access to technology; elevating the quality of information and tools for the professionals who serve people with vision loss; and promoting independent and healthy living for people with vision loss by providing them and their families with relevant and timely resources. In addition, AFB's web site serves as a gateway to a wealth of vision loss information and services. AFB is also proud to house the Helen Keller Archives and honor the over forty years that Helen Keller worked tirelessly with AFB. For more information visit us online at www.afb.org.

Membership –

Dues –

Meetings –

Publications – AFB News (free); Journal of Visual Impairment & Blindness; AFB Press Catalog of Publications (free). AccessWorld™; Subscriptions Tel: (800) 232-3044 or (412) 741-1398.

Name of Organization or Association – American Library Association

Acronym – ALA

Address – 50 E. Huron St.

City – Chicago

State – IL

Zip Code – 60611

Country – US

Phone Number – (800) 545-2433

Fax Number – (312) 440-9374

Email Contact – library@ala.org

URL – http://www.ala.org

Leaders – Keith Michael Fiels, Executive Director

Description – The ALA is the oldest and largest national library association. Its 65,000 members represent all types of libraries: state, public, school, and academic, as well as special libraries serving persons in government, commerce, the armed services, hospitals, prisons, and other institutions. The ALA is the chief advocate of achievement and maintenance of high-quality library information services through protection of the right to read, educating librarians, improving services, and making information widely accessible. See separate entries for the following affiliated and subordinate organizations: American Association of School Librarians, American Library Trustee Association, Association for Library Collections and Technical Services, Association for Library Service to Children, Association of College and Research Libraries, Association of Specialized and Cooperative Library Agencies, Library Administration and Management Association, Library and Information Technology Association, Public Library Association, Reference and User Services Association, Young Adult Library Services Association, and Continuing Library Education Network and Exchange Round Table.

Membership – 65,000 members at present; everyone who cares about libraries is allowed to join the American Library Association.

Dues – Professional rate: $55, first year; $83, second year; third year & renewing: $110 Library Support Staff: $39 Student members: $28 Retirees: $39 International librarians: $66 Trustees: $50 Associate members (those not in the library field): $50.

Meetings – Annual Conference: July 10–15, 2009 – Chicago, IL; June 24–30, 2010 – Washington, DC; June 23–29, 2011-New Orleans, LA//Midwinter Meeting: January 23–28, 2009 – Denver, CO; January 15–20, 2010 – Boston, MA; January 21–26, 2011 – San Diego, CA.

Publications – American Libraries; Booklist; Choice; Book Links.

Name of Organization or Association – American Society for Training and Development

Acronym – ASTD

Address – 1640 King St., Box 1443

City – Alexandria

State – VA

Zip Code – 22313

Country – US

Phone Number – (703)683-8100

Fax Number – (703)683-1523

Email Contact – memberservices@astd.org

URL – http://www.astd.org

Leaders – Tony Bingham, President and CEO

Description – Founded in 1944, ASTD is the worlds premiere professional association in the field of workplace learning and performance. ASTDs membership includes more than 70,000 people in organizations from every level of the field of workplace performance in more than 100 countries. Its leadership and members work in more than 15,000 multinational corporations, small and medium-sized businesses, government agencies, colleges, and universities. ASTD is the leading resource on workplace learning and performance issues, providing information, research, analysis, and practical information derived from its own research, the knowledge and experience of its members, its conferences and publications, and the coalitions and partnerships it has built through research and policy work. ASTD has a board membership of 16 and staff of 90 to serve member needs.

Membership – 70,000 National and Chapter members.

Dues – The Classic Membership ($150.00) is the foundation of ASTD member benefits. Publications, newsletters, research reports, discounts and services and much more, are all designed to help you do your job better. Heres what you have to look forward to when you join: Training and Development – Monthly publication of the Industry. Stay informed on Trends, successful practices, public policy, ASTD news, case studies and more. Performance in Practice- Quarterly newsletter offers articles written by members for members. Hot Topics- ASTDs online reading list gets you up to speed on leading edge issues in the training and performance industry. Database and Archive Access – FREE online access to Trainlit, ASTDs searchable database featuring products reviews, book and article summaries and archived articles. Learning Circuits – Monthly Webzine features articles, departments and columns that examine new technologies and how they are being applied to workplace learning. Human Resource Development Quarterly – In depth studies and reports on human resource theory and practice give you a scholarly look at the training profession. HRDQ is available ONLY online with archives dating back to 1998 ASTD News Briefs – Weekly news briefs relating to the training and performance industry. Special Reports and Research – Trends Report, State of the Industry, Learning Outcomes and International Comparison Report. Training

Data Book – An annual publication, now online, draws on ASTD research and highlights the nature and magnitude of corporate investment in employer-provided training. Research Assistance – ASTD provides an Information Center that can provide you with the research you're looking for while you're on the phone. You can also send you research request through the website. Just provide your member number! Membership Directory – Online directory and searchable by a variety of criteria. Access to the Membership Directory is for Members Only, and is being enhanced for future networking capabilities. Buyers Guide & Consultants Directory – A one stop resource for information on over 600 suppliers of training and performance products and services. We also have several segments that you can add on to your Classic Membership: Membership Plus: Your choice of 12 info lines or four pre-chosen ASTD books. $79.00 Training Professionals: Includes an annual subscription to Info-lines, Pfeiffers Best of Training and the ASTD Training and Performance Yearbook. $130.00 Organizational Development/Leadership Professionals: Includes Pfeiffers Consulting Annual, Leader to Leader and Leadership in Action $200.00 Consulting: Includes annual subscription to C2M (quarterly journal), and Pfeiffers Consulting Annual. $75.00 E-Learning: Includes Training Media Review Online (Database and newsletter that evaluates audio, video, software and online products 6/year email newsletters yr.) and ASTD Distance Learning Yearbook. $175.00.

Meetings – International Conference 2002 – New Orleans, Louisiana May 31– June 6: International Conference 2003 – San Diego, CA May 17–22.

Publications – Training & Development Magazine; Info-Line; The American Mosaic: An In-depth Report of Diversity on the Future of Diversity at Work; ASTD Directory of Academic Programs in T&D/HRD; Training and Development Handbook; Quarterly publications: Performance in Practice; National Report on Human Resources; Washington Policy Report. ASTD also has recognized professional forums, most of which produce newsletters.

Name of Organization or Association – Association for Childhood Education International

Acronym – ACEI

Address – 17904 Georgia Ave., Suite 215

City – Olney

State – MD

Zip Code – 20832

Country – US

Phone Number – (301)570-2111

Fax Number – (301)570-2212

Email Contact – headquarters@acei.org

URL – http://www.acei.org

Leaders – Diane P. Whitehead, Acting Executive Director

Description – ACEI publications reflect careful research, broad-based views, and consideration of a wide range of issues affecting children from infancy through early adolescence. Many are media-related in nature. The journal (Childhood Education) is essential for teachers, teachers-in-training, teacher educators, day care workers, administrators, and parents. Articles focus on child development and emphasize practical application. Regular departments include book reviews (child and adult); film reviews, pamphlets, software, research, and classroom idea-sparkers. Six issues are published yearly, including a theme issue devoted to critical concerns.

Membership – 10,000

Dues – $45, professional; $29, student; $23, retired; $85, institutional.

Meetings – 2009 Annual Conference, March 18–21, Chicago, IL, USA.

Publications – Childhood Education (official journal) with ACEI Exchange (insert newsletter); Journal of Research in Childhood Education; professional focus newsletters (Focus on Infants and Toddlers, Focus on Pre-K and K, Focus on Elementary, Focus on Middle School, Focus on Teacher Education, and Focus on Inclusive Education); various books.

Name of Organization or Association – Association for Computers and the Humanities

Acronym – ACH

Address – [Address]

City – [City]

State – ON

Zip Code – [Zip Code]

Country – [Country]

Phone Number – [phone number]

Fax Number – [fax number]

Email Contact – kretzsh@uga.edu

URL – http://www.ach.org/

Leaders – Executive Secretary, ACH

Description – The Association for Computers and the Humanities is an international professional organization. Since its establishment, it has been the major professional society for people working in computer-aided research in literature and language studies, history, philosophy, and other humanities disciplines, and especially research involving the manipulation and analysis of textual materials. The ACH is devoted to disseminating information among its members about work in the field of humanities computing, as well as encouraging the development and dissemination of significant textual and linguistic resources and software for scholarly research.

Membership – 300

Dues – Individual regular member, US \$65 Student or Emeritus Faculty member, US \$55 Joint membership (for couples), Add US \$7.

Meetings – Annual meetings held with the Association for Literary and Linguistic Computing.

Publications – ACH Publications: – Literary & Linguistic Computing – Humanist.

Name of Organization or Association – Association for Educational Communications and Technology

Acronym – AECT

Address – 1800 N Stonelake Dr., Suite 2

City – Bloomington

State – IN

Zip Code – 47404

Country – US

Phone Number – (812)335-7675

Fax Number – (812)335-7678

Email Contact – pharris@aect.org

URL – http://www.aect.org

Leaders – Phillip Harris, Executive Director; Ward Cates, Board President

Description – AECT is an international professional association concerned with the improvement of learning and instruction through media and technology. It serves as a central clearinghouse and communications center for its members, who include instructional technologists, library media specialists, religious educators, government media personnel, school administrators and specialists, and training media producers. AECT members also work in the armed forces, public libraries, museums, and other information agencies of many different kinds, including those related to the emerging fields of computer technology. Affiliated organizations include the International Visual Literacy Association (IVLA), Minorities in Media (MIM), New England Educational Media Association (NEEMA), SICET (the Society of International Chinese in Educational Technology), and KSET (the Korean Society for Educational Technology). The ECT Foundation is also related to AECT. Each of these affiliated organizations has its own listing in the Yearbook. AECT Divisions include: Instructional Design & Development, Information & Technology Management, Training & Performance, Research & Theory, Systemic Change, Distance Learning, Media & Technology, Teacher Education, International, and Multimedia Productions.

Membership – 2,500 members in good standing from K-12, college and university and private sector/government training. Anyone interested can join. There are different memberships available for students, retirees, corporations and international parties. We also have a new option for electronic membership for international affiliates.

Dues – $99.00 standard membership discounts are available for students and retirees. Additional fees apply to corporate memberships or international memberships.

Meetings – Summer Leadership Institute held each July. In 2007 it will be in Chicago, IL. AECT holds an annual Conference each year in October. In 2007, it will be held in Anaheim, CA.

Publications – TechTrends (6/yr., free with AECT membership; available by subscription through Springer at www.springeronline.com); Educational Technology Research and Development (6/yr., $46 members; available by subscription through Springer at www.springeronline.com); Quarterly Review of Distance Education (q., $55 to AECT members); many books; videotapes.

Name of Organization or Association – Association for Experiential Education

Acronym – AEE

Address – 3775 Iris Avenue, Ste 4

City – Boulder

State – CO

Zip Code – 80301-2043

Country – US

Phone Number – (303)440-8844

Fax Number – (303)440-9581

Email Contact – executive@aee.org

URL – http://www.aee.org

Leaders – Patricia Hammond, Executive Director

Description – AEE is a nonprofit, international, professional organization committed to the development, practice, and evaluation of experiential education in all settings. AEE's vision is to be a leading international organization for the development and application of experiential education principles and methodologies with the intent to create a just and compassionate world by transforming education.

Membership – Nearly 1,500 members in over 30 countries including individuals and organizations with affiliations in education, recreation, outdoor adventure programming, mental health, youth service, physical education, management development training, corrections, programming for people with disabilities, and environmental education.

Dues – $55–$115, individual; $145, family; $275–$500, organizational.

Meetings – AEE Annual Conference in November. Regional Conferences in the Spring.

Publications – The Journal of Experiential Education (3/yr.); Experience and the Curriculum; Adventure Education; Adventure Therapy; Therapeutic Applications of Adventure Programming; Manual of Accreditation Standards for Adventure Programs; The Theory of Experiential Education, Third Edition; Experiential Learning in Schools and Higher Education; Ethical Issues in Experiential Education, Second Edition; The K.E.Y. (Keep Exploring Yourself) Group: An Experiential Personal Growth Group Manual; Book of Metaphors, Volume II; Women's Voices in Experiential Education; bibliographies, directories of programs, and membership directory. New publications since last year: Exploring the Boundaries of Adventure Therapy; A Guide to Women's Studies in the Outdoors; Administrative Practices of Accredited Adventure Programs; Fundamentals of Experience-Based Training; Wild Adventures: A Guidebook of Activities for Building Connections with Others and the Earth; Truth Zone: An Experimental Approach to Organizational Development; Exploring the Power of Solo, Silence, and Solitude.

Name of Organization or Association – Association for Library and Information Science Education

Acronym – ALISE

Address – 65 E. Wacker Place Suite 1900

City – Chicago

State – IL

Zip Code – 60612

Country – US

Phone Number – 312-795-0996

Fax Number – 312-419-8950

Email Contact – contact@alise.org

URL – http://www.alise.org

Leaders – Kathleen Combs Executive Director

Description – Seeks to advance education for library and information science and produces annual Library and Information Science Education Statistical Report. Open to professional schools offering graduate programs in library and information science; personal memberships open to educators employed in such institutions; other memberships available to interested individuals.

Membership – 500 individuals, 69 institutions.

Dues – institutional, sliding scale, $350–$2,500; $150 international; personal, $125 full-time; $75 part-time, $40 student, $60 retired.

Meetings – Tuesday, January 20, through Friday, January 23, 2009 – Denver, Colorado.

Publications – Journal of Education for Library and Information Science; ALISE Directory; Library and Information Science Education Statistical Report.

Name of Organization or Association – Association for Library Collections & Technical Services

Acronym – ALCTS

Address – 50 E. Huron St.

City – Chicago

State – IL

Zip Code – 60611

Country – US

Phone Number – (312)280-5037

Fax Number – (312)280-5033

Email Contact – alcts@ala.org

URL – www.ala.org/alcts

Leaders – Charles Wilt, Executive Director

Description – A division of the American Library Association, ALCTS is dedicated to acquisition, identification, cataloging, classification, and preservation of library materials; the development and coordination of the country's library resources; and aspects of selection and evaluation involved in acquiring and developing library materials and resources. Sections include Acquisitions, Cataloging and Classification, Collection Management and Development, Preservation and Reformatting, and Serials.

Membership – 4,800 Membership is open to anyone who has an interest in areas covered by ALCTS.

Dues – $65 plus membership in ALA.

Meetings – Annual Conference; Chicago, July 9–15, 2009, Washington, DC, June 24–30, 2010, New Orleans, June 23–29, 2011, Anaheim, June 21–27, 2012.

Publications – Library Resources & Technical Services (q.); ALCTS Newsletter Online (6/yr.)

Name of Organization or Association – Association for Library Service to Children

Acronym – ALSC

Address – 50 E. Huron St.

City – Chicago

State – IL

Zip Code – 60611

Country – US

Phone Number – (312)280-2163

Fax Number – (312)944-7671

Email Contact – alsc@ala.org

URL – http://www.ala.org/alsc

Leaders – Diane Foote

Description – Information about ALSC can be found at http://www.ala.org/alsc. Information on ALSCs various awards, including the nationally-known Newbery Medal for authors and the Caldecott Medal for illustrators can be found at http://www.ala.org/alsc. The Association for Library Service to Children develops and supports the profession of children's librarianship by enabling and encouraging its practitioners to provide the best library service to our nations children. The Association for Library Service to Children is interested in the improvement and extension of library services to children in all types of libraries. It is responsible for the evaluation and selection of book and non-book library materials and for the improvement of techniques of library service to children from preschool through the eighth grade or junior high school age, when such materials and techniques are intended for use in more than one type of library. Committee membership is open to ALSC members. Full list of ALSC boards and committees can be found at.

Membership – Over 4,000 members.

Dues – $45 plus membership in ALA; $18 plus membership in ALA for library school students; $25 plus membership in ALA for retirees.

Meetings – National Institute, Fall.

Publications – Children and Libraries: The Journal of the Association for Library Service to Children (3x per year); ALSConnect (quarterly newsletter). ALSC Blog.

Name of Organization or Association – Association for Media and Technology in Education in Canada

Acronym – AMTEC

Address – 3-1750 The Queensway, Suite 1318

City – Etobicoke

State – ON

Zip Code – M9C 5H5

Country – Canada

Phone Number – (403)220-3721

Fax Number – (403)282-4497

Email Contact – wstephen@ucalgary.ca

URL – http://www.amtec.ca

Leaders – Bob Brandes: Past President; Christine Shelton, Pres. ; Wendy Stephens, Sec./Treas.

Description – AMTEC is Canada's national association for educational media and technology professionals. The organization provides national leadership through annual conferences, publications, workshops, media festivals, and awards. It responds to media and technology issues at the international, national, provincial, and local levels, and maintains linkages with other organizations with similar interests.

Membership – AMTEC members represent all sectors of the educational media and technology fields.

Dues – $101.65, Canadian regular; $53.50, student and retiree.

Meetings – Annual Conferences take place in late May or early June. 1999, Ottawa; 2000, Vancouver.

Publications – Canadian Journal of Learning and Technology (a scholarly journal published 3 times a year) Media News (3/yr.); Membership Directory (with membership).

Name of Organization or Association – Association of College and Research Libraries

Acronym – ACRL

Address – 50 E. Huron St.

City – Chicago

State – IL

Zip Code – 60611-2795

Country – US

Phone Number – (312)280-2523

Fax Number – (312)280-2520

Email Contact – acrl@ala.org

URL – http://www.ala.org/acrl

Leaders – Mary Ellen Davis, Executive Director

Description – The Association of College and Research Libraries (ACRL), the largest division of the American Library Association, is a professional association of academic librarians and other interested individuals. It is dedicated to enhancing the ability of academic library and information professionals to serve the information needs of the higher education community and to improve learning, teaching, and research. ACRL is the only individual membership organization in North America that develops programs, products and services to meet the unique needs of academic and research librarians Information on ACRLs various committees, task forces, discussion groups, and sections can be found at. Information on ACRLs various awards can be found at.

Membership – With over 13,000 members, is a national organization of academic and research libraries and librarians working with all types of academic libraries—community and junior college, college, and university—as well as comprehensive and specialized research libraries and their professional staffs.

Dues – $55 plus membership in ALA; $35 plus membership in ALA for library school students and for retirees SECTIONS (two at no charge, additional sections $5 each): African American Studies Librarians (AFAS); Anthropology and Sociology Section (ANSS); Arts Section; Asian, African, and Middle Eastern

Section (AAMES); College Libraries Section (CLS); Community and Junior College Libraries Section (CJCLS); Distance Learning Section (DLS); Education and Behavioral Sciences Section (EBSS); Instruction Section (IS); Law and Political Science Section (LPSS); Literatures in English (LES); Rare Books and Manuscripts Section (RBMS); Science and Technology Section (STS); Slavic and East European Section (SEES); University Libraries Section (ULS); Western European Studies Section (WESS); Women's Studies Section (WSS).

Meetings – ACRL 14th National Conference – March 12–15, 2009, Seattle, WA, Theme: Pushing the Edge: Explore, Engage, Extend.

Publications – List of all print and electronic publications at ACRLog: Blogging for and by academic and research librarians –. ACRL Insider – The mission of the ACRL Insider Weblog is to keep the world current and informed on the activities, services, and programs of the Association of College & Research Libraries, including publications, events, conferences, and eLearning opportunities. ACRL Podcasts – Academic Library Trends & Statistics (annually). Statistics data for all academic libraries reporting throughout the U.S. and Canada. Trends data examines a different subject each year. Available from ALA Order Fulfillment, P.O. Box 932501, Atlanta, GA 31193-2501 and from the ALA Online Store. Choice: Editor and Publisher, Irving E. Rockwood. ISSN 0009-4978. Published monthly. Only available by subscription: $315 per year for North America; $365 outside North America. CHOICE Reviews on Cards: $390 per year for North America – U.S., Canada, and Mexico); $440 outside North America. ChoiceReviews.online: See pricing for site licenses at. College & Research Libraries (6 bimonthly journal issues). Sent to all ACRL members. Subscriptions, $70-US. $75-Canada and other PUAS countries. $80-Other foreign countries. College & Research Libraries News (11 monthly issues, July–Aug. combined). Sent to all ACRL members. Subscriptions: $46-US. $52-Canada and other PUAS countries. $57-Other foreign countries. RBM: A Journal of Rare Books, Manuscripts, and Cultural Heritage (2 issues). Subscriptions, $42-US. $47 Canada and other PUAS countries. $58-Other foreign countries.

Name of Organization or Association – Canadian Library Association/Association canadienne des bibliothèques

Acronym – CLA/ACB

Address – 328 Frank Street

City – Ottawa

State – ON

Zip Code – K2P 0X8

Country – Canada

Phone Number – (613)232-9625

Fax Number – (613)563-9895

Email Contact – info@cla.ca

URL – http://www.cla.ca

Leaders – Linda Sawden Harris, Manager of Financial Services; Judy Green, Manager, Marketing & Communications; Don Butcher, Executive Director

Description – Our Mission CLA/ACB is my advocate and public voice, educator and network. We build the Canadian library and information community and advance its information professionals. Our Values We believe that libraries and the principles of intellectual freedom and free universal access to information are key components of an open and democratic society. Diversity is a major strength of our Association. An informed and knowledgeable membership is central in achieving library and information policy goals. Effective advocacy is based upon understanding the social, cultural, political and historical contexts in which libraries and information services function. Our Operating Principles A large and active membership is crucial to our success Our Association will have a governance structure that is reviewed regularly and ensures that all sectors of the membership are represented. Our Association will be efficiently run, fiscally responsible and financially independent Technology will be used in efficient and effective ways to further our goals. Our Association places a high value on each of our members. Our Association will ensure that its staff are provided with tools and training necessary for them to excel at their jobs. Our Associations strategic plan will be continually reviewed and updated.

Membership – The Associations five constituent divisions are: Canadian Association for School Libraries (CASL), including the School Library Administrators (SLAS) section (approx. 200 members) Canadian Association of College and University Libraries (CACUL), including the Community and Technical College (CTCL) section (approx. 800 members) Canadian Association of Public Libraries (CAPL), including the Canadian Association of Children's Librarians (CACL) section (approx. 650 members) Canadian Association of Special Libraries and Information Services (CASLIS), with chapters in Calgary, Edmonton, Manitoba, Ottawa, Toronto and Atlantic Canada (approx. 590 members) Canadian Library Trustees Association (approx. 180 members).

Dues – $25–$1,000

Meetings – 2009 CLA/ACB National Conference 7 Tradeshow, Montreal, May 29–June 1

Publications – Feliciter (membership & subscription magazine, 6/yr.).

Name of Organization or Association – Close Up Foundation

Acronym – CUF

Address – 44 Canal Center Plaza

City – Alexandria

State – VA

Zip Code – 22314

Country – US

Phone Number – (703)706-3300

Fax Number – (703)706-3329

Email Contact – cutv@closeup.org

URL – http://www.closeup.org

Leaders – Timothy S. Davis, President & CEO

Description – A nonprofit, nonpartisan civic engagement organization dedicated to providing individuals of all backgrounds with the knowledge, skills, and confidence to actively participate in democracy. Each year, Close Up brings 15,000 secondary and middle school students and teachers to Washington, DC for week-long government studies programs. In addition, Close Up produces an array of multimedia civic education resources for use in classrooms and households nationwide, including Close Up at the Newseum, a weekly youth-focused current affairs program C-SPAN.

Membership – Any motivated middle or high school student who wants to learn about government and American history is eligible to come on our programs. No dues or membership fees.

Dues – Tuition is required to participate on Close Up educational travel programs. A limited amount of tuition assistance is available to qualified students through the Close Up Fellowship program. With a designated number of students, teachers receive a fellowship that covers the adult tuition and transportation price. Please contact 1-800-CLOSE UP for more information.

Meetings – Meetings take place during weeklong educational programs in Washington, DC.

Publications – Current Issues (new edition produced annually); The Bill of Rights: A Users Guide; Perspectives; International Relations; The American Economy; Face the Music: Copyright, Art & the Digital Age; documentaries on domestic and foreign policy issues.

Name of Organization or Association – Computer Assisted Language Instruction Consortium

Acronym – CALICO

Address – 214 Centennial Hall, Texas State University, 601 University Dr.

City – San Marcos

State – TX

Zip Code – 78666

Country – US

Phone Number – (512)245-1417

Fax Number – (512)245-9089

Email Contact – info@calico.org

URL – http://calico.org

Leaders – Robert Fischer, Executive Director

Description – CALICO is devoted to the dissemination of information on the application of technology to language teaching and language learning.

Membership – 1,000 members from United States and 20 foreign countries. Anyone interested in the development and use of technology in the teaching/learning of foreign languages are invited to join.

Dues – $65 annual/individual.

Meetings – 2007, Texas State University, San Marcos; 2008, University of San Francisco.

Publications – CALICO Journal (three times a year), CALICO Monograph Series (Monograph V, 2006; Monograph VI, 2007).

Name of Organization or Association – Consortium of College and University Media Centers

Acronym – CCUMC

Address – 1200 Communications Bldg., Iowa State University

City – Ames

State – IA

Zip Code – 50011-3243

Country – US

Phone Number – (515)294-1811

Fax Number – (515)294-8089

Email Contact – ccumc@ccumc.org

URL – www.ccumc.org

Leaders – Executive Director (currently vacant)

Description – CCUMC is a professional group of higher education media personnel whose purpose is to improve education and training through the effective use of educational media. Assists educational and training users in making films, video, and educational media more accessible. Fosters cooperative planning among university media centers. Gathers and disseminates information on improved procedures and new developments in instructional technology and media center management.

Membership – 750 individuals at 325 institutions/corporations: Institutional Memberships – Individuals within an institution of higher education who are associated with the support of instruction and presentation technologies in a media center and/or technology support service. Corporate Memberships – Individuals within a corporation, firm, foundation, or other commercial or philanthrophic whose business or activity is in support of the purposes and objectives of CCUMC. Associate Memberships – Individuals from a public library, religious, governmental, or other organizations not otherwise eligible for other categories of membership. Student Memberships – Any student in an institution of higher education who is not eligible for an institutional membership.

Dues – Institutional or Corporate Membership: $325 for 1–2 persons, $545 for 3–4 persons, $795 for 5–6 persons, $130 each additional person beyond six Student Membership: $55 per person Associate Membership: $325 per person.

Meetings – 2007 Conference, Gainesville Florida, October 18–22, 2007.

Publications – College & University Media Review (journal – semi-annual) Leader (newsletter – 3 issues annually in electronic format).

Name of Organization or Association – Council for Exceptional Children

Acronym – CEC

Address – 1110 N. Glebe Rd. #300

City – Arlington

State – VA

Zip Code – 22201

Country – US

Phone Number – (703)620-3660. TTY: (703)264-9446

Fax Number – (703)264-9494

Email Contact – cec@cec.sped.org.

URL – http://www.cec.sped.org

Leaders – Bruce Ramirez, Executive Director

Description – CEC is the largest international organization dedicated to improving the educational success of students with disabilities and/or gifts and talents. CEC advocates for governmental policies supporting special education, sets professional standards, provides professional development, and helps professionals obtain conditions and resources necessary for high quality educational services for their students.

Membership – Teachers, administrators, professors, related services providers (occupational therapists, school psychologists...), and parents. CEC has approximately 50,000 members.

Dues – $111 a year

Meetings – Annual Convention & Expo attracting approximately 6,000 special educators.

Publications – Journals, newsletters books, and videos with information on new research findings, classroom practices that work, and special education publications. (See also the ERIC Clearinghouse on Disabilities and Gifted Education).

Name of Organization or Association – Education Development Center, Inc.

Acronym – EDC

Address – 55 Chapel St.

City – Newton

State – MA

Zip Code – 02458-1060

Country – US

Phone Number – (617)969-7100

Fax Number – (617)969-5979

Email Contact – emarshall@edc.org

URL – http://www.edc.org

Leaders – Dr. Luther S. Luedtke, President and CEO

Description – Education Development Center, Inc. (EDC) is an international, non-profit organization that conducts and applies research to advance learning and promote health. EDC currently manages 325 projects in 50 countries. Our award-winning programs and products, developed in collaboration with partners around the globe, address nearly every critical need in society, including early child development, K-12 education, health promotion, workforce preparation, community development, learning technologies, basic and adult education, institutional reform, medical ethics, and social justice.

Membership – Not applicable

Dues – Not applicable

Meetings – Not applicable

Publications – (1) Annual Report (2) Mosaic, an EDC Report Series (3) EDC Update, an EDC Newsletter (4) EDC Online Report (5) Detailed Web site with vast archive of publications, technical reports, and evaluation studies.

Name of Organization or Association – Educational Communications, Inc., Environmental and Media Projects of

Acronym –

Address – P.O. Box 351419

City – Los Angeles

State – CA

Zip Code – 90035

Country – US

Phone Number – (310)559-9160

Fax Number – (310)559-9160

Email Contact – ECNP@aol.com

URL – www.ecoprojects.org

Leaders – Nancy Pearlman, Executive Director and Producer

Description – Educational Communications is dedicated to enhancing the quality of life on this planet and provides radio and television programs about the environment. Serves as a clearinghouse on ecological issues. Programming is available on 100 stations in 25 states. These include: ECONEWS television series and ENVIRONMENTAL DIRECTIONS radio series. ECO-TRAVEL Television shows focus on ecotourism. Services provided include a speakers bureau, award-winning public service announcements, radio and television documentaries, volunteer and intern opportunities, and input into the decision-making process. Its mission is to educate the public about both the problems and the solutions in the environment. Other projects include the Ecology Center of Southern California (a regional conservation group), Project Ecotourism, Humanity and the Planet, Earth Cultures (providing ethnic dance performances), and more.

Membership – $20.00 for yearly subscription to the Compendium Newsletter.

Dues – $20 for regular. All donations accepted.

Meetings – -as needed.

Publications – Compendium Newsletter (bi-monthly newsletter) Environmental Directions radio audio cassettes, (1,550 produced to date) ECONEWS and ECO-TRAVEL television series (over 550 shows in the catalog available on 3/4", VHS, and DVD).

Name of Organization or Association – Edvantia, Inc. (formerly AEL, Inc.)

Acronym – Edvantia

Address – P.O. Box 1348

City – Charleston

State – WV

Zip Code – 25325-1348

Country – US

Phone Number – (304)347-0400, (800)624-9120

Fax Number – (304)347-0487

Email Contact – carla.mcclure@edvantia.org

URL – http://www.edvantia.org

Leaders – Dr. Doris L. Redfield, President and CEO

Description – Edvantia is a nonprofit education research and development corporation, founded in 1966, that partners with practitioners, education agencies, publishers, and service providers to improve learning and advance student success. Edvantia provides clients with a range of services, including research, evaluation, professional development, and consulting.

Membership –

Dues –

Meetings –

Publications – The Edvantia Electronic Library contains links to free online tools and information created by staff on a wide array of education-related topics. Visitors to the Edvantia Web site can also access archived webcasts and webinars and sign up for a free monthly newsletter.

Name of Organization or Association – ENC Learning Inc.

Acronym – ENC

Address – 1275 Kinnear Rd

City – Columbus

State – OH

Zip Code – 43212

Country – US

Phone Number – 800-471-1045

Fax Number – 877-656-0315

Email Contact – info@goenc.com

URL – www.goenc.com

Leaders – Dr. Len Simutis, Director

Description – ENC provides K-12 teachers and other educators with a central source of information on mathematics and science curriculum materials, particularly those that support education reform. Among ENCs products and services is ENC Focus, a free online magazine on topics of interest to math and science educators. Users include K-12 teachers, other educators, policymakers, and parents.

Membership – ENC is a subscription-based online resource for K-12 educators. Subscriptions are available for schools, school districts, college and universities, and individuals. Information for subscribers is available at www.goenc.com/subscribe

Dues – None.

Meetings – None.

Publications – ENC Focus is available as an online publication in two formats: ENC Focus on K-12 Mathematics, and ENC Focus on K-12 Science. Each are accessible via www.goenc.com/focus

Name of Organization or Association – Film Arts Foundation

Acronym – Film Arts

Address – 145 9th St. #101

City – San Francisco

State – CA

Zip Code – 94103

Country – US

Phone Number – (415)552-8760

Fax Number – (415)552-0882

Email Contact – info@filmarts.org

URL – http://www.filmarts.org

Leaders – K.C. Price – Interim Executive Director

Description – Service organization that supports the success of independent film and video makers. Some services are for members only and some open to the public. These include low-cost classes in all aspects of filmmaking; affordable equipment rental (including digital video, 16 mm, Super-8, Final Cut Pro editing, ProTools mix room, optical printer, etc.); Resource Library; free legal consultation; bi-monthly magazine Release Print; grants program; year-round events and exhibitions; non-profit sponsorship; regional and national advocacy on media issues, and significant discounts on film- and video-related products and services.

Membership – nearly 3,000

Dues – $45 for "Subscriber" level benefits including bi-monthly magazine, discounts, and access to libraries and on-line databases. $65 for full "Filmmaker" benefits including above plus: significant discounts on classes and equipment rentals, eligibility for non-profit fiscal sponsorship, free legal consultation and filmmaking consultation.

Meetings – Annual membership meeting and regular networking events.

Publications – The award-winning bimonthly magazine Release Print.

Name of Organization or Association – Great Plains National ITV Library

Acronym – GPN

Address – P.O. Box 80669

City – Lincoln

State – NE

Zip Code – 68501-0669

Country – US

Phone Number – (402)472-2007, (800)228-4630

Fax Number – (800)306-2330

Email Contact – npba@umd.edu

URL – http://shopgpn.com/

Leaders – Stephen C. Lenzen, Executive Director

Description – Produces and distributes educational media, video, CD-ROMs and DVDs, prints and Internet courses. Available for purchase for audiovisual or lease for broadcast use.

Membership – Membership not required.

Dues – There are no dues required.

Meetings – There are no meetings. We do attend subject specific conventions to promote our products.

Publications – GPN Educational Video Catalogs by curriculum areas; periodic brochures. Complete listing of GPN's product line is available via the Internet along with online purchasing. Free previews available.

Name of Organization or Association – Health Sciences Communications Association

Acronym – HeSCA

Address – One Wedgewood Dr., Suite 27

City – Jewett City

State – CT

Zip Code – 06351-2428

Country – US

Phone Number – (203)376-5915

Fax Number – (203)376-6621

Email Contact – hesca@hesca.org

URL – http://www.hesca.org/

Leaders – Ronald Sokolowski, Executive Director

Description – An affiliate of AECT, HeSCA is a nonprofit organization dedicated to the sharing of ideas, skills, resources, and techniques to enhance communications and educational technology in the health sciences. It seeks to nurture the professional growth of its members; serve as a professional focal point for those engaged in health sciences communications; and convey the concerns, issues, and concepts of health sciences communications to other organizations which influence and are affected by the profession. International in scope and diverse in membership, HeSCA is supported by medical and veterinary schools, hospitals, medical associations, and businesses where media are used to create and disseminate health information.

Membership – 150

Dues – $150, indiv.; $195, institutional ($150 additional institutional dues); $60, retiree; $75, student; $1,000, sustaining. All include subscriptions to the journal and newsletter.

Meetings – Annual meetings, May–June.

Publications – Journal of Bio Communications; Feedback (newsletter).

Name of Organization or Association – Institute for the Future

Acronym – IFTF

Address – 124 University Avenue, 2nd Floor

City – Palo Alto

State – CA

Zip Code – 94301

Country – US

Phone Number – (650)854-6322

Fax Number – (650)854-7850

Email Contact – info@iftf.org

URL – http://www.iftf.org

Leaders – Dale Eldredge, COO

Description – The Institute for the Future (IFTF) is an independent nonprofit research group. We work with organizations of all kinds to help them make better, more informed decisions about the future. We provide the foresight to create insights that lead to action. We bring a combination of tools, methodologies, and a deep understanding of emerging trends and discontinuities to our work with companies, foundations, and government agencies. We take an explicitly global approach to strategic planning, linking macro trends to local issues in such areas as: * Work and daily life * Technology and society * Health and health care * Global business trends * Changing consumer society The Institute is based in California's Silicon Valley, in a community at the crossroads of technological innovation, social experimentation, and global interchange. Founded in 1968 by a group of former RAND Corporation researchers with a grant from the Ford Foundation to take leading-edge research methodologies into the public and business sectors, the IFTF is committed to building the future by understanding it deeply.

Membership – Become a Member To become a member of IFTF, companies and organizations can join one or more of our membership programs or contract with us for private work. Each membership program offers a distinct set of deliverables at different membership prices and enrollment terms. Please visit the individual program sites for more detailed information on a particular program. For more information on membership contact Sean Ness at sness@iftf.org or 650-854-6322. ∗ Ten-Year Forecast Program ∗ Technology Horizons Program ∗ Health Horizons Program ∗ Custom Private Work.

Dues – Corporate-wide memberships are for one year periods: ∗ Ten-Year Forecast – $15,000/year ∗ Technology Horizons – $65,000/year ∗ Health Horizons – $65,000/year. At present, we do not have university, individual or small-company programs set up. For those companies that support our research programs, we will often conduct custom research.

Meetings – Several a year, for supporting members.

Publications – IFTF blogs ∗ Future Now – http://future.iftf.org – emerging technologies and their social implications ∗ Virtual China – http://www.virtual-china.org – an exploration of virtual experiences and environments in and about China ∗ Future of Marketing – http://fom.iftf.org – emerging technology, global change, and the future of consumers and marketing ∗ Ten-Year Forecast (members only) – http://blogger.iftf.org/tyf – a broad scan of the leading edge of change in business, government, and the global community ∗ Technology Horizons (members only) – http://blogger.iftf.org/tech – emerging technologies and their implications for business, society and family life.

Name of Organization or Association – Instructional Technology Council

Acronym – ITC

Address – One Dupont Cir., NW, Suite 360

City – Washington

State – DC

Zip Code – 20036-1143

Country – US

Phone Number – (202)293-3110

Fax Number – (202)822-5014

Email Contact – cmullins@itcnetwork.org

URL – http://www.itcnetwork.org

Leaders – Christine Mullins, Executive Director

Description – An affiliated council of the American Association of Community Colleges established in 1977, the Instructional Technology Council (ITC) provides leadership, information and resources to expand access to, and enhance learning through, the effective use of technology. ITC represents higher education institutions in the United States and Canada that use distance learning technologies. ITC members receive a subscription to the ITC News and ITC list serv with information on what's happening in distance education, participation in ITCs professional development audio conference series, distance learning grants information, updates on distance learning legislation, discounts to attend the annual e-Learning Conference which features more than 80 workshops and seminars.

Membership – Members include single institutions and multi-campus districts; regional and statewide systems of community, technical and two-year colleges; for-profit organizations; four-year institutions; and, non-profit organizations that are interested or involved in instructional telecommunications. Members use a vast array of ever-changing technologies for distance learning. They often combine different systems according to students needs. The technologies they use and methods of teaching include: audio and video conferences, cable television, compressed and full-motion video, computer networks, fiber optics, interactive videodisc, ITFS, microwave, multimedia, public television, satellites, teleclasses, and telecourses.

Dues – $450, Institutional; $750, Corporate.

Meetings – Annual e-Learning Conference.

Publications – Quality Enhancing Practices in Distance Education: Vol. 2 Student Services; Quality Enhancing Practices in Distance Education: Vol. 1 Teaching and Learning; New Connections: A Guide to Distance Education (2nd ed.); New Connections: A College President's Guide to Distance Education; Digital Video: A Handbook for Educators; Faculty Compensation and Support Issues in Distance Education; ITC News (monthly publication/newsletter); ITC Listserv.

Name of Organization or Association – International Association for Language Learning Technology

Acronym – IALLT

Address – Instr. Media Svcs, Concordia Coll.

City – Moorhead

State – MN

Zip Code – 56562

Country – US

Phone Number – (218)299-3464

Fax Number – (218)299-3246

Email Contact – business@iallt.org

URL – http://iallt.org

Leaders – Claire Bartlett, President; Ron Balko, Treasurer

Description – IALLT is a professional organization whose members provide leadership in the development, integration, evaluation and management of instructional technology for the teaching and learning of language, literature and culture.

Membership – 400 members Membership/Subscription Categories * Educational Member: for people working in an academic setting such as a school, college or university. These members have voting rights. * Full-time Student Member: for full-time students interested in membership. Requires a signature of a voting member to verify student status. These members have voting rights. * Commercial Member: for those working for corporations interested in language learning and technology. This category includes for example language laboratory vendors, software and textbook companies. * Library Subscriber: receive our journals for placement in libraries.

Dues – 1 year: $50, voting member; $25, student; $60, library subscription; $75 commercial. 2 year: $90, voting member; $140 commercial.

Meetings – Biennial IALLT conferences treat the entire range of topics related to technology in language learning as well as management and planning. IALLT also sponsors sessions at conferences of organizations with related interests, including CALICO and ACTFL.

Publications – IALLT Journal of Language Learning Technologies (2 times annually); materials for language lab management and design, language teaching and technology. Visit our website for details. http://iallt.org

Name of Organization or Association – International Association of School Librarianship

Acronym – IASL

Address – PO Box 83

City – Zillmere

State – QLD

Zip Code – 4034

Country – AUSTRALIA

Phone Number – 61 7 3216 5785

Fax Number – 61 7 3633 0570

Email Contact – iasl@kb.com.au

URL – www.iasl-slo.org/

Leaders – Peter Genco-President; Karen Bonanno-Executive Secretary

Description – Seeks to encourage development of school libraries and library programs throughout the world; promote professional preparation and continuing education of school librarians; achieve collaboration among school libraries of the world; foster relationships between school librarians and other professionals connected with children and youth and to coordinate activities, conferences, and other projects in the field of school librarianship.

Membership – 550 plus.

Dues – $50 Zone A (e.g. United States, Canada, Western Europe, Japan) $35 Zone B (e.g. Eastern Europe, Latin America, Middle East) $20 Zone C (e.g. Angola, India, Bulgaria, China) Based on GNP.

Meetings – Annual Conference, Lisbon, Portugal, July 2006.

Publications – IASL Newsletter (3/yr.); School Libraries Worldwide (semi-annual); Conference Professionals and Research Papers (annual).

Name of Organization or Association – International Center of Photography

Acronym – ICP

Address – 1114 Avenue of the Americas at 43rd Street

City – New York

State – NY

Zip Code – 10036

Country – US

Phone Number – (212)857-0045

Fax Number – (212)857-0090

Email Contact – info@icp.org

URL – http://www.icp.org

Leaders – Willis Hartshorn, Dir.; Phyllis Levine, Director of Communications.

Description – Located on a dynamic two-part campus in midtown Manhattan, the International Center of Photography (ICP) stands amongst the nation's foremost museums dedicated to preserving the past and ensuring the future of the art of photography. One of the largest facilities of its kind, ICP presents changing exhibitions of the finest works of some of the most talented photographers in the world. With over 20 exhibitions each year, ICP presents an extensive array of historical and contemporary photographs, revealing the power and diversity of the medium from documentary photography to digital imaging. The School of the International Center of Photography fosters study of the history, techniques, aesthetics, and practices of photography in a wide range of programs: continuing education classes; two full-time certificate programs; a Master of Fine Arts program in collaboration with Bard

College, Master of Arts and Master of Fine Arts degree programs in conjunction with NYU; Digital Media Program; lectures; and symposia.

Membership – 4,430

Dues – Current levels available on request.

Meetings – The ICP Infinity Awards (annual – 2007 is the 23rd)

Publications – Martin Munkacsi; Ecotopia; Atta Kim: ON-AIR; Snap Judgments: New Positions in Contemporary African Photography; African American Vernacular Photography: Selections from the Daniel Cowin Collection; Modernist Photography: Selections from the Daniel Cowin Collection; Young America. The Daguerreotypes of Southworth and Hawes; and others!

Name of Organization or Association – International Council for Educational Media

Acronym – ICEM

Address – Postfach 114

City – Vienna

State – n/a

Zip Code – A-1011

Country – Austria

Phone Number – +43 660 5113241

Fax Number – n/a

Email Contact – lylt@a1.net

URL – www.icem-cime.org

Leaders – John Hedberg – President; Ray Laverty – Secretary General

Description – Welcome to ICEM Our purposes are: * To provide a channel for the international exchange and evaluation of information, experience and materials in the field of educational media as they apply to pre-school, primary and secondary education, to technical and vocational, industrial and commercial training, teacher training, continuing and distance education. * To foster international liaison among individuals and organizations with professional responsibility in the field of educational media. * To cooperate with other international organizations in the development and application of educational technology for practice, research, production, and distribution in this field.

Membership – What are the main advantages of ICEM membership? IICEM membership enables those professionally involved in the production, distribution and use of media in teaching and learning to establish a broad network of contacts with educators, researchers, managers, producers and distributors of educational media from around the world. It also provides opportunities to discuss topics of mutual concern in an atmosphere of friendship and trust, to plan and carry out co-productions, to compare and exchange ideas and experiences, to keep abreast of the latest developments, and to work together towards the improvement of education on an international level. Membership in ICEM includes a subscription to the ICEM quarterly journal, Educational Media International, an entry in the Who's who on the ICEM Webpage, registration at ICEM events and activities either free of charge or at reduced rates, eligibility to engage in working groups or become a member of the Executive Committee, participate at the General Assembly and numerous other advantages. Our purposes are: * To provide a channel for the international exchange and evaluation of information, experience and materials in the field of educational media as they apply to pre-school, primary and secondary education, to technical and vocational, industrial and commercial training, teacher training, continuing and distance education. * To foster international liaison among individuals and organizations with professional responsibility in the field of educational media. * To cooperate with other international organizations in the development and application of educational technology for practice, research, production, and distribution in this field. Who can be a member of ICEM? Members are organizations and individuals who are involved in educational technology in any one of a variety of ways. There are several different types and categories of ICEM members, Individual Members, National Representatives, Deputy Representatives and Coordinators. Individual Members may join ICEM by paying individual membership fees. National Representatives are appointed by their Ministry of Education. National Coordinators are elected by other ICEM members in their country. Regional Representatives and Coordinators represent a group of several countries. ICEM Secretariat, c/o Ray Laverty SG Pf 114 1011 WIEN AUSTRIA E-mail: lylt-at-a1.net

Dues – n/a

Meetings – Annual General Assembly in Autumn; Executive Committee meeting in Spring; Locations vary.

Publications – Educational Media International (quarterly journal) http://www. icem-cime.org/emi/issues.asp Aims & Scope Educational media has made a considerable impact on schools, colleges and providers of open and distance education. This journal provides an international forum for the exchange of information and views on new developments in educational and mass media. Contributions are drawn from academics and professionals whose ideas and experiences come from a number of countries and contexts. Abstracting & Indexing Educational Media International is covered by the British Education Index; Contents Pages in Education; Educational Research Abstracts online (ERA); Research into Higher Education Abstracts; ERIC; EBSCOhost; and Proquest Information and Learning.

Name of Organization or Association – International Recording Media Association

Acronym – IRMA

Address – 182 Nassau St., Suite 204

City – Princeton

State – NJ

Zip Code – 08542-7005

Country – US

Phone Number – (609)279-1700

Fax Number – (609)279-1999

Email Contact – info@recordingmedia.org

URL – http://www.recordingmedia.org

Leaders – Charles Van Horn, President.; Guy Finley, Associate Executive Director

Description – IRMA, the content delivery and storage association, is the worldwide forum on trends and innovation for the delivery and storage of entertainment and information. Founded in 1970, this global trade association encompasses organizations involved in every facet of content delivery. Beginning with the introduction of the audiocassette, through the home video revolution, and right up to today's digital delivery era, IRMA has always been the organization companies have turned to for news, networking, market research, information services, and leadership.

Membership – Over 400 corporations, IRMAs membership includes raw material providers, manufacturers, replicators, duplicators, packagers, copyright holders, logistics providers, and companies from many other related industries. Corporate membership includes benefits to all employees.

Dues – Corporate membership dues based on gross dollar volume in our industry.

Meetings – Annual Recording Media Forum (Palm Springs, CA); December Summit (New York, NY).

Publications – 9X annual Mediaware Magazine; Annual International Source Directory, Quarterly Market Intelligence.

Name of Organization or Association – International Society for Performance Improvement

Acronym – ISPI

Address – 1400 Spring Street, Suite 260

City – Silver Spring

State – MD

Zip Code – 20910

Country – US

Phone Number – 301-587-8570

Fax Number – 301-587-8573

Email Contact – emember@ispi.org

URL – http://www.ispi.org

Leaders – Richard D. Battaglia, Executive Director

Description – The International Society for Performance Improvement (ISPI) is dedicated to improving individual, organizational, and societal performance. Founded in 1962, ISPI is the leading international association dedicated to improving productivity and performance in the workplace. ISPI represents more than 10,000 international and chapter members throughout the United States, Canada, and 40 other countries. ISPI's mission is to develop and recognize the proficiency of our members and advocate the use of Human Performance Technology. This systematic approach to improving productivity and competence uses a set of methods and procedures and a strategy for solving problems for realizing opportunities related to the performance of people. It is a systematic combination of performance analysis, cause analysis, intervention design and development, implementation, and evaluation that can be applied to individuals, small groups, and large organizations.

Membership – 10,000 Performance technologists, training directors, human resources managers, instructional technologists, human factors practitioners, and organizational consultants are members of ISPI. They work in a variety of settings including business, academia, government, health services, banking, and the armed forces.

Dues – Membership Categories Active Membership ($145 annually). This is an individual membership receiving full benefits and voting rights in the Society. Student Membership ($60 annually). This is a discounted individual full membership for full-time students. Proof of full-time enrollment must accompany the application. Retired Membership ($60 annually). This is a discounted individual full membership for individuals who are retired from full-time employment. Special Organizational Membership Categories These groups support the Society at the top level. Sustaining Membership ($950 annually). This is an organizational membership and includes five active memberships and several additional value-added services and discounts. Details available upon request. Patron Membership ($1,400 annually). This is an organizational membership and includes five active memberships and several additional value-added services and discounts. Details available upon request.

Meetings – Annual International Performance Improvement Conference, Fall Symposiums, Professional Series Workshops, Human Performance Technology Institutes.

Publications – Performance Improvement Journal (10/yr.) The common theme is performance improvement practice or technique that is supported by research or germane theory. PerformanceXpress (12/yr.) Monthly newsletter published on-line. Performance Improvement Quarterly PIQ is a peer-reviewed journal created to stimulate professional discussion in the field and to advance the discipline of HPT through publishing scholarly works. ISPI Bookstore The ISPI online bookstore is hosted in partnership with John Wiley & Sons.

Name of Organization or Association – International Society for Technology in Education

Acronym – ISTE

Address – 480 Charnelton Street

City – Eugene

State – OR

Zip Code – 97401

Country – US

Phone Number – 800.336.5191 (U.S. & Canada) 541.302.3777 (Intl.)

Fax Number – 541.302.3780

Email Contact – iste@iste.org

URL – http://www.iste.org

Leaders – Don Knezek, CEO; Cheryl Williams, Co-President; Cathie Norris, Co-President

Description – As the leading organization for educational technology professionals, the International Society for Technology in Education is a professional organization that supports a community of members through research, publications, workshops, symposia, and inclusion in national policy making through ISTE-DC. Home of the National Center for Preparing Tomorrows Teachers to Use Technology (NCPT3), ISTE works in conjunction with the U.S. Department of Education and various private entities to create and distribute solutions for technology integration. ISTEs National Educational Technology Standards (NETS) for students and teachers have been adopted by hundreds of districts nationwide. ISTE is also the home of NECC, the premier U.S. educational technology conference, is a forum for advancing educational philosophies, practices, policies, and research that focus on the appropriate use of current and emerging technologies to improve teaching and learning in K-12 and teacher education.

Membership – ISTE members are leaders. ISTE members contribute to the field of educational technology as classroom teachers, lab teachers, technology coordinators, school administrators, teacher educators, and consultants. ISTE provides leadership and professional development opportunities for its members. In addition to other benefits, ISTE members can participate in ISTE-sponsored invitational events at the National Educational Computer Conference (NECC), join one of ISTEs many Special Interest Groups (SIGs), and test and evaluate the latest in educational technology products and services through the ISTE Advocate Network. ISTE Members also enjoy subscriptions to ISTE Update and "Learning & Leading with Technology" or the "Journal for Research on Technology in Education." In the member's areas of the ISTE Web site, ISTE members can join discussion lists and other online forums for participation, review a database of educational technology resources, network with a cadre of education professionals, and review online editions of ISTE publications.

Dues – Annual dues for individual ISTE members are $58. Membership to SIG communities are $20 for ISTE members. Contact iste@iste.org to become a member. Annual dues for ISTE 100 members are $5,0000. Contact iste100@iste.org for more information. Group discounts are available. To see if you qualify, contact groupdiscounts@iste.org

Meetings – National Educational Computing Conference (NECC).

Publications – ISTEs publications include "ISTE Update" (online member newsletter); "Learning & Leading with Technology;" the "Journal of Research on Technology in Education" (q.; formerly "Journal of Research on Computing in Education"); and books about incorporating technology in the K-16 classroom.

Name of Organization or Association – International Visual Literacy Association, Inc.

Acronym – IVLA

Address – Darrell Beauchamp, IVLA Treasurer, Navarro College, 3200 W. 7th Ave.

City – Corsicana

State – TX

Zip Code – 75110

Country – US

Phone Number – 903-875-7441

Fax Number – 903-874-4636

Email Contact – abbasj@cameron.edu

URL – www.ivla.org

Leaders – Darrell Beauchamp

Description – IVLA provides a multidisciplinary forum for the exploration, presentation, and discussion of all aspects of visual learning, thinking, communication, and expression. It also serves as a communication link bonding professionals from many disciplines who are creating and sustaining the study of the nature of visual experiences and literacy. It promotes and evaluates research, programs, and projects intended to increase effective use of visual communication in education, business, the arts, and commerce. IVLA was founded in 1968 to promote the concept of visual literacy and is an affiliate of AECT.

Membership – Membership of 500 people, mostly from academia and from many disciplines. We are an international organization and have conferences abroad once every third year. Anyone interested in any visual-verbal area should try our organization: architecture, engineering, dance, the arts, computers, video, design, graphics, photography, visual languages, mathematics, acoustics, physics, chemistry, optometry, sciences, literature, library, training, education, etc.

Dues – $40 regular; $20 student and retired; $45 outside United States; corporate memberships available; $500 lifetime membership.

Meetings – Yearly conference usually Oct./Nov. in selected locations.

Publications – The Journal of Visual Literacy (bi-annual – juried research papers); Selected Readings from the Annual Conference; and The Visual Literacy Review (newsletter – 4 times per year).

Name of Organization or Association – Learning Point Associates

Acronym – (none)

Address – 1120 E. Diehl Road Suite 200

City – Naperville

State – IL

Zip Code – 60563-1486

Country – US

Phone Number – (630)649-6500, (800)356-2735

Fax Number – (630)649-6700

Email Contact – info@learningpt.org

URL – www.learningpt.org

Leaders – Gina Burkhardt, Chief Executive Officer

Description – Learning Point Associates, with offices in Naperville, Illinois; Chicago; New York; and Washington, DC, is a nonprofit educational organization with more than 20 years of direct experience working with and for educators and policymakers to transform educational systems and student learning. The national and international reputation of Learning Point Associates is built on a solid foundation of conducting rigorous and relevant education research and evaluation; analyzing and synthesizing education policy trends and practices; designing and conducting client-centered evaluations; delivering high-quality professional services; and developing and delivering tools, services, and resources targeted at pressing education issues. Learning Point Associates manages a diversified portfolio of work ranging from direct consulting assignments to major federal contracts and grants, including REL Midwest, the National Comprehensive Center for Teacher Quality, Great Lakes East Comprehensive Assistance Center, Great Lakes West Comprehensive Assistance Center, The Center for Comprehensive School Reform and Improvement, and the NCLB Implementation Center.

Membership – Not applicable.

Dues – None.

Meetings – None.

Publications – Visit the Publications section of our website.

Name of Organization or Association – Library Administration and Management Association

Acronym – LAMA

Address – 50 E. Huron St.

City – Chicago

State – IL

Zip Code – 60611

Country – US

Phone Number – (312)280-5032

Fax Number – (312)280-5033

Email Contact – lama@ala.org

URL – http://www.ala.org/lama

Leaders – Lorraine Olley, Executive Director; Catherine Murray-Rust, President

Description – MISSION: The Library Administration and Management Association encourages and nurtures current and future library leaders, and develops and promotes outstanding leadership and management practices. VISION: LAMA will be the foremost organization developing present and future leaders in library and information services. IMAGE: LAMA is a welcoming community where aspiring and experienced leaders from all types of libraries, as well as those who support libraries, come together to gain skills in a quest for excellence in library management, administration and leadership. Sections include: Buildings and Equipment Section (BES); Fundraising & Financial Development Section (FRFDS); Library Organization & Management Section (LOMS); Human Resources Section (HRS); Public Relation and Marketing Section (PRMS); Systems & Services Section (SASS); and Measurement, Assessment and Evaluation Section (MAES).

Membership – 4,800

Dues – $50 regular (in addition to ALA membership); $65 organizations and corporations; $15, library school students.

Meetings – ALA Annual Conference 2006, New Orleans, June 22–27; Midwinter Meeting 2007, San Diego, Jan 9–14.

Publications – Library Administration & Management (q); LEADS from LAMA (electronic newsletter, irregular).

Name of Organization or Association – Library and Information Technology Association

Acronym – LITA

Address – 50 E. Huron St.

City – Chicago

State – IL

Zip Code – 60611

Country – US

Phone Number – (312)280-4270, (800)545-2433, ext. 4270

Fax Number – (312)280-3257

Email Contact – lita@ala.org

URL – http://www.lita.org

Leaders – Mary C. Taylor, Executive Director, mtaylor@ala.org

Description – A division of the American Library Association, LITA is concerned with library automation; the information sciences; and the design, development, and implementation of automated systems in those fields, including systems development, electronic data processing, mechanized information retrieval, operations research, standards development, telecommunications, video communications, networks and collaborative efforts, management techniques, information technology, optical technology, artificial intelligence and expert systems, and other related aspects of audiovisual activities and hardware applications.

Membership – LITA members come from all types of libraries and institutions focusing on information technology in libraries. They include library decision-makers, practitioners, information professionals and vendors. Approximately 4,300 members.

Dues – $60 plus membership in ALA; $25 plus membership in ALA for library school students.

Meetings – National Forum, fall.

Publications – LITA Blog. Information Technology and Libraries (ITAL): Contains the table of contents, abstracts and some full-text of ITAL, a refereed journal published quarterly by the Library and Information Technology Association. Technology Electronic Reviews (TER): TER is an irregular electronic serial publication that provides reviews and pointers to a variety of print and electronic resources about information technology. LITA Publications List: Check for information on LITA Guides and Monographs.

Name of Organization or Association – Lister Hill National Center for Biomedical Communications

Acronym – LHNCBC

Address – National Library of Medicine, 8600 Rockville Pike

City – Bethesda

State – MD

Zip Code – 20894

Country – US

Phone Number – (301)496-4441

Fax Number – (301)402-0118

Email Contact – lhcques@lhc.nlm.nih.gov

URL – http://lhncbc.nlm.nih.gov/

Leaders – Clement J. McDonald, MD, Director, ClemMcDonald@mail.nih.gov

Description – The Lister Hill National Center for Biomedical Communications is a research and development division of the National Library of Medicine (NLM). The Center conducts and supports research and development in the dissemination of high quality imagery, medical language processing, high-speed access to biomedical information, intelligent database systems development, multimedia visualization, knowledge management, data mining and machine-assisted indexing. The Lister Hill Center also conducts and supports research and development projects focusing on educational applications of state-of-the-art technologies including the use of microcomputer technology incorporating stereoscopic imagery and haptics, the Internet, and videoconferencing technologies for training health care professionals and disseminating consumer health information. The Centers Collaboratory for High Performance Computing and Communication serves as a focus for collaborative research and development in those areas, cooperating with faculties and staff of health sciences educational institutions. Health profession educators are assisted in the use and application of these technologies through periodic training, demonstrations and consultations. High Definition (HD) video is a technology area that has been explored and developed within the Center, and is now used as the NLM standard for all motion imaging projects considered to be of archival value. Advanced three dimensional animation and photorealistic rendering techniques have also become required tools for use in visual projects within the Center.

Membership – None.

Dues – None.

Meetings – None.

Publications – Fact sheet (and helpful links to other publications) at: http://www.nlm.nih.gov/pubs/factsheets/lister_hill.html

Name of Organization or Association – Medical Library Association

Acronym – MLA

Address – 65 E. Wacker Pl., Ste. 1900

City – Chicago

State – IL

Zip Code – 60601-7246

Country – US

Phone Number – (312)419-9094

Fax Number – (312)419-8950

Email Contact – info@mlahq.org

URL – http://www.mlanet.org

Leaders – Carla J. Funk, MLS, MBA, CAE, Executive Director

Description – MLA, a nonprofit, educational organization, comprises health sciences information professionals with more than 4,500 members worldwide. Through its programs and services, MLA provides lifelong educational opportunities, supports a knowledgebase of health information research, and works with a global network of partners to promote the importance of quality information for improved health to the health care community and the public.

Membership – MLA, a nonprofit, educational organization, comprises health sciences information professionals with more than 4,500 members worldwide. Through its programs and services, MLA provides lifelong educational opportunities, supports a knowledgebase of health information research, and works with a global network of partners to promote the importance of quality information for improved health to the health care community and the public. Membership categories: Regular Membership Institutional Membership International Membership Affiliate Membership Student Membership.

Dues – $165, regular; $110, introductory; $255–$600, institutional, based on total library expenditures, including salaries, but excluding grants and contracts; $110, international; $100, affiliate; $40, student.

Meetings – National annual meeting held every May; most chapter meetings are held in the fall.

Publications – MLA News (newsletter, 10/yr.); Journal of the Medical Library Association (quarterly scholarly publication.); MLA DocKit series, collections of representative, unedited library documents from a variety of institutions that illustrate the range of approaches to health sciences library management topics); MLA BibKits, selective, annotated bibliographies of discrete subject areas in the health sciences literature; standards; surveys; and co-published monographs.

Name of Organization or Association – Mid-continent Research for Education and Learning

Acronym – McREL

Address – 4601 DTC Blvd., Suite 500

City – Denver

State – CO

Zip Code – 80237

Country – US

Phone Number – (303)337-0990

Fax Number – (303)337-3005

Email Contact – info@mcrel.org

URL – http://www.mcrel.org

Leaders – J. Timothy Waters, Executive Director

Description – McREL is a private, nonprofit organization whose purpose is to improve education through applied research and development. McREL provides products and services, primarily for K-12 educators, to promote the best instructional practices in the classroom. McREL houses one of 10 regional educational laboratories funded by the U.S. Department of Education, Institute for Educational Science. The regional laboratory helps educators and policymakers work toward excellence in education for all students. It also serves at the North Central Comprehensive Center, providing school improvement support to the states of Iowa, Minnesota, Nebraska, North Dakota, and South Dakota. McREL has particular expertise in standards-based education systems, leadership for school improvement, effective instructional practices, teacher quality, mathematics and science education improvement, early literacy development, and education outreach programs.

Membership – not a membership organization.

Dues – no dues.

Meetings – annual conference.

Publications – Changing Schools (q. newsletter); Noteworthy (annual monograph on topics of current interest in education reform). Numerous technical reports and other publications. Check website for current listings.

Name of Organization or Association – Minorities in Media

Acronym – MIM

Address – 1800 N. Stonelake Dr. Suite 2

City – Bloomington

State – IN

Zip Code – 47408

Country – US

Phone Number – (703) 993-3669

Fax Number – (313)577-1693

Email Contact – dtolbert@nu.edu

URL – -

Leaders – Denise Tolbert, President

Description – MIM is a special interest group of AECT that responds to the challenge of preparing students of color for an ever-changing international marketplace and recognizes the unique educational needs of today's diverse learners. It promotes the effective use of educational communications and technology in the learning process. MIM seeks to facilitate changes in instructional design and development, traditional pedagogy, and instructional delivery systems by responding to and meeting the significant challenge of educating diverse individuals to take their place in an ever-changing international marketplace. MIM encourages all of AECT's body of members to creatively develop curricula, instructional treatments, instructional strategies, and instructional materials that promote an acceptance and appreciation of racial and cultural diversity. Doing so will make learning for all more effective, relevant, meaningful, motivating, and enjoyable. MIM actively supports the Wes McJulien Minority Scholarship, and selects the winner.

Membership – contact MIM president.

Dues – $20, student; $30, nonstudent.

Meetings –

Publications – Newsletter is forthcoming online. The MIM listserv is a membership benefit.

Name of Organization or Association – Museum of Modern Art, Circulating Film and Video Library

Acronym – MoMA

Address – 11 W. 53rd St.

City – New York

State – NY

Zip Code – 10019

Country – US

Phone Number – (212)708-9530

Fax Number – (212)708-9531

Email Contact – kitty_cleary@moma.org

URL – http://www.moma.org

Leaders – Kitty Cleary

Description – Provides film and video rentals and sales of over 1,300 titles covering the history of film from the 1890s to the present. It also includes an important collection of work by leading video artists and is the sole distributor of the films of Andy Warhol. The Circulating Film and Video Library continues to add to its holdings of early silents, contemporary documentaries, animation, avant-garde, independents and video and to make these available to viewers who otherwise would not have the opportunity to see them. The Circulating Film and Video Library has 16 mm prints available for rental, sale, and lease. Some of the 16 mm titles are available on DVD and videocassette. The classic film collection is not. The video collection is available in all formats for rental and sale. The Library also has available a limited number of titles on 35 mm, including rare early titles preserved by the Library of Congress. They also now distribute some films on art and artists formally handled by the American Federation of the Arts as well as the film work of contemporary artists such as Richard Serra and Yoko Ono.

Membership – no membership.

Dues – 0

Meetings –

Publications – Information on titles may be found in the free Price List and the Films of Andy Warhol brochure, both available from the Library.

Name of Organization or Association – National Aeronautics and Space Administration

Acronym – NASA

Address – NASA Headquarters, 300 E Street SW

City – Washington

State – DC

Zip Code – 20546

Country – US

Phone Number – (202)358-0103

Fax Number – (202)358-3032

Email Contact – education@nasa.gov

URL – http://education.nasa.gov

Leaders – Angela Phillips Diaz, Assistant Administrator for Education.

Description – From elementary through postgraduate school, NASAs educational programs are designed to inspire the next generation of explorers by capturing students interest in science, mathematics, and technology at an early age; to channel more students into science, engineering, and technology career paths; and to enhance the knowledge, skills, and experiences of teachers and university faculty. NASAs educational programs include NASA Spacelink (an electronic information system); videoconferences (60-minute interactive staff development videoconferences to be delivered to schools via satellite); and NASA Television (informational and educational television programming). Additional information is available from the Office of Education at NASA Headquarters and counterpart offices at the nine NASA field centers. Further information may be obtained from the NASA

Education Homepage and also accessible from the NASA Public Portal at See learning in a whole new light!

Membership – n/a

Dues – n/a

Meetings – n/a

Publications – Publications and Products can be searched and downloaded from the following URL – http://www.nasa.gov/audience/foreducators/5-8/learning/index.html

Name of Organization or Association – National Alliance for Media Arts and Culture

Acronym – NAMAC

Address – 145 Ninth Street, Suite 250

City – San Francisco

State – CA

Zip Code – 94103

Country – US

Phone Number – (415)431-1391

Fax Number – (415)431-1392

Email Contact – namac@namac.org

URL – http://www.namac.org

Leaders – Helen DeMichel, Co-Director

Description – NAMAC is a nonprofit organization dedicated to increasing public understanding of and support for the field of media arts in the United States. Members include media centers, cable access centers, universities, and media artists, as well as other individuals and organizations providing services for production, education, exhibition, distribution, and preservation of video, film, audio, and intermedia. NAMACs information services are available to the general public, arts and non-arts organizations, businesses, corporations, foundations, government agencies, schools, and universities.

Membership – 300 organizations, 75 individuals.

Dues – $75-$450, institutional (depending on annual budget); $75, indiv.

Meetings – Biennial Conference.

Publications – Media Arts Information Network; The National Media Education Directory, annual anthology of case-studies "A Closer Look," periodic White Paper reports, Digital Directions: Convergence Planning for the Media Arts.

Name of Organization or Association – National Association for Visually Handicapped

Acronym – NAVH

Address – 22 West 21st St., 6th Floor

City – New York

State – NY

Zip Code – 10010

Country – US

Phone Number – (212) 889-3141

Fax Number – (212) 727-2931

Email Contact – navh@navh.org

URL – http://www.navh.org

Leaders – Dr. Lorraine H. Marchi, Founder/CEO; Cesar Gomez, Executive Director

Description – NAVH ensures that those with limited vision do not lead limited lives. We offer emotional support; training in the use of visual aids and special lighting; access to a wide variety of optical aids, electronic equipment and lighting; a large print, nationwide, free-by-mail loan library; large print educational materials; free quarterly newsletter; referrals to eye care specialists and local low vision resources; self-help groups for seniors and working adults; and educational outreach to the public and professionals.

Membership – It is not mandatory to became a member in order to receive our services. However, your membership helps others retain their independence by allowing NAVH to provide low vision services to those who cannot afford to make a donation. In addition, members receive discounts on visual aids, educational materials and our catalogs. Corporations and publishers may also join to help sponsor our services. Please contact us for more information.

Dues – Membership is $50 a year for individuals. Publishers and corporations interested in membership should contact NAVH.

Meetings – Seniors support group 2 times at month; Seminar on low vision for ophthalmology residents; yearly showcase of the latest in low vision technology, literature and services.

Publications – Free quarterly newsletter distributed free throughout the English-speaking world; Visual Aids Catalog; Large Print Loan Library Catalog; informational pamphlets on vision, common eye diseases and living with limited vision; booklets for professionals who work with adults and children with limited vision.

Name of Organization or Association – National Association of Media and Technology Centers

Acronym – NAMTC

Address – NAMTC, 7105 First Ave. SW

City – Cedar Rapids

State – IA

Zip Code – 52405

Country – US

Phone Number – 319 654 0608

Fax Number – 319 654 0609

Email Contact – bettyge@mchsi.com

URL – www.namtc.org

Leaders – Betty Gorsegner Ehlinger, Executive Director

Description – NAMTC is committed to promoting leadership among its membership through networking, advocacy, and support activities that will enhance the equitable access to media, technology, and information services to educational communities. Membership is open to regional, K-12, and higher education media centers which serve K-12 students as well as commercial media and technology centers.

Membership – Institutional and corporate members numbering approximately 225.

Dues – $100 institutions; $300, corporations.

Meetings – Regional meetings are held throughout the United States annually. A national Leadership Summit is held in the spring.

Publications – Membership newsletter is 'ETIN, a quarterly publication.

Name of Organization or Association – National Commission on Libraries and Information Science

Acronym – NCLIS

Address – 1800 M Street, NW; Suite 350 North Tower

City – Washington

State – DC

Zip Code – 20036-5841

Country – US

Phone Number – (202)606-9200

Fax Number – (202)606-9203

Email Contact – info@nclis.gov

URL – http://www.nclis.gov

Leaders – C. Beth Fitzsimmons, Chairman

Description – A permanent independent agency of the U.S. government charged with advising the executive and legislative branches on national library and information policies and plans. The Commission reports directly to the president and Congress on the implementation of national policy; conducts studies, surveys, and analyses of the nations library and information needs; appraises the inadequacies of current resources and services; promotes research and development activities; conducts hearings and issues publications as appropriate; and develops overall plans for meeting national library and information needs and for the coordination of activities at the federal, state, and local levels. The Commission provides general policy advice to the Institute of Museum and Library Services (IMLS) director relating to library services included in the Library Services and Technology Act (LSTA).

Membership – 16 commissioners (14 appointed by the president and confirmed by the Senate, the Librarian of Congress, and the Director of the IMLS).

Dues – None.

Meetings – Average 2–3 meetings a year.

Publications – n/a

Name of Organization or Association – National Communication Association

Acronym – NCA

Address – 1765 N Street, NW

City – Washington,

State – DC

Zip Code – 22003

Country – US

Phone Number – 202-464-4622

Fax Number – 202-464-4600

Email Contact – dwallick@natcom.org

URL – http://www.natcom.org

Leaders – Roger Smitter, Executive Director

Description – A voluntary society organized to promote study, criticism, research, teaching, and application of principles of communication, particularly of speech communication. Founded in 1914, NCA is a non-profit organization of researchers, educators, students, and practitioners, whose academic interests span all forms of human communication. NCA is the oldest and largest national organization serving the academic discipline of Communication. Through its services, scholarly publications, resources, conferences and conventions, NCA works with its members to strengthen the profession and contribute to the greater good of the educational enterprise and society. Research and instruction in the discipline focus on the study of how messages in various media are produced, used, and interpreted within and across different contexts, channels, and cultures.

Membership – 7,700

Dues – From $60 (Student) to $300 (Patron). Life membership also available.

Meetings – Four regional conferences (ECA, ESCA SSCA, WSCA) and 1 Annual National Conference.

Publications – Spectra Newsletter (mo.); Quarterly Journal of Speech; Communication Monographs; Communication Education; Critical Studies in Mass Communication; Journal of Applied Communication Research; Text and Performance Quarterly; Communication Teacher; Index to Journals in Communication Studies through 1995; National Communication Directory of NCA and the Regional Speech Communication Organizations (CSSA, ECA, SSCA, WSCA). For additional publications, request brochure.

Name of Organization or Association – National Council of Teachers of English: Commission on Media, Assembly on Media Arts

Acronym – NCTE

Address – 1111 W. Kenyon Rd.

City – Urbana

State – IL

Zip Code – 61801-1096

Country – US

Phone Number – (217)328-3870

Fax Number – (217)328-0977

Email Contact – public_info@ncte.org

URL – http://www.ncte.org

Leaders – Kent Williamson, NCTE Executive Director; David Bruce, Commission Director; Mary Christel, Assembly Chair

Description – The NCTE Commission on Media is a deliberative and advisory body which each year identifies and reports to the NCTE Executive Committee on key issues in the teaching of media; reviews what the Council has done concerning media during the year; recommends new projects and persons who might undertake them. The commission monitors current and projected NCTE publications (other than journals), suggests topics for future NCTE publications on media, and performs a similar role of review and recommendation for the NCTE Annual Convention program. Occasionally, the commission undertakes further tasks and projects as approved by the Executive Committee. The NCTE Assembly on Media Arts promotes communication and cooperation among all individuals who have a special interest in media in the English language arts; presents programs and special projects on this subject; encourages the development of research, experimentation, and investigation in the judicious uses of media in the teaching of English; promotes the extensive writing of articles and publications devoted to this subject; and integrates the efforts of those with an interest in this subject.

Membership – The National Council of Teachers of English, with 50,000 individual and institutional members worldwide, is dedicated to improving the teaching and learning of English and the language arts at all levels of education. Members include elementary, middle, and high school teachers; supervisors of English programs; college and university faculty; teacher educators; local and state agency English specialists; and professionals in related fields The members of the NCTE Commission on Media are NCTE members appointed by the director of the group. Membership in the Assembly on Media Arts is open to members and nonmembers of NCTE.

Dues – Membership in NCTE is $40 a year; adding subscriptions to its various journals adds additional fees. Membership in the Assembly on Media Arts is $15 a year.

Meetings – http://www.ncte.org/conventions/ 96th NCTE Annual Convention, November 20–25, 2003, San Francisco, California; 94th NCTE Annual Convention, November 16–21, 2006, Nashville, Tennessee.

Publications – NCTE publishes about 20 books a year. Visit http://www.ncte.org/pubs/books/ and http://www.ncte.org/store. NCTEs journals include Language Arts English Journal College English College Composition and Communication English Education Research in the Teaching of English Teaching English in the Two-Year College Voices from the Middle Primary Voices, K-6

Talking Points Classroom Notes Plus English Leadership Quarterly The Council Chronicle (included in NCTE membership) Journal information is available at http://www.ncte.org/pubs/journals/ The Commission on Media doesn't have its own publication. The Assembly on Media Arts publishes Media Matters, a newsletter highlighting issues, viewpoints, materials, and events related to the study of media. Assembly members receive this publication.

Name of Organization or Association – National EBS Association

Acronym – NEBSA

Address – PO Box 121475

City – Clermont

State – FL

Zip Code – 34712-1475

Country – US

Phone Number – (407)401-4630

Fax Number – (321)406-0520

Email Contact – execdirector@nebsa.org

URL – http://nebsa.org

Leaders – Lynn Rejniak, Chair, Bd. of Dirs.; Don MacCullough, Executive Director

Description – Established in 1978, NEBSA is a nonprofit, professional organization of Educational Broadband Service (EBS) licensees, applicants, and others interested in EBS broadcasting. EBS is a very high frequency television broadcast service that is used to broadcast distance learning classes, two way internet service, wireless and data services to schools and other locations where education can take place. The goals of the association are to gather and exchange information about EBS, gather data on utilization of EBS, act as a conduit for those seeking EBS information, and assist migration from video broadcast to wireless, broadband Internet services using EBS channels. The NEBSA represents EBS interests to the FCC, technical consultants, and equipment manufacturers. The association uses its Web site and Listserv list to provide information to its members in areas such as technology, programming content, FCC regulations, excess capacity leasing and license and application data.

Membership – The current membership consists of Educational Institutions and non-profit organizations that hold licenses issued by the Federal Communications Commission for Educational Broadband Service (EBS). We also have members that have an interest in EBS and members such as manufacturers of EBS related equipment and Law firms that represent Licensees.

Dues – We have two main types of memberships: Voting memberships for EBS licensees only, and non-voting memberships for other educational institutions and sponsors. See the Web site http://www.nebsa.org for details.

Meetings – Annual Member Conference, February/March.

Publications – http://www.nebsa.org

Name of Organization or Association – National Endowment for the Humanities

Acronym – NEH

Address – Division of Public Programs, Media Program, 1100 Pennsylvania Ave., NW, Room 426

City – Washington

State – DC

Zip Code – 20506

Country – US

Phone Number – (202)606-8269

Fax Number – (202)606-8557

Email Contact – publicpgms@neh.gov

URL – http://www.neh.gov

Leaders – Tom Phelps, Acting Director, Division of Public Programs

Description – The NEH is an independent federal grant-making agency that supports research, educational, and public programs grounded in the disciplines of the humanities. The Division of Public Programs Media Program supports film and radio programs in the humanities for public audiences, including children and adults. All programs in the Division of Public Program support various technologies, specifically web sites both as stand alone projects and as extensions of larger projects such as museum exhibitions.

Membership – Nonprofit institutions and organizations including public television and radio stations.

Dues – n/a

Meetings – n/a

Publications – Visit the web site (http://www.neh.gov) for application forms and guidelines as well as the Media Log, a cumulative listing of projects funded through the Media Program.

Name of Organization or Association – National Federation of Community Broadcasters

Acronym – NFCB

Address – 1970 Broadway, Ste. 1000

City – Oakland

State – CA

Zip Code – 94612

Country – US

Phone Number – 510 451-8200

Fax Number – 510 451-8208

Email Contact – ginnyz@nfcb.org

URL – http://www.nfcb.org.

Leaders – Carol Pierson, President and CEO

Description – NFCB represents non-commercial, community-based radio stations in public policy development at the national level and provides a wide range of practical services, including technical assistance.

Membership – 250. Noncommercial community radio stations, related organizations, and individuals.

Dues – range from $200 to $3,500 for participant and associate members.

Meetings – 2002 Charlottesville, VA; 2003 San Francisco; 2004 Albuquerque; 2005 Baltimore; 2006 Portland, OR; 2007 New Orleans.

Publications – Public Radio Legal Handbook; AudioCraft; Community Radio News; Let a Thousand Voices Speak: A Guide to Youth in Radio Projects; Guide to Underwriting.

Name of Organization or Association – National Film Board of Canada

Acronym – NFBC

Address – 1123 Broadway, STE 307

City – New York

State – NY

Zip Code – 10010

Country – US

Phone Number – (212)629-8890

Fax Number – (212)629-8502

Email Contact – NewYork@nfb.ca

URL – www.nfb.ca

Leaders – Dylan McGinty, US Sales Manager; Laure Parsons, US Sales and Marketing Associate

Description – Established in 1939, the NFBCs main objective is to produce and distribute high-quality audiovisual materials for educational, cultural, and social purposes.

Membership – None.

Dues – None.

Meetings – n/a

Publications – n/a

Name of Organization or Association – National Freedom of Information Coalition

Acronym – NFOIC

Address – 133 Neff Annex, University of Missouri

City – Columbia

State – MO

Zip Code – 65211-0012

Country – US

Phone Number – (573)882-4856

Fax Number – (573)884-6204

Email Contact – daviscn@missouri.edu

URL – http://www.nfoic.org

Leaders – Dr. Charles N. Davis, Executive Director

Description – The National Freedom of Information Coalition is a national membership organization devoted to protecting the publics right to oversee its government. NFOICs goals include helping start-up FOI organizations; strengthening existing FOI organizations; and developing FOI programs and publications appropriate to the membership.

Membership – The NFOIC offers active memberships to freestanding nonprofit state or regional Freedom of Information Coalitions, academic centers and First Amendment Centers, and associated memberships to individuals and entities supporting NFOICs mission. Membership information is available on the NFOIC Web page. Achieving and maintaining active membership in all 50 states is the primary goal of NFOIC.

Dues – Membership categories and levels of support are described on the NFOIC Web site.

Meetings – The National Freedom of Information Coalition host an annual meeting and a spring conference.

Publications – The FOI Advocate, an electronic newsletter available for free through email subscription. The FOI Report, a periodic White Paper, published electronically.

Name of Organization or Association – National Gallery of Art

Acronym – NGA

Address – Department of Education Resources, 2000B South Club Drive

City – Landover

State – MD

Zip Code – 20785

Country – US

Phone Number – (202)842-6273

Fax Number – (202)842-6935

Email Contact – EdResources@nga.gov

URL – http://www.nga.gov/education/classroom/loanfinder/

Leaders – Leo J. Kasun Education Resources Supervisory Specialist

Description – This department of NGA is responsible for the production and distribution of 120+ educational audiovisual programs, including interactive technologies. Materials available (all loaned free to individuals, schools, colleges and universities, community organizations, and non-commercial television stations) range from videocassettes and color slide programs to CD-ROMs, and DVDs. All videocassette and DVD programs are closed captioned A free catalog of programs is available upon request. All cd-roms, dvds, utilizing digitized images on the gallery's collection are available for long-term loan.

Membership – Our free-loan lending program resembles that of a library and because we are a federally funded institution we have membership system. Last year we lent programs directly to over one million borrowers. Our programs are available to anyone who requests them which ranges from individuals to institutions.

Dues – None.

Meetings – None.

Publications – Extension Programs Catalogue.

Name of Organization or Association – National PTA

Acronym – National PTA

Address – 541 North Fairbanks Ct, Ste. 1300

City – Chicago

State – IL

Zip Code – 60611

Country – US

Phone Number – (312)670-6782

Fax Number – (312)670-6783

Email Contact – info@pta.org

URL – http://www.pta.org

Leaders – Warlene Gary, Chief Executive Officer

Description – Advocates the education, health, safety, and well-being of children and teens. Provides parenting education and leadership training to PTA volunteers. National PTA partners with the National Cable & Telecommunications Association on the "Taking Charge of Your TV" project by training PTA and cable representatives to present media literacy workshops. The workshops teach parents and educators how to evaluate programming so they can make informed decisions about what to allow their children to see. The National PTA in 1997 convinced the television industry to add content information to the TV rating system.

Membership – 6.2 million Membership open to all interested in the health, welfare, and education of children and support the PTA mission – http://www.pta.org/aboutpta/mission_en.asp

Dues – vary by local unit – national dues portion is $1.75 per member annually.

Meetings – National convention, held annually in June in different regions of the country, is open to PTA members; convention information available on the Website.

Publications – Our Children (magazine) plus electronic newsletters and other web-based information for members and general public.

Name of Organization or Association – National Public Broadcasting Archives

Acronym – NPBA

Address – Hornbake Library, University of Maryland

City – College Park

State – MD

Zip Code – 20742

Country – US

Phone Number – (301)405-9160

Fax Number – (301)314-2634

Email Contact – npba@umd.edu

URL – http://www.lib.umd.edu/NPBA

Leaders – Karen King, Acting Curator

Description – NPBA brings together the archival record of the major entities of noncommercial broadcasting in the United States. NPBAs collections include the archives of the Corporation for Public Broadcasting (CPB), the Public Broadcasting Service (PBS), and National Public Radio (NPR). Other organizations represented include the Midwest Program for Airborne Television Instruction (MPATI), the Public Service Satellite Consortium (PSSC), Americas Public Television Stations (APTS), Children's Television Workshop (CTW), and the Joint Council for Educational Telecommunications (JCET). NPBA also makes available the personal papers of many individuals who have made significant contributions to public broadcasting, and its reference library contains basic studies of the broadcasting industry, rare pamphlets, and journals on relevant topics. NPBA also collects and maintains a selected audio and video program record of public broadcastings national production and support centers and of local stations. Oral history tapes and transcripts from the NPR Oral History Project and the Televisionaries Nal History Project are also available at the archives. The archives are open to the public from 9 A.M. to 5 P.M., Monday through Friday. Research in NPBA collections should be arranged by prior appointment. For further information, call (301)405-9988.

Membership – n/a

Dues – n/a

Meetings – n/a

Publications – n/a

Name of Organization or Association – National Telemedia Council Inc.

Acronym – NTC

Address – 1922 University Ave.

City – Madison

State – WI

Zip Code – 53726

Country – USA

Phone Number – (608)218-1182

Fax Number – (608)218-1183

Email Contact – NTelemedia@aol.com

URL – http://www.nationaltelemediacouncil.org, and www.journalofmedia-literacy.org

Leaders – Karen Ambrosh, President; Marieli Rowe, Executive Director

Description – The NTC is a national, nonprofit professional organization dedicated to promoting media literacy, or critical media viewing and listening skills. This is done primarily through the Journal of Media Literacy, the publication of the National Telemedia Council, as well as work with teachers, parents, and caregivers. NTC activities include publishing The Journal of Media Literacy, the Teacher Idea Exchange (T.I.E.), the Jessie McCanse Award for individual contribution to media literacy, assistance to media literacy educators and professionals.

Membership – Member/subscribers to the Journal of Media Literacy, currently over 500, including individuals, organizations, schools and University libraries across the Globe including Asia, Australia, Europe, North and South America. Our membership is open to all those interested in media literacy.

Dues – Individuals:$35, basic; $50, contributing; $100, patron Organizations/Library: $60 Corporate sponsorship: $500 (Additional Postage for Overseas)

Meetings – No major meetings scheduled this year.

Publications – The Journal of Media Literacy.

Name of Organization or Association – Native American Public Telecommunications

Acronym – NAPT

Address – 1800 North 33rd Street

City – Lincoln

State – NE

Zip Code – 68503

Country – US

Phone Number – (402)472-3522

Fax Number – (402)472-8675

Email Contact – rfauver1@unl.edu

URL – http://nativetelecom.org

Leaders – Shirley K. Sneve, Executive Director

Description – Native American Public Telecommunications (NAPT) supports the creation, promotion and distribution of Native public media. We accomplish this mission by: (1) Producing and developing educational telecommunication programs for all media including public television and public radio. (2) Distributing and encouraging the broadest use of such educational telecommunications programs. (3) Providing training opportunities to encourage increasing numbers of American Indians and Alaska Natives to produce quality public broadcasting programs. (4) Promoting increased control and use of information technologies by American Indians and Alaska Natives. (5) Providing leadership in creating awareness of and developing telecommunications policies favorable to American Indians and Alaska Natives. (6) Building partnerships to develop and implement telecommunications projects with tribal nations, Indian organizations, and native communities.

Membership – No Membership.

Dues – None.

Meetings – None.

Publications – The Vision Maker (e-newsletter).

Name of Organization or Association – Natural Science Collections Alliance

Acronym – NSC Alliance

Address – P.O. Box 44095

City – Washington

State – DC

Zip Code – 20026-4095

Country – US

Phone Number – (202)633-2772

Fax Number – (202)633-2821

Email Contact – ddrupa@burkine.com

URL – http://www.nscalliance.org

Leaders – Executive Director

Description – Fosters the care, management, and improvement of biological collections and promotes their utilization. Institutional members include free-standing museums, botanical gardens, college and university museums, and public institutions, including state biological surveys and agricultural research centers. The NSC Alliance also represents affiliate societies, and keeps members informed about funding and legislative issues.

Membership – 80 institutions, 30 affiliates, 120 individual and patron members.

Dues – Dues: depend on the size of collections.

Meetings – Annual Meeting (May or June).

Publications – Guidelines for Institutional Policies and Planning in Natural History Collections; Global Genetic Resources; A Guide to Museum Pest Control.

Name of Organization or Association – New England School Library Association

Acronym – NESLA

Address – c/o Katrina Palazzolo, Secretary 73 George Road

City – Rocky Hill

State – CT

Zip Code – 06067

Country – US

Phone Number – 860-563-4702

Fax Number – Please email

Email Contact – kandthewaves@mac.com

URL – www.neschoolibraries.org

Leaders – Merlyn Miller, President

Description – An affiliate of AECT, NESLA is a regional professional association dedicated to the improvement of instruction through the effective utilization of school library media services, media, and technology applications. For over 90 years, it has represented school library media professionals through activities and networking efforts to develop and polish the leadership skills, professional representation, and informational awareness of the membership. The Board of Directors consists of departments of education as well as professional leaders of the region. An annual conference program and a Leadership Program are offered in conjunction with the various regional state association conferences.

Membership – NESLA focuses on school library media issues among the six New England states, consequently, membership is encouraged for school library media specialists in this region.

Dues – Regular membership $30. Student /retired membership $15.

Meetings – Annual Leadership Conference and Business Meeting.

Publications – NESLA Views.

Name of Organization or Association – New York Festivals

Acronym – NYF

Address – 260 West 39th Street, 10th Floor

City – New York

State – NY

Zip Code – 10018

Country – USA

Phone Number – 212-643-4800

Fax Number – 212-643-0170

Email Contact – info@newyorkfestivals.com

URL – http://www.newyorkfestivals.com

Leaders – Alisun Armstrong, Executive Director

Description – New York Festivals (NYF) is an international awards company founded in 1957. Recognizing The World's Best Work^{TM} in advertising, programming, design, and marketing, NYF honors creativity and effectiveness in global communications through six different annual competitions. New York Festivals International Film & Video Awards is one of the oldest extant international festivals in the world. Known best for honoring informational, educational and industrial film production, the New York Festivals Film & Video Awards is entering its 50th year of recognizing The Worlds Best Work^{TM} in categories including Documentaries, Business Theatre, Short and Feature Length Films, Home Video Productions, Distance Learning, Slide Productions, and Multi-Screen Productions. Winners are honored in a black-tie event in Manhattan in January. The 2007 International Film & Video Awards will open for entry on July 5th. The Discount Deadline is August 23rd (enter online by that date and get a 10% discount off the entry total), and the final deadline will be September 22. For more information and fees, plus a full list of categories and the rules & regulations, please visit www.newyorkfestivals.com

Membership – No membership feature. The competition is open to any non-broadcast media production.

Dues – n/a

Meetings – n/a

Publications – Winners are posted on our web site at www.newyorkfestivals.com

Name of Organization or Association – Northwest College and University Council for the Management of Educational Technology

Acronym – NW/MET

Address – c/o WITS, Willamette University, 900 State St.

City – Salem

State – OR

Zip Code – 97301

Country – US

Phone Number – (503)370-6650

Fax Number – (503)375-5456

Email Contact – mmorandi@willamette.edu

URL – http://www.nwmet.org

Leaders – Doug McCartney, Director (effective April 14, 2007); Marti Morandi, Membership Chair.

Description – NW/MET is a group of media professionals responsible for campus-wide media services. Founded in 1976, NW/MET is comprised of members from 2 provinces of Canada and 4 northwestern states.

Membership – The membership of NW/MET is composed of individuals who participate by giving time, energy, and resources to the support and advancement of the organization. Full Membership may be awarded to individuals whose primary professional role involves the facilitation of educational technology, who are employed by an institution of higher education located in the NW/MET membership region, and who submit a membership application in which they list their professional qualifications and responsibilities.

Dues – $35

Meetings – An annual conference and business meeting are held each year, rotating through the region.

Publications – An annual Directory and website.

Name of Organization or Association – Northwest Regional Educational Laboratory

Acronym – NWREL

Address – 101 SW Main St., Suite 500

City – Portland

State – OR

Zip Code – 97204

Country – US

Phone Number – (503)275-9500

Fax Number – (503)275-0448

Email Contact – info@nwrel.org

URL – http://www.nwrel.org

Leaders – Dr. Carol Thomas, Executive Director

Description – One of 10 Office of Educational Research and Improvement (OERI) regional educational laboratories, NWREL works with schools and communities to improve educational outcomes for children, youth, and adults. NWREL provides leadership, expertise, and services based on the results of research and development. The specialty area of NWREL is school change processes. It serves Alaska, Idaho, Oregon, Montana, and Washington.

Membership – 856 organizations.

Dues – None.

Meetings – None.

Publications – Northwest Education (quarterly journal).

Name of Organization or Association – OCLC Online Computer Library Center, Inc.

Acronym – OCLC

Address – 6565 Kilgour Place

City – Dublin

State – OH

Zip Code – 43017-3395

Country – US

Phone Number – (614)764-6000

Fax Number – (614)764-6096

Email Contact – oclc@oclc.org

URL – http://www.oclc.org

Leaders – Jay Jordan, President and CEO

Description – Founded in 1967, OCLC is a nonprofit, membership, computer library service and research organization dedicated to the public purposes of furthering access to the worlds information and reducing information costs. More than 60,000 libraries in 112 countries and territories around the world use OCLC services to locate, acquire, catalog, lend and preserve library materials. Researchers, students, faculty, scholars, professional librarians and other information seekers use OCLC services to obtain bibliographic, abstract and full-text information. OCLC and its member libraries cooperatively produce and maintain WorldCat, the worlds largest database for discovery of library materials. OCLC publishes the Dewey Decimal Classification. OCLC Digital Collection and Preservation Services provide digitization and archiving services worldwide. OCLCs NetLibrary provides libraries with eContent solutions that support Web-based research, reference and learning.

Membership – OCLC welcomes information organizations around the world to be a part of our unique cooperative. A variety of participation levels are available to libraries, museums, archives, historical societies, other cultural heritage organizations and professional associations. OCLC membership represents more than 60,000 libraries in 112 countries and territories around the world.

Dues – n/a

Meetings – OCLC Members Council (3/yr.) Held in Dublin, Ohio.

Publications – Annual Report (1/yr.; print and electronic); OCLC Newsletter (4/yr.; print and electronic); OCLC Abstracts (1/week, electronic only).

Name of Organization or Association – Online Audiovisual Catalogers

Acronym – OLAC

Address – n/a

City – n/a

State – n/a

Zip Code – n/a

Country – US

Phone Number – n/a

Fax Number – n/a

Email Contact – neumeist@buffalo.edu

URL – http://www.olacinc.org/

Leaders – n/a

Description – In 1980, OLAC was founded to establish and maintain a group that could speak for catalogers of audiovisual materials. OLAC provides a means for exchange of information, continuing education, and communication among catalogers of audiovisual materials and with the Library of Congress. While maintaining a voice with the bibliographic utilities that speak for catalogers of audiovisual materials, OLAC works toward common understanding of AV cataloging practices and standards.

Membership – 500

Dues – United States and Canada Personal Memberships One year $20.00 Two years $38.00 Three years $55.00 Institutional Memberships One year $25.00 Two years $48.00 Three years $70.00 Other Countries All Memberships One year $25.00 Two years $48.00 Three years $70.00.

Meetings – bi-annual.

Publications – OLAC Newsletter.

Name of Organization or Association – Ontario Film Association, Inc. (also known as the Association for the Advancement of Visual Media/Lassociation pour lavancement des médias visuels).

Acronym – OLA

Address – 50 Wellington St East Suite 201

City – Toronto

State – ON

Zip Code – M5E 1C8

Country – Canada

Phone Number – (416)363-3388

Fax Number – 1-800-387-1181

Email Contact – info@accessola.com

URL – www.accessola.com

Leaders – Lawrence A. Moore, Executive Director

Description – A membership organization of buyers, and users of media whose objectives are to promote the sharing of ideas and information about visual media through education, publications, and advocacy.

Membership – 112

Dues – $120, personal membership; $215, associate membership.

Meetings – OFA Media Showcase, spring.

Publications – Access.

Name of Organization or Association – Pacific Film Archive

Acronym – PFA

Address – University of California, Berkeley Art Museum, 2625 Durant Ave.

City – Berkeley

State – CA

Zip Code – 94720-2250

Country – US

Phone Number – (510)642-1437 (library); (510)642-1412 (general).

Fax Number – (510)642-4889

Email Contact – NLG@berkeley.edu

URL – http://www.bampfa.berkeley.edu

Leaders – Susan Oxtoby, Senior Curator of Film; Nancy Goldman, Head, PFA Library and Film Study Center

Description – Sponsors the exhibition, study, and preservation of classic, international, documentary, animated, and avant-garde films. Provides on-site research screenings of films in its collection of over 7,000 titles. Provides access to its collections of books, periodicals, stills, and posters (all materials are non-circulating). Offers BAM/PFA members and University of California, Berkeley, affiliates reference and research services to locate film and video distributors, credits, stock footage, etc. Library hours are 1 P.M.–5 P.M. Mon.–Thurs. Research screenings are by appointment only and must be scheduled at least two weeks in advance; other collections are available for consultation on a drop-in basis during Library hours.

Membership – Membership is through our parent organization, the UC Berkeley Art Museum and Pacific Film Archive, and is open to anyone. The BAM/PFA currently has over 3,000 members. Members receive free admission to the Museum; reduced-price tickets to films showing at PFA; access to the PFA Library & Film

Study Center; and many other benefits. Applications and more information is available at http://www.bampfa.berkeley.edu/membership_giving/index.html

Dues – $40 indiv. and nonprofit departments of institutions.

Meetings – None.

Publications – BAM/PFA Calendar (6/yr.).

Name of Organization or Association – Pacific Resources for Education and Learning

Acronym – PREL

Address – 900 Fort Street Mall, Suite 1300

City – Honolulu

State – HI

Zip Code – 96813

Country – US

Phone Number – (808)441-1300

Fax Number – (808)441-1385

Email Contact – askprel@prel.org

URL – http://www.prel.org/

Leaders – Thomas W. Barlow, Ed.D., President and Chief Executive Officer

Description – Pacific Resources for Education and Learning (PREL) is an independent, nonprofit 501(c)(3) corporation that serves the educational community in the U.S.-affiliated Pacific islands, the continental United States, and countries throughout the world. PREL bridges the gap between research, theory, and practice in education and works collaboratively to provide services that range from curriculum development to assessment and evaluation. PREL serves the Pacific educational community with quality programs and products developed to promote educational excellence. We work throughout school systems, from classroom to administration, and collaborate routinely with governments, communities, and businesses. Above all, we specialize in multicultural and multilingual environments. From direct instruction to professional development to creation of quality educational materials, PREL is committed to ensuring that all students, regardless of circumstance or geographic location, have an equal opportunity to develop a strong academic foundation. PREL brings together in the Center for Information, Communications, and Technology (CICT) an experienced cadre of specialists in website development and design, educational technology, distance and online learning, multimedia production, interactive software development, writing and editing, graphics, and print production. By combining tested pedagogy with leading edge technology, PREL can create learning materials encompassing a wide variety of subject matter and delivery methods. PREL partners with researchers, schools, evaluators, publishers, and leaders in the learning technology industry to develop state-of-the-art learning tools and technology solutions. There are vast disparities across the Pacific when it comes to school resources, technology access, and bandwidth. PREL's goal is to work effectively in any type of setting in which an application is needed. With routine travel and a staff presence throughout the northern Pacific, PREL has resolved to reach underserved communities, determine their needs, and meet their requirements with the appropriate delivery and dissemination methods. Multimedia, Software, and Website conception, design, and delivery have become critical components of many learning programs. Our projects include development of teacher and student resources and resource kits, learning games, software solutions, and complex interactive database design. Distance Learning Content and Delivery extend educational resources to audiences and individuals outside the classroom setting. Distance options both enhance and exponentially increase learning opportunities. The CICT is a premier provider of distance education, integrating curriculum and technology. High-Quality Publications are a PREL hallmark. PREL produces and distributes numerous high-quality publications for educators, including its research compendium, Research into Practice; Pacific Educator magazine; educational books and videos; and briefs and reports on research findings and current topics of interest.

Membership – PREL serves teachers and departments and ministries of education in American Samoa, Commonwealth of the Northern Mariana Islands, Federated States of Micronesia (Chuuk, Kosrae, Pohnpei, and Yap) Guam, Hawaii, the Republic of the Marshall Islands, and the Republic of Palau. In addition we work with the educational community on the continental United States and countries throughout the world. We are not a membership organization. We are grant funded with grants from the United States Departments of Education, Labor, Health and Human Services, and other federal funding agencies such as the Institute of Museum and Library Services and the National Endowment for the Arts. In addition we have projects in partnership with regional educational institutions. Internationally we have worked with the International Labor Organization and the World Health Organization and are currently working with Save the Children on a US AID project in the Philippines.

Dues – n/a

Meetings – PREL supports the annual Pacific Educational Conference (PEC), held each July.

Publications – Publications are listed on the PREL website at http://ppo.prel.org/. Most are available in both PDF and HTML format. Some recent publications are described below: Focus on Professional Development, A (Research Based Practices in Early Reading Series) A Focus on Professional Development is the fourth in the Research-Based Practices in Early Reading Series published by the Regional Educational Laboratory (REL) at Pacific Resources for Education and Learning (PREL). Because reading proficiency is fundamental to student achievement across all subjects and grades, the preparation of the teachers and administrators who are responsible for providing early reading instruction is of special importance. This booklet examines what research tells us about professional development and about the role that effective professional development plays in improving both teacher performance and student achievement. http://www.prel.org/products/re_/prodevelopment.pdf (902 K) Look and See: Using the Visual Environment as Access to Literacy (Research Brief) This paper describes how the visual environment – what we see when we look – can be used to develop both visual and verbal literacy, including aesthetic appreciation, comprehension, and vocabulary. http://www.prel.org/products/re_/look_see.pdf (1 M) Measuring the Effectiveness of Professional Development in Early Literacy: Lessons Learned (Research Brief) This Research Brief focuses on the methodology used to measure professional development (PD) effectiveness. It examines the needs that generated this research, what PREL did to meet those needs, and lessons that have been learned as a result. In particular, it discusses the development of a new instrument designed to measure the quality of PD as it is being delivered. http://www.prel.org/products/re_/effect_of_pd.pdf (730 K) Pacific Early Literacy Resource Kit CD-ROM (Early Literacy Learning Resources) The Pacific Early Literacy Resource Kit was developed from PRELs research-based work performed with early literacy teachers in US-affiliated Pacific islands. The contents of the Resource Kit represent information, products, and processes we found beneficial as we worked to support literacy teachers in their efforts to improve student literacy achievement. http://www.prel.org/toolkit/index.htm Research Into Practice 2006 (PREL Compendium) This 86-page volume of PRELs annual research compendium brings together articles detailing research conducted during 2005 by PREL. The six articles in this issue focus on putting research findings to work to improve education. http://www.prel.org/products/pr_/compendium06/tableofcontents.asp

Name of Organization or Association – Reference and User Services Association, a division of the American Library Association

Acronym – RUSA

Address – 50 E. Huron St.

City – Chicago

State – IL

Zip Code – 60611

Country – US

Phone Number – (800)545-2433, ext. 4398.

Fax Number – Fax (312)280-5273

Email Contact – rusa@ala.org

URL – http://rusa.ala.org

Leaders – Barbara A. Macikas, Exec. Dir

Description – A division of the American Library Association, RUSA is responsible for stimulating and supporting in every type of library the delivery of reference information services to all groups and of general library services and materials to adults.

Membership – 5,200

Dues – Join ALA and RUSA $120; RUSA membership $60(added to ALA membership); student member $55 ($30 for ALA and $25 for RUSA); retired, support staff or non-salaried $72 ($42 for ALA and $30 for RUSA).

Meetings – Meetings are held in conjunction with the American Library Association.

Publications – RUSQ (q.), information provided on RUSA website at http://rusa.ala.org, RUSA Update, online membership newsletter, select publications.

Name of Organization or Association – SERVE Center @ UNCG

Acronym – We no longer use the acronym

Address – 5900 Summit Avenue, Dixon Building

City – Browns Summit

State – FL

Zip Code – 27214

Country – US

Phone Number – 800-755-3277, 336-315-7457

Fax Number – 336-315-7457

Email Contact – info@serve.org

URL – http://www.serve.org/

Leaders – Ludy van Broekhuizen, Executive Director

Description – The SERVE Center at the University of North Carolina at Greensboro, under the leadership of Dr. Ludwig David van Broekhuizen, is a university-based education organization with the mission to promote and support the continuous improvement of educational opportunities for all learners in the Southeast. The organizations commitment to continuous improvement is manifest in an applied research-to-practice model that drives all of its work. Building on research, professional wisdom, and craft knowledge, SERVE staff members develop tools, processes, and interventions designed to assist practitioners and policymakers with their work. SERVEs ultimate goal is to raise the level of student achievement in the region. Evaluation of the impact of these activities combined with input from stakeholders expands SERVEs knowledge base and informs future research. This rigorous and practical approach to research and development is supported by an experienced staff strategically located throughout the region. This staff is highly skilled in providing needs assessment services, conducting applied research in schools, and developing processes, products, and programs that support educational improvement and increase student achievement. In the last three years, in addition to its basic research and development work with over 170 southeastern schools, SERVE staff provided technical assistance and training to more than 18,000 teachers and administrators across the region. The SERVE Center is governed by a board of directors that includes the governors, chief state school officers, educators, legislators, and private sector leaders from Alabama, Florida, Georgia, Mississippi, North Carolina, and South Carolina. SERVEs operational core is the Regional Educational Laboratory. Funded by the U.S. Department of Educations Institute of Education Sciences, the Regional Educational Laboratory for the Southeast is one of ten Laboratories providing research-based information and services to all 50 states and territories. These Laboratories form a nationwide education knowledge network, building a bank of information and resources shared and disseminated nationally and regionally to improve student achievement. SERVEs National Leadership Area, Expanded Learning Opportunities, focuses on improving student outcomes through the use of exemplary pre–K and extended-day programs.

Membership – None.

Dues – None.

Meetings – None.

Publications – Three titles available in the highlighted products area of website: A Review Of Methods and Instruments Used In State and Local School Readiness Evaluations Abstract: This report provides detailed information about the methods and instruments used to evaluate school readiness initiatives, discusses important considerations in selecting instruments, and provides resources and recommendations that may be helpful to those who are designing and implementing school readiness evaluations. Levers For Change: Southeast Region State Initiatives To Improve High Schools Abstract: This descriptive report aims to stimulate discussion about high school reform among Southeast Region states. The report groups recent state activities in high school reform into six "levers for change." To encourage critical reflection, the report places the reform discussion in the context of an evidence-based decision-making process and provides sample research on reform activities. Evidence-Based Decision making: Assessing Reading Across the Curriculum Intervention Abstract: When selecting reading across the curriculum interventions, educators should consider the extent of the evidence base on intervention effectiveness and the fit with the school or district context, whether they are purchasing a product from vendors or developing it internally. This report provides guidance in the decision making.

Name of Organization or Association – Society for Applied Learning Technology

Acronym – SALT

Address – 50 Culpeper St.

City – Warrenton

State – VA

Zip Code – 20186

Country – US

Phone Number – (540)347-0055

Fax Number – (540)349-3169

Email Contact – info@lti.org.

URL – http://www.salt.org

Leaders – Raymond G. Fox, Pres.

Description – The society is a nonprofit, professional membership organization that was founded in 1972. Membership in the society is oriented to professionals whose work requires knowledge and communication in the field of instructional technology. The society provides members with a means to enhance their knowledge and job performance by participation in society-sponsored meetings, subscription to society-sponsored publications, association with other professionals at conferences sponsored by the society, and membership in special interest groups and special society-sponsored initiatives. In addition, the society offers member discounts on society-sponsored journals, conferences, and publications.

Membership – 350

Dues – $55

Meetings – Orlando Learning Technologies 2004, February 18–20, 2004, Orlando, FL; 2004 Interactive Technologies, August 18–20, 2004, Arlington, VA.

Publications – Journal of Educational Technology Systems; Journal of Instruction Delivery Systems; Journal of Interactive Instruction Development. Send for list of available publications.

Name of Organization or Association – Society for Photographic Education

Acronym – SPE

Address – 126 Peabody Hall, The School of Interdisciplinary Studies, Miami University

City – Oxford

State – OH

Zip Code – 45056

Country – US

Phone Number – (513)529-8328

Fax Number – (513)529-9301

Email Contact – speoffice@spenational.org

URL – www.spenational.org

Leaders – Richard Gray, Chairperson of SPE Board of Directors

Description – An association of college and university teachers of photography, museum photographic curators, writers, publishers and students. Promotes discourse in photography education, culture, and art.

Membership – 1,800 membership dues are for the calendar year, January through December.

Dues – Membership Dues: $90-Regular Membership $50-Student Membership $600-Corporate Member $380-Collector Member (with print) $150-Sustaining Member $65-Senior Member.

Meetings – Denver, CO, March 13–16, 2008.

Publications – Exposure (Photographic Journal) – biannual – Quarterly Newsletter – Membership Directory -Conference Program Guide.

Name of Organization or Association – Society of Photo Technologists

Acronym – SPT

Address – 11112 S. Spotted Rd.

City – Cheney

State – WA

Zip Code – 99004

Country – US

Phone Number – 800-624-9621 or (509)624-9621

Fax Number – (509)624-5320

Email Contact – cc5@earthlink.net

URL – http://www.spt.info/

Leaders – Chuck Bertone, Executive Director

Description – An organization of photographic equipment repair technicians, which improves and maintains communications between manufacturers and repair shops and technicians. We publish Repair Journals, Newsletters, Parts & Service Directory and Industry Newsletters. We also sponsor SPTNET (a technical email group), Remanufactured parts and residence workshops.

Membership – 1,000 shops and manufactures world wide, eligible people or businesses are any who are involved full or part time in the camera repair field.

Dues – $97.50–$370. Membership depends on the size/volume of the business. Most one man shops are Class A/$170 dues. Those not involved full time in the field is $95.50/Associate Class.

Meetings – SPT Journal; SPT Parts and Services Directory; SPT Newsletter; SPT Manuals – Training and Manufacturer's Tours.

Publications – Journals & Newsletters.

Name of Organization or Association – Southwest Educational Development Laboratory

Acronym – SEDL

Address – 211 East Seventh St.

City – Austin

State – TX

Zip Code – 78701

Country – US

Phone Number – (512)476-6861

Fax Number – (512)476-2286

Email Contact – info@sedl.org

URL – http://www.sedl.org

Leaders – Dr. Wesley A. Hoover, Pres. and CEO

Description – The Southwest Educational Development Laboratory (SEDL) is a private, not-for-profit education research and development corporation based in Austin, Texas. SEDL has worked in schools to investigate the conditions under which teachers can provide student-centered instruction supported by technology, particularly computers alone with other software. From that field-based research with teachers, SEDL has developed a professional development model and modules, which resulted in the production of Active Learning with Technology (ALT) portfolio. ALT is a multimedia training program for teachers to learn how to apply student-centered, problem-based learning theory to their instructional strategies that are supported by technologies. Copies of Active Learning with Technology Portfolio and other products used to integrate technology in the classroom can be viewed and ordered online at http://www.sedl.org/pubs/category_technology.html from SEDLs Office of Institutional Communications. SEDL operates the Southeast Comprehensive Center (SECC), funded by the U.S. Department of Education, which provides high-quality technical assistance in the states of Alabama, Georgia, Louisiana, Mississippi and South Carolina. The goals of the SECC are to build the capacities of states in its region to implement the programs and goals of the No Child Left Behind Act of 2001 (NCLB) and to build states capacity to provide sustained support of high-needs districts and schools. SECC works closely with each state in its region to provide access and use of information, models, and materials that facilitate implementation of and compliance with NCLB. SEDLs Texas Comprehensive Center provides technical assistance and support to the Texas Education Agency to assure Texas has an education system with the capacity and commitment to eliminate achievement gaps and enable all students to achieve at high levels.

Membership – n/a

Dues – n/a

Meetings – n/a

Publications – SEDL LETTER and other newsletters and documents are available for free general distribution in print and online. Topic-specific publications related to educational change, education policy, mathematics, language arts, science, and disability research and a publications catalog are available at http://www.sedl.org/pubs on the SEDL Web site.

Name of Organization or Association – Special Libraries Association

Acronym – SLA

Address – 331 South Patrick St.

City – Alexandria

State – VA

Zip Code – 22314

Country – US

Phone Number – 703-647-4900

Fax Number – 703-647-4901

Email Contact – sla@sla.org

URL – http://www.sla.org

Leaders – The Honorable Janice R. Lachance, CEO

Description – The Special Libraries Association (SLA) is a nonprofit global organization for innovative information professionals and their strategic partners. SLA serves more than 11,000 members in 75 countries in the information profession, including corporate, academic and government information specialists. SLA promotes and strengthens its members through learning, advocacy, and networking initiatives. For more information, visit us on the Web at www.sla.org

Membership – 11,500

Dues – Full Membership: USD 160.00 (members earning greater than USD 35,000 in annual salary); USD 99.00 (members earning USD 35,000 or less in annual salary). Student/Retired Membership: USD 35.00.

Meetings – 2006 Annual Conference and Exposition: 11–14 June, Baltimore; 2007 Annual Conference and Exposition: 3–6 June, Denver.

Publications – Information Outlook (monthly glossy magazine that accepts advertising). SLA Connections (monthly electronic newsletter for members and stakeholders).

Name of Organization or Association – Teachers and Writers Collaborative

Acronym – T&W

Address – 520 Eighth Avenue, Suite 2020

City – New York

State – NY

Zip Code – 10018

Country – US

Phone Number – (212)691-6590, Toll-free (888)266-5789

Fax Number – (212)675-0171

Email Contact – bmorrow@twc.org

URL – http://www.twc.org and http://www.writenet.org

Leaders – Amy Swauger, Director

Description – T&W brings the joys and pleasures of reading and writing directly to children. As an advocate for the literary arts and arts education, we support writers and teachers in developing and implementing new teaching strategies; disseminate models for literary arts education to local, national, and international audiences; and showcase both new and established writers via publications and literary events held in our Center for Imaginative Writing. T&W was founded in 1967 by a group of writers and educators who believed that professional writers could make a unique contribution to the teaching of writing and literature. Over the past 40 years, 1,500

T&W writers have taught writing workshops in New York City's public schools. Approximately 700,000 New York City students have participated in our workshops, and we have worked with more than 25,000 teachers. Our wealth of experience, which is reflected in T&W's 80 books about teaching writing, led the National Endowment for the Arts to single out T&W as the arts-in-education group "most familiar with creative writing/literature in primary and secondary schools." The American Book Review has written that T&W "has created a whole new pedagogy in the teaching of English."

Membership – T&W has over 1,000 members across the country. The basic membership is $35; patron membership is $75; and benefactor membership is $150 or more. Members receive a free book or T-shirt; discounts on publications; and a free one-year subscription to Teachers & Writers magazine. (Please see http://www.twc.org/member.htm.).

Dues – T&W is seeking general operating support for all of our programs and program support for specific projects, including: (1) T&W writing residencies in New York City area schools; (2) T&W publications, books and a quarterly magazine, which we distribute across the country; (3) T&W events, including readings for emerging writers and small presses; and (4) T&Ws Internet programs for teachers, writers, and students. Grants to T&Ws Endowment support the stability of the organization and help to guarantee the continuation of specific programs.

Meetings – T&W offers year-round public events in our Center for Imaginative Writing in New York City. For a list of events, please see http://www.twc.org/events.htm

Publications – T&W has published over 80 books on the teaching of imaginative writing, including The T&W Handbook of Poetic Forms; The Dictionary of Wordplay; The Story in History; Personal Fiction Writing; Luna, Luna: Creative Writing from Spanish and Latino Literature; The Nearness of You: Students and Teachers Writing On-Line. To request a free publications catalog, please send email to info@twc.org or call 888-BOOKS-TW. (Please see http://www.twc.org/pubs).

Name of Organization or Association – The George Lucas Educational Foundation

Acronym – GLEF

Address – P.O. Box 3494

City – San Rafael

State – CA

Zip Code – 94912

Country – US

Phone Number – (415)662-1600

Fax Number – (415)662-1619

Email Contact – edutopia@glef.org

URL – http://edutopia.org

Leaders – Milton Chen, PhD., Executive Director

Description – Mission: The George Lucas Educational Foundation (GLEF) is a nonprofit operating foundation that documents and disseminates models of the most innovative practices in our nation's K-12 schools. We serve this mission through the creation of media – from films, books, and magazine to CD-ROMS and DVDs. GLEF works to provide its products as tools for discussion and action in conferences, workshops, and professional development settings. Audience: A successful educational system requires the collaborative efforts of many different stakeholders. Our audience includes teachers, administrators, school board members, parents, researchers, and business and community leaders who are actively working to improve teaching and learning. Vision: The Edutopian vision is thriving today in our country's best schools: places where students are engaged and achieving at the highest levels, where skillful educators are energized by the excitement of teaching, where technology brings outside resources and expertise into the classroom, and where parents and community members are partners in educating our youth.

Membership – All online content and the Edutopia magazine are offered free of charge to educators.

Dues – Free subscription to Edutopia magazine for those working in education.

Meetings – no public meetings; advisory council meets annually; board of directors meets quarterly.

Publications – Edutopia Online: The Foundation's Web site, Edutopia (www.edutopia.org) celebrates the unsung heroes who are making Edutopia a reality. All of GLEF's multimedia content dating back to 1997 is available on its Web site. A special feature, the Video Gallery, is an archive of short documentaries and expert interviews that allow visitors to see these innovations in action and hear about them from teachers and students. Detailed articles, research summaries, and links to hundreds of relevant Web sites, books, organizations, and publications are also available to help schools and communities build on successes in education. Edutopia: Success Stories for Learning in the Digital Age: This book and CD-ROM include numerous stories of innovative educators who are using technology to connect with students, colleagues, the local community, and the world beyond. The CD-ROM contains more than an hour of video footage. Published by Jossey-Bass. Teaching in the Digital Age (TDA) Videocassettes This video series explores elements of successful teaching in the Digital Age. The project grows out of GLEFs belief that an expanded view is needed of all our roles in educating children and supporting teachers. The series explores School Leadership, Emotional Intelligence,

Teacher Preparation, and Project-Based Learning and Assessment. Learn & Live
This documentary film and 300-page companion resource book showcases innovative schools across the country. The film, hosted by Robin Williams, aired on public television stations nationwide in 1999 and 2000. The Learn & Live CD-ROM
includes digital versions of the film and book in a portable, easy-to-use format.
Edutopia Magazine A free magazine which shares powerful examples of innovative and exemplary learning and teaching. Edutopia Newsletter This free, semian-
nual print newsletter includes school profiles, summaries of recent research, and
resources and tips for getting involved in public education. Instructional Modules
Free teaching modules developed by education faculty and professional developers.
They can be used as extension units in existing courses, or can be used independently in workshops. Includes presenter notes, video segments, discussion questions. Topics include project-based learning, technology integration, and multiple
intelligences.

Name of Organization or Association – The International Society of the Learning
Sciences

Acronym – ISLS

Address – n/a

City – n/a

State – n/a

Zip Code – n/a

Country – n/a

Phone Number – n/a

Fax Number – n/a

Email Contact – info@isls.org

URL – http://www.isls.org/

Leaders – Nancy Songer, Executive Officer

Description – The International Society of the Learning Sciences, incorporated as
a non-profit professional society in September, 2002, unites the traditions started by
the Journal of the Learning Sciences, the International Conferences of the Learning Sciences (ICLS), and the Computer-Supported Collaborative Learning Conferences (CSCL) and offers publications, conferences, and educational programs to the
community of researchers and practitioners who use cognitive, socio-cognitive, and
socio-cultural approaches to studying learning in real-world situations and designing environments, software, materials, and other innovations that promote deep and
lasting learning. The society is governed by a Board of Directors elected by the paid-
up membership. Officers of the society include the President (chosen by the Board

of Directors), Past-President, President-Elect, an Executive Officer and a Financial Officer. Much of the work of the society is done by committees whose members are drawn from both the Board and the membership at large.

Membership – Researchers in the interdisciplinary field of learning sciences, born during the 1990s, study learning as it happens in real-world situations and how to better facilitate learning in designed environments – in school, online, in the workplace, at home, and in informal environments. Learning sciences research is guided by constructivist, social-constructivist, socio-cognitive, and socio-cultural theories of learning.

Dues – $109 with one journal and $142 with both journals.

Meetings – The International Conference of the Learning Sciences (ICLS) and The International Conference on Computer-Supported Collaborative Learning (CSCL)

Publications – JLS—Journal of the Learning Sciences Published by LEA and in its 14th volume in 2005, JLS is a multidisciplinary forum for the presentation and discussion of important ideas that can change our understanding of learning and teaching. JLS has been in the top five of most-cited journals in education for the past five years. IJCSCL—International Journal of Computer Supported Collaborative Learning to be published by Springer, IJCSCL goes into its first volume in 2006 and will publish papers reflecting the interests of the international CSCL community. The International Conference of the Learning Sciences (ICLS), first held in 1992 and held bi-annually since 1996, covers the entire field of the learning sciences. The International Conference on Computer-Supported Collaborative Learning (CSCL), held bi-annually since 1995, focuses on issues related to learning through collaboration and promoting productive collaborative discourse with the help of the computer and other communications technologies.

Name of Organization or Association – The NETWORK, Inc.

Acronym – NETWORK

Address – 136 Fenno Drive

City – Rowley

State – MA

Zip Code – 01969-1004

Country – USA

Phone Number – 800-877-5400, (978)948-7764

Fax Number – (978)948-7836

Email Contact – davidc@thenetworkinc.org

URL – www.thenetworkinc.org

Leaders – David Crandall, President

Description – A nonprofit research and service organization providing training, research and evaluation, technical assistance, and materials for a fee to schools, educational organizations, and private sector firms with educational interests. The NETWORK has been helping professionals manage and learn about change since 1969. Our Leadership Skills series of computer-based simulations extends the widely used board game versions of Making Change (tm) and Systems Thinking/Systems Changing(tm) with the addition of Improving Student Success: Teachers, Schools and Parents to offer educators a range of proven professional development tools. Available in 2007, Networking for Learning, originally developed for the British Department for Education and Skills, offers schools considering forming or joining a network a risk-free means of exploring the many challenges.

Membership – none required.

Dues – no dues, fee for service.

Meetings – call.

Publications – Making Change: A Simulation Game [board and computer versions]; Systems Thinking/Systems Changing: A Simulation Game [board and computer versions]; Improving Student Success: Teachers, Schools and Parents [computer based simulation]; Systemic Thinking: Solving Complex Problems; Benchmarking: A Guide for Educators; Networking for Learning; Check Yourself into College: A quick and easy guide for high school students.

Name of Organization or Association – University Continuing Education Association

Acronym – UCEA

Address – One Dupont Cir. NW, Suite 615

City – Washington

State – DC

Zip Code – 20036

Country – US

Phone Number – (202)659-3130

Fax Number – (202)785-0374

Email Contact – kjkohl@ucea.edu

URL – http://www.ucea.edu/

Leaders – Kay J. Kohl, Executive Director, kjkohl@ucea.edu

Description – UCEA is an association of public and private higher education institutions concerned with making continuing education available to all population segments and to promoting excellence in continuing higher education. Many institutional members offer university and college courses via electronic instruction.

Membership – 425 institutions, 2,000 professionals.

Dues – vary according to membership category; see: http://www.ucea.edu/membership.htm

Meetings – UCEA has an annual national conference and several professional development seminars throughout the year. See: http://www.ucea.edu/page02.htm

Publications – monthly newsletter; quarterly; occasional papers; scholarly journal, Continuing Higher Education Review; Independent Study Catalog. With Peterson's, The Guide to Distance Learning; Guide to Certificate Programs at American Colleges and Universities; UCEA-ACE/Oryx Continuing Higher Education book series; Lifelong Learning Trends (a statistical factbook on continuing higher education); organizational issues series; membership directory.

Name of Organization or Association – Young Adult Library Services Association

Acronym – YALSA

Address – 50 E. Huron St.

City – Chicago

State – IL

Zip Code – 60611

Country – US

Phone Number – (312)280-4390

Fax Number – (312)280-5276

Email Contact – yalsa@ala.org

URL – http://www.ala.org/yalsa

Leaders – Beth Yoke, Executive Director; Judy T. Nelson, President

Description – A division of the American Library Association (ALA), the Young Adult Library Services Association (YALSA) seeks to advocate, promote, and strengthen service to young adults as part of the continuum of total library services. Is responsible within the ALA to evaluate and select books and media and to interpret and make recommendations regarding their use with young adults. Selected List Committees include Best Books for Young Adults, Popular Paperbacks for Young Adults, Quick Picks for Reluctant Young Adult Readers, Outstanding Books for the

College Bound, Selected Audiobooks for Young Adults, Great Graphic Novels for Teens and Selected Films for Young Adults. To learn more about our literary awards, such as the Odyssey Award for best audiobook production, and recommended reading, listening and viewing lists go to www.ala.org/yalsa/booklists. YALSA celebrates Teen Tech Week the first full week of March each year. To learn more go to www.ala.org/teentechweek

Membership – 5,500. YALSA members may be young adult librarians, school librarians, library directors, graduate students, educators, publishers, or anyone for whom library service to young adults is important.

Dues – $50; $20 students; $20 retirees (in addition to ALA membership).

Meetings – 2 ALA conferences yearly, Midwinter (January) and Annual (June); one biennial Young Adult Literature Symposium (beginning in 2008).

Publications – Young Adult Library Services, a quarterly print journal YAttitudes, a quarterly electronic newsletter for members only.

Part V
Graduate Programs in North America

Introduction

Pamela Fortner

This section lists graduate programs in Instructional Technology, Educational Media and Communications, School Library Media, and closely related programs. Masters, specialist, and doctoral degrees are combined into one unified list. Program administrators who respond to our request for information provide the data for this section. We routinely include such categories as program description, institutional affiliation, matriculation details, curriculum outlines, selected resources and resident faculty.

One intention of this listing is to provide a record that can be used to make historical comparisons of relevant degree programs over time. However, prospective students and administrators at other institutions should also find this section useful as a means of comparing requirements among similar programs. Information in this section can be considered current as of 2007 for most programs. The editing team would like to thank those respondents who helped assure the currency and accuracy of this current listing by responding to our request for an update.

We are currently in a transition to an online dynamic database-driven system that will improve our ability to maintain the accuracy of the information listed and make it much easier to update our annual listing. Input for the new listing will be editable via the Internet. Readers of this volume are encouraged to furnish new information to the Yearbook editors or directly input data at the AECT web site: http://www.aect.org/Curricula/. The results of our new system will be part of the 2010 *Educational Media and Technology Yearbook*.

P. Fortner (✉)
The University of Georgia, Athens, GA 30602-7144, USA
e-mail: phales@uga.edu

M. Orey et al. (eds.), *Educational Media and Technology Yearbook*,
DOI 10.1007/978-0-387-09675-9_25, © Springer Science+Business Media, LLC 2009

Graduate Programs

Name of Institution – University of Alaska Southeast
Name of Program within institution – Educational Technology
Title/Degree as it appears on official certificate or diploma – Master's in Educational Technology
Name & Title of person administering program – Marsha A. Gladhart
Address – 11120 Glacier Highway, Juneau, AK, 99801, United States
Telephone Number – 907-465-8750
Fax Number – 907-465-2166
E-Mail – marsha.gladhart@uas.alaska.edu
Institution's home page – http://www.uas.alaska.edu
Admittance URL – http://pec.jun.alaska.edu/edtechpec/
PREREQUISITES: Higher Education – Yes
If yes, number of years or degree required – B.A.
Teaching Certificate – Yes
ACCEPTANCE OF TRANSFERS – Yes
MASTER'S PROGRAM DURATION: Number of required Courses – 11
Comprehensive Exam Required? – No
Thesis Required? – No
Continuous Enrollment Required? – No
Other Requirements – Electronic portfolio
Does program culminate in a degree in the field of educational communications and technology? – Yes
Name of the degree – M.ED. in Educational Technology
Is this program part of another degree, certificate, or diploma? – No
OTHER PROGRAMS in educational technology or instructional development fields: Certificate Program available? – Yes
Certificate URL – http://www.educ.state.ak.us/TeacherCertification/#HIGHLY
Specialist Program available? – No
Undergraduate Program available? – No
Doctorate Program available? – No
Program Content – Master's degree
Program Content URL – http://pec.jun.alaska.edu/edtechpec/
Name of Institution – Alabama A & M University

Name of Program within institution – Instructional Technology

Title/Degree as it appears on official certificate or diploma – Curriculum and Instruction

Name & Title of person administering program – Sha Li, EdD

Address – Box 937, Normal, AL, 35762, United States

Telephone Number – 256-372-5973

Fax Number – 256-372-5526

E-Mail – sha.li@email.aamu.edu

Institution's home page – http://www.aamu.edu/

Admittance URL – http://www.aamu.edu/Admission/default.htm

PREREQUISITES: Higher Education – No

If yes, number of years or degree required – B.A.

Teaching Certificate – Yes

Other requirement, ACCEPTANCE OF TRANSFERS – Yes

MASTER'S PROGRAM DURATION: Comprehensive Exam Required – Yes

Thesis Required? – Optional

Continuous Enrollment Required? – Yes

Does program culminate in a degree in the field of educational communications and technology? – No

Is this program part of another degree, certificate, or diploma? – Yes

If yes, name of the degree, certificate, or diploma – Curriculum and Instruction

OTHER PROGRAMS in educational technology or instructional development fields, Certificate Program available? – Yes

Specialist Program available? – No

Undergraduate Program available? – No

Doctorate Program available? – No

Program Content – Master's degree

Program Content URL – http://stuinfo.aamu.edu/shali/home/index.htm

Name of Institution – The University of Alabama

Name of Program within institution – Secondary Curriculum, Teaching and Learning Computers and Applied Technology

Title/Degree as it appears on official certificate or diploma – Master of Arts

Name & Title of person administering program – Dr. Vivian H. Wright

Address – Box 870232, Tuscaloosa, AL, 35487, United States

E-Mail – vwright@bamaed.ua.edu

Institution's home page – http://www.ua.edu

Admittance URL – http://graduate.ua.edu

PREREQUISITES: Higher Education – Yes

If yes, number of years or degree required – B.A.

Teaching Certificate – Yes

ACCEPTANCE OF TRANSFERS – Yes

Comprehensive Exam Required? – Yes
Thesis Required? – No
Continuous Enrollment Required? – No
Does program culminate in a degree in the field of educational communications and technology? – No
Name of the degree – Master of Arts
Is this program part of another degree, certificate, or diploma? – Yes
If yes, name of the degree, certificate, or diploma, OTHER PROGRAMS in educational technology or instructional development fields: Certificate Program available? – No
Specialist Program available? – No
Undergraduate Program available? – No
Doctorate Program available? – PhD
Doctorate URL – http://education.ua.edu/leader/index.html
Program Content – Master's degree
Program Content URL – http://www.bamaed.ua.edu/cat/

Name of Institution – University of South Alabama
Name of Program within institution – Instructional Design and Development
Title/Degree as it appears on official certificate or diploma – PhD or MS in Instructional Design and Development
Name & Title of person administering program – Prof. Jack Dempsey
Address – 3100 University Commons, Mobile, AL, 36688, United States
Telephone Number – 251-380-2861
Fax Number – 251-380-2713
E-Mail – jdempsey@usouthal.edu
Institution's home page – http://www.southalabama.edu/coe/bset/idd/
Number of required Semesters – 6
Comprehensive Exam Required? – Yes
Thesis Required? – No
Continuous Enrollment Required? – Yes
Does program culminate in a degree in the field of educational communications and technology? – Yes
Name of the degree – Instructional Design and Development
Is this program part of another degree, certificate, or diploma? – No
OTHER PROGRAMS in educational technology or instructional development fields: Doctorate Program available? – PhD
Doctorate URL – http://www.southalabama.edu/coe/bset/idd/
Program Content – Master's degree
Program Content URL – http://www.southalabama.edu/coe/bset/idd/

Name of Institution – Arkansas Tech University
Name of Program within institution – Master of Education in Instructional Technology

Title/Degree as it appears on official certificate or diploma – Master of Education

Name & Title of person administering program – Connie Zimmer, Associate Professor of Secondary Education

Address – 308 Crabaugh, Russellville, AR, 72801, United States

Telephone Number – 479-968-0434

Fax Number – 479-964-0811

E-Mail – connie.zimmer@atu.edu

Institution's home page – http://www.atu.edu

Admittance URL – http://graduate.atu.edu

PREREQUISITES: Higher Education – Yes

If yes, number of years or degree required – Bachelor Degree

Teaching Certificate – No

Other requirement – Teaching certificate is required if you are seeking library media licensure

ACCEPTANCE OF TRANSFERS – Yes

MASTER'S PROGRAM DURATION: Number of required Courses – 12

Comprehensive Exam Required? – No

Thesis Required? – Optional

Continuous Enrollment Required? – No

Other Requirements – Action project in educational research

Does program culminate in a degree in the field of educational communications and technology? – Yes

Name of the degree – Master of Education in Instructional Technology

Is this program part of another degree, certificate, or diploma? – No

If yes, name of the degree, certificate, or diploma, OTHER PROGRAMS in educational technology or instructional development fields: Certificate Program available? – No

Specialist Program available? – No

Undergraduate Program available? – No

Doctorate Program available? – No

Program Content – Master's degree

Program Content URL – http://education.atu.edu

Name of Institution – University of Arkansas

Name of Program within institution – Educational Technology

Title/Degree as it appears on official certificate or diploma – Master of Education

Name & Title of person administering program – Dr. Cheryl Murphy, Program Chair

Address – 350 Graduate Education Building, Fayetteville, AR, 72701, United States

Telephone Number – 479-575-5111

E-Mail – cmurphy@uark.edu

Institution's home page – http://uark.edu

Admittance URL – http://www.uark.edu/depts/coehp/ETEC/etec.htm
PREREQUISITES: Higher Education – Yes
If yes, number of years or degree required – Bachelors degree required
Teaching Certificate – No
ACCEPTANCE OF TRANSFERS – No
MASTER'S PROGRAM DURATION: Number of required Courses – 11
Number of weeks long – 15
Comprehensive Exam Required? – Yes
Thesis Required? – No
Continuous Enrollment Required? – No
Other Requirements – Complete degree within 6 years
Does program culminate in a degree in the field of educational communications and technology? – Yes
Name of the degree – Master of Education, Educational Technology
Is this program part of another degree, certificate, or diploma? – No
OTHER PROGRAMS in educational technology or instructional development fields: Certificate Program available? – No
Specialist Program available? – No
Undergraduate Program available? – No
Doctorate Program available? – No
Program Content – Master's degree
Program Content URL – http://www.uark.edu/depts/coehp/ETEC/etec.htm

Name of Institution – University of Arkansas at Little Rock
Name of Program within institution – Learning Systems Technology
Title Degree as it appears on official certificate or diploma – Masters of Education in Learning Systems Technology
Name & Title of person administering program – David S. Spillers, Professor
Address – 2801 S. University, Little Rock Arkansas, AR, 72204, United States
Telephone Number – 501-569-3267
E-Mail – dsspillers@ualr.edu
Institution's home page – http://www.ualr.edu
Admittance URL – http://www.ualr.edu/www/prospective/index.htmlx
PREREQUISITES: Higher Education – Yes
If yes, number of years or degree required – Bachelor's degree
Teaching Certificate – No
ACCEPTANCE OF TRANSFERS – Yes
MASTER'S PROGRAM DURATION: Number of required Semesters – 6
Number of weeks long – 15
Comprehensive Exam Required? – No
Thesis Required? – No
Continuous Enrollment Required? – No
Other Requirements – Comprehensive portfolio

Does program culminate in a degree in the field of educational communications and technology? – Yes
Name of the degree – Learning Systems Technology – M.Ed.
Is this program part of another degree, certificate, or diploma? – No
If yes, name of the degree, certificate, or diploma, OTHER PROGRAMS in educational technology or instructional development fields: Certificate Program available? – No
Specialist Program available? – No
Undergraduate Program available? – Yes
Doctorate Program available? – No
Program Content – Master's degree
Program Content URL – http://edlrlab.ualr.edu/LSTE/

Name of Institution – Arizona State University
Name of Program within institution – Educational Technology
Title/Degree as it appears on official certificate or diploma – Educational Technology
Name & Title of person administering program – James D. Klein
Address – Box 870611, Tempe, AZ, 85287, United States,
Telephone Number – 480 965 3384
Fax Number – 480 965 0300
E-Mail – dpe@asu.edu
Institution's home page – http://coe.asu.edu/psyched/edtech/
Admittance URL – http://coe.asu.edu/psyched/edtech/admission.html
PREREQUISITES: Higher Education – No
If yes, number of years or degree required – Bachelor's
Teaching Certificate – No
ACCEPTANCE OF TRANSFERS – Yes
MASTER'S PROGRAM DURATION: Number of required Semesters – 2
Number of weeks long – 16
Comprehensive Exam Required? – Yes
Thesis Required? – No
Continuous Enrollment Required? – Yes
Other Requirements, Does program culminate in a degree in the field of educational communications and technology? – Yes
Name of the degree – Educational Technology
Is this program part of another degree, certificate, or diploma? – No
OTHER PROGRAMS in educational technology or instructional development fields: Certificate Program available? – No
Specialist Program available? – No
Undergraduate Program available? – No
Doctorate Program available? – PhD
Doctorate URL – http://coe.asu.edu/psyched/edtech/phd.html
Program Content – Master's degree
Program Content URL – http://coe.asu.edu/psyched/edtech/med.html

Name of Institution – Northern Arizona University
Name of Program within institution – M.Ed. in Educational Technology
Title/Degree as it appears on official certificate or diploma – Masters in Education in Educational Technology
Name & Title of person administering program – Dr. Willard Gilbert
Address – Box 5774, Flagstaff, AZ, 86011, United States
Telephone Number – 928-523-7107
Fax Number – 928-523-1929
E-Mail – willard.gilbert@nau.edu
Institution's home page – http://www.nau.edu
Admittance URL – http://www.nau.edu/edtech
PREREQUISITES: Higher Education – Yes
If yes, number of years or degree required – BA or BS
Teaching Certificate – No
ACCEPTANCE OF TRANSFERS – Yes
Number of required Courses – 12
Number of weeks long – 16
Comprehensive Exam Required? – No
Thesis Required? – No
Continuous Enrollment Required? – No
Other Requirements – Students must complete a Capstone course that includes a comprehensive project
Does program culminate in a degree in the field of educational communications and technology? – Yes
Name of the degree – Masters in Education in Educational Technology
Is this program part of another degree, certificate, or diploma? – No
OTHER PROGRAMS in educational technology or instructional development fields: Certificate Program available? – Yes
Certificate URL – http://www.nau.edu/edtech
Specialist Program available? – No
Undergraduate Program available? – No
Doctorate Program available? – No
Program Content – Master's degree
Program Content URL – http://www.nau.edu/edtech

Name of Institution – La Sierra University
Name of Program within institution – Curriculum & Instruction-Technology
Title/Degree as it appears on official certificate or diploma – Master of Arts
Name & Title of person administering program – Dr. Anita Oliver
Address – 4500 Riverwalk Parkway, Riverside, CA, 92515, United States
Telephone Number – (951) 785-2203
Fax Number – (951) 785-2205
E-Mail – aoliver@lasierra.edu
Institution's home page – http://www.lasierra.edu
Admittance URL, REREQUISITES: Higher Education – Yes

If yes, number of years or degree required – Bachelors
Teaching Certificate – No
ACCEPTANCE OF TRANSFERS – Yes
MASTER'S PROGRAM DURATION: Number of required Courses – 15
Number of weeks long – 11
Comprehensive Exam Required? – Yes
Thesis Required? – No
Continuous Enrollment Required? – Yes
Other Requirements – 45 total quarter hours of coursework: 15 Education
  Core 15–18 Educational Technology 12–15 Curriculum and Instruction
**Does program culminate in a degree in the field of educational communi-
cations and technology?** – No
Is this program part of another degree, certificate, or diploma? – Yes
If yes, name of the degree, certificate, or diploma – Master of Arts in Cur-
  riculum and Instruction, Emphasis in Technology
**OTHER PROGRAMS in educational technology or instructional develop-
ment fields: Certificate Program available?** – Yes
Certificate URL – http://lsuonline.org/distance/edtech/
Program Content – Master's degree
Program Content URL – http://lsuonline.org/distance/edtech/

Name of Institution – California State University, Fullerton
Name of Program within institution – MS in Instructional Design and Tech-
  nology
Title/Degree as it appears on official certificate or diploma – MS in Instruc-
  tional Design and Technology
Name & Title of person administering program – Dr. JoAnn Carter-Wells
Address – 800 North State College Blvd., Fullerton, CA, 92834, United States
Telephone Number – 714-278-2842
Fax Number – 714-278-5518
E-Mail – msidt@fullerton.edu
Institution's home page – http://www.fullerton.edu
Admittance URL – http://csumentor.edu
PREREQUISITES: Higher Education – Yes
If yes, number of years or degree required – BA or BS degree
Teaching Certificate – No
ACCEPTANCE OF TRANSFERS – Yes
MASTER'S PROGRAM DURATION: Number of required Terms – 5
Number of weeks long – 15
Comprehensive Exam Required? – No
Thesis Required? – No
Continuous Enrollment Required? – Yes
Other Requirements – cohort membership

Does program culminate in a degree in the field of educational communications and technology? – Yes
Name of the degree – MS in Instructional Design and Technology
Is this program part of another degree, certificate, or diploma? – No
OTHER PROGRAMS in educational technology or instructional development fields: Certificate Program available? – Yes
Specialist Program available? – No
Undergraduate Program available? – No
Doctorate Program available? – No
Program Content – Master's degree
Program Content URL – http://msidt.fullerton.edu

Name of Institution – California State University, Long Beach
Name of Program within institution – Educational Technology, Title/Degree as it appears on official certificate or diploma, M.A. in Education, option in Educational Technology
Name & Title of person administering program – Dr. Ali Rezaei
Address – 1250 Bellflower Blvd., Long Beach, CA, 90840, United States
Telephone Number – 562-985-4517
Fax Number – 562-985-4534
E-Mail – arezaei@csulb.edu
Institution's home page – http://www.csulb.edu/edtech
PREREQUISITES: Higher Education – No
If yes, number of years or degree required – B.A.
Teaching Certificate – No
ACCEPTANCE OF TRANSFERS – Yes
MASTER'S PROGRAM DURATION: Number of required Courses – 11
Number of weeks long – 16
Comprehensive Exam Required? – No
Thesis Required? – Optional
Continuous Enrollment Required? – No
Other Requirements – Option for Comprehensive exam, thesis, or project
Does program culminate in a degree in the field of educational communications and technology? – Yes
Name of the degree – M.A in Education
Option in Educational Technology, Is this program part of another degree, certificate, or diploma? – Yes
If yes, name of the degree, certificate, or diploma – M.A. in Education
OTHER PROGRAMS in educational technology or instructional development fields: Certificate Program available? – No
Specialist Program available? – No
Undergraduate Program available? – No
Doctorate Program available? – No
Program Content – Master's degree
Program Content URL – http://www.csulb.edu/edtech

Name of Institution – California State University Monterey Bay (CSUMB)

Name of Program within institution – Masters in Instructional Sciences and Technology (MIST)

Title/Degree as it appears on official certificate or diploma – M.S. in Info Tech & Comm Design – emphasis in Inst. Sci. & Tech

Name & Title of person administering program – Eric Tao, Ph.D., Director of ITCD

Address – 100 Campus Center, Seaside, CA, 93955, United States

Telephone Number – 831-582-3621

Fax Number – 831-582-4484

E-Mail – mist@csumb.edu

Institution's home page – http://csumb.edu

Admittance URL – http://itcd.csumb.edu/mist

PREREQUISITES: Higher Education – No

If yes, number of years or degree required – B.S. or B.A.

Teaching Certificate – No

ACCEPTANCE OF TRANSFERS – Yes

MASTER'S PROGRAM DURATION: Number of required Terms – 4

Number of weeks long – 60

Comprehensive Exam Required? – No

Thesis Required? – Optional

Continuous Enrollment Required? – Yes

Other Requirements – MIST program requires four terms Summer (first year), Fall, Spring, Summer (Second year) – 15 months in total

Does program culminate in a degree in the field of educational communications and technology? – Yes

Name of the degree – Masters in Instructional Sciences and Technology (MIST)

Is this program part of another degree, certificate, or diploma? – Yes

If yes, name of the degree, certificate, or diploma – M.S. in Info Tech & Comm Design – emphasis in Inst. Sci. & Tech

OTHER PROGRAMS in educational technology or instructional development fields: Certificate Program available? – Yes

Certificate URL – http://itcd.csumb.edu

Undergraduate Program available? – Yes

Undergraduate URL – http://itcd.csumb.edu

Program Content – Master's degree

Program Content URL – http://itcd.csumb.edu/mist

Name of Institution – California State University, Fresno

Name of Program within institution – Educational Technology

Title/Degree as it appears on official certificate or diploma – Master of Arts in Education

Name & Title of person administering program – Roy M. Bohlin

Address – MS2, 5005 N. Maple Avenue, Fresno, CA, 93740, United States

Telephone Number – 559-278-0245
E-Mail – royb@csufresno.edu
Institution's home page – http://www.csufresno.edu/
Admittance URL – http://education.csufresno.edu/applications/PDF_files/Curr_MA_Tech.pdf
PREREQUISITES: Higher Education – Yes
If yes, number of years or degree required – Bachelor's Degree
Teaching Certificate – No
Other requirement – GRE is required for admission
ACCEPTANCE OF TRANSFERS – Yes
MASTER'S PROGRAM DURATION: Number of required Courses – 10
Comprehensive Exam Required? – No
Thesis Required? – No
Continuous Enrollment Required? – No
Other Requirements – A Project may be done instead of a Thesis
Does program culminate in a degree in the field of educational communications and technology? – No
Is this program part of another degree, certificate, or diploma? – Yes
If yes, name of the degree, certificate, or diploma – Master of Arts in Education with an emphasis in Curriculum and Instruction
OTHER PROGRAMS in educational technology or instructional development fields: Certificate Program available? – Yes
Certificate URL – http://education.csufresno.edu/applications/PDF_files/Curr_Tech.pdf
Specialist Program available? – No
Undergraduate Program available? – No
Doctorate Program available? – No
Program Content – Master's degree

Name of Institution – California State University at East Bay
Name of Program within institution – Educational Technology Leadership Program
Title/Degree as it appears on official certificate or diploma – Master of Science in Education
Name & Title of person administering program – Dr. Bijan Gillani
Address – 25800 Carlos Bee Blvd., Hayward, CA 94542, CA, 94542, United States
Telephone Number – 510-885-3027
Fax Number – 510-885-4632
E-Mail – gillani@csuhayward.edu
Institution's home page – http://etleads.csuhayward.edu/
Admittance URL – http://www.csuhayward.edu/campus_contacts/index.html
PREREQUISITES: Higher Education – No
If yes, number of years or degree required – 2 years of college
Teaching Certificate – No

Other requirement, ACCEPTANCE OF TRANSFERS – Yes
MASTER'S PROGRAM DURATION: Number of required Courses – 6
Number of weeks long – 10
Comprehensive Exam Required? – Yes
Thesis Required? – No
Continuous Enrollment Required? – Yes
Does program culminate in a degree in the field of educational communications and technology? – Yes
Name of the degree – M.S. in education
Is this program part of another degree, certificate, or diploma? – Yes
If yes, name of the degree, certificate, or diploma – M.S. Online Teaching & Learning
OTHER PROGRAMS in educational technology or instructional development fields: Certificate Program available? – Yes
Certificate URL – http://edschool.csueastbay.edu/Departments/TED/INDEX.HTML
Specialist Program available? – Yes
Specialist URL – http://etleads.csuhayward.edu
Undergraduate Program available? – No
Doctorate Program available? – No
Program Content – Master's degree
Program Content URL – http://etleads.csuhayward.edu

Name of Institution – San Diego State University
Name of Program within institution – Educational Technology
Title/Degree as it appears on official certificate or diploma – MA
Name & Title of person administering program – Marcie Bober, Department Chair
Address – 5500 Campanile Dr, San Diego, CA, 92182, United States
Telephone Number – 619-594-6378
E-Mail – bober@mail.sdsu.edu
Institution's home page – http://edtec.sdsu.edu
PREREQUISITES: Higher Education – Yes
If yes, number of years or degree required – undergraduate degree required
Teaching Certificate – No
ACCEPTANCE OF TRANSFERS – Yes
MASTER'S PROGRAM DURATION: Number of required Courses – 12
Number of weeks long – 16
Comprehensive Exam Required? – Yes
Thesis Required? – No
Continuous Enrollment Required? – No
Other Requirements, Does program culminate in a degree in the field of educational communications and technology? – Yes
Name of the degree – Master of Arts in Education
Is this program part of another degree, certificate, or diploma? – No

OTHER PROGRAMS in educational technology or instructional development fields: Certificate Program available? – Yes
Certificate URL – http://edtec.sdsu.edu
Specialist Program available? – No
Undergraduate Program available? – No
Doctorate Program available? – PhD
Program Content – Master's degree
Program Content URL – http://edtec.sdsu.edu

Name of Institution – California State Polytechnic University
Name of Program within institution – Educational Multimedia Program
Title/Degree as it appears on official certificate or diploma – MA in education
Name & Title of person administering program – Dr. Shahnaz Lotfipour
Address – 3801 W. Temple Ave, Pomona, CA, 91768, United States
Telephone Number – 909-869-2255
Fax Number – 909-869-5206
E-Mail – slotfipour@csupomona.edu
Institution's home page – http://www.csupomona.edu
PREREQUISITES: Higher Education – Yes
If yes, number of years or degree required – BA or BS
Teaching Certificate – No
Other requirement – Minimum 3.0 GPA in undergraduate and graduate (if applicable) degrees
ACCEPTANCE OF TRANSFERS – Yes
MASTER'S PROGRAM DURATION: Number of required Quarters – 5–8
Number of weeks long – 11
Comprehensive Exam Required? – No
Thesis Required? – Optional
Continuous Enrollment Required? – Yes
Other Requirements, Does program culminate in a degree in the field of educational communications and technology? – Yes
Name of the degree – MA in Education with the emphasis in Educational Multimedia
Is this program part of another degree, certificate, or diploma? – No
OTHER PROGRAMS in educational technology or instructional development fields: Certificate Program available? – Yes
Specialist Program available? – No
Undergraduate Program available? – No
Doctorate Program available? – Ed.D
Doctorate URL – http://www.gse.uci.edu/csu-uci-edd
Program Content – Master's degree
Program Content URL – http://www.csupomona.edu/~gps/em/

Name of Institution – San Jose State University
Name of Program within institution – Instructional Technology Department
Title/Degree as it appears on official certificate or diploma – Master of Arts
Name & Title of person administering program – Robertta H. Barba
Address – One Washington Square, San Jose, CA, 95192, United States
Telephone Number – 408-924-3620
E-Mail – rbarba@email.sjsu.edu
Institution's home page – http://www2.sjsu.edu/depts/it
Admittance URL – http://www2.sjsu.edu/depts/it/fast.html
PREREQUISITES: Higher Education – Yes
If yes, number of years or degree required – Bachelor's
Teaching Certificate – No
ACCEPTANCE OF TRANSFERS – Yes
MASTER'S PROGRAM DURATION: Number of required Courses – 10
Number of weeks long – 15
Comprehensive Exam Required? – Yes
Thesis Required? – No
Continuous Enrollment Required? – Yes
Other Requirements, Does program culminate in a degree in the field of educational communications and technology? – Yes
Name of the degree – Master of Arts
Is this program part of another degree, certificate, or diploma? – No
OTHER PROGRAMS in educational technology or instructional development fields: Certificate Program available? – Yes
Certificate URL – http://www2.sjsu.edu/depts/it/en1.html
Specialist Program available? – No
Specialist URL – http://www2.sjsu.edu/depts/it/en1.html
Undergraduate Program available? – No
Doctorate Program available? – No
Program Content – Master's degree
Program Content URL – http://www2.sjsu.edu/depts/it/ma1.html

Name of Institution – San Francisco State University
Name of Program within institution – Instructional Technologies Department
Title/Degree as it appears on official certificate or diploma – Master of Arts
Name & Title of person administering program – Kim Foreman, Department Chair
Address – 1600 Holloway Ave, San Francisco, CA, 94132, United States
Telephone Number – 415-338-1509
Fax Number – 415-338-0510
E-Mail – kforeman@sfsu.edu
Institution's home page – http://www.sfsu.edu/~itec
Admittance URL – http://www.sfsu.edu/~itec
PREREQUISITES: Higher Education – Yes

Teaching Certificate – No
ACCEPTANCE OF TRANSFERS – Yes
MASTER'S PROGRAM DURATION: Number of required Semesters – 2
Comprehensive Exam Required? – No
Thesis Required? – Optional
Continuous Enrollment Required? – No
Does program culminate in a degree in the field of educational communications and technology? – Yes
Name of the degree – Master of Arts
Is this program part of another degree, certificate, or diploma? – No
OTHER PROGRAMS in educational technology or instructional development fields: Certificate Program available? – Yes
Certificate URL – http://www.sfsu.edu/~itec
Specialist Program available? – Yes
Specialist URL – http://www.sfsu.edu/~itec
Undergraduate Program available? – No
Doctorate Program available? – No
Program Content – Master's degree
Program Content URL – http://www.sfsu.edu/~itec

Name of Institution – California State University San Bernardino
Name of Program within Institution – Instructional Technology
Title/Degree as it appears on official certificate or diploma – M.A. in Education, Option in Instructional Technology
Name & Title of person administering program – Dr. Amy S. C. Leh
Address – 5500 University Parkway, San Bernardino, CA, 92407, United States
Telephone Number – (909) 880-5692
Fax Number – (909) 880-7522
E-Mail – aleh@csusb.edu
Institution's home page – http://www.csusb.edu
PREREQUISITES: **Higher Education** – Yes
If yes, number of years or degree required – Bachelor's Degree
Teaching Certificate – No
Other requirement – Undergraduate GPA 3.0, 3 letters of recommendation, completion of writing req.
ACCEPTANCE OF TRANSFERS – Yes
MASTER'S PROGRAM DURATION: Number of required Quarters – 6
Number of weeks long – 11
Comprehensive Exam Required? – No
Thesis Required? – Optional
Continuous Enrollment Required? – No
Other Requirements – Program must be completed within 7 years
Does program culminate in a degree in the field of educational communications and technology? – Yes
Name of the degree – M.A. in Education Option in Instructional Technology

Is this program part of another degree, certificate, or diploma? – No

OTHER PROGRAMS in educational technology or instructional development fields: Certificate Program available? Yes

Certificate URL – http://soe.csusb.edu/etec/aboutcourses.html#CertificatePrograms

Specialist Program available? – No

Undergraduate Program available? – No

Doctorate Program available? – No

Program Content – Master's degree

Program Content URL – http://soe.csusb.edu/etec

Name of Institution – California State University, East Bay

Name of Program within institution – Online Teaching & Learning

Title/Degree as it appears on official certificate or diploma – MS in Education, Option in Online Teaching & Learning

Name & Title of person administering program – Nan Chico, Ph.D.

Address – 25800 Carlos Bee Blvd., Hayward, CA, 94542, United States

Telephone Number – 510-885-4384

Fax Number – 510-885-4498

E-Mail – nan.chico@csueastbay.edu

Institution's home page – http://www.csueastbay.edu

Admittance URL – http://www.csumentor.edu

PREREQUISITES: Higher Education – No

Teaching Certificate – No

Other requirement – 3.0 GPA in previous 90 quarter credits of BA/BS in any subject

ACCEPTANCE OF TRANSFERS – No

MASTER'S PROGRAM DURATION: Number of required Quarters – 5

Number of weeks long – 10

Comprehensive Exam Required? – No

Thesis Required? – Optional

Continuous Enrollment Required? – No

Does program culminate in a degree in the field of educational communications and technology? – Yes

Name of the degree – MS in Education, Option in Online Teaching & Learning

Is this program part of another degree, certificate, or diploma? – No

OTHER PROGRAMS in educational technology or instructional development fields: Certificate Program available? – Yes

Certificate URL – http://www.ce.csueastbay.edu/certificate/online_teaching/index.shtml?intid=fhome_otlc

Specialist Program available? – No

Undergraduate Program available? – No

Doctorate Program available? – No

Program Content – Master's degree

Program Content URL – http://edschool.csueastbay.edu/departments/olp/index.html

Name of Institution – University of Northern Colorado
Name of Program within institution – Educational Technology
Title/Degree as it appears on official certificate or diploma – MA or PhD in Educational Technology, MA in Educational Media
Name & Title of person administering program – Heng-Yu Ku, Program Coordinator
Address – 512 McKee Hall, Greeley, CO, 80631, United States
Telephone Number – 970 351 2807
Fax Number – 970 351 1622
E-Mail – heng-yu.Ku@unco.edu
Institution's home page – http://www.coe.unco.edu/cebs/edtech
PREREQUISITES: Higher Education – No
If yes, number of years or degree required – BS or BA
Teaching Certificate – No
Other requirement, ACCEPTANCE OF TRANSFERS – Yes
MASTER'S PROGRAM DURATION: Number of required Courses – 10
Number of weeks long – 16
Comprehensive Exam Required? – Yes
Thesis Required? – No
Continuous Enrollment Required? – Yes
Does program culminate in a degree in the field of educational communications and technology? – Yes
Name of the degree – Master of Arts in Educational Technology or Educational Media
Is this program part of another degree, certificate, or diploma? – No
If yes, name of the degree, certificate, or diploma, OTHER PROGRAMS in educational technology or instructional development fields: Certificate Program available? – Yes
Specialist Program available? – No
Undergraduate Program available? – No
Doctorate Program available? – PhD
Doctorate URL – http://www.unco.edu/cebs/edtech
Program Content – Master's degree

Name of Institution – Colorado State University
Name of Program within institution – Adult Education and Training
Title/Degree as it appears on official certificate or diploma – Med
Name & Title of person administering program – Timothy Davies
Address – Education Building, Fort Collins, CO, 80523, United States
Fax Number – 970-491-1317
Institution's home page – http://aet.colostate.edu/
Admittance URL – http://www.admissions.colostate.edu/
PREREQUISITES: Higher Education – Yes
If yes, number of years or degree required – Bachelors
Teaching Certificate – No
ACCEPTANCE OF TRANSFERS – Yes

MASTER'S PROGRAM DURATION: Number of required Semesters – 5
Number of weeks long – 16
Comprehensive Exam Required? – No
Thesis Required? – No
Continuous Enrollment Required? – Yes
Does program culminate in a degree in the field of educational communications and technology? – No
Name of the degree – Adult Education and Training
Is this program part of another degree, certificate, or diploma? – No
Program Content – Master's degree
Program Content URL – http://aet.colostate.edu/

Name of Institution – Metropolitan State College of Denver
Name of Program within institution – School of Professional Studies
Title/Degree as it appears on official certificate or diploma – Bachelor's Degree
Name & Title of person administering program – Dr. Miri Chung
Address – Speer Blvd. and Colfax Ave, Denver, CO, 80217, United States
Telephone Number – (303) 352-4416
Fax Number – (303) 556-5353
E-Mail – mchung3@mscd.edu
Institution's home page – http://www.mscd.edu/~ted
PREREQUISITES: Higher Education – Yes
Teaching Certificate – Yes
ACCEPTANCE OF TRANSFERS – Yes
MASTER'S PROGRAM DURATION: Comprehensive Exam Required? – Yes
Thesis Required? – No
Continuous Enrollment Required? – Yes
Does program culminate in a degree in the field of educational communications and technology? – Yes
Is this program part of another degree, certificate, or diploma? – Yes
Program Content – Master's degree

Name of Institution – Regis University
Name of Program within institution – M.Ed., specialization in Instructional Technology
Title/Degree as it appears on official certificate or diploma – Master of Education, specialization in Instructional Technology
Name & Title of person administering program – Patrick Lowenthal, Assistant Professor
Address – 3333 Regis Boulevard, Denver, CO, 80221-1099, United States
Telephone Number – 1.800.944.7667

E-Mail – plowenth@regis.edu
Institution's home page – http://www.regis.edu
Admittance URL – http://www.regis.edu/sps.asp?page=online.grdeg.med& mode=online
PREREQUISITES: Higher Education – No
If yes, number of years or degree required – Bachelor's Degree Required
Teaching Certificate – No
ACCEPTANCE OF TRANSFERS – Yes
MASTER'S PROGRAM DURATION: Number of required Courses – 10
Number of weeks long – 8 week
Comprehensive Exam Required? – No
Thesis Required? – No
Continuous Enrollment Required? – No
Other Requirements – Research Capstone
Does program culminate in a degree in the field of educational communications and technology? – Yes
Name of the degree – Master of Education, Specialization in Instructional Technology
Is this program part of another degree, certificate, or diploma? – No
OTHER PROGRAMS in educational technology or instructional development fields: Certificate Program available? – Yes
Certificate URL – http://www.regis.edu/sps.asp?page=online.grcert.med& mode=online
Specialist Program available? – No
Undergraduate Program available? – No
Doctorate Program available? – No
Program Content – Master's degree
Program Content URL – http://www.regis.edu/regis.asp?sctn=cur&p1=spsed

Name of Institution – Jones International University
Name of Program within institution – Master of Education
Title/Degree as it appears on official certificate or diploma – Master of Education
Name & Title of person administering program – Dr. Robert W. Fulton, Chair of Education
Address – 9697 East Mineral Avenue, Englewood, CO, 80112, United States
Telephone Number – 1-800-811-5663 (ext. 8498)
Fax Number – 303-784-8547
E-Mail – rfulton@international.edu
Institution's home page – http://www.jonesinternational.edu
Admittance URL – http://www.jonesinternational.edu
PREREQUISITES: Higher Education – Yes
If yes, number of years or degree required – Bachelor's
Teaching Certificate – No
ACCEPTANCE OF TRANSFERS – Yes

MASTER'S PROGRAM DURATION: Number of required Courses – 12
Number of weeks long – 8
Comprehensive Exam Required? – No
Thesis Required? – No
Continuous Enrollment Required? – No
Does program culminate in a degree in the field of educational communications and technology? – Yes
Name of the degree – M.Ed. in e-Learning
Is this program part of another degree, certificate, or diploma? – Yes
OTHER PROGRAMS in educational technology or instructional development fields: Certificate Program available? – Yes
Certificate URL – http://www.jonesinternational.edu
Specialist Program available? – Yes
Specialist URL – http://www.jonesinternational.edu
Undergraduate Program available? – No
Doctorate Program available? – No
Program Content – Master's degree
Program Content URL – http://www.jonesinternational.edu

Name of Institution – University of Colorado at Denver
Name of Program within institution – Information and Learning Technologies
Title/Degree as it appears on official certificate or diploma – MA in Information and Learning Technologies
Name & Title of person administering program – Brent G. Wilson
Address – UCD CB 106; POB 173364, Denver, CO, 80217-3364, United States
Telephone Number – 303-556-4363
Fax Number – 303-556-4479
E-Mail – brent.wilson@cudenver.edu
Institution's home page – http://www.cudenver.edu/ilt
Admittance URL – http://thunder1.cudenver.edu/ilt/id_and_adult_learning/req_admission.htm
PREREQUISITES: Higher Education – Yes
Teaching Certificate – No
ACCEPTANCE OF TRANSFERS – Yes
MASTER'S PROGRAM DURATION: Number of required Semesters – 6
Comprehensive Exam Required? – No
Thesis Required? – No
Continuous Enrollment Required? – Yes
Other Requirements – Professional portfolio
Does program culminate in a degree in the field of educational communications and technology? – Yes
Name of the degree – Information and Learning Technologies
Is this program part of another degree, certificate, or diploma? – Yes
If yes, name of the degree, certificate, or diploma – Brent Wilson

OTHER PROGRAMS in educational technology or instructional development fields: Certificate Program available? – Yes
Certificate URL – http://thunder1.cudenver.edu/ilt/wle/
Specialist Program available? – No
Undergraduate Program available? – No
Doctorate Program available? – PhD
Doctorate URL – http://thunder1.cudenver.edu/ideal/
Program Content – Master's degree
Program Content URL – http://thunder1.cudenver.edu/ilt/

Name of Institution – Graduate School of Education and Allied Professions, Fairfield University
Name of Program within institution – Educational Technology
Title/Degree as it appears on official certificate or diploma – M.A. and C.A.S.
Name & Title of person administering program – Dr. Ibrahim Michail Hefzallah, Chair
Address – 1073 North Benson Rd, Fairfield, CT, 06824, United States
Telephone Number – 203-254-4000
Fax Number – 203-254-4047
E-Mail – ihefzallah@mail.fairfield.edu
Institution's home page – http://www.fairfield.edu
Admittance URL – http://www.fairfield.edu/academic/gradedu/adm_info_01. html
PREREQUISITES: Higher Education – No
If yes, number of years or degree required – Bachelor degree
Teaching Certificate – No
ACCEPTANCE OF TRANSFERS – Yes
MASTER'S PROGRAM DURATION: Number of required Courses – 11
Comprehensive Exam Required? – Yes
Thesis Required? – No
Continuous Enrollment Required? – Yes
Does program culminate in a degree in the field of educational communications and technology? – Yes
Name of the degree – M.A.
Is this program part of another degree, certificate, or diploma? – No
OTHER PROGRAMS in educational technology or instructional development fields: Certificate Program available? – No
Specialist Program available? – Yes
Undergraduate Program available? – No
Doctorate Program available? – No
Program Content – Master's degree
Program Content URL – http://www.fairfield.edu/academic/gradedu/pro_edutech_01.html

Name of Institution – University of Connecticut
Name of Program within institution – Learning Technology
Title/Degree as it appears on official certificate or diploma – Educational Psychology/Educational Technology
Name & Title of person administering program – Michael Young, Ph.D.
Address – 249 Glenbrook Road, Unit 2064, Storrs, CT, 06269, United States
Telephone Number – (860) 486-0182
Fax Number – (860) 486-0180
E-Mail – myoung@uconn.edu
Institution's home page – http://www.epsy.uconn.edu
Admittance URL – http://www.grad.uconn.edu/applications.html
PREREQUISITES: Higher Education – No
Teaching Certificate – No
ACCEPTANCE OF TRANSFERS – Yes
MASTER'S PROGRAM DURATION: Number of required Courses – 9
Comprehensive Exam Required? – Yes
Thesis Required? – No
Continuous Enrollment Required? – Yes
Other Requirements – e-portfolio-based
Does program culminate in a degree in the field of educational communications and technology? – Yes
Is this program part of another degree, certificate, or diploma? – Yes
OTHER PROGRAMS in educational technology or instructional development fields: Certificate Program available? – Yes
Doctorate Program available? – PhD
Program Content – Master's degree
Program Content URL – http://www.education.uconn.edu/dept/epsy/

Name of Institution – University of Bridgeport
Name of Program within institution – Instructional Technology
Title/Degree as it appears on official certificate or diploma – Master of Science Instructional Technology
Name & Title of person administering program – Jerald D. Cole
Address – 126 Park Avenue, Bridgeport, CT, 06601, United States
Telephone Number – 2035764217
Fax Number – 2035764102
E-Mail – jcole@bridgeport.edu
Institution's home page – http://www.bridgeport.edu
PREREQUISITES: Higher Education – No
If yes, number of years or degree required – Bachelors
Teaching Certificate – No
ACCEPTANCE OF TRANSFERS – Yes
MASTER'S PROGRAM DURATION: Number of required Courses – 12
Number of weeks long – 15
Comprehensive Exam Required? – No

Thesis Required? – Optional
Continuous Enrollment Required? – No
Does program culminate in a degree in the field of educational communications and technology? – Yes
Name of the degree – iMSIT
Is this program part of another degree, certificate, or diploma? – No
OTHER PROGRAMS in educational technology or instructional development fields: Certificate Program available? – Yes
Specialist Program available? – Yes
Undergraduate Program available? – Yes
Doctorate Program available? – EdD
Program Content – Master's degree
Program Content URL – http://www.bridgeport.edu/pages/2994.asp

Name of Institution – The George Washington University
Name of Program within institution – Educational Technology Leadership Program
Title/Degree as it appears on official certificate or diploma – Master of Arts in Education and Human Development
Name & Title of person administering program – Dr. Michael Corry, Director, Educational Technology Leadership Program
Address – 2134 G Street NW, Suite 103, Washington, DC, 20052, United States
Telephone Number – Toll Free 1-866-498-3382
Fax Number – 202-994-2145
E-Mail – etladmin@gwu.edu
Institution's home page – http://www.gwu.edu/~etl
PREREQUISITES: Higher Education – Yes
Teaching Certificate – No
ACCEPTANCE OF TRANSFERS – Yes
MASTER'S PROGRAM DURATION: Number of required Courses – 12
Comprehensive Exam Required? – Yes
Thesis Required? – No
Continuous Enrollment Required? – Yes
Does program culminate in a degree in the field of educational communications and technology? – No
Name of the degree – Master of Arts in Education and Human Development
Is this program part of another degree, certificate, or diploma? – No
OTHER PROGRAMS in educational technology or instructional development fields: Certificate Program available? – Yes
Certificate URL – http://www.gwu.edu/~etl/webcertificate
Specialist Program available? – No
Undergraduate Program available? – No
Doctorate Program available? – No
Program Content – Master's degree
Program Content URL – http://www.gwu.edu/~etl

Name of Institution – Florida State University
Name of Program within institution – Instructional Systems
Title/Degree as it appears on official certificate or diploma – Instructional Systems
Name & Title of person administering program – Dr. Bob Reiser, Program Leader
Address – 305, F Stone Building, Department of EPLS, FSU, Tallahassee, FL, 32306, United States
Telephone Number – 850-644-4592
Fax Number – 850-644-8776
E-Mail – rreiser@mailer.fsu.edu
Institution's home page – http://www.epls.fsu.edu
PREREQUISITES: Higher Education – Yes
If yes, number of years or degree required – BS/BA
Teaching Certificate – No
ACCEPTANCE OF TRANSFERS – Yes
MASTER'S PROGRAM DURATION: Number of required Courses – 12
Number of weeks long – 16
Comprehensive Exam Required? – Yes
Thesis Required? – No
Continuous Enrollment Required? – Yes
Other Requirements – Internship
Does program culminate in a degree in the field of educational communications and technology? – Yes
Name of the degree – Masters in Instructional Systems
Is this program part of another degree, certificate, or diploma? – Yes
If yes, name of the degree, certificate, or diploma – Masters Degree in Instructional Systems with a Major in Open and Distance Learning
OTHER PROGRAMS in educational technology or instructional development fields: Certificate Program available? – Yes
Certificate URL – http://www.epls.fsu.edu/is/index.htm
Specialist Program available? – No
Undergraduate Program available? – No
Doctorate Program available? – PhD
Doctorate URL – http://www.epls.fsu.edu/is/doctoral.htm
Program Content – Master's degree
Program Content URL – http://www.epls.fsu.edu/is/msIntro.htm

Name of Institution – Nova Southeastern University
Name of Program within institution – Programs in Instructional Technology and Distance Education
Title/Degree as it appears on official certificate or diploma – Master of Science
Address – 1750 NE 167th St, North Miami Beach, FL, 33162, United States
Telephone Number – 1-800-986-3223

Fax Number – (954) 262-3905
Institution's home page – http://www.nova.edu
Admittance URL – http://www.fgse.nova.edu/itde/admissions.htm
PREREQUISITES: Higher Education – No
If yes, number of years or degree required – Bachelor's
Teaching Certificate – No
ACCEPTANCE OF TRANSFERS – Yes
MASTER'S PROGRAM DURATION: Number of required Terms – 5
Number of weeks long – 15
Comprehensive Exam Required? – No
Thesis Required? – No
Continuous Enrollment Required? – No
Other Requirements – Portfolio
Does program culminate in a degree in the field of educational communications and technology? – Yes
Name of the degree – Master of Science
Is this program part of another degree, certificate, or diploma? – No
OTHER PROGRAMS in educational technology or instructional development fields: Certificate Program available? – Yes
Specialist Program available? – No
Undergraduate Program available? – No
Doctorate Program available? – EdD
Doctorate URL – http://www.fgse.nova.edu/itde/index.htm
Program Content – Master's degree

Name of Institution – University of West Florida
Name of Program within institution – Instructional Technology
Title/Degree as it appears on official certificate or diploma – M.Ed., Instructional Technology
Name & Title of person administering program – Karen Rasmussen, Chair and Associate Professor
Address – 11000 University Parkway, Pensacola, FL, 32514, United States
Telephone Number – 850-474-2484
Fax Number – 850-474-2804
E-Mail – krasmuss@uwf.edu
Institution's home page – http://uwf.edu
Admittance URL – http://uwf.edu/admissions
PREREQUISITES: Higher Education – Yes
Teaching Certificate – No
ACCEPTANCE OF TRANSFERS – Yes
MASTER'S PROGRAM DURATION: Number of required Courses – 12
Number of weeks long – 6–16
Comprehensive Exam Required? – Yes
Thesis Required? – No
Continuous Enrollment Required? – No

Other Requirements – Comprehensive Examination or Technology Showcase

Does program culminate in a degree in the field of educational communications and technology? – Yes

Name of the degree – Instructional Technology

Is this program part of another degree, certificate, or diploma? – No

OTHER PROGRAMS in educational technology or instructional development fields: Certificate Program available? – Yes

Certificate URL – http://cops.uwf.edu/hpt

Specialist Program available? – Yes

Specialist URL – http://cops.uwf.edu/dect

Undergraduate Program available? – No

Doctorate Program available? – EdD

Doctorate URL – http://cops.uwf.edu/dect

Program Content – Master's degree

Program Content URL – http://cops.uwf.edu/dect

Name of Institution – University of Florida

Name of Program within institution – Educational Technology

Title/Degree as it appears on official certificate or diploma – Instruction and Curriculum/Educational Technology

Name & Title of person administering program – Kara Dawson

Address – G518 Norman Hall, Gainesville, FL, 32611, United States

Telephone Number – 352 392-9191

Fax Number – 352 392-9191

E-Mail – kdawson@coe.ufl.edu

Institution's home page – http://www.coe.ufl.edu

Admittance URL – http://www.coe.ufl.edu/Courses/EdTech/index.html

PREREQUISITES: Higher Education – Yes

Teaching Certificate – No

ACCEPTANCE OF TRANSFERS – Yes

MASTER'S PROGRAM DURATION: Number of required Courses – 12

Number of weeks long – 15

Comprehensive Exam Required? – Yes

Thesis Required? – No

Continuous Enrollment Required? – No

Does program culminate in a degree in the field of educational communications and technology? – No

Name of the degree – Educational Technology

Is this program part of another degree, certificate, or diploma? – No

OTHER PROGRAMS in educational technology or instructional development fields: Certificate Program available? – Yes

Certificate URL – http://www.coe.ufl.edu/online/edtech/CertProgram.html

Specialist Program available? – Yes

Undergraduate Program available? – No

Doctorate Program available? – PhD

Program Content – Master's degree
Program Content URL – http://www.coe.ufl.edu/Courses/EdTech/index.html

Name of Institution – Nova Southeastern University
Name of Program within institution – Computing Technology in Education
Title/Degree as it appears on official certificate or diploma – Master of Science
Name & Title of person administering program – Eric S. Ackerman, Ph.D.
Address – 3301 College Avenue, Fort Lauderdale, FL, 33314, United States
Telephone Number – (800) 986-2247
Fax Number – (954) 262-3915
E-Mail – scisinfo@nova.edu
Institution's home page – http://www.scis.nova.edu
Admittance URL – http://www.scis.nova.edu/Admissions/index.html
PREREQUISITES: Higher Education – Yes
If yes, number of years or degree required – Bachelors
Teaching Certificate – No
ACCEPTANCE OF TRANSFERS – Yes
MASTER'S PROGRAM DURATION: Number of required Terms – 4
Number of weeks long – 12
Comprehensive Exam Required? – No
Thesis Required? – Optional
Continuous Enrollment Required? – No
Does program culminate in a degree in the field of educational communications and technology? – Yes
Name of the degree – Master of Science
Is this program part of another degree, certificate, or diploma? – No
OTHER PROGRAMS in educational technology or instructional development fields: Certificate Program available? – No
Specialist Program available? – Yes
Specialist URL – http://www.scis.nova.edu/Doctoral/Academic_Programs/Academic _ Programs _ DCTE.html
Undergraduate Program available? – No
Doctorate Program available? – PhD
Doctorate URL – http://www.scis.nova.edu/Doctoral/Academic _ Programs/Academic _ Programs _ DCTE.html
Program Content – Master's degree
Program Content URL – http://www.scis.nova.edu/Masters/Academic _ Programs/Academic _ Programs _ MCTE.html

Name of Institution – University of South Florida
Name of Program within institution – Instructional Technology Program
Title/Degree as it appears on official certificate or diploma – Curriculum & Instruction with emphasis in Instructional Technology
Name & Title of person administering program – Dr. William A. Kealy

Address – 4202 E. Fowler Avenue EDU162, Tampa, FL, 33620, United States
Telephone Number – 813-974-3533
Fax Number – 813-974-3837
E-Mail – IT@coedu.usf.edu
Institution's home page – http://www.usf.edu
Admittance URL – http://www.coedu.usf.edu/it/curriculum/index.cfm
PREREQUISITES: Higher Education – Yes
If yes, number of years or degree required – Baccalaureate degree for all programs; Master's degree
Teaching Certificate – No
ACCEPTANCE OF TRANSFERS – Yes
MASTER'S PROGRAM DURATION: Number of required Courses – 12
Comprehensive Exam Required? – Yes
Thesis Required? – No
Continuous Enrollment Required? – Yes
Does program culminate in a degree in the field of educational communications and technology? – Yes
Name of the degree – Masters of Education (M.Ed.) in Instructional Technology
Is this program part of another degree, certificate, or diploma? – No
OTHER PROGRAMS in educational technology or instructional development fields: Certificate Program available? – Yes
Certificate URL – http://www.coedu.usf.edu/it/curriculum/certs/index.cfm
Specialist Program available? – Yes
Specialist URL – http://www.coedu.usf.edu/it/curriculum/eds/index.cfm
Undergraduate Program available? – No
Doctorate Program available? – PhD
Doctorate URL – http://www.coedu.usf.edu/it/curriculum/phd/index.cfm
Program Content – Master's degree
Program Content URL – http://www.coedu.usf.edu/it/curriculum/med/index.cfm

Name of Institution – University of Central Florida
Name of Program within institution – Instructional Technology
Title/Degree as it appears on official certificate or diploma – MA Instructional Systems
Name & Title of person administering program – Atsusi Hirumi, Ph.D., Associate Professor, Program Chair
Address – 4000 University Blvd, Orlando, FL, 32816, United States
Telephone Number – 407.823.1760
Fax Number – 407.823.4880
E-Mail – hirumi@mail.ucf.edu
Institution's home page – http://www.ucf.edu
Admittance URL – http://www.ucf.edu/admission.html
PREREQUISITES: Higher Education – No

If yes, number of years or degree required – Bachelors
Teaching Certificate – No
ACCEPTANCE OF TRANSFERS – No
MASTER'S PROGRAM DURATION: Number of required Courses – 13
Comprehensive Exam Required? – – No **Thesis Required?** – – Optional
Continuous Enrollment Required? – No – **Does program culminate in a degree in the field of educational communications and technology?** – Yes
Name of the degree – MA Instructional Technology
Is this program part of another degree, certificate, or diploma? – – Yes
OTHER PROGRAMS in educational technology or instructional development fields: Certificate Program available? – – No
Certificate URL – http://www.ucf.edu/programs/index.html
Doctorate Program available? – PhD
Doctorate URL – http://www.graduate.ucf.edu/acad_progs/index.cfm? SubCatID=123&ProgID=103
Program Content – Master's degree
Program Content URL – http://pegasus.cc.ucf.edu/~instsys/home.html

Name of Institution – University of Central Florida
Name of Program within institution – Instructional Technology
Title/Degree as it appears on official certificate or diploma – MA-Educational Technology
Name & Title of person administering program – Dr. Glenda Gunter
Address – 4000 University Blvd Orlando, FL, 32816, United States
Telephone Number – 407.823.3502
Fax Number – 407.823.4880
E-Mail – ggunter@mail.ucf.edu
Institution's home page – http://pegasus.cc.ucf.edu/~edtech/welcome.html
Admittance URL – http://www.ucf.edu/admission.html
PREREQUISITES: Higher Education – Yes
If yes, number of years or degree required – Bachelor's Degree
Teaching Certificate – Yes
ACCEPTANCE OF TRANSFERS – Yes
MASTER'S PROGRAM DURATION: Number of required Courses – 14
Comprehensive Exam Required? – Yes
Thesis Required? – – No
Continuous Enrollment Required? No
Does program culminate in a degree in the field of educational communications and technology? – Yes
Name of the degree – MA Educational Technology
Is this program part of another degree, certificate, or diploma? – Yes
If yes, name of the degree, certificate, or diploma – Instructional Technology
OTHER PROGRAMS in educational technology or instructional development fields: Certificate Program available? – Yes

Certificate URL – http://edcollege.ucf.edu/mod_depts/prog_page.cfm?Prog
  DeptID=5&ProgID=63
Undergraduate Program available? – No
Doctorate Program available? – PhD
Doctorate URL – http://edcollege.ucf.edu/mod_depts/prog_page.cfm?Prog
  DeptID=9&ProgID=77
Program Content – Master's degree

Name of Institution – University of Georgia
Name of Program within institution – Instructional Technology
Title/Degree as it appears on official certificate or diploma – Instructional
  Technology
Name & Title of person administering program – Robert Maribe Branch
Address – 604 Aderhold Hall, Athens, GA, 30602, United States
Telephone Number – 706 542-3810
Fax Number – 706 542-4032
E-Mail – pschutz@coe.uga.ed
Institution's home page – http://www.uga.edu/
Admittance URL – http://it.coe.uga.edu/
PREREQUISITES: Higher Education – Yes
If yes, number of years or degree required – Bachelor Degree
Teaching Certificate – No
ACCEPTANCE OF TRANSFERS – Yes
MASTER'S PROGRAM DURATION: Number of required Semesters – 4
Number of weeks long – 15
Comprehensive Exam Required? – Yes
Thesis Required? – No
Continuous Enrollment Required? – Yes
**Does program culminate in a degree in the field of educational communi-
  cations and technology?** – Yes
Name of the degree – Instructional Technology
Is this program part of another degree, certificate, or diploma? – No
**OTHER PROGRAMS in educational technology or instructional develop-
  ment fields: Certificate Program available?** – No
Specialist Program available? – Yes
Specialist URL – http://it.coe.uga.edu/program.htm
Undergraduate Program available? – Yes
Undergraduate URL – http://www.coe.uga.edu/gwinnett/iptt/
Doctorate Program available? – PhD
Doctorate URL – http://it.coe.uga.edu/program_doctoral1.htm
Program Content – Master's degree
Program Content URL – http://it.coe.uga.edu/program_master3.htm

Name of Institution – Georgia State University
Name of Program within institution – Instructional Technology

Title/Degree as it appears on official certificate or diploma – Master of Science in Instructional Technology

Name & Title of person administering program – Dr. Stephen W. Harmon

Address – 30 Pryor Street, Atlanta, GA, 30303, United States

Telephone Number – 404-651-2510

Fax Number – 404-651-2546

E-Mail – swharmon@gsu.edu

Institution's home page – http://www.gsu.edu

Admittance URL – http://education.gsu.edu/coe/content/admissions.htm

PREREQUISITES: Higher Education – Yes

If yes, number of years or degree required – Bachelor's

Teaching Certificate – No

ACCEPTANCE OF TRANSFERS – Yes

MASTER'S PROGRAM DURATION: Number of required Courses – 12

Number of weeks long – 15

Comprehensive Exam Required? – Yes

Thesis Required? – No

Continuous Enrollment Required? – No

Does program culminate in a degree in the field of educational communications and technology? – Yes

Name of the degree – Master of Science in Instructional Technology

Is this program part of another degree, certificate, or diploma? – No

OTHER PROGRAMS in educational technology or instructional development fields: Certificate Program available? – No

Specialist Program available? – Yes

Specialist URL – http://edtech.gsu.edu/programs.htm#eds

Undergraduate Program available? – No

Doctorate Program available? – PhD

Doctorate URL – http://edtech.gsu.edu/programs.htm#phd

Program Content – Master's degree

Program Content URL – http://edtech.gsu.edu/programs.htm#ms

Name of Institution – University of Hawaii at Manoa

Name of Program within institution – Educational Technology

Title/Degree as it appears on official certificate or diploma – Master's of Education, Educational Technology

Name & Title of person administering program – Curtis P. Ho, Chair

Address – 1776 University Avenue, Honolulu, HI, 96822, United States

Telephone Number – (808) 956-7671

Fax Number – (808) 956-3905

E-Mail – edtech-dept@hawaii.edu

Institution's home page – http://etec.hawaii.edu

Admittance URL – http://etec.hawaii.edu/curricula.html?p=masters&s=adm-reqs

PREREQUISITES: Higher Education – No

If yes, number of years or degree required – Bachelor's
Teaching Certificate – No
ACCEPTANCE OF TRANSFERS – Yes
MASTER'S PROGRAM DURATION: Number of required Semesters – 4
Number of weeks long – 16
Comprehensive Exam Required? – No
Thesis Required? – Optional
Continuous Enrollment Required? – Yes
Other Requirements – Praxis I Writing Test TOEFL for International Students
Does program culminate in a degree in the field of educational communications and technology? Yes
Name of the degree – Educational Technology
Is this program part of another degree, certificate, or diploma? No
OTHER PROGRAMS in educational technology or instructional development fields: Certificate Program available? – No
Specialist Program available? – No
Undergraduate Program available? – No
Doctorate Program available? – No
Program Content – Master's degree
Program Content URL – http://etec.hawaii.edu/curricula.html

Name of Institution – University of Northern Iowa
Name of Program within institution – Instructional Technology
Title/Degree as it appears on official certificate or diploma – Master of Education
Name & Title of person administering program – Mary Herring
Address – 618 SEC, Cedar Falls, IA, 50614, United States
Telephone Number –319-273-2368
Fax Number – 319-273-5886
E-Mail – mary.herring@uni.edu
Institution's home page – http://www.uni.edu
Admittance URL – http://www.grad.uni.edu/admission/
PREREQUISITES: Higher Education –No
If yes, number of years or degree required – Bachelors degree in any field
Teaching Certificate –No
Other requirement – Transfers accepted from US schools only.
Undergraduate grade point – 3.0 of 4.0
ACCEPTANCE OF TRANSFERS – Yes
MASTER'S PROGRAM DURATION: Number of required Courses – 12
Number of weeks long – 16
Comprehensive Exam Required? – Yes
Thesis Required? – No
Continuous Enrollment Required? – No
Does program culminate in a degree in the field of educational communications and technology? – Yes

Name of the degree – C&I: Instructional Technology; C&I Performance and Training

Is this program part of another degree, certificate, or diploma? Yes

OTHER PROGRAMS in educational technology or instructional development fields: Certificate Program available? – No

Specialist Program available? – No

Undergraduate Program available? – No

Doctorate Program available? – No

Program Content – Master's degree

Program Content URL – http://ci.coe.uni.edu/edtech/index.html

Name of Institution – Iowa State University

Name of Program within institution – Curriculum & Instructional Technology

Title/Degree as it appears on official certificate or diploma – Education with specialization in Curriculum and Instructional Technology

Name & Title of person administering program – Dr. C. Hargrave

Address – Lagomarcino Hall, Ames, IA, 50011, United States

Telephone Number – (515) 294-7021

Fax Number – (515) 294-6206

E-Mail – pkendall@iastate.edu

Institution's home page – http://www.iastate.edu/

Admittance URL – http://www.grad-college.iastate.edu/applying/applying.html

PREREQUISITES: Higher Education – Yes

If yes, number of years or degree required – Bachelors degree

Teaching Certificate – No

Other requirement – An advanced level of general computer literacy

ACCEPTANCE OF TRANSFERS – Yes

MASTER'S PROGRAM DURATION: Number of required Semesters – 4

Number of weeks long – 16

Comprehensive Exam Required? – No

Thesis Required? – Optional

Continuous Enrollment Required? – No

Does program culminate in a degree in the field of educational communications and technology? – Yes

Name of the degree, M.Ed. /M.S.

Is this program part of another degree, certificate, or diploma? – No

OTHER PROGRAMS in educational technology or instructional development fields: Undergraduate Program available? – Yes

Undergraduate URL – http://www.ctlt.iastate.edu/teaching/tech_minor.html

Doctorate Program available? – PhD

Doctorate URL – http://www.ctlt.iastate.edu/teaching/phD.html

Program Content – Master's degree

Program Content URL – http://www.ctlt.iastate.edu/teaching/mastcurr.html

Name of Institution – Boise State University
Name of Program within institution – Instructional & Performance Technology
Title/Degree as it appears on official certificate or diploma – Master of Science in Instructional & Performance Technology
Name & Title of person administering program – Dr. David Cox
Address – 1910 University Drive, Boise, ID, 83725, United States
Telephone Number – 208-426-1312
E-Mail – jfenner@boisestate.edu
Institution's home page – http://www.boisestate.edu
Admittance URL – https://sycamore.boisestate.edu/gradcoll/apply.asp
PREREQUISITES: Higher Education – Yes
If yes, number of years or degree required – 4 year undergraduate degree
Teaching Certificate – No
Other requirements – minimum GPA of 3.0, resume and letter of intent
ACCEPTANCE OF TRANSFERS – Yes
MASTER'S PROGRAM DURATION: Number of required Semesters – 10
Number of weeks long – 16
Comprehensive Exam Required? – Yes
Thesis Required? – No
Continuous Enrollment Required? – No
Does program culminate in a degree in the field of educational communications and technology? – Yes
Name of the degree – Instructional & Performance Technology
Is this program part of another degree, certificate, or diploma? – No
OTHER PROGRAMS in educational technology or instructional development fields: Certificate Program available? – No
Specialist Program available? – No
Undergraduate Program available? – No
Doctorate Program available? – No
Program Content – Master's degree
Program Content URL – http://ipt.boisestate.edu

Name of Institution – Boise State University
Name of Program within institution – Educational Technology
Title/Degree as it appears on official certificate or diploma – Masters of Educational Technology
Name & Title of person administering program – Dr. Lisa Dawley
Address – 1910 University Drivev, Boise, ID, 83725, United States
Telephone Number – 208.426.1966
Fax Number – 208.426.1451
E-Mail – edtech@boisestate.edu
Institution's home page – http://www.boisestate.edu
Admittance URL – http://edtech.boisestate.edu/

PREREQUISITES: Higher Education – No
If yes, number of years or degree required – 4 year undergraduate degree
Teaching Certificate – No
Other requirement – minimum GPA of 3.0, application letter
ACCEPTANCE OF TRANSFERS – Yes
MASTER'S PROGRAM DURATION: Number of required Semesters – 4
Number of weeks long – 16
Comprehensive Exam Required? – Yes
Thesis Required? – Optional
Continuous Enrollment Required? – No
Does program culminate in a degree in the field of educational communications and technology? – Yes
Is this program part of another degree, certificate, or diploma? – Yes
If yes, name of the degree, certificate, or diploma – Educational Technology
OTHER PROGRAMS in educational technology or instructional development fields: Certificate Program available? – Yes
Certificate URL – http://edtech.boisestate.edu
Specialist Program available? – No
Specialist URL – http://edtech.boisestate.edu
Undergraduate Program available? – No
Doctorate Program available? – EdD
Program Content – Master's degree
Program Content URL – http://edtech.boisestate.edu

Name of Institution – Illinois State University
Name of Program within institution – Instructional Technology and Design
Title/Degree as it appears on official certificate or diploma – M.S. (Master of Science)
Name & Title of person administering program – Temba C. Bassoppo-Moyo Ph.D., Associate Coordinator
Address – 5330 DeGarmo Hall, Normal, IL, 61790, United States
Telephone Number – 3094385623
Fax Number – 3094388659
E-Mail – tcbasso@ilstu.edu
Institution's home page – http://www.coe.ilstu.edu/
Admittance URL – http://www.ilstu.edu
PREREQUISITES: Higher Education – Yes
If yes, number of years or degree required – 4
Teaching Certificate – Yes
ACCEPTANCE OF TRANSFERS – Yes
MASTER'S PROGRAM DURATION: Number of required Semesters – 6
Number of weeks long – NA
Comprehensive Exam Required? – Yes
Thesis Required? – Optional
Continuous Enrollment Required? – No

Other Requirements – See Program URL

Does program culminate in a degree in the field of educational communications and technology? – Yes

Name of the degree – Master of Science in Educational Technology

Is this program part of another degree, certificate, or diploma? – No

OTHER PROGRAMS in educational technology or instructional development fields: Certificate Program available? – Yes

Certificate URL – http://www.coe.ilstu.edu/

Specialist Program available? – No

Undergraduate Program available? – No

Doctorate Program available? – No

Program Content – Master's degree

Program Content URL – http://www.coe.ilstu.edu/

Name of Institution – Western Illinois University

Name of Program within institution – Instructional Technology and Telecommunications

Title/Degree as it appears on official certificate or diploma – Instructional Technology and Telecommunications/B.S./M.S.

Name & Title of person administering program – Hoyet H. Hemphill, Ph.D.

Address – 1 University Circle, Macomb, IL, 61455, United States

Telephone Number – (309) 298-1952

Fax Number – (309) 298-2978

E-Mail – hh-hemphill@wiu.edu

Institution's home page – http://wiu.edu/itt/

Admittance URL – http://wiu.edu/itt/potential/potential.htm

PREREQUISITES: Higher Education – Yes

If yes, number of years or degree required – Bachelors for MS program

Teaching Certificate – No

ACCEPTANCE OF TRANSFERS – Yes

MASTER'S PROGRAM DURATION: Number of required Courses – 12

Number of weeks long – 16

Comprehensive Exam Required? – No

Thesis Required? – Optional

Continuous Enrollment Required? – No

Other Requirements – Applied Project or Portfolio Option

Does program culminate in a degree in the field of educational communications and technology? – Yes

Name of the degree – Instructional Technology and Telecommunications

Is this program part of another degree, certificate, or diploma? – No

OTHER PROGRAMS in educational technology or instructional development fields: Certificate Program available? – Yes

Certificate URL – http://wiu.edu/itt/potential/certificates/certificates.htm

Specialist Program available? – No

Undergraduate Program available? – Yes

Program Content – Master's degree
Program Content URL – http://wiu.edu/itt/potential/bsitt/bsitt.htm

Name of Institution – Southern Illinois University at Carbondale
Name of Program within institution – Instructional Design or Instructional Technology
Title/Degree as it appears on official certificate or diploma – MS. in Curriculum and Instruction
Name & Title of person administering program – Sharon Shrock
Address – C&I. SIUC, Carbondale, IL, 62901, United States
Telephone Number – 618.453.4218
Fax Number – 618.453.5654
E-Mail – sashrock@siu.edu
PREREQUISITES: Higher Education – No
Teaching Certificate – No
Other requirement – B.S/ BA required
ACCEPTANCE OF TRANSFERS – Yes
MASTER'S PROGRAM DURATION: Number of required Courses – 12
Comprehensive Exam Required? – No
Thesis Required? – No
Continuous Enrollment Required? – No
Does program culminate in a degree in the field of educational communications and technology? – Yes
Is this program part of another degree, certificate, or diploma? – Yes
OTHER PROGRAMS in educational technology or instructional development fields: Certificate Program available? – No
Specialist Program available? – No
Undergraduate Program available? – No
Doctorate Program available? – PhD
Program Content – Master's degree

Name of Institution – Northern Illinois University
Name of Program within institution – Instructional Technology
Title/Degree as it appears on official certificate or diploma – MSEd or EdD in Instructional Technology
Name & Title of person administering program – Jeffrey B Hecht
Address – 208 Gabel Hall, DeKalb, IL, 60115, United States
Telephone Number – 815-753-9339
Fax Number – 815-753-9388
E-Mail – edtech@niu.edu
Institution's home page – http://www.cedu.niu.edu/etra
PREREQUISITES: Higher Education – Yes
If yes, number of years or degree required – Bachelor's
Teaching Certificate – No
Other requirement – Yes for Library Information Specialist Certification

ACCEPTANCE OF TRANSFERS – Yes
MASTER'S PROGRAM DURATION: Number of required Courses – 13
Comprehensive Exam Required? – Yes
Thesis Required? – No
Continuous Enrollment Required? – No
Other Requirements – Comprehensive Examination is in Portfolio format
Does program culminate in a degree in the field of educational communications and technology? – Yes
Name of the degree – MSEd Instructional Technology
Is this program part of another degree, certificate, or diploma? – No
OTHER PROGRAMS in educational technology or instructional development fields: Certificate Program available? – Yes
Certificate URL – http://www.cedu.niu.edu/etra/slm_program/slm_overview.htm
Specialist Program available? – No
Undergraduate Program available? – No
Doctorate Program available? – EdD
Doctorate URL – http://www.cedu.niu.edu/etra
Program Content – Master's degree
Program Content URL – http://http://www.cedu.niu.edu/etra/it_program/it_overview.htm

Name of Institution – Southern Illinois University Edwardsville
Name of Program within institution – Instructional Design and Learning Technologies (ID<)
Title/Degree as it appears on official certificate or diploma – masters in education
Name & Title of person administering program – Dr. Wayne Nelson
Address – Alumni Hall, Box 1125, Edwardsville, IL, 62026, United States
Telephone Number – 618-650-3277
Fax Number – 618-650-3808
E-Mail – wnelson@siue.edu
Institution's home page – http://www.siue.edu/
Admittance URL – http://www.siue.edu/GRADUATE/
PREREQUISITES: Higher Education – No
Teaching Certificate – Yes
ACCEPTANCE OF TRANSFERS – Yes
MASTER'S PROGRAM DURATION: Number of required Semesters – 4
Number of weeks long – 16
Comprehensive Exam Required? – Yes
Thesis Required? – No
Continuous Enrollment Required? – Yes
Does program culminate in a degree in the field of educational communications and technology? – Yes
Name of the degree – masters in education
Is this program part of another degree, certificate, or diploma? – Yes

If yes, name of the degree, certificate, or diploma – masters in education
OTHER PROGRAMS in educational technology or instructional development fields: Certificate Program available? – No
Specialist Program available? – Yes
Specialist URL – http://www.siue.edu/EDUCATION/ed_leadership/tech.html
Undergraduate Program available? – No
Doctorate Program available? – No
Program Content – Master's degree
Program Content URL – http://www.siue.edu/EDUCATION/ed_leadership/tech.html

Name of Institution – University of Illinois at Urbana-Champaign
Name of Program within institution – Curriculum, Technology, and Education Reform (CTER)
Title/Degree as it appears on official certificate or diploma – Ed.M. (Master of Education)
Name & Title of person administering program – Doe-Hyung Kim, M.A., Project Coordinator
Address – 1310 S. Sixth Street, Rm 226 Education Bldg, Champaign, IL, 61820, United States
Telephone Number – 2172443315
Fax Number – 2172447620
E-Mail – cter-info-L@listserv.uiuc.edu
Institution's home page – http://www.uiuc.edu
Admittance URL – http://cterport.ed.uiuc.edu/admissions_folder/application_procedures_html
PREREQUISITES: Higher Education – Yes
If yes, number of years or degree required – 4
Teaching Certificate – No
ACCEPTANCE OF TRANSFERS – Yes
MASTER'S PROGRAM DURATION: Number of required Semesters – 6
Number of weeks long – 4–16
Comprehensive Exam Required? – No
Thesis Required? – No
Continuous Enrollment Required? – No
Other Requirements – See program URL for technical requirements
Does program culminate in a degree in the field of educational communications and technology? – Yes
Name of the degree – Master of Education
Is this program part of another degree, certificate, or diploma? – Yes
If yes, name of the degree, certificate, or diploma – Master of Education in Educational Psychology
OTHER PROGRAMS in educational technology or instructional development fields: Certificate Program available? – No
Specialist Program available? – No
Undergraduate Program available? – No

Doctorate Program available? – No
Program Content – Master's degree
Program Content URL – http://cter.ed.uiuc.edu

Name of Institution – Ball State University
Name of Program within institution – Library Media and Computer Education
Title/Degree as it appears on official certificate or diploma – Bachelor of Science
Name & Title of person administering program – Patricia F. Beilke, Professor of Library & Information Science & of Secondary Ed.
Address – 2000 West University Avenue, Muncie, IN, 47306-0610, United States
Telephone Number – (765) 285-5477
Fax Number – (765) 285-5489
E-Mail – pbeilke@bsu.edu
Institution's home page – http://www.bsu.edu/
PREREQUISITES: Higher Education – No
Teaching Certificate – No
ACCEPTANCE OF TRANSFERS – Yes
Number of required Semesters – 8
Number of weeks long – 16
Comprehensive Exam Required? – No
Thesis Required? – No
Continuous Enrollment Required? – No
Other Requirements – Graduation from a commissioned secondary school or its equivalent
Does program culminate in a degree in the field of educational communications and technology? – No
Name of the degree – Library Media and Computer Education
Is this program part of another degree, certificate, or diploma? – Yes
If yes, name of the degree, certificate, or diploma – Library Media and Computer Education
OTHER PROGRAMS in educational technology or instructional development fields: Certificate Program available? – No
Specialist Program available? – Yes
Undergraduate Program available? – No
Doctorate Program available? – No
Program Content – Master's degree

Name of Institution – Purdue University Calumet
Name of Program within institution – Instructional Technology
Title/Degree as it appears on official certificate or diploma – Master of Science in Instructional Technology

Name & Title of person administering program – Janet Buckenmeyer, PhD, Program Chair
Address – 2200 169th St., Hammond, IN, 46323, United States
Telephone Number – 219-989-2692
Fax Number – 219-989-3215
E-Mail – buckenme@calumet.purdue.edu
Institution's home page – http://www.calumet.purdue.edu
Admittance URL – http://ssl.adpc.purdue.edu/rgs/plsql/w_apc.disp_intropg
PREREQUISITES: Higher Education – No
If yes, number of years or degree required – Bachelor's
Teaching Certificate – No
ACCEPTANCE OF TRANSFERS – Yes
MASTER'S PROGRAM DURATION: Number of required Semesters – 6
Number of weeks long – 16
Comprehensive Exam Required? – No
Thesis Required? – Optional
Continuous Enrollment Required? – No
Other Requirements – Internship and Project; Professional Portfolio
Does program culminate in a degree in the field of educational communications and technology? – Yes
Name of the degree – Master of Science in Instructional Technology
Is this program part of another degree, certificate, or diploma? – No
OTHER PROGRAMS in educational technology or instructional development fields: Certificate Program available? – No
Specialist Program available? – No
Undergraduate Program available? – No
Doctorate Program available? – No
Program Content – Master's degree
Program Content URL – http://education.calumet.purdue.edu/graduatestudies/tech/index.html

Name of Institution – Purdue University
Name of Program within institution – Educational Technology
Title/Degree as it appears on official certificate or diploma – Masters (or Doctor) of Curriculum and Instruction
Name & Title of person administering program – Tim Newby
Address – 100 N. University St., West Lafayette, IN, 47907-2098, United States
Telephone Number – 765-494-5669
Fax Number – 765-496-1622
E-Mail – edtech@soe.purdue.edu
Institution's home page – http://www.purdue.edu
Admittance URL – http://www.edci.purdue.edu/student/admission.html
PREREQUISITES: Higher Education – No
If yes, number of years or degree required – Bachelors Degree

Teaching Certificate – No
ACCEPTANCE OF TRANSFERS – Yes
MASTER'S PROGRAM DURATION: Number of required Semesters, 32 h, **Comprehensive Exam Required?** – Yes
Thesis Required? – No
Continuous **Enrollment Required?** – No
Other Requirements – Portfolio Integrated Project or Masters Thesis
Does program culminate in a degree in the field of educational communications and technology? – Yes
Name of the degree – Masters of Curriculum and Instruction
Is this program part of another degree, certificate, or diploma? – Yes
OTHER PROGRAMS in educational technology or instructional development fields: Certificate Program available? – Yes
Certificate URL – http://www.edci.purdue.edu/et/license_prg.html
Specialist Program available? – No
Undergraduate Program available? – No
Doctorate Program available? – PhD
Doctorate URL – http://www.edci.purdue.edu/et/phd.html
Program Content – Master's degree
Program Content URL – http://www.edci.purdue.edu/et/ms.html

Name of Institution – Indiana University
Name of Program within institution – Instructional Systems Technology
Title/Degree as it appears on official certificate or diploma – Master of Science in Instructional Systems Technology
Name & Title of person administering program – Chair Instructional Systems Technology
Address – 201 N. Rose Avenue, Education 2276, Bloomington, IN, 47405, United States
Telephone Number – 812-856-8455
Fax Number – 812-856-8239
E-Mail – istdept@indiana.edu
Institution's home page – http://education.indiana.edu/
Admittance URL – http://education.indiana.edu/isthome.html/admit/policy.html
PREREQUISITES: Higher Education – Yes
If yes, number of years or degree required – BA or BS
Teaching Certificate – No
ACCEPTANCE OF TRANSFERS – Yes
MASTER'S PROGRAM DURATION: Number of required Semesters – 4
Number of weeks long – 16
Comprehensive Exam Required? – No
Thesis Required? – No
Continuous Enrollment Required? – No
Other Requirements – capstone project professional portfolio
Does program culminate in a degree in the field of educational communications and technology? – Yes

Name of the degree – MS in Instructional Systems Technology

Is this program part of another degree, certificate, or diploma? – No

OTHER PROGRAMS in educational technology or instructional development fields: Certificate Program available? – Yes

Certificate URL – http://www.indiana.edu/~istde/programs.html#certificate

Specialist Program available? – Yes

Undergraduate Program available? – No

Doctorate Program available? – PhD

Doctorate URL – http://education.indiana.edu/isthome.html/programs/phd/docphd.html

Program Content – Master's degree

Program Content URL – http://education.indiana.edu/isthome.html/programs/masters/mastersresident.html

Name of Institution – Ball State University

Name of Program within institution – Master of Arts in Curriculum and Educational Technology

Title/Degree as it appears on official certificate or diploma – Master of Arts

Name & Title of person administering program – Matthew J. Stuve, Assistant Professor of Educational Technology

Address – 2000 West University Avenue, Muncie, IN, 47306, United States

Telephone Number – (765) 285-5477

Fax Number – (765) 285-5489

E-Mail – mstuve@bsu.edu

Institution's home page – http://www.bsu.edu/

PREREQUISITES: Higher Education – No

If yes, number of years or degree required – Bachelor's degree

Teaching Certificate – No

ACCEPTANCE OF TRANSFERS – Yes

MASTER'S PROGRAM DURATION: Number of required Semesters – 2

Number of weeks long – 16

Comprehensive Exam Required? No, **Thesis Required?** – Optional

Continuous Enrollment Required? No

Other Requirements – 21–24 credit hours of core courses + 9 credit hours from educational technology or curriculum track

Does program culminate in a degree in the field of educational communications and technology? – Yes

Name of the degree – Master of Arts in Curriculum and Educational Technology

Is this program part of another degree, certificate, or diploma? – No

OTHER PROGRAMS in educational technology or instructional development fields: Certificate Program available? – No

Specialist Program available? – Yes

Undergraduate Program available? – Yes

Doctorate Program available? – No

Program Content – Master's degree

Name of Institution – Indiana State University
Name of Program within institution – Master's of Science in Educational Technology
Title/Degree as it appears on official certificate or diploma – Master's of Science in Educational Technology
Name & Title of person administering program – Dr. Susan Powers, Dr. Feng-Qi Lai
Address – College of Education Room 1010, Terre Haute, IN, 47809, United States
Telephone Number – (812) 237-2960
Fax Number – (812) 237-4556
E-Mail – espowers@isugw.indstate.edu
Institution's home page – http://www.indstate.edu
Admittance URL – http://www.indstate.edu/sogs
PREREQUISITES: Higher Education – Yes
If yes, number of years or degree required – Bachelor's degree
Teaching Certificate – No
Other requirement – 2.6 GPA
ACCEPTANCE OF TRANSFERS – Yes
MASTER'S PROGRAM DURATION: Number of required Courses – 4
Comprehensive Exam Required? – No
Thesis Required? – No
Continuous Enrollment Required? – No
Other Requirements – Thirty-three semester hours to graduate. Culminating project or practicum
Does program culminate in a degree in the field of educational communications and technology? – Yes
Name of the degree – Master's of Science in Educational Technology
Is this program part of another degree, certificate, or diploma? – No
OTHER PROGRAMS in educational technology or instructional development fields: Certificate Program available? – Yes
Certificate URL – http://soe.indstate.edu/cimt/mams.htm#top
Specialist Program available? – No
Undergraduate Program available? – No
Doctorate Program available? – PhD
Doctorate URL – http://soe.indstate.edu/cimt/phdprog.htmtop
Program Content – Master's degree
Program Content URL – http://soe.indstate.edu/cimt/mams.htm#top

Name of Institution – Pittsburg State University
Name of Program within institution – Educational Technology
Title/Degree as it appears on official certificate or diploma – Master's Degree in Educational Technology
Name & Title of person administering program – Dr. Sue Stidham

Address – 1701 S. Broadway, Pittsburg, KS, 66762, United States
Telephone Number – 620 235-4507
Fax Number – 620 235-4520
E-Mail – jstidham@pittstate.edu
Institution's home page – http://pittstate.edu
Admittance URL – http://www.pittstate.edu/admit/wheretoapply.html
PREREQUISITES: Higher Education – Yes
If yes, number of years or degree required – Bachelor's Degree
Teaching Certificate – Yes
Other requirement – For Library Media Specialists Licensure
ACCEPTANCE OF TRANSFERS – Yes
MASTER'S PROGRAM DURATION: Number of required Semesters – 6
Number of weeks long – 16/8
Comprehensive Exam Required? – Yes
Thesis Required? – Optional
Continuous Enrollment Required? – No
Other Requirements – Continuous enrollment isn't required but strongly suggested
Does program culminate in a degree in the field of educational communications and technology? – Yes
Name of the degree – Master's Degree in Educational Technology
Is this program part of another degree, certificate, or diploma? – Yes
If yes, name of the degree, certificate, or diploma – http://www.pittstate.edu/ssls/edtech.html
OTHER PROGRAMS in educational technology or instructional development fields: Certificate Program available? – Yes
Certificate URL – http://www.pittstate.edu/ssls/edtech.html
Specialist Program available? – No
Specialist URL – http://www.pittstate.edu/ssls/edtech.html
Undergraduate Program available? – No
Doctorate Program available? – No
Program Content – Master's degree
Program Content URL – http://www.pittstate.edu/ssls/edtech.html

Name of Institution – Fort Hays State University
Name of Program within institution – Master of Science in Instructional Technology
Title/Degree as it appears on official certificate or diploma – Master of Science in Instructional Technology
Name & Title of person administering program – Dr. Robert Howell
Address – 600 Park Street, Hays, KS, 67601, United States
Telephone Number – 785-628-4306
Fax Number – 785-628-4267
E-Mail – bhowell@fhsu.edu
Institution's home page – http://www.fhsu.edu

PREREQUISITES: Higher Education – Yes
Teaching Certificate – No
ACCEPTANCE OF TRANSFERS – Yes
MASTER'S PROGRAM DURATION: Number of required Courses – 12
Comprehensive Exam Required? – Yes
Thesis Required? – No
Continuous Enrollment Required? – Yes
Does program culminate in a degree in the field of educational communications and technology? – Yes
Name of the degree – Master of Science in Instructional Technology
Is this program part of another degree, certificate, or diploma? – No
OTHER PROGRAMS in educational technology or instructional development fields: Certificate Program available? – Yes
Specialist Program available? – No
Undergraduate Program available? – No
Doctorate Program available? – No
Program Content – Master's degree
Program Content URL – http://www.fhsu.edu/techstudies/rhauck

Name of Institution – Emporia State University
Name of Program within institution – Instructional Design and Technology
  Title/Degree as it appears on official certificate or diploma – Master of Science
Name & Title of person administering program – Marcus D. Childress, Chair
Address – 1200 Commercial Street, Campus Box 4037, 328 Visser Hall, Emporia, KS, 66801, United States
Telephone Number – 620-341-5829
Fax Number – 620-341-5785
E-Mail – idt@emporia.edu
Institution's home page – http://www.emporia.edu
Admittance URL – http://idt.emporia.edu
PREREQUISITES: Higher Education – No
Teaching Certificate – No
ACCEPTANCE OF TRANSFERS – Yes
MASTER'S PROGRAM DURATION: Number of required Courses – 12
Number of weeks long – 16
Comprehensive Exam Required? – Yes
Thesis Required? – No
Continuous Enrollment Required? – No
Does program culminate in a degree in the field of educational communications and technology? – Yes
Name of the degree – Master of Science in Instructional Design and Technology
Is this program part of another degree, certificate, or diploma? – No

OTHER PROGRAMS in educational technology or instructional development fields: Certificate Program available? – No

Specialist Program available? – No

Undergraduate Program available? – No

Doctorate Program available? – No

Program Content – Master's degree

Program Content URL – http://idt.emporia.edu

Name of Institution – Western Kentucky University

Name of Program within institution – Library Media Education

Title/Degree as it appears on official certificate or diploma – Master of Science

Name & Title of person administering program – Robert C. Smith, Professor, **Address** – 1906 College Heights Blvd. #71030, Bowling Green, KY, 42101-1030, United States

Telephone Number – 270-745-4607

Fax Number – 270-745-6435

E-Mail – lmeinfo@wku.edu

Institution's home page – http://www.wku.edu

Admittance URL – http://www.wku.edu/graduate/

PREREQUISITES: Higher Education – Yes

Teaching Certificate – No

Other requirement – Teacher certification not required

ACCEPTANCE OF TRANSFERS – Yes

MASTER'S PROGRAM DURATION: Number of required Semesters – 3.5

Number of weeks long – 16

Comprehensive Exam Required? – Yes

Thesis Required? – No

Continuous Enrollment Required? – No

Other Requirements – Admission to the Master of Science in LME (Educational Technology) program requires a GAP score (undergraduate GPA X GRE score) of 2500 and a minimum GRE analytical writing score of 3.5.

Does program culminate in a degree in the field of educational communications and technology? – Yes

Name of the degree – Master of Science

Is this program part of another degree, certificate, or diploma? – No

OTHER PROGRAMS in educational technology or instructional development fields: Certificate Program available? – Yes

Certificate URL – http://www.wku.edu/lme/edutech.html

Specialist Program available? – No

Undergraduate Program available? – No

Doctorate Program available? – EdD

Program Content – Master's degree

Program Content URL – http://www.wku.edu/lme/graduate.html

Name of Institution – Georgetown College
Name of Program within institution – Instructional Technology Endorsement
Title/Degree as it appears on official certificate or diploma – Master of Arts in Education
Name & Title of person administering program – Dr. David Forman
Address – 400 E. College Street, Georgetown, KY, 40324, United States
Telephone Number – 502-863-8176
E-Mail – dforman1@georgetowncollege.edu
Institution's home page – http://www.georgetowncollege.edu/
Admittance URL – http://www.georgetowncollege.edu/departments/education/index.htm
PREREQUISITES: Higher Education – No
If yes, number of years or degree required – B.A. or B.S.
Teaching Certificate – Yes
ACCEPTANCE OF TRANSFERS – Yes
MASTER'S PROGRAM DURATION: Number of required Courses – 14
Comprehensive Exam Required? – No
Thesis Required? – No
Continuous Enrollment Required? – No
Does program culminate in a degree in the field of educational communications and technology? – Yes
Name of the degree – M.A. in Education with Instructional Technology Endorsement
Is this program part of another degree, certificate, or diploma? – Yes
If yes, name of the degree, certificate, or diploma – Instructional Technology Endorsement
OTHER PROGRAMS in educational technology or instructional development fields: Certificate Program available? – No
Specialist Program available? – No
Undergraduate Program available? – No
Doctorate Program available? – No
Program Content – Master's degree
Program Content URL – http://spider.georgetowncollege.edu/education/it

Name of Institution – Morehead State University
Name of Program within institution – Educational Technology
Title/Degree as it appears on official certificate or diploma – Master of Arts in Education - Educational Technology
Name & Title of person administering program – Christopher T. Miller
Address – 401 K Ginger Hall, Morehead, KY, 40351, United States
Telephone Number – 606-783-2855
Fax Number – 606-783-9102
E-Mail – c.miller@morehead-st.edu
Institution's home page – http://www.morehead-st.edu
Admittance URL – https://wwws.morehead-st.edu/aimsweb/application.html

PREREQUISITES: Higher Education – No
If yes, number of years or degree required – Bachelor
Teaching Certificate – Yes
Other requirement – Teaching certificate or proof of educational support position
ACCEPTANCE OF TRANSFERS – Yes
MASTER'S PROGRAM DURATION: Number of required Courses – 12
Comprehensive Exam Required? – Yes
Thesis Required? – No
Continuous Enrollment Required? – Yes
Other Requirements – 750 combined GRE score 2.5 on the GRE analytic writing subtest 2.75 undergraduate GPA Exit exam and portfolio required
Does program culminate in a degree in the field of educational communications and technology? – Yes
Name of the degree – Master of Arts in Education – Educational Technology
Is this program part of another degree, certificate, or diploma? – No
OTHER PROGRAMS in educational technology or instructional development fields: Certificate Program available? – Yes
Certificate URL – http://www.morehead-st.edu
Specialist Program available? – No
Undergraduate Program available? – No
Doctorate Program available? – No
Program Content – Master's degree
Program Content URL – http://www.morehead-st.edu/ci/

Name of Institution University of Massachusetts: Amherst
Name of Program within institution – Educational technology
Title/Degree as it appears on official certificate or diploma – Masters of Education
Name & Title of person administering program – Robert W. Maloy
Address – Room 110 Furcolo Building, Amherst, MA, 01003, United States
Telephone Number – 413-545-0945
Fax Number – 413-545-2879
E-Mail – rwm@educ.umass.edu
Institution's home page – http://www.umass.edu
Admittance URL – http://www.umass.edu/gradschool
PREREQUISITES: Higher Education – Yes
If yes, number of years or degree required – BA required
Teaching Certificate – No
ACCEPTANCE OF TRANSFERS – Yes
MASTER'S PROGRAM DURATION: Number of required Semesters – 4
Number of weeks long – 14
Comprehensive Exam Required? – No
Thesis Required? – No
Continuous Enrollment Required? – No

Other Requirements – Steady progress towards completion of degree
Does program culminate in a degree in the field of educational communications and technology? – Yes
Name of the degree – Masters of Education
Is this program part of another degree, certificate, or diploma? – No
OTHER PROGRAMS in educational technology or instructional development fields: Certificate Program available? – No
Specialist Program available? – No
Undergraduate Program available? – Yes
Undergraduate URL – http://www.umass.edu/itprogram
Doctorate Program available? – EdD
Doctorate URL – http://www.umass.edu/education/departments/tecs/teacher_ed.htm
Program Content – Master's degree
Program Content URL – http://www.umass.edu/education/departments/main_tecs.htm

Name of Institution – Boston University
Name of Program within institution – Educational Media & Technology
Title/Degree as it appears on official certificate or diploma – Ed D, Ed M, CAGS
Name & Title of person administering program – David Whittier, Ed D, Asst. Professor
Address – 2 Sherborn Street, Boston, MA, 02215, United States
Telephone Number – 617-353-3181
Fax Number – 617-353-3924
E-Mail – whittier@bu.edu
Institution's home page – http://www.bu.edu/sed/
Admittance URL – http://emt.bu.edu/program
PREREQUISITES: Higher Education – Yes
If yes, number of years or degree required – Bachelors
Teaching Certificate – No
ACCEPTANCE OF TRANSFERS – Yes
MASTER'S PROGRAM DURATION: Comprehensive Exam Required? – No
Thesis Required? – No
Continuous Enrollment Required? – Yes
Does program culminate in a degree in the field of educational communications and technology? – Yes
Name of the degree – Masters Degree in Educational Media & Technology
Is this program part of another degree, certificate, or diploma? – No
OTHER PROGRAMS in educational technology or instructional development fields: Certificate Program available? – Yes
Certificate URL – http://emt.bu.edu/program
Specialist Program available? – Yes

Undergraduate Program available? – No
Doctorate Program available? – EdD
Doctorate URL – http://emt.bu.edu/program
Program Content – Master's degree
Program Content URL – http://emt.bu.edu/program

Name of Institution – Harvard Graduate School of Education
Name of Program within institution – Technology in Education
Title/Degree as it appears on official certificate or diploma – Ed.M.
Name & Title of person administering program – Joseph Blatt, Program Director
Address – 330 Longfellow Hall, Appian Way, Cambridge, MA, 02138, United States
Telephone Number – 617-495-3541
Fax Number – 617-495-9268
E-Mail – tie@gse.harvard.edu
Institution's home page – http://www.gse.harvard.edu
Admittance URL – http://www.gse.harvard.edu/admissions/
MASTER'S PROGRAM DURATION: Number of required Semesters – 2
Number of weeks long – 39
Comprehensive Exam Required? – No
Thesis Required? – No
Continuous Enrollment Required? – Yes
Other Requirements – Some options for part-time study. Total of 8 courses required
Does program culminate in a degree in the field of educational communications and technology? – Yes
Name of the degree – Ed.M.
Is this program part of another degree, certificate, or diploma? – No
OTHER PROGRAMS in educational technology or instructional development fields: Certificate Program available? – No
Undergraduate Program available? – No
Doctorate Program available? – EdD
Doctorate URL – http://www.gse.harvard.edu/academics.html
Program Content – Master's degree
Program Content URL – http://www.gse.harvard.edu/tie

Name of Institution – University of Maryland, Baltimore County
Name of Program within institution – ISD Training Systems Graduate Program
Title/Degree as it appears on official certificate or diploma – Masters in Education – ISD
Name & Title of person administering program – Dr. Greg Williams
Address – 1000 Hilltop Circle, Baltimore, MD, 21250, United States
Telephone Number – 410-455-6773

Fax Number – 410-455-1322
E-Mail – gregw@umbc.edu
Institution's home page – http://www.umbc.edu
Admittance URL – http://www.umbc.edu/gradschool/admissions/
PREREQUISITES: Higher Education – Yes
If yes, number of years or degree required – Bachelor's Degree
Teaching Certificate – No
ACCEPTANCE OF TRANSFERS – Yes
MASTER'S PROGRAM DURATION: Number of required Courses – 12
Number of weeks long – 13
Comprehensive Exam Required? – Yes
Thesis Required? – No
Continuous Enrollment Required? – Yes
Does program culminate in a degree in the field of educational communications and technology? – No
Name of the degree – Instructional Systems Design
Is this program part of another degree, certificate, or diploma? – Yes
If yes, name of the degree, certificate, or diploma – Education
OTHER PROGRAMS in educational technology or instructional development fields: Certificate Program available? – Yes
Certificate URL – http://continuinged.umbc.edu/isd/gradcert.htm
Specialist Program available? – No
Undergraduate Program available? – No

Doctorate Program available? – No
Program Content – Master's degree
Program Content URL – http://continuinged.umbc.edu/isd/isd-ma.htm

Name of Institution – University of Maryland University College
Name of Program within institution – Master of Distance Education
Title/Degree as it appears on official certificate or diploma – Master of Distance Education
Name & Title of person administering program – Stella Porto
Address – 3501 University Blvd East, Adelphi, MD, 20783, United States
Telephone Number – 301-985-7826
E-Mail – erubin@umuc.edu
Institution's home page – http://www.umuc.edu/mde/
PREREQUISITES: Higher Education – No
If yes, number of years or degree required – B.A.
Teaching Certificate – Yes
ACCEPTANCE OF TRANSFERS – Yes
MASTER'S PROGRAM DURATION: Number of required Courses – 12
Comprehensive Exam Required? – No
Thesis Required? – No
Continuous Enrollment Required? – No

Does program culminate in a degree in the field of educational communications and technology? – Yes
Name of the degree – Master of Distance Education
Is this program part of another degree, certificate, or diploma? – No
OTHER PROGRAMS in educational technology or instructional development fields: Certificate Program available? – Yes
Certificate URL – http://www.umuc.edu/grad/certificates/certif_list.shtml# dist_ed
Specialist Program available? – No
Undergraduate Program available? – No
Doctorate Program available? – No
Program Content – Master's degree
Program Content URL – http://www.umuc.edu/mde/

Name of Institution – University of Maine
Name of Program within institution – Instructional Technology
Title/Degree as it appears on official certificate or diploma – Master's of Education / Instructional Technology
Name & Title of person administering program – Dr. Abigail Garthwait
Address – 108 Shibles Hall, Orono, ME, 04469, United States
Telephone Number – (207) 581-2441
Fax Number – (207) 581-2423
E-Mail – Becky_Libby@umit.maine.edu
Institution's home page – http://www.umaine.edu/
Admittance URL – http://www.umaine.edu/graduate/default.htm
PREREQUISITES: Higher Education – Yes
If yes, number of years or degree required – BA or BS
Teaching Certificate – No
Other requirement – Miller's Analogy, letters of reference, grade point average
ACCEPTANCE OF TRANSFERS – Yes
MASTER'S PROGRAM DURATION: Number of required Courses – 12
Comprehensive Exam Required? – No
Thesis Required? – No
Continuous Enrollment Required? – No
Other Requirements – Practicum and digital portfolio
Does program culminate in a degree in the field of educational communications and technology? – Yes
Name of the degree – Master's of Education / Instructional Technology
Is this program part of another degree, certificate, or diploma? – Yes
If yes, name of the degree, certificate, or diploma – Currently applying to have a degree automatically led to ME endorsement
OTHER PROGRAMS in educational technology or instructional development fields: Certificate Program available? – No
Specialist Program available? – No

Undergraduate Program available? – No
Doctorate Program available? – EdD
Program Content – Master's degree
Program Content URL – http://www.umaine.edu/edhd/academic/grad/edintech. htm

Name of Institution – Eastern Michigan University
Name of Program within institution – Educational Media and Technology
Title/Degree as it appears on official certificate or diploma – Master of Arts in Educational Media and Technology
Name & Title of person administering program – Dr. Nancy L. Copeland, Ed.D
Address – 314R Porter Building, Ypsilanti, MI, 48197, United States
Telephone Number – 734.487.3260
Fax Number – 734.487.2101
E-Mail – ncopeland@emich.edu
Institution's home page – http://www.emich.edu
Admittance URL – http://www.emich.edu/coe/teach_ed/programs/edmt/index. html
PREREQUISITES: Higher Education – No
If yes, number of years or degree required – Bachelor's Degree
Teaching Certificate – No
ACCEPTANCE OF TRANSFERS – Yes
MASTER'S PROGRAM DURATION: Number of required Courses – 11
Comprehensive Exam Required? – No
Thesis Required? – No
Continuous Enrollment Required? – No
Other Requirements – Culminating Research or Development Project
Does program culminate in a degree in the field of educational communications and technology? – Yes
Name of the degree – Master of Arts in Educational Media and Technology
Is this program part of another degree, certificate, or diploma? – No
OTHER PROGRAMS in educational technology or instructional development fields: Certificate Program available? – Yes
Certificate URL – http://www.emich.edu/coe/teach_ed/programs/edmt/index. html
Specialist Program available? – No
Undergraduate Program available? – No
Doctorate Program available? – No
Program Content – Master's degree
Program Content URL – http://www.emich.edu/coe/teach_ed/programs/edmt/ MA_Prog.htm

Name of Institution – Oakland University
Name of Program within institution – Human Resource Development

Title/Degree as it appears on official certificate or diploma – Master of Training and Development

Name & Title of person administering program – Dr. James Quinn, Coordinator, Master of Training and Development Program

Address – 435E Pawley Hall, Rochester, MI, 48309, United States

Telephone Number – 248.370.3041

Fax Number – 248.370.4095

E-Mail – quinn@oakland.edu

Institution's home page – http://www.oakland.edu

Admittance URL – http://www2.oakland.edu/grad/grad2/prog_detail.cfm?ID= MD4900&pth=PD

PREREQUISITES: Higher Education – Yes

If yes, number of years or degree required – Undergraduate degree in any discipline

Teaching Certificate – No

ACCEPTANCE OF TRANSFERS – Yes

MASTER'S PROGRAM DURATION: Number of required Courses – 9

Comprehensive Exam Required? – No

Thesis Required? – No

Continuous Enrollment Required? – No

Does program culminate in a degree in the field of educational communications and technology? – Yes

Name of the degree – Master of Training & Development

Is this program part of another degree, certificate, or diploma? – Yes

OTHER PROGRAMS in educational technology or instructional development fields: Certificate Program available? – No

Specialist Program available? – No

Undergraduate Program available?– Yes

Doctorate Program available? – No

Program Content – Master's degree

Program Content URL – http://www2.oakland.edu/sehs/hrd/

Name of Institution – Wayne State University

Name of Program within institution – Instructional Technology

Title/Degree as it appears on official certificate or diploma – M.Ed.

Name & Title of person administering program – Rita C. Richey

Address – 381 Education, Detroit, MI, 48202, United States

Telephone Number – 313.577.1728

Fax Number – 313.577.1693

E-Mail – rrichey@wayne.edu

Institution's home page – http://www.coe.wayne.edu/InstructionalTechnology/

Admittance URL – http://www.coe.wayne.edu/InstructionalTechnology/admissions-mast.htm

PREREQUISITES: Higher Education – Yes

Teaching Certificate – No

ACCEPTANCE OF TRANSFERS – Yes
MASTER'S PROGRAM DURATION: Number of required Semesters –
12
Number of weeks long – 15
Comprehensive Exam Required? – No
Thesis Required? – No
Continuous Enrollment Required? – No
Other Requirements – Concentration in either Performance Improvement &
Training; K-12 Technology Integration; or Interactive Technologies
**Does program culminate in a degree in the field of educational communi-
cations and technology?** – Yes
Name of the degree – Master of Education
Is this program part of another degree, certificate, or diploma? – No
**OTHER PROGRAMS in educational technology or instructional develop-
ment fields: Certificate Program available?** – No
Specialist Program available? – Yes
Specialist URL – http://www.coe.wayne.edu/InstructionalTechnology/prog-
edsp.htm
Undergraduate Program available? – No
Doctorate Program available? – PhD
Doctorate URL – http://www.coe.wayne.edu/InstructionalTechnology/prog-
doct.htm
Program Content – Master's degree
Program Content URL – http://www.coe.wayne.edu/InstructionalTechnology/
prog-mast.htm

Name of Institution – Bemidji State University
Name of Program within institution – Master of Science with Educa-
tional/Information Communications and Technology
Title/Degree as it appears on official certificate or diploma – Master of Sci-
ence in Education
Name & Title of person administering program – Patricia L. Rogers, Ph.D.
Address – 1500 Birchmont Drive NE, Bemidji, MN, 56601, United States
Telephone Number – 218-755-3781
Fax Number – 218-755-3787
E-Mail – progers@bemidjistate.edu
Institution's home page – http://distance.bemidjistate.edu/index.html
Admittance URL – http://distance.bemidjistate.edu/BMC/Adm.html
PREREQUISITES: Higher Education – Yes
If yes, number of years or degree required – bachelor's degree
Teaching Certificate – No
ACCEPTANCE OF TRANSFERS – Yes
MASTER'S PROGRAM DURATION: Number of required Semesters –
4+
Number of weeks long – 15

Comprehensive Exam Required? – Yes

Thesis Required? – Optional

Continuous Enrollment Required? – Yes

Does program culminate in a degree in the field of educational communications and technology? – Yes

Name of the degree – Master of Science in Education

Is this program part of another degree, certificate, or diploma? – Yes

If yes, name of the degree, certificate, or diploma – certificate in ICT

OTHER PROGRAMS in educational technology or instructional development fields: Certificate Program available? – Yes

Specialist Program available? – No

Undergraduate Program available? – No

Doctorate Program available? – No

Program Content – Master's degree

Program Content URL – http://distance.bemidjistate.edu/BMC/Pro.html

Name of Institution – St. Cloud State University

Name of Program within institution – Information Media

Title/Degree as it appears on official certificate or diploma – Master of Science, Information Media

Name & Title of person administering program – Jeanne Anderson Coordinator

Address – 720 Fourth Avenue South, MC110, St. Cloud, MN, 56301, United States

Telephone Number – 320-308-2062

Fax Number – 320-308-4778

E-Mail – cim@stcloudstate.edu

Institution's home page – http://www.stcloudstate.edu

Admittance URL – http://www.stcloudstate.edu/graduatestudies/

PREREQUISITES: Higher Education – No

Teaching Certificate – No

ACCEPTANCE OF TRANSFERS – Yes

MASTER'S PROGRAM DURATION: Number of required Semesters – 4

Number of weeks long – 15

Comprehensive Exam Required? – No

Thesis Required? – Optional

Continuous Enrollment Required? – Yes

Does program culminate in a degree in the field of educational communications and technology? – Yes

Name of the degree – Master of Science, Information Media

Is this program part of another degree, certificate, or diploma? – No

OTHER PROGRAMS in educational technology or instructional development fields: Certificate Program available? – Yes

Certificate URL – http://www.stcloudstate.edu/cim/graduate/default.asp

Specialist Program available? – No

Undergraduate Program available? – Yes
Undergraduate URL – http://www.stcloudstate.edu/cim/undergraduate/default.
asp
Doctorate Program available? – No
Program Content – Master's degree
Program Content URL – http://www.stcloudstate.edu/cim/graduate/default.asp

Name of Institution – University of Missouri-Kansas City
Name of Program within institution – Learning Technologies
Title/Degree as it appears on official certificate or diploma – Masters Degree
in Curriculum and Instruction
Name & Title of person administering program – Donna Russell, Ph.D.
Address – 309 School of Education, Kansas City, MO, 64110, United States
Telephone Number – 816.235.5871
Fax Number – 816.235.5270
E-Mail – russelldl@umkc.edu
Institution's home page – http://www.umkc.edu/education
Admittance URL – http://www.umkc.edu
PREREQUISITES: Higher Education – Yes
If yes, number of years or degree required – bachelors degree
Teaching Certificate – No
ACCEPTANCE OF TRANSFERS – Yes
MASTER'S PROGRAM DURATION: Number of required Semesters – 4
Number of weeks long – 16
Comprehensive Exam Required? – No
Thesis Required? – Yes
Continuous Enrollment Required? – No
Other Requirements – strong background in basic technology use
**Does program culminate in a degree in the field of educational communi-
cations and technology?** – No
Is this program part of another degree, certificate, or diploma? – No
If yes, name of the degree, certificate, or diploma – Masters Degree in Cur-
riculum and Instruction
**OTHER PROGRAMS in educational technology or instructional develop-
ment fields: Certificate Program available?** – No
Specialist Program available? – No
Undergraduate Program available? – No
Doctorate Program available? – No
Program Content – Master's degree
Program Content URL – http://http://www.umkc.edu/education/CIL/masters/
CILTech.htm

Name of Institution – Southwest Missouri State University
Name of Program within institution – Instructional Media Technology

Title/Degree as it appears on official certificate or diploma – Master of Science in Education

Name & Title of person administering program – Dr. Roger Tipling – IMT Graduate Program Director

Address – 901 S. National, Springfield, MO, 65807, United States

Telephone Number – 417 836-5280

Fax Number – 417 836-6252

E-Mail – RogerTipling@smsu.edu

Institution's home page – http://education.smsu.edu/imt/

Admittance URL – http://http://graduate.smsu.edu/admissions/admissions.htm

PREREQUISITES: Higher Education – No

Teaching Certificate – No

ACCEPTANCE OF TRANSFERS – Yes

MASTER'S PROGRAM DURATION: Number of weeks long – 15

Comprehensive Exam Required? – Yes

Thesis Required? – No

Continuous Enrollment Required? – No

Does program culminate in a degree in the field of educational communications and technology? – Yes

Name of the degree – Instructional Media Technology

Is this program part of another degree certificate, or diploma? – Yes

OTHER PROGRAMS in educational technology or instructional development fields: Certificate Program available? – Yes

Certificate URL – http://graduate.smsu.edu/programs/CertPrograms/ITSpec.htm

Specialist Program available? – No

Undergraduate Program available? – No

Doctorate Program available? – No

Program Content – Master's degree

Program Content URL – http://graduate.smsu.edu/OnlineCatalog/COED/STE_InstMedia.pdf

Name of Institution – University of Missouri – Columbia

Name of Program within institution – Educational Technology

Title/Degree as it appears on official certificate or diploma – Masters, Specialist, or PhD

Name & Title of person administering program – John Wedman

Address – 303 Townsend Hall, Columbia, MO, 65211, United States

Telephone Number – 877-747-5868 (toll free)

Fax Number – 573-884-0122

E-Mail – sislt@missouri.edu

Institution's home page – http://sislt.missouri.edu

Admittance URL – http://gradschool.missouri.edu/apply/

PREREQUISITES: Higher Education – No

If yes, number of years or degree required – Bachelor

Teaching Certificate – No

ACCEPTANCE OF TRANSFERS – Yes
MASTER'S PROGRAM DURATION: Number of required Courses – 10+
Number of weeks long – 8–16
Comprehensive Exam Required? – Yes
Thesis Required? – No
Continuous Enrollment Required? – No
Does program culminate in a degree in the field of educational communications and technology? – Yes
Name of the degree – Master's with emphasis in Educational Technology
Is this program part of another degree, certificate, or diploma? – No
OTHER PROGRAMS in educational technology or instructional development fields: Certificate Program available? – No
Specialist Program available? – Yes
Specialist URL – http://sislt.missouri.edu/edspec.php
Undergraduate Program available? – No
Doctorate Program available? – PhD
Doctorate URL – http://sislt.missouri.edu/phd.php
Program Content – Master's degree
Program Content URL – http://sislt.missouri.edu/edtech.php

Name of Institution – The University of Southern Mississippi
Name of Program within institution – Instructional Technology
Title/Degree as it appears on official certificate or diploma – M.S.
Name & Title of person administering program – Dr. Steve Yuen
Address – 118 College Drive Number5036, Hattiesburg, MS, 39406, United States
Telephone Number – 601-266-4446
Fax Number – 601-266-5957
E-Mail – steve.yuen@usm.edu
Institution's home page – http://www.usm.edu
Admittance URL – http://dragon.ep.usm.edu/~it/
PREREQUISITES: Higher Education – Yes
If yes, number of years or degree required – 4
Teaching Certificate – No
ACCEPTANCE OF TRANSFERS – Yes
MASTER'S PROGRAM DURATION: Number of required Semesters – 4
Number of weeks long – 14
Comprehensive Exam Required? – No

Thesis Required? – Optional
Continuous Enrollment Required? – Yes
Other Requirements – Capstone Project
Does program culminate in a degree in the field of educational communications and technology? – Yes
Name of the degree – Master of Science in Instructional Technology

Is this program part of another degree, certificate, or diploma? – No
OTHER PROGRAMS in educational technology or instructional development fields: Certificate Program available? – No
Specialist Program available? – No
Undergraduate Program available? – No
Doctorate Program available? – No
Program Content – Master's degree
Program Content URL – http://dragon.ep.usm.edu/~it/

Name of Institution – East Carolina University
Name of Program within institution – Master of Education in Instructional Technology
Title/Degree as it appears on official certificate or diploma – M.A.Ed IT; Certificate in Computers in Education
Name & Title of person administering program – Carol A. Brown, Program Coordinator
Address – LTDI Joyner Library 1804, East Carolina University, Greenville, NC, 27858, United States
Telephone Number – 252 328-6621
Fax Number – 252 328-4368
E-Mail – browncar@mail.ecu.edu
Institution's home page – http://www.ecu.edu
Admittance URL – http://www.coe.ecu.edu/LTDI/ma-it.htm
PREREQUISITES: Higher Education – Yes
If yes, number of years or degree required – bachelor's degree
Teaching Certificate – Yes
ACCEPTANCE OF TRANSFERS – Yes
MASTER'S PROGRAM DURATION: Number of required Courses – 13
Number of weeks long – 17
Comprehensive Exam Required? – No
Thesis Required? – Optional
Continuous Enrollment Required? – No
Other Requirements – final portfolio and internship portfolio 1. Final portfolio product; 2. 120 hour internship
Does program culminate in a degree in the field of educational communications and technology? – Yes
Name of the degree – Master of Education in Instructional Technology
Is this program part of another degree, certificate, or diploma? – Yes
If yes, name of the degree, certificate, or diploma – Three available 1. Computers in education, 2. Virtual Reality, 3. Telelearning
OTHER PROGRAMS in educational technology or instructional development fields: Certificate Program available? – Yes
Certificate URL – http://www.coe.ecu.edu/LTDI/online/certificates.htm
Specialist Program available? – Yes
Specialist URL – http://www.coe.ecu.edu/LTDI/CAS1.htm

Undergraduate Program available? – No
Doctorate Program available? – EdD
Doctorate URL – http://ltdi.coe.ecu.edu/edd/
Program Content – Master's degree
Program Content URL – http://www.coe.ecu.edu/LTDI/maed/advising.htm

Name of Institution – Appalachian State University
Name of Program within institution – New Media and Global Education
Title/Degree as it appears on official certificate or diploma – MA in Educational Media: Concentration in New Media and Global Education
Name & Title of person administering program – Roberto Muffoletto
Address – College of Education, Boone, NC, 28608, United States
Telephone Number – 828-262-2277
E-Mail – muffoletto@appstate.edu
Admittance URL – http://edtech.ced.appstate.edu
PREREQUISITES: Higher Education – Yes
If yes, number of years or degree required – 4 year undergrad degree
Teaching Certificate – No
ACCEPTANCE OF TRANSFERS – Yes
MASTER'S PROGRAM DURATION: Number of required Semesters – 5–6
Number of weeks long – 15
Comprehensive Exam Required? – Yes
Thesis Required? – No
Continuous Enrollment Required? – Yes
Other Requirements – English is main language for the online program
Does program culminate in a degree in the field of educational communications and technology? – Yes
Name of the degree – Educational Media
Is this program part of another degree, certificate, or diploma? – Yes
If yes, name of the degree, certificate, or diploma – Educational Media
OTHER PROGRAMS in educational technology or instructional development fields: Certificate Program available? – Yes
Certificate URL – http://edtech.ced.appstate.edu
Undergraduate Program available? – No
Doctorate Program available? – No
Program Content – Master's degree
Program Content URL – http://edtech.ced.appstate.edu

Name of Institution – University of North Carolina at Wilmington
Name of Program within institution – Master of Science in Instructional Technology
Title/Degree as it appears on official certificate or diploma – Master of Science in Instructional Technology
Name & Title of person administering program – Mahnaz Moallem

Address – 601 South College Road, Wilmington, NC, 28403, United States
Telephone Number – 910-962-4183
Fax Number – 910-962-3609
E-Mail – moallemm@uncw.edu
Institution's home page – http://www.uncw.edu/
Admittance URL – http://www.uncw.edu/ed/mit/
PREREQUISITES: Higher Education – Yes
If yes, number of years or degree required – A bachelor's degree from a accredited college
Teaching Certificate – No
Other requirement – Applicants applying for NC Advanced Licensure required to be certified
ACCEPTANCE OF TRANSFERS – Yes
MASTER'S PROGRAM DURATION: Number of required Semesters – 4
Comprehensive Exam Required? – Yes
Thesis Required? – Yes
Continuous Enrollment Required? – Yes
Other Requirements – Requires a minimum of 36 (15 required (core) and 15 selective (focus)) graduate level semester hours beyond the baccalaureate degree –Requires completion of Internship, as part of required core courses – Requires completions of master thesis or master electronic portfolio
Does program culminate in a degree in the field of educational communications and technology? – Yes
Name of the degree – Master of Science in Instructional Technology
Is this program part of another degree, certificate, or diploma? – No
OTHER PROGRAMS in educational technology or instructional development fields: Certificate Program available? – Yes
Certificate URL – http://www.uncw.edu/ed/mit/
Specialist Program available? – No
Undergraduate Program available? – No
Doctorate Program available? – No
Program Content – Master's degree
Program Content URL – http://www.uncw.edu/ed/mit/

Name of Institution – East Carolina University
Name of Program within institution – Master of Science in Instructional Technology
Title/Degree as it appears on official certificate or diploma – Master of Science
Name & Title of person administering program – William Sugar, Program Coordinator
Address – 1805 Joyner Library, Greenville, NC, 27851, United States
Telephone Number – 252.328.1546
Fax Number – 252.328.4368
E-Mail – sugarw@coe.ecu.edu

Institution's home page – http://www.ecu.edu
PREREQUISITES: Higher Education – Yes
If yes, number of years or degree required – Bachelor's degree
Teaching Certificate – No
ACCEPTANCE OF TRANSFERS – Yes
MASTER'S PROGRAM DURATION: Number of required Courses – 12
Comprehensive Exam Required? – No
Thesis Required? – No
Continuous Enrollment Required? – Yes
Does program culminate in a degree in the field of educational communications and technology? – Yes
Name of the degree – Master of Science in Instructional Technology
Is this program part of another degree, certificate, or diploma? – No
OTHER PROGRAMS in educational technology or instructional development fields: Certificate Program available? – Yes
Certificate URL – http://www.coe.ecu.edu/lsit/it
Specialist Program available? – No
Undergraduate Program available? – No
Doctorate Program available? – No
Program Content – Master's degree
Program Content URL – http://www.coe.ecu.edu/lsit/it

Name of Institution – North Carolina State University
Name of Program within institution – Instruction Technology – masters
Title/Degree as it appears on official certificate or diploma – M.Ed. or M.S.
Name & Title of person administering program – Dr. Ellen S. Vasu
Address – Department of C&I, Box 7801, North Carolina State University, Raleigh, NC, 27511, United States
Telephone Number – 919 515-1779
Fax Number – 919-513-1687
E-Mail – ellen_vasu@ncsu.edu
Institution's home page – http://www.ncsu.edu
Admittance URL – http://www2.acs.ncsu.edu/grad/prospect.htm
PREREQUISITES: Higher Education – Yes
If yes, number of years or degree required – For M.Ed. or M.S. – Bachelors
Teaching Certificate – Yes
ACCEPTANCE OF TRANSFERS – Yes
MASTER'S PROGRAM DURATION: Number of required Courses – 12
Number of weeks long – 15
Comprehensive Exam Required? – Yes
Thesis Required? – No
Continuous Enrollment Required? – Yes
Does program culminate in a degree in the field of educational communications and technology? – No

Name of the degree – Instructional Technology

Is this program part of another degree, certificate, or diploma? – Yes

If yes, name of the degree, certificate, or diploma – 077 teaching licensure K-12, 079 teaching endorsement K-12

OTHER PROGRAMS in educational technology or instructional development fields: Certificate Program available? – No

Specialist Program available? – No

Undergraduate Program available? – No

Doctorate Program available? – No

Program Content – Master's degree

Program Content URL – http://ced.ncsu.edu/ci/

Name of Institution – Appalachian State University

Name of Program within institution, Instructional Technology Specialist/Computers

Title/Degree as it appears on official certificate or diploma – MA in Educational Media with a concentration in Instructional Technology Special

Name & Title of person administering program – Dr. Richard Riedl

Address – LES, Boone, NC, 28608, United States

Telephone Number – 828 262-6104

Fax Number – 828 262-6035

E-Mail – riedlre@appstate.edu

Institution's home page – http://www.appstate.edu

Admittance URL – http://www.graduate.appstate.edu/gradstudies/prospective/

PREREQUISITES: Higher Education – Yes

If yes, number of years or degree required – Bachelor's Degree

Teaching Certificate – Yes

ACCEPTANCE OF TRANSFERS – Yes

MASTER'S PROGRAM DURATION: Number of required Courses – 12

Number of weeks long – 15

Comprehensive Exam Required? – Yes

Thesis Required? – No

Continuous Enrollment Required? – Yes

Does program culminate in a degree in the field of educational communications and technology? – Yes

Name of the degree – MA in Educational Media

Is this program part of another degree, certificate, or diploma? – No

OTHER PROGRAMS in educational technology or instructional development fields: Certificate Program available? – No

Specialist Program available? – No

Undergraduate Program available? – No

Doctorate Program available? – No

Program Content – Master's degree

Program Content URL – http://www.ced.appstate.edu/departments/les/programs/instr_tech_gen/it.aspx

Name of Institution – North Carolina State University
Name of Program within institution – Training & Development Program
Title/Degree as it appears on official certificate or diploma – M.Ed. in Training and Development
Name & Title of person administering program – Diane Chapman, Visiting Assistant Professor
Address – 310 Poe Hall, Campus Box 7801, Raleigh, NC, 27695, United States
Telephone Number – 919-513-1568
Fax Number – 919-515-6305
E-Mail – tdonline_info@ncsu.edu
Institution's home page – http://www.ncsu.edu
Admittance URL – http://ced.ncsu.edu/acce/admissions.html#step1
PREREQUISITES: Higher Education – Yes
If yes, number of years or degree required – Bachelor's degree
ACCEPTANCE OF TRANSFERS – No
MASTER'S PROGRAM DURATION: Number of required Courses – 12
Comprehensive Exam Required? – No
Thesis Required? – No
Continuous Enrollment Required? – Yes
Other Requirements – Capstone paper in last semester of course work
Does program culminate in a degree in the field of educational communications and technology? – No
Name of the degree – M.Ed. in Training and Development
Is this program part of another degree, certificate, or diploma? – No
OTHER PROGRAMS in educational technology or instructional development fields: Certificate Program available? – Yes
Certificate URL – http://tdonline.ncsu.edu/programs/tdcertificate.html
Specialist Program available? – No
Undergraduate Program available? – No
Doctorate Program available? – EdD
Doctorate URL – http://ced.ncsu.edu:8480/acce/program_des/acce_edd.htm
Program Content – Master's degree
Program Content URL – http://tdonline.ncsu.edu/programs/medonline.html

Name of Institution – University of North Dakota
Name of Program within institution – Instructional Design & Technology
Title/Degree as it appears on official certificate or diploma – Master of Science/Master of Education: Instructional Design & Technology
Name & Title of person administering program – Richard Van Eck, PhD
Address – Box 7189, Grand Forks, ND, 58202, United States
Telephone Number – (701) 777-3574
Fax Number – (701) 777-3246
E-Mail – richard.vaneck@und.edu
Institution's home page – http://idt.und.edu
Admittance URL – https://apply.embark.com/grad/northdakota/19/

PREREQUISITES: Higher Education – No
If yes, number of years or degree required – B.A., B.S., BFA
Teaching Certificate – No
Other requirement – 18 hours undergraduate education courses required for M.Ed only
ACCEPTANCE OF TRANSFERS – Yes
MASTER'S PROGRAM DURATION: Number of required Courses – 12
Number of weeks long – 15
Comprehensive Exam Required? – No
Thesis Required? – No
Continuous Enrollment Required? – Yes
Does program culminate in a degree in the field of educational communications and technology? – Yes
Name of the degree – Instructional Design & Technology
Is this program part of another degree, certificate, or diploma? – No
OTHER PROGRAMS in educational technology or instructional development fields: Certificate Program available? – Yes
Specialist Program available? – No
Undergraduate Program available? – No
Doctorate Program available? – No
Program Content – Master's degree
Program Content URL – http://idt.und.edu

Name of Institution – Valley City State University
Name of Program within institution – Teaching and Technology
Title/Degree as it appears on official certificate or diploma – Master of Education
Name & Title of person administering program – Patricia L. Rogers, Ph.D.
Address – 101 College Street SW, Valley City, ND, 58072, United States
Telephone Number – 701-845-7196
Fax Number – 701-845-0706
E-Mail – patricia.rogers@vcsu.edu
Institution's home page – http://www.vcsu.edu
Admittance URL – http://www.vcsu.edu/graduate/vp.htm?p=214
PREREQUISITES: Higher Education – Yes
If yes, number of years or degree required – 2
Teaching Certificate – No
Other requirement – community and tech college faculty do not need certificate
ACCEPTANCE OF TRANSFERS – Yes
MASTER'S PROGRAM DURATION: Number of required Semesters – 4
Number of weeks long – 15
Comprehensive Exam Required? – No
Thesis Required? – Optional
Continuous Enrollment Required? – Yes

Other Requirements – complete capstone

Does program culminate in a degree in the field of educational communications and technology? – Yes

Name of the degree – Master of Education

Is this program part of another degree, certificate, or diploma? – No

OTHER PROGRAMS in educational technology or instructional development fields: Certificate Program available? – No

Specialist Program available? – No

Undergraduate Program available? – No

Doctorate Program available? – No

Program Content – Master's degree

Program Content URL – http://www.vcsu.edu/graduate/vp.htm?p=210

Name of Institution – University of Nebraska at Kearney

Name of Program within institution – Instructional Technology

Title/Degree as it appears on official certificate or diploma – MSED Instructional Technology

Name & Title of person administering program – Dr. Scott Fredrickson

Address – 905 West 25th Street, Kearney, NE, 68849, United States

Telephone Number – 308 865 8833

Fax Number – 308 865 8097

E-Mail – fredricksons@unk.edu

Institution's home page – http://www.unk.edu

Admittance URL –
http://www.unk.edu/acad/gradstudies/prospectivestudents/admission/admission.html

PREREQUISITES: Higher Education – No

If yes, number of years or degree required – BS/BA

Teaching Certificate – No

ACCEPTANCE OF TRANSFERS – Yes

MASTER'S PROGRAM DURATION: Number of required Courses – 12

Number of weeks long – 16

Comprehensive Exam Required? – Yes

Thesis Required? – No

Continuous Enrollment Required? – No

Does program culminate in a degree in the field of educational communications and technology? – Yes

Name of the degree – MSED Instructional Technology

Is this program part of another degree, certificate, or diploma? – Yes

OTHER PROGRAMS in educational technology or instructional development fields: Certificate Program available? – No

Specialist Program available? – No

Undergraduate Program available? – No

Doctorate Program available? – No

Program Content – Master's degree

Program Content URL – http://www.unk.edu/acad/gradstudies/PDF/2003-2005gradcatalog.pdf

Name of Institution – Richard Stockton College of New Jersey
Name of Program within institution – Instructional Technology
Title/Degree as it appears on official certificate or diploma – Master of Arts in Instructional Technology
Name & Title of person administering program – Jung Lee, Associate Professor, Program Director
Address – Jim Leeds Road, Pomona, NJ, 08240, United States
Telephone Number – 609-652-4949
Fax Number – 609-652-4858
E-Mail – mait@stockton.edu
Institution's home page – http://www.stockton.edu
Admittance URL – http://admissions.stockton.edu/
PREREQUISITES: Higher Education – Yes
If yes, number of years or degree required – BA degree
Teaching Certificate – No
ACCEPTANCE OF TRANSFERS – Yes
MASTER'S PROGRAM DURATION: Number of required Courses – 11
Comprehensive Exam Required? – No
Thesis Required? – Yes
Continuous Enrollment Required? – No
Other Requirements – GRE General Test
Does program culminate in a degree in the field of educational communications and technology? – Yes
Is this program part of another degree, certificate, or diploma? – No
Program Content – Master's degree
Program Content URL – http://graduate.stockton.edu/mait.html

Name of Institution – Montclair State University
Name of Program within institution – Educational Technology
Title/Degree as it appears on official certificate or diploma – M.Ed. in Educational Technology
Name & Title of person administering program – Dr. Vanessa Domine, Program Coordinator
Address – 1 College Avenue, Montclair, NJ, 07043, United States
Telephone Number – (973) 655-5187
Fax Number – (973) 655-7084
E-Mail – dominev@mail.montclair.edu
Institution's home page – http://www.montclair.edu
Admittance URL – http://www.montclair.edu/applying.shtml
PREREQUISITES: Higher Education – No

If yes, number of years or degree required – bachelor's degree
Teaching Certificate – No
ACCEPTANCE OF TRANSFERS – Yes
MASTER'S PROGRAM DURATION: Number of required Courses – 11
Number of weeks long – 16
Comprehensive Exam Required? – No
Thesis Required? – Optional
Continuous Enrollment Required? – No
Other Requirements – Field experience and capstone project
Does program culminate in a degree in the field of educational communications and technology? – Yes
Name of the degree – Master of Education degree in Educational Technology
Is this program part of another degree, certificate, or diploma? – No
OTHER PROGRAMS in educational technology or instructional development fields: Certificate Program available? – Yes
Certificate URL – http://www.montclair.edu/pages/edmedia
Specialist Program available? – Yes
Specialist URL – http://www.montclair.edu/pages/edmedia
Undergraduate Program available? – No
Doctorate Program available? – No
Program Content – Master's degree
Program Content URL – http://www.montclair.edu/pages/edmedia

Name of Institution – Seton Hall University
Name of Program within institution – School Library Media Specialist
Title/Degree as it appears on official certificate or diploma – Master of Education with a concentration as a School Library Media Specialist
Name & Title of person administering program – Rosemary W. Skeele
Address – College of Education and Human Services, South Orange, NJ, 07079, United States
Telephone Number – 973-761-9393
Fax Number – 973-313-6036
E-Mail – edstudies@shu.edu
Institution's home page – http://www.shu.edu
Admittance URL – http://education.shu.edu/academicprograms/edstudies/profdev/ed_media.html
PREREQUISITES: Higher Education – Yes
If yes, number of years or degree required – Bachelor's degree required
Teaching Certificate – No
Other requirement – Miller Analogy Test or GRE scores; 2 letters of recommendation; resume
ACCEPTANCE OF TRANSFERS – Yes
MASTER'S PROGRAM DURATION: Number of required Semesters – 4
Number of weeks long – 1-15
Comprehensive Exam Required? – No

Thesis Required? – No
Continuous Enrollment Required? – No
Other Requirements – Capstone Project
Does program culminate in a degree in the field of educational communications and technology? – Yes
Name of the degree – MA Education with a concentration in School Library Media Specialist
Is this program part of another degree, certificate, or diploma? – Yes
If yes, name of the degree, certificate, or diploma – New Jersey Certification as a School Library Media Specialist
OTHER PROGRAMS in educational technology or instructional development fields: Certificate Program available? – Yes
Certificate URL – http://education.shu.edu/academicprograms/edstudies/profdev/grad_itcertificate.html
Specialist Program available? – No
Undergraduate Program available? – No
Doctorate Program available? – No
Program Content – Master's degree
Program Content URL – http://education.shu.edu/academicprograms/edstudies/profdev/ed_media.html

Name of Institution – Rochester Institute of Technology
Name of Program within institution – Training and Instructional Design
Title/Degree as it appears on official certificate or diploma – MS Training and Instructional Design
Name & Title of person administering program – C. J. Wallington
Address – 43 Lomb Drive, Rochester, NY, 14623, United States
Telephone Number – 585.475.2893
Fax Number – 585.475.5099
E-Mail – cjwici@rit.edu
Institution's home page – http://www.rit.edu
Admittance URL – http://www.rit.edu
PREREQUISITES: Higher Education – Yes
If yes, number of years or degree required – Bachelors degree
Teaching Certificate – No
Other requirement – Miller Analogies Test, writing sample, resume
ACCEPTANCE OF TRANSFERS – Yes
MASTER'S PROGRAM DURATION: Number of required Quarters – 3
Number of weeks long – 11
Comprehensive Exam Required? – No
Thesis Required? – No
Continuous Enrollment Required? – No
Does program culminate in a degree in the field of educational communications and technology? – Yes
Name of the degree – Training and Instructional Design

Is this program part of another degree, certificate, or diploma? – No

If yes, name of the degree, certificate, or diploma, OTHER PROGRAMS in educational technology or instructional development fields: Certificate Program available? – Yes

Certificate URL – http://www.cepworldwide.com

Specialist Program available? – No

Undergraduate Program available? – No

Doctorate Program available? – No

Program Content – Master's degree

Program Content URL – http://www.rit.eud

Name of Institution – New York Institute of Technology

Name of Program within institution – Instructional Technology

Title/Degree as it appears on official certificate or diploma – Master of Science in Instructional Technology

Name & Title of person administering program – Dr. Sarah McPherson, Coordinator

Address – Northern Blvd, Old Westbury, NY, 11568, United States

Telephone Number – 516687777

Fax Number – 5166867655

E-Mail – smcphers@nyit.edu

Institution's home page – http://www.nyit.edu

PREREQUISITES: Higher Education – Yes

If yes, number of years or degree required – BA,BS

Teaching Certificate – Yes

ACCEPTANCE OF TRANSFERS – Yes

MASTER'S PROGRAM DURATION: Number of required Semesters – 12

Number of weeks long – 15

Comprehensive Exam Required? – No

Thesis Required? – Yes

Continuous Enrollment Required? – Yes

Other Requirements – GPA 3.0, teaching certification

Does program culminate in a degree in the field of educational communications and technology? – Yes

Name of the degree – Master of Science in Instructional Technology

Is this program part of another degree, certificate, or diploma? – No

If yes, name of the degree, certificate, or diploma, OTHER PROGRAMS in educational technology or instructional development fields: Certificate Program available? – No

Specialist Program available? – No

Undergraduate Program available? – No

Doctorate Program available? – No

Program Content – Master's degree

Name of Institution – State University of New York at Potsdam

Name of Program within institution – Educational Technology Specialist

Title/Degree as it appears on official certificate or diploma – Master of Science in Education

Name & Title of person administering program – Dr. Anthony Betrus

Address – 44 Pierrepont Ave, Potsdam, NY, 13676, United States

Telephone Number – 315-267-2670

E-Mail – betrusak@potsdam.edu

Institution's home page – http://www.potsdam.edu

Admittance URL – http://www.potsdam.edu/content.php?contentID=EEF71F54CCBC4B0D4CDC4BBCF6C937FC

PREREQUISITES: Higher Education – Yes

If yes, number of years or degree required – 4-year Undergraduate Degree required

Teaching Certificate – Yes

ACCEPTANCE OF TRANSFERS – Yes

MASTER'S PROGRAM DURATION: Number of required Courses – 13

Number of weeks long – 15

Comprehensive Exam Required? – No

Thesis Required? – Optional

Continuous Enrollment Required? – Yes

Does program culminate in a degree in the field of educational communications and technology? – Yes

Name of the degree – Educational Technology Specialist

Is this program part of another degree, certificate, or diploma? – No

OTHER PROGRAMS in educational technology or instructional development fields: Certificate Program available? – No

Specialist Program available? – No

Undergraduate Program available? – No

Doctorate Program available? – No

Program Content – Master's degree

Program Content URL – http://www.potsdam.edu/ict

Name of Institution – New York University

Name of Program within institution – Educational Communication and Technology

Title/Degree as it appears on official certificate or diploma – M.A. or Ph.D. or Certificate of Advanced Study in Education

Name & Title of person administering program – Dr. Jan L. Plass

Address – 239 Greene Street, Suite 300, New York, NY, 10003, United States

Telephone Number – (212) 998-5520

Fax Number – (212) 995-4041

E-Mail – jan.plass@nyu.edu

Institution's home page – http://education.nyu.edu/education

Admittance URL – http://nyu.edu/education/alt/ectprogram

PREREQUISITES: Higher Education – Yes

If yes, number of years or degree required – Undergrad for M.A.; M.A. for
Ph.D. and Certificate
Teaching Certificate – No
ACCEPTANCE OF TRANSFERS – Yes
MASTER'S PROGRAM DURATION: Number of required Courses – 12
Number of weeks long – 15
Comprehensive Exam Required? – No
Thesis Required? – Yes
Continuous Enrollment Required? – No
Other Requirements – Two foundations courses, Instructional Design for
Media Environments, and Cognitive Science and Educational Technology
I; (2) continuous active status to maintain matriculation when not enrolled in
courses; 24 credits in residency at NYU
**Does program culminate in a degree in the field of educational communi-
cations and technology?** – Yes
Name of the degree – M.A. or Ph.D. in Educational Communication and Tech-
nology
Is this program part of another degree, certificate, or diploma? – No
**OTHER PROGRAMS in educational technology or instructional develop-
ment fields: Certificate Program available?** – Yes
Certificate URL – http://nyu.edu/education/alt/ectprogram
Specialist Program available? – No
Undergraduate Program available? – No
Doctorate Program available? – PhD
Doctorate URL – http://nyu.edu/education/alt/ectprogram
Program Content – Master's degree
Program Content URL – http://nyu.edu/education/alt/ectprogram

Name of Institution – Syracuse University
Name of Program within institution – Instructional Design, Development and
Evaluation
Title/Degree as it appears on official certificate or diploma – MS, PhD
Name & Title of person administering program – Philip Doughty-Chair
Address – 330 Huntington Hall, Syracuse, NY, 13244, United States
Telephone Number – 315-443-3703
Fax Number – 315-443-1218
E-Mail – pldought@syr.edu
Institution's home page – http://syr.edu
Admittance URL – http://idde.syr.edu
PREREQUISITES: Higher Education – No
If yes, number of years or degree required – Bachelors degree
Teaching Certificate – No
ACCEPTANCE OF TRANSFERS – Yes
MASTER'S PROGRAM DURATION: Number of required Semesters –
3-4

Number of weeks long – 13&6
Comprehensive Exam Required? – Yes
Thesis Required? – No
Continuous Enrollment Required? – No
Other Requirements – Portfolio
Does program culminate in a degree in the field of educational communications and technology? – Yes
Name of the degree – MS
Is this program part of another degree, certificate, or diploma? – No
OTHER PROGRAMS in educational technology or instructional development fields: Certificate Program available? – Yes
Certificate URL – http://idde.syr.edu
Specialist Program available? – Yes
Specialist URL – http://idde.syr.edu
Undergraduate Program available? – No
Doctorate Program available? – PhD
Doctorate URL – http://idde.syr.edu
Program Content – Master's degree
Program Content URL – http://idde.syr.edu

Name of Institution – Ithaca College
Name of Program within institution – Communications
Title/Degree as it appears on official certificate or diploma – Communications
Name & Title of person administering program – Gordon Rowland
Address – Roy H. Park School of Communications, Ithaca College, Ithaca, NY, 14850, United States
Telephone Number – 607.274.1031
Fax Number – 607.274.7076
E-Mail – rowland@ithaca.edu
Institution's home page – http://www.ithaca.edu/
Admittance URL – http://www.ithaca.edu/admissions/
PREREQUISITES: Higher Education – Yes
If yes, number of years or degree required – bachelors
Teaching Certificate – No
ACCEPTANCE OF TRANSFERS – Yes
MASTER'S PROGRAM DURATION: Number of required Semesters – 2
Number of weeks long – 15
Comprehensive Exam Required? – Yes
Thesis Required? – Optional
Continuous Enrollment Required? – Yes
Does program culminate in a degree in the field of educational communications and technology? – Yes
Name of the degree – master of science, communications
Is this program part of another degree, certificate, or diploma? – No

OTHER PROGRAMS in educational technology or instructional development fields: Certificate Program available? – No
Specialist Program available? – No
Undergraduate Program available? – Yes
Undergraduate URL – http://www.ithaca.edu/ocld/
Doctorate Program available? – No
Program Content – Master's degree
Program Content URL – http://www.ithaca.edu/rhp/gradcomm/

Name of Institution – Ohio University
Name of Program within institution – Instructional Technology
Title/Degree as it appears on official certificate or diploma – Curriculum and Instruction: Instructional Technology
Name & Title of person administering program – Dr. Teresa Franklin, Associate Professor – IT
Address – 313D McCracken Hall, Athens, OH, 45701, United States
Telephone Number – 740-593-4561
Fax Number – 740-593-0477
E-Mail – franklit@ohio.edu
Institution's home page – http://www.ohio.edu/education/
Admittance URL – http://www.ohio.edu/education/dept/es/it/dept-es-it-msci.cfm
PREREQUISITES: Higher Education – No
If yes, number of years or degree required – Bachelor's for MED admission
Teaching Certificate – No
Other requirement – Master'd Degree for PHD admission
ACCEPTANCE OF TRANSFERS – Yes
MASTER'S PROGRAM DURATION: Number of required Quarters – 7
Number of weeks long – 9
Comprehensive Exam Required? – No
Thesis Required? – Optional
Continuous Enrollment Required? – No
Other Requirements – Degree is Weekend/Online Program with campus visits 3 times per quarter only
Does program culminate in a degree in the field of educational communications and technology? – Yes
Name of the degree – Master's of Education: Computer Education and Technology
Is this program part of another degree, certificate, or diploma? – No
OTHER PROGRAMS in educational technology or instructional development fields: Certificate Program available? – No
Specialist Program available? – No
Undergraduate Program available? – No
Doctorate Program available? – PhD

Doctorate URL – http://www.ohio.edu/education/dept/es/it/dept-es-it-phdsci.cfm

Program Content – Master's degree

Program Content URL – http://www.ohio.edu/education/dept/es/it/dept-es-it-msci.cfm

Name of Institution – The Ohio State University

Name of Program within institution – Educational Technology

Name & Title of person administering program – Rick Voithofer, Associate Professor

Address – 29 W. Woodruff, Columbus, OH, 43210, United States

Telephone Number – 614-247-7945

E-Mail – voithofer.2@osu.edu

Institution's home page – http://ehe.osu.edu/epl/academics/cftqi/technology.cfm

Admittance URL – http://ehe.osu.edu/epl/students/prospectve-stdnts.cfm

PREREQUISITES: Higher Education – No

If yes, number of years or degree required – Bachelors degree

Teaching Certificate – No

ACCEPTANCE OF TRANSFERS – Yes

MASTER'S PROGRAM DURATION: Number of required Quarters – 6

Comprehensive Exam Required? – No

Thesis Required? – Optional

Continuous Enrollment Required? – No

Does program culminate in a degree in the field of educational communications and technology? – Yes

Name of the degree – MA

Is this program part of another degree, certificate, or diploma? – No

OTHER PROGRAMS in educational technology or instructional development fields: Certificate Program available? – No

Specialist Program available? – Yes

Undergraduate Program available? – No

Doctorate Program available? – PhD

Doctorate URL – http://ehe.osu.edu/epl/academics/cftqi/tech-phd.cfm

Program Content – Master's degree

Name of Institution – University of Toledo

Name of Program within institution – Educational Technology

Title/Degree as it appears on official certificate or diploma – Master's Degree in Educational Technology, and Curriculum and Instruction, Ph.D.

Name & Title of person administering program – Dr. Berhane Teclemainaot, Assistant Professor of Educational Technology

Address – 2081 W. Bancroft St., Mail Stop #924, Toledo, OH, 43606, United States

Telephone Number – (419) 530-7979

Fax Number – (419) 530-4309

E-Mail – berhane.Teclehaimanot@utoledo.edu
Institution's home page – http://www.utoledo.edu
Admittance URL – http://gradschool.utoledo.edu
PREREQUISITES: Higher Education – Yes
If yes, number of years or degree required – Undergraduate Degree
MASTER'S PROGRAM DURATION: Number of required Semesters – 6
Number of weeks long – 17
Comprehensive Exam Required? – Yes
Thesis Required? – No
Continuous Enrollment Required? – Yes
Does program culminate in a degree in the field of educational communications and technology? – Yes
Name of the degree – Master's of Educational Technology or Curriculum and Instruction, Ph.D.
Is this program part of another degree, certificate, or diploma? – No
OTHER PROGRAMS in educational technology or instructional development fields: Certificate Program available? – Yes
Certificate URL – http://education.utoledo.edu
Specialist Program available? – No
Undergraduate Program available? – No
Doctorate Program available? – PhD
Doctorate URL – http://gradschool.utoledo.edu
Program Content – Master's degree, **Program Content URL** – http://education.utoledo.edu

Name of Institution – Kent State University
Name of Program within institution – Instructional Technology
Title/Degree as it appears on official certificate or diploma – Instructional Technology
Name & Title of person administering program – David Dalton, Coordinator
Address – 405 White Hall, Kent, OH, 44242, United States
Telephone Number – 330.672.2294
Fax Number – 330.672.2512
E-Mail – ddalton@kent.edu
Institution's home page – http://www.itecksu.org
Admittance URL – http://oss.educ.kent.edu
PREREQUISITES: Comprehensive Exam Required? – No
Thesis Required? – Optional
Continuous Enrollment Required? – No
Does program culminate in a degree in the field of educational communications and technology? – Yes
Name of the degree – Instructional Technology
Is this program part of another degree, certificate, or diploma? – Yes
OTHER PROGRAMS in educational technology or instructional development fields: Certificate Program available? – Yes

Specialist Program available? – No
Undergraduate Program available? – No
Doctorate Program available? – PhD
Program Content – Master's degree
Program Content URL – http://www.itecksu.org

Name of Institution – University of Oklahoma
Name of Program within institution – Instructional Psychology & Technology
Title/Degree as it appears on official certificate or diploma – Ph.D or M.Ed., Department of Educational Psychology
Name & Title of person administering program – Raymond B. Miller
Address – 820 Van Vleet Oval, Collings 321, Norman, OK, 73019, United States
Telephone Number – 405-325-1501
Fax Number – 405-325-6655
E-Mail – rmiller@ou.edu
Institution's home page – http://www.ou.edu
Admittance URL – http://www.ou.edu/education/edpsy/iptwww/programs.html
PREREQUISITES: Higher Education – No
If yes, number of years or degree **required** – Bachelor degree
Teaching Certificate – No
ACCEPTANCE OF TRANSFERS – Yes
MASTER'S PROGRAM DURATION: Number of required Semesters – 4
Number of weeks long – 16
Comprehensive Exam Required? – Yes
Thesis Required? – Optional
Continuous Enrollment Required? – Yes
Other Requirements, Practicum & Internship, **Does program culminate in a degree in the field of educational communications and technology?** – Yes
Name of the degree – Instructional Psychology & Technology
Is this program part of another degree, certificate, or diploma? – No
OTHER PROGRAMS in educational technology or instructional development fields: Certificate Program available? – No
Specialist Program available? – Yes
Specialist URL – http://www.ou.edu/education/edpsy/iptwww/masters.html
Undergraduate Program available? – No
Doctorate Program available? – PhD
Doctorate URL – http://www.ou.edu/education/edpsy/iptwww/phd.html
Program Content – Master's degree
Program Content URL – http://www.ou.edu/education/edpsy/iptwww/masters.html

Name of Institution – Lehigh University
Name of Program within institution – Educational Technology

Title/Degree as it appears on official certificate or diploma – Instructional Design and Development

Name & Title of person administering program – Ward Cates, Professor/Program Coordinator

Address – 111 Research Drive, Bethlehem, PA, 18015, United States

Telephone Number – 610-758-4794

Fax Number – 610-758-3243

E-Mail – ward.cates@lehigh.edu

Institution's home page – http://www.lehigh.edu

Admittance URL – http://www.lehigh.edu/collegeofeducation/main_frameset. htm?admissions/admissions.htm~mainFrame

PREREQUISITES: Higher Education – No

Teaching Certificate – No

ACCEPTANCE OF TRANSFERS – Yes

MASTER'S PROGRAM DURATION: Number of required Courses – 10

Comprehensive Exam Required? – No

Thesis Required? – No

Continuous Enrollment Required? – No

Does program culminate in a degree in the field of educational communications and technology? – Yes

Name of the degree – Instructional Design and Development

Is this program part of another degree, certificate, or diploma? – No

OTHER PROGRAMS in educational technology or instructional development fields: Certificate Program available? – No

Specialist Program available? – No

Undergraduate Program available? – No

Doctorate Program available? – EdD

Doctorate URL – http://www.lehigh.edu/collegeofeducation/degree_programs/ ed_technology/main_frameset.htm

Program Content - Master's degree

Program Content URL – http://www.lehigh.edu/collegeofeducation/degree_ programs/ed_technology/main_frameset.htm

Name of Institution – Seton Hill University

Name of Program within institution – Instructional Design for Technologies Enhanced Learning

Title/Degree as it appears on official certificate or diploma – Master of Education in Instructional Design

Name & Title of person administering program – Dr. Shirley Campbell

Address – 1 Seton Hill Drive, Greensburg, PA, 15601, United States

Telephone Number – 724 830 1007

Fax Number – 724 830 1295

E-Mail – scampbell@setonhill.edu

Institution's home page – http://www.setonhill.edu

PREREQUISITES: Higher Education – Yes

If yes, number of years or degree **required** – Bachelor Degree
Other requirement – Please talk to advising faculty if instructional tech certificate is desired
ACCEPTANCE OF TRANSFERS – Yes
MASTER'S PROGRAM DURATION: Number of required Semesters – 6
Number of weeks long – 15
Comprehensive Exam Required? – No
Thesis Required? – Optional
Continuous Enrollment Required? – Yes
Other Requirements, Thesis or internship option, except Instructional Certificate - requires internship, **Does program culminate in a degree in the field of educational communications and technology?** – Yes
Name of the degree – Master of Education in Instructional Design
Is this program part of another degree, certificate, or diploma? – No
OTHER PROGRAMS in educational technology or instructional development fields: Certificate Program available? – No
Specialist Program available? – Yes
Undergraduate Program available? – No
Doctorate Program available? – EdD
Program Content – Master's degree
Program Content URL – http://www.setonhill.edu/idtel

Name of Institution – Temple University
Name of Program within institution – Instructional and Learning Technology
Title/Degree as it appears on official certificate or diploma – M.Ed.
Name & Title of person administering program – Susan M. Miller
Address – 1301 Cecil B. Moore Ritter Annex 209, Philadelphia, PA, 19122, United States
Telephone Number – 215.204.4497
Fax Number – 215.204.6013
E-Mail – susan.miller@temple.edu
Institution's home page – http://www.temple.edu
Admittance URL – http://ilt.temple.edu/
PREREQUISITES: Higher Education – No
If yes, number of years or degree required – Bachelor's Degree
Teaching Certificate – No
ACCEPTANCE OF TRANSFERS – Yes
MASTER'S PROGRAM DURATION: Number of required Courses – 11
Comprehensive Exam Required? – Yes
Thesis Required? – No
Continuous Enrollment Required? – Yes
Other Requirements – Practicum
Does program culminate in a degree in the field of educational communications and technology? – Yes
Name of the degree – Instructional and Learning Technology

Is this program part of another degree, certificate, or diploma? – No
OTHER PROGRAMS in educational technology or instructional development fields: Certificate Program available? – Yes
Certificate URL – http://ilt.temple.edu
Specialist Program available? – No
Undergraduate Program available? – No
Doctorate Program available? – No
Program Content – Master's degree
Program Content URL – http://ilt.temple.edu

Name of Institution – Penn State Great Valley School of Graduate Professional Studies
Name of Program within institution – Instructional Systems
Title/Degree as it appears on official certificate or diploma – M.Ed. Instructional Systems
Name & Title of person administering program – Doris Lee, Ph.D. Associate Professor, Program Coordinator
Address – 30 E. Swedesford Road, Malvern, PA, 19355, United States
Telephone Number – 610-648-3266
Fax Number – 610-725-5253
E-Mail – ydl1@psu.edu
Institution's home page – http://www.gv.psu.edu/
Admittance URL – http://www.gv.psu.edu/
PREREQUISITES: Higher Education – Yes
Teaching Certificate – No
ACCEPTANCE OF TRANSFERS – Yes
MASTER'S PROGRAM DURATION: Number of required Courses – 12
Number of weeks long – 14wk
Comprehensive Exam Required? – No
Thesis Required? – Optional
Continuous Enrollment Required? – Yes
Other Requirements – There are 10 required courses and a master's paper or 2 additional courses to complete M.Ed.
Does program culminate in a degree in the field of educational communications and technology? – Yes
Name of the degree – M.Ed.
Is this program part of another degree, certificate, or diploma? – No
OTHER PROGRAMS in educational technology or instructional development fields: Certificate Program available? – Yes
Certificate URL – http://wwwgv.psu.edu/Current_Students/Degrees_Certificate
Specialist Program available? – No
Undergraduate Program available? – No
Doctorate Program available? – No
Program Content – Master's degree
Program Content URL – http://gv.psu.edu/Current_Students/Degrees

Name of Institution – Philadelphia University
Name of Program within institution – Instructional Design and Technology
Title/Degree as it appears on official certificate or diploma – M.S. Instructional Design and Technology
Name & Title of person administering program – Dr. Tim McGee
Address – School House Lane & Henry Avenue, Philadelphia, PA, 19144, United States
Telephone Number – 215.951.2872
Fax Number – 215.951.2915
E-Mail – mcgeet@philau.edu
Institution's home page – http://www.;philau.edu/msit
Admittance URL – http://www.philau.edu/graduate
PREREQUISITES: Higher Education – Yes
If yes, number of years or degree required – Bachelors degree
Teaching Certificate – No
ACCEPTANCE OF TRANSFERS – Yes
MASTER'S PROGRAM DURATION: Number of required Courses – 11
Number of weeks long – 15
Comprehensive Exam Required? – No
Thesis Required? – Optional
Continuous Enrollment Required? – No
Other Requirements – GRE, MAT, or GMAT
Does program culminate in a degree in the field of educational communications and technology? – Yes
Name of the degree – M.S. Instructional Design and Technology
Is this program part of another degree, certificate, or diploma? – No
OTHER PROGRAMS in educational technology or instructional development fields: Certificate Program available? – Yes
Certificate URL, http://www.philau.edu/msit/degrees.html, **Specialist Program available?** – Yes
Specialist URL, http://www.philau.edu/msit/degrees.html, **Undergraduate Program available?** – No
Doctorate Program available? – No
Program Content – Master's degree,
Program Content URL – http://www.philau.edu/msit/degrees.html

Name of Institution – East Stroudsburg University
Name of Program within institution – Instructional Technology
Title/Degree as it appears on official certificate or diploma – Master of Education in Instructional Technology
Name & Title of person administering program – Elzar Camper, Jr.
Address – 200 Prospect Street, Rosenkrans Hall-East, East Stroudsburg, PA, 18301, United States
Telephone Number – 570-422-3646
Fax Number – 570-422-3876

E-Mail – elzar.camper@po-box.esu.edu
Institution's home page – http://www3.esu.edu/graduate/default.asp
Admittance URL – http://www3.esu.edu/graduate/forms.asp
PREREQUISITES: Higher Education – No
If yes, number of years or degree required – Bachelors degree
Teaching Certificate – No
ACCEPTANCE OF TRANSFERS – Yes
MASTER'S PROGRAM DURATION: Number of required Courses – 11
Number of weeks long – 15
Comprehensive Exam Required? – No
Thesis Required? – No
Continuous Enrollment Required? – No
Other Requirements – Non teaching instructional technology specialist certification program may be taken concurrently with degree
Does program culminate in a degree in the field of educational communications and technology? – Yes
Name of the degree – Instructional Technology
Is this program part of another degree, certificate, or diploma? – Yes
If yes, name of the degree, certificate, or diploma – Instructional Media Specialist certification
OTHER PROGRAMS in educational technology or instructional development fields: Certificate Program available? – Yes
Certificate URL – http://www3.esu.edu/graduate/Itechnology.index.asp
Specialist Program available? – No
Undergraduate Program available? – No
Doctorate Program available? – No
Program Content – Master's degree
Program Content URL – http://www.esu.edu/grants/gradwebpage/IT.SWF

Name of Institution – Bloomsburg University
Name of Program within institution – Instructional Technology
Title/Degree as it appears on official certificate or diploma – Master of Science in Instructional Technology
Name & Title of person administering program – Dr. Timothy L. Phillips
Address – 400 East Second Street, Bloomsburg, PA, 17815, United States
Telephone Number – 570-389-4875
Fax Number – 570-389-4943
E-Mail – tphillip@bloomu.edu
Institution's home page – http://iit.bloomu.edu
Admittance URL – http://iit.bloomu.edu/dit/pages/forms.htm
PREREQUISITES: Higher Education – Yes
If yes, number of years or degree required – Undergraduate degree, BS or BA
Teaching Certificate – No
ACCEPTANCE OF TRANSFERS – Yes

MASTER'S PROGRAM DURATION: Number of required Semesters – 4
Number of weeks long – 15
Comprehensive Exam Required? – No
Thesis Required? – No
Continuous Enrollment Required? – No
Does program culminate in a degree in the field of educational communications and technology? – Yes
Name of the degree – Master of Science in Instructional Technology
Is this program part of another degree, certificate, or diploma? – No
OTHER PROGRAMS in educational technology or instructional development fields: Certificate Program available? Yes
Specialist Program available? Yes
Specialist URL – http://iit.bloomu.edu/dit/pages/itSpecialist.htm
Undergraduate Program available? – No
Doctorate Program available? – No
Program Content – Master's degree
Program Content URL – http://http://iit.bloomu.edu/dit/pages/corporate.htm

Name of Institution – WIDENER UNIVERSITY
Name of Program within institution – Instructional Technology
Title/Degree as it appears on official certificate or diploma – M.Ed; Ed.D.; Certificate; in Instructional Technology
Name & Title of person administering program – Dr. Kathleen A. Bowes
Address – One University Place, Chester, PA, 19013, United States
Telephone Number – 610-499-4256
E-Mail – Kathleen.A.Bowes@Widener.Edu
Institution's home page – http://www.widener.edu
PREREQUISITES: Higher Education – No
Teaching Certificate – No
ACCEPTANCE OF TRANSFERS – Yes
MASTER'S PROGRAM DURATION: Number of required Courses – 10
Number of weeks long – 14
Comprehensive Exam Required? – No
Thesis Required? – No
Continuous Enrollment Required? – Yes
Does program culminate in a degree in the field of educational communications and technology? – Yes
Name of the degree, Masters of Education in Instructional Technology, **Is this program part of another degree, certificate, or diploma?** – Yes
If yes, name of the degree, certificate, or diploma – Instructional Technology Specialist Certificate
OTHER PROGRAMS in educational technology or instructional development fields: Certificate Program available? – Yes
Specialist Program available? – No
Undergraduate Program available? – No

Doctorate Program available? – EdD
Program Content – Master's degree

Name of Institution – The Pennsylvania State University
Name of Program within institution – Instructional Systems
Title/Degree as it appears on official certificate or diploma – Instructional
   Systems/M.Ed., M.S., D.Ed., Ph.D.
Name & Title of person administering program – Alison Carr-Chellman,
   Professor-In-Charge
Address – 315 Keller Building, University Park, PA, 16802, United States
Telephone Number – 814-865-0473
Fax Number – 814-865-0128
E-Mail – nxc1@psu.edu
Institution's home page – http://www.ed.psu.edu/insys
Admittance URL – http://www.ed.psu.edu/insys/newstudents/application
PREREQUISITES: Higher Education – No
If yes, number of years or degree required – 4 yr. Bachelor's degree, Under-
   grad. GPA-2.75 or >
Teaching Certificate – No
Other requirement – Grad. Record Exam-Minimum Score; TOEFL-550 or >
ACCEPTANCE OF TRANSFERS – Yes
MASTER'S PROGRAM DURATION: Comprehensive Exam Required? –
   Yes
Thesis Required? – No
Continuous Enrollment Required? – No
Other Requirements – Comp. exam required for doctoral degree; thesis req.
   for M.S.-not M.Ed.
**Does program culminate in a degree in the field of educational communi-
   cations and technology?** – Yes
Name of the degree – Instructional Systems-M.Ed., M.S.
Is this program part of another degree, certificate, or diploma? – Yes
**OTHER PROGRAMS in educational technology or instructional develop-
   ment fields: Certificate Program available?** – Yes
Certificate URL – http://www.cde.psu.edu/DE
Specialist Program available? – Yes
Specialist URL – http://www.ide.ed.psu.edu/itsc/dev/
Undergraduate Program available? – No
Doctorate Program available? – PhD
Doctorate URL – http://www.ed.psu.edu/insys
Program Content – Master's degree
Program Content URL – http://www.ed.psu.edu/insys

Name of Institution – University of South Carolina
Name of Program within institution – M. Ed. in Educational Technology

Title/Degree as it appears on official certificate or diploma – Master of Education in Educational Technology

Name & Title of person administering program – Thomas Smyth

Address – 471 University Parkway, Aiken, SC, 30909, United States

Telephone Number – 803-641-3527

Fax Number – 803-641-3698

E-Mail – smyth@usca.edu

Institution's home page – http://edtech.sc.edu

Admittance URL – http://edtech.sc.edu

PREREQUISITES: Higher Education – No

If yes, number of years or degree required – BA/BS

Teaching Certificate – No

ACCEPTANCE OF TRANSFERS – Yes

MASTER'S PROGRAM DURATION: Number of required Semesters – 4.5

Number of weeks long – 15

Comprehensive Exam Required? – No

Thesis Required? – No

Continuous Enrollment Required? – No

Other Requirements – Program Portfolio

Does program culminate in a degree in the field of educational communications and technology? – Yes

Name of the degree – M. Ed. in Educational Technology

Is this program part of another degree, certificate, or diploma? – No

If yes, name of the degree, certificate, or diploma – Tom Smyth

OTHER PROGRAMS in educational technology or instructional development fields: Certificate Program available? – No

Specialist Program available? – No

Undergraduate Program available? – No

Doctorate Program available? – No

Program Content – Master's degree

Program Content URL – http://edtech.sc.edu

Name of Institution – University of South Dakota

Name of Program within institution – Technology for Education and Training

Title/Degree as it appears on official certificate or diploma – M.S. in Technology for Education and Training

Name & Title of person administering program – Leslie Moller

Address – 414 E, Clark St., Vermillion, SD, 57069, United States

Telephone Number – 605-677-5448

Fax Number – 605-677-5438

E-Mail – tet@usd.edu

Institution's home page – http://www.usd.edu/tet/

Admittance URL – http://www.usd.edu/tet/

PREREQUISITES: Higher Education – No

If yes, number of years or degree required – Baccalaureate
Teaching Certificate – No
ACCEPTANCE OF TRANSFERS – Yes
MASTER'S PROGRAM DURATION: Number of required Semesters – 3
Number of weeks long – 15
Comprehensive Exam Required? – Yes
Thesis Required? – No
Continuous Enrollment Required? – No
Other Requirements – Electronic portfolio presentation
Does program culminate in a degree in the field of educational communications and technology? – Yes
Name of the degree – M.S. in Technology for Education and Training
Is this program part of another degree, certificate, or diploma? – No
If yes, name of the degree, certificate, or diploma, OTHER PROGRAMS in educational technology or instructional development fields: Certificate Program available? – No
Specialist Program available? – Yes
Specialist URL – http://www.usd.edu/tet/
Undergraduate Program available? – No
Doctorate Program available? – No
Program Content – Master's degree
Program Content URL – http://www.usd.edu/tet/

Name of Institution – Dakota State University
Name of Program within institution – Educational Technology
Title/Degree as it appears on official certificate or diploma – Master of Science in Education
Name & Title of person administering program – Mark Hawkes
Address – 820 North Washington Ave., Madison, SD, 57042, United States
Telephone Number – 605-256-5274
Fax Number – 605-256-7700
E-Mail – mark.hawkes@dsu.edu
Institution's home page – http://www.dsu.edu/
Admittance URL – http://www.departments.dsu.edu/gradoffice/MSET/Default.htm
PREREQUISITES: Higher Education – Yes
If yes, number of years or degree required – Baccalaureate
Teaching Certificate – No
ACCEPTANCE OF TRANSFERS – Yes
MASTER'S PROGRAM DURATION: Number of required Semesters – 3
Number of weeks long – 15
Comprehensive Exam Required? – No
Thesis Required? – No
Continuous Enrollment Required? – Yes

Other Requirements – Electronic Portfolio Presentation of program products and alignment with program objectives

Does program culminate in a degree in the field of educational communications and technology? – Yes

Name of the degree – Master of Science in Educational Technology

Is this program part of another degree, certificate, or diploma? – No

OTHER PROGRAMS in educational technology or instructional development fields: Certificate Program available? – No

Specialist Program available? – Yes

Specialist URL – http://www.departments.dsu.edu/gradoffice/MSET/courses_descriptions.htm

Undergraduate Program available? – No

Doctorate Program available? – No

Program Content – Master's degree

Program Content URL – http://www.departments.dsu.edu/gradoffice/MSET/Default.htm

Name of Institution – The University of Memphis

Name of Program within institution – Instructional Design and Technology

Title/Degree as it appears on official certificate or diploma – Instructional Design and Technology

Name & Title of person administering program – Deborah L. Lowther

Address – COE: 404 Ball Hall, Memphis, TN, 38152, United States

Telephone Number – 901-678-5645

Fax Number – 901-678-3881

E-Mail – dlowther@memphis.edu

Institution's home page – http://idt.memphis.edu

Admittance URL – http://http://academics.memphis.edu/gradschool/applicant.html

PREREQUISITES: Higher Education – No

If yes, number of years or degree required – Bachelor's Degree

Teaching Certificate – No

ACCEPTANCE OF TRANSFERS – Yes

MASTER'S PROGRAM DURATION: Number of required Courses – 12

Comprehensive Exam Required? – Yes

Thesis Required? – No

Continuous Enrollment Required? – No

Other Requirements – The comprehensive Exam is performance-based

Does program culminate in a degree in the field of educational communications and technology? – Yes

Name of the degree – Instructional Design and Technology

Is this program part of another degree, certificate, or diploma? – No

OTHER PROGRAMS in educational technology or instructional development fields: Certificate Program available? – Yes

Certificate URL – http://http://academics.memphis.edu/gradcatalog0305/cated
    intro.html
Specialist Program available? – Yes
Specialist URL – http://http://academics.memphis.edu/gradcatalog0305/cated
    intro.html
Undergraduate Program available? – No
Doctorate Program available? – EdD
Doctorate URL – http://http://academics.memphis.edu/gradcatalog0305/cated
    intro.html
Program Content – Master's degree
Program Content URL – http://idt.memphis.edu

Name of Institution – University of Tennessee Knoxville
Name of Program within institution – Instructional Technology
Title/Degree as it appears on official certificate or diploma – Doctor of Phi-
    losophy in Education, Master of Science in Education
Name & Title of person administering program – Edward L. Counts, Jr.,
    Ed.D.
Address – Claxton Complex 442, Knoxville, TN, 37996, United States
Telephone Number – 865-974-4246
Fax Number – 865-974-8103
E-Mail – ecounts1@utk.edu
Institution's home page – http://www.utk.edu
Admittance URL – http://admissions.utk.edu/graduate/
PREREQUISITES: Higher Education – Yes
Teaching Certificate – No
ACCEPTANCE OF TRANSFERS – Yes
MASTER'S PROGRAM DURATION: Number of required Semesters – 3
Number of weeks long – 48
Comprehensive Exam Required? – Yes
Thesis Required? – Optional
Continuous Enrollment Required? – No
**Does program culminate in a degree in the field of educational communi-
    cations and technology?** – Yes
Name of the degree – Master of Science in Instructional Technology
Is this program part of another degree, certificate, or diploma? – No
**OTHER PROGRAMS in educational technology or instructional develop-
    ment fields: Certificate Program available?** – No
Specialist Program available? – Yes
Specialist URL – http://ites.tennessee.edu/it2.shtml
Undergraduate Program available? – No
Doctorate Program available? – PhD
Doctorate URL – http://ites.tennessee.edu/it4.shtml
Program Content – Master's degree
Program Content URL – http://ites.tennessee.edu/it1.shtml

Name of Institution – University of Tennessee at Chattanooga
Name of Program within institution – Educational Technology
Title/Degree as it appears on official certificate or diploma – Master of Education
Name & Title of person administering program – Tony Lease
Address – 615 McCallie Ave., Chattanooga, TN, 37403, United States
Telephone Number – 423.425.4171
Fax Number – 423.425.5380
E-Mail – Tony-Lease@utc.edu
Institution's home page – http://www.utc.edu/
Admittance URL – http://www.utc.edu/Administration/HealthEducationAnd
ProfessionalStudies/Graduate_Studies/graduate_studies.html
PREREQUISITES: Higher Education – Yes
If yes, number of years or degree required – undergraduate degree
Teaching Certificate – No
Other requirement – no licensure program
ACCEPTANCE OF TRANSFERS – Yes
MASTER'S PROGRAM DURATION: Number of required Courses – 12
Comprehensive Exam Required? – No
Thesis Required? – Optional
Continuous Enrollment Required? – No
Does program culminate in a degree in the field of educational communications and technology? – Yes
Name of the degree – Master of Education in Elementary or Secondary Ed. w/concentration in Ed. Tech
Is this program part of another degree, certificate, or diploma? – Yes
If yes, name of the degree, certificate, or diploma – Master of Education in Elementary or Secondary Ed.
OTHER PROGRAMS in educational technology or instructional development fields: Certificate Program available? – No
Certificate URL – http://www.utc.edu/Administration/HealthEducationAnd
ProfessionalStudies/Graduate_Studies/graduate_studies.html#tech
Specialist Program available? – Yes
Specialist URL – http://www.utc.edu/Administration/HealthEducationAnd
ProfessionalStudies/Graduate_Studies/graduate_studies.html#tech
Undergraduate Program available? – No
Doctorate Program available? – No
Program Content – Master's degree

Name of Institution – University of North Texas
Name of Program within institution – Computer Education and Cognitive Systems
Title/Degree as it appears on official certificate or diploma – Computer Education and Cognitive Systems
Name & Title of person administering program – Dr. Jon Young

Address – Box 311355, Denton, TX, 76203, United States
Telephone Number – 940-565-2057
Fax Number – 940-565-2185
E-Mail – jyoung@unt.edu
Institution's home page – http://www.cecs.unt.edu/
Admittance URL – http://www.cecs.unt.edu/admissions.jsp
PREREQUISITES: Higher Education – Yes
If yes, number of years or degree required – Bachelors degree
Teaching Certificate – No
ACCEPTANCE OF TRANSFERS – Yes
MASTER'S PROGRAM DURATION: Number of required Courses – 12
Number of weeks long – 15
Comprehensive Exam Required? – No
Thesis Required? – No
Continuous Enrollment Required? – Yes
**Does program culminate in a degree in the field of educational communi-
cations and technology?** – Yes
Name of the degree – Computer Education and Cognitive Systems
Is this program part of another degree, certificate, or diploma? – No
**OTHER PROGRAMS in educational technology or instructional develop-
ment fields: Doctorate Program available?** – PhD
Doctorate URL – http://www.cecs.unt.edu/degrees.jsp
Program Content – Master's degree
Program Content URL – http://www.cecs.unt.edu/degrees.jsp

Name of Institution – Texas A&M University
Name of Program within institution – Educational Technology
Title/Degree as it appears on official certificate or diploma – M.Ed. Educa-
tional Technology Ph.D. Educational Psychology Foundat
Name & Title of person administering program – Dr. Ronald Zellner
Address – MS 4225, College Station, TX, 77843, United States
Telephone Number – 979 845 72776
E-Mail – zellner@tamu.edu
Institution's home page – http://tamu.edu
Admittance URL – http://www.tamu.edu/new/prospective.html
PREREQUISITES: Higher Education – No
If yes, number of years or degree required – Baccalaureate
Teaching Certificate – No
ACCEPTANCE OF TRANSFERS – Yes
MASTER'S PROGRAM DURATION: Number of required Courses – 13
Comprehensive Exam Required? – Yes
Thesis Required? – No
Continuous Enrollment Required? – No
**Does program culminate in a degree in the field of educational communi-
cations and technology?** – Yes

Name of the degree – M.Ed. Educational Technology
Is this program part of another degree, certificate, or diploma? – No
OTHER PROGRAMS in educational technology or instructional development fields: Certificate Program available? – Yes
Certificate URL – https://secure.sbec.state.tx.us/SBECOnline/login.asp
Specialist Program available? – No
Undergraduate Program available? – No
Doctorate Program available? – PhD
Doctorate URL – http://www.coe.tamu.edu/epsy/epf/epfindex.htm
Program Content – Master's degree
Program Content URL – http://edtc.tamu.edu

Name of Institution – The University of Texas at Austin
Name of Program within institution – Instructional Technology Program
Title/Degree as it appears on official certificate or diploma – Curriculum & Instruction
Address – 1 University Station D5700, Austin, TX, 78712, United States
Telephone Number – 512-471-5211
Fax Number – (512)-471-8460
Institution's home page – http://www.utexas.edu/
Admittance URL – http://jabba.edb.utexas.edu/it/
MASTER'S PROGRAM DURATION: Number of required Courses – 12
Comprehensive Exam Required? – No
Thesis Required? – Optional
Continuous Enrollment Required? – Yes
Does program culminate in a degree in the field of educational communications and technology? – Yes
Is this program part of another degree, certificate, or diploma? – No
OTHER PROGRAMS in educational technology or instructional development fields: Doctorate Program available? – PhD
Doctorate URL – http://jabba.edb.utexas.edu/it/
Program Content – Master's degree
Program Content URL – http://jabba.edb.utexas.edu/it/

Name of Institution – Texas Tech University
Name of Program within institution – Educational and Instructional Technology
Title/Degree as it appears on official certificate or diploma – Master, Ed.D. & pending Ph.D
Address – College of Education, Lubbock, TX, 79409, United States
Telephone Number – 806-742-1997
Fax Number – 806-742-2179
Institution's home page – http://www.educ.ttu.edu/edit/
PREREQUISITES: Higher Education – Yes
Teaching Certificate – Yes

ACCEPTANCE OF TRANSFERS – Yes
MASTER'S PROGRAM DURATION: Comprehensive Exam Required? –
  Yes
Thesis Required? – No
Continuous Enrollment Required? – Yes
**Does program culminate in a degree in the field of educational communi-
  cations and technology?** – Yes
Is this program part of another degree, certificate, or diploma? – Yes
**OTHER PROGRAMS in educational technology or instructional develop-
  ment fields: Program Content** – Master's degree

Name of Institution – University of Texas at Brownsville
Name of Program within institution – Educational Technology
Title/Degree as it appears on official certificate or diploma – M.Ed. in Edu-
  cational Technology
Address – 80 Fort Brown, Brownsville, TX, 78520, United States
Institution's home page – http://www.utb.edu
PREREQUISITES: Higher Education – Yes
Teaching Certificate – Yes
ACCEPTANCE OF TRANSFERS – Yes
MASTER'S PROGRAM DURATION: Comprehensive Exam Required? –
  Yes
Thesis Required? – No
Continuous Enrollment Required? – Yes
**Does program culminate in a degree in the field of educational communi-
  cations and technology?** – Yes
Is this program part of another degree, certificate, or diploma? – Yes
**OTHER PROGRAMS in educational technology or instructional develop-
  ment fields: Certificate Program available?** – No
Program Content – Master's degree
Program Content URL – http://edtech.utb.edu

Name of Institution – Texas A&M University-Texarkana
Name of Program within institution – Master of Science in Instructional
  Technology
Title/Degree as it appears on official certificate or diploma – Master of Sci-
  ence in Instructional Technology
Name & Title of person administering program – Dr. Bosede Aworuwa,
  Program Coordinator
Address – 2600 N. Robinson Road, Texarkana, TX, 75505, United States
Institution's home page – http://www.tamut.edu
Admittance URL – http://www.tamut.edu/ited
PREREQUISITES: Higher Education – No
If yes, number of years or degree required – B.A., B.S.

Teaching Certificate – No
ACCEPTANCE OF TRANSFERS – Yes
MASTER'S PROGRAM DURATION: Number of required Semesters –
6-8
Number of weeks long – 15
Comprehensive Exam Required? – Yes
Thesis Required? – No
Continuous Enrollment Required? – Yes
Does program culminate in a degree in the field of educational communications and technology? – Yes
Is this program part of another degree, certificate, or diploma? – Yes
If yes, name of the degree, certificate, or diploma – Has Master Technology Teacher Certificate option
OTHER PROGRAMS in educational technology or instructional development fields: Certificate Program available? – Yes
Certificate URL – http://www.tamut.edu/ited
Specialist Program available? – No
Undergraduate Program available? – No
Doctorate Program available? – No
Program Content – Master's degree

Name of Institution – Brigham Young University
Name of Program within institution – Instructional Psychology and Technology
Title/Degree as it appears on official certificate or diploma – Instructional Psychology and Technology
Name & Title of person administering program – Andrew S. Gibbons, Department Chair
Address – 150-C MCKB, BYU, Provo, UT, 84602, United States
Telephone Number – (801) 422-5097
Fax Number – (801) 422-0314
E-Mail – andy_gibbons@byu.edu
Institution's home page – http://www.byu.edu
PREREQUISITES: Higher Education – No
Teaching Certificate – No
ACCEPTANCE OF TRANSFERS – No
MASTER'S PROGRAM DURATION: Number of required Semesters – 3
Number of weeks long – 16
Comprehensive Exam Required? – Yes
Thesis Required? – Optional
Continuous Enrollment Required? – Yes
Other Requirements – Minimum 36 hours (30 coursework + 6 Thesis or Project
Does program culminate in a degree in the field of educational communications and technology? – Yes

Name of the degree – Master of Science

Is this program part of another degree, certificate, or diploma? – No

OTHER PROGRAMS in educational technology or instructional development fields: Certificate Program available? – No

Specialist Program available? – No

Undergraduate Program available? – No

Doctorate Program available? – PhD

Program Content – Master's degree

Program Content URL – http://www.byu.edu/ipt/index.html

Name of Institution – Utah State University

Name of Program within institution – Instructional Technology

Title/Degree as it appears on official certificate or diploma – Masters of Science in Instructional Technology

Name & Title of person administering program – Byron Burnham

Address – 2830 Old Main Hill, Logan, UT, 84322, United States

Telephone Number – 435-797-0437

Fax Number – 435-797-2693

E-Mail – byron.burnham@usu.edu

Institution's home page – http://inst..usu.edu/

PREREQUISITES: Higher Education – Yes

If yes, number of years or degree required – Bachelors degree required

Teaching Certificate – No

ACCEPTANCE OF TRANSFERS – Yes

MASTER'S PROGRAM DURATION: Number of required Semesters – 5

Comprehensive Exam Required? – No

Thesis Required? – No

Continuous Enrollment Required? – Yes

Other Requirements – Internship or creative project

Does program culminate in a degree in the field of educational communications and technology? – Yes

Name of the degree – Masters of Science in Instructional Technology

Is this program part of another degree, certificate, or diploma? – No

OTHER PROGRAMS in educational technology or instructional development fields: Certificate Program available? – No

Specialist Program available? – Yes

Specialist URL – http://inst.usu.edu/eds/ over.php

Undergraduate Program available? – No

Doctorate Program available? – PhD

Doctorate URL – http://inst.usu.edu/phd over.php

Program Content – Master's degree

Program Content URL – http://inst.usu.edu/masters over.php

Name of Institution – Western Governors University

Name of Program within institution – Learning and Technology

Title/Degree as it appears on official certificate or diploma – Master of Arts in Learning and Technology

Name & Title of person administering program – Vincent E Shrader

Address – 4001 S 700 East Suite 700, Salt Lake City, UT, 84107, United States

Institution's home page – http://www.wgu.edu

Admittance URL – https://www.wgu.edu/wgu/app/app_step0.asp

PREREQUISITES: Higher Education – Yes

If yes, number of years or degree required – B.A.

Teaching Certificate – No

MASTER'S PROGRAM DURATION: Number of required Terms – 5

Number of weeks long – 26

Comprehensive Exam Required? – Yes

Thesis Required? – No

Continuous Enrollment Required? – Yes

Does program culminate in a degree in the field of educational communications and technology? – Yes

Name of the degree – Master of Arts in Learning and Technology

Is this program part of another degree, certificate, or diploma? – Yes

If yes, name of the degree, certificate, or diploma – Master of Education

OTHER PROGRAMS in educational technology or instructional development fields: Certificate Program available? – No

Specialist Program available? – No

Undergraduate Program available? – No

Doctorate Program available? – No

Program Content – Master's degree

Program Content URL – http://www.wgu.edu/education/master_education_learning_technology.asp

Name of Institution – Old Dominion University

Name of Program within institution – Instructional Design and Technology

Title/Degree as it appears on official certificate or diploma – Master of Science in Education

Name & Title of person administering program – Gary R. Morrison

Address – Education 145, Norfolk, VA, 23529, United States

Telephone Number – 757-683-4387

E-Mail – gmorriso@odu.edu

Institution's home page – http://www.odu.edu

Admittance URL – http://admissions.odu.edu/graduate/

PREREQUISITES: Higher Education – Yes

If yes, number of years or degree required – Bachelor

ACCEPTANCE OF TRANSFERS – No

MASTER'S PROGRAM DURATION: Comprehensive Exam Required? – Yes

Thesis Required? – Optional

Continuous Enrollment Required? – No

Does program culminate in a degree in the field of educational communications and technology? – Yes

Name of the degree – Masters of Science in Education

Is this program part of another degree, certificate, or diploma? – Yes

OTHER PROGRAMS in educational technology or instructional development fields: Certificate Program available? – No

Specialist Program available? – No

Undergraduate Program available? – No

Doctorate Program available? – PhD

Doctorate URL – http://www.odu.edu/educ/idt/

Program Content – Master's degree

Program Content URL – http://www.odu.edu/educ/idt/assets/pdf_docs/advising sheet.pdf

Name of Institution – University of Virginia

Name of Program within institution – Instructional Technology

Title/Degree as it appears on official certificate or diploma – Instructional Technology

Name & Title of person administering program – Dr. John Bunch

Address – 405 Emmet Street, Box 400265, Charlottesville, VA, 22904-4265, United States

Telephone Number – 434-924-0834

Fax Number – 434-924-1384

E-Mail – jbb2 s@virginia.edu

Institution's home page – http://curry.edschool.virginia.edu/it

Admittance URL – http://curry.edschool.virginia.edu/admissions/procedures. html

PREREQUISITES: Higher Education – No

Teaching Certificate – No

ACCEPTANCE OF TRANSFERS – Yes

MASTER'S PROGRAM DURATION: Number of required Semesters – 3

Number of weeks long – 15

Comprehensive Exam Required? – Yes

Thesis Required? – No

Continuous Enrollment Required? – Yes

Does program culminate in a degree in the field of educational communications and technology? – Yes

Name of the degree – Master of Education, Instructional Technology

Is this program part of another degree, certificate, or diploma? – No

OTHER PROGRAMS in educational technology or instructional development fields: Certificate Program available? – No

Specialist Program available? – Yes

Specialist URL – http://curry.edschool.virginia.edu/it/prospective/degree_ programs/index.htm

Undergraduate Program available? – No

Doctorate Program available? – PhD
Doctorate URL – http://curry.edschool.virginia.edu/it/prospective/degree_programs/index.htm
Program Content – Master's degree
Program Content URL – http://curry.edschool.virginia.edu/it/prospective/degree_programs/masters/index.htm

Name of Institution – George Mason University
Name of Program within institution – Instructional Technology
Title/Degree as it appears on official certificate or diploma – Curriculum and Instruction
Address – 4400 University Drive, Fairfax, VA, 22030, United States
Institution's home page – http://it.gse.gmu.edu
Admittance URL – http://it.gse.gmu.edu/admissions.htm
MASTER'S PROGRAM DURATION: Comprehensive Exam Required? – No
Thesis Required? – Optional
Continuous Enrollment Required? – Yes
Does program culminate in a degree in the field of educational communications and technology? – Yes
Is this program part of another degree, certificate, or diploma? – No
OTHER PROGRAMS in educational technology or instructional development fields: Certificate Program available? – Yes
Certificate URL – http://it.gse.gmu.edu/programs.htm
Doctorate Program available? – PhD
Doctorate URL – http://gse.gmu.edu/programs/phd/index.htm
Program Content – Master's degree
Program Content URL – http://it.gse.gmu.edu/programs.htm

Name of Institution – Virginia Tech
Name of Program within institution – Instructional Technology
Title/Degree as it appears on official certificate or diploma – Ph. D., Ed. D. and M.S. in Curriculum and Instruction
Name & Title of person administering program – Katherine S. Cennamo, Program Area Leader
Address – 220 WMH, Blacksburg, VA, 24061, United States
Telephone Number – 540-231-5587
Institution's home page – http://www.vt.edu
Admittance URL – http://www.tandl.vt.edu/it/default.html
PREREQUISITES: Higher Education – Yes
If yes, number of years or degree required – Bachelors
Teaching Certificate – No
MASTER'S PROGRAM DURATION: Number of required Courses – 12
Number of weeks long – 15

Comprehensive Exam Required? – Yes
Thesis Required? – No
Continuous Enrollment Required? – No
Does program culminate in a degree in the field of educational communications and technology? – No
Is this program part of another degree, certificate, or diploma? – Yes
If yes, name of the degree, certificate, or diploma – Curriculum and Instruction
OTHER PROGRAMS in educational technology or instructional development fields: Specialist Program available? – Yes
Specialist URL – http://www.tandl.vt.edu/it/default.html
Undergraduate Program available? – No
Doctorate Program available? – PhD
Doctorate URL – http://www.tandl.vt.edu/it/default.html
Program Content – Master's degree
Program Content URL – http://www.tandl.vt.edu/it/default.html

Name of Institution – Concordia University Wisconsin
Name of Program within institution – Educational Technology
Title/Degree as it appears on official certificate or diploma – M.S. in Education - Educational Technology
Name & Title of person administering program – Dr. Bernard Bull
Address, 12800 N Lakeshore Drive, Mequon, WI, 53097, United States
Telephone Number – 262-243-4595
E-Mail – bernard.bull@cuw.edu
Institution's home page – http://www.cuw.edu/AdultEd_Graduate/programs/education/technology/index.html
PREREQUISITES: Higher Education – Yes
If yes, number of years or degree required – A bachelor's degree from an accredited college
Teaching Certificate – No
ACCEPTANCE OF TRANSFERS – Yes
MASTER'S PROGRAM DURATION: Comprehensive Exam Required? – No
Thesis Required? – Optional
Continuous Enrollment Required? – Yes
Other Requirements – Portfolio
Does program culminate in a degree in the field of educational communications and technology? – Yes
Name of the degree – M.S in Education - Educational Technology
Is this program part of another degree, certificate, or diploma? – Yes
OTHER PROGRAMS in educational technology or instructional development fields: Undergraduate Program available? – No
Doctorate Program available? – No
Program Content – Master's degree

Program Content URL – http://www.cuw.edu/AdultEd_Graduate/programs/education/technology/index.html

Name of Institution – University of Wyoming
Name of Program within institution – Instructional Technology
Title/Degree as it appears on official certificate or diploma – Master of Science
Name & Title of person administering program – Dr. John Cochenour
Address – Dept 3374, 1000 E University Ave, Laramie, WY, 82070, United States
Telephone Number – 307-766-3247
Fax Number – 307-766-3237
E-Mail – ask_alt@uwyo.edu
Institution's home page – http://www.uwyo.edu/alt
Admittance URL – http://www.uwyo.edu/alt
PREREQUISITES: Higher Education – No
If yes, number of years or degree required – Bachelor's from an Accredited Institution
Teaching Certificate – No
ACCEPTANCE OF TRANSFERS – Yes
MASTER'S PROGRAM DURATION: Number of required Courses – 11
Comprehensive Exam Required? – Yes
Thesis Required? – No
Continuous Enrollment Required? – Yes
Does program culminate in a degree in the field of educational communications and technology? – Yes
Name of the degree – Instructional Technology
Is this program part of another degree, certificate, or diploma? – No
OTHER PROGRAMS in educational technology or instructional development fields: Certificate Program available? – No
Specialist Program available? – No
Undergraduate Program available? – No
Doctorate Program available? – EdD
Doctorate URL – http://www.uwyo.edu/alt
Program Content – Master's degree
Program Content URL – http://www.uwyo.edu/alt

Name of Institution – Macquarie University
Name of Program within institution – Master of Education
Title/Degree as it appears on official certificate or diploma – Master of Education
Name & Title of person administering program – Dr John Hedberg
Address – Balaclava Road, Macquarie University, 2109, Australia
Telephone Number – +61-2-9850 9894
Fax Number – +61-2-9850 8674

E-Mail – Maree.McEvoy@mq.edu.au
Institution's home page – http://www.mq.edu.au
Admittance URL – http://www.aces.mq.edu.au/educ_home.asp
PREREQUISITES: Higher Education – No
If yes, number of years or degree required – Completed Bachelors degree
Teaching Certificate – No
ACCEPTANCE OF TRANSFERS – Yes
MASTER'S PROGRAM DURATION: Number of required Courses – 8
Number of weeks long – 14
Comprehensive Exam Required? – No
Thesis Required? – No
Continuous Enrollment Required? – Yes
**Does program culminate in a degree in the field of educational communi-
cations and technology?** – No
Name of the degree, Master of Education, **Is this program part of another
degree, certificate, or diploma?** – Yes
**OTHER PROGRAMS in educational technology or instructional develop-
ment fields: Certificate Program available?** – Yes
Specialist Program available? – No
Undergraduate **Program available?** – No
Doctorate Program available? – PhD
Program **Content** – Master's degree

Name of Institution – The University of Sydney
Name of Program within institution – Learning Science and Technology
Title/Degree as it appears on official certificate or diploma – Master of
Learning Science and Technology
Address – Education Building (A35), The University of Sydney, Sydney, NSW,
2006, Australia
Telephone Number – +61 2 9351 4107
Fax Number – +61 2 9036 5205
E-Mail – coco@edfac.usyd.edu.au
Institution's home page – http://www.usyd.edu.au/
Admittance URL – http://www.edsw.usyd.edu.au/future_students/postgraduate/
deg_MLST
PREREQUISITES: Higher Education – Yes
If yes, number of years or degree required – Bachelor's Degree
Teaching Certificate – No
ACCEPTANCE OF TRANSFERS – No
MASTER'S PROGRAM DURATION: Number of required Courses – 8
Comprehensive Exam Required? – No
Thesis Required? – Optional
Continuous Enrollment Required? – No

Other Requirements – 1 year full time, or 2 years part time. Research stream requires a dissertation

Does program culminate in a degree in the field of educational communications and technology? – Yes

Name of the degree – Master of Learning Science and Technology

Is this program part of another degree, certificate, or diploma? – No

OTHER PROGRAMS in educational technology or instructional development fields: Doctorate Program available? – PhD

Doctorate URL – http://coco.edfac.usyd.edu.au/Learn/PhD

Program Content – Master's degree

Program Content URL – http://coco.edfac.usyd.edu.au/Learn/Postgraduate/Courses

Name of Institution – University of Calgary

Name of Program within institution – Educational Technology

Title/Degree as it appears on official certificate or diploma – Specialization in Educational Technology

Name & Title of person administering program – Dr. Michele Jacobsen

Address – 940 Education Tower, 2500 University Drive NW, Calgary, AB, T2N1N, Canada

Telephone Number – 403-220-5675

Fax Number – 403-282-3005

E-Mail – gder@ucalgary.ca

Institution's home page – http://external.educ.ucalgary.ca/gder/

Admittance URL – http://external.educ.ucalgary.ca/gder/technology.html

PREREQUISITES: Higher Education – Yes

If yes, number of years or degree required – Bachelor

Teaching Certificate – No

Other requirement – Industry and/or professional experience

ACCEPTANCE OF TRANSFERS – Yes

MASTER'S PROGRAM DURATION: Number of required Courses – 12

Number of weeks long – 14

Comprehensive Exam Required? – No

Thesis Required? – No

Continuous Enrollment Required? – Yes

Other Requirements – A capstone, exit project - multiple options for completion

Does program culminate in a degree in the field of educational communications and technology? – Yes

Name of the degree – Master of Education, Specialization in Educational Technology

Is this program part of another degree, certificate, or diploma? – No

OTHER PROGRAMS in educational technology or instructional development fields: Certificate Program available? – Yes

Certificate URL – http://external.educ.ucalgary.ca/gder/htdocs/programs

Doctorate Program available? – PhD
Doctorate URL – http://external.educ.ucalgary.ca/gder/padmit.html
Program Content – Master's degree
Program Content URL – http://external.educ.ucalgary.ca/gder/technology.html

Name of Institution – Athabasca University
Name of Program within institution – Master of Distance Education
Title/Degree as it appears on official certificate or diploma – Master of Distance Education
Name & Title of person administering program – Bob Spencer
Address – 1 University Drive, Athabasca, AB, T9S3A3, Canada,
Telephone Number – 780-675-6238
Fax – 780-675-6170
E-Mail – bobs@athabascau.ca
Institution's home page – http://www.athabascau.ca
Admittance URL – http://www.athabascau.ca/calendar/grad/distance_01_01. html
PREREQUISITES: Higher Education – No
If yes, number of years or degree required – undergraduate degree
Teaching Certificate – No
ACCEPTANCE OF TRANSFERS – Yes
MASTER'S PROGRAM DURATION: Number of required Courses – 14
Number of weeks long – 13
Comprehensive Exam Required? – Yes
Thesis Required? – Optional
Continuous Enrollment Required? – Yes
Other Requirements – minimum of 2 courses a year part time
Does program culminate in a degree in the field of educational communications and technology? – No
Name of the degree – Master of Distance Education
Is this program part of another degree, certificate, or diploma? – Yes
If yes, name of the degree, certificate, or diploma – Graduate Diploma in Distance Education (Technology)
OTHER PROGRAMS in educational technology or instructional development fields: Certificate Program available? – Yes
Certificate URL – http://cde.athabascau.ca/programs/agddet.htm
Specialist Program available? – No
Undergraduate Program available? – No
Doctorate Program available? – No
Program Content – Master's degree
Program Content URL – http://cde.athabascau.ca/index.htm

Name of Institution – University of British Columbia
Name of Program within institution – Master of Educational Technology

Title/Degree as it appears on official certificate or diploma – Master of Educational Technology

Name & Title of person administering program – David Roy

Address – 1304-2125 Main Mall, Vancouver, BC, V6T1Z4, Canada

Telephone Number – 604-822-2013

Fax – 604-822-2015,

E-Mail – david.roy@ubc.ca

Institution's home page – http://www.ubc.ca

PREREQUISITES: Higher Education – No

If yes, number of years or degree required – 4-year bachelor's degree, depending on country

Teaching Certificate – No

ACCEPTANCE OF TRANSFERS – Yes

MASTER'S PROGRAM DURATION: Number of required Courses – 10

Number of weeks long – 13

Comprehensive Exam Required? – No

Thesis Required? – No

Continuous Enrollment Required? – No

Does program culminate in a degree in the field of educational communications and technology? – Yes

Name of the degree – Master of Educational Technology

Is this program part of another degree, certificate, or diploma? – No

OTHER PROGRAMS in educational technology or instructional development fields: Certificate Program available? – Yes

Certificate URL – http://www.met.ubc.ca

Specialist Program available? – No

Undergraduate Program available? – No

Doctorate Program available? – No

Program Content – Master's degree

Program Content URL – http://www.met.ubc.ca

Name of Institution – University of British Columbia

Name of Program within institution – Master of Educational Technology

Title/Degree as it appears on official certificate or diploma – Master of Educational Technology

Name & Title of person administering program – Dr. Jim Gaskell, Associate Dean

Address – 2125 Main Mall, Vancouver, BC, V6T1Z, Canada

Telephone Number – 604 822 2013

Fax – 604 822 2015

E-Mail – eplt.educ@ubc.ca

Institution's home page – http://www.ubc.ca

Admittance URL – http://www.met.ubc.ca

PREREQUISITES: Higher Education – Yes

If yes, number of years or degree required – Four-Year Bachelor's Required

Teaching Certificate – No
ACCEPTANCE OF TRANSFERS – Yes
MASTER'S PROGRAM DURATION: Number of required Courses – 10
Number of weeks long – 13
Comprehensive Exam Required? – No
Thesis Required? – No
Continuous Enrollment Required? – Yes
Does program culminate in a degree in the field of educational communications and technology? – Yes
Name of the degree – Master of Educational Technology
Is this program part of another degree, certificate, or diploma? – No
OTHER PROGRAMS in educational technology or instructional development fields: Certificate Program available? – Yes
Certificate URL – http://www.met.ubc.ca,
Program Content – Master's degree
Program Content URL – http://www.met.ubc.ca

Name of Institution – University of New Brunswick
Name of Program within institution – Masters of Education in Instructional Design
Title/Degree as it appears on official certificate or diploma – Masters of Education in Instructional Design
Name & Title of person administering program – Dr. Ellen Rose
Address – Box 4400, Fredericton, NB, E3B5A3, Canada
Telephone Number – (506) 452-6125
Fax – (506) 453-3569
E-Mail – erose@unb.ca
Institution's home page – http://www.unb.ca
PREREQUISITES: Higher Education – Yes
If yes, number of years or degree required – Bachelor of Education
Teaching Certificate – No
ACCEPTANCE OF TRANSFERS – Yes
MASTER'S PROGRAM DURATION: Number of required Courses – 12
Number of weeks long – 13
Comprehensive Exam Required? – No
Thesis Required? – Optional,
Continuous Enrollment Required? – Yes
Does program culminate in a degree in the field of educational communications and technology? – Yes
Name of the degree – Master of Education in Instructional Design
Is this program part of another degree, certificate, or diploma? – No
OTHER PROGRAMS in educational technology or instructional development fields: Certificate Program available? – No
Specialist Program available? – No
Undergraduate Program available? – No

Doctorate Program available? – PhD
Program Content – Master's degree
Program Content URL – http://www.unbf.ca/education/grad/med.htm

Name of Institution – Concordia University
Name of Program within institution – Educational Technology
Title/Degree as it appears on official certificate or diploma – M.A. and Ph.D.
Name & Title of person administering program – Dr. Dennis Dicks
Address – 1455 demaisonneuve Blvd. W., Montreal, QC, PQ, H3G, Canada
Telephone Number – 514-848-2424 x2030
Fax – 514-848-4520
E-Mail – anne@education.concordia.ca,
Admittance URL – http://doe.concordia.ca
PREREQUISITES: Higher Education – No
Teaching Certificate – No
ACCEPTANCE OF TRANSFERS – Yes
MASTER'S PROGRAM DURATION: Number of required Semesters – 4
Number of weeks long – 13
Comprehensive Exam Required? – No
Thesis Required? – Optional
Continuous Enrollment Required? – No
Does program culminate in a degree in the field of educational communications and technology? – Yes
Name of the degree – M.A. and Ph.D.
Is this program part of another degree, certificate, or diploma? – Yes
OTHER PROGRAMS in educational technology or instructional development fields: Certificate Program available? – No
Specialist Program available? – No
Undergraduate Program available? – No
Doctorate Program available? – PhD
Doctorate URL – http://doe.concordia.ca
Program Content – Master's degree

Name of Institution – University of Saskatchewan
Name of Program within institution – Educational Communications and Technology
Title/Degree as it appears on official certificate or diploma – Master of Education
Name & Title of person administering program – Richard A. Schwier
Address – 28 Campus Drive, Saskatoon, SK, s7n0x, Canada
Telephone Number – 306-966-7558
Fax – 306-966-7658
E-Mail – richard.schwier@usask.ca
Institution's home page – http://www.edct.ca
Admittance URL – http://www.edct.ca

PREREQUISITES: Higher Education – No
If yes, number of years or degree required – 4 year bachelor of education or equivalent
Teaching Certificate – Yes
ACCEPTANCE OF TRANSFERS – Yes
MASTER'S PROGRAM DURATION: Number of required Courses – 12
Number of weeks long – 14
Comprehensive Exam Required? – No
Thesis Required? – Optional
Continuous Enrollment Required? – No
Other Requirements – minimum G.P.A. of 70% (B average)
Does program culminate in a degree in the field of educational communications and technology? – Yes
Name of the degree – Master of Education
Is this program part of another degree, certificate, or diploma? – No
OTHER PROGRAMS in educational technology or instructional development fields: Certificate Program available? – No
Specialist Program available? – No
Undergraduate Program available? – No
Doctorate Program available? – No
Program Content – Master's degree
Program Content URL – http://www.edct.ca

Name of Institution – Hebei University
Name of Program within institution – Educational Technology
Title/Degree as it appears on official certificate or diploma – Master of Education, Bachelor of Science
Name & Title of person administering program – Prof. Lixin Zhang
Address – 180 Wusi Road, Baoding, Baoding, 071002, China
Telephone Number – 86-312-5079387
Fax – 86-312-5079387
E-Mail – Zhang_et@hotmail.com
Institution's home page – http://hbu.edu.cn
Admittance URL – http://ce.hbu.cn
PREREQUISITES: Higher Education – Yes
If yes, number of years or degree required – 4
ACCEPTANCE OF TRANSFERS – Yes
MASTER'S PROGRAM DURATION: Number of required Semesters – 6
Number of weeks long – 18
Comprehensive Exam Required? – Yes
Thesis Required? – Yes
Continuous Enrollment Required? – Yes
Does program culminate in a degree in the field of educational communications and technology? – No
Name of the degree – Master of Educational Technology

Is this program part of another degree, certificate, or diploma? – Yes
If yes, name of the degree, certificate, or diploma – Master of Education
OTHER PROGRAMS in educational technology or instructional development fields: Program Content – Master's degree
Program Content URL – http://ce.hbu.cn/zhuanyejieshao.htm

Name of Institution – Beijing Normal University
Name of Program within institution – Educational Technology
Title/Degree as it appears on official certificate or diploma – Ph. D or Ed. D
Name & Title of person administering program – Prof. Ronghuai HUANG
Address – 19 Xinjiekouwai St., Beijing, 100875, China
Telephone Number – +8610 5880 9054
Fax – +8610 5880 0641
E-Mail – huangrh@bnu.edu.cn
Institution's home page – http://www.bnu.edu.cn
MASTER'S PROGRAM DURATION: Comprehensive Exam Required? Yes, **Thesis Required?** – No
Continuous Enrollment Required? –Yes
Does program culminate in a degree in the field of educational communications and technology? – Yes
Is this program part of another degree, certificate, or diploma? – Yes
OTHER PROGRAMS in educational technology or instructional development fields: Program Content – Master's degree

Name of Institution – Educational Technology Institute of Tsinghua University
Name of Program within institution – Master Program of Educational Technology
Title/Degree as it appears on official certificate or diploma – Master of Education
Name & Title of person administering program – Prof. Jiangang Cheng
Address – Tsinghua University, Haidian District, Beijing, Beijing, 100084, China
Telephone Number – 0086-10-62772006
Fax – 0086-10-62789900
E-Mail – chengjg@tsinghua.edu.cn
Institution's home page – http://166.111.92.7
PREREQUISITES: Higher Education – No
If yes, number of years or degree required – 4
Teaching Certificate – No
ACCEPTANCE OF TRANSFERS – No
MASTER'S PROGRAM DURATION: Number of required Semesters – 4
Comprehensive Exam Required? – Yes
Thesis Required? – Yes
Continuous Enrollment Required? – Yes

Does program culminate in a degree in the field of educational communications and technology? – Yes

Name of the degree – Master of Educational Technology

Is this program part of another degree, certificate, or diploma? – Yes

If yes, name of the degree, certificate, or diploma – Master of Education

OTHER PROGRAMS in educational technology or instructional development fields: Program Content – Master's degree

Program Content URL – http://166.111.92.7

Name of Institution – Zhejiang University

Name of Program within institution – Educational Technology

Title/Degree as it appears on official certificate or diploma – MSE, ME, MS

Name & Title of person administering program – Qunli Sheng

Address – 280 Tainmushan Rd, Xixi Campus, Hangzhou, 310012, China

Telephone Number – 86-571-88273656

Fax – 86-571-88273659

E-Mail – bill85@mail.hz.zj.cn

Institution's home page – http://www.ced.zju.edu.cn/jyxx/

Admittance URL – http://www.ced.zju.edu.cn/jyxx/

PREREQUISITES: Higher Education – No

If yes, number of years or degree required – 4 yrs, Bachelor

Teaching Certificate – No

ACCEPTANCE OF TRANSFERS – Yes

MASTER'S PROGRAM DURATION: Comprehensive Exam Required? – Yes

Thesis Required? – Yes

Continuous Enrollment Required? – No

Does program culminate in a degree in the field of educational communications and technology? – No

Is this program part of another degree, certificate, or diploma? – No

OTHER PROGRAMS in educational technology or instructional development fields: Certificate Program available? – No

Specialist Program available? – No

Undergraduate Program available? – Yes

Undergraduate URL – http://www.ced.zju.edu.cn/jyxx/

Doctorate Program available? – No

Program Content – Master's degree

Program Content URL – http://www.ced.zju.edu.cn/jyxx/

Name of Institution – School of ICT in Education, South China Normal University

Name of Program within institution – Department of Educational Technology

Title/Degree as it appears on official certificate or diploma – PhD. MA, BA, EDM

Address – ShiPai, Guangzhou, 510631, China
Telephone Number – +86-(0)20-85213841
Fax – +86-(0)20-85213841
E-Mail – ferc21cn@hotmail.com
Institution's home page – http://et.scnu.edu.cn/
Admittance URL – http://et.scnu.edu.cn/
PREREQUISITES: Higher Education – No
If yes, number of years or degree required – 4
Teaching Certificate – No
ACCEPTANCE OF TRANSFERS – Yes
MASTER'S PROGRAM DURATION: Number of required Semesters – 6
Number of weeks long – 5
Comprehensive Exam Required? – Yes
Thesis Required? – Yes
Continuous Enrollment Required? – Yes
Does program culminate in a degree in the field of educational communi-cations and technology? – Yes
Is this program part of another degree, certificate, or diploma? – Yes
OTHER PROGRAMS in educational technology or instructional develop-ment fields: Certificate Program available? – Yes
Certificate URL – http://et.scnu.edu.cn/
Specialist Program available? – Yes
Specialist URL – http://et.scnu.edu.cn/
Undergraduate Program available? – Yes
Undergraduate URL – http://et.scnu.edu.cn/
Doctorate Program available? – EdD
Doctorate URL – http://et.scnu.edu.cn/
Program Content – Master's degree
Program Content URL – http://et.scnu.edu.cn/

Name of Institution – Université de Poitiers
Name of Program within institution – Master, Ingéniérie des Medias pour l'Education
Title/Degree as it appears on official certificate or diploma – Master
Name & Title of person administering program – Jean-François CERISIER
Address – 95 Avenue du Recteur Pineau, Poitiers, 86022, France
Telephone Number – + 33 (0)5 49 45 32 26
Fax – + 33 (0) 549 45 32 30
E-Mail – master-ime@univ-poitiers.fr
Institution's home page – http://spip.univ-poitiers.fr/masterime
PREREQUISITES: Higher Education – Yes
If yes, number of years or degree required – completion of three years prior to entry in 1st yr
MASTER'S PROGRAM DURATION: Number of required Semesters – 4

Number of weeks long – 40
Comprehensive Exam Required? – Yes
Thesis Required? – Yes
Continuous Enrollment Required? – Yes
Does program culminate in a degree in the field of educational communications and technology? – Yes
Name of the degree – Master Ingéniérie des Medias pour l'Education
Is this program part of another degree, certificate, or diploma? – No
OTHER PROGRAMS in educational technology or instructional development fields: Certificate Program available? – Yes
Certificate URL – http://spip.univ-poitiers.fr/masterime
Undergraduate Program available? – No
Doctorate Program available? – No
Program Content – Master's degree
Program Content URL – http://spip.univ-poitiers.fr/masterime/

Name of Institution – Freie Universitaet Berlin
Name of Program within institution – Qualification Program Media Pedagogy and Media Psychology (including eLearning)
Title/Degree as it appears on official certificate or diploma – Educational Media Specialist
Name & Title of person administering program – Ludwig J. Issing, Prof. Dr.
Address – Malteserstr. 74-100, Berlin, D-12307, Germany
Telephone Number – ++49 30 838 70403
Fax – ++49 30 838 70741
E-Mail – cmr@cmr.fu-berlin.de
Institution's home page – http://cmr.fu-berlin.de
Admittance URL – http://cmr.fu-berlin.de/
PREREQUISITES: Higher Education – Yes
If yes, number of years or degree required – 3
Teaching Certificate – No
Other requirement – BA
ACCEPTANCE OF TRANSFERS – Yes
MASTER'S PROGRAM DURATION: Number of required Semesters – 3
Number of weeks long – 14
Comprehensive Exam Required? – No
Thesis Required? – Yes
Continuous Enrollment Required? – Yes
Other Requirements – admittance only for students registered at the Freie Universitaet Berlin for a major study subject
Does program culminate in a degree in the field of educational communications and technology? – Yes
Name of the degree – Certificate
Is this program part of another degree, certificate, or diploma? – Yes

If yes, name of the degree, certificate, or diploma – Diploma or BA/MA in Education, Psychology, or Communications

OTHER PROGRAMS in educational technology or instructional development fields: Certificate Program available? – No
Specialist Program available? – Yes
Undergraduate Program available? – No
Doctorate Program available? – PhD
Program Content – Master's degree
Program Content URL – http://cmr.fu-berlin.de/

Name of Institution – The Chinese University of Hong Kong
Name of Program within institution – Master of Arts (Information Technology in Education)
Title/Degree as it appears on official certificate or diploma – Master of Arts
Name & Title of person administering program – Prof. Fong-Lok Lee
Address – Faculty of Education, The Chinese University of Hong Kong, Shatin, 0000, Hong Kong
Telephone Number – 852 26096977
Fax – 852 26035622
E-Mail – fllee@cuhk.edu.hk
Institution's home page – http://caite.fed.cuhk.edu.hk/
Admittance URL – http://www.fed.cuhk.edu.hk/course/programme/med.html
PREREQUISITES: Higher Education – Yes
If yes, number of years or degree required – Bachelor
Teaching Certificate – Yes
Other requirement – Postgraduate Diploma of Education or equivalent
ACCEPTANCE OF TRANSFERS – Yes
MASTER'S PROGRAM DURATION: Number of required Semesters – 4
Comprehensive Exam Required? – No
Thesis Required? – Optional
Continuous Enrollment Required? – No
Does program culminate in a degree in the field of educational communications and technology? – Yes
Name of the degree – PhD or EdD
Is this program part of another degree, certificate, or diploma? – No
OTHER PROGRAMS in educational technology or instructional development fields: Certificate Program available? – No
Specialist Program available? – Yes
Specialist URL – http://www.fed.cuhk.edu.hk/adeit/
Program Content – Master's degree
Program Content URL – http://www.fed.cuhk.edu.hk/mait/

Name of Institution – The University of Hong Kong
Name of Program within institution – Information Technology in Education

Title/Degree as it appears on official certificate or diploma – Master of Science in Information Technology in Education

Name & Title of person administering program – Dr Bob Fox

Address – Pokfulam Road, Hong Kong, HK, Hong Kong

Telephone Number – 852-22415856

Fax – 852-25170075

E-Mail – mite@cite.hku.hk

Institution's home page – http://msc.cite.hku.hk/

PREREQUISITES: Higher Education – No

If yes, number of years or degree required – Bachelor

Teaching Certificate – No

ACCEPTANCE OF TRANSFERS – Yes

MASTER'S PROGRAM DURATION: Number of required Terms – 3

Comprehensive Exam Required? – No

Thesis Required? – Optional

Continuous Enrollment Required? – No

Does program culminate in a degree in the field of educational communications and technology? – Yes

Name of the degree – Master of Science in Information Technology in Education

Is this program part of another degree, certificate, or diploma? – No

OTHER PROGRAMS in educational technology or instructional development fields: Certificate Program available? – No

Specialist Program available? – Yes

Specialist URL – http://www.hku.hk/education/pcaes.htm

Undergraduate Program available? – No

Doctorate Program available? – EdD

Doctorate URL – http://www.hku.hk/education/research/EdD.htm

Program Content – Master's degree

Name of Institution – Utrecht University

Name of Program within institution – Learning in Interaction

Title/Degree as it appears on official certificate or diploma – Master of Science

Name & Title of person administering program – Prof. dr. Paul A. Kirschner

Address – Box 80.140, Utrecht, 3508TC, Netherlands

Telephone Number – +31 (0)30 253 4962

Fax – +31 (0)30 253 2352

E-Mail – p.a.kirschner@fss.uu.nl

Institution's home page – http://www.uu.nl

Admittance URL – http://www.internationalmasters.uu.nl/

PREREQUISITES: Higher Education – No

If yes, number of years or degree required – BA or BSc in related field

Teaching Certificate – No

Other requirement – For non-native English speakers - TOEFL score of 580 (computer score 237)

ACCEPTANCE OF TRANSFERS – Yes

MASTER'S PROGRAM DURATION: Number of required Semesters – 4

Comprehensive Exam Required? – No

Thesis Required? – Yes

Continuous Enrollment Required? – Yes

Other Requirements – GPA of at least 3.25 knowledge and skills in reading, writing, and speaking English knowledge of multivariate analysis techniques

Does program culminate in a degree in the field of educational communications and technology? – Yes

Is this program part of another degree, certificate, or diploma? – Yes

OTHER PROGRAMS in educational technology or instructional development fields: Certificate Program available? – No

Specialist Program available? – No

Undergraduate Program available? – Yes

Undergraduate URL – http://www.studiekiezers.nl/index.cfm/site/Bachelor/pageid/7FA95A73-3048-275E-60165A8E5273F868/index.cfm

Doctorate Program available? – PhD

Doctorate URL – http://www.fss.uu.nl/graduateschool/EdSci

Program Content – Master's degree

Program Content URL – http://www.fss.uu.nl/graduateschool/EdSci

Name of Institution – Adam Mickiewicz University

Name of Program within institution – Media Education

Title/Degree as it appears on official certificate or diploma – M.A. (Mgr) of Pedagogy; in an area of media education

Name & Title of person administering program – Prof. Waclaw Strykowski

Address – Slowackiego 20, Poznan, 60-82, Poland

Telephone Number – +48 (61) 8292- 801

Fax – +48 (61) 8411-394

E-Mail – ztka@amu.edu.pl

Institution's home page – http://www.amu.edu.pl/~edu

PREREQUISITES: Higher Education – Yes

Teaching Certificate – Yes

ACCEPTANCE OF TRANSFERS – Yes

MASTER'S PROGRAM DURATION: Number of required Semesters – 5

Number of weeks long – 75

Comprehensive Exam Required? – Yes

Thesis Required? – No

Continuous Enrollment Required? – Yes

Does program culminate in a degree in the field of educational communications and technology? – Yes

Name of the degree – A teacher of computer science

Is this program part of another degree, certificate, or diploma? – No

OTHER PROGRAMS in educational technology or instructional development fields: Doctorate Program available? – EdD
Program Content – Master's degree
Program Content URL – http://elex.amu.edu.pl/ects/wse/ang/edu-se/edu-se.htm

Name of Institution – Taganrog State Pedagogical Institute
Name of Program within institution – Media Education
Title/Degree as it appears on official certificate or diploma – University Diploma and Ed.D.
Name & Title of person administering program – Prof. Dr. Alexander Fedorov
Address – Iniciativnaya, 48, Taganrog, media, Russian Federation
Telephone Number – +7(86344)21753
Fax – +7(86344)21802
E-Mail – tgpi@mail.ru
Institution's home page – http://www.tgpi.ttn.ru
Admittance URL – http://www.tgpi.ttn.ru
PREREQUISITES: Higher Education – Yes
If yes, number of years or degree required – 5 (for University diploma) + 3 (for Ed.D.)
Teaching Certificate – Yes
ACCEPTANCE OF TRANSFERS – No
MASTER'S PROGRAM DURATION: Number of required Semesters – No
Number of weeks long – No
Comprehensive Exam Required? – No
Thesis Required? – No
Continuous Enrollment Required? – No
Other Requirements – No
Does program culminate in a degree in the field of educational communications and technology? – No
Name of the degree – No
Is this program part of another degree, certificate, or diploma? – No
OTHER PROGRAMS in educational technology or instructional development fields: Certificate Program available? – Yes
Certificate URL – http://www.tgpi.ttn.ru
Specialist Program available? – Yes
Specialist URL – http://www.tgpi.ttn.ru
Undergraduate Program available? – Yes
Undergraduate URL – http://www.tgpi.ttn.ru
Doctorate Program available? – EdD
Doctorate URL – http://www.tgpi.ttn.ru
Program Content – Master's degree

Name of Institution – Taganrog State Pedagogical Institute
Name of Program within institution – teachers for schools
Title/Degree as it appears on official certificate or diploma – specialist
(teacher, educator in humanities, languages, etc.), BA, MA, Ed.D.
Name & Title of person administering program – Rector Prof. Dr. Vitaly
Popov
Address – Iniciativna, 48, Taganrog, 347936, Russian Federation
Telephone Number – 7(8634)601812
Fax – 7(8634)605397
E-Mail – rector@tgpi.ttn.ru
Institution's home page – http://www.tgpi.org.ru
Admittance URL – http://www.tgpittn.ru
PREREQUISITES: Higher Education – No
If yes, number of years or degree required – diploma of school (for BA) univ.
dip. (for MA)
Teaching Certificate – No
ACCEPTANCE OF TRANSFERS – Yes
MASTER'S PROGRAM DURATION: Number of required Semesters – 8
Number of weeks long – 16
Comprehensive Exam Required? – Yes
Thesis Required? – No
Continuous Enrollment Required? – Yes
**Does program culminate in a degree in the field of educational communi-
cations and technology?** – Yes
Is this program part of another degree, certificate, or diploma? – Yes
**OTHER PROGRAMS in educational technology or instructional develop-
ment fields: Certificate Program available?** – No
Specialist Program available? – Yes
Undergraduate Program available? – No
Doctorate Program available? – PhD
Program Content – Master's degree

Name of Institution – National Institute of Education
Name of Program within institution – Masters of Arts (Instructional Design
Technology)
Title/Degree as it appears on official certificate or diploma – Masters of Arts
(Instructional Design Technology)
Name & Title of person administering program – A/P Tan Seng Chee
Address – 1 Nanyang Walk, Singapore, SG, Singapore
Telephone Number – 65-6790-3133
E-Mail – sctan@nie.edu.sg
Institution's home page – http://www.nie.edu.sg
Admittance URL – http://eduweb.nie.edu.sg/programme/maidt/index.htm
PREREQUISITES: Higher Education – Yes

If yes, number of years or degree required – Good degree with three years of work experience

Teaching Certificate – No

ACCEPTANCE OF TRANSFERS – No

MASTER'S PROGRAM DURATION: Number of required Semesters – 4

Number of weeks long – 52

Comprehensive Exam Required? – Yes

Thesis Required? – Optional

Continuous Enrollment Required? – Yes

Other Requirements – Part-time

Does program culminate in a degree in the field of educational communications and technology? – Yes

Name of the degree – Masters of Arts (Instructional Design Technology)

Is this program part of another degree, certificate, or diploma? – No

OTHER PROGRAMS in educational technology or instructional development fields: Program Content – Master's degree

Program Content URL – http://eduweb.nie.edu.sg/programme/maidt/index.htm

Name of Institution – Ewha Womans University

Name of Program within institution – Educational Technology

Title/Degree as it appears on official certificate or diploma – B.A., M.A., Ph.D.

Address – 11-1 Daehyun-dong, Seodaemun-gu, Seoul, 120750, Country, South Korea

Telephone Number – +82-2-3277-2670

Fax – +82-2-3277-2728

E-Mail – et2670@hanmail.net

Institution's home page – http://home.ewha.ac.kr/~et

MASTER'S PROGRAM DURATION: Number of required Semesters – 4

Number of weeks long – 16

Comprehensive Exam Required? – Yes

Thesis Required? – Yes

Continuous Enrollment Required? – Yes

Does program culminate in a degree in the field of educational communications and technology? – Yes

Name of the degree – M.A.

Is this program part of another degree, certificate, or diploma? – No

OTHER PROGRAMS in educational technology or instructional development fields: Certificate Program available? – No

Specialist Program available? – No

Undergraduate Program available? – Yes

Undergraduate URL – http://home.ewha.ac.kr/~et

Doctorate Program available? – PhD

Doctorate URL – http://home.ewha.ac.kr/~et

Program Content – Master's degree

Program Content URL – http://home.ewha.ac.kr/~et

Name of Program within institution – Educational Technology
Title/Degree as it appears on official certificate or diploma – Education
Name & Title of person administering program – Insook Lee/Associate Professor
Address – 98 Gunja dong, Gwangjin-gu, Seoul, 143-7, South Korea
Telephone Number – 82-2-3408-3304
Fax – 82-2-3408-3304
E-Mail – edudpt@sejong.ac.kr
Institution's home page – http://graduate.sejong.ac.kr/grad/
Admittance URL – http://graduate.sejong.ac.kr/grad/
PREREQUISITES: Higher Education – Yes
If yes, number of years or degree required – 4
Teaching Certificate – No
ACCEPTANCE OF TRANSFERS – No
MASTER'S PROGRAM DURATION: Number of required Semesters – 2
Number of weeks long – 16
Comprehensive Exam Required? Yes
Thesis Required? Yes
Continuous Enrollment Required? No
Does program culminate in a degree in the field of educational communications and technology? No
Is this program part of another degree, certificate, or diploma? – Yes
If yes, name of the degree, certificate, or diploma – education
OTHER PROGRAMS in educational technology or instructional development fields: Certificate Program available? – No
Specialist Program available? – No
Undergraduate Program available? – Yes
Undergraduate URL – http://graduate.sejong.ac.kr/grad/
Doctorate Program available? – EdD
Doctorate URL – http://graduate.sejong.ac.kr/grad/
Program Content – Master's degree
Program Content URL – http://graduate.sejong.ac.kr/grad/

Name of Institution – Hanyang University
Name of Program within institution – Educational Technology
Title/Degree as it appears on official certificate or diploma – B.A., M.A., Ph.D.
Address – 17 Haendang-dong Seondong-gu, Seoul, 133791, South Korea
Telephone Number – +82-2-2220-1120
Fax – +82-2-2296-2675
E-Mail – sanghee@hanyang.ac.kr
Institution's home page – http://education.hanyang.ac.kr/
MASTER'S PROGRAM DURATION: Number of required Semesters – 4
Number of weeks long – 16
Comprehensive Exam Required? – Yes
Thesis Required? – Yes

Continuous Enrollment Required? – Yes
Does program culminate in a degree in the field of educational communications and technology? – Yes
Name of the degree – M.A
Is this program part of another degree, certificate, or diploma? – No
OTHER PROGRAMS in educational technology or instructional development fields: Certificate Program available? – No
Specialist Program available? – No
Undergraduate Program available? – Yes
Undergraduate URL – http://education.hanyang.ac.kr/
Doctorate Program available? – PhD
Doctorate URL – http://education.hanyang.ac.kr/
Program Content – Master's degree
Program Content URL – http://education.hanyang.ac.kr/

Name of Institution – Keimyung University
Name of Program within institution – Educational Technology
Title/Degree as it appears on official certificate or diploma – MA, PH.D.
Name & Title of person administering program – Wooyong Eom
Address – 1000, Shindang-Dong, Dalseo-Gu, Daegu, 704-701, South Korea
Telephone Number – 82-53-580-5962
Fax – 82-53-580-5162
E-Mail – weom@kmu.ac.kr
Institution's home page – http://education.kmu.ac.kr
Admittance URL – http://www.kmu.ac.kr
PREREQUISITES: Higher Education – Yes
If yes, number of years or degree required – 4
Teaching Certificate – Yes
ACCEPTANCE OF TRANSFERS – Yes
MASTER'S PROGRAM DURATION: Number of required Semesters – 4
Comprehensive Exam Required? – Yes
Thesis Required? – Yes
Continuous Enrollment Required? – No
Does program culminate in a degree in the field of educational communications and technology? – Yes
Name of the degree – MA
Is this program part of another degree, certificate, or diploma? No
OTHER PROGRAMS in educational technology or instructional development fields: Certificate Program available? – No
Specialist Program available? – No
Undergraduate Program available? – No
Doctorate Program available? – PhD
Program Content – Master's degree
Program Content URL – http://education.kmu.ac.kr

Name of Institution – Andong National University
Name of Program within institution – Department of Educational Technology
Title/Degree as it appears on official certificate or diploma – Ph. D., M. Ed., B. Ed
Name & Title of person administering program – Dr. Yong-Chil Yang
Address – 388 Songchung-dong, Andong, Kyungbuk 760-749, 76074, South Korea
Telephone Number – +82-54-820-5580
Fax – +82-54-823-1624
E-Mail – ycyang@andong.ac.kr
Institution's home page – http://edutech.andong.ac.kr/~try/2004-3/
Admittance URL – http://www.andong.ac.kr/
PREREQUISITES: Higher Education – Yes
If yes, number of years or degree required – 4 years for B. Ed.
Teaching Certificate – Yes
ACCEPTANCE OF TRANSFERS – Yes
MASTER'S PROGRAM DURATION: Number of required Semesters – 4
Number of weeks long – 15
Comprehensive Exam Required? – Yes
Thesis Required? – Yes
Continuous Enrollment Required? – No
Does program culminate in a degree in the field of educational communications and technology? – No
Name of the degree – Ph.D
Is this program part of another degree, certificate, or diploma? – Yes
If yes, name of the degree, certificate, or diploma – Ph. D. in Educational Technology
OTHER PROGRAMS in educational technology or instructional development fields: Certificate Program available? – No
Specialist Program available? – No
Undergraduate Program available? – Yes
Undergraduate URL – http://edutech.andong.ac.kr/~try/2004-3/
Doctorate Program available? – PhD
Doctorate URL – http://edutech.andong.ac.kr/~try/2004-3/
Program Content – Master's degree
Program Content URL – http://edutech.andong.ac.kr/~try/2004-3/

Name of Institution – University of Balearic Islands
Name of Program within institution – MÁSTER INTERUNIVERSITARIO EN TECNOLOGÍA EDUCATIVA
Title/Degree as it appears on official certificate or diploma – Master en tecnologia Educativa
Name & Title of person administering program – Dr. Jesus Salinas
Address – Cta. Valldemossa km 7,5, Palma de Mallorca, 07122, Spain

Telephone Number – 34 971173000
Fax – 34 971173190
E-Mail – jesus.salinas@uib.es
Institution's home page – http://www.uib.es
Admittance URL – http://gte.uib.es/master/web/index1.htm
PREREQUISITES: Higher Education – Yes
If yes, number of years or degree required – 4
Teaching Certificate – Yes
ACCEPTANCE OF TRANSFERS – Yes
MASTER'S PROGRAM DURATION: Number of required Semesters – 4
Comprehensive Exam Required? – No
Thesis Required? – Optional
Continuous Enrollment Required? – Yes
Does program culminate in a degree in the field of educational communications and technology? – Yes
Is this program part of another degree, certificate, or diploma? – No
OTHER PROGRAMS in educational technology or instructional development fields: Certificate Program available? – No
Doctorate Program available? – EdD
Doctorate URL – http://www.sre.urv/doctorado/
Program Content – Master's degree
Program Content URL – http://gte.uib.es/master/web/index1.htm

Name of Institution – University of Geneva
Name of Program within institution – MALTT
Title/Degree as it appears on official certificate or diploma – Master of Science in Learning and Teaching Technologies
Name & Title of person administering program – Prof. Dr. Mireille Bétrancourt
Address – 54 route des Acacias, Carouge, 1227, Switzerland
Telephone Number – 41 22 379 9375
Fax – 41 22 379 9379
E-Mail – Mireille.Betrancourt@tecfa.unige.ch
Institution's home page – http://tecfa.unige.ch/
Admittance URL – http://tecfa.unige.ch/maltt
PREREQUISITES: Higher Education – Yes
If yes, number of years or degree required – bachelor (3 years, 180 ECTS or equivalent)
Teaching Certificate – No
Other requirement – Candidates have to present a project (2-3 pages), show some IT skills
ACCEPTANCE OF TRANSFERS – Yes
MASTER'S PROGRAM DURATION: Number of required Semesters – 4
Number of weeks long – 15
Comprehensive Exam Required? – No

Thesis Required? – Yes

Continuous Enrollment Required? – Yes

Other Requirements – This program is organized in "blended" format (3x1 weeks/semester). Being able to attend these sessions. Understand french (important papers and MA thesis can be done in English)

Does program culminate in a degree in the field of educational communications and technology? – Yes

Name of the degree – Master of Science in Learning and Teaching Technologies

Is this program part of another degree, certificate, or diploma? – No

OTHER PROGRAMS in educational technology or instructional development fields: Certificate Program available? – No

Specialist Program available? – No

Undergraduate Program available? – No

Doctorate Program available? – PhD

Program Content – Master's degree

Program Content URL – http://tecfa.unige.ch/maltt

Name of Institution – University of Lugano

Name of Program within institution – Master of Science in Communication, major in Education and Training

Title/Degree as it appears on official certificate or diploma – Master of Science in Communication, major in Education and Training

Name & Title of person administering program – Lorenzo Cantoni, Prof. & Luca Botturi, Ph.D.

Address – via G. Buffi 13, Lugano, 6900, Switzerland

Telephone Number – +41 91 912 46 74

Fax – +41 91 912 46 47

E-Mail – luca.botturi@lu.unisi.ch

Institution's home page – http://www.met.unisi.ch/en/index.htm

Admittance URL – http://www.unisi.ch/master-iscrizione.htm

PREREQUISITES: Higher Education – Yes

If yes, number of years or degree required – bachelor, 3 years

Teaching Certificate – No

ACCEPTANCE OF TRANSFERS – Yes

MASTER'S PROGRAM DURATION: Number of required Semesters – 4

Number of weeks long – 56

Comprehensive Exam Required? – No

Thesis Required? – Yes

Continuous Enrollment Required? – No

Does program culminate in a degree in the field of educational communications and technology? – Yes

Name of the degree – Master of Science in Communication, major in Education and Training

Is this program part of another degree, certificate, or diploma? – No

OTHER PROGRAMS in educational technology or instructional development fields: Doctorate Program available? – PhD
Doctorate URL – http://www.unisi.ch/en/index/formazione/phd.htm
Program Content –Master's degree
Program Content URL – http://www.met.unisi.ch/en/index.htm

Name of Institution – National Pingtung University of Education
Name of Program within institution – Educational Technology
Title/Degree as it appears on official certificate or diploma – M.Ed.
Name & Title of person administering program – Chung-wei Shen
Address – 4-18 Ming-seng Road, Pingtung, Taiwan
Telephone Number – (08)7236147
Fax – (08)7236147
E-Mail – cwshen@mail.npue.edu.tw
Institution's home page – http://et.npue.edu.tw
PREREQUISITES: Higher Education – Yes
Teaching Certificate – No
ACCEPTANCE OF TRANSFERS – Yes
MASTER'S PROGRAM DURATION: Number of required Courses – 38
Comprehensive Exam Required? – No
Thesis Required? – Yes
Continuous Enrollment Required? – No
Does program culminate in a degree in the field of educational communications and technology? – No
Is this program part of another degree, certificate, or diploma? – No
OTHER PROGRAMS in educational technology or instructional development fields: Certificate Program available? – No
Specialist Program available? – No
Undergraduate Program available? – No
Doctorate Program available? – No
Program Content – Master's degree

Name of Institution – National Chiayi University
Name of Program within institution – Graduate Institute of Educational Technology
Title/Degree as it appears on official certificate or diploma – M.Ed.
Name & Title of person administering program – Lin Ching Chen
Address – 85 Wenlong, Mingsuin, Chiayi Hsien, 62113, Taiwan
Telephone Number – 886-5-2263411, ext.1511
Fax – 886-5-2062328
E-Mail – lingin@mail.ncyu.edu.tw
Institution's home page – http://www.etech.ncyu.edu.tw
Admittance URL – http://www.ncyu.edu.tw
PREREQUISITES: Higher Education – Yes
Teaching Certificate – Yes

ACCEPTANCE OF TRANSFERS – No

MASTER'S PROGRAM DURATION: Number of required Semesters – 4

Comprehensive Exam Required? – No

Thesis Required? – Yes

Continuous Enrollment Required? – No

Does program culminate in a degree in the field of educational communications and technology? – Yes

Name of the degree – M.Ed.

Is this program part of another degree, certificate, or diploma? – No

OTHER PROGRAMS in educational technology or instructional development fields: Undergraduate Program available? – Yes

Undergraduate URL – http://www.etech.ncyu.edu.tw

Program Content – Master's degree

Program Content URL – http://www.etech.ncyu.edu.tw

Name of Institution – National Hsin-chu University of Education

Name of Program within institution – Graduate Institute of e-Learning Technology

Title/Degree as it appears on official certificate or diploma – Master of Education

Name & Title of person administering program – Chair, Ding-Ming Wang

Address – No. 521, Dan-Da Road, Hsin-chu City, 30014, Taiwan

Telephone Number – +886-3-521-3132~7900

Fax – +886-3-561-0207

E-Mail – elt@mail.nhcue.edu.tw

Institution's home page – http://www.nhcue.edu.tw/~elt/

Admittance URL – http://www.nhcue.edu.tw/

PREREQUISITES: Higher Education – No

If yes, number of years or degree required, Bachelor or Associate Bachelor

Teaching Certificate – No

ACCEPTANCE OF TRANSFERS – Yes

MASTER'S PROGRAM DURATION: Number of required Semesters – 4

Number of weeks long – 18

Comprehensive Exam Required? – No

Thesis Required? – Yes

Continuous Enrollment Required? – No

Does program culminate in a degree in the field of educational communications and technology? – No

Is this program part of another degree, certificate, or diploma? – No

OTHER PROGRAMS in educational technology or instructional development fields: Certificate Program available? – No

Specialist Program available? – No

Undergraduate Program available? – No

Doctorate Program available? – PhD

Doctorate URL – http://www.nhcue.edu.tw/%7Egdee/welcomenglish.htm

Program Content – Master's degree
Program Content URL – http://www.nhcue.edu.tw/~elt/curriculum.htm

Name of Institution – Chulalongkorn University
Name of Program within institution – Faculty of Education
Title/Degree as it appears on official certificate or diploma – M.Ed./ Ph.D.
Name & Title of person administering program – Dr. Bunroeng Nieamhom
Address – Phayathai Road, Patumwan, Bangkok, 10330, Thailand
Telephone Number – 66 2 218 2644
Fax – 66 2 218 2644
Institution's home page – http://www.chula.ac.th
PREREQUISITES: Higher Education – No
If yes, number of years or degree required – Bachelor Degree
Teaching Certificate – Yes
Other requirement – graduated in Education field or have experiences in the
    filed of Ed Tech.
ACCEPTANCE OF TRANSFERS – Yes
MASTER'S PROGRAM DURATION: Number of required Semesters – 4
Comprehensive Exam Required? – Yes
Thesis Required? – Yes
Continuous Enrollment Required? – Yes
**Does program culminate in a degree in the field of educational communi-
    cations and technology?** – Yes
Name of the degree – M.Ed. in Audio Visual Communications
Is this program part of another degree, certificate, or diploma? – No
**OTHER PROGRAMS in educational technology or instructional develop-
    ment fields: Certificate Program available?** – No
Specialist Program available? – No
Undergraduate Program available? – Yes
Doctorate Program available? – PhD
Program Content – Master's degree

Name of Institution – Mahasarakham University
Name of Program within institution – Educational Technology and Commu-
    nications
Title/Degree as it appears on official certificate or diploma – M.Ed., Ph.D.
Name & Title of person administering program – Assoc. Prof. Dr. Chaiyot
    Ruangsuwan
Address – Mahasarakham University, A. Muang, Maha Sarakham, 44000,
    Thailand
Telephone Number – 66-4372-1764
Fax – 66-4372-1764
E-Mail – chaiyot@aetthailand.org
Institution's home page – http://www.msu.ac.th
PREREQUISITES: Higher Education – Yes

If yes, number of years or degree required – Bachelor Degree

Teaching Certificate – No

ACCEPTANCE OF TRANSFERS – Yes

MASTER'S PROGRAM DURATION: Number of required Semesters – 4

Comprehensive Exam Required? – Yes

Thesis Required? – Yes

Continuous Enrollment Required? – Yes

Does program culminate in a degree in the field of educational communications and technology? – Yes

Name of the degree – M.Ed.

Is this program part of another degree, certificate, or diploma? – No

OTHER PROGRAMS in educational technology or instructional development fields: Certificate Program available? – No

Undergraduate Program available? – Yes

Undergraduate URL – http://www.edu.ac.th

Doctorate Program available? – PhD

Doctorate URL – http://www.edu.ac.th

Program Content – Master's degree

Program Content URL – http://www.edu.ac.th

Name of Institution – Ankara University (Faculty of Educational Sciences)

Name of Program within institution – Curriculum & Instruction (Educational Technology)

Title/Degree as it appears on official certificate or diploma – Educational Technology

Name & Title of person administering program – Prof. Dr. Hafize Keser

Address – Cebeci Kampusu, Ankara, 06590, Turkey

Telephone Number – 90 (312) 363 3350

Fax – 90 (312) 363 6145

E-Mail – dekanlik@education.ankara.edu.tr

Institution's home page – http://www.education.ankara.edu.tr

Admittance URL – http://www.ankara.edu.tr

PREREQUISITES: Higher Education – Yes

If yes, number of years or degree required – 4 years

Teaching Certificate – No

Other requirement – Foreign Language

ACCEPTANCE OF TRANSFERS – Yes

MASTER'S PROGRAM DURATION: Number of required Courses – 8

Number of weeks long – 16

Comprehensive Exam Required? – No

Thesis Required? – Yes

Continuous Enrollment Required? – Yes

Does program culminate in a degree in the field of educational communications and technology? – Yes

Name of the degree – Educational Technology

Is this program part of another degree, certificate, or diploma? – Yes
If yes, name of the degree, certificate, or diploma – Curriculum & Instruction
  (Program of Educational Technology)
**OTHER PROGRAMS in educational technology or instructional develop-
  ment fields: Certificate Program available?** – No
Specialist Program available? – No
Undergraduate Program available? – Yes
Undergraduate URL – http://www.education.ankara.edu.tr
Doctorate Program available? – PhD
Doctorate URL – http://www.education.ankara.edu.tr
Program Content – Master's degree

Name of Institution – Hacettepe University
Name of Program within institution – Computer Education & Instructional
  Technology
Title/Degree as it appears on official certificate or diploma – MSc in Com-
  puter Education and Instructional Technology
Name & Title of person administering program – Petek Askar
Professor of Instructional Technology
Address – Bilgisayar ve Ogretim Teknolojileri Egitimi, Beytepe/ANKARA,
  06532, Turkey
Telephone Number – 90-312-297 71 76
Fax – 90-312-297 71 76
E-Mail – paskar@hacettepe.edu.tr
Institution's home page – http://www.ebit.hacettepe.edu.tr/
Admittance URL – http://www.fenbilimleri.hacettepe.edu.tr/english.htm
PREREQUISITES: Higher Education – Yes
If yes, number of years or degree required – 4 years
Teaching Certificate – No
Other requirement – LES 50, or a combined GRE score of 1100 on the Anal.
  and Quant.; TOEFL Comp. 187
ACCEPTANCE OF TRANSFERS – No
MASTER'S PROGRAM DURATION: Number of required Courses – 7
Comprehensive Exam Required? – Yes
Thesis Required? – Yes
Continuous Enrollment Required? – Yes
**Does program culminate in a degree in the field of educational communi-
  cations and technology?** – Yes
Name of the degree – MSc in Computer Education and Instructional
  Technology
Is this program part of another degree, certificate, or diploma? – No
**OTHER PROGRAMS in educational technology or instructional develop-
  ment fields: Certificate Program available?** – No
Specialist Program available? – No
Undergraduate Program available? – Yes

Undergraduate URL – http://www.ebit.hacettepe.edu.tr/Bolumumuz/bilgi/bolu
mumuz_eng.htm
Doctorate Program available? – No
Program Content – Master's degree
Program Content URL – http://www.fenbilimleri.hacettepe.edu.tr/dersler/
btoyon.htm

Name of Institution – Middle East Technical University
Name of Program within institution – Computer Education and Instructional
Technology
Title/Degree as it appears on official certificate or diploma – Computer Edu-
cation and Instructional Technology
Name & Title of person administering program – M. Yasar OZDEN, Pro-
fessor
Address – CEIT, Faculty of Education, ODTU/ ANKARA, ANKARA, 06531,
Turkey
Telephone Number – 90-312-210 4061
Fax – 90-312-210 10 06
E-Mail – myozden@metu.edu.tr
Institution's home page – http://ceit.metu.edu.tr
Admittance URL – http://www.fbe.metu.edu.tr/
PREREQUISITES: Higher Education – Yes
If yes, number of years or degree required – 4
Teaching Certificate – No
Other requirement – LES=50, 50(LES)+%15(GPA)+%35 interview
MASTER'S PROGRAM DURATION: Number of required Courses – 7
Comprehensive Exam Required? – No
Thesis Required? – Yes
Continuous Enrollment Required? – Yes
**Does program culminate in a degree in the field of educational communi-
cations and technology?** – Yes
Is this program part of another degree, certificate, or diploma? – Yes
If yes, name of the degree, certificate, or diploma – MSc in Computer Edu-
cation and Instructional Technology
**OTHER PROGRAMS in educational technology or instructional develop-
ment fields: Certificate Program available?** – No
Undergraduate Program available? – Yes
Undergraduate URL – http://www.catalog.metu.edu.tr/compedu.php
Doctorate Program available? – PhD
Doctorate URL – http://www.catalog.metu.edu.tr/compedu.php
Program Content – Master's degree
Program Content URL – http://www.catalog.metu.edu.tr/compedu.php

Name of Institution – Anadolu University
Name of Program within institution – Computer Education and Instructional
Technology

Title/Degree as it appears on official certificate or diploma – Masters of Education

Name & Title of person administering program – Ferhan Odabasi

Address – College of Education, Eskisehir, 26000, Turkey

Telephone Number – 90-222-3350580 ext:3519

E-Mail – fodabasi@anadolu.edu.tr

Institution's home page – http://www.egtbe.anadolu.edu.tr/eindex.htm

PREREQUISITES: **Higher Education** – Yes

If yes, number of years or degree required – 4 years

ACCEPTANCE OF TRANSFERS – Yes

MASTER'S PROGRAM DURATION: **Number of required Semesters** – 4

Number of weeks long – 15

Comprehensive Exam Required? – No

Thesis Required? – Yes

Continuous Enrollment Required? – Yes

Does program culminate in a degree in the field of educational communications and technology? – Yes

Name of the degree, Is this program part of another degree, certificate, or diploma? – No

OTHER PROGRAMS in educational technology or instructional development fields: Undergraduate Program available? – Yes

Undergraduate URL – http://www.egt.anadolu.edu.tr/eindex.htm

Doctorate Program available? – EdD

Doctorate URL – http://www.egtbe.anadolu.edu.tr/eindex.htm

Program Content – Master's degree

Name of Institution – Anadolu University

Name of Program within institution – Distance Education

Title/Degree as it appears on official certificate or diploma – Masters of Distance Education

Name & Title of person administering program – Levend Kilic

Address – Open Education Faculty, Eskisehir, 26470, Turkey

Telephone Number – 90-222-335-6580

Fax – 90-222-335-6580

E-Mail – lkilic@anadolu.edu.tr

Institution's home page – http://www.sosbe.anadolu.edu.tr/eindex.htm

PREREQUISITES: Higher Education – Yes

Teaching Certificate – Yes

ACCEPTANCE OF TRANSFERS – Yes

MASTER'S PROGRAM DURATION: **Number of required Semesters** – 4

Number of weeks long – 15

Comprehensive Exam Required? – No

Thesis Required? – Yes

Continuous Enrollment Required? – Yes

Does program culminate in a degree in the field of educational communications and technology? – No

Is this program part of another degree, certificate, or diploma? – No

OTHER PROGRAMS in educational technology or instructional development fields: Certificate Program available? – No

Specialist Program available? – No

Undergraduate Program available? – Yes

Undergraduate URL – http://www.egt.anadolu.edu.tr/eindex.htm

Doctorate Program available? – EdD

Doctorate URL – http://http://www.egtbe.anadolu.edu.tr/eindex.htm

Program Content – Master's degree

Name of Institution – University of Manchester

Name of Program within institution – MEd: ICT in Education

Title/Degree as it appears on official certificate or diploma – Masters in Education: Information and Communications Technology in Education

Name & Title of person administering program – Dr. Andrew Whitworth

Address – Humanities Devas Street, University of Manchester, Oxford Road, Manchester, M13 9PL, United Kingdom

Telephone Number – +44 161 275 7843

Fax – +44 161 275 3528

E-Mail – andrew.whitworth@manchester.ac.uk

Institution's home page – http://www.manchester.ac.uk

Admittance URL – http://www.manchester.ac.uk/postgraduate/howtoapply/

PREREQUISITES: Higher Education – Yes

If yes, number of years or degree required – Undergrad degree 2:2 or above (or equivalent)

Other requirement – Recommended but not obligatory

ACCEPTANCE OF TRANSFERS – Yes

MASTER'S PROGRAM DURATION: Number of required Semesters – 2

Comprehensive Exam Required? – No

Thesis Required? – Yes

Continuous Enrollment Required? – No

Does program culminate in a degree in the field of educational communications and technology? – Yes

Name of the degree – MEd: ICT in Education

Is this program part of another degree, certificate, or diploma? – No

OTHER PROGRAMS in educational technology or instructional development fields: Certificate Program available? – No

Specialist Program available? – No

Undergraduate Program available? – No

Doctorate Program available? – PhD

Program Content – Master's degree

Program Content URL – http://www.education.manchester.ac.uk/postgraduate students/taughtprogrammes/courseunit,17068,en.htm

Part VI
Mediagraphy: Print and Non-Print Resources

Introduction

Jinn-Wei Tsao and Chad Galloway

Contents

This resource lists journals and other resources of interest to practitioners, researchers, students, and others concerned with educational technology and educational media. The primary goal of this section is to list current publications in the field. The majority of materials cited here were published in 2007 or mid-2008. Media-related journals include those listed in past issues of EMTY, as well as new entries in the field. A thorough list of journals in the educational technology field has been updated for the 2008 edition using Ulrich's Periodical Index Online and journal Websites. This chapter is not intended to serve as a specific resource location tool, although it may be used for that purpose in the absence of database access. Rather, readers are encouraged to peruse the categories of interest in this chapter to gain an idea of recent developments within the field. For archival purposes, this chapter serves as a snapshot of the field of instructional technology publications in 2007. Readers must bear in mind that technological developments occur well in advance of publication and should take that fact into consideration when judging the timeliness of resources listed in this chapter.

Selection

Items were selected for the Mediagraphy in several ways. The EBSCO Host Databases were used to locate most of the journal citations. Others were taken from the journal listings of large publishing companies. Items were chosen for this list when they met one or more of the following criteria: reputable publisher, broad circulation, coverage by indexing services, peer review, and coverage of a gap in the literature. The author chose items on subjects that seem to reflect the instructional technology field as it is today. Because of the increasing tendency for media

J.-W. Tsao (✉)
The University of Georgia, Athens, GA 30602-7144
e-mail: miketsao@uga.edu

M. Orey et al. (eds.), *Educational Media and Technology Yearbook*,
DOI 10.1007/978-0-387-09675-9_27, © Springer Science+Business Media, LLC 2009

producers to package their products in more than one format and for single titles to contain mixed media, titles are no longer separated by media type. The author makes no claims as to the comprehensiveness of this list. It is, instead, intended to be representative.

Obtaining Resources

Media-related periodicals: The author has attempted to provide various ways to obtain the resources listed in this Mediagraphy, including telephone and fax numbers, Web and postal addresses, as well as email contacts. Prices are also included for individual and institutional subscriptions. The information presented reflects the most current information available at the time of publication.

ERIC Documents: As of December 31, 2003, ERIC was no longer funded. However, ERIC documents can still be read and copied from their microfiche form at any library holding an ERIC microfiche collection. The identification number beginning with ED (for example, ED 332 677) locates the document in the collection. Document delivery services and copies of most ERIC documents can also continue to be available from the ERIC Document Reproduction Service. Prices charged depend on format chosen (microfiche or paper copy), length of the document, and method of shipping. Online orders, fax orders, and expedited delivery are available.

To find the closest library with an ERIC microfiche collection, contact: ACCESS ERIC, 1600 Research Blvd, Rockville, METHOD 20850-3172; (800) LET-ERIC (538-3742); email: acceric@inet.ed.gov

To order ERIC documents, contact:

ERIC Document Reproduction Services (EDRS)
7420 Fullerton Rd, Suite 110, Springfield, VA 22153-2852
(800) 433-ERIC (433-3742); (703) 440-1400
Fax: (703) 440-1408
E-mail: service@edrs.com

Journal articles: Photocopies of journal articles can be obtained in one of the following ways: (1) from a library subscribing to the title, (2) through interlibrary loan, (3) through the purchase of a back issue from the journal publisher, or (4) from an article reprint service such as UMI.

UMI Information Store, 500 Sansome St, Suite 400
San Francisco, CA 94111
(800) 248-0360 (toll-free in U.S. and Canada); (415) 433-5500 (outside U.S. and Canada)
E-mail: orders@infostore.com

Journal articles can also be obtained through the Institute for Scientific Information (ISI).

ISI Document Solution
P.O. Box 7649
Philadelphia, PA 19104-3389
(215) 386-4399
Fax: (215) 222-0840 or (215) 386-4343
E-mail: ids@isinet.com

Arrangement

Mediagraphy entries are classified according to major subject emphasis under the following headings:

- Artificial Intelligence, Robotics, and Electronic Performance Support Systems
- Computer-Assisted Instruction
- Distance Education
- Educational Research
- Educational Technology
- Information Science and Technology
- Instructional Design and Development
- Learning Sciences
- Libraries and Media Centers
- Media Technologies
- Professional Development
- Simulation, Gaming, and Virtual Reality
- Special Education and Disabilities
- Telecommunications and Networking

Mediagraphy

Artificial Intelligence, Robotics, and Electronic Performance Support Systems

Artificial Intelligence Review. Springer Science+Business Media, 333 Meadowlands Pkwy, Secaucus, NJ 07094. www.springer.com/journal/10462, tel: 800-777-4643, fax: 201-348-4505, journals-ny@springer.com [8/yr; $320 indiv, $771 inst] Publishes commentary on issues and development in artificial intelligence foundations and current research.

AI Magazine. Association for the Advancement of Artificial Intelligence, 445 Burgess Dr, Suite 100, Menlo Park, CA 94025. www.aaai.org/Magazine, tel: 650-328-3123, fax: 650-321-4457, info08@aaai.org [4/yr; $35 student, $95 indiv, $190 inst] Proclaimed "journal of record for the AI community," this magazine provides full-length articles on research and new literature, but is written to allow access to those reading outside their area of expertise.

International Journal of Robotics Research. Sage Publications, 2455 Teller Rd, Thousand Oaks, CA 91320. ijr.sagepub.com, tel: 800-818-7243, fax: 800-583-2665, journals@sagepub.com [12/yr; $192 indiv (print), $1465 inst (online), $1595 inst (print), $1628 inst (online + print)] Interdisciplinary approach to the study of robotics for researchers, scientists, and students. The first scholarly publication on robotics research.

Journal of Intelligent and Robotic Systems. Springer Science+Business Media, 333 Meadowlands Pkwy, Secaucus, NJ 07094. www.springer.com/journal/10846, tel: 800-777-4643, fax: 201-348-4505, journals-ny@springer.com [12/yr; $806 indiv, $1574 inst] Main objective is to provide a forum for the fruitful interaction of ideas and techniques that combine systems and control science with artificial intelligence and other related computer science concepts. It bridges the gap between theory and practice.

Journal of Interactive Learning Research. Association for the Advancement of Computing in Education, P.O. Box 1545, Chesapeake, VA 23327-1545. www.aace.org/pubs/jilr, tel: 757-366-5606, fax: 703-997-8760, info@aace.org [4/yr; $25 for AACE student members, $55 AACE members (discount available

M. Orey et al. (eds.), *Educational Media and Technology Yearbook*, DOI 10.1007/978-0-387-09675-9_28, © Springer Science+Business Media, LLC 2009

for ordering multiple AACE journals), $175 inst] Publishes articles on how intelligent computer technologies can be used in education to enhance learning and teaching. Reports on research and developments, integration, and applications of artificial intelligence in education.

Knowledge-Based Systems. Elsevier, Inc., Customer Service Dept, 6277 Sea Harbor Dr, Orlando, FL 32887-4800. www.elsevier.com/locate/knosys, tel: 877-839-7126, fax: 407-363-1354, journalcustomerservice-usa@elsevier.com [8/yr; $186 indiv, $1163 inst] Interdisciplinary applications-oriented journal on fifth-generation computing, expert systems, and knowledge-based methods in system design.

Minds and Machines. Springer Science+Business Media, 333 Meadowlands Pkwy, Secaucus, NJ 07094. www.springer.com/journal/11023, tel: 800-777-4643, fax: 201-348-4505, journals-ny@springer.com [4/yr; $275 indiv, $673 inst] Discusses issues concerning machines and mentality, artificial intelligence, epistemology, simulation, and modeling.

Computer-Assisted Instruction

AACE Journal. Association for the Advancement of Computing in Education, P.O. Box 1545, Chesapeake, VA 23327-1545. www.aace.org/pubs/aacej, tel: 757-366-5606, fax: 703-997-8760, info@aace.org [4/yr; $35 student, $95 indiv] Publishes articles dealing with issues in instructional technology.

CALICO Journal. Computer Assisted Language Instruction Consortium, 214 Centennial Hall, Texas State Univ, San Marcos, TX 78666. calico.org, tel: 512-245-1417, fax: 512-245-9089, info@calico.org [3/yr; $65 indiv, $50 K-12 or community college teacher, $40 students or senior citizen, $105 inst] Provides information on the applications of technology in teaching and learning languages.

Children's Technology Review. Active Learning Associates, 120 Main St, Flemington, NJ 08822. www.childrenstechnology.com, tel: 800-993-9499, fax: 908-284-0405, lisa@childrenssoftware.com [12/yr; $64 online, $108 online + print] Provides reviews and other information about software to help parents and educators more effectively use computers with children.

Computers and Composition. Elsevier, Inc., Customer Service Dept, 6277 Sea Harbor Dr, Orlando, FL 32887-4800. www.elsevier.com/locate/compcom, tel: 877-839-7126, fax: 407-363-1354, journalcustomerservice-usa@elsevier.com [4/yr; $69 indiv, $353 inst] International journal for teachers of writing that focuses on the use of computers in writing instruction and related research.

Computers & Education. Elsevier, Inc., Customer Service Dept, 6277 Sea Harbor Dr, Orlando, FL 32887-4800. www.elsevier.com/locate/compedu, tel: 877-839-

7126, fax: 407-363-1354, journalcustomerservice-usa@elsevier.com [8/yr; $341 indiv, $1749 inst] Presents technical papers covering a broad range of subjects for users of analog, digital, and hybrid computers in all aspects of higher education.

Computers in Education Journal. American Society for Engineering Education, Computers in Education Division, Port Royal Square, P.O. Box 68, Port Royal, VA 22535. www.asee.org/about/publications/divisions/coed.cfm, tel: 804-742-5611, fax: 804-742-5030, ed-pub@crosslink.net [4/yr; $20 student, $69 indiv, inst prices vary] Covers transactions, scholarly research papers, application notes, and teaching methods.

Computers in Human Behavior. Elsevier, Inc., Customer Service Dept, 6277 Sea Harbor Dr, Orlando, FL 32887-4800. www.elsevier.com/locate/comphumbeh, tel: 877-839-7126, fax: 407-363-1354, journalcustomerservice-usa@elsevier. com [6/yr; $267 indiv, $1370 inst] Scholarly journal dedicated to examining the use of computers from a psychological perspective.

Computers in the Schools. Haworth Press, Inc., 10 Alice St, Binghamton, NY 13904-1580. www.haworthpress.com/web/CITS, tel: 800-354-1420, fax: 215-625-2940, haworthorders@taylorandfrancis.com [4/yr; $109 indiv, $610 inst] Features articles that combine theory and practical applications of small computers in schools for educators and school administrators.

Converge. e.Republic, Inc., 100 Blue Ravine Rd, Folsom, CA 95630. www. convergemag.com, tel: 800-940-6039, fax: 916-932-1470, subscriptions@ govtech.net [4/yr; free] Explores the revolution of technology in education.

Dr. Dobb's Journal. CMP Media, P.O. Box 1126, Skokie, IL 60076. www.ddj. com, tel: 888-847-6188, fax: 902-563-4807, drdobbsjournal@halldata.com [12/yr; $11.99; free to qualified applicants] Articles on the latest in operating systems, programming languages, algorithms, hardware design and architecture, data structures, and telecommunications; in-depth hardware and software reviews.

eWEEK. Ziff Davis Media Inc., 28 E 28th St, New York, NY 10016-7930. www.eweek.com, tel: 888-663-8438, fax: 847-564-9453, eweek@ziffdavis.com [36/yr; $195 (print), free online] Provides current information on the IBM PC, including hardware, software, industry news, business strategies, and reviews of hardware and software.

Information Technology in Childhood Education Annual. Association for the Advancement of Computing in Education, P.O. Box 1545, Chesapeake, VA 23327-1545. www.aace.org/pubs/itce, tel: 757-366-5606, fax: 703-997-8760, info@aace.org [1/yr] Scholarly trade publication reporting on research and investigations into the applications of instructional technology.

Instructor. Scholastic Inc., 557 Broadway, 5th Floor, New York, NY 10012. teacher.scholastic.com/products/instructor, tel: 866-436-2455, fax: 386-447-2321, instructor@palmcoastd.com [8/yr; $8 (8 issues), $14.95 (16 issues)]

Features articles on applications and advances of technology in education for K-12 and college educators and administrators.

Interactive Learning Environments. Taylor & Francis Group, Customer Services Dept, 325 Chestnut St, Suite 800, Philadelphia, PA 19106. www.tandf. co.uk/journals/titles/10494820, tel: 800-354-1420, fax: 215-625-2940, customerservice@taylorandfrancis.com [3/yr; $127 indiv, $376 inst (online), $396 inst (print + online)] Explores the implications of the Internet and multimedia presentation software in education and training environments.

Journal of Computer Assisted Learning. Blackwell Publishing, Journal Customer Services, 350 Main St, Malden, MA 02148. www.blackwellpublishing.com/ journals/JCA, tel: 800-835-6770, fax: 781-388-8232, orders@ames.blackwell publishing.com [6/yr; $193 individual (print + online), $1027 inst (online), $1189 inst (print + online)] Articles and research on the use of computer-assisted learning.

Journal of Educational Computing Research. Baywood Publishing Co., Inc., 26 Austin Ave, Box 337, Amityville, NY 11701-0337. www.baywood. com/journals/previewjournals.asp?id=0735-6331, tel: 800-638-7819, fax: 631-691-1770, info@baywood.com [8/yr; $176 indiv, $467 inst] Presents original research papers, critical analyses, reports on research in progress, design and development studies, article reviews, and grant award listings.

Journal of Educational Multimedia and Hypermedia. Association for the Advancement of Computing in Education, P.O. Box 1545, Chesapeake, VA 23327-1545. www.aace.org/pubs/jemh, tel: 757-366-5606, fax: 703-997-8760, info@aace.org [4/yr; $25 for AACE student members, $55 AACE members (discount available for ordering multiple AACE journals), $175 inst] A multidisciplinary information source presenting research about and applications for multimedia and hypermedia tools.

Journal of Research on Technology in Education. International Society for Technology in Education, 180 West 8th Ave., Suite 300, Eugene, OR 97401. www.iste.org/jrte, tel: 800-336-5191, fax: 541-302-3778, iste@iste.org [4/yr; $155] Contains articles reporting on the latest research findings related to classroom and administrative uses of technology, including system and project evaluations.

Language Resources and Evaluation. Springer Science+Business Media, 333 Meadowlands Pkwy, Secaucus, NJ 07094. www.springer.com/journal/10579, tel: 800-777-4643, fax: 201-348-4505, journals-ny@springer.com [4/yr; $230 indiv, $651 inst] Contains papers on computer-aided studies, applications, automation, and computer-assisted instruction.

Learning and Leading with Technology. International Society for Technology in Education, 180 West 8th Ave., Suite 300, Eugene, OR 97401. www.iste.org/LL, tel: 800-336-5191, fax: 541-302-3778, iste@iste.org [8/yr; $100] Focuses on the use of technology, coordination, and leadership; written by educators for educators. Appropriate for classroom teachers, lab teachers, technology coordinators, and teacher educators.

MacWorld. Mac Publishing, Macworld Subscription Services, P.O. Box 37781, Boone, IA 50037. www.macworld.com/magazine, tel: 800-288-6848, fax: 515-432-6994, subhelp@macworld.com [12/yr; $19.97] Describes hardware, software, tutorials, and applications for users of the Macintosh microcomputer.

OnCUE. Computer-Using Educators, Inc., 387 17th St, Suite 208, Oakland, CA 94612. www.cue.org/oncue, tel: 510-814-6630, fax: 510-444-4569, cueinc@cue.org [4/yr; free to CUE members; not sold separately] Contains articles, news items, and trade advertisements addressing computer-based education.

PC Magazine. Ziff Davis Media Inc., 28 E 28th St, New York, NY 10016-7930. www.pcmag.com, tel: 212-503-3500, fax: 212-503-4399, pcmag@ziffdavis.com [12/yr; $14.97] Comparative reviews of computer hardware and general business software programs.

Social Science Computer Review. Sage Publications, 2455 Teller Rd, Thousand Oaks, CA 91320. ssc.sagepub.com, tel: 800-818-7243, fax: 800-583-2665, journals@sagepub.com [4/yr; $115 indiv (print), $537 inst (online), $585 inst (print), $597 inst (online + print)] Interdisciplinary peer-reviewed scholarly publication covering social science research and instructional applications in computing and telecommunications; also covers societal impacts of information technology.

Wireless Networks. Springer Science+Business Media, 333 Meadowlands Pkwy, Secaucus, NJ 07094. www.springer.com/journal/11276, tel: 800-777-4643, fax: 201-348-4505, journals-ny@springer.com [6/yr; $599 inst] Devoted to the technological innovations that result from the mobility allowed by wireless technology.

Distance Education

American Journal of Distance Education. Taylor & Francis Group, Customer Services Dept, 325 Chestnut St, Suite 800, Philadelphia, PA 19106. www.ajde.com, tel: 800-354-1420, fax: 215-625-2940, customerservice@taylorandfrancis.com [4/yr; $64 indiv (online + print), $233 inst (online), $246 inst (online + print)] Created to disseminate information and act as a forum for criticism and debate about research on and practice of systems, management, and administration of distance education.

Journal of Distance Education. Canadian Network for Innovation in Education, BCIT Learning & Teaching Centre, British Columbia Institute of Technology, 3700 Willingdon Ave, Burnaby, BC, V5G 3H2, Canada. www.jofde.ca, tel: 604-454 2280, fax: 604-431-7267, journalofde@gmail.com [at least 2/yr; $40 (print);

free online] Aims to promote and encourage scholarly work of empirical and theoretical nature relating to distance education in Canada and throughout the world.

Journal of Library & Information Services in Distance Learning. Haworth Press, Inc., 10 Alice St, Binghamton, NY 13904-1580. www.haworthpress.com/web/JLISD, tel: 800-354-1420, fax: 215-625-2940, haworthorders@taylorandfrancis.com [4/yr; $48 indiv $150 inst] Contains peer-reviewed articles, essays, narratives, current events, and letters from distance learning and information science experts.

Journal of Research on Technology in Education. International Society for Technology in Education, 180 West 8th Ave., Suite 300, Eugene, OR 97401. www.iste.org/jrte, tel: 800-336-5191, fax: 541-302-3778, iste@iste.org [4/yr; $155] Contains articles reporting on the latest research findings related to classroom and administrative uses of technology, including system and project evaluations.

Open Learning. Taylor & Francis Group, Customer Services Dept, 325 Chestnut St, Suite 800, Philadelphia, PA 19106. www.tandf.co.uk/journals/titles/02680513, tel: 800-354-1420, fax: 215-625-2940, customerservice@taylorandfrancis.com [3/yr; $98 indiv, $293 inst (online), $309 inst (print + online)] Academic, scholarly publication on aspects of open and distance learning anywhere in the world. Includes issues for debate and research notes.

Educational Research

American Educational Research Journal. Sage Publications, 2455 Teller Rd, Thousand Oaks, CA 91320. aer.sagepub.com, tel: 800-818-7243, fax: 800-583-2665, journals@sagepub.com [4/yr; $50 indiv (print + online), $265 inst (online), $288 inst (print), $294 inst (print + online)] Reports original research, both empirical and theoretical, and brief synopses of research.

Educational Research. Taylor & Francis Group, Customer Services Dept, 325 Chestnut St, Suite 800, Philadelphia, PA 19106. www.tandf.co.uk/journals/titles/00131881, tel: 800-354-1420, fax: 215-625-2940, customerservice@taylorandfrancis.com [4/yr; $165 indiv, $463 inst (online), $488 inst (print + online)] Reports on current educational research, evaluation, and applications.

Educational Researcher. Sage Publications, 2455 Teller Rd, Thousand Oaks, CA 91320. edr.sagepub.com, tel: 800-818-7243, fax: 800-583-2665, journals@sagepub.com [9/yr; $50 indiv (print + online), $284 inst (online), $309 inst (print), $315 inst (print + online)] Contains news and features of general significance in educational research.

Journal of Interactive Learning Research. Association for the Advancement of Computing in Education, P.O. Box 1545, Chesapeake, VA 23327-1545. www.aace.org/pubs/jilr, tel: 757-366-5606, fax: 703-997-8760, info@aace.org [4/yr; $25 for AACE student members, $55 AACE members (discount available for ordering multiple AACE journals), $175 inst] Publishes articles on how intelligent computer technologies can be used in education to enhance learning and teaching. Reports on research and developments, integration, and applications of artificial intelligence in education.

Learning Technology. IEEE Computer Society, Technical Committee on Learning Technology. lttf.ieee.org/learn_tech, tel: (+64) 6-350-5799 (x2090), fax: (+64) 6-350-5725, kinshuk@ieee.org [4/yr; free] Online publication that reports developments, projects, conferences, and findings of the Learning Technology Task Force.

Meridian. North Carolina State University, College of Education, Poe Hall, Box 7801, Raleigh, NC 27695-7801. www.ncsu.edu/meridian, meridian_mail@ncsu.edu [2/yr; free] Online journal dedicated to research in middle school educational technology use.

Research in Science & Technological Education. Taylor & Francis Group, Customer Services Dept, 325 Chestnut St, Suite 800, Philadelphia, PA 19106. www.tandf.co.uk/journals/titles/02635143, tel: 800-354-1420, fax: 215-625-2940, customerservice@taylorandfrancis.com [3/yr; $313 indiv, $1510 inst (online), $1590 inst (print + online)] Publication of original research in the science and technological fields. Includes articles on psychological, sociological, economic, and organizational aspects of technological education.

Educational Technology

Appropriate Technology. Research Information Ltd., Grenville Court, Britwell Rd, Burnham, Bucks, SL1 8DF, United Kingdom. www.researchinformation.co.uk/apte.php, tel: 44 (0) 1628 600499, fax: 44 (0) 1628 600488, info@researchinformation.co.uk [4/yr; $315] Articles on less technologically advanced, but more environmentally sustainable, solutions to problems in developing countries.

British Journal of Educational Technology. Blackwell Publishing, Journal Customer Services, 350 Main St, Malden, MA 02148. www.blackwellpublishing.com/journals/BJET, tel: 800-835-6770, fax: 781-388-8232, orders@ames.blackwellpublishing.com [6/yr; $185 indiv (print + online), $981 inst (online), $1136 inst (print + online)] Published by the National Council for Educational Technology, this journal includes articles on education and training, especially theory, applications, and development of educational technology and communications.

Canadian Journal of Learning and Technology. Canadian Network for Innovation in Education (CNIE), 260 Dalhousie St., Suite 204, Ottawa, ON, K1N 7E4, Canada. www.cjlt.ca, tel: 613-241-0018, fax: 613-241-0019, cjlt@ucalgary.ca [3/yr; $95 indiv, $115 inst] Concerned with all aspects of educational systems and technology.

Educational Technology. Educational Technology Publications, Inc., 700 Palisade Ave, P.O. Box 1564, Englewood Cliffs, NJ 07632-0564. www.bookstoread. com/etp, tel: 800-952-2665, fax: 201-871-4009, edtecpubs@aol.com [6/yr; $179] Covers telecommunications, computer-aided instruction, information retrieval, educational television, and electronic media in the classroom.

Educational Technology Abstracts. Taylor & Francis Group, Customer Services Dept, 325 Chestnut St, Suite 800, Philadelphia, PA 19106. www.tandf.co.uk/journals/titles/02663368, tel: 800-354-1420, fax: 215-625-2940, customerservice@taylorandfrancis.com [1/yr; $563 indiv, $1446 inst (online), $1523 inst (print + online)] An international publication of abstracts of recently published material in the field of educational and training technology.

Educational Technology Research & Development. Springer Science+Business Media, 333 Meadowlands Pkwy, Secaucus, NJ 07094. www.springer.com/journal/11423, tel: 800-777-4643, fax: 201-348-4505, journals-ny@springer.com [6/yr; $148 indiv, $280 inst] Focuses on research, instructional development, and applied theory in the field of educational technology.

International Journal of Technology and Design Education. Springer Science+Business Media, 333 Meadowlands Pkwy, Secaucus, NJ 07094. www.springer.com/journal/10798, tel: 800-777-4643, fax: 201-348-4505, journals-ny@springer.com [3/yr; $189 indiv, $352 inst] Publishes research reports and scholarly writing about aspects of technology and design education.

Journal of Computing in Higher Education. Springer Science+Business Media, 333 Meadowlands Pkwy, Secaucus, NJ 07094. www.springer.com/journal/12528, tel: 800-777-4643, fax: 201-348-4505, journals-ny@springer.com [3/yr; $130 inst] Publishes scholarly essays, case studies, and research that discuss instructional technologies.

Journal of Educational Technology Systems. Baywood Publishing Co., Inc., 26 Austin Ave, Box 337, Amityville, NY 11701-0337. www.baywood.com/journals/previewjournals.asp?id=0047-2395, tel: 800-638-7819, fax: 631-691-1770, info@baywood.com [4/yr; $324 inst] Deals with systems in which technology and education interface; designed to inform educators who are interested in making optimum use of technology.

Journal of Interactive Media in Education. Open University, Knowledge Media Institute, Milton Keynes MK7 6AA United Kingdom. www-jime.open.ac.uk, tel: 44 (0) 1908 653800, fax: 44 (0) 1908 653169, jime@open.ac.uk [Irregular; free]

A multidisciplinary forum for debate and idea sharing concerning the practical aspects of interactive media and instructional technology.

Journal of Science Education and Technology. Springer Science+Business Media, 333 Meadowlands Pkwy, Secaucus, NJ 07094. www.springer.com/journal/10956, tel: 800-777-4643, fax: 201-348-4505, journals-ny@springer.com [6/yr; $205 indiv, $906 inst] Publishes studies aimed at improving science education at all levels in the U.S.

MultiMedia & Internet@Schools. Information Today, Inc., 143 Old Marlton Pike, Medford, NJ 08055-8750. www.mmischools.com, tel: 800-300-9868, fax: 609-654-4309, custserv@infotoday.com [6/yr; $44.95] Reviews and evaluates hardware and software. Presents information pertaining to basic troubleshooting skills.

Science Communication. Sage Publications, 2455 Teller Rd, Thousand Oaks, CA 91320. scx.sagepub.com, tel: 800-818-7243, fax: 800-583-2665, journals@sagepub.com [4/yr; $149 indiv (print), $633 inst (online), $689 inst (print), $703 inst (online + print)] An international, interdisciplinary journal examining the nature of expertise and the translation of knowledge into practice and policy.

Social Science Computer Review. Sage Publications, 2455 Teller Rd, Thousand Oaks, CA 91320. ssc.sagepub.com, tel: 800-818-7243, fax: 800-583-2665, journals@sagepub.com [4/yr; $115 indiv (print), $537 inst (online), $585 inst (print), $597 inst (online + print)] Interdisciplinary peer-reviewed scholarly publication covering social science research and instructional applications in computing and telecommunications; also covers societal impacts of information technology.

TechTrends. Springer Science+Business Media, 333 Meadowlands Pkwy, Secaucus, NJ 07094. www.springer.com/journal/11528, tel: 800-777-4643, fax: 201-348-4505, journals-ny@springer.com [6/yr; $94 indiv, $105 inst] Targeted at leaders in education and training; features authoritative, practical articles about technology and its integration into the learning environment.

T.H.E. Journal. 1105 Media, P.O. Box 2170, Skokie, IL 60076. www.thejournal.com, tel: 866-293-3194, fax: 847-763-9564, THEJournal@1105service.com [12/yr; $29, free to those in K-12, free online] For educators of all levels; focuses on a specific topic for each issue, as well as technological innovations as they apply to education.

Information Science and Technology

Canadian Journal of Information and Library Science. University of Toronto Press, Journals Division, 5201 Dufferin St, Toronto, ON, M3H 5T8, Canada. www.utpjournals.com/cjils/cjils.html, tel: 416-667-7777, fax: 416-667-7881, journals@utpress.utoronto.ca [4/yr; $75 indiv, $109 inst] Published by the

Canadian Association for Information Science to contribute to the advancement of library and information science in Canada.

EContent. Information Today, Inc., 143 Old Marlton Pike, Medford, NJ 08055-8750. www.econtentmag.com, tel: 800-300-9868, fax: 609-654-4309, custserv@infotoday.com [10/yr; $115] Features articles on topics of interest to online database users; includes database search aids.

Information Processing & Management. Elsevier, Inc., Customer Service Dept, 6277 Sea Harbor Dr, Orlando, FL 32887-4800. www.elsevier.com/locate/infoproman, tel: 877-839-7126, fax: 407-363-1354, journalcustomer service-usa@elsevier.com [6/yr; $311 indiv, $1768 inst] International journal covering data processing, database building, and retrieval.

Information Services & Use. IOS Press, Nieuwe Hemweg 6B, 1013 BG Amsterdam, The Netherlands. www.iospress.nl/html/01675265.php, tel: 31-20-688-3355, fax: 31-20-620-3419, info@iospress.nl [4/yr; $115 indiv (online), $455 inst (online), $503 inst (print + online)] An international journal for those in the information management field. Includes online and offline systems, library automation, micrographics, videotex, and telecommunications.

The Information Society. Taylor & Francis Group, Customer Services Dept, 325 Chestnut St, Suite 800, Philadelphia, PA 19106. www.tandf.co.uk/journals/titles/01972243, tel: 800-354-1420, fax: 215-625-2940, customerservice@taylorandfrancis.com [5/yr; $155 indiv, $400 inst (online), $422 inst (print + online)] Provides a forum for discussion of the world of information, including transborder data flow, regulatory issues, and the impact of the information industry.

Information Technology and Libraries. American Library Association, Subscriptions, 50 E Huron St, Chicago, IL 60611-2795. www.lita.org/ital, tel: 800-545-2433, fax: 312-944-2641, membership@ala.org [4/yr; $65] Articles on library automation, communication technology, cable systems, computerized information processing, and video technologies.

Information Today. Information Today, Inc., 143 Old Marlton Pike, Medford, NJ 08055-8750. www.infotoday.com/it, tel: 800-300-9868, fax: 609-654-4309, custserv@infotoday.com [11/yr; $82.95] Newspaper for users and producers of electronic information services. Includes articles and news about the industry, calendar of events, and product information.

Information Technology Management. Idea Group Publishing, 701 E Chocolate Ave, Suite 200, Hershey, PA 17033-1240. www.igi-pub.com/journals/details.asp?id=200, tel: 866-342-6657, fax: 717-533-7115, cust@idea-group.com [2/yr; $70 indiv, $90 inst] Designed for library information specialists, this bi-annual newsletter presents current issues and trends in information technology presented by and for specialists in the field.

Internet Reference Service Quarterly. Haworth Press, Inc., 10 Alice St, Binghamton, NY 13904-1580. www.haworthpress.com/web/IRSQ, tel: 800-354-1420, fax: 215-625-2940, haworthorders@taylorandfrancis.com [4/yr; $74 indiv, $190 inst] Discusses multidisciplinary aspects of incorporating the Internet as a tool for reference service.

Journal of Access Services. Haworth Press, Inc., 10 Alice St, Binghamton, NY 13904-1580. www.haworthpress.com/web/JAS, tel: 800-354-1420, fax: 215-625-2940, haworthorders@taylorandfrancis.com [4/yr; $69 indiv, $190 inst] Explores topics and issues surrounding the organization, administration, and development of information technology on access services and resources.

Journal of the American Society for Information Science and Technology. John Wiley & Sons, Ltd., Subscription Dept, 111 River St, Hoboken, NJ 07030-5774. www.asis.org/jasist.html, tel: 201-748-6645, fax: 201-748-5915, subinfo@wiley.com [14/yr; $1999 inst (print), $2197 inst (online), $2354 inst (print + online)] Provides an overall forum for new research in information transfer and communication processes, with particular attention paid to the context of recorded knowledge.

Journal of Database Management. Idea Group Publishing, 701 E Chocolate Ave, Suite 200, Hershey, PA 17033-1240. www.idea-group.com/journals/details.asp?id=198, tel: 866-342-6657, fax: 717-533-7115, cust@igi-global.com [4/yr; $125 indiv, $445 inst (online), $495 inst (print + online)] Provides state-of-the-art research to those who design, develop, and administer DBMS-based information systems.

Journal of Documentation. Emerald Group Publishing Limited, 875 Massachusetts Ave, 7th Floor, Cambridge, MA 02139. www.emeraldinsight.com/jd.htm, tel: 888-622-0075, fax: 617-354-6875, america@emeraldinsight.com [6/yr; $929] Focuses on theories, concepts, models, frameworks, and philosophies in the information sciences.

Journal of Internet Cataloging. Haworth Press, Inc., 10 Alice St, Binghamton, NY 13904-1580. www.haworthpress.com/web/JIC, tel: 800-354-1420, fax: 215-625-2940, haworthorders@taylorandfrancis.com [4/yr; $72 indiv, $210 inst] Gives library cataloging experts a system for managing Internet reference resources in the library catalog.

Resource Sharing & Information Networks. Haworth Press, Inc., 10 Alice St, Binghamton, NY 13904-1580. www.haworthpress.com/web/RSIN, tel: 800-354-1420, fax: 215-625-2940, haworthorders@taylorandfrancis.com [4/yr; $50 indiv, $275 inst] A forum for ideas on the basic theoretical and practical problems faced by planners, practitioners, and users of network services.

Instructional Design and Development

Human-Computer Interaction. Taylor & Francis Group, Customer Services Dept, 325 Chestnut St, Suite 800, Philadelphia, PA 19106. www.tandf.co.uk/journals/titles/07370024, tel: 800-354-1420, fax: 215-625-2940, customerservice@taylorandfrancis.com [4/yr; $69 indiv (online + print), $588 inst (online), $619 institution (online + print)] A journal of theoretical, empirical, and methodological issues of user science and of system design.

Instructional Science. Springer Science+Business Media, 333 Meadowlands Pkwy, Secaucus, NJ 07094. www.springer.com/journal/11251, tel: 800-777-4643, fax: 201-348-4505, journals-ny@springer.com [6/yr; $298 indiv, $650 inst] Promotes a deeper understanding of the nature, theory, and practice of the instructional process and the learning resulting from this process.

International Journal of Human-Computer Interaction. Taylor & Francis Group, Customer Services Dept, 325 Chestnut St, Suite 800, Philadelphia, PA 19106. www.tandf.co.uk/journals/titles/10447318, tel: 800-354-1420, fax: 215-625-2940, customerservice@taylorandfrancis.com [6/yr; $110 indiv (online + print), $893 inst (online), $940 inst (online + print)] Addresses the cognitive, social, health, and ergonomic aspects of work with computers. It also emphasizes both the human and computer science aspects of the effective design and use of computer interactive systems.

Journal of Educational Technology Systems. Baywood Publishing Co., Inc., 26 Austin Ave, Box 337, Amityville, NY 11701-0337. www.baywood.com/journals/previewjournals.asp?id=0047-2395, tel: 800-638-7819, fax: 631-691-1770, info@baywood.com [4/yr; $324 inst] Deals with systems in which technology and education interface; designed to inform educators who are interested in making optimum use of technology.

Journal of Instructional Delivery Systems. Learning Technology Institute, 50 Culpeper St, Warrenton, VA 20186. www.salt.org/salt.asp?ss=1&pn=jids, tel: 540-347-0055, fax: 540-349-3169, info@lti.org [4/yr; $45 indiv, $40 lib] Devoted to the issues, problems, and applications of instructional delivery systems in education, training, and job performance.

Journal of Interactive Instruction Development. Learning Technology Institute, 50 Culpeper St, Warrenton, VA 20186. www.salt.org/salt.asp?ss=1&pn=jiid, tel: 540-347-0055, fax: 540-349-3169, jiid@lti.org [4/yr; $45 indiv, $40 lib] A showcase of successful programs that will heighten awareness of innovative, creative, and effective approaches to courseware development for interactive technology.

Journal of Technical Writing and Communication. Baywood Publishing Co., Inc., 26 Austin Ave, Box 337, Amityville, NY 11701-0337. www.baywood.com/journals/previewjournals.asp?id=0047-2816, tel: 800-638-7819, fax: 631-691-1770, info@baywood.com [4/yr; $81 indiv, $324 inst] Essays on oral and written communication, for purposes ranging from pure research to needs of business and industry.

Journal of Visual Literacy. International Visual Literacy Association, Dr. Constance L. Cassity, IVLA Executive Treasurer, Northeastern State University, 3100

E New Orleans St, Broken Arrow, OK 74014. plato.ou.edu/˜jvl, tel: 918-449-6511, cassityc@nsuok.edu [2/yr; $30 student, $60 indiv] Explores empirical, theoretical, practical, and applied aspects of visual literacy and communication.

Performance Improvement Journal. John Wiley & Sons, Inc., 989 Market St, 5th Floor, San Francisco, CA 94103. www.ispi.org/publications/pij.htm, tel: 888-378-2537, fax: 888-481-2665, jbsubs@jbp.com [10/yr; $75 indiv (print), $275 inst (print), $303 (print + online)] Promotes performance science and technology. Contains articles, research, and case studies relating to improving human performance.

Performance Improvement Quarterly. International Society for Performance Improvement, 989 Market Street, San Francisco, CA 94103-1741. www.ispi.org/publications/piq.htm, tel: 888-378-2537, fax: 888-481-2665, jbsubs@jbp.com [4/yr; $45] Presents the cutting edge in research and theory in performance technology.

Training. V N U Business Publications, 70 Broadway, New York, NY 10003. www.trainingmag.com, tel: 800-255-2824, fax: 612-333-6526, edit@trainingmag.com [12/yr; $79] Covers all aspects of training, management, and organizational development, motivation, and performance improvement.

Learning Sciences

International Journal of Computer-Supported Collaborative Learning. Springer Science+Business Media, 333 Meadowlands Pkwy, Secaucus, NJ 07094. www.springer.com/journal/11412, tel: 800-777-4643, fax: 201-348-4505, journals-ny@springer.com [6/yr; $360 inst] Promote a deeper understanding of the nature, theory and practice of the uses of computer-supported collaborative learning.

Journal of the Learning Sciences. Taylor & Francis Group, Customer Services Dept, 325 Chestnut St, Suite 800, Philadelphia, PA 19106. www.tandf.co.uk/journals/journal.asp?issn=1050-8406&linktype=44, tel: 800-354-1420, fax: 215-625-2940, customerservice@taylorandfrancis.com [4/yr; $64 indiv, $612 inst (online), $645 inst (print + online)] Provides a forum for the discussion of research on education and learning, with emphasis on the idea of changing one's understanding of learning and the practice of education.

Libraries and Media Centers

Collection Building. Emerald Group Publishing Limited, 875 Massachusetts Ave, 7th Floor, Cambridge, MA 02139. www.emeraldinsight.com/cb.htm, tel: 888-622-0075, fax: 617-354-6875, america@emeraldinsight.com [4/yr; $1499] Provides well-researched and authoritative information on collection maintenance and development for librarians in all sectors.

Computers in Libraries. Information Today, Inc., 143 Old Marlton Pike, Medford, NJ 08055-8750. www.infotoday.com/cilmag/default.shtml, tel: 800-300-9868, fax: 609-654-4309, custserv@infotoday.com [10/yr; $99.95] Covers practical applications of microcomputers to library situations and recent news items.

The Electronic Library. Emerald Group Publishing Limited, 875 Massachusetts Ave, 7th Floor, Cambridge, MA 02139. www.emeraldinsight.com/el.htm, tel: 888-622-0075, fax: 617-354-6875, america@emeraldinsight.com [6/yr; $679] International journal for minicomputer, microcomputer, and software applications in libraries; independently assesses current and forthcoming information technologies.

Government Information Quarterly. Elsevier, Inc., Customer Service Dept, 6277 Sea Harbor Dr, Orlando, FL 32887-4800. www.elsevier.com/locate/govinf, tel: 877-839-7126, fax: 407-363-1354, journalcustomerservice-usa@elsevier.com [4/yr; $165 indiv, $521 inst] International journal of resources, services, policies, and practices.

Information Outlook. Special Libraries Association, Information Outlook Subscriptions, 331 S Patrick St, Alexandria, VA 22314-3501. www.sla.org/io, tel: 703-647-4900, fax: 703-647-4901, magazine@sla.org [12/yr; $125] Discusses administration, organization, and operations. Includes reports on research, technology, and professional standards.

The Journal of Academic Librarianship. Elsevier, Inc., Customer Service Dept, 6277 Sea Harbor Dr, Orlando, FL 32887-4800. www.elsevier.com/locate/jacalib, tel: 877-839-7126, fax: 407-363-1354, journalcustomerservice-usa@elsevier. com [6/yr; $118 indiv, $317 inst] Results of significant research, issues, and problems facing academic libraries, book reviews, and innovations in academic libraries.

Journal of Librarianship and Information Science. Sage Publications, 2455 Teller Rd, Thousand Oaks, CA 91320. lis.sagepub.com, tel: 800-818-7243, fax: 800-583-2665, journals@sagepub.com [4/yr; $88 indiv (print), $528 inst (online), $575 inst (print), $587 inst (online + print)] Deals with all aspects of library and information work in the United Kingdom and reviews literature from international sources.

Journal of Library Administration. Haworth Press, Inc., 10 Alice St, Binghamton, NY 13904-1580. www.haworthpress.com/web/JLA, tel: 800-354-1420, fax: 215-625-2940, getinfo@haworthpress.com [8/yr; $184 indiv, $705 inst] Provides information on all aspects of effective library management, with emphasis on practical applications.

Library & Information Science Research. Elsevier, Inc., Customer Service Dept, 6277 Sea Harbor Dr, Orlando, FL 32887-4800. www.elsevier.

com/locate/lisres, tel: 877-839-7126, fax: 407-363-1354, journalcustomer service-usa@elsevier.com [4/yr; $139 indiv, $395 inst] Research articles, dissertation reviews, and book reviews on issues concerning information resources management.

Library Hi Tech. Emerald Group Publishing Limited, 875 Massachusetts Ave, 7th Floor, Cambridge, MA 02139. www.emeraldinsight.com/lht.htm, tel: 888-622-0075, fax: 617-354-6875, america@emeraldinsight.com [4/yr; $429] Concentrates on reporting on the selection, installation, maintenance, and integration of systems and hardware.

Library Hi Tech News. Emerald Group Publishing Limited, 875 Massachusetts Ave, 7th Floor, Cambridge, MA 02139. www.emeraldinsight.com/lhtn.htm, tel: 888-622-0075, fax: 617-354-6875, america@emeraldinsight.com [10/yr; $549] Supplements Library Hi Tech and updates many of the issues addressed in-depth in the journal; keeps the reader fully informed of the latest developments in library automation, new products, network news, new software and hardware, and people in technology.

Library Journal. Reed Business Information, 360 Park Avenue South, New York, NY 10010. www.libraryjournal.com, tel: 800-588-1030, fax: 712-733-8019, LJLcustserv@cds-global.com [20/yr; $149.99] A professional periodical for librarians, with current issues and news, professional reading, a lengthy book review section, and classified advertisements.

Library Media Connection. Linworth Publishing, Inc., 3650 Olentangy River Rd., Suite 250, Columbus, Ohio 43214. www.linworth.com/lmc, tel: 800-786-5017, fax: 614-884-9993, linworth@linworthpublishing.com [7/yr; $69] Journal for junior and senior high school librarians; provides articles, tips, and ideas for day-to-day school library management, as well as reviews of audiovisuals and software, all written by school librarians.

The Library Quarterly. University of Chicago Press, Journals Division, Journals Division, P.O. Box 37005, Chicago, IL 60637. www.journals.uchicago.edu/LQ, tel: 877-705-1878, fax: 877-705-1879, subscriptions@press.uchicago.edu [$25 students (online), $42 indiv (print or online), $47 indiv (print + online), inst prices vary] Scholarly articles of interest to librarians.

Library Resources & Technical Services. American Library Association, Subscriptions, 50 E Huron St, Chicago, IL 60611-2795. www.ala.org/ala/alcts/alcts.cfm, tel: 800-545-2433, fax: 312-944-2641, membership@ala.org [4/yr; $75] Scholarly papers on bibliographic access and control, preservation, conservation, and reproduction of library materials.

Library Trends. Johns Hopkins University Press, P.O. Box 19966, Baltimore, MD 21211-0966. www.press.jhu.edu/journals/library_trends, tel: 800-548-1784, fax: 410-516-6968, jrnlcirc@press.jhu.edu [4/yr; $78 indiv (print or online), $78 inst (online), $128 inst (print)] Each issue is concerned with one aspect of library and information science, analyzing current thought and practice and examining ideas that hold the greatest potential for the field.

Public Libraries. American Library Association, Subscriptions, 50 E Huron St, Chicago, IL 60611-2795. www.ala.org/ala/pla/plapubs/publiclibraries/publiclibraries.cfm, tel: 800-545-2433, fax: 312-944-2641, membership@ala.org [6/yr; $50] News and articles of interest to public librarians.

Public Library Quarterly. Haworth Press, Inc., 10 Alice St, Binghamton, NY 13904-1580. www.haworthpress.com/web/PLQ, tel: 800-354-1420, fax: 215-625-2940, haworthorders@taylorandfrancis.com [4/yr; $60 indiv, $265 inst] Addresses the major administrative challenges and opportunities that face the nation's public libraries.

Reference and User Services Quarterly. American Library Association, Subscriptions, 50 E Huron St, Chicago, IL 60611-2795. rusq.org, tel: 800-545-2433, fax: 312-944-2641, membership@ala.org [4/yr; $65] Disseminates information of interest to reference librarians, bibliographers, adult services librarians, those in collection development and selection, and others interested in public services.

The Reference Librarian. Haworth Press, Inc., 10 Alice St, Binghamton, NY 13904-1580. www.haworthpress.com/web/REF, tel: 800-354-1420, fax: 215-625-2940, haworthorders@taylorandfrancis.com [4/yr; $218 indiv, $940 inst] Each issue focuses on a topic of current concern, interest, or practical value to reference librarians.

Reference Services Review. Emerald Group Publishing Limited, 875 Massachusetts Ave, 7th Floor, Cambridge, MA 02139. www.emeraldinsight.com/rsr.htm, tel: 888-622-0075, fax: 617-354-6875, america@emeraldinsight.com [4/yr; $459] Dedicated to the enrichment of reference knowledge and the advancement of reference services. It prepares its readers to understand and embrace current and emerging technologies affecting reference functions and information needs of library users.

School Library Journal. Reed Business Information, 360 Park Avenue South, New York, NY 10010. www.slj.com, tel: 800-595-1066, fax: 712-733-8019, sljcustserv@cds-global.com [12/yr; $129.99] For school and youth service librarians. Reviews about 4,000 children's books and 1,000 educational media titles annually.

School Library Media Activities Monthly. Libraries Unlimited, Inc., 88 Post Road W, Westport, CT 06881. www.schoollibrarymedia.com, tel: 800-225-5800, fax: 203-454-8662, Deborah.Levitov@lu.com [10/yr; $55] A vehicle for distributing ideas for teaching library media skills and for the development and implementation of library media skills programs.

School Library Media Research. American Library Association and American Association of School Librarians, Subscriptions, 50 E Huron St, Chicago, IL 60611-2795. http://www.ala.org/ala/aasl/aaslpubsandjournals/slmrb/school

library.cfm, tel: 800-545-2433, fax: 312-944-2641, membership@ala.org [annual compilation; free online] For library media specialists, district supervisors, and others concerned with the selection and purchase of print and non-print media and with the development of programs and services for preschool through high school libraries.

Teacher Librarian. The Scarecrow Press, Inc., 4501 Forbes Blvd, Suite 200, Lanham, MD 20706. www.teacherlibrarian.com, tel: 800-462-6420, fax: 800-338-4550, editor@teacherlibrarian.com [5/yr; $54 prepaid, $59 billed] "The journal for school library professionals"; previously known as Emergency Librarian. Articles, review columns, and critical analyses of management and programming issues.

Media Technologies

Broadcasting & Cable. Reed Business Information, 360 Park Avenue South, New York, NY 10010. www.broadcastingcable.com, tel: 800-554-5729, fax: 712-733-8019, bcbcustserv@cdsfulfillment.com [51/yr; $199.99] All-inclusive newsweekly for radio, television, cable, and allied business.

Communication Abstracts. Sage Publications, 2455 Teller Rd, Thousand Oaks, CA 91320. www.sagepub.com/journalsProdDesc.nav?prodId=Journal200918, tel: 800-818-7243, fax: 800-583-2665, journals@sagepub.com [6/yr; $333 indiv (print), $1557 inst (print)] Abstracts communication-related articles, reports, and books. Cumulated annually.

Educational Media International. Taylor & Francis Group, Customer Services Dept, 325 Chestnut St, Suite 800, Philadelphia, PA 19106. www.tandf.co.uk/journals/titles/09523987, tel: 800-354-1420, fax: 215-625-2940, customerservice@taylorandfrancis.com [4/yr; $121 indiv, $453 inst (online), $477 inst (print + online)] The official journal of the International Council for Educational Media.

Historical Journal of Film, Radio and Television. Taylor & Francis Group, Customer Services Dept, 325 Chestnut St, Suite 800, Philadelphia, PA 19106. www.tandf.co.uk/journals/titles/01439685, tel: 800-354-1420, fax: 215-625-2940, customerservice@taylorandfrancis.com [4/yr; $356 indiv, $971 inst (online), $1023 inst (print + online)] Articles by international experts in the field, news and notices, and book reviews concerning the impact of mass communications on political and social history of the 20th century.

International Journal of Instructional Media. Westwood Press, Inc., 118 5 Mile River Rd, Darien, CT 06820-6237. www.adprima.com/ijim.htm, tel: 203-656-8680, fax: 212-353-8291, PLSleeman@aol.com [4/yr; $181.20] Focuses on quality research on ongoing programs in instructional media for education, distance learning, computer technology, instructional media and technology, telecommunications, interactive video, management, media research and evaluation, and utilization.

Journal of Educational Multimedia and Hypermedia. Association for the Advancement of Computing in Education, P.O. Box 1545, Chesapeake, VA 23327-1545. www.aace.org/pubs/jemh, tel: 757-366-5606, fax: 703-997-8760, info@aace.org [4/yr; $25 for AACE student members, $55 AACE members (discount available for ordering multiple AACE journals), $175 inst] A multidisciplinary information source presenting research about and applications for multimedia and hypermedia tools.

Journal of Popular Film and Television. Heldref Publications, 1319 18th St NW, Washington, DC 20036-1802. www.heldref.org/jpft.php, tel: 866-802-7059, fax: 205-995-1588, jpft@heldref.org [4/yr; $56 indiv (online), $59 (print + online), $129 inst (print or online), $155 (print + online)] Articles on film and television, book reviews, and theory. Dedicated to popular film and television in the broadest sense. Concentrates on commercial cinema and television, film and television theory or criticism, filmographies, and bibliographies. Edited at the College of Arts and Sciences of Northern Michigan University and the Department of Popular Culture, Bowling Green State University.

Learning, Media & Technology. Taylor & Francis Group, Customer Services Dept, 325 Chestnut St, Suite 800, Philadelphia, PA 19106. www. tandf.co.uk/journals/titles/17439884, tel: 800-354-1420, fax: 215-625-2940, customerservice@taylorandfrancis.com [4/yr; $398 indiv, $1416 inst (online), $1491 inst (print + online)] This journal of the Educational Television Association serves as an international forum for discussions and reports on developments in the field of television and related media in teaching, learning, and training.

Media & Methods. American Society of Educators, 1429 Walnut St, Philadelphia, PA 19102. www.media-methods.com, tel: 215-563-6005, fax: 215-587-9706, info@media-methods.com [5/yr; $35] The only magazine published for the elementary school library media and technology specialist. A forum for K-12 educators who use technology as an educational resource, this journal includes information on what works and what does not, new product reviews, tips and pointers, and emerging technologies.

Multichannel News. Reed Business Information, 360 Park Avenue South, New York, NY 10010. www.multichannel.com, tel: 888-343-5563, fax: 712-733-8019, mulcustserv@cdsfulfillment.com [51/yr; $169.99] A newsmagazine for the cable television industry. Covers programming, marketing, advertising, business, and other topics.

MultiMedia & Internet@Schools. Information Today, Inc., 143 Old Marlton Pike, Medford, NJ 08055-8750. www.mmischools.com, tel: 800-300-9868, fax: 609-654-4309, custserv@infotoday.com [6/yr; $44.95] Reviews and evaluates hardware and software. Presents information pertaining to basic troubleshooting skills.

Multimedia Systems. Springer Science+Business Media, 333 Meadowlands Pkwy, Secaucus, NJ 07094. www.springer.com/journal/00530, tel: 800-777-4643, fax: 201-348-4505, journals-ny@springer.com [6/yr; $599 inst] Publishes original research articles and serves as a forum for stimulating and disseminating innovative research ideas, emerging technologies, state-of-the-art methods and tools in all aspects of multimedia computing, communication, storage, and applications among researchers, engineers, and practitioners.

Telematics and Informatics. Elsevier, Inc., Customer Service Dept, 6277 Sea Harbor Dr, Orlando, FL 32887-4800. www.elsevier.com/locate/tele, tel: 877-839-7126, fax: 407-363-1354, journalcustomerservice-usa@elsevier.com [4/yr; $130 indiv, $1149 inst] Publishes research and review articles in applied telecommunications and information sciences in business, industry, government, and educational establishments. Focuses on important current technologies, including microelectronics, computer graphics, speech synthesis and voice recognition, database management, data encryption, satellite television, artificial intelligence, and the ongoing computer revolution.

Professional Development

Journal of Computing in Teacher Education. International Society for Technology in Education, Special Interest Group for Teacher Educators, 180 West 8th Ave., Suite 300, Eugene, OR 97401. www.iste.org/jcte, tel: 800-336-5191, fax: 541-302-3778, iste@iste.org [4/yr; $122] Contains refereed articles on preservice and inservice training, research in computer education and certification issues, and reviews of training materials and texts.

Journal of Technology and Teacher Education. Association for the Advancement of Computing in Education, P.O. Box 1545, Chesapeake, VA 23327-1545. www.aace.org/pubs/jtate, tel: 757-366-5606, fax: 703-997-8760, info@aace.org [4/yr; $25 for AACE student members, $55 AACE members (discount available for ordering multiple AACE journals), $175 inst] Serves as an international forum to report research and applications of technology in preservice, inservice, and graduate teacher education.

Simulation, Gaming, and Virtual Reality

Simulation & Gaming. Sage Publications, 2455 Teller Rd, Thousand Oaks, CA 91320. sag.sagepub.com, tel: 800-818-7243, fax: 800-583-2665, journals@sagepub.com [4/yr; $131 indiv (print), $603 inst (online), $657 inst (print), $670 inst (online + print)] An international journal of theory, design, and research focusing on issues in simulation, gaming, modeling, role-playing, and experiential learning.

Special Education and Disabilities

Journal of Special Education Technology. Council for Exceptional Children, Technology and Media Division, 1110 N. Glebe Road, Arlington, VA 22201-5704. www.tamcec.org/jset/index.htm, tel: 405-325-1533, fax: 405-325-7661, jset@ou.edu [4/yr; $60 indiv, $129 inst, free online] Provides information, research, and reports of innovative practices regarding the application of educational technology toward the education of exceptional children.

Telecommunications and Networking

Canadian Journal of Learning and Technology. Canadian Network for Innovation in Education (CNIE), 260 Dalhousie St., Suite 204, Ottawa, ON, K1N 7E4, Canada. www.cjlt.ca, tel: 613-241-0018, fax: 613-241-0019, cjlt@ucalgary.ca [3/yr; $95 indiv, $115 inst] Concerned with all aspects of educational systems and technology.

Computer Communications. Elsevier, Inc., Customer Service Dept, 6277 Sea Harbor Dr, Orlando, FL 32887-4800. www.elsevier.com/locate/comcom, tel: 877-839-7126, fax: 407-363-1354, journalcustomerservice-usa@elsevier.com [18/yr; $1882 inst] Focuses on networking and distributed computing techniques, communications hardware and software, and standardization.

EDUCAUSE Review. EDUCAUSE, 4772 Walnut St, Suite 206, Boulder, CO 80301-2536. www.educause.edu/er, tel: 303-449-4430, fax: 303-440-0461, ersubs@educause.edu [6/yr; $30] Features articles on current issues and applications of computing and communications technology in higher education. Reports on EDUCAUSE consortium activities.

International Journal on E-Learning. Association for the Advancement of Computing in Education, P.O. Box 1545, Chesapeake, VA 23327-1545. www.aace.org/pubs/ijel, tel: 757-366-5606, fax: 703-997-8760, info@aace.org [4/yr; $25 for AACE student members, $55 AACE members (discount available for ordering multiple AACE journals), $175 inst] Reports on current theory, research, development, and practice of telecommunications in education at all levels.

The Internet and Higher Education. Elsevier, Inc., Customer Service Dept, 6277 Sea Harbor Dr, Orlando, FL 32887-4800. www.elsevier.com/locate/iheduc, tel: 877-839-7126, fax: 407-363-1354, journalcustomerservice-usa@elsevier.com [4/yr; $67 indiv, $343 inst] Designed to reach faculty, staff, and administrators responsible for enhancing instructional practices and productivity via the use of information technology and the Internet in their institutions.

Internet Reference Services Quarterly. Haworth Press, Inc., 10 Alice St, Binghamton, NY 13904-1580. www.haworthpress.com/web/IRSQ, tel: 800-354-

1420, fax: 215-625-2940, haworthorders@taylorandfrancis.com [4/yr; $74 indiv, $190 inst] Describes innovative information practice, technologies, and practice. For librarians of all kinds.

Internet Research. Emerald Group Publishing Limited, 875 Massachusetts Ave, 7th Floor, Cambridge, MA 02139. www.emeraldinsight.com/intr.htm, tel: 888-622-0075, fax: 617-354-6875, america@emeraldinsight.com [5/yr; $2679] A cross-disciplinary journal presenting research findings related to electronic networks, analyses of policy issues related to networking, and descriptions of current and potential applications of electronic networking for communication, computation, and provision of information services.

Online. Information Today, Inc., 143 Old Marlton Pike, Medford, NJ 08055-8750. www.infotoday.com/online, tel: 800-300-9868, fax: 609-654-4309, custserv@infotoday.com [6/yr; $119] For online information system users. Articles cover a variety of online applications for general and business use.

Index

Printed in the United States
148072LV00003BA/1/P